Egypt

Handbook for Travellers; Upper Egypt, With
Nubia as Far as the Second Cataract and the
Western Oases
Volume 2

By Karl Baedeker

ISBN: 978-1-63923-621-3

Printed: January 2023

Published and Distributed By:
Lushena Books
607 Country Club Drive, Unit E
Bensenville, IL 60106
www.lushenabks.com

ISBN: 978-1-63923-621-3

PREFACE.

The present volume forms the second part of the Editor's *Handbook for Egypt*, the first part of which has reached a second edition in 1880.

The materials upon which this Handbook to Upper Egypt is chiefly founded were contributed principally by *Professor Georg Ebers* of Leipsic, and *Professor Johannes Dümichen* of Strassburg, and their work, which was mainly finished in 1877, has been revised, augmented, and brought up to date in all practical details by *Professor August Eisenlohr* of Heidelberg, who has twice visited Egypt for this express purpose. To Prof. Ebers the editor is indebted for the account of the Nile-voyage as far as and including Philæ; Prof. Dümichen contributed the descriptions of the temples of Denderah and Edfu, of the town of Keneh, and of the caravanroutes thence viâ the quarries of Ḥamâmât to Ḳoṣêr on the Red Sea; while the routes in Lower Nubia and to the Western Oases are wholly from the pen of Prof. Eisenlohr.

The practical introduction to the first volume, and the sections on the geography, history, and art of Egypt, there published, apply of course also to the districts of Upper Egypt. The special introduction to the present volume dea s chiefly with the Nile voyage and the necessary prepa at o s for it, preceded by a brief survey of the chief steamer-routes between Egypt and Europe and a note on the new Egyptian monetary system, introduced since the publication of the Handbook to Lower Egypt. A list of works on Egypt is added, and, to obviate the necessity of too frequent references to the first volume, also a chronological list of the rulers of Egypt down to the close of the Ptolemaic period, and a selection from the royal cartouches of most frequent occurrence in Upper Egypt. Finally the Arabic Alphabet is given, showing the system of transliteration adopted in this Handbook.

The Maps and Plans have been an object of especial care. The former are based upon the large maps of *Kiepert, Lepsius,* and *Linant;* the latter chiefly upon the plans of *Lepsius,* though with the necessary additions and corrections, while some have been specially prepared by Prof. Eisenlohr.

HEIGHTS above the sea-level and other measurements are iven in English feet or miles.

Though nearly every page of the Handbook has been compiled from personal observation and experience, and although the conservative East is not nearly so liable to changes as the more progressive West, the Editor makes no claim to absolute accuracy in every detail; and he will feel indebted to any traveller who, from personal experience, may be able to indicate errors or omissions in the Handbook. The same remark applies equally to the PRICES and various items of expenditure mentioned in the volume. The expense of a tour is much more directly affected by the circumstances of the moment and the individuality of the traveller in the East than in Europe; though it may here be added that the arrangements of Messrs. Cook and Gáze (pp. XIV, XV), of which most visitors to Upper Egypt will avail themselves, offer a comparative immunity against extortion. A carefully drawn up contract will similarly protect those who prefer to hire a dhahabîyeh for themselves.

CONTENTS.

Maps.

Plans.

Vignettes.

Asterisks
are used as marks of commendation.

INTRODUCTION.

I. Steamer Routes between Europe and Egypt.

Fuller details as to the steamers in the Mediterranean are given in the first volume of the Handbook (pp. 7-10). The following resumé of the principal routes embodies the most recent alterations.

A. From England direct. Steamers of the PENINSULAR AND ORIENTAL STEAM NAVIGATION Co. ('P. & O.'), leaving London every week, for India or Australia, sail viâ Gibraltar, Malta, and Brindisi (see below) in 12-13 days to *Port Saïd* (fares 1st cl. 19*l.*, 2nd cl. 11*l.*, return-tickets 29*l.*, 17*l.*) and *Isma'îlîyeh* (20*l.*, 12*l.*, return 30*l.*, 18*l.*), whence a special train is run to *Cairo* on the arrival of the steamer. Passengers for *Alexandria* change at Brindisi to the fortnightly steamer thence (see below; fares from London, 18*l.*, 10*l.*, return 27*l.*, 10*l.*). The steamers from London touch fortnightly at *Naples* (see p. xii). Return-tickets are valid for 3 months.

Steamers of the ORIENT AND PACIFIC Co. ('Orient Line'), leaving London every alternate week, sail viâ Gibraltar and Naples to *Isma'îlîyeh*. Thence by rail to *Alexandria* (fares 1st cl. 21*l.*, return-ticket, valid for 6 months, 33*l.*) or to *Cairo* (20*l.*, return 32*l.*).

Steamers of the *Papayanni Line*, *Moss Line*, *Anchor Line*, and *Ocean Line* sail from Liverpool to Alexandria at irregular intervals (fare about 15*l.*).

OVERLAND ROUTES FROM LONDON TO MEDITERRANEAN PORTS. *Brindisi* may be reached from London in about 59 hrs., either viâ Paris and Mont Cenis (fares 1st cl. 12*l.* 8*s.* 6*d.*, 2nd cl. 9*l.*, 1*s.*), or viâ Bâle and the St. Gotthard (fares 12*l.* 5*s.* 6*d.*, 8*l.* 17*s.* 6*d.*), or in 49 hrs. by the P. & O. Express leaving London every Frid. afternoon (fare, including sleeping berth, 16*l.* 18*s.*; tickets obtainable only of Sleeping Car Co., 122 Pall Mall, S.W., or the P. & O. Co., 122 Leadenhall St., E.C.). — *Genoa* is 30¼ hrs. from London viâ Paris and Turin (fares 7*l.* 16*s.*, 5*l.* 16*s.*), or 36 hrs. viâ Bâle and the St. Gotthard (fares 8*l.* 2*s.*, 5*l.* 19*s.*). — *Venice* is 42 hrs. from London either viâ Paris and Mont Cenis (fares 9*l.* 1*s.*, 6*l.* 14*s.*) or viâ Bâle and the St. Gotthard (fares 8*l.* 15*s.*, 6*l.* 8*s.*). — *Marseilles* is 25-28 hrs. from London, according to route selected between London and Paris (fares 1st cl. 5*l.* 19*s.* 7*d.*-7*l.* 6*s.* 9*d.*, 2nd cl. 4*l.* 9*s.* 4*d.*-5*l.* 10*s.* 6*d.*). A 'Mediterranean Express' leaves Paris for Marseilles etc. three times a week in winter, once a week in summer; passengers from London by this train pay 4*l.* 0*s.* 1*d.* in addition to the ordinary 1st cl. fare.

B. From Mediterranean Ports. P. & O. STEAMERS, in connection with the P. & O. Express (see above), leave *Brindisi* every Sun. evening for *Port Saïd* (fares 1st cl. 10*l.*, 2nd cl. 7*l.*) and *Isma'îlîyeh* (fares 11*l.*, 8*l.*). — Steamers of the same company leave

Venice every alternate Frid. at 2 p.m., for *Ancona* (weather permitting) and *Brindisi* (arriving on Sun.). They leave Brindisi on Mon. at 2 a.m. (in direct connection with Sun. morning express from Bologna) and reach *Alexandria* on Tues. morning (72 hrs. from Brindisi). Return from Alexandria every alternate Mon. at 3 p.m. Fares from Venice or Ancona, 1st cl. 10*l.*, 2nd cl. 7*l.*, from Brindisi, 9*l.*, 6*l.;* return-ticket from Venice to Alexandria, valid for 3 months, 15*l.*, 11*l.* — P. & O. Steamers also leave *Naples* every alternate Sat. for Port Sa'id (10*l.*, 7*l.*) and Isma'ilîyeh (11*l.*, 8*l.*).

'ORIENT LINE' STEAMERS leave *Naples* every alternate Sun. at midnight for Port Sa'id; returning thence every alternate Wednesday.

The steamers of the MESSAGERIES MARITIMES leave Marseilles every alternate Frid. at 4 p.m. for *Alexandria* direct (no longer touching at Naples), arriving on Wed. morning. Return from Alexandria every alternate Saturday. Fares, 1st cl. 300, 2nd cl. 210 francs.

The steamers of the SOCIETÀ FLORIO-RUBATTINO (Navigazione Generale Italiana) leave *Genoa* every Mon. at 9 a.m., touch at *Leghorn*, *Naples* (leaving Wed. 7.30 p.m.), and *Messina*, and reach *Alexandria* at midnight on Monday. Return from Alexandria every Sat. at 3 p.m., waiting, however, for the steamer from Massowah.

The NORTH GERMAN LLOYD steamers sail from *Genoa* every alternate Mon., from *Brindisi* the following Wed., reaching *Port Sa'îd* on Saturday. Return from Port Sa'id every alternate Saturday. Fares: from Genoa, 1st cl. 400, 2nd cl. 240 marks; from Brindisi, 240 or 175 marks.

The AUSTRIA-HUNGARIAN LLOYD steamers from *Trieste* to Alexandria now sail viâ Brindisi, and no longer viâ Corfu. Leaving Trieste every Frid. at midday, they reach *Brindisi* on Sat. at 9 p.m. or sooner, proceed thence on Sun. at 5 a.m., and reach *Alexandria* on Wed. at 5 a.m. Fare from Brindisi, 1st cl. 88, 2nd cl. 59 florins in gold. The 'Thalia' and 'Euterpe' are the best ships on this line; some of the others are poor. Second-class passengers have to sleep in the saloon.

All the steamers now lie beside the quay at Alexandria, so that landing in small boats, as described in our first volume, has now become a thing of the past.

II. Monetary System.

The information as to the Egyptian monetary system given on pp. 4, 5 of our first vol., has to be supplemented by the statement that the Egyptian Government has recently issued new silver coins and some gold coins, and that these now form the only legal currency throughout the whole country, where their value is uniform. The unit of reckoning is still the *Piastre* (Arabic *Ghirsh*, plur. *Ghrush*). The *Egyptian Pound* is divided into 100 piastres or 1000 *Millièmes*.

ARABIC NAME.	Value in Egyptian Money		Value in British Money		Value in French Money		Value in German Money	
	Piastres	Millième	Shillings	Pence	Francs	Centimes	Marks	Pfennige
Gold Coins.								
Gineh Masri (Egypt. pound £ E.)	100	1000	20	6	25	95	20	80
Nusseh Masri (half an Egypt. pd.)	50	500	10	3	13	—	10	40
Silver Coins.								
Riyal Masri.	20	200	4	1	5	20	4	16
Nusseh Riyál	10	100	2	—	2	60	2	10
Rub'a Riyál.	5	50	1	—	1	30	1	5
Ghirshên (double piastre)	2	20	—	5	—	52	—	42
Ghirsh (piastre)	1	10	—	$2^{1}/_{2}$	—	26	—	21
Nickel Coins.								
Nusseh Ghirsh	$^{1}/_{2}$	5	—	1	—	13	—	10
2 Millième.	$^{2}/_{10}$	2	—	$^{1}/_{2}$	—	5	—	4
1 Millième.	$^{1}/_{10}$	1	—	$^{1}/_{4}$	—	$2^{1}/_{2}$	—	2

In COPPER there are also pieces of $^{1}/_{2}$ and $^{1}/_{4}$ Millième (called also *2 Para* and *1 Para* pieces, from the old system), but these are used only for bakshish by tourists.

The difference between *Tariff-piastres* and *Current-piastres* has been legally abolished; but it still lingers among shopkeepers, so that purchasers should be careful to ascertain in which reckoning the prices of goods are stated.

The *Pound Sterling* (*Gineh inglisi*) is worth 97 piastres 5 millième; the French *Twenty Franc piece* (*Bint*, derived from Napoleon Bonaparte) 77 pias. $1^{1}/_{2}$ mill.; the *Turkish Pound* (£ T.; *Mejidiyeh*) $87^{3}/_{4}$ piastres. A 'purse' is equivalent to 500 piastres or about 104s.

Before starting on the Nile-journey travellers are recommended to provide themselves with at least 40 or 50 francs' worth of small Egyptian coins (especially $^{1}/_{2}$ piastres, 1 and 2 millième-pieces, and copper). Even in Cairo a commission is charged on the exchange.

III. The Nile Journey.

The ascent of the Nile may be made either by *Steamer* or by *Dhahabîyeh*. The former is recommended to those who have not more than three or four weeks to devote to a visit to the Nile valley and the monuments of the Pharaohs; and in fact for the immense majority of travellers, especially for those who do not belong to a party, the steamers are the only practicable means of making the journey. Travellers, however, who desire to make a closer acquaintance with the country, who have abundance of time (to Assuân and back at least 7-8 weeks), and who are indifferent to a considerable increase of expense, should hire a dhahabîyeh (p. xix).

The company met with on board the steamers is generally unexceptionable, though, of course, it is always wise to use some little exertion to secure an agreeable and sympathetic cabin-companion. The trunks to be taken into the cabins should be small and handy,

for the accommodation is somewhat limited. Greater care is required
in the choice of companions for the dhahabîyeh-voyage, for the close
and constant intercourse in rather narrow quarters and for perhaps two months at a time is apt to produce somewhat strained relations between those who are not originally sympathetic. The
'dhahabîyeh devil', indeed, is famous in Egypt for causing those
who have embarked as friends to disembark as foes. In especial travellers with scientific aims should avoid travelling with those who
have no particular interest in the gigantic remains of antiquity, and
who are thus constantly wishing to push on hurriedly from sheer
ennui. In all cases it is prudent to distribute the various cabins
and seats on the divân by lot before starting.

A government tax of 100 pias. (20s. 6d.) is levied upon all visitors to
the monuments of Upper Egypt, to be devoted to the maintenance of such
monuments. The tax may be paid and cards admitting to the temples etc.
obtained at the Museum of Gizeh or at Cook's or Gaze's Office.

A. The Steamboat Voyage.

The steamers belonging to Messrs. Thomas Cook & Son (offices,
see p. xv) are the best on the Nile, as well in point of comfort and
cleanliness, as in point of organization and attentive service. Cook's
Tourist Steamers between Cairo and Assuân start every alternate
Tuesday from the middle of November till the end of December,
and every Tuesday from that date until the middle of March, spending 20 days on the voyage to Assuân and back. Extra-steamers
are also run at the most crowded time; while two special excursions
are organized in the course of the season, allowing four weeks for
the double voyage. The three-weeks service is carried on by the
steamers *Rameses the Great*, *Rameses*, *Prince Mohammed Ali*,
Tewfik, and *Prince Abbas*, of which the two first are the best. The
fare is 50l., or for occupants of the two superior cabins, specially
adapted for invalids, 60l. The four-weeks steamer is named *Sethi*;
fare 65l. The fares include provisions (wine etc. excepted), all
necessary travelling expenses, donkeys, English saddles for ladies,
boats to cross the river, the services of dragomans and guides, and
bakshish to guides. The donkey-boys, however, usually look for
a small bakshish from the traveller, who is also expected to bestow
a gratuity upon the attendants on board the steamer. The tax
levied by the Egyptian Government (see above) is also not included
in the fares. Each traveller is entitled to ship 200 *lbs.* of personal
luggage not exceeding 2 cubic mètres in measurement. A physician
is carried on each steamer, whose services, if required, are paid for
in addition to the fare. A deposit of 10l. must be paid on taking
a ticket at Cook's offices in Europe. The name, sex, and nationality
of the passenger must be inserted at the time of booking. Tickets
are not transferable except with Messrs. Cook's consent. If a traveller be prevented by exceptional circumstances from joining the
steamer for which he has booked he may proceed with the following

steamer if there is a berth free. After that, however, the ticket becomes invalid, without any recourse against Messrs. Cook.

In 1889-90 Messrs. Cook also organized a MAIL STEAMER SERVICE
between Assiût, the railway terminus, and Assuân (4 days up,
3 days down), starting from Assiût on Wed. and Sat. mornings in
connection with the day-trains leaving Bûlâk ed-Dakrûr on Tues.
and Frid. mornings; and returning from Assuân on Mon. and Thurs.
afternoons in connection with the train leaving Assiût for Bûlâk
ed-Dakrûr on Frid. and Mon. evenings. The names of the mail-
steamers are *Cleopatra*, *Nefertari*, *Amenartas*, and *Hatasoo*. In
1891 a mail-steamer also sailed every Sat. direct from *Cairo* viâ
Assiût to Assuân, in some respects to be preferred to the others.
This steamer touches at Benihasan (visit to the tombs), reaches
Assiût on Tues. evening, and proceeds thence on Wed. morning (as
above). The fare from Cairo is 23*l.* to Assuân and back (14 days,
or 18 days if the direct steamer from Cairo be taken) and 20*l.* to
Luxor and back (11 days), including 1st cl. fare from Cairo to
Assiût, transfer of baggage at Assiût, provisions on board the
steamers, and 3-4 days' hotel accommodation at Luxor. Incidental
expenses for sight-seeing, donkeys, guides, etc. are not included in
these fares. About $1^1/_2$ day is spent at Assuân, and on the return-
voyage 3 hrs. are spent at Edfu and $2^3/_4$ hrs. at Keneh-Denderah.
Kôm Ombo, Esneh, and Luxor are night-stations, and travellers who
desire to visit the temples at these places must do so by torch-light.
Passengers may also spend additional time at any of the stations en
route continuing their journey by later steamers, and paying the
fare from stage to stage (to Luxor 2.94*l.E.*, to Assuân 5*l.E.*) together
with 10*s.* per day for food on board the steamers. These mail-
steamers enable travellers to visit the chief points in Upper Egypt
at a less expenditure of time and money than the tourist steamers.
No one should omit the voyage to Assuân, while Sakkârah may be
visited from Cairo. The life on board these vessels is often lively;
and the scenes at the numerous landing-places are frequently
highly entertaining. The mail-steamers touch at the following
stations: *Abutîg, Nekheleh, Sedfeh, Temeh, Meshteh, Tahtah, Mara-
ghah, Shendawîn, Sohâg, Akhmîm, Menshîyeh, Girgeh, Beliâneh,
Abu Shûsheh, Shêkh Amrân, Farshût, Kasr es-Saiyâd, Deshneh,
Keneh, Kûs, Nakâdeh, Kamûleh, Luxor, Erment, Esneh, Basalîyeh,
Edfu, Sebû'ah, Kôm Ombo, Darâwi,* and *Assuân.*

Detailed information as to all these steamers, as well as the dhahabîyehs mentioned on p. xix, will be found in *Cook's Programme*, published annually, 6*d.* post free, and obtainable at any of Cook's offices:
London, Ludgate Circus; *Alexandria*, Place Méhémet Ali; *Cairo*, Cook's
Pavilion, next door to Shepheard's Hotel.

The well-equipped steamers of the *Thewfikieh Nile Navigation Co.*
(managing director, *Rostowitz-Bey*) afford another excellent means
of ascending the Nile. Messrs. **Henry Gaze & Son** (London,
142 Strand; Alexandria, Place de l'Eglise; Cairo, opposite Shep-

heard's Hotel) are the sole agents. The tourist-steamers *Memphis*, *El-Khedevie*, and *El-Kahireh* leave Cairo every alternate Wed., for Assuân and back (21 days; fare 42*l*.), on conditions similar to those of Messrs. Cook.   Special thirty-days expeditions are organized twice during the season (fare 55*l*.).   The company also owns the *Shellal* (26 berths), *Luxor* (25 berths), *Karnak* (19 berths), *Denderah* (14 berths), *Edfou, Philœ*, and *Elephantine* (8 berths each) for smaller parties.   Messrs. Gaze & Son have also arranged a series of seventeen-day tours, starting (by train) from Cairo every fourth day from the end of November to the end of March, and proceeding by steamer from Assiût to Assuân and back; fare from Cairo and back, including 4 days' hotel accommodation at Luxor, 26*l*.

Dhahabîyehs belonging to the Thewfikieh Co., see p. xix.

DAILY ITINERARY OF COOK'S THREE-WEEKS STEAMERS.

Passengers who prefer to proceed by rail from Cairo to Assiût (not recommended) are provided on request with a 1st cl. railway ticket by Messrs. Cook.

1st Day.   Leave Cairo at 10 a.m., starting from the landing-stage above the iron-bridge near *Ḳaṣr en-Nîl*. At midday *Bedrashên* is reached, where donkeys are in readiness to convey passengers to the site of *Memphis:* the Step-Pyramid of Sakḳârah, Serapeum, Maṣṭaba of Ti, and Pyramid of Unas; in all about 3 hrs. (comp. *Baedeker's Lower Egypt*, pp. 371 seq.).   In the evening the steamer proceeds to *Kafr el-'Ayât* (36 M. from Cairo).

2nd Day.   Steam to (106 M.) *Maghâghah*, where there is one of the largest sugar factories in Egypt (comp. p. 6), lighted by gas. Sugar manufacturing begins about the beginning of January.

3rd Day.   Steam to *Benihasan* (p. 12), whence the *Speos Artemidos* and the tombs of Ameni-Amenemha and Khnumhotep are visited (p. 14). — Thence to (182 M.) *Rôdah*.

4th Day.   Steam to (250 M.) *Assiût* (p. 31).

5th Day.   Visit Assiût and neighbourhood.   In the afternoon steam to (294 M.) *El-Maraghât* (p. 48).

6th Day.   Steam past *Beliâneh* (Abydos is visited on the return journey) to (388 M.) *Deshneh* (p. 72).

7th Day.   Steam to *Keneh*, whence the *Temple of Denderah* (p. 79) is visited.   Thence to (450 M.) *Luxor* (p. 101), which is reached about 5 p.m.

8th Day.   Visit the *Temple of Ḳurnah*, the *Tombs of the Kings*, and the *Temple of Der el-baḥri* (pp. 196 seq.); 8 a.m. to 4.30 p.m.

9th Day.   Excursion to *Karnak* (3 hrs.; p. 115); in the afternoon, the *Temple of Luxor* (p. 109).

10th Day.   Visit the Ramesseum (p. 158), the *Tombs of Shêkh 'Abd el-Ḳurnah* (p. 190), the *Temple of Dêr el-Medîneh* (p. 188), and the *Pavilion* and *Temple of Medînet Habu* (p. 171), where lunch is served about noon.   Return viâ the *Colossi of Memnon* (p. 153).

11th Day.   Steam to (4½ hrs.) *Esneh* (p. 231), where a short visit to the temple is paid, then (4 hrs. more) to (515 M.) *Edfu* (p. 243), where the temple is visited.

12th Day. Steam viâ *Gebel Silsileh* (p. 255) and *Kôm Ombo* (¹/₂ hr.'s halt; p. 260) to (583 M.) Assuân (p. 266), which is reached about 4 p.m. Visit to the island of *Elephantine* (p. 271) before dinner.

13th Day. *Assuân*, its bazaars, etc. Expedition to the tombs on *Mount Grenfell* (p. 269) recommended.

14th Day. Expedition into the desert on donkey or camel. Then cross to the island of *Philœ* (p. 281), where lunch is served. Passengers afterwards descend to the *First Cataract* in a small boat, and ride back to Assuân on donkeys from the Nubian village of Mahâdah. Or they may shoot the cataract (p. 279).

15th Day. The return voyage is begun, Luxor being reached before dark.

16th Day. Karnak may be revisited; or the travellers may inspect the Necropolis of Thebes at their own expense. Arrangements should be made the day before with the dragoman or. manager. The steamer starts again at noon, and reaches *Ḳeneh* (p. 72) in the evening.

17th Day. Steam to *Beliâneh*, where donkeys are in readiness to convey travellers to *Abydos* (p. 53).

18th Day. *Assiûṭ* is reached in the afternoon. Train thence to Cairo if desired.

19th Day. Steam to *Gebel eṭ-Ṭêr* (p. 7), sometimes visiting the sugar-factory at Rôḍah (p. 18).

20th Day. Arrival at *Cairo*. Passengers may remain on board until after breakfast on the following morning. ·

The FOUR WEEKS' TOUR (usually in the beginning of Jan. and the beginning of Feb.) is much preferable to the above hurried visit. About ¹/₂ day is devoted to *Bedrashên, Memphis*, and *Sakkârah* (instead of 3 hrs.), ¹/₂ day to *Benihasan* (instead of 4 hrs.), 2¹/₂ days to *Assiûṭ* (instead of ¹/₂ day), ¹/₂ day to the Coptic Convents of *Dêr el-Abyaḍ* and *Dêr el-Aḥmar*, several hours to *Akhmîm* and to *Ḳeneh*, 1 day to *Denderah* (instead of ¹/₂ day), 5¹/₂ days to *Thebes* (instead of 3¹/₂ days), several hours to *Esneh*, 5 hrs. to *el-Kâb*, ¹/₂ day to *Edfu*, ¹/₂ day to *Gebel Silsileh*, ¹/₂ day to *Kôm Ombo* (where a night is spent), 3 days (instead of 2) to *Assuân, Elephantine*, and *Philœ*, 1 day to *Abydos* (instead of ³/₄ day), and a morning to *Tell el-Amarnah*. The steamers, being smaller, have the advantage of conveying a less numerous party. Timely application for a berth is strongly recommended. The itinerary is as follows: —

1st Day. To *Bedrashên* as on p. xvi. Excursion to *Memphis* (see Vol. I.).

2nd Day. To *Benisuéf* (p. 5) or *Feshn* (p. 6).

3rd Day. To *Benihasan* (p. 12).

4th Day. Excursion to the *Speos Artemidos* and the tombs of *Ameni*, *Khnumhotep*, etc. — In the afternoon to *Gebel Abu Fêdah* (p. 28).

5th Day. To *Assiûṭ* (p. 31), arriving about noon.

6th Day. To *Sohâg* (p. 48).

7th Day. Excursion to the Coptic convents of *Dêr el-Abyaḍ* and *Dêr el-Aḥmar* (p. 49). In the afternoon to *Girgeh* (p. 52), with a short halt at *Akhmîm* (p. 49).

8th Day. To *Ḳeneh* (p. 72).

9th Day. Excursion to *Denderah* (p. 79), lunching in the temple.

10th Day. To *Luxor* (p. 109), visiting the temple in the afternoon.

11th Day. Excursion to *Ḳurnah* (p. 196), the *Ramesseum* (p. 158), *Dêr el-baḥri* (p. 223), and the *Tombs of the Kings* (p. 199), as on the 8th Day of the three weeks' tour.

12th Day. No settled programme; comp. Day 16, p. xvii.

13th Day. Excursion to *Shêkh ʿAbd el-Ḳurnah* (p. 190), *Dêr el-Medîneh* (p. 188), *Medînet Hâbu* (p. 171), the *Colossi of Memnon* (p. 153); as on Day 10, p. xvi.

14th Day. Visit to *Karnak* (p. 115), lunching in the temple.

15th Day. Steam to *Esneh* (p. 231), visiting the temple in the evening.

16th Day. To *El-Ḳâb* (p. 236) and in the evening to *Edfu*.

17th Day. Visit to the temple of *Edfu* (p. 243), then to *Gebel Silsileh* (p. 255).

18th Day. Visit the quarries in the morning, then steam to *Assuân* (p. 266), making a short halt at *Kôm Ombo* (p. 260).

19th Day. No settled programme.

20th Day. *Philæ* (p. 281) and the *First Cataract* (p. 278), as on Day 14, p. xvii.

21st Day. *Elephantine* (p. 271), and *Tombs of Mekhu, Saben, Ranubkaunekht,* and *Si Renput* (p. 269); or to *Philæ* again, on previous arrangement with the manager. — In the afternoon steam to *Kôm Ombo* (p. 260).

22nd Day. To *Luxor* (p. 101), arriving about 4 p.m.

23rd Day. Excursions in Thebes to suit the travellers' tastes.

24th Day. To *Beliâneh* (p. 53).

25th Day. Excursion to *Abydos* (p. 53); lunch in the temple.

26th Day. To *Assiût* (p. 31).

27th Day. Excursion to the tombs on the hill of *Assiût* (p. 32); in the afternoon, steam to *Ḥagg el-Kandîl* (p. 22).

28th Day. Excursion to the caves of *Tell el-Amarnah* (p. 22). In the afternoon steam to *Minyeh* (p. 9) and visit to the sugar-factory there if the river is high enough.

29th Day. Arrival in *Cairo*.

Holders of Cooks' tickets may break their journey at Luxor or Assuân either on the way up or the way down (after previous arrangement with Cooks' manager in Cairo), and proceed by a subsequent steamer, if there are vacant berths. The mail-steamers, usually less crowded than the others, may be used in descending the stream. In all these deviations from the usual tours, very strict adherence to the terms of the special arrangement is exacted. Travellers are strongly recommended to time their voyage so as to arrive at Luxor 3-4 days before full moon; for moonlight adds a peculiar charm to a visit to the ruins here and at Assuân.

Passengers by steamer should beware of the risk of catching cold by leaving the windows of their cabin open. They should also avoid placing themselves too near the edge of the deck; and it is well to remember (*e.g.* when shaving) that the steamers frequently run aground, especially above Luxor. Liability to delay through this last fact, makes it impossible to be sure of reaching Cairo in time to make connection with the ocean-steamers.

For the Mail and Tourist Steamers between the First and Second Cataract Philæ to Wadi Ḥalfah), see p. 299.

b. The Dhahabîyeh Voyage.

Though the voyage in a **Dhahabîyeh** demands much more time and money than the steamboat-voyage, on the other hand it offers the only means of a satisfactorily close examination of the country and its monuments. A party of 4-5 persons will be found advisable, especially as the expense is not much more than for 1-2 persons.

A large selection of good dhahabîyehs is to be found at Cairo, on the left bank of the Nile both above and below the new bridge at Bûlâ. Travellers who take the train from Cairo to Assiût should despatch their boat from Cairo about a fortnight in advance, for there are no good dhahabîyehs either at Assiût or farther up at Luxor and Assuân. In Cairo the best dhahabîyehs are those belonging to Messrs. Cook & Son (*'Isis'*, *'Osiris'*, *'Horus'*, *'Hathor'*, *'Nephthis'*, and *'Ammon-Ra'*, costing 130*l*. per month) or Messrs. Gaze & Son (*'Sesostris'*, *'Cheops'*, *'Herodotus'*, and *'Hope'*, 110*l*. per month). Other good craft, with the monthly hire, are as follows: *'Diamond'* (100*l*.), *'Eva'* (80*l*.), *'Admiral'* (85*l*.), *'Timsah'* (90*l*.), *'London'*, *'Luxor'*, *'Philæ'* (each 75*l*.), *'India'* (85*l*.), *'Alma'*, *'Nubia'*, *'Zenobia'*, *'Gamila'* (each 90*l*.), *'Lotus'* (70*l*.), *'Meermin'*, *'Manhattan'* (each 75*l*.), *'Griffin'* (80*l*.), *'Zingara'* (65*l*.), and *'Vittoria'* (55*l*.).

These prices include the hire of the dhâhabîyeh and its full equipment and the wages of the reîs or captain and the crew. For the services of a dragoman, cook, and attendant, and for provisions, saddles, and all the incidental expenses of excursions (excluding bakshîsh), the price per day and per pers. is calculated thus: —

	Cook	Gaze	Dragoman
Party of 2, each pers.	33*s*.	35*s*.	30*s*.
- - 3 - -	28*s*.	27*s*.	24*s*.
- - 4 - -	24*s*.	25*s*.	20*s*.
- - 5 - -	22*s*.	20*s*.	18*s*.
- - 6 or more,	20*s*.	16*s*.	16*s*.

Thus for a voyage of 60 days from Cairo to Assuân and back, including the payment of a dragoman and all provisions (except·wine, etc.), Cook charges 590*l*. for a party of 5 (*i.e.* 118*l*. each pers., or 39*s*. 4*d*. each per day). For smaller parties, the cost per head is considerably more. A three months' voyage in the 'Manhattan' (the property of a dragoman) costs 485*l*. for a party of 4 (*i.e.* 6*l*. 10*s*. per day, or 32*s*. 6*d*. each pers. per day). The inclusive charge for Cook's excellent steam-dhahabîyeh *'Nitocris'* (5 berths) is 400*l*. per month, a sum that will not appear exorbitant when the time saved by steaming is taken into account.

Those who employ Cook's or Gaze's dhahabîyehs are relieved from all trouble in the matter of engaging a dragoman (quite indispensable to the traveller who speaks no Arabic) or purchasing provisions. And there are the additional advantages that the stores of meat, fowls, vegetables, and fruit can be replenished en route from the steamers, and that, in case of head-winds, the small *Steam Towing Launches* belonging to these firms, may be hired for 6-8*l*. per day.

The chartering of a private dhahabîyeh is much cheaper though much more troublesome. The first step is to engage a *Dragoman*, not without a careful enquiry as to his record at the consulate and from the hotel-keepers, and an examination of the testimonials from previous travellers. There are about 90 dragomans in Cairo, all more or less intelligent and able, but scarcely a half of the number are trustworthy. Most of them speak English or French, and a few speak Italian.

The following are well spoken of: *Hassan Speke*, *Ahmed Ramadan*, *Ibrahim Solem*, *Ahmed Abderrahim* (owner of the Manhattan, p. xix), *Hasan Bibars*, *Salim Sadjar*, *Bishai Awad*, *Abdullah Abdelkhalik* (all these Egyptians); *Saleh* (a Nubian); *Michael Galt*, *Anton Sapienza* (Maltese); *Mansûr*, *Lewiz Mansûr*, *Daeybis Fadúl*, *Elias Telhany*, and *Elias Abusháya* (Syrians). It cannot be too strongly impressed upon the traveller that it is essential for him to show from the very beginning that he is and intends to remain the master. Even the best dragomans are inclined to patronize their clients, a tendency which must at once be quashed.

The next step is to select a suitable dhahabîyeh assisted by the dragoman. A contract is then made with the dragoman, either entrusting him with the entire preparations, or assigning to him only the duty of engaging and paying the reʿis and crew, while the traveller retains the commissariat department in his own hands. The reʿis or steersman is a most important functionary upon whose skill during the often stormy passage the safety of the vessel depends. The crew number from 8 to 12 according to the size of the dhahabiyeh. The vessel is either hired by the day (for 2 pers. 5-6*l.*, 3 or 4 pers. 6-7*l.*) or chartered for the whole return-voyage to Assuân (for 2 pers. 300-350*l.*, 3 or 4 pers. 350-400*l.*). In the former case the dragoman will try to travel as slowly as possible to protract his engagement; in the latter case he will press on, so as to save boat-hire and board. The latter arrangement is preferable, but the right of halting for 15-20 days in the course of the journey should carefully be stipulated for. The dragoman must also provide donkeys and camels for the excursions. Farther details are indicated in the following draft-contracts, in which it is believed that nothing of importance has been overlooked. The contract must be signed at the traveller's consulate, either with the dragoman alone if he has undertaken the whole of the arrangements, or with the dragoman and reʿis, when the traveller has hired the dhahabîyeh and pays board to the dragoman.

Contract with the Dragoman. — Mr. X. and his travelling companions on the one hand, and the Dragoman Y. on the other, have mutually entered into the following contract: —

(1) The Dragoman Y. binds himself to conduct Mr. X. and his party from Cairo to Assuân (or Wâdi Halfah), and back, for the sum of ....pounds sterling.

(2) The Dragoman Y. shall exclusively defray the whole travelling expenses of the party, including the hire of the dhahabîyeh, sufficiently manned, and equipped to the satisfaction of Mr. X., the entire cost of food, service, lighting, pilotage, watching the boat, and all charges for donkeys, donkey-boys, camels, and guides.

(3) The Dragoman Y. shall provide a good bed with moustiquaire

(mosquito-curtains) for each member of the party, with all necessary bed and table linen, table-equipage, and implements in good condition. Each person shall have two clean towels every four days, a clean table-napkin every second day, and clean sheets once a week.

(4) The Dragoman Y. undertakes the entire provisioning of Mr. X. and his party. The following meals shall be served daily: 1. Breakfast, consisting of tea, coffee, or chocolate (at the travellers' option), bread, butter, biscuits, eggs, marmalade (or whatever the traveller is accustomed to); 2. Lunch, consisting of . . . . 3. Dinner, consisting of . . . . [The traveller may adjust the bill of fare to his taste, but it may be remarked that Nile-voyagers usually enjoy an excellent appetite, and that a choice of several dishes affords an agreeable variety without adding much to the cost. For lunch 2-3 courses are usually demanded, and for dinner, soup, 3 courses, and desert.] All the dishes shall be well-cooked and properly served. Fresh bread shall be baked every second day. For each guest invited by the travellers to breakfast the dragoman shall receive 3 fr., for each guest at dinner 4 fr.

(5) A lighted lamp shall be affixed outside the dhahabîyeh at night.

(6) A small boat in good condition shall accompany the dhahabîyeh, and shall be at all times at the disposal of the travellers, with the necessary crew. Two or more sailors shall accompany the travellers when the latter desire to land, and shall serve as watches or porters when required.

(7) The dhahabîyeh shall be maintained in a good and efficient condition. The deck shall be washed every morning.

(8) The Dragoman Y. is responsible for the maintenance of order among the crew; and he shall take care that both the crew and the attendants are quiet at night so as not to prevent the travellers from sleeping.

(9) When the wind is unfavourable, the dhahabîyeh shall be towed on the way upstream or rowed on the way downstream.

(10) The Dragoman Y. is alone responsible for any damage that may occur to the dhahabîyeh or the small boat.

(11) No passenger or goods shall be received on board without the express permission of Mr. X.

(12) The travellers reserve to themselves the right of halting for 15-20 days in the course of the voyage, without extra charge, at such times and places as they may select. Halts of less than 2 hrs. shall not be reckoned; but the travellers will not avail themselves of this exception oftener than once a day.

(13) The travellers shall have the right of halting for more days than are stipulated for in paragraph 12, on condition of paying 20 fr. each pers. for each extra day, in addition to the boat-hire. Thus if the dhabahiyeh has been hired for 30*l.* per month or 25 fr. per day, a party of 3 pers. would pay for each extra day 3×20+25=85 fr.

(14) If the dhahabîyeh reaches a spot during the night, at which the Dragoman Y. has been instructed to stop, a halt must be made; and the day's halt to be reckoned to the traveller shall not begin until sunrise.

(15) The Reïs shall have the right of halting for 24 hours on two occasions for the purpose of baking bread for the crew. These periods (48 hrs.) shall not be reckoned against the traveller; nor shall any other halt not expressly commanded by Mr. X., whether due to bad weather or any other cause, be so reckoned. The halt for baking shall be made at Assiût, and not at Girgeh (comp. p. 52).

(16) One-third of the stipulated price shall be paid to the Dragoman Y. before the commencement of the voyage; one-third during the voyage; and the remaining third on its completion. [Or one-half before the voyage is begun and one-half on its completion.]

(17) In the event of disputes or differences in carrying out this contract, Mr. X. and the Dragoman Y. bind themselves to submit unconditionally such disputes or differences to the arbitration of the consul, before whom it has been signed.

(18) The voyage shall begin on such and such a day.

Then follow the signatures of the traveller and the dragoman.

Contract with the Reꞌis. Mr. X. on the one hand, and the Reꞌîs Y. on the other have mutually entered into the following contract: —

(1) The Reꞌîs V., owner (or captain) of the dhahabîyeh named Z., now anchored at Bûlâk (or Ramleh), agrees to hire that vessel with all necessary equipments in good condition to Mr. X. for a voyage to Upper Egypt, for the price of n pounds sterling for the first month, and n pounds sterling for each day thereafter. [If the traveller desires to pass the cataract as described on p. 273, he must ascertain whether the dhahabîyeh is fit for the passage, and in that case add to paragraph 1: The Reꞌîs Y. declares the dhahabîyeh fit for passing the first cataract. Mr. X. shall in no wise be responsible for any damage sustained by the dhahabîyeh in passing the cataract.]

(2) The Reꞌis Y. binds himself to present the dhahabîyeh in the best-possible condition for sailing. The mast, sails, and rudder shall be strong and in good condition. The crew shall consist of (at least) 6-8 able-bodied and experienced sailors and a second reꞌis or steersman.

(3) A good and efficient small boat (fellukah) shall accompany the dhahabîyeh, and shall at all times be at the disposal of Mr. X., with at least three sailors as crew, either for excursions, for hunting, or other object.

(4) When the wind is favourable the voyage shall be continued during the night, when Mr. X. desires it. When the wind is unfavourable, the dhahabîyeh shall be towed from sunrise to sunset.

(5) The Reꞌis Y. shall cause the dhahabîyeh to halt or to start at such times as Mr. X. shall direct. He binds himself to select safe and proper anchorages. Mr. X.'s express permission must be obtained before any of the sailors shall be allowed to quit the dhahabîyeh for some hours, either to go to market, to visit their friends, or for any other purpose.

(6) The dhahabîyeh shall be washed daily, special care being bestowed upon the after-deck, on which Mr. X. travels. A good and efficient awning adapted to shade the after-deck shall be provided, and shall be rigged on Mr. X.'s request, unless the state of the wind prevents it. The Reꞌis shall cause a lighted lamp to be hung outside the dhahabîyeh at night.

(7) No passengers or persons other than the crew, and no goods shall be received on board the dhahabîyeh without the express permission of Mr. X. Mr. X. has the right of receiving on board as many companions and as much luggage as he chooses.

(8) When the traveller desires to spend some time on shore (*e.g.* at Thebes or Philæ), the Reꞌis shall direct at least two sailors to act as guards over the tent, or temple, or other place where the traveller may spend the night.

(9) The Reꞌis and crew shall at all times be obliging and respectful to Mr. X. and his party. Two sailors shall be at all times at the disposal of the travellers to accompany them on shore and to carry provisions, books, boxes, a ladder, or whatever shall be required.

(10) During the absence of the travellers from the dhahabîyeh, the Reꞌis binds himself to maintain it in good condition, and to take charge of any possessions left by the travellers on board. He binds himself also to indemnify the travellers for any of their possessions that may be stolen or injured while under his charge.

(11) The travellers shall be responsible for all damage done to the dhahabîyeh through their fault, but they shall on no account be liable for damage arising from any other cause whatever. If the Reꞌîs is prevented by any cause, not due to the fault of the travellers, from continuing the voyage, the travellers shall pay only for as many days as the voyage has actually lasted.

(12) Fees charged for the passage of the bridge at Cairo and the first cataract, by the dhahabîyeh shall be paid by the hirer. [These fees are fixed by Egyptian officials according to the size of the dhahabîyeh.]

(13) Mr. X. and the Reꞌis Y. bind themselves to submit all disputes which may arise as to the carrying out of this contract to the arbitration of the consul in whose presence it has been signed.

Travellers who know some Arabic or who are already acquainted with Egypt and its people may dispense with a dragoman, engaging only a *Camp-Servant* (about 4*l.* a month, with 1-2*l.* bakshish) and a *Cook* (5-6*l.* a month and 1-2*l.* bakshîsh). The former, who must understand some European language as well as Arabic, will assist in the search for a good dhahabîyeh; and the advice of the hotel-keeper will also be found of use. The hire of the boat will be at least 15*l.* per month, and the wages of the Re'is and about 12 rowers 20-21*l.*, with 40-50*s.* bakshish, in all 36-38*l.*

The Contract with the Servant may be as follows: The Servant Y. binds himself for a payment of —, to accompany Mr. X. on his journey to Nubia (or elsewhere) in the capacity of camp-servant (or cook), and farther binds himself to discharge willingly and attentively the services that may be demanded of him by Mr. X. and his party.

Provisions. The following firms may be recommended from the writer's personal experience to those travellers who attend to their own commissariat: *Walker & Co.*, Ezbekîyeh 16-20, for preserved meats and other eatables; *Nicola Zigada*, beside Shepheard's Hotel, for eatables and wine; *E. J. Fleurant*, opposite the Crédit Lyonnais, for French and Austrian wine. The following list of articles taken by a party of three for two months voyage, will assist the traveller to select his fare.

2¹/₅ lbs. of tea in tins
15 lbs. of coffee
1 bag of green coffee
1 tin of cocoa
1 doz. tins of condensed milk
1 tin of tapioca
2 tins of Julienne soup
7 lbs. of maccaroni soup
11 lbs. of maccaroni
45 lbs. of rice
1 pot of extract of meat
1 bottle of ket soup
2 tins of condensed vegetables
4 tins of green peas
6 tins of French beans
6 tins of white beans
1 tin of arrowroot
11 lbs. of biscuits
13 lbs. of bacon
15 lbs. of ham
2 tins of ox-tongue
3 tins of preserved meat
1 bottle of Worcester sauce
1 bottle of pickles
18 small boxes of sardines
12 large boxes of sardines
2 bottles of olives
7 lbs. of dried apricots
10 lbs. of plums (in tins)
1 box of figs
1¹/₂ lb. of candied lemon-peel
2¹/₅ lbs. of Malaga raisins
1 lb. of sultana raisins
2¹/₂ lbs. of currents
1 bag of maize flour
2 casks of flour

48 lbs. of salt (in tins)
2 bottles of essences
1 packet of spice
1 tin of pepper
2 bottles of vinegar
3 bottles of salad-oil
1 bottle of mustard
1 bottle of French mustard
2 packets of gelatine
2 barrels of potatoes
1 Cheshire cheese
2 Dutch cheeses
11 lbs. of syrup
15 lbs. of loaf-sugar
15 lbs. of butter in ¹/₄ lb. tins
17 lbs. of butter in ¹/₂ lb. tins
20 packets of candles
1 bottle of lamp-oil
1 barrel of paraffin-oil
1 box of toilet-soap
4 bars of soap
1 tin of soda
1 packet of starch
Blacking and blacking-brushes
3 packets of paper
2 packets of matches
Wood and charcoal
Corkscrew
2 knives for opening tins
1 tin of knive-powder
Baking-powder
String and rope

Wine, etc.

60 bottles of Medoc at 2 fr. per bot.
36   -   - Medoc supérieur at 3 fr.

35 bottles of red Voslauer }
25   -   - white   - } at 2½ fr.
20   -   - beer
1 bottle of brandy   1 bottle of cognac

1 bottle of whiskey
1   -   - vermuth
A little champagne for festivals and the reception of guests.

A hanging-lamp, bought in the Muski for 20 fr., suspended over the saloon-table, and a pack of playing-cards were found very convenient.

The above stores, purchased for 28*l*., not only were amply sufficient, but 70s. worth was returned to the dealers at the end of the voyage. For no one should omit to make an arrangement entitling him to return unused stores (at a reduction of about 10% on the original price) and to have the agreement entered on the invoice.

Other stores, such as eggs, fresh beef, buffalo-meat, mutton, poultry, oranges, lemons, etc., are taken only in small supplies, it being easy to replenish the larder en route, either from the steamers or still better from the markets on the banks, where prices are moderate. The cook makes the purchases and submits his accounts.

Average prices. Fowl, 4-9 piastres, according to quality; fat turkey, 45-62; hen-turkey 22-36; pair of pigeons 4-8; sheep 128-350; 16 eggs, 5-8; rotl (about 15 oz.) of butter 9-13; rotl of beef, 5-8; rotl of mutton 4-5 piastres.

Various kinds of provisions, including some delicacies, are to be obtained from the bakkáls or small dealers of *Minyeh*, *Assiût*, *Keneh*, *Luxor*, *Esneh*, and *Assuân*.

Tobacco for chibouques may be obtained in the bazaars, also at Assiût, Keneh, and Esneh; the best mixture is ½ *Gebeli* and ½ *Kûráni*. The best Turkish tobacco (Stambûli) and cigarettes may be bought in Cairo from *Nestor Gianachis* and *E. Zalichi & Jaconomu* in the Muski, *Volterra Frères* at the post-office, and *Cortessi*, Ezkebîyeh, next the Café de la Bourse. Good cigars are also kept by Cortessi; those to be obtained en route are bad.

Medicine. Comp. Vol., I. pp. 15, 473. Some Antipyrine, 50 gr. of quinine, some laudanum, a supply of zinc or other eye-wash, rhubarb, etc. should not be forgotten.

Clothing and Equipment. Clothes such as are worn in autumn at home are the best for the Nile. Boots must be stout and water-tight. Slippers, bathing-shoes for the clayey Nile baths, both thick and thin stockings, flannel shirts, a broad-brimmed hat, a warm overcoat, and a substantial rug should not be forgotten. A sun-umbrella and kufiyeh, a silk handkerchief or muffler, blue or grey spectacles, and a leathern cushion stuffed with horse-hair will also be found useful. Saddles, which may be hired in Cairo, should be taken, especially if ladies are of the party, for the donkeys hired at the various points do not always have saddles. — Explorers should provide themselves with a long and strong ladder; as well as a magnesium lamp or magnesium-wire (to be obtained in Cairo). — Photographic apparatus should be brought from home, for chemicals are either not obtainable or very dear in Egypt, and good dry plates are scarcely to be obtained. The plate should not be more than 8 to 10 inches at the largest. The traveller should superintend the custom-house examination in person.

Fowling-pieces and ammunition (including Lefaucheux cartridges) may be bought in Cairo, but not higher up, where only coarse gun-powder can be obtained.

Letters. The letter-post, even in Upper Egypt, is both rapid and punctual. From Cairo to Thebes letters take three days, being forwarded to Assiût by rail and thence by steamer. Passengers going beyond Cairo should instruct| the porter of the hotel to forward letters to some fixed point. Cook's manager does this for Cook's tourists. The post goes on even beyond Assuân.

IV. Works on Egypt.

A good selection of books is one of the necessities of the traveller in Egypt. The steamer sometimes steams for an entire day without passing anything of special interest; and the dhahabîyeh-traveller, when his vessel is being slowly towed against an adverse wind, will gladly fall back upon reading when he is tired of walking along the bank with a gun on the chance of a shot. A considerable number of the chief books upon Egypt have been mentioned in Vol. l., pp. 201, 202; a few more are named here; while other special works are referred to in the descriptions of some of the principal monnments (e.g. pp. 83, 95, 244, 255, etc.). For authorities on the Western Oases see pp. 344, 348.

HISTORICAL, DESCRIPTIVE, AND SCIENTIFIC WORKS.

Bell, C. F. Moberley, From Pharaoh to Fellah; London, 1888.
Brugsch, H., Egypt under the Pharaohs, transl. from the German by P. Smith, 1874; condensed and revised ed., by M. Broderick, London, 1891.
Dor, V. E., L'instruction publique en Egypte; Paris, 1872.
Dümichen (J.) and Meyer, Geschichte des Alten Ægyptens; Berlin, 1877 (specially useful for the ancient geography).
Klunzinger, C. B, Upper Egypt; its people and products; London, 1877.
Lane, Account of the Manners and Customs of the modern Egyptians; new ed., London, 1872.
Lane-Poole, Stanley, Social Life in Egypt; London, 1884.
Mariette-Bey, The Monuments of Upper Egypt; transl. Alexandria, 1877.
Maspero, G., Egyptian Archæology, transl. by Amelia B. Edwards; London, 1887.
Sandwith, F. M., Egypt as a winter-resort; London, 1889.

TRAVELS IN EGYPT.

Du Camp, Maxime, Le Nil, Egypte, et Nubie; 4th ed., Paris 1877.
Edwards, Amelia B., A Thousand Miles up the Nile; London, 1877.
Edwards, Amelia B., Pharaohs, Fellahs, and Explorers; London, 1891.
Lepsius, R., Discoveries in Egypt, Ethiopia, and Sinai, transl. by K. R. H. Kennedy; London, 1852.
Loftie, W. J., A Ride in Egypt from Sioot to Luxor; London, 1879.
Oxley, W., Egypt and the Wonders of the Land of the Pharaohs, 1884.
Rhind, A. H., Thebes, its Tombs and their Tenants; London, 1862.
Rhoné, A., L'Egypte à petites journées; Paris, 1877.
Stuart, H. Villiers, Nile Gleanings; London, 1880.
Stuart, H. Villiers, Egypt after the War; London, 1883.
Taylor, Bayard, Life and Landscape from Egypt to the Negro Kingdoms of the White Nile, 2nd ed., London, 1855.
Warner, Chas. Dudley, My Winter on the Nile; new ed., London, 1881.
Classical scholars visiting Egypt should provide themselves with the 2nd book of *Herodotus*, the 17th book of *Strabo*, and the first book of *Diodorus Siculus*.
A very complete bibliography of Egypt will be found in *Prince Ibrahim-Hilny's* Literature of Egypt and the Soudan from the earliest times to the year 1885 inclusive; 2 vols. fol., London, 1886-87.

V. Chronological List of Rulers of Egypt to the end of the Ptolemaic period.

3892-2380.	The Primæval Monarchy.
Lepsius 3892. Mariette 5004. Wilkinson 2700.	I. DYNASTY *(Thinites)*. Mena, Greek (in Manetho) Menes. Teta. Atet, Gr. Athotis. Ata, Gr. Uenephes. Hesep-ti, Gr. Usaphaïdes. Mer-ba-pen, Gr. Miebidos. Sam-en-ptah, Gr. Semempses. Keb-hu, Gr. Bieneches.
L. 3639.	II. DYNASTY *(Thinites)*. But'au, Gr. Boethós. Kakau, Gr. Kaiechos. Bannutru, Gr. Binothris. Ut'nas, Gr. Tlas. Sent, Gr. Sethenes. Neferkara, Gr. Nephercheres. Sokar-nefer-ka, Gr. Sesochris. Hat'efa, Gr. Cheneres.
L. 3338.	III. DYNASTY *(Memphites)*. T'at'aï, Gr. Necherophes. Nebka. T'eser, Gr. Tosorthros. Teta. Set'es. T'eserteta, Gr. Tosertasis. Abtes, Gr. Aches. Neferkara. Nebkara. Huni.
L. 3124. W. 2450.	IV. DYNASTY *(Memphites)*. Snefru, Gr. Soris. Khufu, Gr. Cheops. Ratet-f. Khafra, Gr. Chephren. Menkaura, Gr. Mykerinos. Aseskaf.
L. 2840.	V. DYNASTY *(Elephantines*, according to Lepsius *Memphites)*. Userkaf, Gr. Usercheres. Sahurā, Gr. Sephres. {Kaka. {Neferarkara.

Aseskara.
{Neferkhara, Gr. Nephercheres.
{Akauhor.ᵛ
Ra-en-user An, Gr. Rathures.
Men-kau-hor, Gr. Mencheres.
Assa Tetkara, Gr. Tancheres.
Unas,· Gr. Onnos.

L. 2744. | VI. DYNASTY *(Memphites)*.
Teta, Gr. Othoes.
{Userkara.
{Atī.
{Pepi I., Gr. Phios.
{Merira. .
{Mentu-em-saf, Gr. Methusuphis.
{Merenra.
{Pepi II.
{Neferkara, Gr. Phiops.
Neitakrit, Gr. Nitocris (Queen).

VII. DYNASTY *(Memphites)*.

L. 2522. | VIII. DYNASTY *(Memphites)*.

IX. DYNASTY *(Heracleopolites)*.

X. DYNASTY *(Heracleopolites)*.

L. 2423. | XI. DYNASTY *(Diospolites, Thebans)*.
Antef.
Antef-sa — Ra-ha-hor-apu-ma.
Antef — Ra-tat-har-hi-ma.
Mentuhotep I. — Ra-neb-hotep.
Mentuhotep II. — Ra-neb-taui.
Mentuhotep III. — Ra-neb-kher.
Sankhkara.

2380-1276. | **The Middle Monarchy.**

L. 2380. | XII. DYNASTY *(Diospolites)*.
W. 20·0. | Amenemha I. — Ra-sehotep-ab.
Usertesen I. — Ra-kheper-ka.
Amenemha II. — Ra-nub-kau.
Usertesen II. — Ra-kha-kheper.
Usertesen III. — Ra-kha-kau.
Amenemha III. — Ra-en-mat.
Amenemha IV. — Ra-ma-kheru.
Sebek-neferu (Queen).

L. 2136. | XIII. DYNASTY *(Diospolites)*.
Rakhutaui.
Ameni.
Sebekhotep I. — Ra-sekhem-uat′-taui.

Ra-smenkh-ka.
Sebekhotep II. — Ra-sekhem-uat'-taui.
Neferhotep — Ra-kha-sekhem.
Sebekhotep III. — Ra-kha-nefer.
Sebekhotep IV. — Ra-kha-hotep.
Sebekhotep V. — Ra-kha-ankh.
Anāh — Ra-men-khau.
Sebekemsaf I. — Ra-sekhem-uat'-khau.
Sebekemsaf II. — Ra-sekhem-se-sheti-taui.
Rahotep — Ra-sekhem-uah-kha.

XIV. DYNASTY *(Khoïtes)*.

XV. DYNASTY *(Hyksos)*.

XVI. DYNASTY *(Hyksos)*.
Set-āa-peh-ti — Nubti.
Apepi I. — Ra-āa-user.
Apepi II. — Ra-āa-ab-taui.
Ra-ian.

L. 1684.

XVII. DYNASTY *(Diospolites)*.
Raskenen I. — Tau-āa.
Raskenen II. — Tau-āa-ken.
Kames — Ra-uat'-kheper.

L. 1591.
W. 1520.

XVIII. DYNASTY *(Diospolites)*.
Ahmes — Ra-neb-pehti.
Ahmes neferatri.
Amenhotep (Amenophis) I. — Ra-sar-ka. Queen:
 Aahhotep.
Tutmes I. — Ra-āa-kheper-ka.
Tutmes II. — Ra-āa-kheper-en.
Hatasu-Khnumt-amen — Ramaka (Queen).
Tutmes III. — Ra-men-kheper.
Amenhotep II. — Ra-āa-kheperu.
Tutmes IV.
Amenhotep III. — Ra-ma-neb. Queen: Tii.
Amenhotep IV. — Khu-en-aten.
Ra-ankh-kheperu.
Amen-tut-ankh — Ra-kheperu-neb.
Ai — Ra-ma-ar-kheperu.
Horemheb Amonmeri — Ra-sar-kheperu, sotep-en-Ra.

L. 1443.
W. 1340.

XIX. DYNASTY *(Diospolites)*.
Ramses I. — Ra-men-pehti.
Seti I. — Ra-ma-men. .
Ramses II. — Ra-userma-sotep-en-Ra.
Merenptah — Hotep-hi-ma.
Seti II. — Ra-user-kheperu.
Siptah — Khu-en-ra. Queen: Ta-usert.

1276-340.	**The New Empire.**

<table>
<tr><td>L. 1276.
W. 1200.</td><td colspan="2">XX. DYNASTY (Diospolites).
Set-nekht — Ra-user-khau.
Ramses III. hak-an — Ra-userma-meramen.
Ramses IV. to XIII.</td></tr>
<tr><td>L. 1091.
W. 1085.</td><td>XXI. DYNASTY (Tanites).
Si-Mentu, Gr. Smindes.
Pisebkhannu I.
Pisebkhannu II.</td><td>(Thebans.)
Herhor.
Piankhi.
Pinozem I.
Ramenkheper.
Pinozem II.</td></tr>
<tr><td>L. 961.
W. 990.</td><td colspan="2">XXII. DYNASTY (Bubastites).
Sheshenk I., the Sesonchis of the Greeks.
Osorkon I., Gr. Osorthon, the Zerah of the Bible.
Takelut I.
Osorkon II.
Sheshenk II.
Takelut II.
Sheshenk III.
Pimai.
Sheshenk IV.</td></tr>
<tr><td>L. 787.
W. 818.</td><td colspan="2">XXIII. DYNASTY (Tanites).
Osorkon III.
Piankhi, King of Ethiopia, conquers Egypt.</td></tr>
<tr><td>L. 729.</td><td colspan="2">XXIV. DYNASTY (Saïtes).
Bek-en-renf, Gr. Bocchoris.</td></tr>
<tr><td>L. 716.
M. 715.
W. 714.</td><td colspan="2">XXV. DYNASTY (Ethiopians).
Shabaka, Greek Sabacon, the Soa of the Bible.
Shabataka.
Tabarka, Gr. Tarkos, the Tirhakah of the Bible, Tar-ku-u of the Assyrian inscriptions.</td></tr>
<tr><td>664-525.
662-610.
610-594.
594-589.
589-564.
564-526.
526-525</td><td colspan="2">XXVI. DYNASTY (Saïtes).
Psammetikh (Psamtik) I.
Nekho, Egyptian Nekau.
Psammetikh II., Gr. Psammis, or Psammuthis.
Uahbra, Gr. Uaphris or Apries, the Hophrah of the Bible.
Aahmes II., Gr. Amasis.
Psammetikh III.</td></tr>
<tr><td>525-362.
525-521.
521-486.
486-465.
465-425.
425-405.
405-362.</td><td colspan="2">XXVII. DYNASTY (Persians).
Cambyses.
Darius I.
Xerxes I.
Artaxerxes I.
Darius II. Nothos.
Artaxerxes II. Mnemon.</td></tr>
</table>

527-399.	XXVIII. DYNASTY *(Saïtes)*. Amyrtæus, Egyptian Amen-rut. Khabash.
399-378.	XXIX. DYNASTY *(Mendesites)*. Nepherites I., Egypt. Naifâurut. Achoris, Egypt. Hakar-khnumma. Psammuthis, Egypt. Psimut.
378-340.	XXX. DYNASTY *(Sebennytes)*. Nektanebus I., Egypt. Nekht-hor-heb. Teos or Takho. Nektanebus II., Egypt. Nekht-nebf.
362-330.	XXXI. DYNASTY *(Persians)*.
362-340.	Artaxerxes III. Ochus.
337-330.	Darius III. Codomannus.
332-323.	ALEXANDER THE GREAT.
323-317.	Philippus Aridæus.
323-310.	Alexander II.
323-30 B.C.	**Period of the Ptolemies.**
323-286.	Ptolemy I. Soter, Son of Lagus (consort Berenice I.).
286-247.	Ptolemy II. Piladephus (consort Arsinöe).
247-222.	Ptolemy III. Euergetes (Berenice II.).
222-205.	Ptolemy IV. Philopator.
205-182.	Ptolemy V. Epiphanes (Cleopatra I.).
182.	Ptolemy VI. Eupator.
182-146.	Ptolemy VII. Philometor (Cleopatra II.).
171.	Ptolemy VIII.
171-117.	Ptolemy IX. Euergetes II., Physkon (Cleopatra II. and III.).
117-81.	Ptolemy X. Soter II., Lathyrus (Cleopatra IV. and Selene).
106-87.	Ptolemy XI. Alexander (Berenice III.).
81-80.	Ptolemy XII. Alexander II. (Berenice III.).
80-52.	Ptolomy XIII. Neos Dionysos, Auletes (Cleopatra V. Tryphæna).
52-47.	Ptolemy XIV. and
52-30.	Cleopatra VI. (mistress of Cæsar and Antony).
47-44.	Ptolemy XV.
44-30.	Ptolemy XVI. Cæsarion.
30.	OCTAVIANUS conquers Egypt and makes it a Roman province.

VI. Frequently recurring Names of Egyptian Kings.†

Selection by Prof. Ebers in Leipsic.

Mena. (Menes). 1.

Snefru 4.

Khufu (Cheops) 4.

Khafra (Chephren) 4.

Men-kaura (Mycerinus) 4.

Tat-ka-ra (Tancheres) 5.

Assa. 5.

Teta. 6.

Rameri. 6.

Pepi. 6.

Nefer-kara. 6.

Antef 11.

Amenemha I. 12.

Usertesen I. 12.

Amenemha II. 12.

Usertesen II. 12.

Usertesen III. 12.

Amenemha III. 12.

Amenemha IV. 12.

Sebek-hotep. 13.

Set Shalati. Hyksos. (Salatis).

Apepa. Hyksos. (Aphobis).

† The numbers placed after the names are those of the different dynasties.

NAMES OF KINGS.

xxxii

The life-dispensing favourite of (the god) Set.

Rasqe-nen.

Aahmes (Amosis). 18.

Amenhotep (Amenophis) I. 18.

Tutmes (Tuthmosis) I. 18.

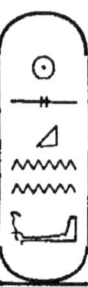  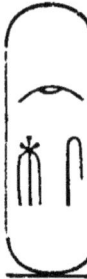 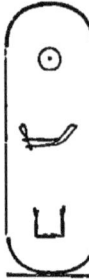 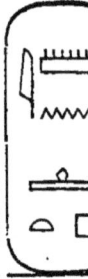  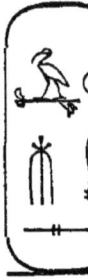

Hatasu. 18.

Tutmes III. 18.

Amenhotep II. 18.

Amenhotep III. 18.

  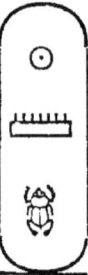 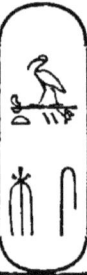  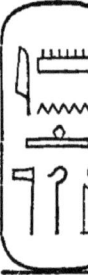  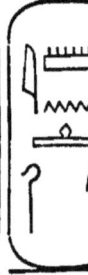

Amenhotep IV. (Khu-en-aten) 18.

Hor-em-heb (Horus) 18.

Ramses I. 19.

Seti I. (favourite of Ptah) 19.

    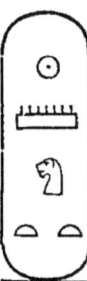  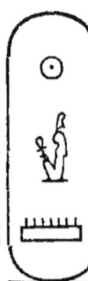  

Ramses II., favourite of Ammon, and his father Seti I., the Sesostris of the Greeks.

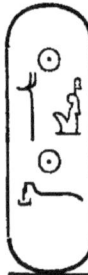   

Prince Khaemus.

Sesetsu (Sesostris.)

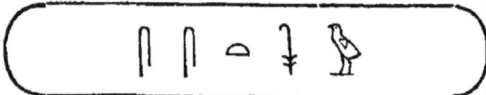

NAMES OF KINGS.

Merenptah I. (Menephthes). 19.

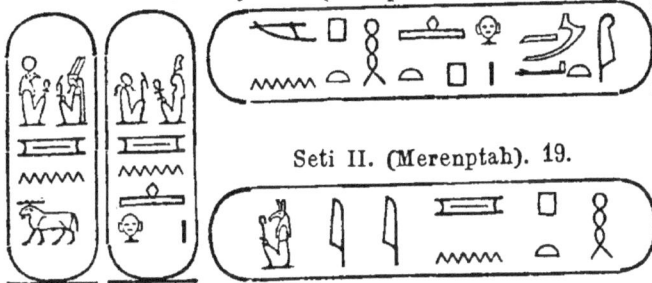

Ramses III. 20.

Seti II. (Merenptah). 19.

Ramses IV. 20. Ramses V. 20. Ramses VI. 20. Ramses VII. 20.

     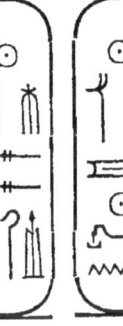  

Ramses VIII. 20. Ramses IX. (Leps. Ramses XI.) 20. Ramses X. (Leps. Ramses IX.) 20. Ramses XI. (Leps. Ramses XII.) 20.

   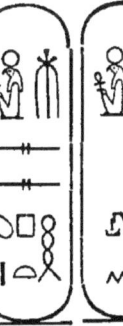    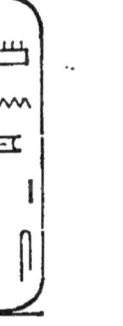

Ramses XII. (Leps. Ramses XIII.) 20.

Sheshenk (Sesonchis) I. 22.

Sheshenk IV. 23.

  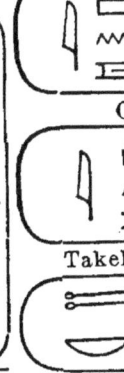 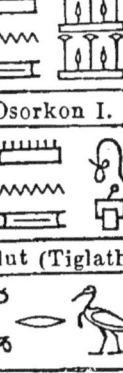

Osorkon I. 22.

Bokenranf (Bocchoris). 24.

Takelut (Tiglath) I. 22.

Shabak (Sabaco). 25.

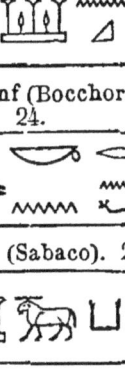 

Tabarka. 25.

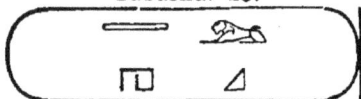

Queen Ameniritis.

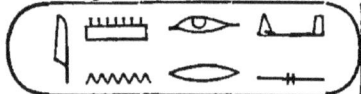

Piankhi.

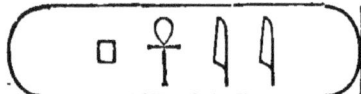

Psammetikh I. 26. Nekho 26. Psammetikh II. 26.

Uahphrahet (Uaphris. Hophrah). 26.

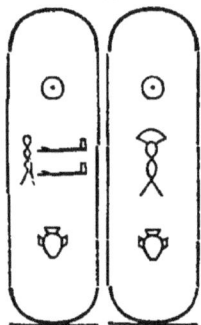

Aahmes II. (Amasis). 26.

Kambatet (Cambyses) 27.

Ntariush (Darius). 27.

Darius. 27.

Khesherish (Xerxes). 27.

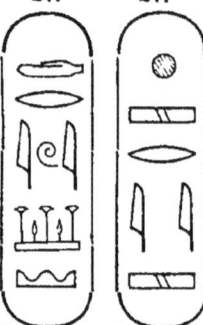

Amenrut (Amyrtæus). 28.

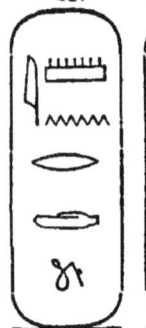

Nekht-nebf (Nectánebus). 30.

Alexauder I. 32.

Philippus Aridæus. 32.

Ptolmis (Ptolemy I. Soter). 33.

Ptolemy II. Philadelphus I. 33.

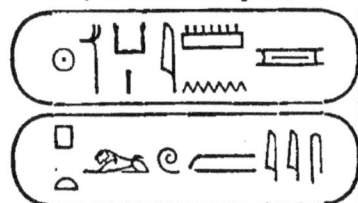

Queen Arsinoë. 33.

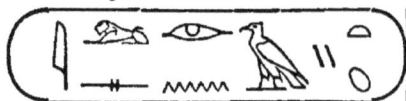

Ptolemy III. Euerge-
tes I. 33.

Queen
Berenice
II. 33.

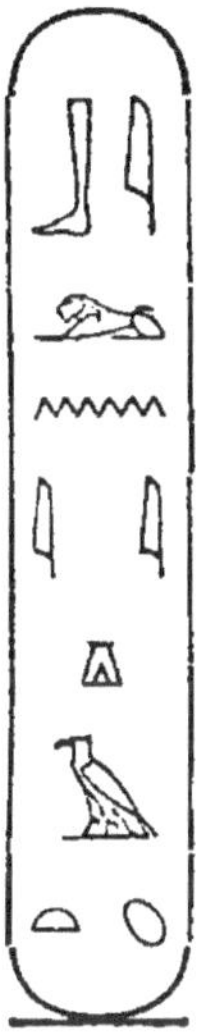

Ptolemy IV. Philopa-
tor I. 33.

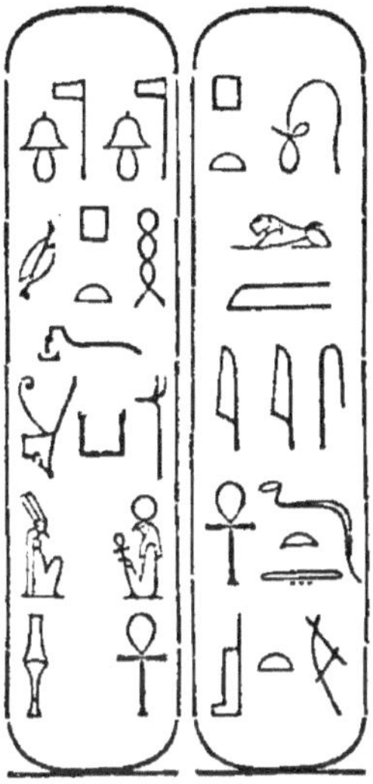

Ptolemy V. Epi-
phanes. 33.

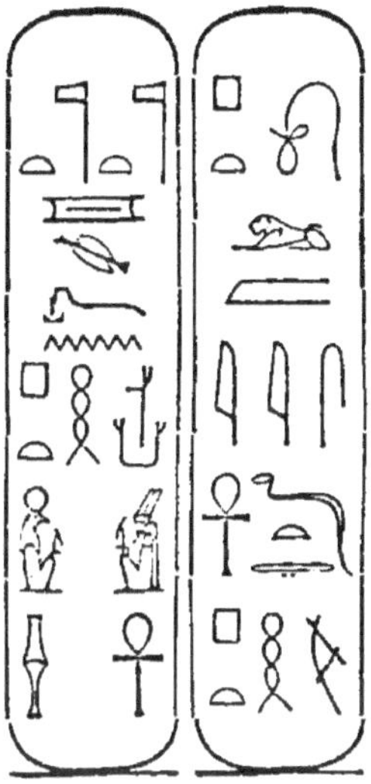

Ptolemy IX. Euerge-
tes II. (Physcon).
33.

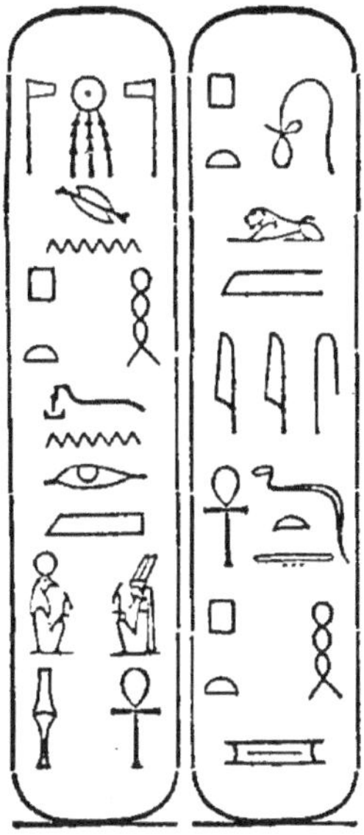

Seven Ptole-
maic prin-
cesses of
the name
of Cleo-
patra occur.

Ptolemy X. Soter II
or Philometor II.
usually known as La-
thyrus. 33.

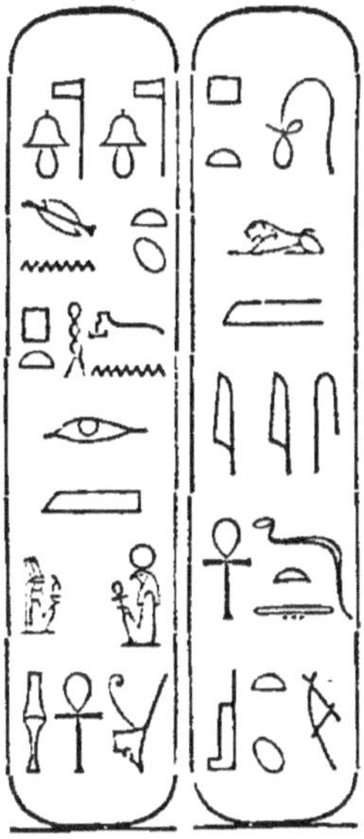

Cleopa-
tra VI.,
mistress
of Cæ-
sar and
Anto-
ny.
33.

Cleopatra VI., with Cæsarion, her son by Cæsar, and nominal co-regent. 33.

Autocrator (absolute monarch) and Kisaros (Cæsar). Epithets of all the emperors. 34.

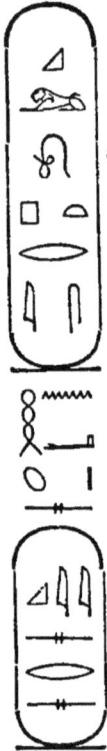

The famous Cleopatra and her son Cæsarion.

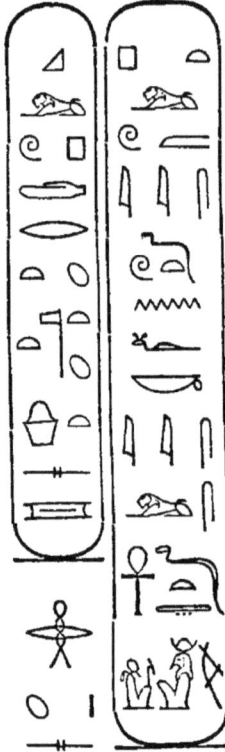

Cleopatra and her son Cæsarion, her co-regent.

 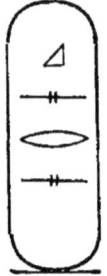

Cæsar Augustus 34.   Tiberius. 34.

Caius Caligula. 34.   Claudius. (Tiberius). 34.   Nero. 34.   Vespasian. 34.   Domitian. 34.   Trajan. 34.

 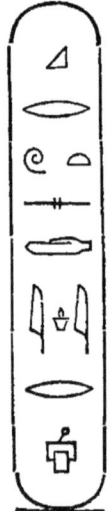    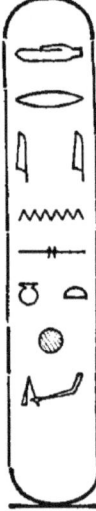

Hadrian. 34. Antoninus Pius. 34. Aurelius. 34. Commodus. 34. Severus. 34. Antoninus (Caracalla). 34. Geta. 34. Decius. 34.

VII. The Arabic Alphabet.

1.	Elif, Alef	ا		accompanies an initial vowel, and is not pronounced except as a hiatus in the middle of a word.
2.	Bâ	ب ﺒ	b	} as in English.
3.	Tâ	ت	t	
4.	Thâ	ث	th	as *th* in 'thing', but generally pronounced *t* or *s*.
5.	Gîm	ج	g / j	in Syria and Arabia like the French *j* (sometimes also like the English *j*), but pronounced *g* (hard) in Egypt
6.	Ḥâ	ح	ḥ	a peculiar guttural *h*, pronounced with emphasis at the back of the palate.
7.	Khâ	خ	kh	like *ch* in the Scotch word 'loch', or the harsh Swiss German *ch*.
8.	Dâl	د	d	as in English.
9.	Dhâl	ذ	dh	as *th* in 'the', but generally pronounced *d* or *z*.
10.	Rê	ر	r	like the French or German *r*.
11.	Zê, Zên	ز	z	
12.	Sîn	س ﺲ	s	} as in English
13.	Shîn	ش	sh	
14.	Ṣâd	ص	ṣ	emphasised *s*.
15.	Ḍâd	ض	ḍ	} both emphasised by pressing the tongue firmly against the palate.
16.	Ṭâ	ط	ṭ	
17.	Ẓâ	ظ	z̧	an emphatic *z*, now pronounced like No. 11 or No. 15.
18.	ʿÊn	ع ﻊ	ʿ	a strong and very peculiar guttural
19.	Ghên	غ ﻎ	gh	a guttural resembling a strong French or German *r*.
20.	Fê	ف	f	as in English
21.	Ḳâf	ق	ḳ	emphasised guttural *k*, replaced by the natives of Lower Egypt, and particularly by the Cairenes, by a kind of hiatus or repression of the voice.
22.	Kâf	ك	k	
23.	Lâm	ل	l	
24.	Mîm	م	m	
25.	Nûn	ن	n	} as in English.
26.	Hê	ه	h	
27.	Wau	و	w	
28.	Ye	ي	y	

1. From Cairo to Assiût.

Comp. Maps, pp. 2, 8.

a. By Railway.

229 M. The railway-station, *Bûlâk ed-Dakrûr*, which is also the start-ing-point of the direct line to Têh el-Bârûd and Alexandria, is situated on the W. bank of the Nile, 3 M. from Cairo (connection with main railway-station in prospect). Carriage from the hotel to the station 4 fr.; for heavy luggage a second carriage is necessary, as the baggage-waggons cannot be implicitly relied on. Passengers should be at the station early, as the processes of ticket-taking and luggage-weighing are by no means expeditious. The first-class carriages are, of course, the most comfortable from a European point of view, and first-class passengers are allowed to take with them in their compartment all their smaller articles of baggage and even trunks. The natives almost invariably travel second-class, and those who wish to make a nearer acquaintance with the country and the people should, perhaps, select a second-class compartment, in spite of its offering less resistance to the incursion of the yellow desert sand (comp. *Baedeker's Lower Egypt*, p. 371). — FARES to Assiût: 1st class 171.8 piastres (Turkish), 2nd class 114.5 pias., 3rd class 57¹/₂ pias. Payment at the station may be avoided by previously buying vouchers at the agencies of either Cook or Gaze, and exchanging them at the railway-station through the dragoman of the agency. The trains start (1891) at 8.30 a.m., 3 p.m. (for Wastah and intermediate stations), and 7 p.m. (Tues. & Frid. only). Those who wish to go on at once by steamboat from Assiût should take the morn-ing train on the preceding day (see Introduction, p. xvi; and comp. Cook's or Gaze's Tourists' Programme). The journey to Assiût takes nominally 10 hrs., but the trains are generally late. A time-table showing the names of stations in French and Arabic and giving distances in English miles is published by Penasson of Alexandria and may be bought at the ticket-offices. Trav-ellers should provide themselves with a supply of meat, bread, and wine, as no stoppage is made for dinner; eggs, bread, water (glass necessary) are offered for sale at the stations. Seats should at first be taken on the *right* side for the sake of the view of the Pyramids; from Minyeh onwards the left side is preferable, for the views of the Nile valley and Benihasan. — The railway follows the course of the Nile pretty closely, and a sufficient idea of the views from the carriage-windows may be obtained from the account of the dhahabîyeh voyage below. The following is a list of the rail-way-stations, nearly all of which are also steamer-stations. For descrip-tions, see the text. Stations: *Gîzeh, Hawamdîyeh;* 14 M. (¹/₂ hr. from Cairo) *Bedrashên* (p. 2); 51 M. (1³/₄ hr. from Bedrashên) *El-Wastah* (p. 4; halt of 6 min.), the junction of the line to the Fayûm (R. 2, p. 34); *Ashment* (to the right, in the distance, the pyramid of *El-Lahûn*); *Bûsh* (p. 5); 71 M. **Benisuéf** (p. 5; rail. stat. ³/₄ M. from the Nile); 84¹/₂ M. *Bibeh* (p. 6), the junction of a branch-line used for the transportation of sugar-cane; 93 M. *Feshn* (p. 6); 106 M. *Maghâghah* (p. 6); 117 M. *Abu Girgeh* (p. 6); *Maṭâyeh,* with a handsome bridge over a canal (left); 128 M. *Kolosaneh* (p. 7); 131 M. *Samallût* (p. 7); 148 M. **Minyeh** (p. 9); *Abu Kerkâs;* 173 M. *Rodah* (p. 18); 178 M. *Melawi el-'Arîsh* (p. 22); *Dêr Mauâs* (to the left or E., *Tanuf,* with the mound marking the site of *Tanis Superior,* not to be confused with Tanis in the Delta); 190 M. *Dêrût esh-Sherîf* (p. 28); *Beni-Korrah;* 210 M. **Monfalût** (p. 29); *Beni-Husên;* 229 M. Assiût (p. 31).

b. By the Nile.

252 M. Arrangements, see Introduction, p. xiii.

As soon as a favourable wind springs up (which, however, has sometimes to be waited for for hours), the dhahabîyeh is cast off and poled out into the middle of the channel. The sailors accompany the hoisting of the lateen sail with a lusty chorus, and if one of the brisk 'Etesia' blows, which Herodotus mentions as driving boats up the Nile, the long pointed craft flies quickly along, passing in rapid succession the Khedive's palace and the barracks of Kaṣr en-Nil, Kaṣr el-ʿAin, the island of Rôḍah with its palaces (on the E. bank), and the châteaux of Gezîreh and Gizeh (W. bank). Old Cairo lies on the E. bank, and beyond it rise the Moḳaṭṭam Mts., with the citadel and Ṣtabl ʿAntar, a ruined Arab fort on the S. end of one of their spurs; on the W. is the group of pyramids at Gizeh. To the left (E. bank) farther on, are the quarries and hamlets of Ṭurah and Maʿṣarah (see *Baedeker's Lower Egypt*, p. 403). Opposite, on the W. bank, rise the pyramids of Abuṣîr, Saḳḳârah, and Dahshûr. Near the bank, to the left, amidst a fine grove of palms, is a Coptic convent, and adjacent is a gun-factory, begun by Ismaʿil Pasha, but never finished.

The steamer remains for some hours at **Bedrashên** (rail. stat., p. 1), where asses are kept ready for a visit to Memphis, Saḳḳârah, etc. (comp. *Baedeker's Lower Egypt*, R. 4). Opposite, on the right bank of the Nile, lies Ḥelwân (ibid, p. 404), frequented as a watering-place. — On the bank at *Kafr el-ʿAyât* (W. bank; rail. stat.), where the steamer lays to for the night, are some ancient constructions which may have belonged to the *Canal of Menes*. The unimportant pyramids of *Lisht* lie to the right, while the singularly shaped pyramid of *Mêdûm* (the so-called 'False Pyramid') becomes more and more prominent.

Riḳḳah, on the W. bank, is the starting-point of the excursion to the *Pyramid* and *Mastabas of Mêdûm* (asses with poor saddles may be procured at the village; 2 fr. and bakshish).

The PYRAMID AND MASTABAS OF MÊDÛM, the oldest monuments in the world, deserve a visit, which may be accomplished from Riḳḳah in about 6 hrs. (railway travellers may perform it in about the same time from the el-Wasṭah station; comp. p. 1). Crossing the railway, we proceed on donkey-back in about 1¼ hr. to the pyramid, which rises close to the cultivated country on the soil of the desert, 1½ M. to the N. of the village of *Mêdûm*. This appears to be the oldest of the local names handed down to us, as it is met with on the mastabas of the early period of Snefru.

The **Pyramid of Mêdûm** is so different from all the other structures of the kind that it is called by the Arabs '*El-Haram el-Kaddâb*', or '*the false pyramid*'. From a large heap of rubbish which covers its base, the smooth and steep upper part of the structure rises in three different stages at an angle of 74° 10', and is still preserved to a height of 122 ft. The first section is 69 ft., and the second 20½ ft., while the third, now almost entirely destroyed, was once 32 ft. in height. The outer walls consist of admirably jointed and polished blocks of Moḳaṭṭam stone. The holes in one of the surfaces were made by Lepsius and Erbkam when they examined the pyramid, the construction of which afforded them an admirable clue to the principle upon which the others were built (Vol. I., p. 350). The Pyramid of Mêdûm was never completed; the heap of debris at its base consists of the material which once filled the angles of the different sections, so as to give the pyramid a smooth surface. The pyramid was pillaged as early as in the time of the 20th Dynasty. It was opened in 1881 by Maspero, who found a long corridor and a chamber without sarcophagus. Perhaps in this pyramid *Snefru*, the first king of the

THE NILE
from
ro to Feshn.including the Fayûm
and the
Pyramids.

1:1000000.

0   10   20   30
Kilometres.
0   5   10   15   20
English Miles.

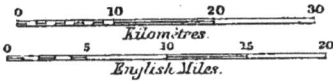

ames of Railway Stations are underlined.

HELIOPOLIS
Tannis
Shubrah
Kufir Embábeh
Abbásiyeh
Abu Roâsh
Bâlâk
Pyram.
ed-Dakrûr
Gizeh
CAIRO
Nasr
el-Afkah
G. Mokattam
Pyram. of
Gizeh
El Basâtin
Zâniyet el-Aryân
Pyr. Shubermen
Turrah
Pyram.
El Masarah
Abusir
Sulphur Baths
Bedroshen
Sakkârah
Pyr.
MEMPHIS
Helwân
Pyram.
Esh-Shôbak
Et-Tebén
Dahshûr
Megdûneh
Barnashi
Sherâfeh
Kafr Hannâid
kebir
Belideh
Gemâzeh
Bebbit
seghir
Tahmeh
Menshiyeh
Kafr el-Ayât
Kafr Lisht
el-Aruâz
Pyr. of Lisht
Wâdinê el Eshker
el-Mohârrakah
Gezireh
Menivet-el-Kaid
Gergiah
Gibibât
Dîmeh
er-Rodhâh
el-Kattâri
Sûlheveh
Tâmiyeh
Rikkah
Atfîh
Medinet Nimrûd
Bonka
Ruba'at
Pyr. Medûn
Gezîret el-K
Sennoris
Masarah
en-Nâsir
Senhûr
Tirseh
el-Atf
Abuksa
Gebelieh
Sirsino
el-Magtûb
Zûwieh
Beshuai
Fidimin
Nalsatiéh
el-Ahsâs
el-Wastah
Korman
Abu Gomsheh
Senru
Minshat
Seleh
Abu Rádi
Kerimât
Kasr Gebali
Telubin
Biharm
el-Elâm
Arbien
Masrat el Kati
Kôm Adrigeh
Agamieh
Medinet el Fayûm
Nawâmis
el-
Nezleh
ARSINOE
Tabhur
Demô
Nemûn
Mâr Antonio
Kasr el-Benât
Desiyeh
Bigig
Pyr. of Hauâra
Abusir
(Capt.Monast.
ûn
Atamneh
Sawâfineh
Illahan
G.
Ashment
Kefr Mograni
Madileh
Abusir
Abu Kandil
Rebiât
Behabsh
Saward
Shidmô
Zeribeh
Bûsh
Medinet Ma'di
Kalamseh
Sedement
Belefieh
enawiyeh
Medinet Garak
Talûn
Akhnâs
Medineh
Benisuêf
Bir Koresh
Talût
(HERAKLEOPOLIS)
Tizment
Barâd
Beraweh
Tensâh
el-Mutaniyeh
G. Gubêh
Nanah
Ghurâb
Deshâsheh
Kômbûsh
et-Tahâh
Dashût
el-Balankah
Senhûr
Tahalebisheh
Rayâd
Nezleh
el-Kubra
Nezleh
Dibeh
Sedô
Menkatin
el-Mesurah
el-Harabshén
el-Fôkah
Saft Rashin
Gemhûr
Feshn
G. et-Têr
in

4th Dyn., was buried, as in the neighbouring tombs persons related to him are interred.

The **Mastabas of Médûm**, which were opened by Mariette, lie to the N. of the pyramid. These were the tombs of the relations of Snefru (4th Dyn.), and in many respects resemble the mausolea of Sakkârah which bear the same name. The façades of the most important of them are partly uncovered. The street of tombs, which is now accessible, presents the appearance of a hill-side covered with masonry, incrusted with stucco, and provided with ante-chambers. The mouth of each tomb is towards the E.; the leaning external walls are generally of Nile bricks, richly embellished with the linear patterns which afterwards formed the favourite decorations of the sides of the sarcophagi (which were imitations of the tomb-façades). The vestibule is in most cases comparatively large, but the inner corridors are narrow, slope downwards, and are covered with representations in a remarkably simple and antiquated style. The archaic character of the scenes and of the hieroglyphics proves the great antiquity of these monuments. The influence of the hieratic canon is already traceable here, but it does not appear to have hampered the efforts of the artists as much as it did at a later age. The admirably preserved colours are also less conventional than those seen in later monuments.

The first open tomb which we reach from the S., was that of Prince (Erpa Ha) *Nefermât,* who lived in the reign of King ⌒ Teta. (There were 3 kings of this name, in the 1st, 3rd, and 6th Dynasty). On the left wall of the corridor leading to the tomb-chamber, we see the deceased in a sitting posture, and on the right wall he is represented standing, with his wife behind him. Adjacent are men and women presenting offerings, as in the mastabas of Ti and Ptahhotep. The flesh-tint of the men is red, and that of the women pale yellow, and this circumstance, especially in a monument of this early period, is important as tending to prove the Asiatic origin of the Egyptian nobles. The features of the persons represented are of the Caucasian, and not of the Ethiopian type. Among the villages belonging to Nefermât, which offered gifts, there appears on the left the name of the district of [hieroglyphs] *i.e.* '*Metun* of the cattle'. Metun is the oldest form of the name Médûm. From the neck of the ox, which represents the victim, flows a black stream of blood. On the right side we find among others a district named that 'of the white sow', which proves that pigs were reared in Egypt as early as the time of Snefru. The pig in this group is very true to nature [hieroglyphs]. In the name of the district *Hat en Sek,* or 'place of the ploughing', the most ancient form of the plough is used as a determinative symbol. The advanced condition of industrial pursuits, showing that the Egyptians already practised the art in which, according to Pliny, they afterwards excelled, is proved by the character of the dress worn by the women represented on the right side of the first passage, consisting of black and white cotton stuff, with pleasing patterns on the borders. He tells us that they were not in the habit of painting the materials for their dress, but of dipping them in certain fluids. They were coloured with boiling dyes, and came out impressed with a pattern. Although the boilers contained one colour only, it is said to have imparted several different tints to the stuffs dyed in them. — In·order to impart a durable colour to the larger figures represented here, an entirely unique process was employed. The outlines were engraved on the stone, while the surfaces enclosed by them were divided into deeply incised squares, which were filled with stucco of different colours, the flesh-tint of the men being red, that of the women yellow, and the colour of the robes being white, etc.

A little farther to the N. is the tomb of *Atet*, the wife of Nefermât. On the architrave over the doorway we see the husband of the deceased engaged in snaring birds, while a servant presents the spoil to the mistress of the house, whose complexion is of a brilliant yellow. On the outside wall, to the left, we observe the cattle of the deceased browsing on reeds. On the right stands Nefermât, who, as the inscription informs us, 'caused this monument to be erected to his gods in indestructible characters'. Among the domestic animals are several cattle of very bright colours. We also notice a gazelle held by the horns by a butcher, who is cutting off its head. Offerings of wine were also made at this early period. In the passage leading to the Serdâb is a group of labourers busily at work. The hunting-scenes are curious, and, notwithstanding their simplicity, remarkably true to nature. Among them is a greyhound seizing a gazelle by the leg, and another carrying a long-eared hare.

A few paces to the N.E. is another maṣṭaba built of well-hewn blocks of limestone. The hieroglyphics and low reliefs, resembling those in the tomb of Ti at Saḳḳârah, are admirably executed. The deceased interred here was named *Khent*, and his wife *Mara*. Traversing the vestibule and a narrow passage, we reach a tomb-chapel with a sacrificial table; in the passage, on the right, is a handsome male figure with a lasso, and on the left are stone-masons, engaged in making sarcophagi. On the left, in the innermost niche of this tomb, we perceive the deceased, and on the right, his wife. We next come to a ruined maṣṭaba, and to another tomb, half excavated, which was constructed for *Rahotep*, a son of Snefru, one of the highest civil and military dignitaries of the kingdom, and his wife *Nefert*, a relation of the royal family. The statues of this married couple, who died young, or at least are so represented, which are now among the principal treasures of the museum of Gîzeh, were found here. Farther to the W. are several other tombs, now covered up.

On the right bank, opposite Riḳḳah and about 1$^1/_2$ M. from the river, lies the hamlet of **Aṭfiḥ**, with some mounds of earth and debris representing the ancient *Aphroditopolis*, the territory of which, according to Strabo, adjoined that of Acanthus (Dahshûr), while its capital lay on the Arabian bank of the Nile. A town of Aphrodite must also be one of Hathor, the Egyptian goddess of love, to whom the white cow, which Strabo says was worshipped here, was sacred; it was the capital of *Matennu*, the 22nd nome of Upper Egypt. Its hieroglyphic name was *Tep ahe*, head of the cow.

In the Christian period (ca. 310 A.D.) Aphroditopolis gained some celebrity from *St. Anthony*, who fixed his hermitage in the mountains to the E. of the town, beside a well and a group of palms. So many pilgrims of every class, age, and sex sought out the holy man, that a regular posting route, with relays of camels, was laid out across the desert. St. Anthony, however, fled from his admirers and buried himself deeper in the mountains. But while he thus shook off his earthly visitants, he could not so easily escape those extraordinary tempters from spirit-land, at which Callot has taught us to smile, though to St. Anthony himself, as well as to St. Hilarion and other similarly persecuted anchorites, the contest was one of bitter earnest. The Coptic convent of Mâr Antonios (P. 5), a few leagues higher up, on the E. side of the Nile, still sends supplies to the convent of St. Anthony, situated in the heart of the Arabian Desert (P. 6).

After passing a few small islands, we now reach (W. bank) el-**Wastah** (pp. 1 and 36; post-office and Arab telegraph at the, rail. stat., $^1/_4$ M. from the Nile), where passengers bound for the Fayûm leave the dhahabîyeh and betake themselves to the train (see R. 2). El-Wastah is pleasantly situated in a grove of palms and is surrounded with fields of clover.

Visitors to the Fayûm may regain el-Wastah on the following day at 10.15 a.m. or at 4.16 p.m., by leaving Medinet el-Fayûm at 9 a.m. or 2.53 p.m. An extra day allows a visit to the Labyrinth and the Pyramid of Hawârah (p. 39). In this case the dhahabiyeh should not be sent on in advance, but should be ordered to await the traveller's return. — The pyramid and tombs of *Mêdûm* may also be visited from el-Wastah (see p. 2).

A small canal, beginning near the village of *Zâwiyeh* (W. bank), runs out of the Nile into the *Bahr Yûsuf* (p. 28).

Farther up, in the latitude of Áhnâs el-Medineh and Beniṣuêf, there seems to have been another deep channel connecting the [river with the Bahr Yûsuf. These four channels enclosed an inland which has been identified with the *Heracleopolitan Nome*, unanimously described by Greek authorities as an island. Strabo, who visited it on his way to the Fayûm, after leaving the nome of Aphroditopolis, calls it 'a large island', and relates that in the city of Heracleopolis the ichneumon was worshipped, the deadliest foe of the crocodile, held sacred in the neighbouring nome of Arsinoë; for, he tells us, it crawls down the throat of the sleeping monster and devours its entrails. The large mounds of debris at *Ahnâs el-Medineh*, the *Umm el-Kimâm* ('mother of rubbish-heaps') of the Arabs, have been identified with Heracleopolis; they lie 11 M. to the W. (inland) of Beniṣuêf. The old name of the town was *Khinensu*, from which *Ahnâs* is derived through the Coptic *Hnes*. The ram-horned god *Horshaf*, the prince of terrors, was also worshipped here. A few columns still stand, here, and other monuments may be buried under the debris. Systematic excavations are to be undertaken. At present Ahnâs need scarcely be visited except by those who approach the Fayûm from Beniṣuêf.

On the W. bank the mountains recede a little from the Nile, but on the E. bank their steep and lofty spurs frequently extend down to the bank in rising picturesque forms. None of the Nile-villages before Beniṣuêf need be mentioned. On the E. bank stands the Coptic convent of *Mâr Antonios* (see p. 4). About 2 M. inland (right) from *Zêtûn* (W. bank) lies the hamlet of *Bûsh* (rail. stat., p. 1), which is inhabited by Copts and thus has some interest for those who wish to study these direct descendants of the ancient Egyptians in a community of some size.

Beniṣuêf, on the W. bank, the first place in Upper Egypt (rail. stat., p. 1; stat., ³/₄ M. from the Nile), is a town of 10,000 inhab., pleasantly situated between the railway and the river. It contains a post and telegraph office and is the capital of a province of the same name, which contains 169 villages and about 220,000 inhabitants. To the left of the rail. station is the Mudîrîyeh, or residence of the mudir or governor. The houses or rather huts of this provincial capital are, however, constructed merely of Nile mud. The linen-manufacture for which this place was celebrated in the middle ages has greatly declined, but there are several sugar-plantations and a small bazaar. To the left of the railway is a fine grove of palms.

A road which was much frequented before the completion of the railway, leads from Beniṣuêf into the *Fayûm* (p. 34), and travellers with a tent and plenty of time might still hire camels, asses, or horses here and proceed to *Medinet el-Fayûm* viâ *el-Lahûn* ('gate' of the Fayûm'), where the Bahr Yûsuf enters the Fayûm, and *Hawârah*. By using the railway for the return-journey and giving up Birket el-Ḳurûn, this excursion can be made in 3-4 days.

Another road, traversing the *Wâdi Bayâd*, which opens near the village of *Bayâd*, on the E. bank of the Nile, opposite Beniṣuêf, leads through

the desert to the Convents of SS. Anthony and Paul, a few leagues
from the Red Sea.   The brotherhood of St. Anthony's Convent occupies
the highest rank among the religious societies of the Monophysite Con-
fession; and the Patriarch, or head of the Coptic community, must be
selected from their number. A visit to the convents, however, does not
compensate for the fatigue and trouble it involves.

As far as Minyeh the space between the E. bank and the hills
remains narrow, the limestone rocks frequently abutting on the river
in unbroken walls or rounded bluffs. Few villages are seen on this
bank, but the fertile alluvial tract on the W. side, 10-12 M. in width,
is thickly populated and carefully cultivated, exhibiting in profusion
all the cereals that grow on the Nile, date-palms, and sugar-cane.
The huge sugar plantations present a busy scene in November, when
the sweet juice is collected from the canes and conveyed to the
factories, which are a monopoly of the Khedive and follow each other
in rapid succession. These factories are connected by the railway,
and short branch-lines, used in harvest-time only, run from them
to the plantations lying farther to the W. Their lofty chimneys
impart a very modern-industrial appearance to the ancient land of
the Pharaohs. Large barges full of sugar-canes and others with
fellahin going to work in the factories are met on the river. Most
of the higher officials in the factories are Europeans. The juice is
expressed from the cane and then refined by being boiled twice in
closed vessels. In an average year about 25,000 tons of sugar are
produced in Egypt; in 1889 the value of the sugar exported
amounted to 509,000*l.*.

The boat passes two large islands. On the W. bank lie *Balankah*
and *Bîbeh* (rail. stat., p. 1), with large sugar-factories. The channel now contracts, and numerous islets are passed. *Feshn* (rail. stat.,
p. 1), on the W. bank, is 1½ M. from the river. Near the village
of *el-Hibeh*, on the E. bank, about 4 M. farther up, are the ruins of
the town of **Kheb** or *Khebi*, which belonged to the nome of Aphrodite (p. 5). These include well-preserved riparian structures of the
time of the Pharaohs and some massive walls made of bricks,
bearing two different stamps. One of these bears the name of the
local goddess, 'Isis of Kheb', and the prænomen of Tutmes IH. (18th
Dyn.); the other, discovered by H. Brugsch in 1853, reads 'The
high-priest of Ammon, Pishem the just, governor of the towns of
Urkhenu and Isem-kheb'.

On the E. bank rises the *Gebel Shêkh Embârak*. The steamer
stops at **Maghâghah**, a pleasant place on the W. bank, with acacias,
palms, and large sugar-works (post and telegraph office at the rail.
stat., p. 1). The Nile-channel is very wide here (several islands);
farther on both banks are flat. At *Abu Girgeh* (rail. stat., p. 1),
with sugar-factories, the railway runs close to the river.

About 12 M. to the E. of Abu Girgeh, on the *Bahr Yûsuf*, in the nome
of *Sep*, lies the town of **Behnesah**, on the site of the ancient *Oxyrrhynchus*
(Demotic; profane name *Pe-mzat*, Coptic Ⲡⲉⲙ̄ϫⲉ, Greek Πέμπτη), now
represented only by a few desolate heaps of debris. The fish *Oxyrrhyn-*

chus, a species of Mormyrus (Arab. Mizdeh), was held in such high honour here, that the inhabitants refused to eat any fish caught by a hook, lest the hook might previously have injured an Oxyrrhynchus. In the neighbouring town of Cynopolis (see below) the dog was held in equal honour, and Plutarch relates how a 'very pretty quarrel', the settlement of which required the intervention of the Romans, arose between the two towns, owing to the facts that the citizens of each had killed and dined on the sacred animals of the other. Juvenal gives an account of a similar strife between Ombos and Tentyra (p. 207). On the introduction of Christianity Oxyrrhynchus became so "full of convents that monkish songs were heard in every quarter". Convent jostles convent all round, forming as it were a second town of monks. In the 5th cent. the diocese of Oxyrrhynchus is said to have contained 10,000 monks and 12,000 nuns. In the town itself were 12 churches. Under the Arabs it is known only as Behnesah. In the Mameluke period it was still of some importance, but it has since steadily declined. From Behnesah the desert-route leads to the 'small oasis' of *Baḥriyeh*, also known as the *Oasis of Behnesah* (comp. p. 343).

About 4 M. above Abu Girgeh, close to the E. bank of the Nile, are the insignificant remains of **Shêkh el-Fadhl**, near which is *Hamathah*. Father Sicard's discovery of a large number of dog-mummies here proves that we are standing on the site of the necropolis of *Cynopolis* (Κυνῶν πόλις), the 'city of the dogs', which, as the above story indicates, must have adjoined Oxyrrhynchus. Strabo's words are: 'Next come the Cynopolitan nome and Cynopolis, where Anubis is worshipped and dogs are held sacred and fed with consecrated meat'. Several trough-like hollows and clefts have been found here, some of which, in the rocks, are of considerable size; but no inscriptions have been discovered. Cynopolis itself, according to Ptolemy, lay on an island in the Nile, but no traces of it are now visible. Opposite, $1^1/_4$ M. from the W. bank, lies the village of *el-Kês*.

Kolosaneh (rail. stat., p. 1), on the W. bank, has a large palm-grove. Opposite (E. bank) lies *Surarîyeh*. To the N. and S. quarries are worked in the limestone rock. — Among the rocks here is a small temple (not very easily found), bearing the names of Seti II. and of Merenptah Hotepher-ma, supposed to be the Pharaoh of the Exodus (19th Dyn.). The kings are offering sacrifices to the triad of Sebek, Hathor, and Horus, and representations of Sebek (with the head of a crocodile), Hathor, and Ramses III. may be made out on the external wall of the grotto, facing the spectator. The inscriptions are very indistinct but are couched in the usual form of thanksgiving to the gods for the blessing of a long reign.

On the W. bank lies **Samallût**, with a handsome railway-station (p. 1), sugar-factories, palms, and fields of clover. A little farther to the S., on the E. bank, rise the steep rocky sides of the **Gebel eṭ-Ṭêr** ('bird-mountain'), with an extensive flat top bearing the Coptic convent of **el-Bukêr**.† Those who wish to visit the mountain should disembark just before reaching it and ascend on the N.

† Now generally called *Dêr el-Bukrah*, from a windlass (bukrah) used in drawing water. But the name is probably derived from the old legend of the Bukir bird.

side. The excursion, which has no great interest except for the fine
view of the Nile valley, takes 1½-2 hrs. Other convents of a similar
kind (see, *e.g.*, p. 51) can be reached more easily. The convent,
also named *Dêr Sitteh Maryam el-ʿAdhrah* or convent of Lady Mary
the Virgin, consists of a group of miserable huts, occupied not only
by the monks but by laymen with their wives and children, and
looks like a fortified village. Most of the monks employ themselves
in making shoes. The underground chapel in which service is held
is uninteresting. The institution is very old, and curious tales are
told of it by Makrizi, Kazwini, Suyuti, and other Arabic writers.

'This convent', says Makrizi, 'is ancient, overlooks the Nile, and is
reached by a staircase hewn in the hill; it lies opposite Samlut'. Then,
following el-Shâboshti, he narrates how it is visited by pilgrims from all
quarters and lies on the 'hill of the caverns'. 'At one point of the hill',
he continues, 'is a narrow fissure, and on the saint's day of the convent
all the bukir-birds† in the neighbourhood come flying to this fissure,
flocking together in a huge crowd and making a tremendous din. One
after the other in constant succession thrusts its head into the cleft, and
utters a scream, until one comes whose head sticks fast and connot be
withdrawn. The victim then beats its wings against the rocks until it
dies, after which all the other birds depart and leave the rock in solitude
and silence. 'This', adds the writer, 'is now a thing of the past'. Similar
legends are found in antiquity. The Pharaohs, on ascending the throne,
let birds loose to bear the tidings to the four quarters of the globe. Herodotus and Ælian tell of feathered ambassadors dispatched in this way from
Egypt, and to this category apparently belongs the myth of the birds of
Memnon, which on certain days visited the grave of the Son of the Dawn,
who fell before Troy, cleansed it with their beaks, and besprinkled it with
water by dipping their feathers in the stream. Though this legend may
have originated in Asia, it was afterwards, like Memnon himself (p. 154),
transplanted to the Nile.

The Wâdi et-Têr (E. bank) leads from the Gebel eṭ-Têr to the S.E.
About 1½ M. to the S. of its mouth is the village of *Ṭehneh el-Ṭahûnah*
('Tehneh of the mill'). Before reaching it we pass the ancient *Hitân el-*
ʿagûs, or 'walls of the old woman', probably erected as a barrier to the
desert-hurricanes. At Ṭehneh, which is about ¾ M. from the Nile, are two
groups of tombs, that to the N. belonging to the latest period at which rock-
tombs were constructed on the Nile, while that to the S. belongs to the
early epoch of the ancient kingdom. The necropolis to which these tombs
belonged is supposed to be that of the town of *Akoris*, mentioned by Ptolemy alone and belonging to the nome of Cynopolis. Mounds mark the
site of the ancient town. Beyond rise the rocks, containing tombs of the
time of the Ptolemies and several short Greek inscriptions. One sepulchral chapel, containing some singular representations of a late date, is
interesting. The colours on the ceiling have faded, but the paintings on
the walls are still distinguishable. In front, on the left wall, stands the
deceased, in Roman costume; opposite, on the right wall, he appears again,
offering a sacrifice, as a sign that though in the Roman service or at least
of Roman tastes he yet reveres the gods of his ancestors. The representations of these deities occur on all four walls of the chamber and are
so numerous that they must include the local divinities, not only of Akoris,
but also of all the other places in the nome, of which the deceased, whose
name is not decipherable, may have been nomarch. The only inscriptions
extant are on the inner side of the door. Higher up on the rock-walls are
two horses in the Roman style, held by men. Between the two were other
sculptures, the subjects of which are no longer recognisable. The first-

---

† This bird is described by Suyuti as black and white, with a black
neck, ringed near the head, black wing-feathers, and the ability to swim.

mentioned figures have been supposed to be Castor and Pollux, or two
Roman emperors, but they rather resemble horses brought as tribute, like
the groups in the pediment of the Stele of Piankhi. Farther to the S.
is a colossal image, carved out of the rock, of Ramses III. sacrificing to
the god Sebek. The inscriptions in the very ancient group of tombs to
the S. are in such bad preservation that their date can only be guessed
at from their general style.

Minyeh (*Minyet-ibn-Khasîb;* rail. stat., p. 1), on the W. bank,
a well-built and handsome town with 15,900 inhab., is the seat of
the mudir of a district containing 281 villages and 315,000 inhabitants. There is a telegraph-office at the railway-station, and adjacent is the post-office, the director of which speaks Italian. At the
hospital is a physician who has studied in Europe. The town possesses two hotels and a large and curiously painted Arab café, in
which ghawâzi sing in the evening. Parts of the street running
along the river are planted with trees, and in the stream many
steamers and dhahabîyehs lie at anchor. The bazaars and the
Greek bakkals' (small dealers) possess large stocks of goods. In the
Bazaar street is an Austrian watchmaker and clothier, and among
the houses on the river is an Italian tailor. The palace of the mudir
is a plain and lightly-built structure. The large sugar-factory is
the oldest in Egypt, and a visit to it during the sugar-harvest is of
great interest; most of the officials are French and very obliging.
Market-day in Minyeh presents a very gay and characteristic picture
of Oriental life. There are no public buildings or monuments of
any interest, but the houses of the richer merchant, in spite of their
plain exterior, are often fitted up with great comfort. A glance
into one of their courts will show what a rich and varied life exists
in the interior of houses which from the outside look like miserable huts.

It is uncertain what place of the Pharaohs' time Minyeh represents;
but the assertion of Leo Africanus that it was founded by the Arabs may
well be doubted. Among the facts which render it improbable are the
old masonry on the river (towards the S.), the ancient architectural fragments immured in one of the mosques, a Coptic inscription, and the very
name of the town, which is derived, not from the Arabic, but from the
old-Egyptian dialect. Its Coptic name is ⲙⲟⲟⲛⲏ (*Moone*) and this, as
Brugsch has demonstrated, is derived from the old-Egyptian *Mena-t.* This
name, however (in full *Mena-t Khufu,* 'nurse of Cheops'), belonged to a
place which lay nearly opposite to the present Minyeh, on a site still
marked by a few remains. At a later date Mena-t was probably transferred, under the name of Minyeh, from the right bank of the Nile to the
left, where, presumably, some of the inhabitants had previously settled.
To this day the inhabitants of Minyeh maintain a close connection with
the E. bank of the Nile, conveying their dead for burial to *Zâwiyeh,* surnamed *el-Métin* (*i.e.* 'of the dead'), 5 M. to the S.

EXCURSION TO BENIHASAN, 15 M. (see p. 12). After making enquiries
as to the security of the route, the traveller hires an ass, ferries to the
right bank of the Nile, and ascends the river viâ *Zâwiyet el-Métin* (P. 10)
and *Kôm el-Ahmar* (p. 10). Instead of returning to Minyeh, he should
continue to follow the right bank of the Nile to the (10½ M.) *Ruins of
Antinoë,* now *Shêkh 'Abâdeh* (p. 19) and cross the river thence to *Rôdah*
(P. 18). This is a long but interesting day's journey. Accommodation
at Rôdah may be obtained on application at the railway-station (p. 1).

Opposite Minyeh, on the E. bank, lies *Kôm el-Kafarah,* where some ancient tombs, ·perhaps belonging to the 12th or 13th Dynasty, have lately been discovered.

Zâwiyet el-Mêtin and **Kôm el-Aḥmar** ('the red rubbish-mound'), situated on the E. bank, 5-6 M. above Minyeh, may be visited together. We first reach the village of *Zâwiyeh,* near which are the estate and beautiful garden of the venerable Abu Sultan Pasha. Between the village and Kôm el-Aḥmar, about 1/2 M. from the latter, lies the fine cemetery of the citizens of Minyeh (p. 9), with its numerous domed tombs and chapels. Thrice yearly, in the months of Regeb, Shawwâl, and Dhilḥiggeh †, at the time of full moon, funereal festivals, lasting several days, are celebrated here. Among the ceremonies observed are the offering of dates to the dead, which recalls the funereal offerings of the ancient Egyptians, and the presentation of palm-branches, recalling the Oriental symbolism of early Christianity, still familiar in our churches. A few minutes' walk towards the S. brings us to the red mound of pottery and rubbish known as *Kôm el-Aḥmar,* which runs parallel with the Nile. Climbing over this we reach the burial-vaults of the primæval monarchy, which are situated among the Arabian hills, with their gates towards the river.

The tombs are unfortunately in bad preservation, and some of them have been destroyed by violence, the stones being removed for use in building. It is uncertain of what town this was the necropolis, but it undoubtedly belonged to the 16th nome of Upper Egypt, named *Mah* or *Mahet* (gazelle), in which the gazelle was held sacred. In this nome also lay the towns of Heben and Nefrus, the chief deity of which was represented as a sparrow-hawk standing on a gazelle, accompanied by Hathor, Horus, and Khnum. Some of the tombs are still open to visitors. The lower ones are small and dilapidated, including one that was richly adorned with statues. Similar figures, hewn in the living rock, are still distinguishable on the façade and in the rear of the chapel. Farther up is the tomb of *Nefersekhru,* royal secretary and superintendent of the storehouses of Upper and Lower Egypt, which still contains some good sculptures. This tomb, in the rear of which are three niches, appears to have been constructed under the 18th Dynasty. Among its contents are sacrificial lists and scenes like those in the vaults of ʿAbd el-Kurnah: Osiris under a canopy; corpse crossing the Nile, accompanied by female mourners; the deceased in the midst of his family. The tomb of *Khunes,* a relative of the Pharaohs, situated farther to the S. and lower down, is of earlier origin and in all probability belongs to the ancient kingdom. The scenes of agriculture and navigation in this tomb, reproduced by Lepsius, are now scarcely ʲvisible. From the upper tombs we obtain a splendidly varied view of the Nile, its fertile valley and the town of Minyeh, with the red mounds of debris in the foreground, while to the N. stretches the sandy desert, from which the domed tombs of Zâwiyet el-Mêtîn rise like a group of tents. On the mound of Kôm el-Aḥmar lies a colossal figure, 70 ft. long, without an inscription.

Benihasan and **Speos Artemidos,** 15 M. from Minyeh and 162 M. from Cairo, an important steamboat-station.

---

† These months cannot be reproduced by the names of our months, as they pass through all the seasons of the solar year. Thus a festival which is celebrated this year in summer will take place 15 years hence in winter.

The 'three weeks' steamer halts here 3-4 hrs., while the 'four weeks' steamer remains overnight and leaves the entire forenoon for a visit to Speos Artemidos and Benihasan. The excursion begins at Speos Artemidos, which lies to the S. (1/2 hr. on donkey-back), whence we proceed towards the N. to (1/2 hr.) the foot of the tombs of Benihasan. We then walk to (10 min.) the S. graves and descend to Nos. 2 (Khnum-hotep) and 1 (Ameni-Amenemha) of the N. tombs, where the asses are in waiting to take us back to the steamer (3/4 hr.). Travellers ascending the river in a dhahabîyeh should land at Benihasan, ride to Speos Artemidos, and send the dhahabîyeh on to meet them near the village of *Benihasan el-Ahmar*. Those descending the stream save a little time by landing at a point somewhat nearer the tombs of Benihasan, almost opposite Benihasan el-Kadim (P. 12).

Speos Artemidos ('grotto of Artemis'), known to the Arabs as *Stabl 'Antar* ('stable of Antar'; comp. p. 33), is reached from the steamboat-landing, where asses are in waiting, in 1/2 hr. The route crosses fields and sand, finally ascending considerably. On the way carefully rolled cat-mummies are offered for sale, which have retained the unmistakeable odour of cats for thousands of years. The cat was sacred to the goddess Pasht ⟨ ⟩, whom the Greeks identified with Artemis. The *Temple* of this goddess, hewn in the rock, consists of a vestibule and of an inner chamber connected with the vestibule by a corridor. Above the door of the vestibule is a long inscription of the time of the 18th Dynasty, which celebrates the goddess Pasht and also speaks, under the name of Amu, of the Hyksos in Avaris who from ignorance of the god Ra destroyed the ancient temples.

The temple itself was founded by Tutmes III. and renewed by Seti I. Of the 8 pillars which supported the vestibule all have been destroyed except two in the front row, which bear inscriptions and royal cartouches on their W. and E. sides only. On the W. side of the recumbent pillar to the right Champollion saw the name of Tutmes III. ⟨ ⟩. All the other cartouches are those of Seti I., who is described as the favourite of the goddess *Pasht*, the mistress of ⟨ ⟩ *Matennu* or the dweller in the mountain ⟨ ⟩ *Ánt*. On the rear-wall of the vestibule are some interesting representations. To the left is Pasht in the guise of a mighty sorceress, stretching out her left hand to king Seti I., behind whom, sitting in an attitude of benediction, is the god Ammon-Ra. To the extreme left is the small figure of the god Thoth, lord of Hermopolis. Appropriate inscriptions are also furnished. To the right, in three rows, are the deities of Speos Artemidos (12 figures), beginning with *Mentu* and *Tum*, in front of whom is *Thoth*, who conveys to the local gods the command of Ammon-Ra that Seti I. shall be raised to the throne of Horus. In the doorway to the next chamber are a long inscription and a representation of the king offering a cynocephalus. In the rear-wall is a niche (naos) with the cartouche of Seti I.

To the W. of the Speos Artemidos is a second grotto (perhaps merely a cat's tomb), on the outside of which are the interesting cartouches of *Alexander II.*, son of Roxana, and six scenes representing the king in the company of the gods.

The dragomans now hurry on to ($^1/_2$ hr.) Benihasan, where we ascend to the S. tombs. These, however, have been almost entirely destroyed, and the only one of any interest is No. 7, the tomb of *Kheti*, which contains hunting-scenes and fine clustered columns. Passing on we soon reach (8 min.) the highly interesting N. tombs of *Ameni* (No. 1) and *Khnum-hotep* (No. 2); comp. pp. 14-18.

The necropolis of **Benihasan** is one of the most interesting in all Egypt, not only on account of the remarkable architectural features of the 12th Dyn. seen here, but also for the manifold representations of scenes from the domestic life of the Egyptians at that early era.

The journey from the Nile to the tombs takes from $^3/_4$ hr. to $1^1/_4$ hr. according to the height of the water and the landing-place selected. Asses, with good saddles, 1-1$^1/_2$ fr. Candles, and if possible magnesium wire, should be taken to light the tombs. The route leads towards the bare limestone hills, at first through groves of palms and then across sand. The ancient *Benihasan* †, *Benihasan el-Kadim* ('the old'), now deserted, lies to the right; the modern village is to the S. of the usual landing-place. On reaching the limestone hills we see the remains of a dilapidated path, supported by masonry, and ascend over debris to the horizontal hill-path, to the W. of which stretch the tombs.

Before the traveller enters the tombs to inspect the representations within, he should examine the columns at the entrance. At first sight everyone will set these columns down as unmistakeable examples of the Doric order; but the indisputable testimony of the inscriptions informs us that they date, not from the Ptolemaic period, but from the invasion of the Hyksos, in the 12th Dyn., between B.C. 2000 and B.C. 3000.

Champollion named them *Proto-Doric* or *Pre-Doric Columns.* Since him many authorities, with these columns as their starting-point, have tried to establish the kinship of the early Greek order with the architecture of Egypt and to prove that the former was derived from the latter. These views, however, aroused keen op-

---

† The place was deserted 30 or 40 years before the visit of the French Expedition, because the inhabitants wished a wider space for cultivation near their village, which they accordingly rebuilt farther to the S. The story that the villagers were expelled by Ibrahim Pasha and exterminated for robbery is a fabrication, although it is true that many of them were executed for this crime.

position, partly because they overshot the mark, and partly because they ignorantly confounded forms peculiar to these rock-tombs with those represented in the entirely independent field of architecture above ground. The connoisseurs and students of Greek art, blinded by their love for the object of their study, refused to allow that a single feature of Hellenic architecture had arisen anywhere but on

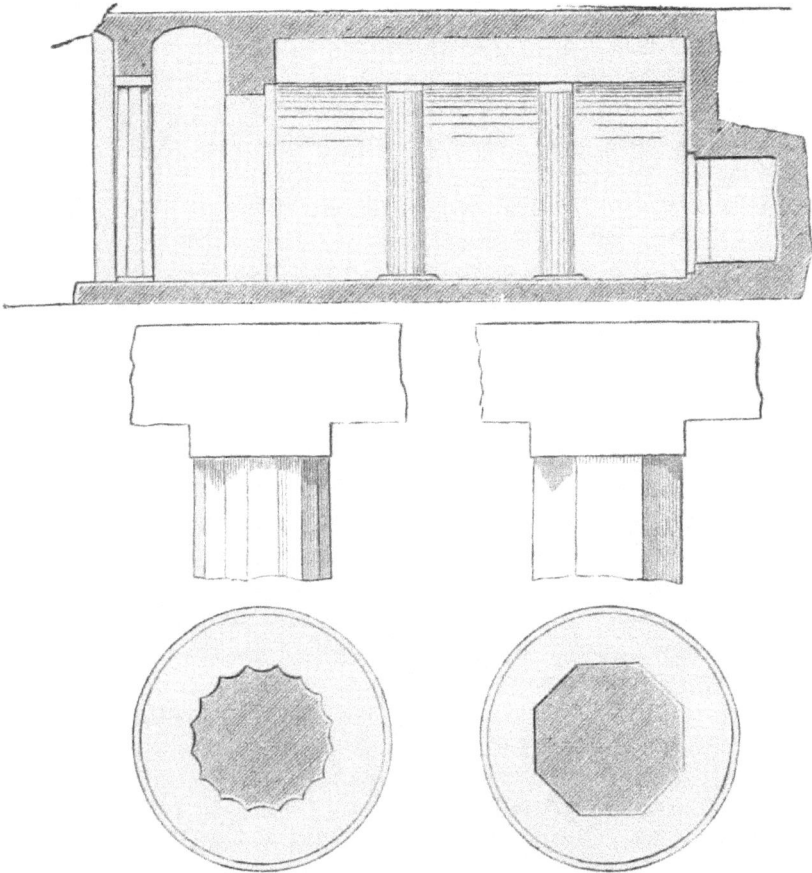

Section of Tomb and Columns of Benihasan.

Grecian soil, and stigmatised Egyptian architecture as 'barbaric' without taking the trouble to investigate its claims. Finally, however, Lepsius, equally at home in both fields, stepped into the fray and his second masterly essay may be taken as the last word on the subject. He shows that the development culminating in the polygonal fluted columns of Benihasan can be traced step by step in the cavern-structures of the Egyptians of the ancient kingdom, and he also shows that, though the Doric Column of the Greeks is known to us only in its fully developed form, some inexplicable features in the Doric order are not only justified, but even necessary

in its Egyptian counterpart†. The columns of Beniḥasan consist,
like the Doric column, of a basis, an octagonal or sixteen-sided
shaft with 16 or 20 flutes, a capital, and an abacus. The echinus
or chymatium is, however, wanting. While the swelling or entasis
on some Doric columns, and also the annuli or rings at the top of
the shaft, have hitherto met with no sufficient explanation, the
same features appear as natural and necessary parts of the so-called
'plant column' of Egypt. The architects of the Nile aimed consciously
at a reproduction of the stem of a plant, and as the capitals repro-
sented a bunch of buds it was natural that the cords which fastened
them should not be absent. Their number is five; and the 3 or
5 annuli at the top of a Doric column, erroneously explained as incisions made for the ropes used in hoisting it to its place, are
simply an inheritance from the Egyptian column. The idea of the
annuli, as of the entire Doric column, is of Egyptian origin, though
the perfect Greek column, with the beautiful transition-member
formed by the echinus, is far from a mere imitation. 'The Greek
column has become an entirely new form, animated by a new principle proper to itself, which has thoroughly mastered the hetero-
geneous elements from without and blended them in a new unity.'
In farther emphasis of the importance of these columns in the history of art, we may remind the reader that the earliest Doric columns known to us date from about the time that the *Psamtikidae*
(p. xxix) were not only allowing the Greeks to enter the valley of
the Nile but were inviting them to settle there, and that the columns of Beniḥasan are 1500 years older than this. The columns of
Beniḥasan are indeed nothing more than the pillars in the Temple
of the Sphinx and the Maṣṭaba (*Baedeker's Lower Egypt*, pp. 365,
379) provided with flutes and chamfered edges.

The two tombs of chief interest, the farthest to the N., are easily
recognised by the beautiful polygonal columns at their entrances.
The donkey-drivers make directly for them, paying no attention to
the others. The numbering begins at the N. end.

Tomb 1. The exterior of the pronaos or vestibule is distinguished by two fine octagonal columns, bearing a flat vault hewn
out of the rock. Four sixteen-edged columns, with narrow fluting,
stand in the interior of the tomb-chamber and appear to bear the
three beautifully painted arches of the ceiling, which are hewn in
the form of shallow barrel vaulting. The side-columns touch the
right and left walls of the nearly square chamber, in the rear of
which opens a recess containing the statues (much dilapidated) of
the deceased and his two wives. The usual long shaft leading to
the bottom of the tomb and the chamber for the corpse at the end
of it are also present. This is the tomb of *Amenemha* or *Ameni*,

† Some details on this matter will be found in the section devoted
to Egyptian art in the first volume of this Handbook (p. 160).

the son of the Lady Hannu, who was one of the chief dignitaries
of the kingdom, bore the title of an *erpa ha* or prince, governed
the nome of Maḥ in time of peace, and commanded a division of
the army in war. To the left and right of the entrance he is depicted on a throne with lions' feet, holding his commander's baton in
his hand. Inside the door are two well-preserved inscriptions,
cut in the stone. That to the right (S.) informs us that Amenemha
departed this life in the 43rd year of Usertesen I., corresponding
to the 25th year of the governorship of Ameni. He undertook all
his wars 'sailing up-stream': — *i.e.* he campaigned only against
the dwellers of the S., the 'miserable Kushites', as they are called
in the inscription. In those days the arms of the Pharaohs had not
yet been carried towards the E. The Sinai peninsula, with its
mines, is the only district in this direction which excited the Egyp-
tion lust of conquest. From his southern campaigns Amenemha
brought home much gold and other booty. The inscription to the
left (N.) also mentions a victorious campaign towards the S., but
is of special interest for the light it throws on the truly human
feelings of this bye-gone time. Amenemha describes his occupa-
tions in time of peace as follows (beginning at the fourth line from
below): 'I cultivated the entire nome of Maḥ with many work-
people. I troubled no child and oppressed no widow, neither did
I keep a fisherman from his fishing or a herdsman from his herd.
There was no head of a village whose people I had taken away for
compulsory labour, and there was no one unhappy in my days or
hungry in my times. When, however, a famine arose, I tilled all
the fields in the nome of Maḥ, from its S. to its N. boundary, and
gave nourishment and life to its inhabitants. So there was no one
in the nome who died of hunger. To the widow I allowed as much
as to the wife of a man, and in all that I did I never preferred the
great man to the small one. When the Nile rose again and everything flourished — fields, trees, and all else — I cut off nothing
from the fields'.

The paintings in the interior of the tomb-chamber proper are
unfortunately very much faded, and they have also been considerably injured, especially in recent years. Some figures of warriors which still remain, armed with club and axe or club and lance,
have a foreign appearance, as their skin is of a lighter colour than
that of the Egyptians, and their hair and beards are red.

Tomb No. 2 is that of *Khnumhotep*, the son of Nehera. It owes
its origin to a member of a family of high rank, in which the office
of governor of Maḥ seems to have been hereditary for several generations. Amenemha I., Usertesen I., and Amenemha II., the first
kings of the 12th Dyn., showered titles and dignities with a free
hand on this family, which in return clung to the royal line with
peculiar loyalty and affection. By a wonderful piece of good fortune
we are able to reproduce the entire family-tree of this family, in

which the names of women fill a very important rôle. Amenemha II. *Ra-nub-kau* 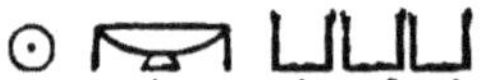 created Khnumhotep governor of the E. nomes, and as the heir of his maternal grandfather made him priest of Horus and Pasht in the town of Menât Khufu (Minyeh).

The portico or vestibule of this tomb deserves particular attention, as it not only possesses proto-Doric columns resembling those of Tomb 1, but also shows some architectural forms, which seem intended to reproduce the beams and rafters of buildings above ground. The cornice projects strongly above the architrave and is supported by fine laths hewn, like all the rest of the structure, out of the living rock. The resemblance of these laths to the mutules of the Doric order is not especially striking in itself, but taken in conjunction with other points of similarity is, perhaps, worthy of mention. — The interior of Khnumhotep's tomb is richly adorned with paintings. Most of the representations were painted on a thin layer of stucco, with which the limestone walls were coated. At the foot, however, is a long inscription cut in the rock, in lines of a greenish colour, $2^{1}/_{2}$ ft. high. [In 1890 the royal names were cut out of the rock by some vandal hand and offered for sale.] From this inscription we receive information about the family of Khnumhotep, who owed the greater part of his dignities to his maternal grandfather, about his relations with Amenemha II., who, at the intercession of his mother, made him a royal governor, and about the benefits he had conferred on his government and its people and the honour he had done to the gods of his nome and the manes of his forefathers.

The paintings have unfortunately suffered so much in the last 30 or 40 years, that the subjects of some of them are now almost indistinguishable. Most of them, however, were copied by Lepsius, Rosellini, Wilkinson, and others, while they were still in fair preservation; and they have furnished most important contributions to our knowledge of the private life of the ancient Egyptians. In the uppermost row of paintings, above the door, was represented the festival of the opening of the tomb of Khnumhotep. 'The heaven opens', says the inscription, 'as the god (*i.e.* the deceased transformed into Osiris) steps forth'. To the right, lower down, we see the colonnades of Khnumhotep's dwelling, with servants measuring and registering his treasures and (farther on) bringing his corn into the barns. Two of the lower rows show the operations of ploughing, harvesting, and threshing. Still lower down is a Nile-boat, bearing the mummy of the deceased, as the inscription informs us, to Abydos (the grave of Osiris), while the high-priest imparts his blessing. Below is a representation of the vintage and of the gathering of fruit and vegetables. The cattle in the water and the fishing scene (at the foot) vividly recall the similar scenes in the Maṣṭaba of Ti. To the left of the door, high up, are seen the processes of preparing clay for pottery and sawing wood; in the second row

Khnumhotep appears in a litter, inspecting his potters and carpenters. Some of the latter are felling palm-trees and others are building a boat for the journey to Abydos (see below). The most interesting of the scenes of artizan life in the lower rows are the representations of women baking and weaving, under the supervision of eunuchs. — The entire *Rear Wall* is occupied by a tastefully arranged representation of the water-sports in which the deceased took delight. A forest of papyrus reeds grows by the water-side, thickly peopled by all kinds of furred and feathered game. To the right and left Khnumhotep is depicted in his boat, accompanied in one instance by his wife Khuti, who is painted a lighter colour. Here he transfixes large river-fish, there he holds the birds he has brought down by his darts. Above are birds caught in a net. In the river swim characteristically drawn fish, and crocodiles and hippopotami are also seen. A man who has fallen into the water is being hauled out again. The dominant idea of the chase is farther carried out in the representations of a hawk seizing a gaily-plumaged bird and an ibis capturing a butterfly.

The *N. Wall* (to the left on entering) is the most important of all, as upon it is the celebrated picture of a Semitic race bringing cosmetics (mestem) and other presents to Khnumhotep. In the lowest row, to the right, are seen the secretaries of Khnumhotep, receiving the report of the steward of the cattle, who is followed by the herds and shepherds. Just above this is Khnumhotep himself, represented on a scale three times as large as the other figures and accompanied by three dogs and a man with sandals, bearing a staff. In the 4th row from below, on a level with the head and shoulders of this huge figure, is represented a curious procession. Neferhotep, the secretary, and another Egyptian lead towards the governor a number of foreign people in gay-coloured garments, whose sharply cut features, hooked noses, and pointed beards unmistakeably proclaim their Semitic nationality. This Asiatic visit seems to have been one of the signal events in the life of the nomarch. Neferhotep hands his master a document from which we learn that the strangers knocked at the door of Egypt in the 9th year of king Usertesen II. Prince Absha, the leader of the foreigners, leads a gazelle and bows to the ground. The next Asiatic leads an antelope. Four armed men march in front of the harem, which consists of four women and three children. Two of these ride upon an ass, which also bears implements for weaving. The women wear brightly coloured raiment of a curious cut. The clothes and loin-cloths of the men are also brilliantly coloured. A heavily-laden ass is followed by a lute-player and a warrior armed with club, bow, and quiver. The inscription, beginning above the figure of the secretary Neferhotep, is as follows: 'Arrival of those bringing the eye-salve mestem (kohl or antimony). He (*i.e.* Neferhotep) introduces 37 Amus'. The Amus were a Semitic race of Asiatic origin in the N.E. of Egypt. We have here, as it were, the advance guard of the invasion of the Hyksos, towards the end of the 12th Dynasty. The Hyksos, named 'Amu' in an inscription in the neighbouring Speos Artemidos (p. 11), consisted of isolated tribes, who purchased permission to enter Egypt by tribute, crossed its boundaries, and finally penetrated to the interior. The chief Absha here bows before the Egyptian; his successors carried things with a high hand and bent the Egyptians under their yoke. — The flock of ostriches behind the last Amu belongs to the series of pictures on the left side of the wall, representing Khnumhotep, accompanied by his dogs, slaying wild beasts with bow and arrows. Below is a flock of geese and a fowling-scene. In the second row from the foot are bulls fighting and scenes of cattle-tending.

The *S. Wall* (to the right) is occupied by processions of servants bringing gifts for the dead, a frequent subject in these representations, and the offering of animals in sacrifice. Before one altar is the figure of Khnumhotep, before another his wife Khuti, daughter of Pent.

The traveller will find many of the above scenes now defaced beyond recognition, but he should not let this deter him from walking a little farther to the S. and entering some of the other tombs. That of *Kheti*, one of the nearest (No. 7), easily recognised by the three pairs of columns supporting the roof, contains interesting, though half-obliterated representations of the innumerable gymnastic and fencing exercises and games of the ancient Egyptians. Girls are seen throwing the ball from one to another, and men ponder carefully over a game of draughts. The *Hunting Scenes* are of linguistic value, as the names of the different animals are written above them. Among these was a stag, now totally effaced. Mechanics are depicted at work here and elsewhere. — Travellers who see the tombs of the new kingdom at Thebes, after having visited the graves of Benihasan, will be astonished at the vastness of the impression made upon the life and sentiment of the Egyptians by the Hyksos period. At Benihasan everything recalls the tombs in the Pyramids, and the subjects of representation are drawn wholly from this earth; under the New Empire scenes of the future life and representations of the gods are also given. We should also notice that the horse, so common in later times, never appears under the early empire. The forms of the columns, including the beautiful lotus capitals (see *Baedeker's Lower Egypt*, p. 164), are of the greatest interest. The proto-Doric column is seen here in all stages of development. The plain pillar, the octagonal pillar, the octagonal and sixteen-sided columns, with and without flutes, all occur at Benihasan side by side and may be looked upon as practical illustrations of the section upon the *Cavern Building* of the Egyptians in the introduction to *Lower Egypt* (p. 160).

At **Rôḍah** (rail. stat., p. 1), an important place on the W. bank,

with post and telegraph offices, several mosques, and a large sugar
factory, the railway approaches close to the river. The factory is
said to contain a stone with a hitherto unpublished Greek inscription.

About 1 M. inland (W.) from Rôḍah, between the Baḥr Yusuf and
the Nile, lie the ruins of the once famous **Ashmunên.** The ancient
Egyptian name was *Khimunu* ☰☰ ☰☰ ⊙ ⊗, while the Greeks called
it *Hermopolis*, the town of *Hermes-Thoth*, the god of writing and science,
whose chief sanctuary was situated here. Hence the town was also named
Pa Teḥuti, or town of Thoth. Hermopolis Magna was the capital of the
Hermópolitan nome of Upper Egypt. The name Ashmunên is derived,
according to Quatremère (Mémoires Géographiques, I., pp. 490 et seq.),
from the fact that the town embraced two different communities, one
on the site of the present ruins, the other, with a harbour, on the Nile.
Among the plates of the French Expedition are two views of a fine
Portico of the Ptolemaic period, with two rows of six columns each
(Antiquités IV, Pl. 50, 51). The columns were 55 ft. high, and the portico
was 124½ ft. long and 29½ ft. wide. In Minutoli's 'Journey to the Oasis
of Jupiter Ammon' (Plate XIV) a view is given of one of the columns,
with the cartouche of Philippus Aridæus, one of the successors of
Alexander the Great, who was a native of Ashmunên. The remains of
the temple were used in building a saltpetre factory.—At *Gebel Tunah*,
near Hermopolis, is a tablet (much dilapidated) with an inscription of
the sun-worshipper *Khu-en-aten*, who lived on the opposite bank of the
river (comp. Tell el-Amarnah, p. 22).

Nearly opposite Rôḍah, on the E. bank, 11 M. from Beniḥasan,
lies the village of *Shêkh 'Abâdeh*, with the ruins of **Antinoë.**
Hadrian erected a new town in honour of his favourite Antinous
on the site of the Egyptian town of *Besa*, where the handsome
youth is said to have drowned himself, to fulfil the oracle which
predicted a heavy loss to the emperor and so to prevent a more
serious disaster. The village lies on the bank amid palms of unusual size and beauty, and to the S. of it is a brook, now dry
except after rain, which must formerly have flowed through the
town. The remains of public buildings of the Egyptian period are
scanty. The French Expedition saw a triumphal arch, a theatre,
and two streets flanked with columns, the one running N. and S.
and leading to the theatre; the other at right angles leading to the
city-gate and the hippodrome. A lofty column bore an inscription
of Alexander Severus (A.D. 222). To-day, however, there are few
remains either of Greek or Roman times. Among the palms lies a
fine Corinthian capital. The marble belonging to the 'very fine gate
of the Corinthian order' that Pococke saw here and figured in his
book was burned to make lime for building the sugar-factory at
Rôḍah. The extensive ruins of the ancient town lie to the E. of the
village of Shêkh 'Abâdeh. The streets and ground-plans of the
houses are still recognisable. The rooms were small and the walls
were made mainly of Nile bricks. There are, however, some underground apartments of flat Roman bricks, reached by stone staircases. Near the scanty ruins of one of the largest buildings lies a
basin of white marble, which must have had a circumference of
at least 23 ft.

Those who are interested in Christian antiquities should follow the E. bank from Shêkh 'Abâdeh towards the S.† In about ³/₄ hr., after passing some ruins of a late epoch, we reach the **Dêr Abu Hennis** (Convent of St. John), called also simply *ed-Dêr*. In the days of the Mameluke persecutions the Christians are said to have lived here and at Shêkh 'Abâdeh in comparative security, as the Arabs believed that no Mohammedan could exist here on account of the evil spirits. At present there are more fellahin here than Copts. There is little to be seen at ed-Dêr. The crypt, in which divine service is held, is said to date from the time of the Empress Helena. By ascending the hill at the back of the houses, we reach, to the left of the ravine, some cave-like quarries, which were fitted up as Christian chapels and were embellished at an early date with sculptures. The main chamber contains paintings of saints and scenes from the New Testament, but those in one of the side chapels (Raising of Lazarus, Wedding at Cana, etc.) are better. To judge from their style these interesting pictures are not earlier than the 6th cent. A.D. Among the Coptic monks who resided here (from the 4th cent. onwards) were Victor and his brother Koluthus, Silvanus, and Macarius; and the tombs of the last two are still shown. The adjoining quarry was begun by Amenhotep III.

About ³/₄ hr. beyond Dêr Abu Hennis we reach **Dêr en-Nakhleh**, the 'convent of the date-palms'. To reach the *Tomb *with the representation of the transportation of a Colossus*, we cross the dry water-course beyond the houses, ascend the hill on the left side, and near the top reach a path on which, a little to the right, the grave is situated. Guides may be procured for a few paras. Travellers descending the river should visit the tomb from *Bersheh*, above which towers the rocky *Gebel Shêkh Sa'îd* (with a shekh's tomb), in which the tomb in question is hollowed out. The whole district belonged to the nome of Un or Hermopolis. The representation in this tomb is highly interesting as being the only one that gives us an idea of the processes used by the Egyptians in moving their colossal statues.

The Arabs thought it impossible that mere human strength could move such huge burdens, and hence a legend grew up among them that the subjects of the Pharaohs were giants, who knew how to move masses of rock with their magical staves. Even the men of the present day, at whose command stand forces of which the ancient Egyptians never even dreamed, are astounded at their achievements in this direction and feel inclined to solve the problem by ascribing to them the use of technical aids, which we have no evidence that they possessed. The principles of the pulley and the lever seem to have been unknown to them; and obstacles, which seem to us to demand imperatively the application of steam and machinery, were overcome by enormous multiplication of sheer human power.

---

† The dhahabîyeh should be sent on to Bersheh, in order to allow time for a visit to the picture of the transportation of an Egyptian statue (see above). About 4-5 hrs. are necessary to see comfortably all the points on this route.

The colossal figure within this tomb represents Kaï, son of Tot-hotep, a high-priest, a steward of the mysteries of the word of God, a privy chamberlain (superintendent of the works in the inner palace), and the head of a nome. His paternal grand-mother was a daughter of Usertesen I., the second king of the 12th Dynasty, and he was also connected with the royal family on the mother-side. He was likewise related to the family of Nehera and Khnum-hotep (see p. **15**).

The successful transportation of the statue figured in his tomb was one of the chief events in the life of Kaï. The scene shows us an image, 13 ells in height, securely fastened to a sled. Small cushions are inserted to prevent the polished stone from being injured by the ropes. To the sled are attached four strong cables, each manned by 43 workmen (in all 172), the 'young men', as the inscriptions inform us, 'of the W. and E. of the nome'. On the lap of the figure stands a man clapping his hands, probably the leader and time-giver of the song of the workmen, whose task was facilitated by rhythmical movement. To this day in Egypt and elsewhere the same custom is observed wherever the strength of many men is united in some common exertion, as in the sailor's chant in raising the anchor or hoisting sail. A man facing the time-keeper knocks two wooden stamps together, obviously to transmit the proper time to those too far off to hear distinctly the hand-clapping of the leader. On the prow of the sled, behind the rings to which the ropes are fastened, stands a man pouring water on the ground to prevent the heavily loaded sled from taking fire by friction. Water-carriers stand ready to refill the empty pitcher. These are followed by other labourers bearing notched beams, for laying under the sledge when necessary. Three bailiffs or stewards, with sticks, are each attended by four men, who seem from their simple costume to be foremen, stone-masons, or extra-hands. At the top are depicted seven well-equipped companies of infantry, marching in stiff military order towards the advancing colossus. The officers bear tridents resembling those in the usual representations of Neptune, which may either have been used as field-standards or for driving the cowardly into action.

This highly instructive representation shows, among other points, how unlimited was the authority of the nomarch over the people of his nome and how freely, not to say extravagantly, he could apply human labour in effecting his ends. One is tempted to pity the corvée labourers and to forget how ends which seem petty or even obnoxious to one generation may have seemed to their ancestors worthy of an unlimited expenditure of time, blood, and wealth. In the time of the pyramid-building 12th Dynasty it was accounted a noble and reputable thing to erect the hugest and most durable monuments. The mass of the people, who seem to have regarded the might of their oppressors in the same light as we regard the workings of destiny, were proud to have had a share in the erection of any specially important monument. Similar considerations are suggested by scenes in the tombs of the pyramids, and the inscription accompanying the above-described picture gives us chapter and verse for the accuracy of this view. It runs as follows: 'Transport of the thirteen-ell statue made of stone from Hatnub. Behold, the way by which it was to be transported was of extraordinary difficulty. Truly difficult was also the toil of the people in drawing the mighty mass along it, in dragging (the colossus) in hewn stone. I ordered the bands of young men to march and prepare the way for it, with watchmen, carpenters, and so forth. The most important were among them. The order was issued that men of a strong arm should go forth to fetch it. My heart was full of content, and my fellow-citizens all rejoiced. The scene was extremely beautiful to witness; the old man leans on the youth, the strong withstood the weak-hearted and timid. They thus became so strong that each one effected as much as a thousand. And behold, this statue

of hewn stone went forth out of the mountain, more unutterably grand
to witness than all things else. Transport-ships equipped with all magnificence, the choicest of my young men and soldiers. My children followed
me arrayed in festal ornaments, and the inhabitants of my nome, singing songs of praise, celebrated my arrival in the fortress of this town'.

The other representations in this tomb offer nothing unusual. Much
has been destroyed and defaced, principally by the monks, who tried to
sanctify the pagan work and drive the devil from it by marking it with
the sign of the cross.

Below this tomb is another of the 12th Dynasty, belonging according
to the inscriptions to the royal chamberlain Aha.

On the W. bank, 1 M. from the Nile, is **Melawi el-'Arish** (rail.
stat., p. 1), a small town with 10,000 inhab., where fowls, eggs,
etc., may be procured cheaply (large market on Sun.). In the vicinity are many large palms and also sugar-plantations. Farther
on, on the E. bank, at the foot of the hill of the same name (p. 20),
lies **Shêkh-Sa'id**, with tombs of the old empire, including those of
priests of Khufu, Userkaf, and Pepi.

We next reach the ruins of **et-Tell** and the grottoes of **Tell el-
Amarnah**, two very interesting points on the E. bank, at which the
'four weeks' steamer stops for a few hours on its return-journey.
The best plan is to disembark at et-Tell, visit the remains of the
old town, return to the dhahabîyeh, and sail to *Hagg el-Ḳandîl*, where
donkeys for the visit to the grottoes are more easily obtained than
at et-Tell. We pass to the right of the village of *et-Tell*, ¹/₄ M.
from the river, and at the point where the cultivated land ends we
turn due S. (to the right). After passing the ruins of a large building (probably a temple), now consisting of the foundations only and
nearly indistinguishable, we turn to the right from the path to visit the numerous relics of public and private buildings of all kinds.
There are larger and finer ruined temples in other parts of Egypt,
but nowhere else do we obtain so excellent an idea of the actual
dwelling-places of the citizens. It looks as if the hand of deity had
bodily removed this large town (more than 1 M. long from N. to S.)
from the surface of the earth, leaving nothing but the foundations
to tell the after-world that many thousands of human beings once
lived and worked, suffered and rejoiced on this waste spot. The
lines of the streets may be followed and ground-plans traced; but
the demands of cultivation are steadily effacing the remains.

Tell el-Amarnah. Whether we proceed by land from et-Tell
or disembark at Hagg el-Ḳandil, we have to ride towards the hills
to the E., in which, even from a distance, we discover the gates of
the celebrated tombs of Tell el-Amarnah. In either case it is advisable
to have a guide. On the way we should not omit to visit the recently
discovered grave of the sun-worshipper *Khu-en-aten* (Amenhotep IV., see below). Of the two groups of tombs that to the N. is
the more interesting and the more easily accessible.

An interesting and not yet fully explained epoch of Egyptian history
is illustrated here by a large number of paintings and inscriptions. In
the Historical Introduction to our first vol. an account is given of both
Amenhotep III. and his son and successor Amenhotep IV. The first, a

mighty prince both in war and peace, was a pious worshipper of Ammon, whose name, indeed, forms part of his own (Amen-hotep). Amenhotep IV., on the other hand, turned his back on his father's religion and on the increasingly spiritual conception of Ammon (the 'Hidden One') and the other ancient gods. discarded his name 'Peace of Ammon', became exclusively a sun-worshipper, and named himself **Khu-en-aten**, *i.e.* 'Reflection of the Sun's Disc'. It is an interesting but doubtful question whether Amenhophis IV., in his rôle of reformer, intended to resuscitate, as 'a patriotic restorer of the old cult', the simple sun-worship from which the religion of the Egyptians had originally taken its rise; or whether he was moved by the Semitic influences, which are so noticeable all over the country after the expulsion of the Hyksos, to become an adorer of the orb of day and to introduce a religious ceremonial that recalled the practices of the Asiatic courts rather than the more dignified usages of the 'Sublime Porte' of Egypt. Portraits of historical personages often cast a clearer light on their character than piles of written documents, and the numerous representations of Amenhotep IV. encountered in these tombs show that he was a sickly man, a fanatic, and an enthusiast. [The portrait-statue of him in the Louvre suggests similar conclusions.] He also, as the inscriptions inform us, stood under the influence of his mother, who was not of royal birth and seems to have encouraged her son's tendency to prefer the old popular religion to the elaborately developed creed of the priests. His work was distinctly reactionary and could not long survive him. Almost everywhere we see his successors scratching out his name as a sign of their disapproval and contempt. Where it still stands intact we may conclude that it was overlooked. The fact that the portrait-like reliefs of men in these tombs, as well as the horses and buildings, appear more true to nature than in any other Egyptian monument may be due to the greater liberty of divergence from the hieratic canon allowed in a reign which was so unfavourable to the priestly dogmas. These reliefs excited the special admiration of the Greeks. A Hellene who visited them inscribed his name as admiring the art of the priestly stone-cutters (τέχνην θαυμάζων τῶν ἱερῶν λαοτόμων). Besides the palaces and tombs of Tell el-Amarnah, Khu-en-aten also built a large *Benben* or temple at Thebes, the blocks of which were used for the pylon of King Horus. He also erected a temple in Heliopolis, the remains of which are still extant, and probably another in Memphis. He is himself depicted on a pylon in Soleb (Nubia).

Quite recently a new light has fallen on the history of Amenhotep IV. and his predecessor through the discovery of several hundred tablets with cuneïform inscriptions in the large Temple, or rather Palace, of Tell el-Amarnah†, which narrate the intercourse of the Kings of Babylon with Amenhotep III. and Amenhotep IV. To the former King Dushratta of Mitanni gave his daughter Tadukhepa in marriage; and her dowry is stated on one of the tablets. Other tablets contain letters from Palestine and Syrian vassals to the King of Egypt, and diplomatic notes from King Burnaburiash to Amenhotep IV., concluding a treaty of peace and asking for the hand of his daughter. Most of the tablets are now in the Asiatic Museum at Berlin, but many are in the British Museum and a few at Gizeh.

N. Group. The tombs in each group are marked with red numbers, running from N. to S. Most of the tombs are entered from a small fore-court, and the doorways of many are adorned with concave cornices. The door leads into an oblong apartment, communicating with a wide sepulchral chapel, with a small burial-recess in the background. The ornamentation of the ceiling is very varied. Columns with bud-capitals occur frequently, some

---

† Some authorities believe that these tablets were found in the tomb of Amenhotep IV. (see above).

of them unfinished, and the colouring of the reliefs is sometimes in wonderful preservation. The mummy shafts, in spite of their great depth, have all long since been despoiled of their contents. In the very first tomb we find a representation of the king and his family offering a sacrifice to the sun's disc. The disc is encircled with the Uræus-snake and furnished with several arms, stretching downwards; the hands are symbolic of energy, liberality, and the creative faculty. Dwarfs (then, as later, a favourite royal plaything), fan-bearers, and bowing courtiers stand below. In front is the provost-martial with his baton. To the left of the first grave, on the hill, is the *Tomb of Pentu* (No. 2), which is in a very ruinous condition. Farther on to the left is that of *Rameri* (No. 3), with a finely worked exterior. On the left wall of the second chamber of this tomb is a military scene, which we do not hesitate to describe as the most realistic representation found hitherto in any Egyptian grave. The lean figure of the Pharaoh, above whom the sun spreads its arms, stands in his war-chariot and drives the fiery steeds, the introduction of which Egypt owes to the Hyksos. Sâis (out-runners) with long staves run in front of the chariot, towards the crowd of people offering sacrifice and bending to the ground in adoration. Standard-bearers and soldiers clear the way for the rapidly advancing procession, just as the mounted kavasses still do for the carriage of the Khedive. The king appears once more followed by his children, who also drive their own chariots. The procession hastens towards the royal palace, which covers the right part of the rear-wall of the chapel and also part of the right wall, affording us a clearer idea of an Egyptian palace than any other scene of the kind. It has long been established that neither the royal princes nor even the Pharaohs themselves lived in the temples. On the contrary they used to build themselves airy châteaux of light materials, with doors opening on shady galleries and colonnades. Gardens with fountains and water-basins surrounded the building, near which were also out-houses, stables, and well-stocked storehouses, in quantity corresponding to the huge number of the dependents of the royal family. The great entrance-door is dignified with double rows of bud columns, and red standards wave from lofty flag-staffs. Above one of the side-doors is a round window similar to those which the French call œil-de-bœuf. The palace is adjoined by a sepulchral chapel, supported by columns and containing figures of the king's ancestors, honoured by rich sacrificial offerings; at the door is a choir, singing pious songs of remembrance to the accompaniment of the harp, and taking its time from the hand-clapping of the leader (a custom still preserved in Egypt). — In the first chamber of Tomb 7 (right wall, p. 26) is a representation of the Temple of the Solar Disc, with a large peristyle court surrounded by a colonnade. Pillars resembling Caryatides decorate the walls, and above all tower the lofty pylons with their hollow cornice.

Not only are the subjects of these representations of great interest, but the character of the architectural drawing itself should be noticed. It is something between a sketch-plan and a finished picture. The ground-plan is clearly indicated, but at the same time an idea is given of the appearance of the external elevation of the building. Clearness and truthful reproduction of details are aimed at here as zealously as in the figure-drawing. The ground-plan is first sketched in, and then the outlines of the façades, and even the doors and trees are added so far as the space allows.

The forms of the persons represented vary considerably from those seen in tombs elsewhere. Almost all have the same thickset body and lean neck that characterize the king. The figure of the latter is, of course, a portrait; and it is possible that the courtly artists burdened the subjects with the weaknesses of the prince so that his deformities might not appear as anything unusual. Amenhotep IV. was certainly not a foreigner; but his mother Tii may have been one, and may have installed her fellow-countrymen at the Egyptian court. Even the highest dignitaries have un-Egyptian features. Among these is the royal favourite Merira, who is represented on the right wall of Tomb 3, as literally overwhelmed with the golden necklaces, rings, and orders, which the Pharaohs of the 18th Dynasty delighted to shower on their loyal adherents; he stands in front of the royal family, the members of which are attended by fan-bearers and courtiers of all kinds. 'Let him receive gold', says the inscription, 'on his neck, on his back, and on his feet'. Secretaries make a note of the donations and write out the royal patents, which are also mentioned elsewhere. The fourth necklace is being hung round the neck of Merira, while the fifth and sixth are handed to him by two officials; a third attendant holds three golden rings. The Urma, to whom this favourite belonged, were, in addition to their other dignities, the most learned physicians and high-priests of Heliopolis (mentioned in the inscription). The sickly prince naturally pays the highest honours to his physician, one of the Urma priests. Another of these priests, named Khui, is mentioned in the Ebers Papyrus as having prepared a famous eye-salve, and it is possible that Amenhotep IV. may have been blind or, at least, threatened with blindness. His outstretched neck suggests the attitude of a blind man, and in the song of one of the priestesses by the door-post of the same tomb occur the words : 'The lord of goodness arises . . . . No other one opens his countenance, healing his eyes with his beams'.

Tomb 4 contained the remains of the 'truth-loving' *Auhmes*, the royal secretary, adjutant of the fan-bearers, and first lord of the bedchamber. Here we find one of the great dignitaries celebrating the glory of the sun. He praises the beauty of the setting of the lord of the lords and princes of the earth, at sight of whom the elect break forth into rejoicing, at whose rising and setting the whole earth and all lands sing songs of praise. The praise of the king is interwoven with the hymn to the sun: 'Thou givest me honour before the king all my days. A worthy burial after a long life in this land of the light-region of the sun's disc was accorded to me. I fulfil the span of my life. I fulfil my life in the completeness of a servant of the good god, who is free to ascend every throne he likes. I am a vassal of the king'. Then follows a list of the titles of Aahmes.

Tomb 6 contains representations of columns, the shafts of which are encircled at regular intervals by rings resembling the tissue enveloping the joints of reeds. The capital consists of several erect bell-flowers, with dependent buds held together by a ring.

The *Tomb of Huia* (No. 7), the keeper of the treasury, also contains much that is interesting. The Temple of the Sun, on the right wall of the first chamber, has already been mentioned. The king is shown seated upon a lion-guarded throne, illuminated by the solar rays, and borne by several courtiers. Before and behind are noble youths with large and small fans. The same chamber contains another striking and well-preserved scene, representing the studio of the sculptor *Auta*, director of the portrait-sculptors (lit. 'givers of life') of the king's mother Tii. A well-executed statue of this powerful but unlovely princess is being coloured by the master himself, while two younger sculptors (s-ankh) give the finishing touches to the head and legs. The sacrificial scenes are of the usual type. — The name of Khu-en-aten has been almost everywhere obliterated from the cartouches. The solar disc with the arms appears frequently as a kind of talisman, sometimes above the single hieroglyphics. While demanding devoted loyalty from his subjects, the king seems to have enjoyed the most affectionate and happy relations with his wife and daughters, in whose names we recognise an echo of his own (Aten). The wife is named 'Beauty of the Solar Disc, the beauteous Dame Aït'; the daughters are Merit Aten, the darling of the sun; Aten makt, the ward of the sun; Ankh-s en pa Aten, she who lives through the sun; Aten nefra' ta shera, beauty of the sun; the little Aten bekt, servant of the sun, and so on. Tii, the mother of the king, is already known to us (see above).

The *S. Tombs*, 1¼-1½ hr. from the N. group, are not so well preserved. The graves formerly stood open, and only those parts under cover have escaped serious injury. In 1883 Maspero dug deeper into the already opened graves, and opened some for the first time, such as that of Mahu (p. 27). The cartouches of Khu-en-aten are not scratched out in the newly uncovered tombs. Of special interest are the recently discovered vaulted passages with steps, leading downwards, which are unlike any other Egyptian construction. It is evident that these were the actual burial-places. Skulls of bodies which had not been embalmed have been found

here. The northernmost tomb (No. 3 of Lepsius) shows us the king
and his family standing on a daïs, below which foreign captives
are depicted. The royal pair receives rich tribute. Those bringing
the gifts are Egyptians. *Aï*, to whom the tomb belongs, is adorned
with necklaces on account of the abundance of his contributions.
Numerous servants carry the sacks and bottles to the open cellar-
door, in front of which, in a bending attitude, is a bailiff with a
staff. It is possible that the cellar belongs to Aï, and that the gifts
are royal bounties to him. — The next grave to the S., on a projecting hill, was excavated in 1883. It was destined for *Mahu*, a
commander of the royal police, and scenes from his life (Arrest of
mountaineers, Escort of the king's equipage, etc.) are depicted on
the walls of the first chamber (esp. to the right of the entrance).
In the right side-wall is a door bearing a prayer in behalf of Mahu
to Aten-Ra (the radiating solar disc). — The next tomb, that of
the royal official *Tutu*, contains (to the right of the entrance) the
almost complete text of a hymn, sung by a priest in praise of the
sun : 'The breath of the wind', says the hymn, 'enters their nostrils,
and Thy gift it is that they have being. All flowers bloom and
grow in their beds, and they flourish at Thy uprising. Festal joy
arises at the sight of Thy countenance. All quadrupeds hurry along
on their feet, all the birds in their nests flutter their wings in joy'.
This tomb also possesses a 'papyrus' column, of unusually careful
workmanship and elaborate ornamentation. The basis of the capital is encircled, among the leaves, by a Uræus-serpent; and at
the upper end of the shaft, below the richly-adorned band repla-
cing the annuli, are singular decorations consisting of sacrificial
gifts, including many birds in groups of five. — To the S., at a
little distance, lies the tomb designated by Lepsius as No. 1. This
also is dedicated to a high dignitary named *Aï*, perhaps the same
as in Tomb 3. On the entrance-wall to the right is represented a
festival, which some interpret as that of an order, while others take
it for the marriage of Aï, fan-bearer and commander of cavalry, to
the royal nurse. The king, denoted by the disc, his wife, and his
daughters stand on a dais. The courtiers, from the charioteers to
the military officers and fan-hearers, receive with deep obeisances
the decorations which the Pharaoh, the queen, and the princesses
throw down to them. The foremost dignitary already wears six
necklaces, and the lady behind him is just adding a fifth to the
four she already possesses. A troop of dancers enlivens the proceedings by energetic leaps and contortions, and secretaries make
a note of the donations. To the S. are several other graves, including those of *Apii* and *Ramses*, the latter a general and chamberlain of Amenhotep III. To the N.N.W. of these tombs lay the huge
residence of the singular king Khu-en-aten, which was perhaps
destroyed by the same generation that obliterated his name from
the cartouches.

Beyond Hagg el-Ḳandil the Nile-voyager passes several small villages, but neither they nor the scanty ruins of the Pharaonic epoch near them deserve a visit.

In a ravine near *el-Hawâtah* (E. bank) stands a stele with a hieroglyphic inscription, discovered by the late Mr. Harris, British consul at Cairo and excellently versed in Egyptian antiquities. Farther on we skirt an island and reach the point on the W. bank, between the villages of *el-Gezîreh* (*i.e.* 'island') and *el-Manduruh*, where the **Baḥr Yûsuf** or *Joseph's Canal*, an arm of the Nile, diverges from the main stream to water the agricultural districts of the Libyan bank, the Fayûm (p. 35) etc. The name of Joseph, was given to it by the Arabs, who recognise in the son of Jacob the type of all administrators. It probably owes its regulation if not its origin to Amenemha III., of the 12th Dynasty. Extensive works are now in progress to furnish the W. part of the Libyan bank with water from a point higher up the Nile, near Assiûṭ.

About 5 M. below the divergence of the Baḥr Yûsuf, at some distance from the Nile, lies **Dérût esh-Sherif** (rail. stat., p. 1). About $1^1/_4$ M. above (S. of) the fork, on the E. bank, are some brick ruins, and $1^1/_4$ M. farther to the S. are the mounds of *Dêr el-Ḳuṣêr*, probably the site of the ancient *Pescla*. This is the N. boundary of the dûm-palms, which, however, do not attain their full development till farther up, between Assiûṭ and Ḳeneh, where we see many fine specimens (p. 70). The Arabian Mts., rising in precipitous rocky walls, approach the river. Swallows, ducks, and other birds inhabit the caves in the porous rock on the banks, and fly in and out in screaming crowds. The cliffs on the right bank of this part of the Nile are known as **Gebel Abu Fêdah.** The stream below them is considered the most dangerous part of the channel between Cairo and Assuân. Violent winds blow round the crags, and numerous sandbanks impede navigation.

The Arabs tell that a ship-master of Ḳeneh, having safely arrived at Bûlâk, was asked by his friends how he had passed the Gebel Abu Fêda. 'Quite easily', was his rejoinder, 'there's no danger there'. An old man who overheard him remarked: 'From your own words I see that you do not know this mountain'. 'I know it as well as my own eyes', said the boatman. 'When I return to Ḳeneh I must pass it once more. If my vessel suffers any damage in doing so, I will pay you 10,000 piastres, on condition that you pay me the like sum if I pass safely. But I give you due warning that I know the Gebel Abu Fêdah perfectly well'. The old man accepted the wager, and the ship-master had his boat bound with iron, engaged the best sailors, and set forth. As he approached the Gebel the boat was assailed at first by one wind, and afterwards by four storm-winds, each blowing from a different quarter. The ship, in spite of its iron fastenings, was cast upon the rocks and went to pieces; and the vainglorious re'is, as he scrambled ashore with nothing saved but his life, cried: 'Gebel Abu Fêdah, I never knew you till now'. Numerous similar stories are related of these cliffs. And no wonder, for nothing can be more mysterious and spectral than their appearance at twilight, when the dark swarms of birds fly towards the rocks and disappear as suddenly as if engulfed by it.

The hill contains many rock-tombs, which have not yet been carefully investigated. Travellers who wish to do so will find the hill not a very arduous climb. In descending they may strike the river at a point a little farther to the S. and row thence to the dhahabîyeh.

On the W. bank, 3 M. from the river, lies **el-Ḳusîyeh,** now an insignificant fellah town, representing the ancient *Kusae,* in which, according to Ælian, Venus Urania and her cow (*i.e.* Hathor nebt pet Hathor, the mistress of heaven) were worshipped. No inscriptions have been found in Ḳusîyeh itself, but elsewhere the name of Hathor occurs as the Lady of Kesi. From Kesi came the Coptic **Ⲕⲱⲥ-Ⲕⲟⲩ** (kōs-koō), and thence was derived the Arabic Ḳusîyeh.

At *el-Harîb,* on the E. bank, are the ruins of an ancient Egyptian town, at the mouth of a Wâdi ascending to the Arabian mountains. The walls, provided in places with window-openings, are high, but fragments of demotic inscriptions show them to be of late date. Small caves in the rocks contain bones from mummies of men and cats.

Monfalût, on the W. bank (rail. stat., see p. 1), an important town with 13,200 inhab., is the seat of a Coptic bishop and contains several fine villas and gardens and a bazaar. Its market is much frequented on Sun., and it also prossesses a sugar-factory and a distillery, where date-brandy ('araḳi) is made, partly for local consumption by the Copts and partly for export. The town lies close to the river, which must here have greatly encroached on the W. bank since the close of last century. The Arabs translate Monfalût as 'Lot's place of banishment'.

To the S.W. of Monfalût lies **Beni 'Adin,** where in 1798 a collision took place between the troops of General Desaix and the Arabs. In the following year, just after the arrival of a caravan from Darfûr, General Davoust destroyed it as a nest of rebels, taking the women prisoners. Mohammed 'Ali united his army here in 1820. The journey to the oasis of *Farâfrah* (p. 348) is frequently begun here. The first station to the N.W. is the convent of *Maragh,* containing 50 Coptic monks.

Esh-Shekilkil, a small village on the E. bank, lies on a narrow strip of fertile land between the Nile and the S. end of the rocky Gebel Abu Fêdah. It is the starting-point for a visit to the Crocodile Grotto of **Ma'abdeh.** A guide, who may be procured in the village of Shekilkil, is necessary to show the best way over the stony hill and to point out the entrance to the cavern, which easily escapes the eyes of even practised searchers. Lantern and ropes are also necessary, and a few strong sailors to handle the latter. Ladies should not attempt this excursion. The distance is about $4^1/_2$ M., and most of the way is up a steep hill. We first proceed towards the N.W. to the ($^1/_2$ hr.) village of *el-Ma'abdeh,* and thence to the N.E. towards the hill, the plateau of which we reach in $^3/_4$ hr. A walk of $^1/_2$ hr. towards the S. then brings us to the grotto. The entrance is in the shape of a hole 12 ft. deep, into which we are lowered by ropes, a guide previously descending to aid in landing. We then creep on all-fours for some distance through the dust of ancient mummies, and after some time

ascend a branch to the left. The passage in a straight direction
chiefly contains human mummies, while that to the left is packed
with mummiès of crocodiles. Some of these are of great size, and
in other cases bundles of 25 baby-crocodiles are put up together.
Baskets of bast contain crocodile-eggs, with the shells, containing the embryo, still unbroken. After some time we reach a more
spacious part of the grotto, where it is possible to stand erect. It is
not improbable that the cave had a second entrance on the other
side of the hill, but this has not yet been discovered. Great care
should be exercised in using the lights; two Frenchmen who acci-
dentally set fire to the mummy-bandages were suffocated by the
smoke and burned to ashes. It was here that Mr. Harris found
the celebrated papyrus MS. containing fragments of Homer's Iliad,
which was held in the hand of the mummy of a man wearing a
coronal of gold. The enormous number of *Crocodile Mummies*
found here will astonish no one who knows the following passage
in the trustworthy 'Abdellaṭif (12th cent.): 'Among the animals
peculiar to Egypt the crocodile must not be forgotten, which occurs
in great numbers in the Nile, particularly in the S. part of Sa'id
(Upper Egypt) and in the vicinity of the cataracts. There they
swarm like worms in the water of the river and around the cliffs
that form the cataracts'. In his time there were still crocodiles in
the Delta. These animals are now totally extinct on the lower Nile;
none has been seen for many years between Cairo and Gebel Abu
Fêdah, and they are becoming very rare between the latter point
and Assuân, mainly, it is said, owing to the noise of the steamboats. Even between the First and Second Cataracts they are now
rare, though 20 years ago they were very frequent.

The road to Assiûṭ, which we encountered on our visit to et-Tell
(see p. 22), leads across the Gebel Abu Fêdah and reaches the Nile
at *Beni Mohammed*, near the S. base of this hill. In the hill beyond
Beni Moḥammed are some tombs of the 6th Dyn., with uninteresting and half-effaced representations of agricultural and other
scenes. In the valley lies the Coptic convent *Dêr el-Gebrai*, containing a Greek inscription (discovered by Mr. Harris) in the shape
of a dedication of the camp of the Lusitanian Cohort, which served
under Diocletian and Maximian, to Zeus, Hercules, and Nike (Vic-
toria). In the desert, between the convent and the hills, are some
scanty fragments of walls of brick, which seem to have belonged
to the fortified camp.

Between Monfalût and Assiûṭ (26 M. by water, 17 M. by land)
the Nile makes several great bends, which occasion a good deal of
delay to navigation. The generally favourable N.E. wind here
sometimes blows broadside on, and sometimes even against us. The
greatest curves are at *Bâkir el-Menḳabâd* and *el-Amrâg*. El-
Menḳabâd, Coptic *Man Kapot* ('potters' village'), situated on an
artificial arm of the Nile, has long been famous for its pottery. To

the S. of it lies *Benîb* (or *Ebnûb*) *el-Ḥammâm*, inhabited by Copts. The mountains of the E. bank now recede, and the foot-hills of the Libyan chain approach the river, on the banks of which grow several fine groups of sycamores. The minarets of Assiût now come into sight, and numerous dredgers are seen at work in the canals. We land at *el-Ḥamrah*, the palm-enclosed harbour of Assiût, with its steamers and other boats.

Passengers by railway reach Assiût in the evening after dark, as the train is not due till 6.30 p.m. and is generally late. Those who do not wish to spend a day here, in order to see the town and the neighbouring tombs (p. 32), should at once transfer themselves and their luggage to the steamer (dragoman of the steamboat agents at the station). The path to el-Hamrah (see above), a walk of about 20 min. (donkeys for hire), leads along the railway track, and, as it is not lighted, a man should precede the party with a lantern. The train, however, often runs right down to the harbour. On reaching the steamer the traveller should at once make sure that all his baggage has been brought aboard.

Assiût, *Asyût*, or *Siût* (*New* Hotel, kept by G. *Benois*, near the station, 12*s.* per day, not very good), 252 M. from Bûlâḳ, is one of the oldest and now one of the most important towns on the Nile, containing 31,600 inhab., a railway station, and steamboat, post, and telegraph offices. There are British, American, French, German, and Austrian consular representatives. The public baths are well fitted up. The Egyptian Mission of the American Presbyterians (100 stations, 26 churches, 97 schools) has one of its stations here, with interesting schools for girls and boys. The sacred name of the place, *Pa anub* ('town of the wolf-headed Anubis') or *Pa ap ḥeru kemū* ('S. town of the way-opener', *i.e.* Anubis) gave rise to its Greek name of *Lycopolis* (see below). Its secular name, even in the ancient kingdom, was   *Saut*, Coptic *Siōut*. No other town, except Mêdûm, has preserved its ancient name with so little change. With the exception of a few fragments of columns, nothing remains of the living quarters of the ancient town, but the older part of the necropolis contains some very interesting relics of early times.

Plotinus, the greatest of the Neo-Platonic philosophers (205-270 A. D.), was born here in the beginning of the 3rd cent., and his system was not uninfluenced by the priestly doctrines of his native town. From the beginning of the 4th cent. onwards Christianity was dominant in the town and neighbourhood. Pious believers took refuge in the caves of the necropolis to live a life of penitence apart from the world. One of these, *John of Lycopolis*, at the end of the 4th cent., bore the reputation of a saint and even of a prophet. Theodosius sent an embassy to him to enquire the outcome of the civil war. The anchorite foretold a complete but bloody victory, and this prophecy was fulfilled in the victory of Theodosius over Eugenius at Aquileia in 394 A.D. The life of the saint of Lycopolis was written by his friends Rufinus and Palladins. The grotto that he occupied cannot now be distinguished from the numerous others in the hills; but the rocky chamber of another hermit of the name of John can be identified in the vicinity of Benihasan, for he wrote on the wall the Coptic phrase: 'make prayers for me miserable. I am John'. Towards the end of his life St. John of Assiût lived in the Convent of the Seven Hills, at the top of the ridge, which was named after him the Convent of St. John the Less. Maḳrizi relates that St. John, at the bidding of his teacher, once planted and watered a piece of dry wood, and that a fruit-tree sprang up, called the 'Tree of Obedience', yielding fruit for the monks.

From very early times Assiûṭ was considered the northernmost point of the *Thebaid*.

The steamers and dhahabîyehs are met at *el-Hamrah* by donkey boys with well-saddled donkeys and by sellers of pottery, which can nowhere in Egypt be obtained better than here. The fine pottery of Assiûṭ, especially its bottles and pipe-bowls, is justly celebrated and forms an important article in its export trade, which also deals in linen, embroidered leather goods, ostrich feathers and other products of the Sûdân, natron, soda, and corn. It has, however, lost part of its commercial importance since the great caravans from W. Africa have frequented other routes and places. Large trains of camels still come from Dârfûr and Kordofân, generally encamping at Beni 'Adin (p. 29), 19 M. to the N.W. of Assiûṭ. The vicinity of Assiûṭ is one of the best-cultivated districts in the valley of the Nile, the fertile strip between the Libyan and Arabian Mts. here attaining a width of 12 M. The province of Assiûṭ, the mudir of which resides here, contains 234 villages with 583,596 inhab. (incl. the oases of *Khârgeh* and *Dâkhel*). Near the harbour are several large palm-gardens, in which also grow pomegranate, fig, and other fruit-trees. These gardens are let at enormous prices and produce rich harvests of fruit.

Those who have $2^1/_2$-3 hrs. to spare should not omit to ride through the town and to the tombs on the slopes of the Libyan limestone hills, not only for the sake of the antiquities, but to see the busy Oriental life in the bazaars and to enjoy the view from the graves. Candles and matches must not be forgotten. To visit Assiûṭ from the dhahabîyeh and to ride through it takes about 1 hr. The town lies about $3/_4$ M. from the river and is reached from the harbour by an embanked road shaded with beautiful trees. Outside the town lie the long government buildings. The streets are full of busy life, especially on Sundays, when the people of the neighbourhood flock into the market. Oriental wares are cheaper in the bazaars of Assiûṭ than at Cairo, but European goods are dearer. The better houses are of burned brick, the meaner of sun-dried Nile bricks. The façades on the street are generally unimposing, but a glance into one of the courts of the bigger houses will show that the wealthy merchants of Assiûṭ are not indifferent to comfort and display. The main street intersecting the town from E. to W. is nearly 3 M. long.

Necropolis of Ancient Lycopolis. To reach this from the harbour we require at least $3/_4$ hr. Riding through part of the town, we diverge from the main street at the point where it bends to the right and proceed to the left, through the cultivated land and across a handsome bridge, to the foot of the Libyan hills. The dark openings of the tombs and caves are conspicuous at a distance in the abrupt sides of the mountain, below which lies the new Arab cemetery. On the way, especially in the forenoon, we often meet funeral processions, resembling, with their wailing women and water-distributors, those of Cairo, but producing a much more solemn effect through the absence of the bustle of the crowded streets and the presence of the deserted city of the dead. Nowhere, not even in Cairo, are the funeral songs so strange and weird as here, or sung by such deep and tuneful voices.

At the foot of the hill we dismount and follow the good path which leads to the most interesting tombs. A tomb below, near the Arab cemetery, is unimportant. Mighty grandees of the ancient empire, who filled the highest secular and ecclesiastical offices, hewed huge vaults in the rocks here for the reception of their mummies. Other tombs, smaller and less elaborately decorated, belong to simple burghers of a later period; and there are also holes in the rock for mummies of the jackal, which was sacred to Anubis Apheru, the local deity of Assiût. It is this animal that the Greeks in this instance wrongly called Lykos or wolf (whence Lycopolis), but a few genuine wolf-bones have also been discovered here. Mummified dogs, kittens, and birds of prey have been found, wrapped in linen bands and sometimes adorned with gilding. Those who do not object to creep into some of the dusty and ill-smelling holes will still easily find fragments of sacred animals. The jackal, along with the Uræus-snake, flaunted proudly on the standard of this nome, the chief town of which was the capital of the whole of Upper Egypt in the time of the ancient empire.

The path, which is well-made though somewhat steep, leads us first to a large rock-hall, the ceiling of which is roughly hewn in the form of a vault and still bears traces of blue stars painted on a yellow ground. Sadly defaced inscriptions, in the style of the ancient empire, cover the walls. The hieroglyphics on the door are half obliterated, but enough remains to show that this was the grave of *Ḥap-Zefa*, son of Dame At àt, a high-priest, and governor of S. Egypt. The Arabs call it *Iṣṭabl 'Antar*, or the stable of Antar, a hero of tradition (comp. their name for the Speos Artemidos at Benihasan, p. 11). The *View from this tomb is very fine. The fertile land and the Nile enclosed by the limestone hills of Libya and the Arabian mountains in the distance form a quiet but by no means monotonous setting for the beautiful town of Assiût with its eleven minarets and its environment of palm-gardens. The view is still grander from the higher tombs. The second chamber of this tomb is covered with important inscriptions. To the right on entering is one of 64 lines, which cannot be read without the aid of a long ladder and a good lantern. It contains ten articles from the code relating to the worship of the dead, determining, amongst other things, the sacrificial gifts for the statues of the deceased. These were translated first by Maspero and afterwards by Erman, while the revised text has been published by *F. L. Griffith* (1889). To the left is another almost illegible inscription, engraved, like a palimpsest, above an older text and referring to Hap-Zefa; on the same side are cartouches of Usertesen I.

Higher up, to the right (N.), is a row of three tombs close to each other, the northernmost of which has been destroyed. The second is the *Kahf el-ʿAsâkir*, or Soldiers' Tomb, so named from the rows of warriors on its S. wall. On the right side of this tomb is a long and partly effaced inscription, referring not only to *Kheti*, father of Tef āb, the owner of the tomb, but also to King Merikara (12th Dyn., acc. to Maspero, of the 10th or Heracleopolitan Dyn.), in whose reign Kheti lived.

The adjoining tomb (to the left or S.; No. 3) contains a long inscription referring to *Tef āb*, a high-priest of Apheru (Anubis), lord of Assiût. A little farther to the S. is the tomb (No. 2) of another *Hap-Zefa*, son of Aï and headman of the district of Atef-kheut.

The geological formation of this hill of tombs is very interesting, especially on account of the numerous specimens of *Callianasse nilotica* and other fossils found on its upper part. The limestone is so hard that it emits sparks, and flints occur in considerable quantity.

Among the curiosities of Assiût there must not be forgotten the small piece of water standing between the river and the town, the ancient legend of whose effect upon virgins is still half seriously related. Paul Lucas is probably the first author who mentions it, and Michaelis devotes a paragraph to it in his edition of Abulfeda's Description of Egypt (A. 189): 'De quo stagno fingunt Siutenses, ejus potu signa virginitatis eripi, unde excusatas habent novas nuptas virginitatem non prodentes, si stagni aquam degustarunt. Felix certe inventum, nec despero tales in vicina aliarum quoque et Europae urbium, quod felix faustumque virginibus sit, fontes'.

At *Beni Mohammed el-Kufûr*, opposite Assiût, are several important tombs of the 6th Dynasty, belonging to nomarchs and (probably) relatives of King Pepi.

2. The Fayûm.
Comp. Map, p. 2.

A TOUR THROUGH THE FAYÛM, including a visit to the Labyrinth, the site of Lake Mœris, the Birket el-Kurûu with its abundant wildfowl, and the ruins in its neighbourhood, takes 6-8 days, and requires a tent, a dragoman, and a supply of provisions. A dragoman charges 30-40 fr. a day for each person, according to the requirements of his employers, and for that sum he is bound to provide them with a tent, provisions (wine excepted), and donkeys, or other means of conveyance, and to pay railway fares and all other expenses. A written contract (comp. p. xx), specifying the places to be visited, the points where some stay is to be made (on which occasions a reduced charge per day should be stipulated for), and other particulars, should be drawn up before starting. Those who intend to visit Medinet el-Fayûm and its immediate environs only, and who do not object to rough quarters for one or two nights, may dispense with a dragoman and a tent, but should be provided with a moderate supply of food. An introduction to the mudîr will be of great service in enabling the traveller to procure the necessary horses or donkeys, which the inhabitants are often unwilling to hire (comp. pp. 37, 42).

Since the completion of the railway this excursion has usually been undertaken from Cairo, but it may also be combined with a visit to Sakkârah. It was formerly usual to visit the Fayûm in connection with a journey up the Nile, but this plan entails needless expense, as the boat and its crew have to be paid for while lying idle for several days. If, however, the traveller prefers this plan, he disembarks at Wastah and sends on his dhahabîyeh to Benisuêf, which he afterwards reaches by railway.

RAILWAY from Cairo to Medinet el-Fayûm (*Ligne de la Haute-Egypte*), 75 M., in about 4 hrs. The trains are often late. — A train starts daily at 8.30 a.m. from the Bûlâk ed-Dakrûr station, reaching Wastah (p. 1) at 10.38 a.m. (halt of 20 min.; change carriages) and Medinet el-Fayûm at 12.16 p.m. A second train starts from Bûlâk ed-Dakrûr at 3 p.m., reaching Wastah at 5.29, where the train leaving Assiût at 8.30 a.m. arrives at 4.25 p.m. From Wastah the Fayûm train proceeds at 5.45 p.m., reaching Medineh at 7 p.m. — From Medinet el-Fayûm the line goes on to Senhûr, but for a visit to the Birket el-Kurûu horses must be brought from Medîneh (comp. p. 42). — A train leaves Medinet-el-Fayûm daily at 9 a.m., reaching Wastah at 10.15 a.m. and Bûlâk ed-Dakrûr at 1.15 a.m.

SITUATION AND HISTORY OF THE FAYÛM. In the great plateau of the *Libyan Desert*, which rises 300-400 ft. above the sea-level, is situated the province of the FAYÛM (from the ancient Egyptian 'Phiom', *i.e.* marsh or lake district), the first of the oases (p. 343), which is usually considered to belong to the valley of the Nile, and is justly celebrated for its extraordinary fertility (p. 36). This tract is in the form of an oval basin, 840 sq. M. in area, and supports a population of 200,000 souls; it is enclosed by the Libyan hills, which are here of moderate height, and lies about three-fifths of a degree to the S. of Cairo. It enjoys a remarkably fine climate, and has but rarely been visited by the plague. This 'land of roses' is still one of the most beautiful parts of Egypt, and more than any other part of the Nile valley deserves the well known epithet of 'the gift of the Nile', bestowed on Egypt by Herodotus, as it is entirely indebted for its fertility to the waters of the Nile with which it is artificially irrigated. The *Bahr Yûsuf* (p. 28), a channel 207 M. in length, which is more probably a natural branch of the river, artificially adapted, than a canal, diverges from the Nile to the N. of Assiût, and flows through a narrow opening in the Libyan chain into the Fayûm, where it divides into numerous ramifications, abundantly watering the whole district. One of its branches runs towards the N., skirting the E. slopes of the Libyan hills. At the point where the Bahr Yusûf enters the Fayûm, the district forms a plateau of moderate height, descending towards the W. in three gradations towards the Birket el-Kurûn, a long, narrow lake, extending from S.W. to N.E. On the easternmost and highest part of the oasis the Labyrinth and Lake Mœris (pp. 39, 40) were once situated; the central part yields the luxuriant crops for which the province is famous; while the westernmost part chiefly consists of sterile desert land. To the W. and N. of the Birket el-Kurûu rise precipitous limestone hills, beyond which lies the immense sandy desert of Sahâra. The Fayûm must have been reclaimed from the desert at a very early period, probably during the early empire, in the reign of Amenemha III., as monuments of his period indicate that he was perhaps the first of the Pharaohs who sought to regulate the whole course of the Nile. On the Upper Nile Prof. Lepsius has found Nilometers constructed by that monarch, and in the Fayûm, on the site of the Labyrinth, a number of blocks of stone inscribed with his name. The Greeks called him *Ameris*, or *Mœris*, and believed that the lake known to them as 'Lake Mœris', which they regarded as a marvel of engineering skill, was named after him. The word *meri*, however, is the Egyptian for lake or overflow, so that the great basin of the Fayûm was simply 'the lake'; and it was from his exertions in connection with the irrigation works that Amenemha obtained the name of Mœris. We learn from several inscriptions, and from a papyrus roll treating of the Fayûm, that the province was known in the time of the Pharaohs as *Ta shet*, or the lake-land, and that Lake Mœris was called *hun-t*, signifying the discharge or posterior lake. On its bank rose the celebrated Labyrinth, which was probably renewed by the Bubastite monarchs of the 22nd Dynasty. About the same period the town of Crocodilopolis, situated on Lake Mœris, and afterwards called Arsinoë after the wife of Ptolemy Philadelphus, was so extended and embellished by Osorkon I. that it is called the 'city of Osorkon I.' in the inscription on the celebrated

2 *

stele of Piankhi. The whole province was at first called the lake-land, then the district of Crocodilopolis, and lastly the Arsinoite Nome. The deity most highly revered here was the crocodile-headed Sebek, the reptile sacred to whom was carefully tended in Lake Mœris. At the same time the voracious and dangerous monster, notwithstanding the reverence paid to it on account of its connection with the inundation, was also regarded as Typhonic, and the Crocodilopolitan nome was therefore passed over in the lists of nomes. — At the period preceding that of the Psamtikides of the 26th Dynasty the Labyrinth appears to have been used as a hall for great imperial assemblies. At the period of the Ptolemies and the Romans the products of the Fayûm were much extolled. 'The Arsinoite Nome', says Strabo, 'is the most remarkable of all, both on account of its scenery and its fertility and cultivation. For it alone is planted with large, full-grown, and richly productive olive-trees, and the oil is good when carefully prepared; those who are neglectful may indeed obtain oil in abundance, but it has a bad smell. In the rest of Egypt the olive-tree is never seen, except in the gardens of Alexandria, where under favourable circumstances they yield olives, but no oil. Vines, corn, podded plants, and many other products also thrive in this district in no small abundance'. — Strabo's description is still applicable at the present day. The oranges and mandarins, peaches, olives, figs, cactus fruit, pomegranates, and grapes grown here are much esteemed, and the beautiful, rich-coloured red roses of the gardens of the Fayûm, which were once so lavishly strewn at the banquets of Cleopatra, still thrive here. At the station of Medinet el-Fayûm small phials of attar of roses, of inferior quality, are frequently offered for sale. Isma'il Pasha devoted special attention to this favoured part of his dominions. The fields, which are watered by means of wheels of peculiar construction, yield rice, sugar, cotton, flax, and hemp, besides the usual cereals. The beginning of November is probably the season at which the traveller will obtain the most distinct idea of the fertile character of the district. — The *Inhabitants* are fellâhin, or tillers of the soil, and Beduins. To the latter race belong the poor fishermen who inhabit the banks of the Birket el-Kurûn. Many of the peasants also call themselves 'Arabs', and the wealthier of them are generally well mounted.

From Cairo to **el-Wastah** (51 M.), see p. 1. Travellers coming from Cairo change carriages here; stay of 20 min. in the forenoon, 17 min. in the afternoon.

The branch-line to the Fayûm runs towards the W., across cultivated land, to the village of *Abu Râdi*, beyond which it traverses a desert tract for 35 min., and then crosses the low and bleak Libyan chain of hills, reaching its highest point at a level of 190 ft. above the sea. We then descend, cross the *Bahr el-Wardân*, which flows towards the Bahr Yûsuf from the N., and then the watercourse of *el-Bats* (p. 38), and near the station of (19 M.) *el-Adweh* (69 ft.), on the right, we again perceive cultivated land. On the left is a cemetery with the dilapidated tombs of several shêkhs. Numerous palm-branches are placed by the tombstones as tokens of affection. On the right stretches an ancient dyke, which once may have belonged to the embankment of Lake Mœris (p. 40). We pass the station of *el-Maslûb*, traverse rich arable land, and soon reach (23½ M.) —

Medînet el-Fayûm, the 'town of the lake-district', situated to the S. of the site of *Crocodilopolis-Arsinoë*, the ancient capital of the province (*Hôtel du Fayoûm*, 10s. daily; with a letter of introduction from Cairo quarters may also be obtained at the American

mission-station or at the house of the Italian curé). It contains
about 40,000 inhab., and is a not unpleasing specimen of an Egyptian town. Between the station and the town we observe a peculiar,
undershot sâḳiyeh, or water-wheel driven by the water itself. The
very long covered bazaar contains nothing of special interest. The
traveller, even if unprovided with an introduction, should pay a
visit to the mudir, who will protect him from extortion in case of
any difficulty with the owners of horses and others (comp. p. 34).
A broad arm of the Baḥr Yûsuf (p. 35) flows through the middle
of the town. The mosque of *Ḳait Bey*, on the N. side of the town,
now somewhat dilapidated, is the only interesting building of the
kind. It contains numerous antique columns, brought from the
ancient Arsinoë, some of which have shafts of polished marble with
Arabic inscriptions, and Corinthian and other capitals. Below the
mosque, on the bank of the Baḥr Yûsuf, are some remains of ancient
masonry. No ancient inscriptions have been discovered here, but
the walls of some of the houses contain fragments which must
have belonged to ancient temples. At the W. end of the town the
Baḥr Yûsuf radiates into numerous branches, which water the
country in every direction. The dilapidated mosque of *Ṣofi* situated
here forms a picturesque foreground.

To the N. of the town are the extensive ruins of **Crocodilopolis-
Arsinoë**, which has been entirely destroyed. The site is now called
Kôm Fâris. Many antiquities, both of the Roman and the Christian
period, have been found here, including numerous small terracotta
lamps and many thousand fragments of papyri, intermixed with
pieces of parchment. Most of the papyri are Greek (among them
fragments of Homer, Euripides, Thucydides, also of a Christian
catechetical book), many are Arabic from the 2nd cent. of the Hegira down to 943 A.D.; and others are in Coptic, Pehlevi, Sassa-
nide-Persian, and Meroitic-Ethiopian characters. Several fragments
in hieratic and hieroglyphic characters, the oldest from the time of
Ramses III. (about 1300 B.C.), have also been discovered. As the
writings are for the most part tax-papers, it has been supposed that
they belonged to a tax office of the town of Crocodilopolis, where
old papyri also were used. A large number of the papyri found
here were acquired by Consul Travers for the Berlin Museum, and
even a larger number by Theod. Graf and Archduke Rainer for the
Austrian Museum of Art and Industry at Vienna. The very extensive cemetery of the town, with its picturesque tombstones, covers
part of the site of the ancient city; the highest of the mounds of
rubbish command a survey of the whole of the Fayûm. At the N.
end of the ruins, about 1¹/₄ M. from Medîneh, M. Schweinfurth
discovered the remains of a large temple with a pylon, in front of
which is a sitting figure of Amenemha I., the founder of the 12th
Dyn., and inside several slabs with the name of Ramses the Great.
A head with Hyksos features, now in the museum of Gizeh, has

also been found here. According to Mr. Flinders Petrie, the temple
proper, which was 490 ft. wide and had a double colonnade, belongs to the 26th Dynasty.

The village of Bihamu, about 4 M. to the N. of Medîneh, was
doubtless once situated on the bank of Lake Mœris. It still contains
some shapeless ruins of ancient origin, destitute of inscription, but supposed to be the remains of the pyramids which according to Herodotus
once stood in the lake. They are now called *Kursi Far'ân*, or chair of
Pharaoh, and resemble dilapidated altars rising above other fragments of
solid masonry. If they were once pyramids, the greater part of them
must have been removed, as the walls are now but slightly inclined
inwards. Distinct traces of the water in which they once stood are to
be seen on their bases, and they are still surrounded by remains of
walls, the purpose of which is unknown.

In the fields near **Ebgîg**, or *Bègîg*, 2½ M. to the S.W. of Medîneh, lies
a fine obelisk, broken into two parts, which must have once been at least
46 ft. in height (route to it rough and dirty). Like other obelisks, it is,
horizontally, of oblong rectangular shape, and its summit is rounded.
The inscriptions, which are damaged at many places, inform us that the
monument was erected by Usertesen I., who also founded the obelisk
of Heliopolis (Vol. I., p. 333), and belonged to the same family (12th Dyn.)
as Amenemha III., the founder of the Labyrinth. — A visit to Bîhamu
and Ebgîg is chiefly interesting to archæologists, and perhaps to bota-
nists also.

EXCURSIONS. A whole day is required for a visit to the *Pyramid
of Hawârah* and the *Labyrinth.*(horse 10, donkey 5 fr.). The route
leads at first for ³/₄ hr. along the bank of the Baḥr Yûsuf. The first
village of any importance is *Uhâfeh*. Our path traverses well cultivated land with numerous water-wheels. The corn and cotton
fields are shaded by numerous sycamores, lebbeks, palms, and
other trees. About ¹/₂ hr. from Uhâfeh, and beyond two smaller
villages, we reach a bridge of ancient brick masonry. Traversing
the slightly undulating tract a little farther, we reach the *Baḥr
Belâh Mâh* ('river without water'), also called *el-Bats*, a deep channel, extending in a wide curve, and terminating near the N.E. end
of the Birket el-Ḳurûn (p. 43). In winter the water, which trick-
les down from its lofty banks, forms a few scanty pools. At the
bottom of the channel grow reeds and tamarisks. The S. bank
rises at places nearly perpendicularly to a height of 26 ft., so that
the sequence of the strata of the soil is distinctly observable. We
now ascend the plateau (the highest in the province, 88 ft. above
the sea level) on which lies **Hawâret el-Ḳaṣab** or *Hawâret el-
Makta*, a considerable village, with a mosque (reached in 1³/₄ hr.
from Medinet el-Fayûm). The traveller may apply to the Shêkh-el-
Beled (prefect of the village) for a guide to the pyramid of Hawârah.
If the water is high, and the canals have to be avoided, we have
to make a circuit of nearly 2 hrs. to the Labyrinth, but by riding
through the water, where necessary, it may be reached in ³/₄ hour.

The longer route is preferable, as it passes several relics of
antiquity. A little beyond the village rises the bridge of *Kanâtir
el-Agani*, the ten buttresses of which rest on a foundation of massive stone. We continue to ride along an ancient embankment, and

thus reach the *Katasantah* structure, which consists of a terrace of six carefully jointed steps of large and well-hewn blocks, but bears no inscription whatever. We cross the *Bahr el-Wardän*, which now intersects the ruins near the Pyramid of Hawârah, and which is sometimes called by the Arabs *Bahr el-Melekh* or *Bahr esh-Sherki*, i.e. river of the East. On the E. side lies the mass of buildings, which, according to Lepsius, was probably the *Labyrinth* (see below). In order to obtain a survey of these interesting ruins the traveller is recommended to ascend at once the **Pyramid of Hawârah.** This consists of unburnt bricks of Nile mud mixed with straw (Vol. I., p. 370), and, when its sides were perfect, covered an area of upwards of 116 sq. yards. It has been ascertained that the nucleus of the structure is a natural mass of rock, 39 ft. in height. The dilapidated summit is easily reached in a few minutes by a flight of well-worn steps. The entrance to the pyramid, on the S. side, was discovered in 1889 by Mr. Flinders Petrie. The tomb chamber is 22 ft. long, 8 ft. wide, and 6 ft. high; it was covered with three large slabs of stone and contained two sarcophagi, one of them of polished sandstone without inscription, and fragments of an alabaster vase with the name of Amenemha III. The chamber was filled with water to a depth of 3 ft.

Towards the S. we observe a congeries of chambers and passages of unburnt bricks, bounded by the Bahr esh-Sherki, and pronounced by Lepsius to be the right side of the **Labyrinth,** and the only part of it which is to some extent preserved. On the other side of the Pyramid there was doubtless a similar collection of rooms which has now disappeared; and several other structures beyond them, of which traces still remain, must have once existed there. The whole Labyrinth must have been in the shape of a horseshoe. Between the wing of the Labyrinth which still exists, and that which has disappeared, lies an extensive space strewn with broken pottery, in the middle of which are large fragments of a magnificent ancient temple. The base of the shaft of a small papyrus column, and a capital of the same order, both in the red stone of Assuân, with sculptured stalks and foliage, are worthy of notice. Some blocks disinterred here bearing the name of Amenemha III. have again been covered with sand. Several large blocks of limestone are also observed in the middle of this large court of the Labyrinth. The inscriptions are almost entirely destroyed, but faint traces of painting, and the symbols ⌒

(âa) and 𓄿 (n), are still recognisable. From the traces still existing, the whole structure would appear to have occupied an area of 8800 sq. yds., and the large inner court an area of about 60 acres.

The Ancient Labyrinth. According to Brugsch, the Greek name Labyrinthos, which has been differently interpreted, is derived from 'erpa', or 'elpa-robunt', i. e. the 'Temple of the mouth of the Lake'. The inscriptions found here by Lepsius prove that it was founded by Amenemha III. of the 12th Dynasty. Herodotus declares that the Laby-

rinth, which was afterwards reckoned as 'one of the wonders of the
world', was so vast as to surpass all the buildings of the Greeks taken
together and even the Pyramids themselves. For the best description
we are indebted to Strabo, who visited the Labyrinth in person. He
says: 'There is also the Labyrinth here, a work as important as the
Pyramids, adjoining which is the tomb of the king who built the Labyrinth. After advancing about 30-40 stadia beyond the first entrance of
the canal, there is a table-shaped surface, on which rise a small town
and a vast palace, consisting of as many royal dwellings as there were
formerly nomes. There is also an equal number of halls, bordered with
columns and adjoining each other, all being in the same row, and forming one building, like a long wall having the halls in front of it. The
entrances to the halls are opposite the wall. In front of the entrances
are long and numerous passages which have winding paths running
through them, so that the ingress and egress to each hall is not
practicable to a stranger without a guide. It is a marvellous fact that
each of the ceilings of the chambers consists of a single stone, and
also that the passages are covered in the same way with single slabs
of extraordinary size, neither wood nor other building material having
been employed. On ascending the roof, the height of which is incon-
siderable, as there is only one story, we observe a stone surface consisting of large slabs. Descending again, and looking into the halls, we may
observe the whole series borne by twenty-seven monolithic columns. The
walls also are constructed of stones of similar size. At the end of this
structure, which is more than a stadium in length, is the tomb, consisting of a square pyramid, each side of which is four plethra (400 ft.) in
length, and of equal height. The deceased, who is buried here, is called
Ismandes. It is also asserted that so many palaces were built, because it
was the custom for all the nomes, represented by their magnates, with
their priests and victims, to assemble here to offer sacrifice and gifts to the
gods, and to deliberate on the most important concerns. Each nome
then took possession of the hall destined for it. Sailing about a hundred
stadia beyond this point, we next reach the town of Arsinoë', etc. This
description of Strabo is confirmed by the contents of two papyri, one of
which is in the museum of Gizeh, the other in private possession (Mr.
Hood). The deities of 66 districts are enumerated here, 24 of whom belong to Upper Egypt, 20 to Lower Egypt, and 22 to the Fayûm.

It is very doubtful whether we should consider these buildings
of Nile bricks as remains of the ancient Labyrinth, or rather as
tombs. Certainly nothing is left that recalls in any way the splendour of the old 'wonder of the world'. Except some blocks of limestone, nothing remains of the extensive structures once erected
here, save the pyramid 'at the end of the labyrinth'.

To the N. of the pyramid Mr. Flinders Petrie discovered some mummy
coffins with carefully painted heads (now in London). Of still greater
value are the portraits found at *el-Rubayât*, 13 M. to the N.E. of Medinet el-Fayûm, which were purchased and brought to Europe by M. Theo-
dore Graf.

Lake Mœris. The object of Lake Mœris, which has long since been
dried up, was to receive the superfluous water in the case of too high
an inundation, and to distribute its contents over the fields when the
overflow was insufficient. Strabo describes Lake Mœris in the following terms: 'Owing to its size and depth it is capable of receiving the
superabundance of water during the inundation, without overflowing the
habitations and crops; but later, when the water subsides, and after the
lake has given up its excess through one of its two mouths, both it and
the canal retain water enough for purposes of irrigation. This is accomplished by natural means, but at both ends of the canal there are also
lock-gates, by means of which the engineers can regulate the influx
and efflux of the water.' The lock-gate, which in ancient times admitted the water conducted from the Nile by the canal into the lake,

was probably situated near the modern *el-Lahûn* (see below), the name of which is supposed to be derived from the old Egyptian '*Ro-hun*' or '*Lo-hun*', *i.e.* 'the mouth of the lake', and the site of which was probably once occupied by the town of Ptolemaïs.

There is a difference of opinion as to the *Situation and Form of the Ancient Lake.* Linant-Bey, arguing from the considerable difference of level between the two lakes, maintains that the Birket el-Kurûn (Lake of the Horns, p. 43) could never have formed part of Lake Mœris, as was formerly supposed, and he assigns to the latter a much smaller area than was attributed to it under the earlier theory. · Placing it farther to the S.E., nearer to the Labyrinth and el-Lahûn, he makes its boundary-line run towards the S.S.W. of Medinet el-Fayûm to the *Birket el-Gharak*, and intersect the desert of *Shêkh Ahmed*, where the ancient height of the water, which far exceeds the level attained in modern times, has left its traces; it then leads to *Kalamshah*, turns to the N. to *Dêr*, and then to the E. and S.E. to *Dimishkineh*, follows the embankment of *Pillawâneh*, and passes *Hawâret el-Kebîr* and the bridge of *el-Lâhûn* (see below). Hence the boundary leads by *Dimmo* towards the N.E. to *Seleh*, and thence to the W. to *Bihamu* (p. 38); then again to the S., and thus returns to Medinet el-Fayûm. — A somewhat fatiguing journey of 2-3 days will enable the traveller to complete this circuit of the bed of the lake, which is now dried up. Recently, however. Mr. F.Cope Whitehouse, relying upon the great circumference assigned by Herodotus (II, 149) to the lake, of 3600 stadia (reduced by Linant to 360) or about 335 M. (Pliny says' 230 M.), and upon measurements made by himself on the spot, ascribes a considerably larger area to the lake than Linant, and maintains that it extended on the S.W· to the *Wâdi Rayân.* It is not improbable that in ancient times nearly the whole of the Fayûm could be laid under water, so that even the Birket el-Kurûn belonged to Lake Mœris, but that the entire system was meant for the watering of the Fayûm alone and not of the Nile valley or the Delta. Considering that the bed of the lake must annually have been raised by the deposit of Nile mud, it follows, that as soon as the raising of the embankments and the removal of the mud were discontinued, the lake must have become unserviceable, especially after the lock-gates at el-Lahûn fell to decay, each opening of which, as Diodorus informs us, cost 50 talents (*i.e.* about 11,250*l*.?). The discharge of the superfluous water probably ran through the Bahr Belâh Mâh, which has already been mentioned (p. 38), or through the Wâdi Nezlch (p. 42), both of which fall into the Birket el-Kurûn. The ancient conjecture, that the latter discharged part of its water into the Sahârâ (or, as Herodotus says, the 'Libyan Syrte'), was not an unnatural one.

A visit to the **Pyramid of el-Lahûn** or **Illahûn** is only interesting to those who are desirous of convincing themselves of the truth of Linant's hypothesis, and to make the circuit of the boundaries of the old bed of the lake (see above). The pyramid, which is built of Nile bricks, may be reached from Hawâret el-Kaṣab in 4-5, or from the Labyrinth in 3-4 hours. It has been recently been opened by Fraser. The discovery of an alabaster altar with the name of Usertesen II. renders it probable that the pyramid was built by that monarch. A smaller pyramid lies to the N.E. The remains of the ancient embankments, which were tolerably well preserved in the time of the Khalifs, are not without attraction. Those who are interested in hydraulic engineering should also inspect the entrance of the Bahr Yûsuf into the Fayûm.

About ¹/₂ M. to the E. of the pyramid of el-Lahûn, Mr. Flinders Petrie discovered a temple in 1889, and close beside it the ruins of the town *Ha-Usertesen-hotep*, now called *Kahun.* The latter was founded by Usertesen II (12th Dyn.) for the labourers on his pyramid. Among the articles found here were pottery, flint and copper implements of the 12th Dyn., numerous papyri of the same period, a statuette of Si-Sebek (13th Dyn.), a wooden stamp of Apepi, and a large wooden door of Osorkon I.

Gurob, 1¹/₂ M. to the W.S.W. of Illahûn and close to the edge of the desert, owed its origin to Tutmes IH., who built a temple there. Many of the inhabitants were foreigners. Mr. Petrie discovered here fragments

of pottery of the time of Tutankhamon and Ramses II., resembling the
most ancient potsherds found at Mycenæ. The coffin of Amentursha,
discovered here, is now at Oxford. The pottery bears Egyptian stamps,
but also letters of the Cyprian, Phœnician, and other alphabets.

Birket el-Kurûn and *Kaṣr Kurûn* (tent, horses, provisions, etc.,
comp. p. 34). The Railway from Medînet el-Fayûm viâ *Ṣenru* and
Abu Gonsheh to (15 M.) *Abuksah* (see below) and thence to *Ṣenhûr* and (7¹/₂ M.) *Tirseh* is used almost exclusively for the conveyance of sugar-cane to the manufactories of the Khedive. Travellers going by railway (one train daily from Medineh to Abuksah,
starting about noon, and performing the journey in about 1 hr.)
must take horses with them for the continuation of their journey.
The following routes are all practicable, but the third is to be
preferred: —

(1) We proceed by land viâ *Nezleh* (where boats must be ordered
for the passage of the lake) to *Kaṣr Kurûn;* then by water to
Dîmeh, and again by water to the S. bank of the lake, situated in
the latitude of *Ṣenhûr*, which lies about 4 M. inland. The horses
should be sent on from Kaṣr Kurûn to the lake (unless the somewhat refractory guides refuse to obey), in order that we may ride
to Ṣenhûr, and thence to Medinet el-Fayûm. Four or five days are
required for the excursion; the points of interest are mentioned in
the third route. The road from Nezleh (see below) to Kaṣr Kurûn
(4 hrs.) leads through the desert, past the remains of a small temple,
called by the Arabs *Kaṣr el-Benât*, or 'Maidens' Castle'.

(2) If the traveller renounces Dimeh and Kaṣr Kurûn, and is
satisfied with the sport to be obtained in the Baḥr el-Wâdi, he may
easily make the excursion in 2¹/₂-3 days. On the first day the route
skirts the railway (see above) to (2 hrs.) *Ṣenrû;* it then leads
through a plantation of opuntia, the growth of which is so gigantic
that it almost resembles a forest, and across a sandy tract overgrown
with tamarisks to (2 hrs.) **Abuksah**, situated on a hill, and commanding a fine survey of the lake and the Libyan mountains. At
the N. base of the hill near the railway station (see above) is a sugar
manufactory, superintended by a Frenchman, who accords a kind reception to travellers. We now proceed to the S.W. across meadows,
and through a somewhat marshy district, to (2¹/₂ hrs.) *Absheh*, situated close to *Nezleh*. (The traveller is recommended to spend the
night in a tent rather than among the Beduins.) Next day we follow the valley of the *Baḥr el-Wâdi* (or *Baḥr Nezleh*), which is
bounded by large mud-hills, to the lake (2¹/₂ hrs.), where we spend
the middle of the day. (The numerous dead fish on the bank of the
lake render its proximity unpleasant; boats are to be had from the
Beduins.) In the evening we return to Absheh, and on the third
day to Medinet el-Fayûm.

(3) Four days at least are required for the somewhat longer
route viâ Senhûr and the lake to Kaṣr Kurûn, if the traveller wishes
to visit Dimeh, and shoot on the lake. The route first skirts the

railway and the villa of Maḥmûd Bey, and then passes the tomb of
a shêkh, where a draught of good water is offered to the traveller
by a dervish. A number of dry ditches must be crossed, and also
several canals, where the traveller on horseback will hardly escape
from wetting his feet when the water is high; if he rides on a
donkey, he should get the Arabs to carry him and his saddle across.
The fields which we pass are remarkably well cultivated, and the
eye rests with pleasure on trees of various kinds, including fine
olives in the gardens, with hedges of cactus. The vegetation is most
luxuriant in the neighbourhood of *Fidmîn*, a village picturesquely
situated on a slope, but inhabited by a thievish population. The
Baḥr eṭ-Ṭâḥûneh ('mill river'), one of the broader canals, must be
crossed here. Beyond this point the country is, at places, green and
well irrigated, and at others dry and sterile. One part of the route,
which is flanked by luxuriant gardens of olives, pomegranates, and
figs, is very muddy. After a ride of fully three hours we reach the
locks and the bridge *Kanâṭir Ḥasan*. The large body of water of
the canal, which is conducted from the Baḥr Yûsuf, here falls into
a channel, which, with many ramifications, conveys it to the fields
of Ṣenhûr.

The large village of Ṣenhûr (rail. station, see p. 42) lies on the
border of the second plateau of the province. Those who visit Hawârah (p. 38) reach the first plateau, while the second is crossed on
the way to Ṣenhûr; the third lies at our feet when looking down on
the Birket el-Ḳurûn from the great *Kôm*, i.e. the ruin-strewn hill
to the N. of the village. The handsome house of the Shêkh el-
Beled offers good accommodation, and even quarters for the night.
The traveller should make a bargain here for a boat with the shêkh
of the fishermen. About 30 fr. for the day, and a baḳshish for the
rowers (of whom 6-8 are necessary for speed), are demanded.

Ṣenhûr stands on the site of an ancient, and not unimportant,
town, of which large heaps of ruins still remain. Roman walls are
traceable in many places. A large building has recently been excavated by the peasants for the sake of obtaining the hard bricks
of which it is built, but part of it has already been removed. No
remains of columns or inscriptions have been met with.

From Ṣenhûr to the Birket el-Ḳurûn takes about 1¹/₂ hr. The route
leads through sugar-plantations. We reach the lake near the peninsula
known as *el-Gezireh*, on which stands a heap of ruins. A short distance
to the W. are the scanty remains of *el-Ḥammâm*. The traveller, after
having ridden to the lake, should not forget to order his horses, which
return to Ṣenhûr, to await him for the return-journey at the spot where
he has quitted them, or to order them to meet him in good time on the
bank of the lake by Nezleh (see p. 42).

The **Birket el-Ḳurûn** ('lake of the horns') owes its name to
its shape, which resembles that of slightly bent cows' horns. It
measures 34 M. in length, and, at its broadest part, is about 6¹/₂ M.
wide. It is situated on the same level as the Mediterranean, and
its depth averages 13 ft. The greenish water is slightly brackish

(scarcely fit for drinking), and abounds in fish, some of which
are very palatable. The right of fishing is let by government, and
the whole of the fishermen dwelling on the banks of the lake are
in the service of the lessee, who receives one-half of the catch.
The boats (merkeb) are very simply constructed, being without
deck or mast; the traveller must take up his quarters on the floor-
ing in the stern; none of the boats have sails, for, as the fish always go in the same direction as the wind, the fishermen have to
row against the wind in order to catch them. Numerous pelicans,
wild duck, and other water-fowl, frequent the lake. The banks
are extremely sterile; on the N. side are barren hills of considerable
height. In the middle of the lake rises a mass of rock, resembling
a table, and serving as a landmark. Near the S. bank, from E. to
W., lie the villages of Kafr Tamîyeh, Tirseh, Ṣenhûr, Abuksah, Beshuai, and Abû Gonsheh; the ruins of Dîmeh are situated on the N.
bank, but there are no other villages of importance. A the S.W.
end of the lake is the promontory of Khashm Khalîl, overgrown
with tamarisks and reeds, the creeks of which afford good landing-
places. Ascending thence across the desert, we reach the temple in
about $1^1/_4$ hours. The fishermen object to pass the night on the
bank in the neighbourhood of Ḳaṣr Ḳurûn, being afraid of the Beduins and the 'Afrît' (evil spirits).

Ḳaṣr Ḳurûn is a tolerably well preserved temple, probably of
the Roman, or, at the earliest, of the Ptolemaic period. Before
reaching it we observe numerous traces of an ancient town,
which has now disappeared. The ground is strewn with blocks
of hewn stone, burnt bricks, broken pottery, and fragments of
glass. A circular foundation wall indicates the site of an ancient
cistern, while other walls seem to have belonged to vineyards. The
walls of the temple consist of carefully hewn blocks of hard limestone. This temple, like almost all the shrines in the oases, was
dedicated to the ram-headed Ammon-Khnum, as is proved by the
only two figures of this deity which still exist. They stand opposite
to each other at the highest part of the posterior wall of the upper
story of the open roof.

The temple is 20 yds. in width across the façade, and 29 yds. in length.
The entrance, facing the E., is approached by a lofty and carefully constructed platform, 14 yds. in length, forming a fore-court, on the S. side
of which rises a massive structure resembling a tower. Adjoining the
façade of the temple, to the W. of the entrance door, rises a massive,
semicircular projection, resembling the half of a huge column. On the
lower floor are the apartments of the temple which were dedicated to
worship, divided into a triple prosekos, and leading to the Sekos or sanctuary. In the first three rooms the ground slopes down towards the sanctuary, which, built in the form of a cella, adjoins the third room of the
prosekos, and (as in the case of other temples) was divided into three
small rooms at the back. The sanctuary is flanked by two narrow passages, each of which is adjoined by three rooms. The rooms of the prosekos also have adjacent chambers from which we may enter the cellars,
or ascend by two flights of steps to the upper floor with its different apartments, and thence to the roof, whence we obtain an extensive view of the

remains of the ancient city, of the lake, and the desert. Each gate of this curious building is surmounted by a winged disc of the sun; and over the doors leading into the second and third rooms of the prosekos and into the sanctuary, instead of the ordinary concave cornice, there is a series of Uræns snakes, which, with their outstretched heads and bendng necks, together form a kind of cornice. The names of several travellers are engraved on the stone of the first room, including those of Paul Lucas, R. Pococke, Jomard, Roux, d'Anville, Coutelle, Bellier, Burton, Belzoni, Hyde, and Paul Martin. Ḳaṣr Kurûn has also been visited by Lepsius. There are no ancient inscriptions remaining.

To the E. of the large temple are situated two smaller Roman temples, in tolerable preservation, the larger of which, situated 300 paces from the smaller, is not without interest. Its walls (18 ft. by 19 ft.) consist of good burnt bricks, and its substructures of solid stone; the cella terminates in a niche resembling an apse; on each of the side-walls are two half-columns, which, as the fragments lying on the ground show, belong to the Ionic order. There are also some less important ruins covering an extensive area, but nothing has been found among them dating from an earlier period than the Roman. The construction of the walls, the architectural forms, and many coins found here, are Roman; and none of those small relics of the period of the Pharaohs, which are usually found so abundantly among the ruins of Egypt, have been discovered here. This was perhaps the site of the ancient *Dionysias*, a town which probably sprang up on the ruins of a Roman military station, situated on the extreme western side of Egypt. On the outskirts of the ruins are walls which perhaps belonged to gardens; there must also have been once an aqueduct for the purpose of supplying the inhabitants and their gardens with water.

From Ḳaṣr Ḳurûn to Dîmeh is one day's journey. **Dimeh** is situated opposite to the point at which we approach the lake from Ṣenhûr. The scanty ruins on the S. bank of the lake (*El-Ham= mâmah*, etc.), are not worthy of a visit; but the ruins of Dimeh, although no inscriptions have been found there, present some attraction. A street, 400 yds. in length, formerly embellished with figures of lions, leads to a platform on which an important temple once stood. The numerous blocks scattered about here, resembling millstones, and apparently artificially rounded, are discovered on closer inspection to be of natural formation. The paved court was surrounded by a brick wall, and the temple itself contained several apartments; a peristyle, with columns now in ruins, led to the entrance. Notwithstanding the imperfect state of the ruins, they suffice to prove, that a town of very considerable importance, perhaps the ancient *Bacchis*, once stood here.

3. From Assiût to Beliâneh.

Comp. Map, p. 8.

107 M. STEAMBOAT upstream in 7 hrs., downstream in 6½ hrs. The mail-steamer stops for the night at Girgeh, both in ascending and descending. The length of the DПAНABÎYEH VOYAGE depends upon the wind. With a favourable wind it takes about twice as long as the steamboat voyage; to *Sohâg* 4 hrs., thence to *Girgeh* 6 hrs., and thence to *Beliâneh* 3 hrs., in all about 13 hrs.

The voyage from Assiût to Akhmîm leads through an extremely fertile and well-cultivated district. Well-tilled fields, broader on the W. than on the E., adjoin both banks of the river, and are shaded by fine palms and Nile acacias, especially near the riverside villages. Here, as in most of Egypt, large quantities of pigeons are kept by the peasants, chiefly for the sake of their droppings, which form the only manure used in the fields, the dung of the cattle being dried and used as fuel. Large pigeon-houses, not unlike pylons, are visible in all the villages, and huge flocks of pigeons are seen wheeling in the air or settling like a dark cloud on the fields. Most of these pigeons are of the common grey species, and attain a considerable size, but many pretty little reddish-grey turtle doves are also seen. The traveller is at liberty to shoot these birds, which in the form of a pigeon-pie with olives form a most acceptable addition to his larder, but he should exercise this liberty with discretion and not rob the harmless fellâḥ of too many of his feathered friends. The pigeons really consume more than they produce, so that their encouragement by the fellâḥin is rightly regarded as a serious mistake in their husbandry.

Those who are interested in Egyptian agriculture may utilise the opportunity of an unfavourable wind to go ashore here. Formerly convent after convent occupied this district, and the gardens of the monks, according to Maḳrîzi, made it possible for the traveller to walk continually in the shade. A few convents still remain, such as the *Dêr er-Rîfeh* (W. bank), on the slope of the Libyan hills, 8 M. to the S.W. of Assiût, with the tomb of Tutus, son of Rahotep and commander of the archers, and other ancient Egyptian graves. The inscriptions prove that *Shas-hotep*, the capital of the Hypselite nome, lay in this vicinity, and it may perhaps be identified with the modern *Shuteb*. Of the Christians who resided here in the 11th cent. we are told that they spoke Greek as well as Coptic. Interesting Coptic MSS. may still reward the searcher in all these convents.

The traveller need not break his journey between Assiût and Akhmîm, as even the antiquarian will derive little profit from the scanty remains on this part of the river. *Wastah*, nearly opposite Assiût, perhaps occupies the site of the ancient *Contralycopolis*. In the *Gebel Rokhâm*, to the E. of the villages of *el-Ghorêbiyeh* and *Natafeh*, is an alabaster quarry.

15 M. **Butig** or **Abutig** (steamboat and mail station), an agricultural town on the W. bank with 10,800 inhab. and a small harbour filled with Nile-boats, lies in the ancient Hypselite nome. The present name is probably derived from the conversion of the ancient Egyptian name *Ha-abeti* into the similarly-sounding Greek name of Ἀποθήκη (Apotheke; Coptic Tapothyke), *i.e.* Storehouse, an admirable name for the chief town of a district so fertile in grain. Among the Hellenes it was generally known as *Abotis*.

At *Bedâri*, on the E. bank, 2 M. from the river, are some rude rock-tombs without inscriptions. On the W. bank follow the mail steamboat-stations *Sedfeh* and *Temeh*.

By following the Arab hills we reach, 5¹/₂ M. from Sedfeh, *Râhineh*, with four large quarries in the hard limestone rock and some tombs of the old empire with roughly cut calyx-capitals and half-effaced sculptures. Similar tombs are found at *Shêkh Gâber* and *Dêr*, a little to the S.E. Near *Hamaniyeh*, in the steep side of the rocky hill, are three grottoes, one above another, containing ancient tombs with inscriptions and representations, belonging to the royal officials Afa and Kakes. In antiquity the place was named *Ka-khent* ⊔𝍫 ◠⊗ (Upper Ḳâu; see below).

14¹/₂ M. **Ḳâu el-Kebîr**, situated in the plain on the E. bank, is surrounded by a ring of hills, containing rock-tombs with sculptures and large quarries with some demotic representations. The few inscriptions refer to the old empire. Stamped bricks found in the mounds of debris belonged to the buildings of the 18th Dynasty. The quarries contain ornaments and representations of the Roman period. Ḳâu el-Kebir stands on the site of the ancient *Antæopolis*, capital of the Antæopolitan nome, in which the hero Antæus and other deities were worshipped. An inscription found here reads: Ἀνταίῳ καὶ τοῖς συννάοις Θεοῖς, 'to Antæus and his divine colleagues'. In ancient Egyptian it was called the 'Nome of the two Gods', probably in commemoration of the contest between Seth and Horus. According to the myth Antæus, son of Poseidon and Gæa, was a giant of immense strength, whom Osiris, on his journey through the world to introduce the vine and the culture of grain, appointed his vicegerent over the land bordering on Ethiopia and Libya. Busiris was governor of the land to the E. Antæus used his giant's strength to overcome and slay strangers, and Hercules had to try conclusions with him when he landed in Libya to steal the cattle of Geryon. After a violent struggle, Hercules succeeded in strangling his huge opponent. The deciding contest between Typhon (Seth) and Osiris, or rather Horus, son and representative of Osiris, took place, according to the version of the legend adopted by Diodorus, at Antæopolis, although the inscriptions, and notably the great Horus text of Edfu, relate that the struggle raged from one end of the Nile valley to the other. The Egyptian name of Ḳâu was ⌒◺𝕀⊗ *Tu ka*, or 'town of the lofty mountain', whence is derived the Coptic *Tkou*. It was also known as β⤻⏝◠⊗ *Zez*. According to Golenischeff Antæus was an Egyptian mountain-god (from *ant* = mountain), whom the Greeks compared with their Dionysus. A representation of Antæus mentioned by Wilkinson, in which he appears with his head, like Helios, surrounded with rays, and accompanied by the goddess Nephthys, has recently been re-discovered by Golenischeff in the N.E. angle

of the hill behind Ḳâu el-Kebir. Two of the piers of the grotto in
which the representation occurs, bear pictures of Antæus.

. At the beginning of the present century an interesting temple stood
on the site of the old town, of which the last column was washed away
by the Nile in 1821. Jomard, who described this temple during the French
Expedition, when the water already lapped its foundations, foretold its
fate. The temple was dedicated by Ptolemy Philometor and his wife
Cleopatra to Antæus and was restored by Marcus Aurelius Antoninus and
his colléague Verus (164 A.D.). This information was conveyed by a
double inscription, in Greek and in hieroglyphics, over the portal. The
bulls of the hieroglyphic inscription 𓃾𓃾𓃾 (*Ḳâu*) probably
denoted the name of the town. The temple was built of limestone and
was at least 225 ft. long, 52 ft. wide, and 51 ft. high. Its entrance faced
the river. The 18 columns, which were arranged in 3 rows, were 37 ft.
high, with a diameter of 27¹/₄ ft., and ended in palm-leaf capitals. If the
gigantic blocks that Jomard found on the ground were really parts of
the ceiling, they exceeded in size those of Karnak, which now excite
our astonishment. One of them was 32 ft. long, 4³/₄ ft. high, and 5¹/₄ ft.
thick, and must have weighed at least 48 tons.

To the S. of Ḳâu el-Kebir the Nile makes a bend to the W. and
forms an island by dividing into two branches. On the W. arm (W.
bank), to the N. of the island, lies *Ḳâu el-Gharbi* (W. Ḳâu), the
seat of a rebellion in 1865, which had important consequences for
all the inhabitants of Upper Egypt and about which the Oriental
facility in forming tradition has already woven numerous legends.†
The fellâhin scarcely venture to utter the name (Aḥmed Ṭayib) of
the hero of this uprising, but speak of him with bated breath as a
Messiah, who will one day return. He is said to be still living, in
Abyssinia. High up on the S. side of the hill of Ḳâu are some
more rock-tombs.

12¹/₂ M. *Sâhel*, on the W. bank, is the station for the town of
Taḥtah, situated 2 M. inland, with 3000 inhab. and a frequented
cattle-market.

On the E. bank, a little higher up, rises the *Gebel Shêkh el-
Harîdeh*, with ancient quarries and (high up) tombs hewn in the
rock, the openings of which are visible from the river. The material
of which the temple of Antæopolis was built was procured in the
large quarries on the S. side of the mountain, and consists of a
hard, fine-grained, grey shell-limestone, which smells unpleasantly
when rubbed but admits of a splendid polish. — The next steamboat stations are *el-Maraghât* and *Shendawîn*, both on the W. bank.
A large market is held in the latter every Saturday. On the E. bank
of the stream, which here encloses several islands, are some rock-
tombs, without inscriptions.

26¹/₂ M. **Sohâg** (*Hôtel du Nil*, on the river-bank; British and
American consular agents), on the W. bank, has recently become
the seat of the mudir in place of Girgeh and contains a very handsome government-building. The Mudîrîyeh contains 521,413 inhab.

---

† For details of the revolt of Aḥmed Ṭayib and its suppression, see
Lady Duff Gordon's *Letters from Egypt* (London 1866. 1875),

and is 650 sq. M. in extent. The *Canal of Sohâg*, which leads hence to Assiût, keeps to the W. and is intended to convey the water of the rising Nile as far as possible towards the Libyan Desert.

On this canal lies *Etfeh (Itfu)*, the ancient *Aphroditopolis*, so named from the sandals (tcb) made out of the skin of Seti. About 2 M. from Etfeh is the Red Convent, *Dêr el-Ahmar*, also called *Dêr Abu Bishâi*. Those who wish to visit the Red Convent and the similar White Convent (one of the regular excursions of the passengers by the 'four weeks' steamer) may hire asses at Sohâg and ride viâ *Demnu* towards the Libyan Desert. The old church of the convent, a basilica with nave and aisles, is a very ancient structure of brick, with elaborate capitals and a richly articulated apse. The outer walls, decreasing in thickness towards the top, and the concave cornice above the portal, are interesting for|their reminiscence of ancient Egyptian art. Abu Bishâi, the founder of the convent, is said by Wansleb to have been a penitent robber, and he afterwards acquired such a reputation for sanctity that, according to Makrîzi, 3000 monks placed themselves under his care. The recluse after whom the White Convent (*Dêr el-Abyad* or *Dêr Abu Shanudi*) was named, is stated to have been one of his pupils. It lies at the foot of the mountains, farther to the S.E., and may perhaps be rather called a Christian village than a convent, as husbands, wives, and children live here in families. The walls of the church are built of hewn stone, probably taken from the adjacent ruins of *Athrîbis* (Shêkh Hamed), dating from the Ptolemaic and Roman imperial periods. It dates at latest from the 5th cent. and is a basilica with nave and aisles. The columns vary in height and thickness, and the capitals are partly of later date. The chancel ends in three vaulted apses. The cupolas are adorned with poor frescoes, and the other decorations are also wretched. — In the hills to the W. of the White Convent are a few late rock-tombs, one of which, according to the inscription, is that of Ermius, son of Archibius.

6½ M. Akhmim, a steamboat and mail station on the E. bank, also reached from Sohâg by a shorter land-route. is a thriving little town with about 10.000 inhab., including 1000 Christians, some of whom are Roman Catholics, with a chapel of their own. The weekly market on Wed. is much frequented, and the bazaar is well-stocked. The numerous cotton mills produce the cloth for the blue shirts of the fellâhin and for the long *shâla* (pl. *shâlât*), or shawls with fringes, which the poorer classes wear on state occasions and for protection against cold. These articles, which have been made here since the time of Strabo, are extraordinarily cheap. Akhmim stands on the site of *Khemmis* or *Panopolis*, generally held to be the most ancient town on the Nile, though this honour probably belongs to the venerable This-Abydos, on the W. bank (p. 53). The deity specially venerated here was the form of Ammon Generator known as Ammon Khem, also called at a later date *Min*, an appellation formed by dropping the Khem and abbreviating the Amen. Thus it is called Σμιν, *i.e.* belonging to Min. For a figure of this deity, who appears in the most ancient texts, see *Baedeker's Lower Egypt*, p. 137. Diodorus, who among other classical writers gives us much information about Khemmis-Panopolis, calls it Χεμμω, whence proceed the Coptic *Shmin* and the Arabic *Ekhmîm* or *Akhmîm*. Its profane name on the monuments is *Apu*.

Herodotus (II, 91) distinguishes the citizens of Khemmis as the only Egyptians who favoured Greek customs and relates that they erected a

temple to Perseus, worshipped him with Hellenic rites, and held games
in his honour. The citizens claim'ed Perseus as a native of their town
and told the garrulous Halicarnassian that he had visited Khemmis, when
on his way to Libyä in pursuit of the Gorgon's head, and had recognised
them as his kinsmen. A statue of him stood in the temple. From time
to time the hero revisited Khemmis, leaving, as a sign of his presence,
his sandals, which were two ells long; the finding of these was considered a portent of good fortune. The festival of pole-climbing, celebrated in honour of Khem, probably suggested his identification with the
Greek Pan. — It is obvious that Perseus has been confused with Horus,
the destroyer of Typhon-Seth. Among the various forms assumed by the
'Libyan Monster' in his long battle with Horus was that of a dragon or
serpent, while Horus, like Perseus, was supported by wings in his en-
counter; hence the mistake of Herodotus. In any case he is excusable
for seeking in Egypt the home of Perseus, whose genealogy may be traced
back to Io. † It is an interesting fact that a later author states that the
Persea tree was first planted in Egypt by Perseus. As no goat-footed
deities have been so far discovered in the Egyptian cult, it is somewhat
difficult to explain how Khem came to be identified with Pan, unless on
account of his Priapian characteristics. The Pans and satyrs at Khemmis
first received and disseminated the news of the death of Osiris, and hence,
says Plutarch, the sudden dread and confusion of a multitude is called
panic. Akhmim is thus the true home of *Panic Fear.* A white bull and a
black cow were sacred to Khem. He appears in the triad along with the
child Horus and Isis Sekhet, surnamed t-erpa (trepha), whence the Greeks
may have formed the name Triphis. Tryphæna was also a cognomen of
some of the queens of the Ptolemaic line.

Khemmis still flourished in the Roman period, and its ancient
and famous temple was finally completed in the 12th year of Trajan.
After Christianity established itself here, the vicinity of Panopolis
became crowded with convents. Nestorius, Bishop of Constantinople, who had been banished to the oasis of Hibeh (Khârgeh,
Egypt. Heb, p. 352) on account of his disbelief in the divine
motherhood of the Virgin Mary, was attacked there by the plundering Blemmyes, and carried captive into the Thebaïd, where he
surrendered himself to the prefect of Panopolis, to avoid a charge
of wilful flight. He died in Panopolis-Akhmûn. Even after the
conquest of Egypt by Islâm, the temple of the 'great town' of
Akhmîm was, as Abulfeda and other Arabs relate, among the most
important remains of the days of the Pharaohs. Edrisi gives the
following account of it: 'At Akhmim we see the building called the
Barba (*i.e.* Perpa, Coptic for temple), which the first Hermes erected
before the flood . . . . . (of many ancient temples) that of Akhmim
is the most enduring and also the most remarkable for the beauty
of its sculpture. In truth we find represented in it not a few stars
only, but also various arts and artists, along with numerous inscriptions. The building lies in the midst of Akhmim'. Since this
account a great part of the town must have vanished, as the temple
ruins now lie outside it, to the N. They are neither extensive nor
beautiful, but are of interest to the savant, because they belonged,

† Danaë, the mother of Perseus, was the daughter of Acrisius, son
of Abas, son of Lynceus and Hypermnestra. Lynceus was the son of
Aigyptos, and Hypermnestra was the daughter of Danaos, from whom
the line runs up through Belos, Libye, and Epaphos (Apis) to Io.

as the above-mentioned Greek inscription informs us, to the old
temple of Pan, who is here represented in an ithyphallic form. Almost all the inscriptions are rapidly becoming effaced, and the same
fate is overtaking a circle divided into twelve parts and supposed to
be intended for the Zodiac. Of the second temple of Khemmis,
which Herodotus describes as dedicated to Perseus, the only remains are a few stones of the 18th Dynasty and some scanty fragments of a building of the Ptolemaic and Roman period. These are
reached by the water when the Nile overflows its banks and are
gradually being swept away.

In 1884 Maspero discovered an extensive *Necropolis* adjoining a Coptic
monastery among the mountains to the N.E. of Akhmim. Thousands of
mummies have been taken thence and some of them were sent to Europe.
A visit to this necropolis is well worth undertaking. The best plan is
to secure the company of *Khalil-Sakkar*, keeper of the Egyptian Museum,
and ride with him to the N.E., in the direction of the mountains. On
a hill beyond the village of (³/₄ hr.) *el-Hawaisheh* we see the deserted Coptic
monastery, round which, in a wide circle, lie the tombs, now mostly
destroyed. They date from the 6th Dynasty (Pepiseneb, Khemankhteta,
Ankhu, etc.) down to the Greek and Roman period. The grave of Tutu,
son of Sit asra (daughter of Osiris), with liturgical inscriptions, is well
preserved (1885). Most of the mummies found here were in good preservation, and many contained rolls of papyrus. Among them were many
priests (āt) and priestesses (āhī) of Khem, whose genealogies are carried
up for eight or ten generations.

The town of Akhmim has now become the seat of an active
trade in mummies. Objects of considerable interest and value may
often be obtained from the dealers in antiquities, but relic-hunters
should not try to make purchases in the presence of the keeper of
the museum.

Continuing our journey up the Nile, we soon see, close to the
E. bank, a conspicuous convent-village, resembling a fortress. On
account of its whitewashed walls the sailors call it **Dêr el-Abyad**,
a name that properly belongs to the monastery mentioned at p. 49,
which lies much farther to the W. About 50 men, women, and
children occupy the convent, which has little of a religious character in its mode of life. The pretty little church, built of light
and dark bricks, is lighted by cupolas, the largest of which is above
the nave. The nave is separated from the aisles by wooden screens.
The Hêkel, or Holy of Holies, at the E. end, is carefully enclosed.
In the nave, below the dome, stands the reading-desk of the priests,
and at the W. end of the church, separated from the priests, are
the seats for the laity. The paintings are wretched, and there are
no old MSS.; but the church is an excellent specimen of a Coptic
place of worship and is worth visiting, especially as it is only
5 min. walk from the river. The monks are very obliging and are
grateful for a small donation (1 fr., 1s., or more). — *Thomu*, which
was occupied by a Roman garrison, must have lain in this neighbourhood.

5¹/₂ M. **el-Menshiyeh**, a steamboat and mail station on the
W. bank, is merely a peasants' town, with very few houses of a

better class. It was probably founded by Soter I. and in the time
of the Pharaohs it was called *Neshi* and *Pasebek (Crocodilopolis)*,
afterwards *Pse-ptulmaios;* under the Ptolemies it was known as
Ptolemaïs-Hermiu Pasui (dwelling of the crocodile). The officials
of Abydos also resided here. The mounds and river-walls at Menshiyeh (no inscriptions) are certainly extensive, but still it is difficult, when face to face with them, to credit the statement of the
usually trustworthy Strabo : 'farther on is the town of Ptolemais,
the largest in the Thebaïd and not inferior in size to Memphis. Its
constitution is drawn up in the Hellenic manner'. The Ptolemaic
kings who died here received the same honours as the manes of the
Pharaohs at Abydos. According to Leo Africanus Menshîyeh was
the seat of an African prince named Hawára. Numerous antiquities
have been found here lately.

Before we reach Girgeh the mountains on the Arabian bank
approach close to the stream. At several points are rock-tombs,
either wholly destitute of inscriptions or with none but obliterated
specimens.

12½ M. **Girgeh**, on the W. bank, is a steamboat-station, with
post and telegraph offices ; the tourist-steamers stop for the night
here.

Girgeh, which is 336 M. from Bûlâk and 235 M. from Assuân, has
been from time immemorial the station where the Nile-boatmen halt to
bake a new supply of bread. As, however, this operation takes 24 hrs.
(a supply for several weeks being necessary), and as Girgeh is not a convenient place for so long a stoppage, the traveller is advised to make a
contract in Cairo before starting to the effect that the halt for baking be
made at Assiût or Keneh and not in Girgeh. No re'is will give up this
privilege, unless he has been previously bound down to do so in writing.
The customs of the Nile boatmen are almost as unchangeable as those of
the desert Arabs. The only suitable way in which to fill up a halt of 24 hrs.
at Girgeh would be to make an excursion to the temple of Abydos, but
this is much more conveniently reached from Beliâneh (p. 53). A day
can be very profitably spent at either Assiût or Keneh, in the latter case by
a visit to the noble temple of Denderah (comp. the Contract at p. xxi).

Girgeh, which contains 14,900 inhab., preceded Assiût as the
capital of Upper Egypt, but is now merely the chief place in the
province of Girgeh, while the seat of the Mudîrîyeh is at Sohâg
(p. 48). It becomes more probable every day that Girgeh occupies
the site of the ancient *This* (hieroglyph. *Teni*), in which the god
Anhur (Greek Onouris) was specially worshipped (comp. p. 53).
Some ancient tombs of the 6th Dynasty exist here, including one
of the time of Merenptah ; and a little to the N. are some other
graves of the ancient kingdom. Many of the present inhabitants
are Copts. Outside the town lies a Roman Catholic convent, which
is probably the oldest but one in Egypt; the abbot is a member of
the Fraternity of the Holy Sepulchre. The name of the town is
Christian, being that of St. George or Girges, the patron-saint of
the Coptic Christians, a representation of whom, in his combat with
the dragon, is present in almost every Coptic church. St. George

was canonised on April 23rd, 303 A.D.; and even as early as the
5th and 6th cent. we find him a favourite saint of the Egyptians.
Leo Africanus says that the Coptic brothers of St. George at Girgeh
were very wealthy and tells how they provided travellers with
what was necessary on their journey and sent rich gifts for the poor
to the Patriarch at Cairo. To this day several of the Coptic families
at Girgeh are very rich, possessing large estates; preëminent among
these is that of Bothrus. The town looks very picturesque as seen
from the river. The Nile makes a sharp bend here, and the effect
is as if the W. bank, on which the town stands, was at right angles
to the E. bank. The Arabian mountains rise like walls, and the
four tall minarets of the town, on the opposite bank of the Nile,
seem to vie with them in height. A picturesque group on the
river-brink is formed by an old and dilapidated mosque and a tall
minaret beside it. Many of the houses in the town are built of
burnt brick and decorated with glazed tiles. The bazaar resembles
those of other Nile towns. — *From Girgeh to Abydos* ('Arâbat el-
Madfûneh), 12-13 M., see below. — At *Meshaïk*, on the E. bank,
above Girgeh, scholars will find interesting remains of a temple
bearing the names of Amenhotep III. and Ramses II. Some very
ancient graves of priests of This have also been found there.

8 M. *Beliâneh*, on the W. bank, is a mail-station and the starting-point from which passengers on both the 'three weeks' and
the 'four weeks' steamer make the excursion to Abydos (see below).
Excursion to the *Western Oases*, see R. 35.

4. Abydos.

Beliâneh is now the usual starting-point for a visit to *'Arâbat
el-Madfûneh (Abydos)*, which lies about $8^1/_2$ M. to the S.W., inland from the river. This highly interesting excursion, which should
on no account be omitted, involves a ride of 2 hrs. (there and back
4 hrs.). The donkeys at Beliâneh are bad and provided only with
loose rugs or straw-mats instead of saddles, and those at Girgeh
are no better. At Abydos accommodation may be obtained in the
house of *Salîbeh*, keeper of the antiquities.

The track crosses the large *Canal of Rênaneh*, traverses a fertile
district dotted with numerous villages, and finally leads over part
of the Libyan Desert. Fine view of the mountain-chain running
towards the Nile. The ancient **Abydos** lay in advance of this chain,
on a site which may confidently be called the cradle of the earliest
line of the Pharaohs.

Menes, the first king of Egypt, is said to have been a Thinite, *i.e.* an
inhabitant of the nome of *This* (Egypt. *Teni*). Adolf Schmidt, in his
'Forschungen auf dem Gebiet des Alterthums', tries to prove that This
(Teni) lay near *el-Kherbeh*, a little to the N. of Abydos, while Pococke
seeks it at *el-Birbeh* (the temple), 3 M. to the W. of Girgeh (comp. p. 52).
If, as Ebers has suggested, the earliest Asiatic immigrants into Egypt
entered the Nile valley from the S., viâ Arabia and the Strait of Bâb el-

Mandeb, they could have found no more suitable spot for a settlement than the neighbourhood of Abydos, where the fertile W. bank of the Nile expands and offers easy cultivation and excellent dwelling-sites, removed from all danger of inundation. This is the most ancient town in Egypt, and its neighbour Abydos cannot have been much younger, for even in the time of the early empire it is frequently spoken of as a holy city. It possessed the most famous grave of Osiris, of which it was believed that burial in its vicinity or consecration in its sanctuary went far in ensuring a favourable judgment in the world to come. From an early period the grandees of the land caused their mummies to be brought hither — often, however, for a limited time only, directing that, as soon as the wished-for blessings had been received from Osiris, the bodies should be carried back to their ancestral burial-grounds. Mariette has proved that the town itself (Egypt. *Abtu*) was never of any great extent. The extant ruins extend from el-Kherbeh on the N.W. to 'Arâbat el-Madfûneh on the S.E. If, however, Abydos was small in the number of its citizens, it was great through the importance of the gods worshipped in its temples. Each of the 42 nomes of Egypt possessed its temple of Osiris; but none of them, except that of Sokar in. Memphis, rivalled in sanctity that of Abydos. The testimony of the monuments is confirmed by the classical writers. Herodotus left Upper Egypt undescribed, because Hecatæus had already treated of it, but we quote the celebrated passage in which the trustworthy Strabo speaks of Abydos : 'Above it (Ptolemaïs) lies Abydos, the site of the *Memnonium*, a wonderful palace of stone, built in the manner of the Labyrinth, only somewhat less elaborate in its complexity. Below the Memnonium is a spring, reached by passages with low vaults consisting of a single stone and prominent by their extent and mode of construction. This spring is connected with the Nile by a canal, which flows through a grove of Egyptian thorn-acacias, sacred to Apollo. Abydos seems once to have been a large city, second only to Thebes, but now it is a small place, etc.' Abydos is also mentioned by Plutarch, Athenæus, Stephanus of Byzantium, Ptolemy, Pliny, and others. Ammianus Marcellinus speaks of the oracle of the god Besa, which flourished here.

The ordinary traveller, especially when he has at his disposal only the 8 hrs. allowed by the steamer, will confine himself to the Memnonium of Seti I. (Pl. I) at 'Arâbat el-Madfûneh and the sadly dilapidated Temple of Ramses II. (Pl. II). The remains of the so-called Temple of Osiris at *el-Kherbeh* (Pl. III) and the adjacent site of Mariette's excavations in the ancient necropolis among the Libyan hills are rapidly becoming less and less interesting through the steady encroachment of the desert sand.

The Memnonium of Seti I.

This noble structure, which, from the time of Strabo onwards, has been visited and described by so many travellers, did not become fully known to the modern world till Mariette Bey, with characteristic judgment and perseverance and supported by the generosity of the Khedive, began in 1853 the task of freeing it from the sand. His plan of isolating the building by digging a trench round and preventing new accumulations of sand was not carried wholly into effect, but still, with the exception of portion of the outside of the N. wall of the second court, there is now no part of the temple where inscriptions are likely to be found that does not stand open to the explorer. The difficulty of the excavations was much increased by the fact that the back part of the temple was buried in the slope of the hill, in such a way that it looked like a gigantic sepulchral chapel forming the vestibule to a mighty rock-tomb in the bowels of the mountain. Mariette believes, and probably with justice, that this peculiarity of the Memnonium explains the name

of the adjoining village, 'Arâbat el-Madfûneh, *i.e.* 'Arâbat of the buried'. Possibly the last portion of the name may refer to Osiris, whose grave here attracted so many pilgrims, and Madfûn (masc.) may be a translation of the old name of the temple-quarter of Abydos. In spite of the most lavish expenditure of time, money, and labour, the excavators failed to find either the spring mentioned by Strabo or the tomb of Osiris, and yet the latter must lie close to the part of the ruins called *Kôm es-Sulṭân*, near the holy hill of Abydos so often mentioned in the inscriptions.

Mariette derives the name *Memnonium* from that of its founder Seti Ra-men-ma or Men-ma-ra. This, however, is undoubtedly wrong, and Lepsius was the first to show that the Egyptian word *Mennu* 𓉫𓉐 or 𓉫 𓈖𓈖𓈖 𓅓 , applied to any large monument or memorial, whether architectural or plastic, led the Greeks to describe every palatial structure of the ancient Egyptians as a Μεμνόνιον (Memnonion) or palace of *Memnon*. Perhaps they first heard the name Menuu given to the colossal figures of Amenhotep III. at Thebes (p. 153) and were attracted by its resemblance in sound to the name of the son of Eos who fell before Troy; hence they called the figures, afterwards so celebrated, statues of Memnon, and saw Memnonia, or palaces of the same hero, in some of the large memorial buildings described as Mennu. The fact that the Hellenes did not apply this name to all the great buildings of Egypt, but only to some of the temples of W. Thebes and to the sanctuary of Seti at Abydos, may be explained by the supposition that in the time of the Pharaohs these buildings monopolised the epithet of Menun, just as the fortress of the Conqueror in London is known as the Tower *par excellence* among the numerous towers of that city. The temple of Seti became known as the Memnonium or Palace of Memnon in the Alexandrine period, and a natural consequence was the conversion of the name *Abtu* into the similarly sounding *Abydos* or *Abydus*, the name of a town of Troas on the Hellespont, not far from the burial-place of Memnon. By degrees the Asiatic hero, son of Tithonus and Eos and ally of Priam (comp. p. 154), was converted into an Ethiopian, and the lively imagination of the Greeks transferred the Asiatic legends to Egypt and adapted them to Egyptian conditions. Thus they related that Tithonus sent an Ethiopian army to aid his son against Troy. These soldiers, however, heard of the death of Memnon at Abydos in Upper Egypt and retraced their steps, after hanging their garlands on the acacias in the holy grove at the Memnonium. Birds were fabled to have sprung from the ashes of Memnon, and reappeared on certain days every year, removed all impurities from his grave, dipped their wings in the Aesopos, which flows into the Propontis at Cyzicns, and sprinkled the grave with the water. At a later date these birds were said to come from Ethiopia. Finally it was asserted that the Egyptian Abydos had been founded by colonists from its Asiatic namesake.

The Memnonium of Abydos is not an ordinary divine or religious temple like those of Denderah, Karnak, and Edfu, but is rather one of the series of sepulchral sanctuaries of which mention is made at p. 170 of *Baedeker's Lower Egypt.* The numerous representations and inscriptions that cover its walls are mostly of a very general nature. They tell us, however, that the building they adorn was primarily intended for funereal purposes. As already mentioned, the bodies of numerous princes and grandees were brought here to participate in the blessings that were supposed to emanate from the sacred tomb of Osiris. The Pharaohs nowhere offered sacrifices to the manes of their forefathers more gladly than at Abydos, and prayers were put up here to the Osiris-kings of the ancient house of the Pharaohs just as at the neighbouring Ptolemaïs divine honours were paid to the deceased princes of Macedonian origin. — It was natural enough that in a sanctuary devoted to purposes of this kind no boisterous festivals or ceremonies should take place, and we are not surprised to learn that neither singer nor flute-player nor lute-player was allowed within its walls.

The great building of Abydos, at first sight, impresses neither by its size nor by its beauty. The walls consist of fine-grained limestone, while a harder material (sandstone) has been selected for the columns, architraves, door-posts, and other burden-bearing parts. The foundations are nowhere more than $4^1/_2$ ft. thick, and the platforms on which the columns rest are equally shallow. Numerous blocks have become disjointed, owing, as Mariette has shown, to the giving way of the dove-tails of sycamore wood with which they were fastened. The inscriptions of Seti and the earlier ones of his son and successor show great purity of style, but this quality disappears in the later texts of the latter. It has been established that a sanctuary of some importance stood at Abydos even in the days of the ancient empire, and indeed we hear of its restoration in that remote epoch. Our witness is a stele, now in the Louvre, on which Ameniseneb, a priest and architect, who lived in the reign of Usertesen I. (12th Dyn.), records the fact that he renewed the colouring and inscriptions in the temple of Abydos from top to bottom. This probably means the building of which some fragments, belonging to the 12th Dynasty, are seen to the N. of the Memnonium (see p. 67). Under the Hyksos the ancient sanctuary was entirely neglected, and the only record here of the 18th Dynasty, which was almost wholly absorbed by its wars and foundations in Thebes, is an inscription of Tutmes III. Seti I., however, of the 19th Dynasty, built an entirely new temple, and his son Ramses II. completed the adornment that his father left unfinished. The ground-plan of the structure is unusual, and differs materially from that of other great Egyptian temples. Among the features, however, which it has in common with these are the pylons, a first and second fore-court, hypostyle halls, and a sanctuary. The last, however, is much more richly articulated than usual. The wing to the S. (to the left on entering) forms an accurate right angle with the main edifice. The whole structure is in the shape of a mason's square.

We enter the temple from the N.E. The first pylon and the walls enclosing Court A are in ruins. Court B, which opens to the S. on the temple proper, is in better preservation. The sons and daughters of Ramses II. were represented on the right and left walls, but the figures and inscriptions have been almost effaced. In spite of the fact that all the inscriptions and representations here refer to Ramses II., it has been proved through the discovery by Mariette of a dove-tail (see above) bearing the name of Seti I., that the

latter founded this N. part of the temple and left merely the decoration of it to his son. — The façade of the temple is of very
unusual form. A row of 12 limestone columns stand a short distance in advance of the temple wall, forming with it a kind of
pronaos. In the time of Seti seven doors, corresponding to the seven
chambers of the sanctuary (see below), pierced the rear-wall, which
was adorned with a cornice of its own. On ceremonial occasions
the processions in honour of the king seem to have entered by the
door to the extreme left; the next served for processions to Ptah,
the third for Harmachis, the fourth for Ammon, the fifth for Osiris,
the sixth for Isis, and the seventh for Horus. Ramses, however,
walled up six of these doors, leaving the central one alone, the
decoration of which had been begun by Seti, as the main entrance
to the temple. A small door in the Horus gateway, to the extreme
right, is still open. The pillars bear huge figured representations
and a few inscriptions, which refer to Seti I. as deceased and introduce Ramses II. in the company of Ammon-Ra, Osiris, Horus, and
other gods. The hieroglyphics inform us that Ramses erected this
part of the temple in honour of his father, one phrase, for instance,
reading: 'The king of Upper and Lower Egypt, the Lord of the
Barbarians (Nine Nations), to make great the name of his father'.
The entrance-wall behind the pillars confirms this pious filial wish
beyond the shadow of a doubt. In the wall, to the left of the main
entrance, is a large and conspicuous inscription in 95 vertical lines,
which, after the lists of kings, must be called the most important
in Abydos. It consists of two parts. In the first Ramses relates
how, on coming to Abydos, he found his father's work unfinished
and resolved to carry it to a conclusion. The grandees rejoiced at
this resolution, and workmen and artists of every kind were summoned to aid in the task. In the second part Pharaoh recalls to his
consciousness all the honours he had paid and the gifts he had
presented to his father. The gods show him favour on account of
his pious acts and advance, one by one, to bestow upon him the
richest gifts of heaven: strength, fearlessness, victory, immortality,
etc. A picture accompanying the inscription represents Ramses,
with a crown on his head, offering sacrifices to the goddess Ma and
to a triad consisting of Osiris, Isis, and his father Seti I., who takes
the place of Horus. Recently deceased, Seti appears as the youthful
god, the victorious opponent of the might of Death, who will soon
become Osiris, after subduing all his enemies beneath his feet. On
one of the pillars, indeed, Seti is already described as the 'royal
Osiris'. The inscription dates from the first year of the single
rule of Ramses and from the time of his first journey to Thebes,
when he erected statues of his father in the city of Ammon
and in Memphis. At Abydos he first undertook the restoration of
his father's monumental structures in the necropolis, on the spot
specially sacred to Osiris Unnefer. After mentioning other restora-

tions, the inscription continues as follows, with special reference to this temple: 'For lo, while the temple of Ra-ma-men (*i.e.* Seti I.) was still building both back and front, Seti ascended to heaven, before his Memnonium (Mennn) was completed. The columns had not yet been placed upon their bases, the statue lay on the ground and was not yet finished off, when he (Seti) became acquainted with the tomb (the 'golden room', the principal chamber of Seti's tomb at Bibân el-Mulûk), etc. Then said His Majesty to the seal-bearer by his side : Summon the courtiers, the military commanders, and their fellows, and also the whole multitude of architects and librarians. When these were conducted before His Majesty, pressing their noses in the dust and their knees to the earth, they broke out into rejoicing and smelled the ground (*i.e.* prostrated themselves). They raised their arms, praising His Majesty, and prayed to this benignant deity, celebrating his perfection'. Then follow emphatic expressions of worship, addressed to the king. 'Then spoke His Majesty unto them and said: I summoned you before me on account of a plan that has entered my mind. I have seen the buildings of the necropolis and the tombs that are at Abydos, and also those who have to work there. Truly nothing has been restored since the time of their lord unto the present day. But when a son finds himself on the throne of his father, shall he not renew the monument (Menun) of his begetter? . . . From childhood until now I have been a prince. He gave me the earth as a gift, and while I was yet in the egg the great ones of the earth prostrated themselves before me. . . . I have called my father to a new life in gold (*i.e.* as a statue) in the first year of my exaltation. I have given orders that his temple be adorned and I have made sure his possession of the land . . . I have offered him sacrifices. . . . And now, when his building stood in my power, I watched over all the labours connected with it . . . . I enlarged and renewed his palatial structure. I did not neglect his foundations, as wicked children do, who do not respect their father . . . I built anew the walls of the temple of my begetter. I presented before him the man whom I had selected to superintend the works. . . I erected pylons in front of it, I have covered his house with clothing (sculptures), I have adorned its columns and provided stones for the foundations. A finished work was the monument, doubly as glorious as at first. It is (named) after my name and after the name of my father, for, as the son, so is also the father'. In the following sentences Ramses is praised as a model son and the highest gifts of the gods are assured to him. 'Since the sun-god Ra there has never been a son who has accomplished what thou hast. . . . Thou, thou workest, thou renewest one monument to the gods after another, according to the command of thy father Ra'. The whole world obeys him and brings him offerings. After the grandees have finished their oration, he once more orders the officials, masters, artists, labourers, and all others engaged in the

building operations to construct the sanctuary of his father in the
necropolis and to hew out his statue. Sacrifices and festivals are
richly provided for. The rest of the inscription assumes more and
more the character of a hymn, like those mentioned at p. 258 and
elsewhere.

The above will suffice to show the filial piety, with which Ramses,
at least in the earlier part of his reign, strove to complete and restore the work of his father. But the remains of the building constructed by him near the Temple of Seti at Abydos (p. 67) prove
that he also founded a large Memnonium for himself in the district
sanctified by the tomb of Osiris.

INTERIOR OF THE TEMPLE.

1. *The Hypostyle Halls and the Sevenfold Sanctuary.*

From the Pronaos, containing the above inscription, two doors
only now lead into the interior of the temple: the main entrance
in the middle and a narrow door to the extreme right. The First
Hypostyle Room (Pl. C), a long but narrow apartment, makes
a solemn and imposing impression. The roof, part of which has
fallen in, is supported by 24 columns, arranged in two rows and in
groups of four. The slender shafts are surmounted by capitals in
the form of papyrus buds. Seti I. did not complete the plastic decoration of the room. Ramses began new sculptures instead of those
begun by his father, apparently forgetting the great filial piety he
arrogates to himself in the above-quoted inscription (p. 58).
Whether it was that the zeal of the son abated along with his grief
for his father, or that the priestly sculptors thought it better to celebrate a living prince rather than a dead one, the fact remains that
it is Ramses alone who is here depicted and the temple itself is
simply called the temple of Abydos, not, as in the earlier inscriptions, that of Ra-ma-men (*i.e.* Seti). The sculptures preserved here
are of mediocre workmanship, and the inscriptions and representations, almost wholly dealing with Ramses and his reception of
gifts from the different gods, are generally uninteresting even for
the scholar. On the right wall, near the second chamber, is a series
of gods, consisting of *Ra, Shu* (the giver of all delight) and his
sister *Tefnut* (giver of health), *Seb* (giver of life and strength),
Osiris, Horus (giver of every victory), *Isis* (giver of life and strength),
the great god *Apheru* (Anubis), and *Nut*, who imparts the fulness of
salvation. — The six lists of the nomes of Egypt, on the lower part
of the walls, are also interesting. As elsewhere, the districts are
represented as bearded male figures with the emblem of the nome
(a piece of surveyed ground, ▦) and a standard bearing the
symbol of the special district. As the lists here have no annota-
tions, they are of less value than those at Denderah and elsewhere.
They indicate that it was customary for all the districts of the land
to pay their vows and bring gifts to the gods of a special sanctuary.

The Second Hypostyle Room (Pl. D) resembles the first, but is higher, deeper, and in all respects of more importance. Seti I. began it and his artists executed both the architectural details and the plastic adornment with the carefulness and purity of style that marks all their work. The son has here left unchanged the name of the father, which occurs at every point. Three rows of twelve columns each support the architrave, on which rest the roofing slabs, and are arranged in six groups, each of six columns. Between the groups access is afforded to the vaulted chambers in the wall facing us as we enter. The first two of the three rows of columns have papyrus-bud capitals. Beyond the second row the floor of the temple is considerably raised, forming a platform from which the vaulted chambers are entered. Upon this platform stands the third row of columns, the cylindrical shafts of which are entirely destitute of capitals, but bear huge blocks of stone forming an abacus for the support of the architrave. This peculiarity is simply explained by the fact that the columns in the third row are shorter than the others, owing to their raised platform, so that the architect, by omitting the capital, brings the abacus of all on the same level and avoids the unpleasant effect which different elevations of the architrave would make on the eye. When processions of worshippers filed in and out, performing pious ceremonies, this hall must have presented a very imposing spectacle. Inscriptions below the openings leading from the first hall to the second inform us they were formerly filled with doors of bronze (asem). The inscriptions and representations on the walls and columns repeat themselves wearisomely and are of little general interest. Here we see the king receiving from the gods such attributes of the royal dignity as the crooked sword or the scourge and crook (symbols, perhaps, of the royal duties of incentive on the one side and restraint on the other); there we behold him offering burnt-offerings to a single god, a triad, or a group of gods. If the king is receiving gifts, he is generally represented on his knees; when he sacrifices, he leans slightly forward, holding the burnt-offering in the left hand and libations in the right. Sometimes he is seated, receiving the blessings of the gods; he appears thus in the fine picture on the N. *Wall* of the second room, with Isis, Amenti, and Nephthys in front, and the goddess Ma and Renpet behind. His profile is evidently a faithful likeness and is everywhere portrayed with great artistic skill. The unusual handsomeness of this king is still recognisable in his mummy at Gizeh. The sacrificial implements should also be noted. Censers like that in his hand have been found, but in bronze, while his were doubtless of gold. They are in the form of an arm, the hand holding a small vessel from which the smoke of the incense arises. The handle shows the carefully executed sparrow hawk's head of Horus. The libation vessel was in the form of a golden lotus flower, with small vases rising above the open corolla, from which essences were poured out in honour of the god. The framework of each scene, the mouldings separating the lines of hieroglyphics, and the hieroglyphic symbols themselves are all executed with inimitable care. The side-walls of this hall, to the right and left, and the walls near the gates leading to the chapels, bear symbolic representations, like those in the first hall, of the nomes of Upper and Lower Egypt.

At a considerable interval, beyond the third row of columns in the second hall, and on the same level with them, is a series of SEVEN VAULTED CHAMBERS or CHAPELS, forming the **Sanctuary** of the Memnonium. The metal doors with which they were once closed have long since disappeared. In the piers separating the doors are rectangular niches, which probably contained images either of the deities to whom the chapels were dedicated or of King Seti. Each chapel is vaulted and the vaults are profusely and beautifully decorated with stars and the name Ra-ma-men (prænomen of Seti I.). Dedicatory inscriptions on three of the vaults prove that Osiris must be regarded as the chief divinity of the temple. It must be noted that the roofs of these chapels are not vaulted in the strict architectural signification of that word; they consist rather of blocks of stone cut in a round fashion and crowned by a key-stone which is hollowed out in the interior. The chapels were dedicated (beginning from the left) to the king, Ptah, Harmachis, Ammon, Osiris, Isis, and Horus. All the chief figures in the Osiris cycle of gods are represented here with the exception of Seth, the antagonist of Osiris, and his wife Nephthys. With them is associated the king who has become Osiris (see p. 57). Ptah, who becomes Sokar-Osiris when regarded in his relations to life beyond the grave, is of course represented. In the place of honour in the midst of the seven is Ammon, 'who is the *only one* and whose years flourish among the gods', who is 'loftier in his ideas than any other god', 'to whose feet the gods crawl, recognising their lord and master', who is 'lord of eternity and creator of the unending', of whom indeed the other gods may be regarded as attributes. To the right and left of Ammon are two groups of three. To the right are Osiris, Isis, and Horus; to the left are Ptah the primæval, the lord of the past; Harmachis, who announces the new day rising in the East, who struggles for the victory of life over death, and assures the future triumph of good over evil; and King Seti, the temporal incarnation of divine power in the present, in the sphere of human activity. — To these gods, conceived as filling these chapels with their presence, were brought the mummies, to be sanctified for their eternal home. The way to the different chapels was indicated on the very threshold of the temple, where Seti I., as we have seen, constructed seven doors in the rear-wall of the pronaos. Most of these, however, were closed by Ramses, probably to intensify and preserve the secret and mysterious character of the temple. But the paths to the different chapels are still easily distinguishable, partly from the plan of the building, partly by the representations and inscriptions; for from each of the seven doors a processional approach led through the two hypostyle halls straight to tho entrance of the corresponding chapel; while the representations on the columns flanking each approach refer only to the deity to whom the chapel at the end of it was dedicated. In the vaulted chapels, amid the fumes of incense and the murmuring of muffled singing, waited the ministering priests of the sanctuary, pouring out libations and uttering benedictions as the processions wound along the aisles, either bearing a mummy to be sanctified or consisting of a group of privileged laymen bringing offerings to the Osiris gods for the soul's welfare of the deceased.—The dedications are inscribed on the door-posts in the traditional forms and with little variation. Similar vaults occur at Benihasan and Dêr el-Bahri, and also in the lids of the sarcophagi in the museum at Gizeh. In each case the monuments to which they belong serve funerary purposes; the shape of the vault is, however, intended to represent the vault of heaven, which the Osiris-soul has to traverse, and they are usually decorated with stars. An inscription preserved on one of the vaults of the sanctuary informs us that the Pharaoh erected this structure for his father Osiris in the interior of the temple of Ra-ma-men and fitted up the chapel to resemble the heaven of the ninefold deities, imitating its constellations, etc.

The internal fitting up and appearance of the chapels vary little. As the middle place had to be assigned to Ammon, the chief of the gods, it was necessary to mark the special dignity of Osiris, to whom indeed the temple was consecrated, by making his chapel (Pl. d) wider than the others. The rear-walls of the latter are, in each case, occupied by two niches, with a lotus-flower between them, from which rises the slender form of Osiris, symbolising the blossoming of the soul in a 'happier sphere'. In the back-wall of the sanctuary of Osiris, however, is a door, leading to a structure (Pl. E) which, including the adjoining smaller columned chambers, is as wide as the whole sanctuary. This was the scene of the mysterious rites celebrated in honour of the Divine-Deceased (Osiris, whose name even the Greek Herodotus shrank from breathing) by the esoteric priests of the highest class (see *Baedeker's Lower Egypt*, p. 124). The inscriptions in the chapels inform us that the priestly processions†, which came from all parts of the kingdom, made a complete circuit of the chapel, keeping to the right wall on entering and returning to the door along the left wall. Thirty-six rites or ceremonies had to be performed during this circuit. First came a recitation to prove the worthiness of the worshipper to approach the holy place and the image of the god. Then the veil was lifted. The worshipper was next allowed to witness the investiture of the god by the priests with his fillets, garments, ornaments, and the attributes of his divine power. Not before this was accomplished did the pilgrim prostrate himself in adoration, bringing drink-offerings, libations, and burnt-offerings. The hymns to be sung at these ceremonies are all prescribed, and the pictorial representations show how the gods were to be clothed and in what attitudes they were to be worshipped. Possibly all these rites were performed only by the priests of

† In the inscriptions the expression invariably used for the processions is the *King*, who is regarded as the embodiment and representative of all his subjects.

the temple. In any case the chapels are too small to have admitted more
than the heads of the deputations from other parts of Egypt. Great weight
is laid upon the sacred number seven, as shown in the number of the
chapels themselves and in the seven heads of sparrow-hawks represented
in each. That the king should appear as the seventh object of worship
along with six gods is undoubtedly unusual; but it may be explained by
the fact that Seti built the seventh chapel, not for the adoration of himself while alive, but for a future period when he hoped to be merged in
Osiris. Neither Seti nor his son could avoid the interment of their mummies near the royal residence of Thebes; but it may be assumed that their
earthly remains received consecration at Abydos, and that the Memnonium
of Seti is to be regarded as a cenotaph, in which the *Name* of Pharaoh,
as a symbol of the king himself, was to be honoured and preserved. The
Pharaohs of the early empire possessed similar monuments here. These,
however, fell into decay during the Hyksos period; and Seti was enabled
to do what unfavourable times had hindered his predecessors from doing
— *i.e.* to build a new and costly Memnonium, in which a place was re-
served, near the tomb of Osiris, for the *Names* of his royal ancestors. In
the arches above the niches in the rear-wall of the chapels are several
representations of the king offering his *Name*, symbolised by the cartouche
or ring ⬭ which surrounded royal names. In this way Abydos
came to be the most important place for the preservation of lists of kings.
The columned aisle leading to Seti's Chapel (Pl. a) contains inscriptions
and representations relating to the king alone and showing us his relationship to the gods in its proper light. On the walled-up door to the first
hall we see Thoth, the Reason or Intelligence, the god of the sciences and
of historical records, offering a sacrifice in front of an image of the king
(the latter unfortunately much damaged). The inscription reads 'I, Thoth,
the dweller in Abydos, come to thee on account of thy greatness and thy
glory. For the sake of thy sanctity as king, for the sake of thy might
and thy constancy on earth, and to make thee great', etc. — On the columns of the first hall the king is represented as sacrificing and receiving
the attributes of the kingdom from Thoth, Anubis Apheru, Horus the son
of Isis, and Henmutef. the high priest of Abydos. The paintings on the
S. wall of the same hall show us the king as a boy, held in the arms of
Isis and suckled at the divine breasts of the Hathors. They admit him
to the place of Horus, that he may increase in strength and ascend the
throne of Osiris as a man. Hathor, the queen-deity of Heliopolis in Abydos, calls herself the mother of his beauty, and says to him: 'Thou hast
been nourished by my milk, thou who art adorned with the crown of Upper
Egypt'. The Hathor of Denderah calls herself his nurse, who raised her
arms to embrace his beauty. On the left side of the door farthest to the
left, also leading to the second hall, we see the king, wearing a helmet,
while Thoth pours over his head the signs of life and dominion. To the
right the king appears with the richly decorated royal crown, holding the
sceptre and scourge in his hands. The priest Henmutef burns incense before him, and the Nile brings him gifts, of which he is the producer. The
king has now passed from the boy Horus to the man Osiris; Henmutef
says: 'I burn incense to thee and to thy name, O Osiris, King Ra-ma-men'.
The words put in the mouth of the Nile are: 'I bring to thee in my arms
the superfluity as an offering, O King, lord of both worlds!' On the sides
of the columns facing the aisle leading to the royal chapel are represented
Anubis-Apheru handing to the king the attributes of constancy and might;
Thoth, either pouring the water of life and dominion over the king, or
addressing him in set speech, with a roll in his left hand; Henmutef ex-
horting him, sacrificing to him, and reaching him the sign of approval
⌒, thus reminding us of the passage in Diodorus which tells us that
it was the duty of the priests to praise and warn the kings. The king
has instituted festivals in honour of Horus, and Horus in return throws
him the symbol of life. Isis, holding in her hand the lotus-staff, entwined
by the Uræus-serpent, also invests him with life, which here as elsewhere included life beyond the grave, which the Egyptians termed the
true life. On the S. wall of the second hall Seti is represented as seated

on the throne of Osiris. In front of him stands Horus, 'the avenger of his father', investing him with immortality, while behind is the jackal-headed Apheru (Anubis), ready to protect him from danger. Above the dedicatory inscription, Thoth, the god of divine eloquence, promises Osiris Ra-ma-men that the Cycle of the Nine Gods will endue him with ever-lasting life. In the chapel itself the representations are very numerous. The king, in one, appears as a sphinx, resting on a base bearing the names of six nations that he has conquered, A somewhat singular scene represents standard-bearers with the ensigns of the nomes, personifying the emblems of life, constancy, and power in threefold repetition; these, like the inscriptions between the standard-poles, teach us that Seti was endued with courage, length of days, uninterrupted safety and strength, victory, abundance, and the kingdom of Egypt for life. It would be weari-some to enumerate the multitude of other inscriptions of a similar tenour. Among the 22 representations in the king's chapel, many of which are in a very dilapidated condition, the most noteworthy is one in which the king appears on the throne of Osiris, embraced by the goddesses Nekheb (Eileithyia) and Buto. Thoth and Horus draw tighter the stems of the plants symbolising Upper and Lower Egypt, which enfold the sign of union sam. Safekh, the goddess of history, behind Thoth, inscribes the name of the king. In another scene Seti is seated on a throne supported by three figures in the form of Horus and three in the form of Anubis. Un-der a canopy adorned with Uræus-serpents appears the state barge of the king, probably a representation of the vessel kept in this temple and borne on high in the processions. Similar representations of the ship in which the Sun-God was supposed to traverse the heavens have been found made of bronze or the precious metals and may be seen in the museum at Gizeh (see *Baedeker's Lower Egypt*) and elsewhere. Below are canopi (Vol. I., p. 301), in front sacrificial offerings, and behind Thoth and Henmutef. — We observe that everything here refers to the king, whose name recurs in weari-some iteration, and who here receives back again as Osiris the offerings he had himself made, during his mortal life, to Osiris and thus to his future self, the Osiris-apotheosis of his soul.

A door in the *Osiris Chapel* (Pl. e), the third from the right wall, leads to the rear-structure (Pl. E) mentioned at p. 62. Though the structure is in a very ruinous state, its ground-plan can easily be made out. A colon-nade, the roof of which, once supported by 10 columns, has fallen to the ground, stood in direct connection with the Osiris chapel. It contains 47 re-presentations, some of which are almost wholly effaced. By the wall, to the right on entering, lay three small chambers adorned with fine sculpture. The first of these (Pl. i) is dedicated to Horus, the second (Pl. k) to Osiris, the third (Pl. l) to Isis. Behind them lay another room (Pl. h). In the wall to the left on entering Room E is a door leading to a room (Pl. m) with four columns, which was adjoined by three smaller apartments (Pl. n, o, p). Though the most sacred mysteries were celebrated in this suite of rooms, they offer little that is novel; the implements of the priests were kept in the side-rooms. Here, no doubt, many a spectacle was prepared which, when displayed in the Osiris chapel, filled the pious worshippers with awe and wonder.

SOUTH BUILDING. APARTMENT WITH THE TABLET OF THE KINGS. — This building consists of a series of rooms, all more or less ruinous and most of them roofless, a court, and some smaller chambers. The most important, to which a visit should be paid, even if all the others be omitted, is a long (65 ft.) and low Corridor (Pl. s), entered from the left side of the second hypostyle hall, between the second and third row of columns. The flat ceiling is adorned with a rich network of ornamentation, combining the name

of the king, the symbol of the 'panegyric tent' [symbol], and a number
of stars. A dedicatory inscription, dividing the ceiling into two
parts, records that 'this Memnonium was erected in the temple of
Abydos to his forefathers and all the cycles of gods of heaven and
earth, by the king, lord of the diadems, who is born again, who
surpasses all in strength and annihilates the barbarians, the victorious Horus, who appears in new glory, bearing sway over the
barbarians in all countries, the king of Upper and Lower Egypt,
who achieves noble deeds, the lord of both worlds, Ra-ma-men.
He erected to them these venerated sanctuaries outside the Necropolis, building them of stone and inlaying them with gold, in
an everlasting work outlasting human life, etc.' — By the right
wall on entering the corridor from the second hypostyle is the celebrated *Tablet of Abydos, consisting of three long rows of royal

shields or cartouches [symbol], before which Seti and his son Ramses II.

stand in adoration. The praying king raises his right hand and holds
a censer in his left hand; the boy-prince, standing in front of him,
still bears the lock of youth, hanging over his temples. In his
raised hands he bears written rolls. The adjoining inscription reads:
'Recitation of songs of praise by Prince Ramses, son and firstborn of
the king who loves him'. Above the shields is another inscription,
which describes the king's offering as made to Ptah-Sokar-Osiris,
the lord of the sarcophagus in the Memnonium of Abydos and *(uah
khet)* the royal forefather of Seti. He enumerates his gifts: 1000
loaves of bread, 1000 barrels of beer, 1000 cattle, 1000 geese,
1000 incense-offerings, 1000 oil-offerings, 1000 pieces of cloth,
1000 garments, 1000 barrels of wine, 1000 holy offerings. The
figure 1000 here, which occurs in almost all sacrificial lists and also
in other formulæ, is not, of course, to be taken literally but simply
as equivalent to many. The king, as we see, brings his youthful
son into the hall dedicated to his ancestors, where the earlier rulers
of Egypt, under the symbol of their name, dwell beside the tomb
of Osiris. He teaches the boy to offer rich gifts, such as hereafter
he would wish offered to his own manes. It is beyond doubt that
Seti was still living when this inscription was set up, and yet
he already adds his own name to those of his predecessors; it
occupies the whole of the lowest row (the third from the top) of the
royal table, being repeated 19 times with prefix and affix. The
living Seti provides for the future Osiris and for his worship at the
holy grave. — In the first volume of this Handbook (p. 85) it has
been shown that the establishment of the chronology of the Egyptian
kings was rendered possible only by a collation of the lists of Manetho
with the lists of Pharaohs preserved in the monuments. Among
the latter none approaches in importance the royal tablet of the

Memnonium at Abydos, which contains no fewer than 76 cartouches, only two of which are slightly injured. The tablet from the temple of Ramses (p. 68), now in London, contains 16 entire and 2 half destroyed cartouches, while the list of Sakkârah, discovered by Mariette, has 39 whole and 3 damaged cartouches.

Mena, *i.e.* Menes, the first historic king of Egypt, heads the list. The names following his are those of the most prominent monarchs, at least those whose legitimacy was unquestionable. The Heracleopolitans and the Hyksos are naturally left out, but other rulers, of whom we possess monuments, have also been apparently deemed unworthy of inclusion in this important roll of honour. The merit of first observing and publishing this inestimable historical document belongs to Prof. Dümichen.

On the *left* wall of the corridor we again meet Seti and the youthful Ramses. The father holds a censer in his left hand, while the son, adorned with the priestly panther-skin, pours a libation on the altar in front of him. The titles of the right wall re-appear here. The inscription, which the royal pair faces, contains in systematic order the names of these objects of worship, with their homes, whom Seti has honoured with sacrificial gifts. The sculpture in this corridor, consisting of alto-reliefs on the fine-grained limestone, is all executed with the greatest delicacy. In the centre of the right wall a door leads into a narrow Chamber (Pl. t), vaulted in the same manner as the sanctuaries (p. 61), and preceding the stair (Pl. u) which leads to the hill at the back of the temple. The inscriptions here are in excellent preservation, being injured only in a few places; the adjoining figures of Seti and Ramses show the latter arrived at manhood and the throne. Safekh, the goddess of history, 'the great mistress of books', addresses her darling son Seti. The ceremony of foundation, which we find more fully represented and described in the Ptolemaic temples, is also depicted here. The praises of the king are sung, and his merits are, at the command of Ra, to be committed to writing by the goddess of history. Thoth also congratulates the king in the emphatic manner usual to such inscriptions, and promises him an eternal existence and the stability of his kingdom for hundreds of thousands of years. Thoth is named the tongue of Ra and lord of the speech of the prophet of truth. This staircase was completed while Ramses shared the throne of his father as co-ruler.

The other rooms of this part of the building are all more or less in ruins. From the S. end of the kings' gallery we enter a kind of peristyle *Court* (Pl. G), with seven columns, which perhaps was never completed. The sculptures and hieroglyphics are not very carefully executed and appear 'en creux' instead of in high relief. The most interesting scenes are those on the lower part of the walls, representing the slaughter of the cattle, gazelles, and antelopes which Seti had so lavishly vowed (in the adjoining king's gallery)

to the gods of the temple. Some of the resisting oxen are remarkably
true to nature. Probably the sacrificial animals were actually slain
in this court, a conclusion strengthened by the broken pottery found
here by Mariette and the two springs of turbid water. A well has
also been discovered outside the E. wall of the temple, which may
be the spring described by Strabo.

The Room marked F on the plan is the most interesting of the
other apartments in this wing. The entrance to it is on the left
(S.) side of the space between the sanctuary and the third row
of columns in the second hypostyle hall. The door leading to it is
named 'the great door of Ra-ma-men (*i.e.* Seti), the favourite of
Sokar'. To this deity, Osiris-Sokar or Ptah-Sokar-Osiris, keeper of
the realm of shades, this room is consecrated, though other gods,
such as Nefer Tum, Horus, and Thoth are also represented here.
The king appears in the act of offering sacrifice. To the extreme
right on entering, on the wall between the doors, are reliefs of
richly adorned Nilometers, the symbols of the state of stability
and permanence aimed at by Pharaoh; the inscriptions inform
us that they were dedicated to the Osiris of the under-world, Ptah-
Sokar-Tatunen, who was worshipped in the Memnonium of Abydos.
On the entrance-wall, to the right of the door, is the bark of Sokar,
and a list is given of the titles of this god of the many aliases,
who was revered in so many different spots. The form of the three
columns preserved here is peculiar. The cylindrical shafts, which
bear the abacus without any transitional member, are flattened at
the points where their periphery would touch an exscribed square,
and hence their section is in the shape of an octagon with four
straight and four curved sides. — The doors to the right, on each
side of the above-mentioned Nilometers, lead into two oblong rooms
with vaulted ceilings, which have partly fallen in (Pl. q, r). — The
other apartments of this wing contain nothing of special interest.
They are all ruinous, and five of them cannot be entered except from
the outside. — In visiting the Memnonium of Abydos, the traveller
should bear in mind that he has to do with a cenotaph, dedicated
to the manes of a king apotheosised as Osiris and to his forefathers;
and he should also remember that the site of the building was determined by the belief that the souls of those who had been 'sanctified' near the Holy Tomb could look forward with confidence to the
highest joys of the world to come.

MONUMENTS TO THE NORTH. Not only Seti, but also his son has
erected a cenotaph to himself near the tomb of Osiris. To reach
this Sepulchral Temple of Ramses II. we turn towards the N. and
skirt the margin of the desert for a few minutes. It is in a very
ruinous state, but still presents many features of interest. The
ground-plan of a peristyle court, several rooms, and the sanctuaries
beyond them can still be traced; but the average height of the remaining walls is only 5-6 ft. The picture of ruin presented to us

here is all the more striking from the obvious pains of the founder to make a costly and enduring monument. Where Seti contented himself with limestone, Ramses made lavish use of granite, Oriental alabaster, and black graywacke. The remaining fragments show that Ramses erected obelisks of granite in front of his cenotaph, and that caryatide-like figures of Osiris, now long since shattered, stood at the sides of the first peristyle court. Plastic ornamentation was freely used and so richly painted that the colours have to this day clung to some of the fragments. Ramses followed the example of his father in consecrating a chamber to the manes of his ancestors. In 1818 Mr. Bankes discovered in the chamber to the left (E.) of the first octostyle room a royal list of eighteen names, two of which were partly destroyed, and the relics of these tablets are still *in situ.* M. Mimant, the French Consul General, tore down the walls on which the important cartouches were represented and sent the stones to Paris, whence they passed by purchase to the British Museum. Almost no inscription has been left intact here. We learn, however, that Ramses was much more anxious than his father to record his own achievements. Not a few names of peoples and towns which he subdued or captured may still be discerned among the ruins.

The visitor will gladly arrest his steps by the representation of a grand procession, which is to be found inside the great court, to the right and left of the entrance. The procession, beginning at the N.W. corner of the hall, which was formerly surrounded with Osiris-pillars, extends over the whole of the N. wall. Four temple officials are represented, one described as a secretary, two with leopard-skins as priests of Osiris and of the house of Ramses Meriamon Khnumt Abdu (connected with Abydos), and the fourth as Korbub. Animals, some living and some dead, are brought to them for sacrifice. Among these are antelopes, geese, and oxen of extraordinary size and fatness. On the right side of the fore-court are similar scenes, in which the procession is still more grandly equipped. Here appear the royal war-chariot, numerous officials, and negroes, while incense is burned before the statue of the monarch. The colouring of these figures is surprisingly well preserved.

On the outside of the temple, N. side, is an inscription relating to the Kheta war, discovered by Eisenlohr in 1870; unfortunately only the lower parts of lines are preserved. Adjacent, to the W. and N., are representations of events in the Kheta war, similar to those of the Ramesseum at Thebes. The exterior of the S. wall is covered with a long inscription, recounting the building of the temple, of which the following is a translation. 'Behold his Majesty, Life, Salvation, and Health, the beloved son representing his father Unnofer and making him a beautiful and lordly dwelling, built for eternity of white, good, fair stone, the two great pylons of finished workmanship, the door-ways of syenite. The doors therein of bronze, plated with real electrum; the great seat (*i.e.* the inner sanctuary) of alabaster; its sanctuary covered with granite, and its exalted seat of sep tep, the meshen (cradle) for its cycle of gods. His exalted father lies within, even as Ra is united with heaven; his lordly portrait is by him that begat him, even as Horus on the throne of his father. He has daily multiplied the offerings for all times, for the feasts of the seasons and the feasts of the year, the feasts for each day for himself. He filled the temple with all things, a super-abundance of gifts of nourishment, bulls, calves, oxen, geese, incense, wine, and fruit, filling it with labourers, enriching it with fields, pre-senting cattle, filling the storehouse with superabundance, the barns reaching to heaven, the servants of the domains of the offering being the captives of his brave sword. His treasure-house filled with all gems, with silver and gold in bars, the storehouse full of all things sent as tribute from all countries. He has constructed numerous canals, and has planted timber of all sorts, fragrant plants from the land of Punt; he has done all this, the son of Ra, the lord of the diadems, the beloved of Osiris and of the gods the lords of Abydos'.

Like the temple of Seti, that of his son Ramses was also a sanctuary dedicated to Osiris, though in each case the predominant feature is the glorification of the monarch in his apotheosis as Osiris. Mariette was therefore on a wrong tack when he saw a special temple of Osiris in the enclosure (Pl. III; p. 52) to the N., near the village of *El-Kherbeh*, and spent much time and money in an attempt to find the actual grave of Osiris. Obviously this was merely an older sanctuary, erected by the kings of the 12th and 13th Dynasties on the site of a still more ancient temple. [Two steles in the Louvre, numbered C 11 and C 12, and the great stele of Mentuhotep, now in the museum of Gizeh, give us information concerning these buildings.] Nowadays this temple is a mere heap of rubbish, and the few interesting 'finds' made here, such as the statues of Usertesen I. and Usertesen III., and some inscriptions of the time of Tutmes III., have been sent to the museum of Gizeh. The same institution received the many hundred steles found partly on the site of this temple and partly in the Necropolis of **Abydos**. Three such cemeteries are distinguished. The first, containing tombs of the New Empire, from the 19th Dynasty downwards, lies to the S. of the temples of Seti I. and Ramses II. Another (Nécropole du Centre) lies to the W. of the path leading from the temple of Ramses II. to the so-called temple of Osiris, and contains graves mainly of the 6th and 11th Dynasties. Here was found the historically valuable tablet of Una (see *Baedeker's Lower Egypt*, p. 307), who accompanied three successive rulers of the 6th Dynasty in their campaigns. The third or N. necropolis, to the W. of the so-called temple of Osiris, contains numerous graves of the 12th and 13th Dynasties, but also many of the new empire. Among the interesting steles found here were those of a Neferhotep of the 13th Dynasty and of Sheshonk, the latter erroneously pronounced by H. Brugsch to have been a Persian satrap. The pyramidal struc-tures found in the N. and central cemeteries are also interesting. Still farther to the W. lies a quadrangular enclosure surrounded by a lofty wall and named *Shunet ez-Zebib* (Pl. IV; p. 52; magazine of the Zibebes), which probably served as a place of defence against the incursions of the Beduins of the Great Oases. A *Coptic Convent* (Pl. V; p. 52) to the N.E. of this point, dating from the year 1306 of the Coptic era, scarcely repays a visit.

5. From Beliâneh to Keneh (*Denderah*).

Comp. Map, p. 8.

56 M. STEAMBOAT in 4½ hrs. COmp. p. 45.

Between Beliâneh and Keneh the *Dûm Palm* (Hyphæna the-
baica) becomes more and more common, generally occurring in
groups and increasing in size and beauty as we travel southwards
(comp. p. 28). It is a fan-leaved palm of moderate height, dividing
into two parts at the upper end of the stem and sometimes repeat-
ing this bifurcation two or three times. It extends far to the S. of
Egypt, and whole forests of it are found on the upper Nile. Its
large nuts contain a soft and fibrous pulp, which is edible and
tastes like sweet cake; while various objects are made out of the
hard rind. Its timber and bast are also of considerable industrial
value.

The ancient *Lepidotum* must have lain on the E. bank of the
river opposite Beliâneh; but, though described by Ptolemy as a
large town, no trace of it remains. The Lepidotus (the Cyprinus
lepidotus of Geoffroy, and Cinex dentex of Savigny) was held here
in high honour, though, according to Plutarch, it was one of the
fishes that swallowed the Phallus of Osiris and was hence generally
regarded with special abhorrence.

From Beliâneh to Keneh the Nile valley lies almost due E. and
W. About 4 M. from the S. bank lies *Samhûd*, on ancient rubbish-
mounds. *Nagi-Hamadi*, also on the S. bank, 19 M. from Beliâneh,
is the station for **Farshût,** 3 M. to the S., now an uninteresting
village with a large sugar-factory belonging to the Khedive.

So late as the 18th cent. this was still the seat of the great shêkh,
who was the head of the *Favâris* (pl. of Fâris, here pron. Havâris), or
tribes of mounted Arabs on the left bank of the Nile. The comparative
width of the river-plain makes horse-breeding an important occupation
among these tribes, and their shaggy grey dogs are also celebrated. The
latters are frequently seen guarding the flocks of sheep, and are easily
distinguishable from the worthless and cowardly curs that haunt the
streets of the towns and villages. When encouraged to attack by their
owners, these brave animals are exceedingly dangerous antagonists. —
From Farshût to the *Great Oasis*, see R. 35.

9½ M. **Hôu** (W. bank) and **Kaṣr es-Ṣaiyâd** (E. bank) lie nearly
opposite one another, at one of the sharpest bends in the stream.
Hôu, a large but miserable-looking village, was the home of Shêkh
Selîm, who died a few years ago, at a very advanced age, after
sitting stark naked on the bank of the Nile for 53 years; he was
regarded by pious Moslems with great honour and was deemed to
possess great powers in helping navigation and barren women. His
grave here is covered with Arabic inscriptions and votive gifts in
the form of small boats.

Those who wish to visit the scanty ruins of the ancient **Diospolis
Parva** traverse the village in the direction of the mountains, cross two
deep ditches, near which stand the finely built piers of a ruined
bridge, and reach (25 min.) a large mound of debris, known as *Gebel Hôr*
(*i.e.* Horus). This is the only remnant of the ancient Diospolis, with the
exception of a fragment of a temple of the Ptolemies in the village,

where, too, some stones bearing the cartouches of Ptolemy Philometor project from the ground in a clear space. Nothing of interest is to be seen here except one of the largest and oldest lebbek-trees in Egypt. The extensive cemetery contains numerous Cufic inscriptions. Hieroglyphic inscriptions have been found in grottoes in a hill to the W. of the town.

Kasr es-Saiyâd (mail steamer station) marks the site of the ancient **Chenoboskion**, which is mentioned by Ptolemy, by Stephanus of Byzantium, and in the Itinerary of Antonine, and belonged to the *Nomos Panopolites.* No remains are visible except a few fragments of the river wall, with an unimportant Greek inscription of the Roman period. It owes its name, meaning 'geese pasture' (Χηνο-βοσχεῖον, Copt. ⲩⲉⲛⲉⲥⲏⲧ, from the ancient Egyptian *Geese lake*), to the fact that immense quantities of geese, a favourite food and sacrificial offering of the old Egyptians, were reared here. Its propinquity to the home of Menes (This-Abydos) makes it seem quite natural that graves of hoar antiquity (6th Dynasty) should be found in the neighbourhood. These are reached from the village of Kasr es-Saiyâd in about $1^1/_4$ hr. Donkeys, but no saddles, may be obtained, through the Shêkh el-Beled. We first ride through a well-tilled district, cross a bridge over a canal which waters the district, pass the village of *Isbah*, and reach the Arab hills. The ancient tombs, constructed of light-coloured and unusually fine-grained limestone, now come in sight; they date from the reigns of Pepi, Morira, and Raneferka, all of the 6th Dynasty. The large tomb situated farthest to the left contains representations and inscriptions which are identical in style with those in the most ancient part of the Necropolis of Memphis. The ceiling was left rough-hewn. Some of the small inscriptions cut in the living rock near the entrance are in Coptic. The representations on the inside of the entrance-wall have been almost wholly destroyed, but some ships may be distinguished to the right of the door. On the right wall are figures bearing funereal gifts and a large sacrificial table. The rear-wall is divided into two distinct portions, as the left side of the tomb has been pushed much farther into the rock than the right. In the latter are two niches. That to the right contains an image of the deceased, one of the chief dignitaries under the Pharaoh Raneferka, named *Zuta* . From the second niche, farther to the left, a mummy-shaft descends obliquely; adjacent is a Coptic inscription. In the deeply recessed rear-wall of the left side are four smaller niches, probably intended for the coffins of members of Zuta's household deemed worthy of special honour. — The next tomb, farther to the right, is of even greater interest than the one just described. It belonged to an official named *Atkhenu*, who lived in the reigns of Pepi, Merira, and Raneferka, and was not only engaged in the construction of the pyramids of these monarchs, but was also a distinguished warrior. The pyramids were named 'Good Place'.

'Fine Ascent', and 'Scene of Life' [hieroglyphs]

The names of the three kings and their pyramids were found in the inscriptions to the right and left of the entrance (outside). The tomb is in the form of a rectangle, with the mummy-shaft opening in the back-wall. The representation of Atkhenu, to the left of the entrance, is very lifelike and derives peculiar interest from the fact that the grandees of the early period are seldom represented, as here, in full military activity. Our hero, another Una (see *Baedeker's Lower Egypt*, p. 307), lifts the arm vigorously to strike his foe. The mode of wearing the hair and headdress, seen both in this figure and that of Atkhenu's wife, is unusual. Atkhenu was a rich man, possessing, according to the inscriptions, 2350 oxen. On the left side of the rear-wall are represented several scenes from the private life of the deceased. Cattle are being slaughtered, cooks are busy at their work, etc. Above the door leading to the mummy-shaft we see a large altar, adjoining which is a long but much damaged inscription. — The smaller tombs in the vicinity are less interesting. Several Coptic inscriptions testify that anchorites found retreats in these tombs during the Christian period. We are now approaching the region which, in the time of Pachomius, was most thickly populated with monks and anchorites.

Farther on we pass a fine mountain-mass, which looks especially imposing by afternoon light, and see several thriving villages, often situated close to the river. *Deshneh,* a steamboat-station on the N. bank, 13 M. from Kaṣr eṣ-Ṣaiyâd, is situated on the ruins of an ancient town.

The site of the celebrated **Tabenna**, which lay between Hôu (Diospolis) and Denderah (Tentyra), must be sought for either here or close to Keneh. It belonged to the nome of Tentyra and its Coptic name was *Tabenneseh*, which may be translated 'place of the Isis palms'. The Greeks supposed that 'nesi' meant νῆσος (nesos) or island, and hence it comes that the town of *Tabennesus*, situated on the mainland, is generally spoken of as the *Island of Tabenna*. It is said that the Arabs name it *Gezîret el-Gharb* or *Isle of the West*, but no support of this could be found on the spot. St. Jerome relates that at the end of the 4th cent. no fewer than 50,000 monks assembled in the district of Tabennesus to celebrate the Easter Festival. All of these followed the rule of Pachomius and belonged either to the chief monastery (Monasterium Majus) or to the smaller cœnobia, laurae, and anchorite cells dependent on it. It is marvellous that the temple of Denderah (p. 80), so close to this community of fanatics, should have been left almost intact. Perhaps the explanation is that at the time the monks settled here the strife about dogmas aroused much more excitement in the ecclesiastical breast than the dislike of heathen gods that had long since become harmless.

56 M. (17 M. from Deshneh) **Keneh** (steamer-station), a town with 15,400 inhab., lies on the E. bank of the Nile at the point where the river, suddenly abandoning its northward course, turns to the W., almost at right angles. It is the capital of the fifth Mudîrîyeh of Upper Egypt, which is 597 sq. M. in extent and contains a population of 406,858. The Greek name of the town was Καινήπολις or 'Newtown'.

At the time of the pilgrimage to Mecca Keneh presents a very lively scene, as it is then frequented by large numbers of the participators in that great religious picnic. The spiritual and material wants of the pious *Hedjâdj* are catered for by six spacious mosques, numerous coffee-houses, and a large number of places of amusement, among the attractions of which Egyptian dancing-girls are prominent. For the rest Keneh differs little in general character from the other towns of Upper Egypt. The traveller should not fail, however, to see the most valuable piece of land near Keneh, which is about one Feddàn (3500 sq.yds.) in area and yields an excellent variety of potter's clay that has made Keneh pottery, like that of Assiût, famous throughout the country. Keneh has a special reputation for its *Kulal* (pl. of Kulle), or cool porous water-bottles, and for its *Ballâs* and *Zîr*, large vessels used in carrying, purifying, and preserving water. In some of the early Egyptian inscriptions figures of the Ballâs and Zîr appear as distinctive symbols, in the exact forms in which they are made to-day. Hundreds of thousands of these clay vessels are annually exported from Keneh in boats of a primitive but not unpractical description, constructed for the purpose, in which they are piled up in pyramidal form, fastened together with ropes made of the bast of the date-palm and attached to rectangular frames. A trustworthy report fixes the number sent away in 1860 at 900,000. Considerable activity is also manifested in the manufacture of kiln-dried pottery, generally either red or black, used for chibouk-heads, bottles, pitchers, vases, drinking-vessels, etc., of every size and shape. The almost invariably graceful forms and tasteful decorations of these utensils may be unreservedly set down as a bequest from ancient Egypt.

6. Routes through the Eastern Desert.

Keneh is a place of some importance as the starting-point of the caravans traversing the Arabian desert to *Kosér* (p. 77) and as an emporium of the trade of Upper Egypt with the coast-districts of the Red Sea. It consequently affords a good opportunity of making a short and comparatively easy desert journey, as the interesting excursion to Kosèr can be made without any very great privation or danger. The caravan-route leads viâ *Hammâmât*, traversing the rocky Arabian Desert, which is not only of great scenic grandeur but also full of interest for the naturalist and the archæologist. Kosèr, a port on the Red Sea, is about 110 M. from Keneh, and the journey can be made comfortably in four, or at most five days.

These desert-routes were important even in antiquity for the trade with the seaports and the land of *Punt* (Arabia) on the one side and the valuable quarries in the mountains of the Arabian Desert on the other. Spices and other costly products were sent across the desert to Keneh, at first on donkey-back and afterwards on camels, while green breccia and several varieties of granite were sent down to the sea in return. The most important points on the Red Sea, named from N. to S., were *Myos Hormos* (now *Abu Sar el-Kibli*), in the latitude of Monfalût; *Leukos Limen*, now *Kosér*; and *Berenike*, in the latitude of Assuân. The route from Keneh to Myos Hormos leads to the N.E., and a short detour may be made through the *Wâdi Fatireh*, with its granite-quarries, and past the Roman town and colony of *Hydreuma* or *Fons Trajanus*, which lies in the latitude of Ḳâu, about 3 days' journey from Keneh. Outside the walls lie a temple and other buildings, and some large columns and Greek inscriptions have been found in the quarries, which were worked chiefly in the time of Hadrian and Trajan. About two days' journey farther to the N. is *Gebel Dukhân* ('smoke mountain'). the ancient porphyry quarries of which were worked by the Romans. Here are the ruins of an Ionic temple of the time of Trajan (never completed), some remains of an irregularly built town, and two large water-reservoirs. The old route led hence to *Myos Hormos*, the harbour of which has been silted up and is now practically useless. Travellers making for the Sinai Peninsula journey to the N. from the porphyry quarries for two or three days more, and cross by boat to *Tûr* (see *Baedeker's Lower Egypt*, p. 515). Those who undertake one of these journeys should study the 'Reisebriefe' of Lepsius and Wilkinson's well-known work.

A much more interesting journey than that to Gebel Dukhân is the trip to *Ḳosêr*, or at least to *Wâdi Ḥamâmât*, where there are numerous Egyptian inscriptions. For the journey (there and back) 10-11 days should be allowed, and Egyptologists will probably want 2-3 days more. It is generally undertaken from Keneh, but we may also choose the old route from *Ḳuft* (Koptos, p. 98), or we may start from Luxor. The first two routes unite at *el-Ḳarn* and are joined at *Laḳêtah* by that from Luxor. The necessary camels may be obtained in Keneh with the aid of one of the consular agents (comp. p. 72). The route from Keneh (telegraph-wires from Ḳûs to Ḳosêr) leads first through the villages of *Shêkh Reḳâb*, *Dômeh*, and *Ḳum 'Imrân*, which follow each other in quick succession, the first on the left, the other two on the right side of the road. The first night is generally spent at the caravanserai of **Bir 'Ambar**, about 3½ hrs. from Keneh, where the lofty palms and shady sycamores and mimosæ offer a most inviting halting-place. The large caravanserai was erected at the expense of an Ibrahim Pasha for the use of the Ḳosêr caravans and the Mecca pilgrims. The structure comprises several separate buildings, covered with dome-shaped roofs and surrounded by courts and colonnades. It has no owner and is free to everyone to use as he likes. As nothing is done to keep it in repair, it is rapidly falling into decay, like most of the Oriental buildings of the kind, and threatens soon to be a complete ruin. In the deserts of Upper Egypt the temperature at night is so mild, even in winter, that strong and healthy persons may safely sleep in the open air if warmly wrapped up; and for various reasons this is preferable to a night in the caravanserai. Those, however, who prefer to take their chances in the interior should not fail to make the most minute examination of the room in which they intend to sleep, in order to clear out the vermin with which it is almost certain to be infested; scorpions and venomous snakes are by no means uncommon visitants.

It is the duty of the *Khabîr*, or guide in charge of the caravan, to see that everyone and everything are ready betimes in the morning, so that a sufficiently early start may be made to cover the ground allotted to each day's march. He is held responsible for the safe conduct of the entire party, and expects implicit obedience to his marching orders. We soon turn our backs on the verdant green district bordering the Nile and enter the barren desert, almost entirely destitute of vegetation, which lies between the great river and the coast of the Red Sea. The first part of the route is very unedifying. We advance steadily, ascending almost imperceptibly, through a monotonous plain, intersected in all directions by small undulating heights. All around us extends the interminable yellowish gray, sun-bleached rocks of the desert; not a trace of organic life is visible, not a single green tree or shrub. At the hill of **el-Ḳarn** ('the horn'), which rises to the left of the caravan-route, about midway between *Bir 'Ambar* and *Laḳêtah*, the road from Keneh is joined by that from *Ḳuft*. Not Keneh but *Koptos*, the modern Ḳuft, a little to the S., was the starting-point of the road constructed by the ancient Egyptians for the traffic between the Thebaïd and the Red Sea. From this point onwards we therefore follow one of the most ancient trading routes known. From the hieroglyphics on the rocks and temple-walls at Ḥamâmât we learn that the ancient Koptos road formed a link, as early as 3000 years before our era, in the intercourse carried on between the Nile valley and Arabia, viâ the desert and the sea.

We now ride in a S.E. direction through a dreary district, in which the only variety is afforded by an occasional *Mobwala* or *Mahatta*. The Mobwalas are simply spaces covered with camel's dung, easily distinguished from the surrounding soil by their darker colour and their smooth, cement-like surface. They occur on every great caravan route at regular intervals and are of the utmost importance as sign-posts showing the road. Hence no khabir or camel-driver passes one of these places without giving his camels an opportunity to contribute their quota to the maintenance of the Mobwala. The *Mahattas* or halting-places are $7^{1}/_{2}$-9 M. apart and serve also as measures of distance. The swift-running camels take their name from the number of mahattas they can reach in one day. Thus a camel which can cover 10 mahattas, *i.e.* 75-90 M., in one day is known as an *'Ashari* (runner of 'ten'). Other milestones of the desert are afforded by the skeletons of camels, horses, and asses, and by small cairns above the remains of unfortunate travellers who have [lost their lives in this dreary waste.

The Koṣêr caravans usually pass the second night in the village of La-kêtah (9 hrs. from Kuṭṭ and Bîr 'Ambar, $12^{1}/_{2}$ hrs. from Keneh), which is chiefly inhabited by *'Ababdeh;* it is also a halting-place for caravans coming in the opposite direction. The small oasis has two wells, five palms, a small piece of tilled ground, a few mud-huts, and a half-ruined Arab caravanserai. It is a characteristic specimen of a desert-village and offers much to interest the stranger. It is a place of great comfort and convenience to the traveller, as its resources include the materials for a solid and satisfying supper in the shape of mutton, goat's flesh, poultry, eggs, etc. The dogs here are great thieves, and care should be taken to leave nothing within their reach at night. Near the chief well are some fragments of a Greek inscription of the reign of Tiberius Claudius.

The first Roman military station, the **Hydreuma**, now called by the Arabs *Ḳaṣr el-Benât* ('castle of the maidens'), is 3 hrs. from Lakêṭah. It lies to the S. of the caravan route and forms an oblong 125 ft. in length and 101 ft. in breadth. The wall inclosing the oblong, formed of layers of sandstone without cement, was $6^{1}/_{2}$ ft. high. Within the wall lie 20 small chambers opening on a rectangular inner court, the only exit from which is on the N. side. No water is now procurable here. To the N. of the path, opposite the ruin of the Hydreuma, stands a rock of sandstone with numerous graffiti in Greek, Coptic, Arabic, Himyaritic, and Sinaitic characters.

At a distance of about 2 hrs. from the Hydreuma the rocks close in and form a winding pass or gateway named *Muṭraḳ es-Selâm*. On the *Gebel Abu Kû'eh* ('father of the elbow'), the rock at the entrance to the pass, are more graffiti. Older than those at Ḳaṣr el-Benât; one of them contains the name of the religious reformer Amenhotep IV. We now approach the fine rocky scenery through which the second part of the Koṣêr route leads. In the distance, to the right, rise the S. foot-hills of the *Hamâmât Mts.*, while nearer and in front are the S.W. spurs. Throughout the whole of the Nile valley from Cairo to Philæ the traveller encounters no such picturesque scenery as he sees in traversing the magnificent rocky formations of this part of the Egyptian-Arabian desert. Even the imposing granite cliffs of the Shellâl islands and the quarries of Assuân pale before the rocky mass of the *Hamâmât*, rising to a height of 4200 ft. The outliers of the range consist of a yellow sandstone, followed by the red 'Nubian' sandstone, resembling that of the Black Forest, while the great central mass is composed of granite.

Beyond the Muṭraḳ es-Selâm the hills again diverge. Among them, to the N. of the caravan-route, lies a second Roman station, with a filled-in well. About 2 hrs. farther on the hills of reddish-yellow sandstone give place to loftier and almost black hills of breccia, through the valleys of which, now wide and now narrow, the caravan winds its way. Beginning with the black mountains and stretching among them for a long way is the Wâdi Ḥamâmât, where the green breccia was quarried in the most ancient times. In 1 hr. more we reach the *Bîr Ḥamâmât,* a well 16 ft. in diameter, with a stone coping. Near the well are the remains of a Roman wall, and between the two are five unfinished sarcophagi, some completely shattered. Near the well begins a series of short graffiti, including an inscription of *Phra em heb,* a superintendent of labourers, and representing Ammon with a ram's head bearing the Atef crown. The cartouche of Seti II. is also met with. About 1 hr. farther on are longer inscriptions. In the first a miner named *Art en benipe* is mentioned and the

symbol of the crow-bar ┃ is given. The numerous inscriptions of the

old empire found here, belonging to the 5th, 6th, 11th, 12th, and 13th Dynasties, have been published by Lepsius (Part II. of his 'Denkmäler') and have recently been completed by W. Golenischeff. They begin with kings *Tetkara-Assa* and *Unas* of the 5th, and *Userkara* and *Pepi* of the 6th Dynasty. The most interesting of all is the inscription of the 8th year of *Sankh kara,* in which a military expedition from Koptos to Ḳoṣêr is recorded; it gives the names of the stations, mentions the digging of two cisterns, and relates the passage from Tuà (the early name of Ḳoṣêr) to the 'Holy Land' (*i.e.* Arabia). The name of Rohannu also occurs. Among the later inscriptions of the 20th Dynasty may be mentioned one of the 3rd year of Ramses ('Denkmäler' of Lepsius, III, 219; transl. in Brugsch's 'History of Egypt', Eng. transl., Vol. 2, pp. 175 et seq.). We learn from this inscription that in the part of this desert named *Rohannu*

lay a special district of the Ḥamâmât Mts.

known as Pa tu en bekhen, or the 'Bekhen

Mts.', so called from the *Bekhen* found there, a dark-green, almost black, and exceedingly hard diorite, which was highly prized by the Egyptian sculptors. This region is figured in the fragments of a map of the time of Ramses II. now preserved in the museum of Turin; and from it it would seem that gold also was procured in the Bekhen Mts. In the treasury of the temple of Medinet Habu we find mention made of gold from Kush

(Ethiopia), Teb (Edfu), Nubit (Ombos) and . By this last we

should undoubtedly understand gold brought by the Koptos trading route, but not gold obtained there. The Turin Museum possesses the plan of another map of a gold-mining region (of the time of Seti I.), the gold from which seems to have been carried over the caravan-route ending opposite *Edfu.* The inscriptions in the so-called Temple of Redêsîyeh (more properly Wâdi 'Abbâs; see p. 253) treat of the water-supply on this route to the gold mines.

In the great inscription of Ramses IV. a complete list is given of all the higher and lower officials, as well as of all the workmen, including 800 Aperiu (from the desert to the E. of the Delta), who had been sent to the quarries by command of the king. The total number amounts to 8368 souls, for whose support commissariat columns were constantly on the move between Koptos and Bekhen. At line 18 we read: 'Total 8368. Provisions for these were brought upon ten waggons, and six yoke of oxen were attached to each waggon in going from Egypt to the Bekhen Mts.' — Among the later inscriptions is one of the time of Darius, giving the genealogy of 25 architects. Xerxes and Artaxerxes are also mentioned in the inscriptions of Persian officials.

Just beyond the quarries the route turns from the N.E. to the S. and passes the ruins of *el-Fawâkhir,* an old mining site. Those who wish to continue their journey to the Red Sea have still two short days' marches ahead of them, the route leading through the *Wâdi Rôṣafah* to *Bêdah* (*Bir el-Inglis)* and thence through the *Wâdi Ambagi* to **Kosêr** or **Kosseir**, on the Arabian Gulf, the *Leukos Limen* (White Harbour) of the Ptolemies and the *Tua* of the ancient Egyptians. About 4 M. to the N. the scanty remains of *Old Kosêr*, corresponding to the harbour of *Philotera*, the ancient *Aennum*, which was named thus in honour of the sister of Ptolemy Philadelphus. Kosêr is now an unimportant town of about 3000 inhab., with a quay, a wooden mole 400 ft. long, two mosques, and several bazaars. The small houses are all whitewashed. The only edifices of any size are the government buildings erected by Mohammed 'Ali opposite the mole, the adjacent custom-house, and a large grain-magazine, also belonging to the Egyptian government.

In going from Kosêr towards the Nile the Beduins sometimes prefer another and more southerly route than that through the Wâdi Hamâmât. This diverges from the route above described at the *Bir el-Inglis* in the *Wâdi Bêdah* (see above) and leads at first through the winding *Wâdi Kabr el-Khâdim*, afterwards passing the *Gebel Nuhâs* and through the pass of *Rî'at el-Ghazâl* into the *Wâdi Ghazâl*. To the right rise the conical *Gebel Daghanîyeh* and *Gebel Moshâghir*. We next follow the *Wâdi Homûdah*, which farther on takes the name of *Wâdi el-Homr* from the fine *Gebel Homr*, which flanks it on the right. The night is spent at *Moilah*, a village with water and a few huts of the 'Ababdeh. At the *Gebel Wâkif* we cross the *Tarîk e'dahrâwi*, a road running from N. to S., and farther on reach *Amârah*, with another well and more 'Ababdeh huts. Thence our route lies through the *Wâdi Nûr* and the *Wâdi Kash* to the *Bir el-Kash*, a dried-up well, beyond which we pass numerous quarries of green breccia. Beyond the passes of *Rî'at el-Khêl* (sandstone formation) and *Rî'at el-Hamrah* we reach the Mobwala (see p. 75) or *Râs âsfar*, whence we go on through the *Wâdi Mâghlat* to *Mobwalat Khôr el-Ghîr*. Lastly we proceed viâ *Gâhrat e'Dab'ah* to *Lakêtah* (p. 75), where our route unites with the more northerly one already described.

Caravans on the way from Kosêr to Esneh take a route still farther to the S., viâ the well of *Darfâwi*. The N. route from *Nukhêl* to Keneh is now seldom used.

The journey to *Berenike*, on the Arabian Gulf in 24° N. lat., and to the emerald mines $^1/_2$° to the N. of it, is seldom undertaken. We may start from Keneh or Koptos, diverging at Lakêtah from the route to Kosêr, or we may begin at a point opposite Edfu (Contra-Apollinopolis) or Redêsîyeh (p. 253). On both routes traces of old watering stations are discernible. Both Pliny and the Itinerary of Antonine (3rd cent. A.D.) give a list of the ancient stations, with their distance from each other in Roman miles. The list in the Itinerary is as follows: Phœnicon 27, Didymo 24, Afrodito 20, Kompasi 22, Jovis 23, Aristonis 25, Phalacro 25, Apollono 23, Kabalsi 27, Kænon Hydreuma 27, Berenike 18 — in all 271 Roman miles = about 250 English miles.

Golenischeff took 11 days from Redêsîyeh (p. 253) to Berenike, and returned thence to Assuân in 8 days. 1st Day. *Bîr Abbâd* (3 hrs.), in the *Wâdi Miâh*, an ancient station with quarry-marks like those at el-Hôsh, near Silsileh (p. 254). — 2nd Day. Temple of Seti I. at Redêsîyeh (p. 253), with rock-inscriptions of the 18-19th Dynasties. — 3rd Day. More masons' marks discovered. Ancient station of *Abu Greiah*, with 2 cisterns (not to be confounded with the place of the same name near Berenike). — 4th Day. Descent through the *Wâdi Bêzah*, with its acacias (selem and seyâl, Acacia Ehrenbergiana and A. nilotica). From this point a diverging route leads direct to the emerald mines of the Wâdi Zahârah (see below). We cross the *Wâdi Higelig*. On the rocks to the right are rude representations of giraffes, camels, and ibexes. Remains of an ancient station named *Samunt*, with a cistern and chambers, occur in the same Wâdi. We next enter the broad green *Wâdi Moëlheh*, and steer for the *Gebel Mugef*, near which is a spring of excellent water. — 5th Day. Through huge granite rocks to groups of ten and twenty rude stone huts, probably built by miners. View of Gebel Zabârah. On a rock to the right is a view of an Egyptian bark, with sails and rudder. Farther on is a ruined station, with the remains of a stone hut. Near this point our route is joined by the route from Kuft (Keptes), which Col. Colston followed in 1873. [Beyond (9 hrs.) Lakêṭah (p. 75), Col. Colston's route led viâ (6½ hrs.) *Marut*, (3 hrs.) a high-lying well, *ed-Dagbag*, two old wells (8½ hrs.), *Bezah* (2 hrs.), and *Wâdi Gerf* (6½ hrs.).] — 6th Day. Ancient station of *ed-Dueîg*, with contreforts, chambers, and a large cistern, opening on the N.E. Adjacent is another smaller building. About 3 hrs. farther on we cross the watershed between the Nile and the Red Sea. Two more cisterns. We pass the granite hill of *Abu Hâd.* — 7th Day. Descent into the *Wâdi Gemâl*. Station in the form of a right-angled triangle. Two round cisterns. Lateral valley diverging towards the emerald mines. The mountains (*Gebel Abyad*) now rise to the right, instead of, as previously, to the left. — 8th Day. We proceed through the *Wâdi Abyad* and the *Wâdi Higelîg*, leaving the *Gebel Hamâta* to the right; then along the *Wâdi Râmît*. On a height in the *Wâdi Husûn* are some curious shékhs' graves, in a circular form. — 9th Day. Seven other circular tombs; the well of *el-Haratrah* lies to the right; old structure of a large cistern in the *Wâdi el-Hasîr*. Through the *Wâdi Amrugûm* to the *Wâdi Lâhemi*, which descends from the mountain of that name, crosses our route, and proceeds in windings to the Red Sea. The last station is *Abu-Greîah*, comprising several buildings, the largest of which, 60 paces long and 47 paces wide, contains the remains of rooms. Another building seems to have been a reservoir for rain water. — 10th Day. Arrival at the ruins of the old temple of Berenike.

The town of Berenike (*Berenice*), situated in the same latitude as Assuân, was founded in B.C. 275 by Ptolemy Philadelphus, who revived the commerce of the Red Sea by the establishment of several new ports. The town, which was named by Ptolemy after his mother, survived for 400 or 500 years. The ruins, still extant, surround the *Temple*, which faces the E.N.E. In front is a fore-court 28½ ft. in width and 12 ft. in depth, which was adjoined by the temple proper (inner length 31 ft.), comprising two rows of apartments. The central apartment, with somewhat sloping sides, seems to have been the main one, as its right and left walls and also the outside of the entrance-wall (to the left) bear traces of paintings, representing a king sacrificing to various deities. The name of the Emp. Tiberius, sacrificing to the god Khem, appears here. The representation on the left outside-wall shows an emperor (probably Hadrian) appearing before a goddess, who seems to be, from the legend,

the tutelary deity of the green (uaz) emerald mine. To the left

of this main apartment is a covered corridor, with a window, and adjacent is a staircase leading to the roof. The temple was cleared from rubbish in 1873 by Purdy Pasha, an American in the Egyptian service.

The Emerald Mines, which were visited last century by Bruce (1768 -73) and in this century by Cailliaud (1815-18), Belzoni, and Beechey, were worked by the Arabs, according to Makrîzi, down to the year 760 of the Hegira (1370 A.D.), after which they were abandoned. Moḥammed 'Ali made an unavailing attempt to reopen them. They lie partly in the *Wâdi Sakêt* and partly on the *Gebel Zabârah*, 14 M. to the N.E. They are best visited from Contra Apollinopolis, but may, like Berenike, be approached by following the coast of the Arabian Gulf from Koṣêr. The first route diverges from the road to Berenike at *Phalacro*. Between Contra-Edfu and the mines are three old stations. At the first of these is the name of a sun-worshipping king of the 18th Dynasty. Close to the second, 13 hrs. from the Nile, is a temple hewn in the rock, the *Temple of Redêsiyeh* (so called after the place of that name on the Nile; see p. 253), which Seti I. dedicated to Ammon. No precious stones are now found in the emerald mines. To the S. of the *Gebel Zabârah* lies the village of *Sakêt*, with the huts of miners and a rock-hewn temple, with a few Greek inscriptions. Among these is a reference to Serapis and the Isis of Senskis.

7. Denderah.

Both the 'Three Weeks' and the 'Four Weeks' Tourist Steamers stop at Denderah in ascending the river, the first halting 3 hrs., the second a whole day. The mail-steamer also halts here for a few hours in descending the river.
For a visit to the temple the steamboats and dhahabîyehs moor at the bank opposite Keneh. The distance to the temple (about 2 M.) is easily accomplished in ½ hr. by the well-equipped donkeys standing in readiness. Those who wish to make a prolonged stay may procure the necessary conveniences for a night in the temple from the keeper 'Ali Effendi, who lives in Keneh. The Arabs, however, are afraid of the ''afrit' or ghosts. The visitor should not fail to be provided with candles or (better still) a magnesium lamp for exploring the crypts and other parts of the temple.

The capital of the 6th nome of Upper Egypt (Âa-ti, 'the district of the place of the presentation of gifts') appears in the inscriptions under several names. The two most frequent of these are

Ân, 'the town of columns', and the secular name *Ta-rir*

or *Ta en ta-rir*, 'the town of the district enclosed by ramparts'. From the latter are derived the Greek *Tentyra* and the modern **Denderah**.

We follow the bank of the Nile towards the N., through palm-trees, and then proceed to the W. through well-tilled fields, passing (right) a farm-enclosure guarded by yelping dogs; or we may ride at once towards the W. in the direction of the Gate of Augustus (p. 88) and proceed thence to the N., passing a door with unfilled cartouches, to the N. entrance, where the cards of admission (see Introd., p. xiv) are shown. The wall enclosing the temple is formed of Nile bricks, and there is another entrance on the W. side. The total enclosure is 317 yds. long and 306 yds. wide, and besides the large temple of Hathor contains a small sanctuary dedicated to Isis and a so-called 'birth-honse' (see below). The N. door, which is in a straight line with the temple, is only 15° to the E. of N.; but in the temple-inscriptions it is always spoken of as the E. entrance, while the long sides of the temple are called the N. and S. sides. In the following description we follow the true geographical position. The N. gate was built under the Emp. Domitian, who is here named Germanicus. On the side next the temple appears the name of Nerva Trajanus, also with the epithets of Germanicus and Dacicus.

From the N. gate a modern brick passage leads to the temple. To the left of this passage lies a building deep-sunken in the debris and wanting its front. Round it ran a colonnade, the capitals of which, with the dwarf-like figure of the god Besa, project from the sand. The remains include a rather large vestibule (33 ft. by 16½ ft.), a long central room, two narrow side-rooms, some small chambers, and the fragments of a staircase (to the right). This building is dedicated to the birth of Horus, with whom the son of each successive monarch is compared. Similar *Birth-Houses* (Egypt.

▭ 𓀭 𓌉 pa-mes), called by Champollion Mameisi (Copt., 'place of birth'), occur in many other Egyptian temples (pp. 253, 289, etc.). The cartouches of *Autokrator Kisres*, which Hathor presents to Horus Sam taui, have been supposed to refer to Augustus; but the fact that the latter had no son makes this very doubtful. The 'birth-house' also contains the names of Trajan and Hadrian, to whom it probably owes its existence. The paintings represent the care of the young Horus, who is nursed and ministered to by goddesses and women with cows' heads. — We now proceed to the temple, either by ascending over the heaps of rubbish, or by returning to the N. gate and walking thence in a straight direction.

**Temple of Hathor at Denderah.

This interesting and much-admired building was dedicated to *Hathor*, the Egyptian Venus. The *Portico* (Pl. E), which is supported by 24 columns, is 139 ft. in breadth. Each of the columns has a capital formed of four heads of Hathor, with cows' ears, surmounted by a house, in reference to the meaning of Hathor, *Hat* (*i.e.* house) *of Horus*. The columns next the entrance show an open door. The six columns in the front row, three on each side of the entrance, are united by balustrades. The rubbish round the temple reaches to the balustrades in front and nearly to the roof on the E. side; hence the floor of the temple appears sunken and is reached by a flight of wooden steps. Originally, however, the temple stood level with the ground, and its present appearance, like that of the temples of Esneh and Edfu, is due to the accumulated rubbish of centuries. In accordance with the plan of other temples, a colonnade and a pylon should stand in front of this portico; but perhaps the means to add these were not forthcoming. The date of the temple is given by a Greek inscription of three lines, which runs round the cornice on the exterior of the building and reads as follows:

ΥΠΕΡ. ΑΥΤΟΚΡΑΤΟΡΟΣ. ΤΙΒΕΡΙΟΥ. ΚΑΙΣΑΡΟΣ. ΝΕΟΥ. ΣΕΒΑΣΤΟΥ. ΘΕΟΥ. ΣΕΒΑΣΤΟΥ. ΥΙΟΥ. ΕΠΙ. ΑΥΛΟΥ. ΑΥΙΛ-ΛΙΟΥ. ΦΛΑΚΚΟΥ.

ΗΓΕΜΟΝΟΣ. ΚΑΙ. ΑΥΛΟΥ. ΦΩΛΥΙΟΥ. ΚΡΙΣΠΟΥ. ΕΠΙΣΤΡΑ-ΤΗΓΟΥ. ΣΑΡΑΠΙΩΝΟΣ. ΤΡΥΧΑΜΒΟΥ. ΣΤΡΑΤΗΓΟΥΝΤΟΣ. ΟΙ. ΑΠΟ. ΤΗΣ. ΜΗΤΡ

ΟΠΟΛΕΩΣ. ΚΑΙ. ΤΟΥ. ΝΟΜΟΥ. ΤΟ. ΠΡΟΝΑΟΝ. ΑΦΡΟΔΕΙ-ΤΗΙ. ΘΕΑΙ. ΜΕΓΙΣΤΗΙ. ΚΑΙ. ΤΟΙΣ. ΣΥΝΝΑΟΙΣ. ΘΕΟΙΣ. L [Κ. ΤΙΒ] ΕΡΙΟΥ. ΚΑΙΣΑΡΟ[Σ ΑΘΥΡ ΚΑ]

'Under the rule of the Emp. Tiberius, and under the prefect Aulus

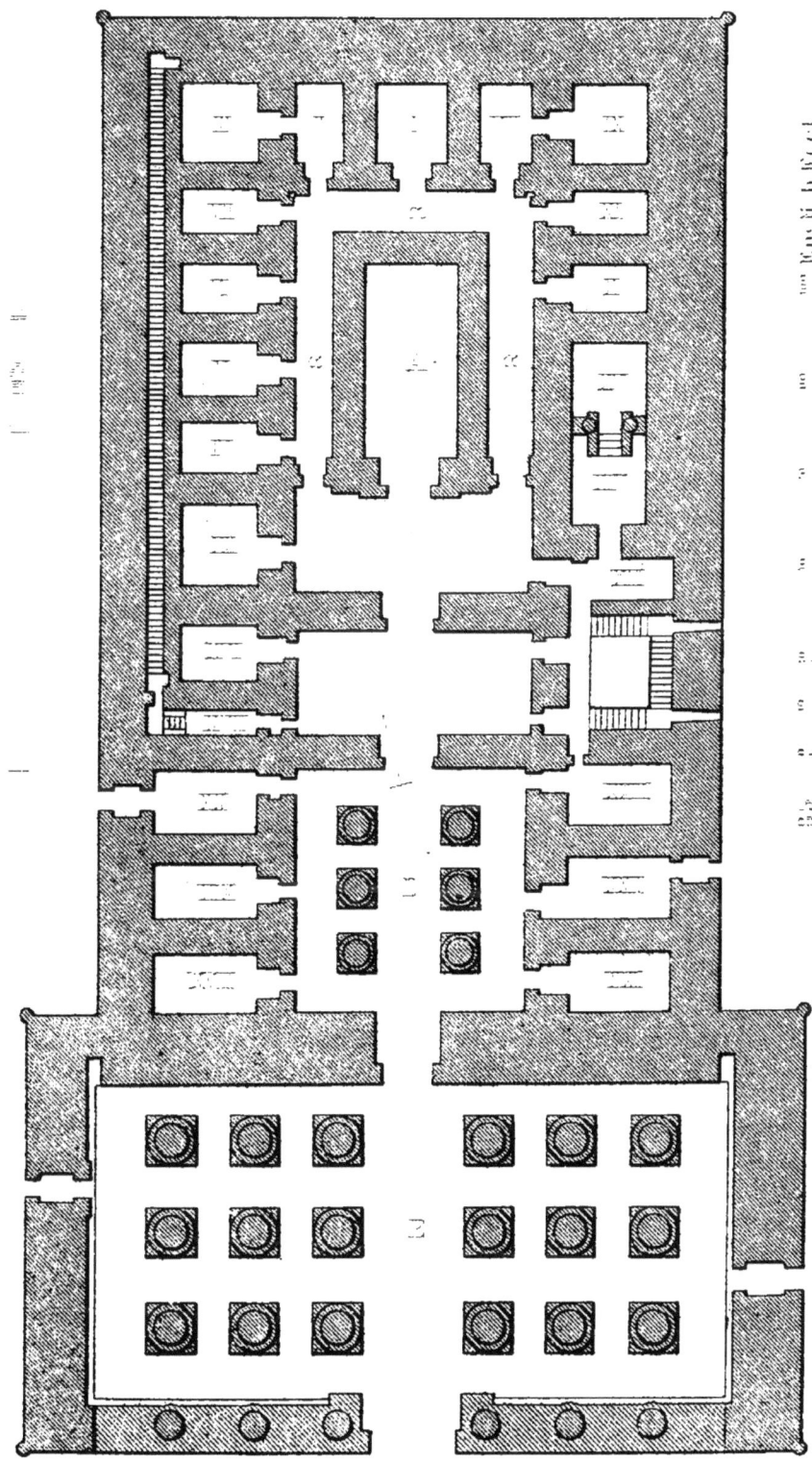

Avillius Flaccus, the governor Aulus Fulvius Crispus, and the district-governor Sarapion Trychambos, the inhabitants of the capital and of the nome dedicated the Pronaos to the great goddess Aphrodite and her fellow-gods, in the twentieth (?)'year of the Emp. Tiberius . . . .' An inscription recently found by. Dümichen on the E. side of the temple informs us that this outer wall of the temple was decorated in the second year of the Emp. Tiberius Claudius (42 A.D.). There are, however, many representations of the Emp. Nero both inside and outside the temple. The crypts of the temple date from the reigns of Ptolemy X., Ptolemy XI., and Ptolemy XIII. (Soter II.; Ptolemy Alexander; Neos Dionysos). The inscriptions running round the temple refer to Ptolemy XVI. Cæsarion and the Emp. Augustus. On the exterior of the rear-wall of the temple appears Ptolemy Kisres, accompanied by Cleopatra VI. and the little Cæsarion; the inscription is Ptulmis, surnamed Kisres. In both cases the Cæsarion referred to is apparently the son of Cæsar and Cleopatra. The temple would thus seem to owe its present form to the last of the Ptolemies and the first Roman emperors. It is, however, obvious that the site was previously occupied by older temple buildings, going back to the earliest period of Egyptian history. King Pepi of the 6th Dynasty is repeatedly represented in the crypts. In one of these crypts (No. 9) the ancient building plan of Denderah is mentioned twice. The first of these mentions occurs in the description of an excursion of the goddess to Edfu on the first of Epiphi: 'The great building-plan (senti) of Ant (Denderah) was found written in ancient characters on hide, of the time of the successors of Horus. Found in the interior of the wall of the royal palace in the time of King Pepi'. Another passage reads: 'The great plan of Denderah, a restoration of the monument made by King Ramenkheper (Tutmes III.), after it was found in ancient characters of the time of King Khufu'. The priests of Tentyra thus ascribed the foundation of their temple to Khufu and Pepi. There are, however, stones bearing the names of Amenemha I., Tutmes III., Tutmes IV., Ramses II., and Ramses III., all of whom probably either built or restored parts of the old temple.

If we compare the temple of Denderah with a similar structure of the earlier period, such as the temple of Abydos or the great national sanctuary of Karnak, we find it not less beautiful in its own way, though of course far from competing with these gigantic structures in magnificence or extent. Its chief characteristics are a fine symmetry of proportions and dignified adaptation to its purposes. A happy blending of Egyptian seriousness with Grecian grace, which meets us unmistakably at every turn, has a peculiarly pleasing effect, and we feel much more at home in the halls of the Hathor of Tentyra than in the great hall of the god of Thebes, with its forest of gigantic columns. Neither the figures nor the inscriptions sculptured on the walls compare in masterly execution with

those in the tombs of the ancient kingdom or with those peculiar
to the times of a Seti or a Tutmes; but we cannot refuse our admiration even to these products of later Egyptian art. Here and
there (as in several chambers of the upper story) we meet specimens of hasty and poor workmanship; but as a rule the sculpture
of Denderah is pleasing and harmonious in style and executed with
a care that does not overlook the smallest detail. The eye is uniformly pleased by the harmony of the whole with its details and by
the great variety of composition which manifests itself in spite of
the prescribed form to which the artist was confined.

Neither the general architectural scheme of the temple as a whole
nor the style of the details shows any essential variation from those
that may be traced in the earlier Egyptian temples. The first
apartment, here as elsewhere, is a handsome *Hypostyle Hall* (Pl. E),
open in front, with 24 massive columns supporting the roof (comp.
p. 93). Next follows a room with six columns (Pl. D), with three
apartments to the left (xviii, xix, xx) and three to the right
(xxi, xxii, xxiii), from the last of which (xxiii) a passage leads
to the festal chambers beside Hall B. The next room (Pl. C),
with no columns, has apartments xvi and xvii on the left. A
fourth hall (Pl. B), adjoined on the left by a single apartment
(xii) and on the right by the suite of three festal chambers (xiii,
xiv, xv), leads to the Adytum (Pl. A), a long narrow room in
which the sacred boats were kept. From the passage (Pl. *a*) which
encircles the latter, entrances lead into eleven side-chambers (left
iv, v, vi, vii, iii, ii, right viii, ix, xi, x), which are grouped
round the main chamber (Pl. I) behind room A. There are also a
number of secret passages (crypts), constructed in the hollow wall
of the temple on the E., W., and S. sides. These passages, which
are difficult of access, are in three stories, one above another (comp.
p. 96). Finally from the central hall C, doors lead on the right
and left to the two stairs which ascend to the roof of the temple
(comp. pp. 91, 97).

The Egyptians had special names for each hall and side-chamber,
for each corridor and staircase, for each door and window, in fact
for each part, great or small, of the more or less complicated temples.
In not a few cases these names explain the use of the different
rooms; but the only certain information as to the special nature of
the various apartments is obtained from the *Inscriptions*, which
are arranged as a kind of ornamental border above and below the
paintings on the wall, much like the borders seen sometimes on old-
fashioned wall-papers. These inscriptions, which are of the greatest
importance both for the history of architecture and for the explanation of the temple-cult, usually have their contents arranged in the
same order. The name of the king, with all his titles and official
epithets, is first mentioned, followed by the statement that he built,
repaired, completed, or adorned such and such a room, or such and

such a staircase, the name of which is in each case given, followed
by as full a description of the room in question and of what took
place there, as space will allow. Prof. Dümichen uncovered the
inscription at the foot of the exterior wall of the temple in 1875
(p. 97), and found that, as at Edfu, the names and dimensions of
the chambers lying to the north were inscribed on the N. side, and
on the S. side those of the chambers lying to the south. He has
published the inscription with a translation †.

In our description, we begin with the *Hypostyle Hall* or **Khent
Hall* (Pl. E). The first large hall of an Egyptian temple frequently
bore the name [hieroglyphs] *Khent, i.e.* front room, as is the case here, at
Edfu, at Philae, and elsewhere. It has several other names as well.
Apparently with reference to the astronomical representations which
adorn both halves of the ceiling, it is frequently named in the inscriptions [hieroglyphs] *'Nut usekh ur t'* i.e. Great Hall of
the Goddess Nut, who as the symbol of the vault of heaven was represented as a tall woman bending her face towards the earth and
letting her arms hang down [hieroglyphs]. A colossal representation of this
figure is met with twice on the ceiling of the hypostyle room at
Denderah, and it is repeated twice more, in the apartment marked
XV. on the plan and in the central Osiris-room on the N. side of
the temple-roof. In the two last instances it occupies the entire
surface of the ceiling. Astronomical representations, whether simply
golden stars scattered promiscuously on a blue ground, or actual
copies of the constellations as seen at some particular time, have
been adopted as a suitable ceiling-decoration in nearly every Egyptian temple and tomb. The two names above given are by far the
commonest for this first room, but it is also called 'the seat of Osiris,
Horus, and Isis', and it is named in the inscriptions 'the dwelling
of Hathor, the house of the sistrum-playing, the house in which the
tambourine is sounded, the seat of the rapture of joy, the birth-
place of the celestial goddess Nut'. The hall is 143 ft. broad, 80 ft.
deep, and about 50 ft. high.

On festal occasions the image of the goddess was conveyed in her
boat to this Hall of Heaven, to meet there the sun-god, her father.
The decorative designs in this room chiefly consist, after the ancient
Egyptian custom, of representations of the royal builders of the
temple. The Roman emperors Augustus, Tiberius, Caligula, Claudius,
and Nero are in turn depicted, each bearing some dedicatory gift
for Hathor or some other of the gods worshipped at Denderah. The
central wall-spaces between the columns to the right and left of the
main portal are each occupied with four designs, referring to the

---

† *Baugeschichte des Denderatempels*, Strassburg, 1877.

entrance of the ruler into the sanctuary and to the ceremony of incense, to which he must submit in the first chamber according to the prescribed ritual. In the first we see the king (Nero) quitting his palace, preceded by five banners with sacred figures, while the high-priest (named Anmut-f) offers incense before him. In the second design, Horus and Thoth sprinkle the king with the symbols of life; in the third, the goddesses of the south *(Nekheb)* and of the north *(Uaz)* present him with the white crown and the crown 'Nefert'; in the fourth and last, the king is conducted before Hathor by the gods Month of Thebes and Tum of Heliopolis. Admission into the temple proper was not granted to him until after this ceremony had been gone through, the sacred garment assumed, and the purification by incense and holy water completed. The representations referring to these, and the explanatory inscriptions, are quite in the same manner as those we have already noted in the earlier temples of the time of Tutmes and Ramses.

The sculptured ornamentation on the ceiling, dealing with astronomical subjects, is divided into a W. and an E. half. The figures in the W. section are turned towards the N. (outside), those of the other to the S. (inside). Each section is divided into three bands, most of which consist of two or more rows. The exterior bands of each section correspond to each other, as do also the central and inner bands. Between the two sections is another band, containing 10 sun-discs and 11 vultures, explained by Prof. Lauth as referring to the 21st year of the reign of Tiberius. — The exterior bands, which are embraced by a tall figure of the goddess of the heavens, contain the twelve signs of the Zodiac in their upper rows; to the right those of the N. sky (lion, serpent instead of the virgin, balances, scorpion, archer, goat), to the left or S., those of the S. sky (water-carrier, fishes, ram, bull, twins, crab). In this row appear also the principal constellations (Orion, Sirius, Sothis) and five planets (Saturn, Mars, Jupiter, Venus, and Mercury). Mingled with the other figures are the gods of the twelve hours of night, on the E. side in ascending order (I to XII), and on the W. side in descending order.
·   The second rows of the exterior bands each contain 18 ships, with the 'Decani' or presidents of the weeks, mentioned elsewhere in other inscriptions. This long series begins in the W. section and ends in the E. section. The second bands, both on the right and left, consist of two rows each. At the four ends of the upper rows are the four Winds, with expanded wings, which are adjoined on the right (next the entrance) by four figures of gods referring to Ra, and on the left by four similar figures referring to Tum, the god of evening. Then follows a series of 'Decani', beginning in the W. and continued in the E. section, consisting of the above-mentioned thirty-six 'Decani' arranged in twelve groups of three, each conducted by a president usually in the form of a serpent. The lower rows of the central bands contain, on the right (W.) the twelve hours of the

night, on the left (N.) the twelve hours of the day, each with their eponymous divinities.

The interior band on the W. side exhibits three designs referring to the moon, which is here represented as ⟨eye⟩ 'uza', eye. In the first are the 14 days of the waning moon, in the second the 14 days of the waxing moon, represented by 14 divinities ascending a flight of steps, while the victorious Thoth appears as a fifteenth divinity beyond the moon-disc. Finally appears Osiris as the moon-god, seated with Isis and Nephthys in a boat, floating above the symbol of the sky ⟨glyph⟩, which is supported by four female forms. -- In the E. section the interior band exhibits the course of the sun-disc through the 12 hours of the day, represented by 12 boats. In each disc appears the figure of the divinity to which the particular hour was sacred.

On the W. side of the hall, between the second and third row of columns (to the right of the entrance), and on the E. side between the third and fourth row (on the left) are *Side-Entrances*, through which the sacrificial offerings used to be brought into the hall (com. p. 88).

Of the three *Prosekos Halls* which we next enter, by far the largest is the hexastyle first hall, the —

Hall of the Appearance (Pl. D), called in the inscriptions *usekh kha* or Hall of the Appearance, and 'Hall of the Appearance of Her Highness', *i.e.* Hathor, the golden-rayed. The inscription at the foot of the external wall gives the measurement of this hall as 26 ells square, which closely coincides with its actual size, $45\frac{1}{2}$ ft. square. On festal days the image of the mighty sun-goddess was carried in solemn procession from its place in the holy of holies, and was not seen by the multitude assembled in the vestibule until it reached this hall, when the lofty double doors were thrown open. Hence probably the name of the hall.

It is a remarkable fact that except in the Khent Hall, the secret passages, and Room xx (p. 88), the cartouches of the kings in all the interior rooms of the temple remain empty. In Room xx the accompanying royal cartouches are found: 'Lord of the rulers, chosen by Ptah', and 'Kaisaros, ever-living, beloved by Ptah and Isis'. The latter, which is also found on the exterior W. wall of the temple, probably refers to Augustus, though the same designation was also used for Caligula, Claudius, and Nero. On the E. external wall of the temple at Denderah and in the temple of Isis at Phi-

lae, Augustus is constantly indicated by the accompanying car-touches '*Autokrator Kisres*'. The temple was probably built in the unsettled times of the later Ptolemies, and the priests were there-fore left in doubt whether to fill in the cartouches with the name of Ptolemy or of Augustus.

The representations on the walls and columns, many of which well deserve special attention, exhibit here also the Egyptian ruler worshipping Hathor or some other of the divinities revered in her temple. They illustrate several most remarkable ceremonies, which the king performed according to the prescribed ritual in presence of the images of the gods in the temple. We have seen reason to be-lieve that the sculptured decorations of all the temple-chambers were executed about the end of the period of the Ptolemies and the beginning of the Roman empire. (The sculptures in some of the chambers in the sunk-floor and in several of the higher secret pas-sages, date from the reigns of Ptolemies X., XI., and XIII.) Yet in spite of that, the entire adornment on the walls is arranged according to early Egyptian patterns; so that the ceremonies here depicted were not first introduced under the empire, and probably no Roman emperor ever took part in these ceremonies in this temple of Hathor. The walls of the temple at Denderah exhibit exclusively *Early Egyp-tian Manners and Customs*. What we here learn are the ceremonies imposed by the priesthood on the early Egyptian monarch who de-sired to worship the goddess. Thus in a representation to the right of the entrance the king appears twice over in the same design. First we see him, clad in a long robe and carrying a staff, entering the hall, preceded by the priest wearing the panther-skin and sprinkling incense on the burning censer. Next we see him stand-ing before the image of Hathor, his robe laid aside; bending for-ward he goes through the motion of cleaving the earth with the short hand-plough in his hand, because it was an immemorial custom that the Egyptian king should turn the first sod on the site of a temple. (In the explanatory inscription here, as elsewhere, this ceremony is named '*bai ta*', cleaving of the ground.) The king also smote the first blow with the hammer at the laying of the foun-dation-stone, and shaped the first brick for the enclosing walls, which were usually built of unburned bricks of Nile-mud dried in the sun. All these ceremonies performed by *early* Egyptian monarchs at the foundation of a temple, are here faithfully recorded according to early models, both in visible shape and by explanatory in-scriptions. They are also recorded in the lowest of the four rows on the W. and E. exterior walls of the temple. In the temple of Horus at Edfu the king is represented performing similar cere-monies.

Another picture, also referring to the founding of a temple, appears on the immediately adjoining wall. Here the king once more appears before Hathor, bearing in his hand the building-tool *khus.* The ceremony is named in the inscription '*the Building of the Temple*'; and the words placed in the mouth of the king and arranged above the Khus run: 'I have built the monument, the great one, as a perfect building to all eternity'. The ceremony represented in the following design also refers to the building of the temple. The king, kneeling before Hathor, is shown shaping the first burned brick for the girdle-wall of the temple. As has already been mentioned in the description of the cult of Hathor, that goddess is frequently extolled in the inscriptions at Denderah as the goddess of joy, at whose festival wine flowed freely and the air was fragrant with incense and all the perfumes of Arabia. Thus, as the inscriptions here inform us, the king mingles grains of incense and wine with the material out of which he moulds the brick. On both sides of the portal admitting to the hall are two long inscriptions, each consisting of 14 vertical lines, and containing a list of all the names under which the great Hathor was worshipped at Denderah and elsewhere in Egypt. This is followed by a list of the chief gods and divine geniuses, those of the temple at Edfu being named in greatest detail; and finally comes a list of the sacred serpents of Denderah, which were probably not kept in the temple itself, but in the adjoining sacred groves.

We now enter the *Side Chambers*, of which there are three on each side. All are of the same size, defined in the inscription on the E. external wall as $11^1/_3$ ells long and $6^1/_2$ ells broad. The first on the left side (Pl. xviii) was called *Ast.t*, or in the fuller form (shown *e.g.* on one of the staircase-walls)

Asi.t. The inscriptions here clearly indicate that the incense, so lavishly used at the sacred festivals, was compounded in this room according to strictly observed recipes in which all kinds of sweet-smelling ingredients were employed; and that the holy oils and ointments for the various ceremonies were also here prepared. We may therefore name this apartment the *Temple Laboratory.* † All the designs and inscriptions on the four walls of this apartment refer to the incense prepared and preserved here; to the oils and ointments used in the temple services; and to the various ingredients of which they were composed. Two seven-lined vertical inscriptions on the two parts of the entrance-wall contain what is to a certain extent a summarized description of the representations on the adjoining walls to the right and left. On each wall are two representations, *i.e.* four

---

† Chemistry derives its name from the land of *Khem*, called 'black land' from the dark colour of its soil.

in all. They exhibit the royal builder of the laboratory worshipping before Hathor, Isis, Hathor with the Horus of Edfu, and Isis with Horus Samtani. In two of the designs the king is accompanied by one of the lords of the laboratory, once with the divine *Master of Anointing*

Mazet, once with *Horus, the lord of the labo-*

ratory   , in the other two, by a goddess and two ram's-

headed divinities, who also stand in some relation to the work of the laboratory. Both the king and his companions offer some of the costly perfumes of the laboratory to the gods above named.

The room next the laboratory (Pl. xix) is named in the inscrip-

tions here found simply   *Sahi*, which means 'assembly-

room', 'room', 'hall', 'apartment'. An indication as to its former use is afforded by the representations on the walls, which depict the king offering the first fruits of the fields, plants, flowers, and fruits, to Hathor and her fellow-divinities. Several times in the accompanying inscriptions Hathor is extolled as 'she who produces all things', 'the nourishment-giving', 'she who provides food and drink, from whom everything comes that heaven bestows or the earth brings forth'. From these representations and inscriptions it may safely be concluded that this room was specially dedicated to the great Hathor as the deity who bestowed life and created and preserved all things, and that the offerings intended for Hathor were placed here on her festal day.

The next room (Pl. xx) is called in the inscriptions

Her-āb, i.e. 'the inner central room', or the *Middle Room*, probably because it lay between Hall D and the E. side-entrance of the temple, which opened into this room (comp. p. 89, Room xxii, on the opposite side). From the inscriptions we learn that it was used for the reception of the offerings which were brought into the temple by the side-entrance. It has been mentioned above (p. 85) that in a representation in this room (beside the door of exit) the royal cartouches above the monarch worshipping Hathor have been filled in with the official name of Augustus, whereas elsewhere the cartouches are left vacant.

On the opposite (W.) side of the hall are the side-chambers xxi, xxii, and xxiii. The last two appear from their representations and inscriptions to have been used for precisely the same purposes as the corresponding chambers on the E. side. The first (Pl. xxi), however, to the right of the entrance, is shown by its adornment and its inscriptions to have been one of the two treasuries of the temple. It bears the name ⌶ *i.e. Silver Room,* and its representations and inscriptions refer almost exclusively to the precions metals and precious stones, or to various kinds of ornaments for the divine images or other costly temple-utensils made of the precious materials deposited here. In the doorway the monarch is represented in the act of entering, and presenting to ،Hathor a jewel-casket, which a hieroglyphic inscription at the monarch's feet states to contain gold, silver, lapis-lazuli, and malachite. The goddess thanks the prince for his offering, with the words: 'I bestow upon thee the mountains to produce for thee stones to be a delight for all to see'.

The MARGINAL INSCRIPTIONS afford farther information as to the former use of this room. The lower marginal inscription, in the half running from right to left, is as follows: 'He has built the *Silver Chamber* for the golden one, as a building for eternity, he has adorned it with a multitude of stones, with all the wonderful gems of the mountains, so as to use them for all manner of work in the temple of Denderah'. In the other half the inscription reads: 'He has built the *lordly abode* for the Hathor of Tentyris, as a noble monument for eternity. He has furnished it with precious stones and all the products of the mountains, so as to use them for all manner of work in the *Gold Chamber.* These were required to make of them the furnishing there, according to the sacred precepts for the execution of the work for the Thrice a day (*i.e.* for the sacrificial ceremonies that took place thrice a day). All the noticeable gems are placed in its interior as the threefold beautiful, on both sides of the Princess's silver-chamber, which is furnished with its requirements, according to the precepts of the ancients referring thereto'. The room here and elsewhere named the *Gold Chamber* is in the central story of the temple, and is entered from the W. staircase. In this room, if we have interpreted the inscriptions aright, were made all kinds of statuettes, necklaces and bracelets for the sacred images, amulets, and other precious articles used in the temple-services, by goldsmiths working according to strictly prescribed rules and under the immediate control of the high priests. Possibly, however, such articles were only repaired here.

The lower part of the wall of the silver chamber is decorated with a representation of considerable geographical importance. At the farther end, on the wall to the right of the entrance, appears the emperor offering 'a golden necklace set with precious stones' to Isis, who is accompanied by Horus, and on the opposite wall the emperor again appears with a similar ornament before Hathor and the sun-god Horus-Samtani. In each case the monarch is followed by thirteen men carrying offerings, all of whom are typical representatives of foreign tribes, some from the mountain-districts of Upper and Lower Nubia, some from the districts lying to the E. and W. of the Nile valley. The name of the home of each is inscribed over his head. and over the casket or vase which each bears in his hands appears the name of its contents, among which are silver, gold, electrum, malachite, lapis-lazuli, mineral dye-stuffs, and other precious products of the mineral kingdom.

The second room on the right or W. (Pl. XXII) shares with Room xx (p. 88) the name *Middle Room,* because it has two entrances, one from Hall D, the other from without. According to the exterior marginal inscription this was the room set apart for the libations, and the door from the outside is named in an inscription on its exterior, 'the portal for the entrance of the priest of the libations, with the ewer for the Mistress of the gods'. This room also has an interesting geographical representation on the lower part of the wall, in which seven water-districts of Lower Egypt, conducted by the ruler of Lower Egypt, are seen approaching Hathor and Horus. — The third room (Pl. XXIII) on this side is named in the marginal inscriptions 'the room for the Mistress in the town of the House of Hathor', 'the room of the hall that lies behind the hall of the altar', and 'the divine hall of the Golden One, the daughter of the sun, (lying) on the left side, where the left stair-case (is situated)'. The chief exit from this room leads into Hall D, while another smaller door (to the left of the entrance) admits to a narrow passage communicating at one end with the Hall of the Altar (Pl. C), and at the other with the *Staircase* (p. 91) leading hence to the roof. Farther on this passage leads to the 'Chief Festal Room' (Pl. XIII; comp. p. 94). Mariette included Room XXIII in the suite of festal chambers, because it has direct communication with the festal Hall XIII and Rooms XIV and XV lying behind the latter.

Proceeding now in our course through the temple of Hathor, we next enter the central Prosekos Hall, or **Hall of the Altar** (Pl. C) as it is termed in the inscriptions . It is about 45 ft. wide and 18 ft. deep. The E. inscription on the external temple-wall states that the ceremonies of the 'offering of the divine things' (sacrifices) were carved in this room, along with the gods of the sacrificial altar; and the W. inscription names it the 'resting-place of the Mistress of the Goddesses'. The inscriptions on the upper and lower margins afford additional information as to the orginal purpose of the room, its decorations, and the festivals cele-brated within it. The upper inscription, in the half running from right to left, is as follows: 'He has built the Hall of the Altar for the Princess adorned with the vulture and the Uræus-crown, the wise goddess. It resembles heaven, with its lord the sun-god. He has richly loaded the altar for the revered goddess within it. — The gods are carved within it, as is seemly; the sacred offerings are laid at the foot of her throne with the ceremonies appropriate to the cult of Hathor. The names of the gods and the names of the place are inscribed on one of the walls in it, and the serpent-deities of Denderah are likewise recounted within it'. The last sentence refers to a list beside the door to the side-room XVIII, which re-counts the names of the temple of Denderah and its chief rooms, the deities worshipped there along with Hathor, and the titles of the priests and priestesses; details by name the sacred ponds, groves, trees and serpents of the temple-enclosure, and the sacred boats of Hathor used at the festivals; mentions the day of the chief festival at Denderah; and concludes with the name of the temple-domains and that of the territory behind it in the nome of Tentyris. The representations on the walls correspond to the marginal inscriptions. Thus over the portal by which we enter is a double representation of the ruler of Egypt. In one case he stands before the altar of Hathor, in the other before that of Isis, performing the ceremonies of offering incense and libation. This he does in his capacity as chief pontiff, as the accompanying inscription implies: 'The sun, the son of the sun (the emperor Augustus), as priest of the incense ('lord at the seat of fragrance'), offering incense to his mother, and as priest of the libations, holding the vessel of libation'. The rear-wall opposite bears several representations of the monarch express-ing his homage in offerings to Hathor, who is accompanied by Horus or her son Ahi.

The first side-door, to the left of the entrance to Hall C, admits us to a narrow *Ante-room* (Pl. XVII), named ⌂⌂⌂ *i.e.* *Staircase-Room*, in the inscriptions. At the farther end are four steps, beyond which a door, opening on the right, leads into the large STAIRCASE HALL, whence an easy stone staircase ascends straight to the roof. This hall is in complete darkness as it 'is roofed over and admits no light from the sides. Another ascent to the roof is found on the opposite or W. side of Hall C, reached by a door to the right of the entrance to that room, and also by a smaller approach from Room XXIII (comp. p. 90). This second ascent is not by a straight and dark flight of steps, but by a kind of spiral staircase, with ten rectangular bends to the right, lighted by means of openings piercing the wall diagonally and widening towards the interior. The representations and inscriptions in the ante-rooms to the right and left and on the walls of both staircases refer exclusively to the entrance to the halls and the ascent of the staircases on the *Great New Year's Festival*. On that occasion the ceremonial procession of the priests with the images of Hathor and her fellow-gods, after completing the circuit of the lower rooms, ascended to the roof of the temple, in order that 'the goddess Ha-thor might be united with the beams of her father Ra, on this noble day, the festival day of the beginning of the year'.

The most comprehensive idea of the festival is given by the representations on the two walls (each about 115 ft. long) of the straight *East Staircase*, which begins from Room XVII. The left wall presents us with a view of the procession ascending from the lower rooms of the temple, so that it is advisable to begin our inspection at the top of the staircase. An explanatory inscription of 13 lines closes with the following words: 'She comes at her beautiful festival, the festival of the beginning of the year, that her spirit may unite in the heavens with her father (the sun-god Ra). The goddesses are festive, the goddesses are joyful, when the right eye unites with the left eye. She rests on her throne in the place for beholding the sun's disc, when the bright one unites with the bright one. Her cycle of gods is at her right hand and at her left; she protects her beloved son, the sun (*i.e.* not the sun-god but his earthly representative, the reigning king of Upper and Lower Egypt)'. The abovementioned union of the right eye with the left eye, *i.e.* of the sun with the moon, at which the New Year's festival at Denderah took place, is one of the astronomical epochs of the calendar veiled in mythological language by the Egyptian priests. We next discern upon poles 'the images of a jackal and of an ibis, the symbols of Anubis as guide of the dead and of the god Thoth, which are described in an eight-lined vertical inscription, after which the explanatory inscription is closed by five more lines, as follows: 'O Hathor, thou ascendest the staircase in the town of the double-sweet life, in order to gaze upon thy father on the day of the New Year's festival. Thou betakest thyself to the roof of thy temple in company with thy cycle of gods. The Bukenkenu of Denderah are before thee, to avert harm from thy path, to purify thy way, to cleanse thy road from evil, at the double union in the sun's room on thy temple-roof, whose doors are opened to thee. Thou takest thy place on thy throne opposite the sun-god with his beams, at thy sides thy terrible attendant spirits on the seats of Hathor's Outlook on the Sun's Disc (a name of the temple of Denderah). Ancestral mother of the gods, thou unitest thyself with thy father Ra in thy festal chamber (*i.e.* probably the small kiosque-like pavilion on the roof of the temple)'. The above-mentioned Bukenkenu were images borne upon poles — small figures of gods and goddesses, sacred animals, and other symbolical objects — which were carried in front of solemn processions. Then follow representations of the persons taking part in the procession; the king and queen of Egypt, and priests and priestesses, some carrying the Bukenkenu (thirteen in number) or holding the prescribed offerings in their hands, and some personating different gods and goddesses, and wearing masks representing lions, bulls, oxen, etc. Among the latter may be pointed out the lion-headed person (No. 16 in order), walking behind the chief master of ceremonies who is chanting a hymn engraved on the tablet in his hand; the priestess (No. 24), bearing a cow's head as representing the milk-yielding Isis-cow, 'who nourishes the mothers with what comes from her breasts'; and the two priests (Nos. 28, 29) with bulls' heads, representing Apis and Mnevis, the two sacred bulls of Memphis and Heliopolis. The rear of the procession is brought up by men bearing the sacred shrines with the divine images. First comes the shrine with the chief image at Denderah, that of the goddess Hathor, then the ten shrines of her fellow-gods, among whom were three other images of Hathor, four of Horus, and one each of Ahi, Osiris, and Isis.

The *Second Side - Room* (Pl. xvi) on the left side of Hall C, is named in the inscriptions 'the ante-chamber belonging to·the Hall of the Altar'; while in the exterior marginal inscriptions it is called ✕ *Seḥ ṭua*, interpreted by Dümichen as *Room of Purification.* It was probably used in the preparations for the festival ceremonies that took place in the adjoining Hall of the Altar; and among its inscriptions in honour of Hathor is one that seems to indicate that the temple at Denderah is to be regarded as a replica of a celebrated temple of the sun-god of Heliopolis, of which however no trace now remains. Here a reference is made to the gilding and painting of the sculptured ornamentation, which are so often mentioned in the inscriptions. A careful examination of the walls in some of the rooms will still detect traces here and there of this painting.

We now pass through the central portal in the rear-wall of Hall C, and enter the last of the Prosekos Halls. This is the **Hall of the Cycle of Gods** (Pl. B), named.in the inscriptions *Usekh paut neteru,* or *Hir āb, i.e.* Middle Hall. The whole of the sculptures and inscriptions in this room refer to Hathor in her capacity as goddess of light, who has her seat in the sun's disc rising from the horizon, and who was as such represented under the figure of an hawk with a woman's head in the middle of the disc rising on the sun-mountain. (With this we may compare the representation of the goddess above the central portal in the rear-wall, *i.e.* above the entrance to the Adytum A.)

The adjoining room to the left (Pl. xii) is named in the inscriptions *i.e.* the *Cloth Room* or *Wardrobe.* It was the repository for the sacred wreaths and garments, with which the images of Hathor and her fellow-gods were adorned at the festivals celebrated in the temple and sometimes at the great new year's festival. According to the sculptures and inscriptions the prepared perfumes were also placed here. One half of the room was devoted to the garments, the other to the sacred perfumes. Over the latter presided the divine Mazet, previously mentioned among the managers of the manufacture of the incense and anointing oil as one of the lords of the laboratory (p. 88); over the former Hathotcp, god of woven fabrics, with his companion the goddess Tai, held sway. The sculptured ornamentation on the walls is also arranged in harmony with this division of the room.

The opposite side-door on the right side of the hall, leads to three connected Rooms (Pl. xiii, xiv, and xv), which to a certain extent form a special enclosed sanctuary, within the large temple. We see here (1) the small temple (Pl. xv), open in front and somewhat higher than the two preceding rooms, and entered by a portal between two Hathor columns, approached by seven steps; (2) the unroofed fore-court (Pl. xiv); and (3) the small ante-room (Pl. xiii), forming a connecting link between the staircase and Room xxiii as well as between Halls C and B. The name ⸤hieroglyphs⸥ *i.e.* Chief Festal Chamber, is occasionally bestowed upon all three rooms in the inscriptions, both on account of the preparations here made for the chief festival at Denderah, the great new year's festival on the morning of Thoth 1st, and on account of the preliminary celebration before this festival, which was also conducted in this suite of rooms with great splendour by the priests of Hathor, 'on the day of the Night of the Child in his Cradle' ⸤hieroglyphs⸥, *i.e.* the 4th Epagomene or intercalated day, on the night of which the closing festival of the Egyptian year began. Most of the representations and inscriptions refer to these festivals. Besides this common name each of the three apartments had a special name. No. xv was called ⸤hieroglyphs⸥ *i.e.* 'Room of the Bright Light', after the large and beautiful painting on the roof. As on the two halves of the ceiling of Hall E (p. 83), the heavenly vault is here personified as a woman with pendent arms, the 'celestial Nut, the bearer of the light-beam'. She is here depicted with the sun rising from her lap, its beams covering the sun-mountain placed in the centre and surrounding with their splendour the head of Hathor, which is represented with radiating tresses as resting upon the sun-mountain.

The entrance-chamber adjoining the uncovered fore-court (Pl. xiv), and affording also communication with the W. staircase (p. 91), is indicated by its sculptured ornamentation as a second treasure-chamber. Like Room xxi (p. 88) it was named ⸤hieroglyphs⸥ *i.e.* Silver Chamber; and it was also called the 'store-room'.

We now return to Hall B in order to visit thence the innermost part of the temple, 'the hidden secret chambers', as they are called in the inscriptions, the rooms of the *Sekos*. These consist of the Adytum, or *Holy of Holies*, occupying the centre, and the 11 side-rooms around it, i to vi on the right, viii to xi on the left. The entrances to these are from the corridor α, which surrounds the Adytum on three sides and is reached from Hall B by the two doors on the right and left.

The **Holy of Holies** was the central hall A, which was named

⌐⌐ ◠
⟨▦⟩ ◯ , the 'Dwelling of the golden one', or the 'Chamber of the

golden-beaming one' — 'of the noble — of the beautiful — of the
goddess', also 'the room of the great throne' — 'the repository of
the sacred boat', the 'sanctuary' †. Here the lord of Egypt alone
is depicted. He, the living type of the beautiful Horus, the son of
the sun, the child of Hathor (as the Pharaoh is frequently named
in this temple of Hathor), the visible representative of the deity,
and as ruler of Egypt the incorporation of all the temporal interests
of the state, he it was alone, to judge from the representations and
inscriptions, whose sacred person might enter the holy of holies and
in solitude commune with the deity. Only once a year was this
permitted even to him, at the great festival of the New Year. We
here see the monarch opening the door of the sacred cella, closed
with a sealed band of byblos. He breaks the seal and removes the
strip of byblos *(sesh tebtu* and se*ker atera)*, he places his hands in
the two rings on the door and thrusts back the bolts, ascends the
steps leading to the cella, and finally gazes upon the hidden figure
of the goddess, and offers his homage. Other designs exhibit the
monarch performing the prescribed ceremonies of offering incense
before the two sacred boats of Hathor and her companion, Horus of
Edfu, and before the boats of Isis and her companion Osiris. The
portable boats *(Tes-nefru, i.e.* 'the bearers of beauties'), which are
here depicted on the side-walls, formerly stood in Room A, and
held the shrines in which were the sacred images of the deities.
The shrines were carried in solemn processions by the priests,
sometimes without the boats, as *e.g.* at the new year's festival represented on the staircase (p. 91), and sometimes standing in the
boats.

The *Side-rooms* of the Adytum are, as mentioned above, entered
from corridor *α.* Behind the Adytum, to the S., lies No. 1, the
Large Chamber, the largest and most sacred of these side-rooms.
The sanctity of this chamber is evidenced by the painting, in which
the king is portrayed exactly as in the Adytum itself, ascending the
steps to the shrine of Hathor, breaking the seal, and opening the
doors, grasping the handles in his hands. Noteworthy also are the
representations of the king offering vases of wine to Hathor and
to Ahi, her son, in each case followed by a harp-playing goddess of
the north and of the south. Two other pictures represent *Pepi,* the
original builder of the temple (p. 81), kneeling before Hathor,
bearing Ahi in his hands, and the later builder with a mirror before
the goddess in a double shrine. The inscriptions give the dimensions of these images and state that they were made of gold, so that

---

† Mariette recognises only a store-room in this Hall A, and places
the Adytum proper in Room I behind Hall A *(Dendérah, Description
Générale,* p. 148).

they were probably preserved in this room or its recesses. The room is also named the *Chief Apartment* and the *Dwelling of Hathor.* — Room·II is called the *Vase Room.* The wall-sculptures shew the· king offering vases to the goddess. — Room III is· the *Sistrum Room,* with corresponding representations. — Room IV (immediately to the left of the entrance to the corridor α) is the *Room of the Restoration of the Body.* — Room V is named the *Birthplace* (meshlon). Here Isis was brought to bed in· the form of a black and red woman. A large representation shows Thoth and Khnum, and the king and queen before Isis and Nephthys. — Room VI was the *Sokar Room,* in which Osiris-Sokar renewed his limbs. The adjoining. Room VII also belonged to the worship of Osiris. It is named *Sam taui,* 'union of the two lands', because, according to an inscription 'the rays of his son unite in it with his body at the noble new year's festival'.

Room VIII, on the right side of the Adytum, was called the *Chamber of Flames.* Hathor is here represented as the goddess Sekhet, who exterminates evil with fire. — Room IX·is the *Throne-room of Ra.* He're the monarch before Horus transfixes the crocodile with his lance, symbolizing the slaying.of his enemies. — The first door on the right side of corridor α admits to Room X, named after its sculptures· the *Room of Ahi* (son of Hathor), but also *Room of Purifying:* — Room XI adjoining is the *Room of the Mena Necklace.* A design in the doorway shows the king presenting the necklace to Hathor.

We have now concluded the survey of the apartments on this floor. Before ascending to the roof of the temple, we should visit two of the subterranean chambers which claim attention not only for their remarkable construction but also for the fresh tints of their paintings.

The temple at Denderah contains; no fewer than 12 **Crypts** (or 14 if we reckon separately the parts of those that are divided), constructed in the thickness of the temple-walls, and lying both above and below the level of the temple-floor; some isolated, others in two or three stories. The walls of these are no less richly adorned with sculpture than the rooms we have already inspected. They were doubtless used for storing the precious articles and images required for the temple - services. Their decorations date from the reign of Ptolemy XIII. Auletes (81-52 B.C.), and are therefore older than the decorations of the temple proper, which were finished under the Roman emperors from Augustus to Nero. The arrangement and entrances of these passages in the different stories are shown in the small Plans II, III, and IV. Some are approached by narrow flights of steps descending from the temple-pavement and formerly concealed by movable stone-slabs; others we enter by climbing or creeping through very narrow openings, sometimes low down, sometimes high up close to the roof, but always in the inner wall of the

THE CRYPTS OF THE TEMPLE AT DENDERAH.

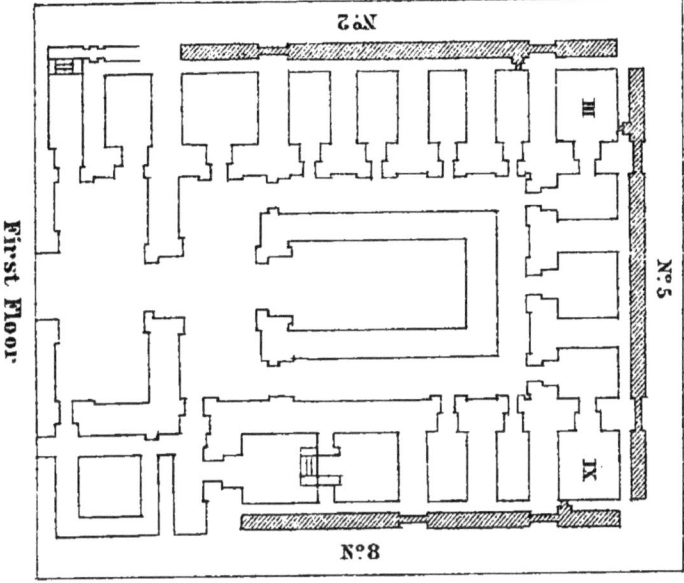

First Floor.

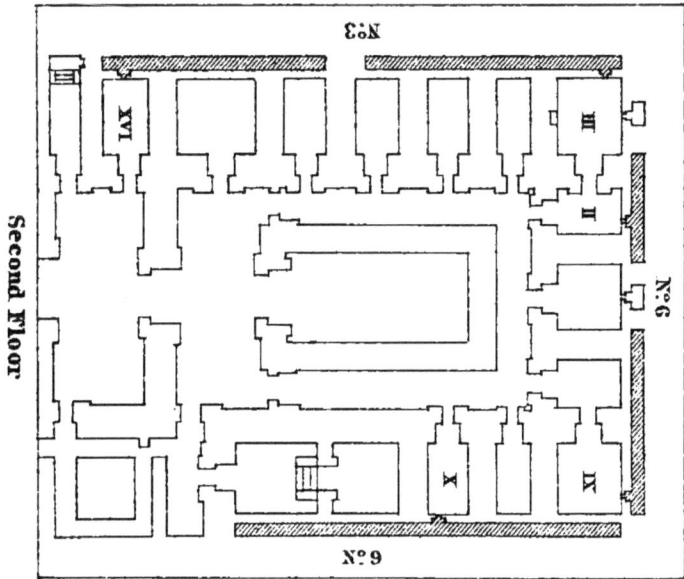

Second Floor.

THE SUBTERRANEAN CRYPTS.

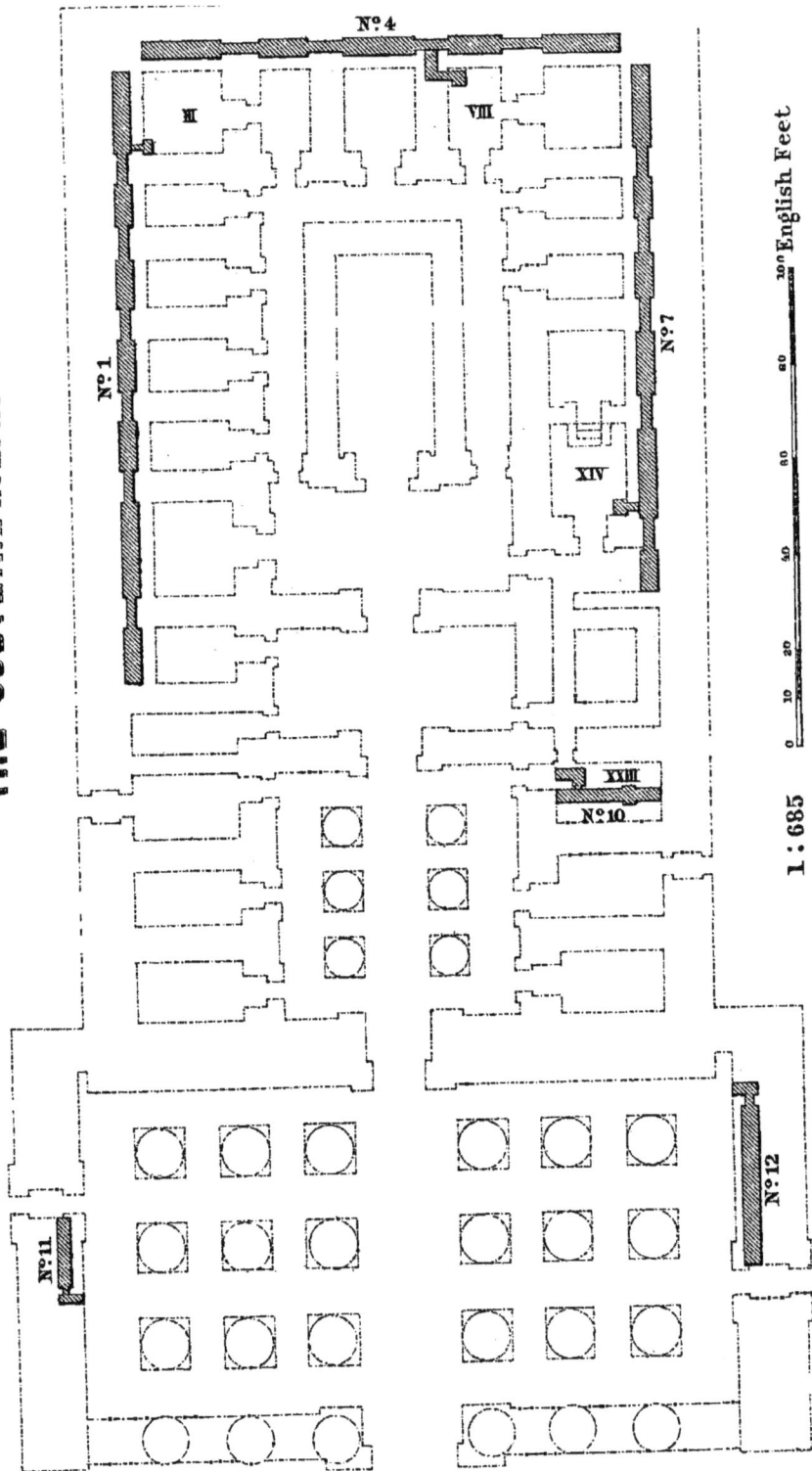

III

VIII

N° 4

N° 1

N° 7

XIV

XXIII

N° 10

N° 11

N° 12

1 : 685

0   10   20   40   60   80   100 English Feet

corresponding temple room. Six of the twelve crypts are beneath the ground-level, and of these two are in the first hypostyle hall E (Nos. 11 and 12 in Pl. II). The entrance to crypt No. 10 is in Room XXIII, adjoining Hall D. Of the remaining three subterranean crypts (Nos. 1, 4, 7), the first is only accessible by a flight of steps descending from crypt No. 2, which lies above it and is entered by an opening in the wall of Room VII. The discomforts of the climb are compensated in this case by the sight of two crypts, the lower one, the largest of all, consisting of 7 chambers, and the upper one adorned with representations and inscriptions in unusually good preservation. No. 4, entered from Room VIII, and No. 7, from Room XIV, are closed with doors, which the temple-keeper will open on request. Good stone stairs lead to both, and no visitor should fail to visit at least these two crypts. Magnesium wire or a lamp will be found useful in examining the painted walls. On the staircase leading to No. 4 occurs a mention of a festival celebrated on the 4th Epagomene day, and within the crypt is a painting of king Pepi, kneeling and offering a golden statue of. Ahi. All these statues, whose dimensions are given, were probably kept in the crypts. Still more important are the inscriptions in crypt No. 9 (mentioned on p. 81), which is entered by a very narrow hole high up in Room x. The calendar-dates of festivals instituted by Tutmes III. (1700 B.C.) are here found. Mention is also made of the fact that the ancient plan of the temple under Cheops was re-discovered in the reign of King Pepi (6th Dyn.).

We now ascend one of the staircases mentioned on p. 91 to the **Temple Roof**. Caution must be observed on account of the holes made in the roof to admit light and air to the rooms below. At the S.W. angle of the roof stands a small open pavilion, supported by 12 columns, which played an important part during the solemn procession at the festival of the new year (p. 91). We pass through this pavilion in passing from the E. staircase to the W. chambers. The W. staircase, which ascends in successive flights, leads past a room in the middle story, probably used as a workshop for restoring and repairing the statues and utensils of the temple. Six chambers on the roof, three on the W. and three on the E., the first in each case being unroofed, were used in the worship of the slain and risen Osiris, as curious representations indicate. The second room on the E. side formerly contained the famous *Zodiac of Denderah*, now in the Bibliothèque Nationale at Paris.

Finally a walk round the outside of the temple will be found interesting. The *Inscriptions*, so frequently referred to above, which contain the names and dimensions of the various apartments of the temple, were laid bare by Prof. Dümichen in 1875, and after being copied were again covered up. The projecting lions' heads on the sides of the building, probably intended to carry off the rain-water, should be noticed. At the left corner of the rear-wall is a *Portrait*

of Cleopatra, with the sistrum and the Mena-necklace. Before his
mother stands Ptolemy Kisres, or Caesarion, the son of Caesar, offering incense. Both are worshipping Isis and her son Horus.

Behind the temple of Hathor is a Temple of Isis, consisting of a
vestibule and three chambers. The unattractive and uninteresting building, which is partly covered with rubbish, owes its origin to the emperor
Augustus. The gate facing the E. bears the Egyptian cartouches of Claudius
and Nero, and two Greek inscriptions on the entablature mention the
21st year of Tiberius. This gateway marks the limit of the temple area
in this direction; and about 10 min. farther on we reach another gate,
which apparently belonged to another temple-precinct. It bears the cartouche of Antoninus.

8. From Keneh to Thebes (Luxor).

47 M. STEAMBOAT in about 5 hrs. Cook's mail-steamer halts for
2½ hrs. at Keneh on Wed. and Sat. mornings on its downward voyage,
and crosses thence to Denderah.

Keneh, see p. 72. The steamer passes three islands. On the
W. bank lies the village of *Ballâs*, with clay-deposits from which
most of the 'Keneh pottery' is made (p. 73). Balâlis (pl. of Ballâs,
named after the village), Kúlal (pl. of Kúlle), and other kinds of jars,
some of considerable size, lie on the banks awaiting shipment.

12½ M. (E. bank) **Kuft**, the ancient *Koptos*, nearly opposite
Ballâs. Though now of no importance, this place was down to the
time of the Khalifs a populous and thriving trading-town.

Even in antiquity a canal, mentioned by Strabo and still
traceable, led from the Nile to the walls of the town, past which the
Canal of Senhur (p. 100) now flows. One of the stones of the bridge
is said to bear the name of an Antef (11th Dyn.); and there is also
a Greek inscription from the same place, of the 8th year of Trajan
and dedicated to the tricoloured Isis. To the S. of the town and on
the road leading to the desert are various remains of ancient buildings. One of these is a square pillar of red granite, bearing a
dedication by Tutmes III. to Ammon Ra, and apparently a relic
of a temple built by that monarch. Still farther to the S. is a
narrow passage, with inscriptions of the reign of Caius Caligula,
dedicated to Khem Ra of Koptos upon his Staircase (comp. p. 178).
The stair-case with 14 ascending and 14 descending steps typifies
the waxing and waning moon (comp. p. 85). The boat of Khem,
borne by four priests, is here depicted, and beside it is an address
to the priests of Khem upon his Staircase. The most considerable
relic of antiquity, a fragment of black granite, probably part of
an altar, lies to the N. It comprizes an exaltation of Khem, Isis,
and Heh (eternity) by Ptolemy XIII. Neos Dionysus.

Koptos is mentioned on very early monuments and also by Greeks
and Romans at a late period. Theophrastus, Pausanias, Athenæus, Plutarch,
Josephus, Ælian, Lucian, Stephanus of Byzantium, Agatharchides, Pliny,
Ammianus Marcellinus, Apuleius, and many other authors, all mention
it, proving the widely-spread fame of the city. It was especially famous
for its commerce. The trade-route, which now leads from Koṣêr on the
Red Sea to Keneh, formerly ended at Koptos, where Nile-boats received

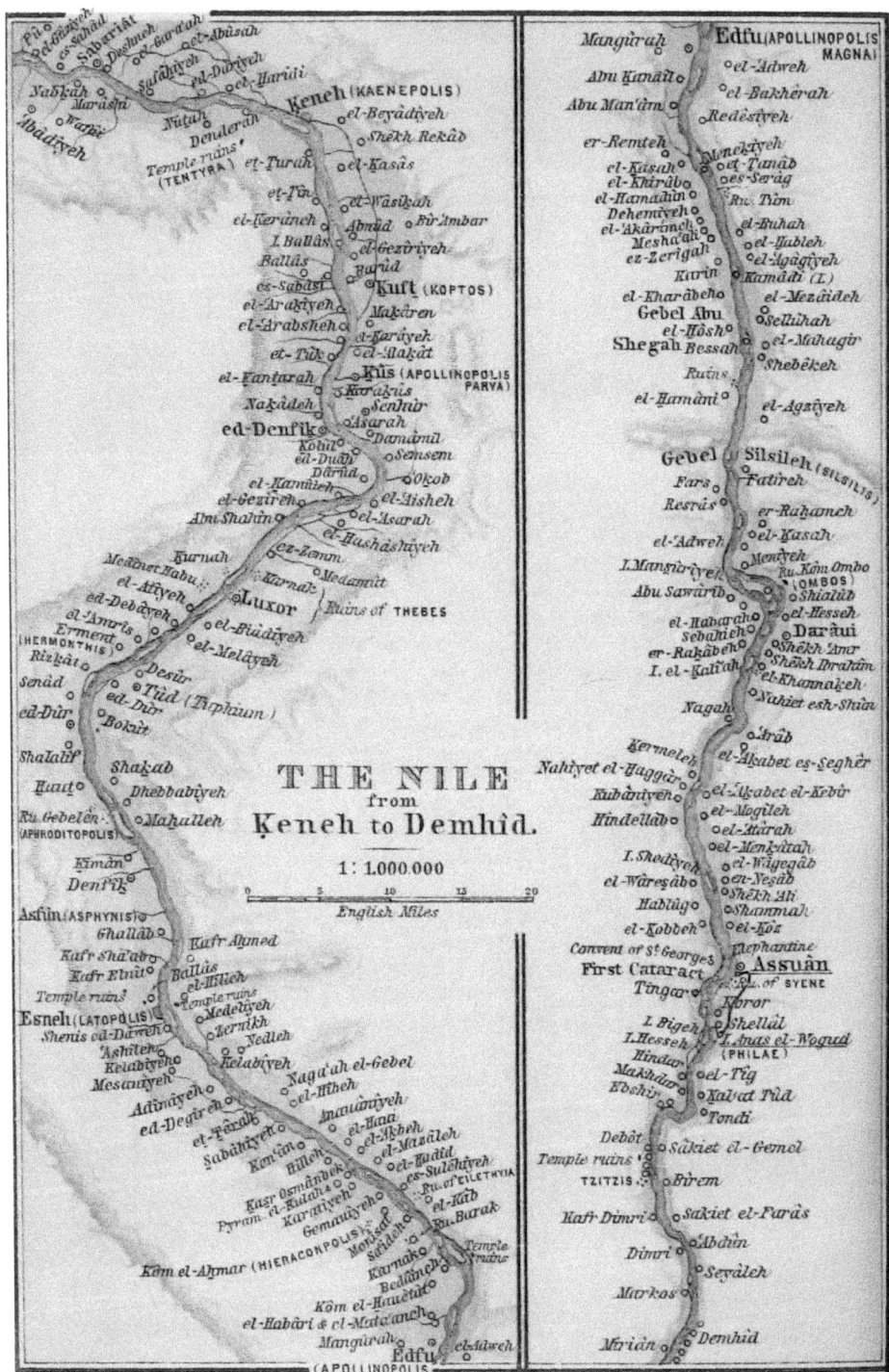

THE NILE
from
Ḳeneh to Demhîd.

1 : 1.000.000

0   5   10   15   20
English Miles

the goods transported hither on camels, or, at an earlier period, on asses, as is expressly mentioned in the great Harris Papyrus (Ramses III., 1320 B.C.). The desert-route to Koṣêr unites with that from Keneh at el-Karn before Laḳêtah (p. 75). Koptos early became an emporium for many kinds of goods. Inscriptions of the 6th Dyn. are found by the side of the old trade-route to the Red Sea at the Wâdi Hamâmât (p. 76). In a tomb at Benihasan belonging to Ameni, a princely official under the 12th Dyn., is an inscription recording the treasures brought by Ameni to Koptos in the train of the crown-prince Usertesen. Koptos was the capital of the fifth nome of Upper Egypt, which bore two hawks on its banner. Its

name appears in hieroglyphics as   *Kebt* and   *Kebti;*

in Coptic it is *Keft* and *Kebto;* in Greek Κοπτος, Κοπτις, Κοφτός, etc. The Arabic Keft corresponds to the Coptic Keft. The deity chiefly worshipped here from a very early period was Khem Min (Vol. I., p. 138), whose wife was called Isis, and son Horus. Osiris also had a burial-place here (Ha nub, 'Gold house'), in which a part of his body (called Kab) was preserved. The book of magic, the search for which is narrated in the demotic romance of Setnau, was sunk in the Nile at Koptos. A medical leather-roll found at Koptos, and now in the British Museum, is said to have been written in the reign of Khufu or Cheops (4th Dyn.). Koptos was fortified as early as the 12th Dynasty; for the wealthy city and eth routes leading to it required to be defended against the warlike tribes who lurked between the Nile and the Arabian mountains, and who, even under the Roman emperors, were a source of danger. Guards were especially necessary at this point, for there is no doubt that a considerable number of Phœnician merchants had settled in Keptes at a very early date along with the Egyptians, and were engaged in importing the products of Arabia, and at a later date even those of India, which were conveyed viâ Arabia to the Egyptian Red Sea ports afterwards called Berenike and Leukos Limen, and thence across the desert to the Nile. The green breccia, used for many buildings even under the Romans, was quarried at Hamâmât, on the desert-route to Keptes. It is even probable that Kebt-town or Keft-town means 'place of the Phœnicians', for the Phœnicians were named Keft or Kaft in Egyptian. Strabo and Pliny expressly state that the population of the town was mixed, containing both Egyptian and Arabic (*i.e.* Semitic) elements. The hieroglyphic name of the town

also occurs with the determinative-sign of the post , which is only used

after the names of foreign places or of places in which foreigners were conspicuous. The reports of Plutarch, Ælian, etc., concerning the strange cults at Keptes farther indicate that a considerable Semitic community dwelt in the town, and was regarded with hostility by their Egyptian neighbours. Ælian's statement that the inhabitants of Koptos worshipped the crocodile (Seth) and crucified the hawk (Horus) can only refer to these Semites. The true Egyptians revenged themselves by throwing an ass from a rock (as Plutarch narrates), because Typhon (Seth) was red-haired and of the colour of an ass. Red-haired men (and many red-haired Semites are represented on the monuments) were despised, and like all foreigners were stigmatized as 'Typhonic'. Many non-Egyptians are commemorated at the sides of the trade-route from the Red Sea to Koptos; names of Persian kings are nowhere more numerous.

The camp of the Beduins, who hired their camels to the caravans and escorted them through the desert, must have anciently existed within the circuit of the town. These Arabs appear to have been the instigators of a great insurrection in Upper Egypt, which broke out under Diocletian in 292 A.D., and led to the siege and destruction of Koptos. The town revived somewhat under the Khalifs, but finally decayed with the gradual transference of the Egyptian trade to the route from Koṣêr to Keneh.

About 7 M. above Koptos, on the E. bank, lies **Kûs** (mail-

steamer station), now an insignificant village, occupying the site of
the ancient *Apollinopolis Parva.* According to Abulfeda (d. 1331)
this town was second in size only to Fostât (Cairo), and was the
chief centre of the Arabian trade. To-day heaps of ruins are the
only remains. A few stones with fragmentary inscriptions have
been built into the houses of the town; and the mosque contains
a basin formed of a single stone, with the name of Ptolemy Philadelphus upon it. A pylon, which stood here 30 years ago but has
now disappeared, bore a Greek inscription, announcing that 'Queen
Cleopatra and King Ptolemy, the great gods and Philometors, and
their children dedicated the temple to the god Arueris and to the
deities worshipped along with him'. Arueris is the earlier Horus,
usually identified by the Greeks with Apollo, whence the name of
the town Apollinopolis. The modern name Kûs appears to be

derived from the Egyptian ŏ ŏ ‾‖‾ ⌒ ⊗ *Keskes.* Near *Senhur* (E. bank),

3 M. to the S. of Kûs, Prisse d'Avennes discovered the ruins of a
small temple of Isis, in which the Horus of Apollinopolis, Khem-
Min of Koptos, the triad of Thebes'(Ammon-Ra, Muth, and Khunsu),
and other gods, were also worshipped. To the E. of Senhur passes
the canal of Senhur (p. 98), which begins above Thebes and
extends N. to Keneh. In the 12th cent. B.C. Kûs was notorious for
the number of its scorpions. Numerous Christians dwell here and
also in *Nakâdeh*, on the W. bank of the Nile, about 3 M. to the S.W.
Nakâdeh (mail-station), with numerous dove-cotes, a Coptic and a
Roman Catholic church, has old and narrow streets, but presents
a picturesque appearance from the river. The traveller who lands
here near sunset on a Sunday or festival (recommended) will be
pleasantly surprised to hear the sound of church-bells. The churches
themselves are uninteresting. Great success has attended the
labours of Christian missionaries here and still more in Kûs; and
a considerable proportion of the Coptic community (including the
worthy and learned bishop of Kûs) have embraced Protestantism.
The missionaries of the United Presbyterian Church of North
America have also had considerable success at Luxor, Esneh, and
other towns in Upper Egypt, their converts, however, being exclusively from among the Copts, never the Mohammedans.
Demetrius II., patriarch of the Copts (d. 1870), excommunicated
both the converts and the missionaries. In 1866 he instigated a
persecution of the proselytes, whom he sought to terrify by fines,
stripes, and imprisonment; and he destroyed the publications of
the missionaries (who have a printing-press of their own) wherever
he could lay hands upon them. The British and American consuls
thereupon interfered energetically on behalf of their fellow-
believers, and now the Coptic Protestants enjoy complete immunity
from every form of religious persecution.

Between Naḳadeh and Luxor (E. bank) the Nile makes a bend, beginning at *ed-Denfîk* (W. bank), after which we continue in a S.W. direction. — *Kamûleh*, a mail steamer station on the W. bank, formerly possessed extensive plantations of sugar-cane. In 1824 it was the residence of Shêkh Aḥmed, and of 'Ali Kâshef Abu-Ṭarbûsh, who bravely defended it against the insurgents. — On the E. bank, about 3¹/₂ M. from the river, lies the temple of *Medamût.* The ruins are not without interest, but it is better to visit them later from Luxor (p. 151) if time permit, than to interrupt the journey so near Thebes.

On the left bank, as we draw near Thebes, rise high limestone hills, presenting precipitous sides to the river, from which, however, they are separated by a strip of fertile land. The right bank is flatter, and the Arabian hills retreat farther into the distance. Before reaching the point where the W. chain projects a long curved mass of rock towards the river, we see to the left first the great obelisk, and the pylons of the temple of Karnak, half-concealed by palm-trees. When we clear the abrupt profile of the W. cliffs and new formations are visible at its foot, we may catch a distant view of Luxor towards the S.E. None of the buildings on the W. bank are visible until the steamer has ascended as high as Karnak; then first the Colossi of Memnon and afterwards the Ramesseum come into view. The telegraph-posts and wires, which here obtrude themselves upon the view, seem strangely out of place beside the majestic relics of Egypt's golden period. As we gradually approach Luxor, we distinguish the flags flying above the white houses on the bank and from the consular dwellings, and the re'îs applies himself to find a suitable anchorage beside the other dhahabîyehs, which are always to be found here. Those who desire to keep by themselves may first halt off Luxor, lay in provisions and other necessaries, visit Karnak, and then land on the W. bank. In this case the re'îs will probably raise objections, and the sailors (for whom a sheep should be bought, as they have tasted no meat on the voyage) prove mutinous, so that watchmen will be necessary.

9. Thebes.

Arrival. The three-weeks tourist steamers halt for three days (8th, 9th, and 10th) at Luxor on the upward journey; the four-weeks steamers for five days. Travellers by the mail-steamers and by Gaze's seventeen days steamers spend 3-4 days in a hotel. — The *Quay* lies in front of the Luxor Hotel (see below); porters await the arrival of the steamers. Travellers should see that all their luggage is landed and conveyed to the hotel, and should not quit the quay till this is done. — *Post Office* beside the Karnak Hotel; *Telegraph Office* (line viâ Keneh) near the Luxor Hotel.

Hotels. *Luxor Hotel*, with a fine large garden in which several interesting stones are placed, pens. per day 15s. or 19fr. in Jan. and Feb., 13s. or 16¹/₂fr.: the rest of the year (bottle of Medoc 4s., bottle of beer 2s. 6d.), cheaper for Egyptologists and those making a stay of some time. Pension includes morning coffee, lunch about noon, supplied also to those making excursions, and a substantial dinner about 6 p.m. The rooms are clean but not luxurious. The manager of the hotel, which belongs to Messrs. Thos. Cook & Son, is M. *Pagnon.* — *KARNAK HOTEL, ¹/₂ M. lower down on a terrace on the river, also belonging to Messrs. Cook, with similar charges. — GRAND HOTEL THEWFIKIEH (Messrs. Gaze & Son), pens. 12s., wine from 2s.

Consular Agents. British and Russian: *Aḥmed Effendi*, who frequently gives 'fantasîyas' (p. 103) and Arabian dinners. American: *Ali Mûrad.* German: *Moḥarb Todrus.* All the consuls sell antiquities; best from Todrus.

Distribution of Time. The ruins of the city of the hundred gates are so huge, so widely scattered, and so profoundly interesting, that at least 5-6 days are necessary to inspect the chief points alone. Those who are specially interested in Egyptology will of course devote a much longer time to Thebes; weeks or even months may be spent in a careful study of its monuments and tombs. — Cook's tourist-programme devotes the 1st day to the temple of Seti I. at Kurnah and the Tombs of the Kings, the return being made at the choice of the tourist either direct or over the hill to Dêr el-Baḥri, the Ramesseum, and the Colossi of Memnon. — 2nd day: Temple of Karnak; Luxor in the afternoon. — 3rd day: Ramesseum, Tombs of Shêkh 'Abd el-Kurnah, Dêr el-Medineh, Medinet Habu, and Colossi of Memnon. Those who are fatigued by the previous excursions should at least make an effort to proceed to Medînet Habu where the party lunches (and in the interval visit Dêr el-Medineh). — A moonlight ride to Karnak may be taken (at the tourist's private expense) on one of the evenings.

Those who are at liberty to arrange their time for themselves will find the following programme of a *Three Days' Visit* convenient.

1st day. Luxor and Karnak (E. bank). Though visitors are sometimes advised to reserve this, the most gigantic of the monuments, to the last, it is really desirable to visit Karnak first of all, before fatigue has begun. The traveller who visits Karnak on the first day proceeds then to view the other lions, with the satisfactory feeling that Thebes has fulfilled his highest expectations; and he will not fail to take a later opportunity|, by moonlight or at any free time, to return to refresh and confirm his first impression. Visitors should ride early to Karnak, while the temple of Luxor, easily reached in a few minutes from the dhahabîyeh, may be reserved for an afternoon-visit.

2nd day. Cross the river early, visit the Colossi of Memnon, the Ramesseum, Medinet Habu, and Dêr el-Medineh, in the morning if possible, if time permit also one of the tombs in the part of the Necropolis of Thebes known as Kurnet Murraï, and finally some of the Tombs of Shêkh 'Abd el-Kurnah. The view at sunset from this point is of incomparable beauty and interest.

3rd day. Cross the river early, visit the temple of Seti I. at Kurnah, ride to the valley of the Tombs of the Kings (Bibân el-Mulûk) with the famous graves of the Pharaohs, then cross the ridge which divides the latter from the other valleys of the Necropolis, and visit the terrace-temple of Dêr el-Baḥri and some of the tombs of el-Asasîf. A visit to the Tombs of the Queens may ¡be combined with an expedition to Medînet-Habu. Other less important monuments may be included according to their situation.

The *Four days'* programme of Gaze's steamers is still better: — 1st day. Luxor and Karnak. 2nd day. Temple of Seti I., Tombs of the Kings, Dêr el-Baḥri, and the Ramesseum. 3rd day. Colossi of Memnon, Medinet Habu, Dêr el-Medineh, and Shêkh 'Abd el-Kurnah. 4th day. Great temple of Karnak.

A *Five days'* visit may be spent as follows. — 1st day. Visit the temple at Luxor and the great temple of Ammon at Karnak. — 2nd day. On the W. bank, Colossi of Memnon, Medinet Habu; Dêr el-Medineh. — 3rd day. Ramesseum; Tombs of Shêkh 'Abd el-Kurnah; terrace-temple of Dêr el-Baḥri; el-Asasif; Drah Abu'l Neggah. — 5th day. Second visit to Karnak; visit to the various side-temples and pylons; excursion to Medamût (p. 151) if desired.

District
of
THEBES.
1 : 45.500
500   1000   1500
Yards.

Tombs of the Kings
(West Valley)
Tombs of the Kings
Dêr el-bahri
North
Asasif
Shêkh Abd
el-Kurnah
Tombs of the
Queens
Dêr el-Medineh
Kurnet
Murrai
South Asasif
Ramesseum
Kôm el-Hêtân
Medinet
Habu
Kasr el-Agûz
Colossi of Men
Remains of ancient
Dykes
New Channel
Birket Hâbu
Dykes
Later
Tombs

*O*ther claims upon the traveller's time will be made in Thebes. If he have paid a visit to one of the consular-agents, he will be invited to a *Fantasiya*, and if he have brought good introductions, the fantasîya will be preceded by a dinner. Among the modern Arabs the word 'fantasîya' is applied to every kind of amusement, from the aimless discharging of muskets, to the greatest festivity. In the present connection it signifies an evening party, at which the chief entertainment is the more or less skilful dancing of hired ghawâzi, and which is recommended especially to gentlemen who have not before seen anything of the kind. Chibouks, cigarettes, coffee, and liqueurs are offered to the guests.

Antiquities. The traveller in Thebes is frequently tempted to purchase antiquities. Half the population of Luxor is engaged in traffic with antiquities, and the practice of fabricating scarabæi and other articles frequently found in tombs is by no means unknown to the other half. Many of the articles offered for sale are so skilfully imitated that even experts are sometimes in doubt as to their genuineness; the ordinary traveller seldom or never secures an authentic specimen. Only as many piastres as they ask shillings should ever be offered to the importunate hawkers of antiquities at the temples and tombs. Those who desire a genuine memorial of antiquity should apply to the director of the hotel or to one of the above named consular agents. Even in this case, however, absolute certainty is not attainable; for though honourable traders themselves, the consular agents are liable to be deceived in the purchases they make. Caution should be observed in the purchase of unopened *Papyrus Rolls;* for dishonest vendors are in the habit of pasting torn fragments of papyrus (frequently found in tombs) upon canes so as to present the appearance of genuine papyrus-rolls. Egyptian antique bronzes, with artificial rust, are made wholesale in Trieste, Paris, and Hanau; Cairo and Luxor have the best factories for the fabrication of antiques in terracotta and carved wood. Valuable and genuine antiques may, however, still be obtained in Luxor by those who are prepared to spend money. The prices are high; 3*l.* being now charged for a genuine scarabæus. Good and reliable specimens. including papyri, may be obtained from Mohammed M'hasseb and 'Abd el-Megîd.

Photographs. Good photographs are produced by *A. Beato* in Luxor; but even in Shepheard's and other hotels in Cairo, excellent photographs of Egyptian temples are sold at moderate prices. Those by *H. Béchard* are distinguished for artistic taste; those by *Sébah* are also good. — Photographs of the *Royal Mummies* (p. 230) about 1*s.* 6*d.* each.

Guides and Donkeys. A guide is of great assistance in saving time. The charge is 4-5 fr. per day, or more for a large party. Guides on the E. bank are not allowed to serve on the W. bank, and vice versâ. The following guides may be recommended: On the right bank (for Karnak), *Hasan Ahmed, Sedan,* and *'Abd el-Megid;* on the left (W.) bank, *'Ali,* who can take good rubbings ; *Mohammed 'Ali, Ahmed Gorgâr, 'Abd al-Mansûr, Ismai'il Husên, Khalifeh* and his son *Selim, Ahmed 'Abd er-Rasûl,* etc.

The DONKEYS on the E. side of Thebes are good and have good saddles. To Karnak 1 fr. or 1*s.*, and as much more when the traveller is called for or keeps the ass for the day. On the W. side the donkeys, which are much more heavily worked, are not so good, but they are fairly well saddled. Charge 2 fr. per day. The hotels on the E. bank provide donkeys; on the W. bank they must be ordered beforehand. — Little girls with water-bottles run after the traveller, especially on the W. bank, keeping up with the donkeys with tireless agility. One should be selected and repaid with a few piastres on the return. The attractive faces of these merry children sometimes vividly recall the portraits of Egyptian women of the time of the Pharaohs.

Sport. Sportsmen may have an opportunity of shooting a jackal, the best time and place being at and after sunset near Bîbân el-Mulûk or the Ramesseum. An experienced hunter is to be found at the Luxor Hotel. Hyenas are sometimes shot on the Karnak side. In March numerous quail are found here.

Literature. The following are the chief authorities for ancient Thebes :

— *Mariette*, Karnak, Etude topographique et archéologique. Leipzig, 1875.
— *Brugsch*. Reiseberichte, 1855. — *E. de Rougé*, Etudes des monuments du
massif de Karnak, in the 'Mélanges d'Archéologie égyptienne et assyrienne'.

On each side of the Nile, here interrupted by three islands,
stretches a wide belt of fertile land, bounded both on the E. and
W. by ranges of hills, displaying a bolder and more definite formation than is usually the case with the mountains that flank the
river-valley. On the E., the ridge, overtopped by finely shaped
peaks, retires farther from the stream than on the W. The fertile
strip ends as abruptly at the foot of the barren limestone-cliffs
as a lawn adjoining a gravel-walk in a garden. Most of the ruined temples are situated in the level district and are reached by
the waters of the Nile when the inundations are at their highest;
while the tombs are hewn in the flanks of the hills, where their
dark openings are so numerous, that the E. slope of the Libyan
range might be aptly compared to a piece of cork or to a honeycomb.
Viewed from the river, the site of ancient Thebes presents the appearance of a wide mountain-girt basin or valley richly endowed with
the gifts of never-failing fertility. Nature here revels in perpetual
youth, while the most enormous edifices ever reared by mortal hand,
though grey, desolate, and succumbing to the common fate of all
human handiwork, yet compel the admiration of posterity for the
wonderful race that has left such mighty memorials of its existence
— memorials that have indeed been injured but not annihilated in
the flight of thousands of years. The verdant crops and palms which
everywhere cheer the traveller as soon as he has quitted the desert,
the splendid hues that tinge the valley every morning and evening,
the brilliant, unclouded sunshine that bathes every object in the
winter season, and the inspiring feeling that every hour is enriching
the imagination with new and strange pictures, wholly prevents in
Thebes the rise of that melancholy which so often steals over the
mind in presence of the relics of by-gone greatness and of vanished
magnificence.

The various monuments are situated as follows. On the right
(E. bank) rises the Temple of Luxor, now occupied by dwellings,
and to the N. are the immense ruins of Karnak, formerly connected
with it. Beyond these monuments lay the streets of ancient Thebes.
Farther to the N. is another extensive temple-site at Medamût,
which must be regarded as occupying the site of a suburb of Thebes.
On the left (W.) bank was the Necropolis, with vaults in the rock
and many mortuary temples. Each of these had its large annexe
for the priesthood, schools, or libraries. The temples were adjoined
by groves and lakes, and from ancient commercial contracts we
gather that one quarter of the citizens dwelt here. Nearer the
mountains stood the houses of the embalmers, refuges for visitors
to the necropolis, shops for the sale of numerous articles which the
Egyptians were accustomed to bring as offerings to their ancestors,
stables for the sacred animals, and slaughter-houses for the cattle

brought to be sacrificed. The landing-place on the other bank, opposite Karnak, was united with the temple of Kurnah by rows of
sphinxes. As the ancient pilgrim continued on his way towards the
N.W. and crossed the hill of the cemetery now called el-Asasif, he
came in sight of the rocky amphitheatre which enclosed the terraced
precincts of the temple of Dêr el-Baḥri. Northwards from Kurnah a
well-made route led to the valley of the Tombs of the Kings, now
called Bibân el-Mulûk, which could also be reached by a shorter
though more fatiguing mountain-path from el-Asasif. Between the
entrance of the valley of the Kings' Tombs and el-Asasif and close
to the mountain lay the necropolis known as Drah Abu'l Neggah.
Thence following the edge of the fertile strip towards the S.W. we
reach the magnificent Ramesseum. Behind rises the mountain-ridge.
The tombs on its E. slope, partly occupied as dwellings by the
fellaḥin, belong to the village now called Shêkh 'Abd el-Kurnah.
As we gaze down upon the plain from the higher-lying graves, the
Colossi of Memnon are conspicuous in the midst of the fertile belt.
Behind these are the prominent ruins, known as Kôm el-Ḥêṭân,
rising near the central point of an imaginary line connecting the
Ramesseum with the temple of Medinet Habu, the magnificent
Memnonium of Ramses III. Turning from Medinet Habu to the
S.W., we reach a small temple of the Ptolemies; to the N., near
the mountains, lies the valley with the Tombs of the Queens; and
skirting the line of hills to the N.W. we reach the scanty tomb-
remains of Kurnet Murraï, to the W. of which lies a valley with
the small but interesting temple of Dêr el-Medineh. Two points
are of special value for taking one's bearings. One is the summit
of the mountain lying between el-Asasif and Bibân el-Mulûk; the
other is the door of either of two tombs at Shêkh 'Abd el-Kurnah.
One of the tombs, in which Lepsius lived, is known to the guides as
Ḳaṣr Lepsius; the other was inhabited by Ebers, who is remembered
by the fellaḥin as Abu Bûlos (Father of Paul).

The name THEBES is probably the Greek form of the Egyptian
Uabu, with the feminine article t prefixed, *i.e.*
Tuabu. The Hellenes, familiar with the name Thebes (Θῆβαι), which
was borne by cities in Bœotia, Attica, Thessaly, Cilicia, near Miletus
in Asia Minor, etc., believed that in Tuabu they had met it once
more. Possibly, however, the name may be derived from the words
âpt âsu, which were applied to the temples on the E.
bank at least. Among the Greeks the town was known as Διόσπολις,
a translation of *Pa-amen*, city of Ammon, also called *Diospolis
Megale* or *Diospolis Magna* to distinguish it from Diospolis Parva
or Hôu (p. 70).

The famous capital of Upper Egypt was certainly founded under the ancient empire, but whether earlier than the 11th Dyn.,

of which tombs have been found, is open to question. Hardly any traces of earlier monuments have been discovered. The earliest prosperity of Thebes dates from the eclipse of the first flourishing period of Memphis. Previously it was named the southern *On*, in distinction to Heliopolis, the northern *On*. A legend, known to us, however, only from inscriptions of a later date, narrates that Osiris was born here. Such a myth can scarcely have been invented in later times, for from the beginning of the New Empire onwards, Osiris fell into a position quite subsidiary to the other gods of Thebes, especially to Ammon-Ra with whom Muth and Khunsu formed a triad. Only in connection with the worship of the dead did Osiris retain his leading rank. Among goddesses a Hathor seems to have enjoyed especial honour from the earliest times; and even till a comparatively late date the nome *Phathyrites* (the Pathros of the Bible), of which Thebes was the flourishing capital, was called after her the 'Hathor district'. Under the early empire the afterwards gigantic city was not conspicuous. It is seldom mentioned, and even under the 13th Dyn. *Assiût-Lycopolis* (p. 31) is described as the chief town of Upper Egypt. When the Hyksos invaded the Nile valley, the legitimate princes, who had ruled from the Mediterranean to the Cataracts, were driven to the south. Here they reigned during several inglorious centuries, until Raskenen and King Aahmes (p. xxxi) arose and under the banner of Ammon of Thebes expelled the strangers. The succeeding princes, won important victories not only on Egyptian soil but also in Asia, always fighting under the auspices of Ammon with whom was joined the Ra of Lower Egypt, and who, as we have seen (Vol. I., p. 138), was speedily placed at the head of all the national gods. The liberation of the country was directed from Thebes, and that city continued for centuries to be the favourite seat of the Pharaohs, and the reservoir into which flowed the untold treasures exacted as tribute or brought as booty from Asia to Egypt. A large share of this wealth was bestowed upon Ammon. The magnificent and gigantic temple, erected at this period to the god, is still one of the chief sights of Thebes. The grandees of the kingdom esteemed it an honour to become priests of Ammon, the schools beside his temples flourished, and the kings offered their richest gifts to this god, from whom they expected a surer fulfilment of their petitions than from any other. Thus Thebes became the city of Ammon, the *No* or *No-Amon* of Scripture and the *Diospolis* of the Greeks. Victory over foes was the burden of every prayer of the Pharaohs at this culminating period of Thebes, and the warriors led out by the monarchs were drilled under the eye of the god. In the introductory remarks on the history of Egypt mention has already been made of the great warrior-princes who placed Thebes at the zenith of its fame, and in the description of the various monuments reference will again be made to them. Here it may be added that the fame of the huge city early reached the ears even of the Greeks. In a possibly interpolated passage of the

Iliad (IX, 379-384), Achilles, enraged with Agamemnon, assures
Ulysses that he will never more unite in council or in deed with the
great Atrides: —

"Ten times as much, and twenty times were vain; the high pil'd store"
"Of rich Mycenæ, and if he ransack wide earth for more,"
"Search old Orchomenus for gold, and by the fertile stream"
"Where, in Egyptian Thebes, the heaps of precious ingots gleam,"
"The hundred-gated Thebes, where twice ten score in martial state"
"Of valiant men with steeds and cars march through each massy gate."
(Blackie's Translation.)

The epithet ἑκατόμπυλος, *i.e.* 'hundred-gated', here used by
Homer, was also applied by later classical authors to Thebes. Diodorus,
Strabo. Pliny, and Bato of Sinope all make use of it, referring,
however, to the pylons of the temples in the capital of Upper Egypt.
With the rising importance of the god and with the increase of his
wealth, of which they had the disposal, the archpriests of Ammon
gradually grew to regard themselves as the chief persons in the
state; and, after the way had been prepared by a series of weak
princes, they succeeded in usurping the throne and by their rule
prepared the ruin of Egyptian power. From the 20th Dyn. onwards,
Thebes began to decay. Ramses III. indeed adorned the left bank
especially with elaborate buildings; but his immediate successors
did no more than hew out for themselves deep and richly carved
graves in the valley of the Kings' Tombs, and the princes of Lower
Egypt who succeeded the priests of Ammon of the 21st Dyn. were
the less able to bestow attention upon Thebes, the more eagerly
they strove to adorn their homes in the Delta with gorgeous structures. Yet even these princes did not wholly abandon Thebes, and
they did not omit to inscribe pretentious reports of their mighty
acts on the walls of the temple of Ammon. The armies of the Assyrians penetrated as far as Thebes and plundered it; the Ethiopians
planted their rule here and honoured Ammon with buildings and
inscriptions; the princes of the 26th Dyn. did for Saïs what the
princes of the 18th and 19th Dyn. had done for the city of Ammon,
but they also paid their homage to the great god of Thebes by
erecting smaller buildings there. The invading army of Cambyses
ascended as far as Upper Egypt, but seems to have done little or
no damage at Thebes. Nectanebus I., one of the native Egyptian
princes who maintained themselves against the Persians, found
time and means to add a handsome pylon to the temple of Ammon.
Alexander the Great and the princes of the house of the Lagidae
probably found Thebes still a great though decadent city, and they
assisted to embellish it, as many buildings dating from the period
of the Ptolemies still attest. After the 22nd Dyn. the treasures of
Ethiopia had ceased to enrich Thebes; and when the harbour of
Alexandria began to attract to itself the produce of Egypt brought
from the Red Sea to the Nile valley, the vessels of Koptos, with
their lading of Indian and Arabian goods, but seldom found their
way S. to the great city of Ammon. Thebes still remained con-

spicuous as a city of temples and priests, but its inhabitants declined in wealth. It may be easily conjectured that these, formerly
the chief among the citizens of Egypt, bore but ill the fate which
now placed them far behind the Alexandrians. Strangers sat on the
throne of Ra, and cared not to take the trouble to visit in person
the remote Diospolis, the coronation-town of the Pharaohs, who
had been accustomed to make a triumphal entry after each victory
and to offer thanks to Ammon. The earlier noble Lagidae were succeeded by worthless rulers, whose extravagant tastes forced them
to drain the resources of the Thebaïd and other provinces. Under the gluttonous Euergetes II. and his consort Cleopatra Cocce
the Alexandrians rose in revolt and expelled Alexander I., the
king's son. The citizens of the capital of Upper Egypt dared also
to rise in the attempt to win back their lost independence; and
they refused to lay down their arms even when Ptolemy Soter II.
(Lathyrus) was recalled from banishment by the Alexandrians and
was universally recognized in Lower Egypt. The army of Lathyrus
besieged the town, whose inhabitants bravely defended themselves
in the huge temples, each of which served as a fortress. Finally,
however, Thebes was stormed; its treasures were plundered and
its venerable monuments terribly mutilated. Thenceforward Thebes
is only mentioned as a goal of inquisitive travellers, who under the
Roman emperors were attracted to the Nile by two monuments in
particular — the pyramids and the musical colossus of Memnon on
the W. bank at Thebes. Diodorus (60 B.C.) and Strabo (24 B.C.)
describe Thebes as it was after the destruction. The latter found
only a few relics on each side of the Nile, just as the traveller of
to-day does. An earthquake, no common occurrence in Egypt,
had done more than the hand of the fierce warrior to destroy the
monuments of thousands of years. In 27 or 24 B.C. a convulsion
of this nature wrought such havoc that Eusebius declared, though
not without exaggeration, that the Egyptian Thebes had been
levelled with the ground. In the absence of some such natural
force, we should be tempted to declare that the annihilation of
many parts of the monuments of Thebes must have been a task
only less difficult than their construction. At many points, especially in the temple at Karnak, the injury is plainly to be ascribed
to human hands. The representations, dating from the period of
the Ptolemies, within the second main pylon, to the left as we approach the large hypostyle hall, have been removed with axes or
hammers. Some smaller injuries, especially to the names of the
kings, were due to political reasons, as when Tutmes III., after he
obtained the sole power, destroyed the cartouches of his too ambitious sister and guardian; others are to be ascribed to the evil habit
of certain Pharaohs of appropriating the monuments of their predecessors by substituting their own names for those of the real
builders; and yet others had religious causes, as when the name of

Seth was obliterated at various epochs. The introduction of Christianity and the edicts of Theodosius were followed by the destruction of many pagan statues and the obliteration of many pagan inscriptions. At all events the new religion and the closing of the
temples dedicated to the ancient gods removed all possibility of
anything being done to preserve the monuments of the Pharaohs.
The Nile, which annually overflowed as far as the temple of Karnak
in particular, and the saline exudations of the soil, wrought harm;
jackals and other animals sought shelter in the subterranean chambers; many tombs, at first occupied by Christian hermits, were converted into peasants' dwellings; Christian churches were erected in
the temple-halls, and houses were built between the columns of the
temple at Luxor. Carefully hewn blocks and slabs were removed
from the monuments, which were used as quarries, and many
limestone details were thrown into the furnace and reduced to
lime. Whither the enormous population of the hundred-gated
Thebes betook itself is unknown. A few widely-scattered villages
alone now represent of the giant city. These have given names to
the various edifices and tombs, whose holy names might only be
uttered with pious awe in the time of the Pharaohs. The ruins of
Thebes remained long forgotten. On the revival of learning classical
students recalled their fame; Pococke rediscovered, described them
and drew them; and finally the publications of the great French
Expedition revealed to astonished Europe how much of the ancient
magnificence of the Pharaohs had survived to our time. Each
succeeding scientific expedition made its longest halt here and
found here its richest rewards. The names of Champollion, Wilkinson, Lepsius, and other Egyptologists are familiar words on the
site of ancient Thebes; and Mariette, who carried on excavations
under the auspices of the Khedive, must also be mentioned.

A. THE EAST BANK AT THEBES.

10. The Temple of Luxor.

The name of Luxor is derived from the Arabic *el-Ḳaṣr*, pl. *el-
Ḳuṣûr*, and means 'the castles', having reference to the extensive
temple in which part of the village of Luxor was built, and which
is adjoined by another part. The mosque still stands within the
temple. The house of the British consul, as well as the so-called
Ḳaṣr Fransâvi, and other buildings, which formerly stood here,
have been removed within the last few years, the S. side of the
temple laid free, and the interior cleansed. The chief entrance on
the N., with the pylons and their obelisks still on their ancient site,
is also to be thoroughly excavated. Seen from the river, the temple
now presents a highly imposing appearance, previously interfered

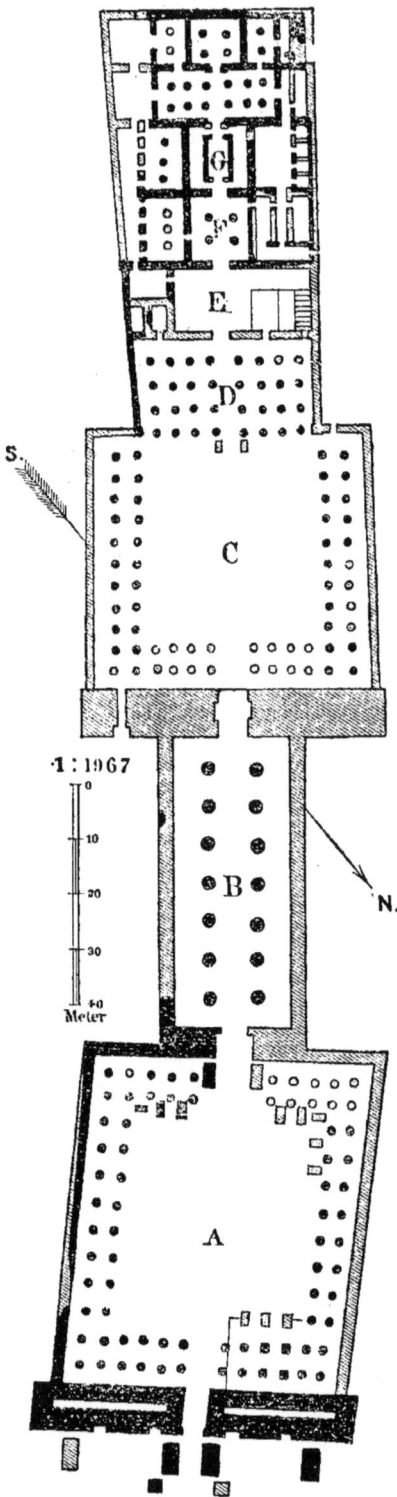

with by modern buildings. The house of Moharb Todrus, the German consular agent (p. 102), lies farther to the N., near the landing-place, where traces of an ancient construction may be seen, which is unfortunately disappearing before the annual inundations, and not far from the principal pylon. To the left of the main pylon is the village, with a shop, kept by a Greek, at which provisions of all kinds and porter, ale, candles, etc. may be purchased. Farther to the N.E. dwell numerous ghawâzi.

The removal of later buildings from the *Temple of Luxor has rendered it easy to reconstruct its ground-plan (see opposite), and to see that its erection was gradual and more or less affected by the existence of still earlier buildings. The general main axis of the temple lies from S.W. to N.E.; but the axis of the N. portion deviates considerably from the direction of that of the S. portion, partly on account of the shape of the river-bank, partly because it was desired to have the pylons at Luxor corresponding to those of Karnak. A careful examination indeed reveals three different axial directions. These deviate from the true meridian, at an angle of 41′ 21″ on the S., and at an angle of 51° on the N. As was the custom, the part of the temple containing the sanctuary (the S. part) was built first, including the large peristyle hall. This took place in the 18th Dyn. under Amenhotep III., while the W. portions were added by Ramses II. From the obelisks to the back of the sanctuary, the total length of the temple is 284 yds. Later kings, including some of the Ptolemies, placed inscriptions with their names on the ancient buildings. The PRINCIPAL PYLON is easily recognized by the obelisks and colossi at its portal. The visitor who places himself in front of this perceives at once that rubbish and earth conceal one-half of the sloping façade which is richly adorned with carvings and inscriptions now sadly damaged. Like all pylons, the one before us consists of two truncated pyramids with an entrance-door between them. The latter was 55 ft. in height. The side-towers, which rose about 20 ft. higher, were crowned with an elegant concave cornice, which has now almost completely disappeared, and were framed with the astragal. The entrance-door is completely ruined. Under the cornice is a conspicuous *Inscription* in large letters, which may be traced also on the architrave of the peristyle court, wherever it has remained visible and entire. This inscription contains a dedication, intimating that Ramses II. built this imposing edifice for his father Ammon-Ra, the king of the Gods. On each side of the entrance were two monolithic *Colossi*, 40 ft. in height; the most easterly has disappeared, the three others are half-buried in rubbish. In front of the central figures, though not quite symmetrically placed, rose two *Obelisks* of pink granite, one of which (the W.) now adorns the Place de la Concorde at Paris. It is to be hoped that a crack, which has been noticed in the monument from the days of antiquity, will not lead to its destruction under the influence of a northern climate. This W. obelisk was smaller than its E. neighbour which is still standing; and the ancient architects endeavoured to counteract this inequality by giving the smaller obelisk a higher base than the other, and placing it a little farther forward. The inscriptions on the obelisk still standing at Luxor are clearly and finely cut in the stone and are perfectly legible. They name Ramses the Pharaoh, with many pretentious titles, as the founder of this gorgeous building erected in honour of Ammon in southern Thebes (Apt res). The faces of these obelisks, like those of most others, are slightly convex, as the priestly architects observed that a flat surface was apt to appear concave in a strong light. Details supplied by the French engineers give a vivid idea of the enormous weight that had to be handled in the erection of an obelisk, although the Paris obelisk is comparatively small; considerably larger obelisks are to be seen at Karnak. The W. obelisk of Luxor is 75 ft. high, its base is $7^1/_2$ ft. square, and its weight is upwards of 212 tons.

The exterior walls of the pylons of nearly every Egyptian temple are adorned with representations referring to victories granted by the gods of the sanctuaries to the royal builders. At Luxor these representations refer to victories granted by Ammon to Ramses II. The rich sculpture with which the broad walls of the pylons were covered has suffered severely from the hand of time. At several places the *Reliefs en creux*, deeply cut in the stone, are practically

rubbed out. On the left (E.) wing, however, the life-like figure of
the king, shooting arrows from his chariot, and the fine rearing
horses of his chariot, are still clearly to be distinguished. On the
right (W.) wall also a good deal may be made out. The king is here
represented in his camp. He has dismounted from his chariot, which
waits for him, and has seated himself upon his throne. His officers
await his instructions, and farther in the background the troops
rest in their camp. The inscriptions are much injured, but it can
be made out from them that they were graven in the stone chiefly
in honour of Ramses II.'s victory over the Kheta (Aramæans) and
their allies. In the 5th year of the king, on the 9th Payni, the fortress of Katesh on the Orontes was stormed. The river and the
contest on its banks are still distinguishable. The *Epic of Pentau*r
in 90 vertical lines, covers the lower part of the W. wing and part
of the E. wing; some of it has recently been uncovered, the rest is
still concealed by rubbish. This poem was the national epos, the
Iliad, of the ancient Egyptians. It occurs twice on the E. bank at
Thebes — on the N. side of the pylon at Luxor and on the S. side
of the temple of Karnak (here also partly concealed by earth). It is
also found, though in a very fragmentary condition, on the N. wall
of the temple of Ramses II. at Abydos (discovered first by Eisenlohr), and in the most complete (hieratic) form in the *Papyrus
Raifet* (now in the Louvre) and the *Papyrus Sallier III.* (now in
the British Museum).

The poetic text on the pylons at Luxor is followed by a prose
text, dealing mainly with the arrival of two hostile spies, who gave
out at first that the Kheta had fled into the land of Khirabu (Helbon or Aleppo) to the N. of Tunep, but who on being scourged revealed the real lurking-place of the enemy to the N.W. of Katesh.
The king hastily recalled the Egyptian troops, but too late to prevent his camp being suddenly attacked on the S. by the Kheta. The
Egyptians were surrounded, and only the personal bravery of the
king secured the final victory. This prose inscription, preserved in
full at the Ramesseum and in the temple of Abu-Simbel, describes
the same event as the poem of Pentaur, though it dates it a month
later.

The most important and finest episodes according to the restoration
of the text by E. de Rougé are as follows. 'Then the miserable and
worthless Kheta with his numerous allies lay hidden behind the fortress
of Katesh. His majesty found himself alone (with his servants). The
legion of Ammon marched after him; the legion of Ra passed through
the valley to the S. of the fortress of Shabtun and marched forwards
. . . . In the centre was the legion of Ptah, supported by the fortress
of Arnam; the legion of Sutekh (Seth-Typhon) went upon its way.
The king had summoned all the leaders of his army, who were in the
valleys of the land of Amaur. The miserable and worthless prince of the
Kheta was in the midst of his soldiers; and for fear of His Majesty dared
not prepare himself to battle. Yet he ordered forward his archers and
his chariots, that were more in number than the sand of the sea shore. Three
men were in each chariot, and they had united themselves with the warriors
of the land of the Kheta, expert with all weapons. He remained hidden

behind the fortress of Katesh. Then they pressed forth on the S. side of
Katesh and attacked the centre of the legion of Ra, which was on the
march, and having no warning was unprepared for the battle. The archers
and chariots gave way before them. His Majesty alone had made a halt
to the N. of the fortress Katesh, on the W. bank of the Orontes. News
was brought to His Majesty of what had happened. And behold, the king
rose up like his father Mont (the god of war); he seized his weapons and
put on his armour, like Baal in his hour. The noble horses that bore his
majesty ('Victory for Thebes' was their name) came forth from the stable
of Ramses, the beloved of Ammon. and the king dashed in his attack
into the midst of the miserable Kheta. *He was alone and no other was
with him.* And as he hastened on before the eyes of those that followed
him, *he found himself surrounded by 2500 chariots of war*, (cut off) from
his return by all the warriors of the miserable Kheta and the numerous peoples that accompanied them; by the people of Arados, Mysia,
and Pisidia (Aratu, Masa, Pidasa). Each of their chariots bore three men,
and they had all united themselves. 'No prince was with me, no general,
no commander of the archers or chariots. My soldiers have deserted me,
and my knights have fled before them; not one of them has made a stand
to fight by my side'. Then spoke his majesty: 'Who art thou, O father
Ammon? does a father forget his son? Have I ever undertaken anything
without thee? Have I not walked and do I not stand ever according to
thy words? Never have I trespassed thy commands . . . What are these
Semites to thee? Ammon renders the godless helpless. Have I not offered
to thee countless sacrifices? Through me thy holy dwelling was filled
with my captives. I have built thee a temple for millions of years, and
I furnish thy store-houses with all my goods. I brought the whole
world to thee to enrich thy possessions; 3000 oxen I sacrificed to thee on
all manner of sweet-smelling wood. I have not failed to make thy fore-
court. Stone pylons I erected for thee, and I myself erected the flag-staffs
before them. I caused obelisks to be brought from Elephanta, and it was
I who caused stones of eternal duration to be brought. For thee ships
plough the deep and bring to thee the tribute of the nations. Surely a
wretched fate awaits him who resists thy commands, but happiness will
be to him who knows thee. I beseech thee, O father Ammon, look upon
me here in the midst of countless peoples who are strange to me. All
nations have united themselves against me, *and I am alone and no one
is with me.* My numerous soldiers have deserted me; no one of my
knights looked out upon me when I called them; none of them heard
my voice. But I believe that Ammon is of more value to me than a
million of soldiers, than a hundred thousand knights and a hundred
thousand brothers and young sons, even were they gathered together in
one place. The work of multitudes of men is as nothing, Ammon out-
weighs them all. This have I accomplished, O Ammon, according to the
counsel of thy mouth, and have not exceeded thy commands. Behold,
I have paid honour to thee to the uttermost ends of the earth'. My voice
sounded to Hermonthis and Ammon came at my cry. He gave me his
hand, I uttered a cry of joy, and he spoke behind me: "I hasten to thine
aid, O Ramses, my son, beloved of Ammon. I am with thee". — In the
farther course of his speech. Ammon says: "Not one of them (the foe)
finds his hand to fight; their hearts have vanished from their breasts for
fright; their arms have become weak. They are no longer able to launch
their arrows, and strength fails them to hold their spears. I thrust them
into the water, so that they fall in like the crocodile. They lie prone, one
upon another, and I spread death in their midst. I will not that one
should look behind him or that another should turn himself. He who
falls there shall not rise again". The king of course, as the epos goes on
to narrate, completely vanquished the Asiatics allied against him, after
hard fighting and after his charioteer himself had lost courage. — Finally
the prince of the Kheta sends a messenger with a letter. His submission
is accepted; and Ammon greets the Pharaoh returning in triumph.

The general impression produced by the pylon with its obelisks, colossi, and the various subsidiary details, is still not unimposing; and the whole entrance to the temple at Luxor is unusually picturesque, perhaps on account of the very abundance of small details which are unrestrainedly placed here side by side with the huge and dignified.

Beyond the principal pylon was the **Great Peristyle Court** (Pl. A), which was entirely surrounded by a double row of columns (twelve pairs on each of the four sides). It measures 185 ft. in length and 167 ft. in breadth. This hall was at one time completely built up, but the W. side at least has now been laid bare. The most recent excavations have revealed a portico, dating from Ramses II., on the inner side of the N.W. wall of the court. The architectonic purport of this portico, which is somewhat lower than the court and has three clustered columns, is not apparent. Between the inner row of columns on the S. side of the court arrows and shields of Ramses II. were placed. A mosque situated within this court prevents the excavation of the E. wall, and considerably mars the general effect. Ramses II. founded the court, but the Ethiopian Sabako wrote his name on the portal, while Ptolemy Philopator wrote his on several of the abaci. On the S. side this court was terminated by a smaller *Pylon*, beyond which, though not with the same axis (see above), is a **Colonnade** (Pl. B), 58 yds. long, built under the 18th Dynasty. The last is in tolerably good preservation and contributes essentially to the dignified appearance of the ruins of Luxor when viewed from the river-bank or still more from the island crossed on the way to visit the monuments of W. Thebes. Seven couples of columns, nearly 42 ft. in height, with calyx-capitals, still support a heavy architrave above a lofty abacus. The whole was built by Amenhotep III., but King Horus, Seti I., and Seti II. have also recorded their names upon it. The marvellous play of colour shown by this colonnade with its deep, heavy shadows when the setting sun sheds a rosy light upon the E. sky, is nowhere excelled. The **Second Peristyle Court** (Pl. C) had double rows of columns on its N., E., and W. sides. These, belonging to the order of sculptured papyrusbud columns, are specially effective as seen from the river-bank. The court was 48 yds. long and 55 yds. broad, and ends in a *Hypostyle Hall* (Pl. D), the roof of which was borne by 32 sculptured bud-columns arranged in 4 rows of 8. The two sphinxes at the entrance bear the name of Sebekhotep II. (13th Dyn.). This hall was barely 20 yds. deep and 35 yds. wide, and for some unexplained reason its E. wall forms an acute angle (instead of a right angle) with the S. wall of the preceding peristyle court. The *Open Space* (Pl. E), which we next find, is entered from the river side, and is specially commended to the traveller's attention. The ancient entrance to the sanctuary-chambers has here been altered into a kind of apsidal recess, bounded on the right and left by two granite Corinthian columns. The court in front of this was used as a church

in later Christian times, and the fine ancient sculptures were covered with lime and gaudily painted in the early Christian style.

Beyond this space were the series of chambers forming the
Sanctuary, now accessible only from the side next the river. This
is certainly the most ancient part of the temple, and unusually
clearly-cut hieroglyphics inform us that it was built by the same
monarch who reared the Colossi of Memnon, *i.e.* by Amenhotep III.
The first *Room* (Pl. F), with four columns, contains a series of representations of homage and sacrifice before Ammon Generator,
and in the chamber to the E. of it (Pl. n) are represented the confinement of the mother of the king (Mut-em-ua) and the nursing of
the infant Amenhotep. Beyond Room F is the *Holy of Holies* (Pl. G).
It is doubtful whether Assyrians or Persians destroyed the original
sanctuary, but at all events after the Macedonians had conquered
Egypt and after the death of Alexander the Great, it was restored
in the name of Alexander II., for whom Ptolemy Soter I. ruled
as 'satrap'. Alexander boasts in the dedicatory inscription of having restored the work of Amenhotep. The last rooms of this part of
the temple have now also been excavated, and contain various fine
sculptures of the 18th Dynasty. Ammon of Thebes, especially in
his ithyphallic form as the productive power, appears everywhere
as the chief deity of the temple, receiving sacrifices and bestowing
gifts. In the chamber adjoining the last square hall traces have
been found of a staircase ascending to the roof of the temple.

11. Karnak.

Travellers who arrive at Luxor in the morning should devote the
afternoon to a first visit to Karnak; if they arrive in the evening they
should spend on it the next morning. Karnak is about 1/2 hr's. ride from
Luxor; ass 1 fr., for the whole day 2 fr. Guides (2s.; p. 103), who speak
a little broken English, are useful to save time on a first visit, but they
are not indispensable. The donkey-boys and temple-keepers also speak
broken English. A visit to Karnak by moonlight is exceedingly attractive,
but travellers are advised not to make it alone, even although there is
nothing to fear from robbers.

Next to the Tombs of the Kings, Karnak is by far the most interesting part of ancient Thebes. Even under the Pharaohs the group
of temples here was considered the most striking creation of an age
peculiarly famous for architectural achievements. Centuries have
here destroyed much, yet there is no other building in the world
that can match the dimensions of the temple of Ammon at Karnak.
The brilliant life that once enlivened these halls with colour and
sound has long slept in silence beneath the dust. Could it be recalled by some magician's wand it would present to the beholder a
dazzling and bewildering scene of unique splendour; but it may
be questioned whether the admiration and interest commanded by
the temple in its uninjured and frequented days could equal the
pure enjoyment which is awakened in the breast of the sympathetic

beholder by the building now, ruined but with its whole plan and theory still clear and intelligible. There is nothing now to distract the eye from the lines and forms of the temple; and the pomp of banners and the clouds of incense are replaced by the magic of dignified antiquity. Amidst these hoary ruins, we realize the short-ness of our mortal span and recognize the evanescence of human greatness and splendour.

· Starting from the great pylon of the temple of Luxor, we pro-cecd to the E., then follow the street with the Greek shops, and leaving the houses of the ghawàzi and the hill with the tomb of the shêkh to the right, hold towards the N. We soon arrive at the first ruins of Karnak, and finally, if we have followed the W. route, reach an imposing row of *Kriosphinxes, i.e.* sphinxes with the bo-dies of lions and the heads of rams. Near this point, to the S. of the temple, are two almost parallel *Processional Avenues* flanked with sphinxes, one uniting the temple of Muth (p. 148) with the S. pylons (p. 147), the other leading from the temple of Luxor to the temple of Khunsu (p. 148). These two avenues were connected with each other by a third cross-avenue of sphinxes. We follow the left (W.) avenue, the flanking sphinxes of which are carved in the grand style and are placed close to each other. Between the legs of each is a statuette with the name of Amenhotep III. (Ra-ma-neb). This leads us to the handsome but almost too slender *Pylon XII,* erected by Ptolemy III. Euergetes I., with a winged sun-disc in the casement, with boldly-spread pinions. In the time of the Lagidae additional pylons, corresponding to this one, were placed at the ex-treme corners of the temple. That on the N. side (p. 143) is still in admirable preservation. Inside the portal Euergetes is represented in Egyptian style though clad in Greek costume. To the right of the lowest representation on the left side, the king appears sacri-ficing to Khunsu. Between these are the hawk of Horus, the vul-ture of Nekheb, and the ibis of Thoth, which are also represented flying, to bear to the world intelligence of the battles, victories, and wisdom of the prince. The inscriptions record that this pylon was dedicated to Khunsu of Thebes. Another avenue of sphinxes follows, beyond which rises the *Temple of Khunsu* (Pl. V.), a hand-some building on which, however, we now bestow only a passing glance (comp. p. 148). About 200 paces towards the W. bring us to the *First Main Pylon (el-bâb el-kebîr),* which faces the river. We here begin our description of the temple.

I. The Great Temple of Ammon.
a. General View. The First Main Pylon.

As we stand before the massive pylons of the largest group of buildings at Karnak, we may cast a glance at the rows of Kriosphinxes which led from the temple-portal to the Nile. Between these rows

Plan of the Temple of Ammon

First Pylon
Great Pylon
Southern Pylons
... of the Temple of Khonsu
... Peristyle Court
... of Seti II Monolith?
... of Ramses III
... Hypostyle Hall
Great Court of the Temple of Ammon
Sanctuary of the Temple of Ammon
... of Buildings of the 12th Dyn.
Colonnade of Thotmes ...
Sanctuary of Thotmes III
Building of the Temple of Thotmes III
Great Hall of Ramses ...
... of Ramses II
... of Isis
Great Temple
... of Ptah

a Portique des Bubastites
b Antechamber of the Sixth Pylon
c Doorway of the Second Pylon
d N. Door of the Hypostyle Hall
e S. Door of the Hypostyle Hall
f Antechamber of the Third Pylon
g Small Obelisk of Thotmes I

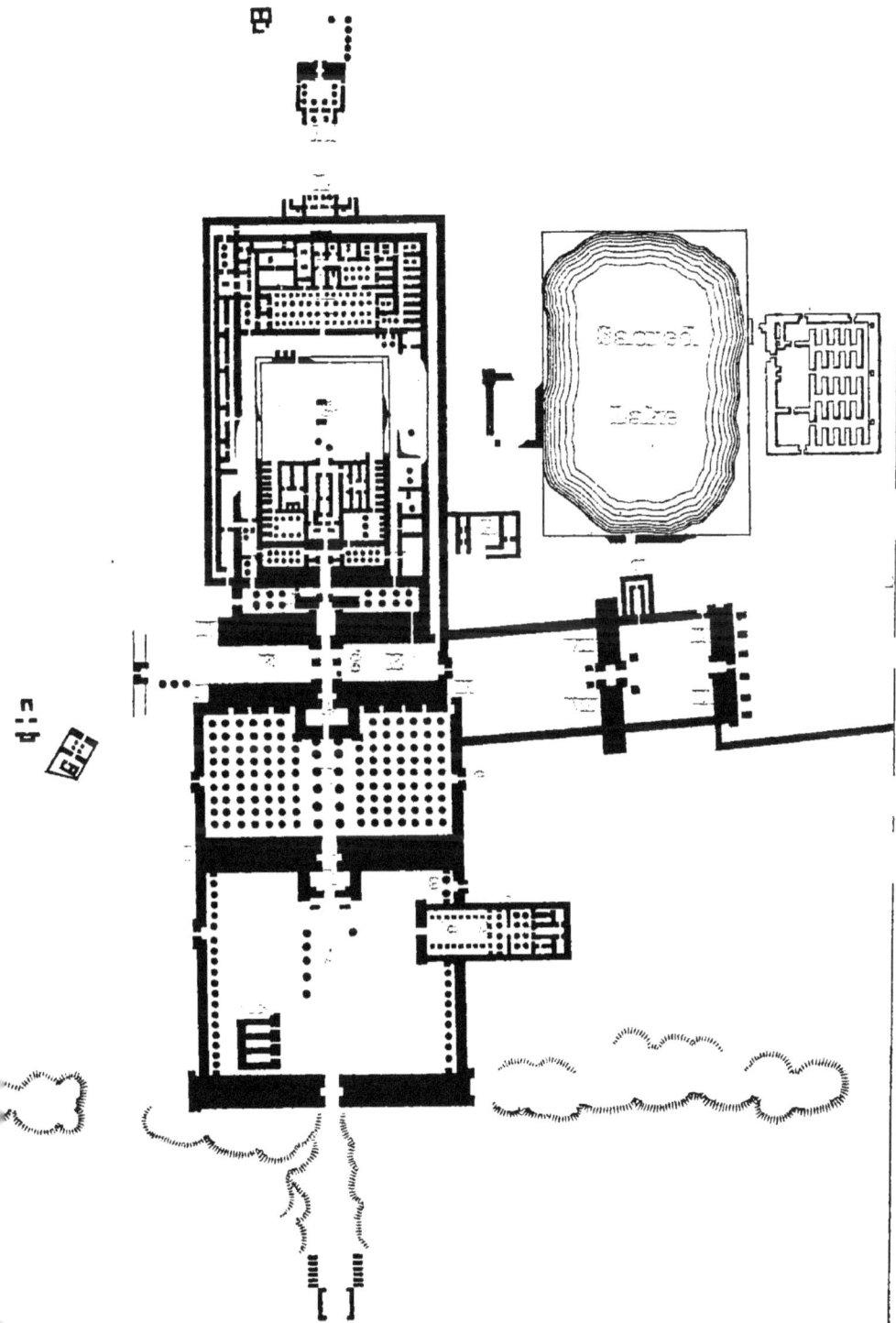

Sacred
Lake

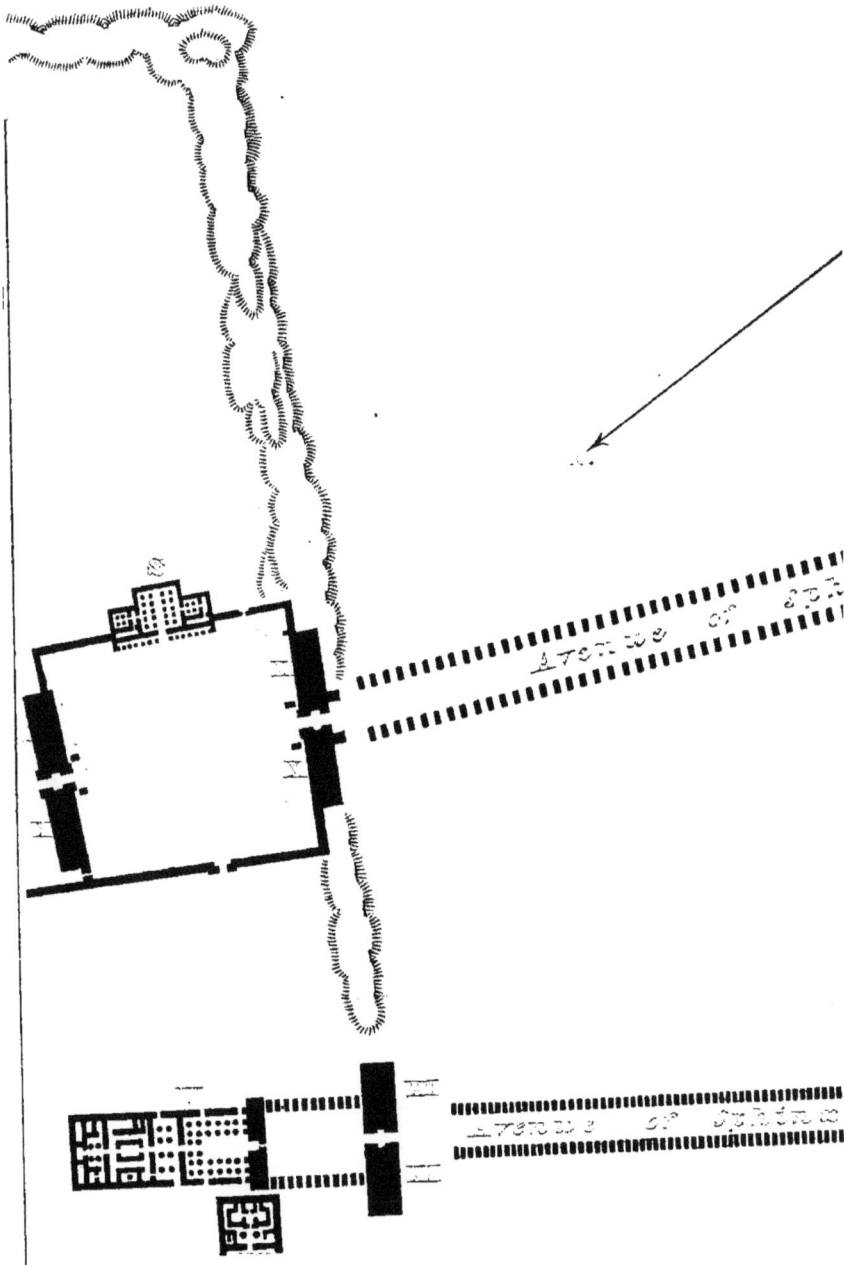

AVENUE OF RAMS

AVENUE OF SPHINXES

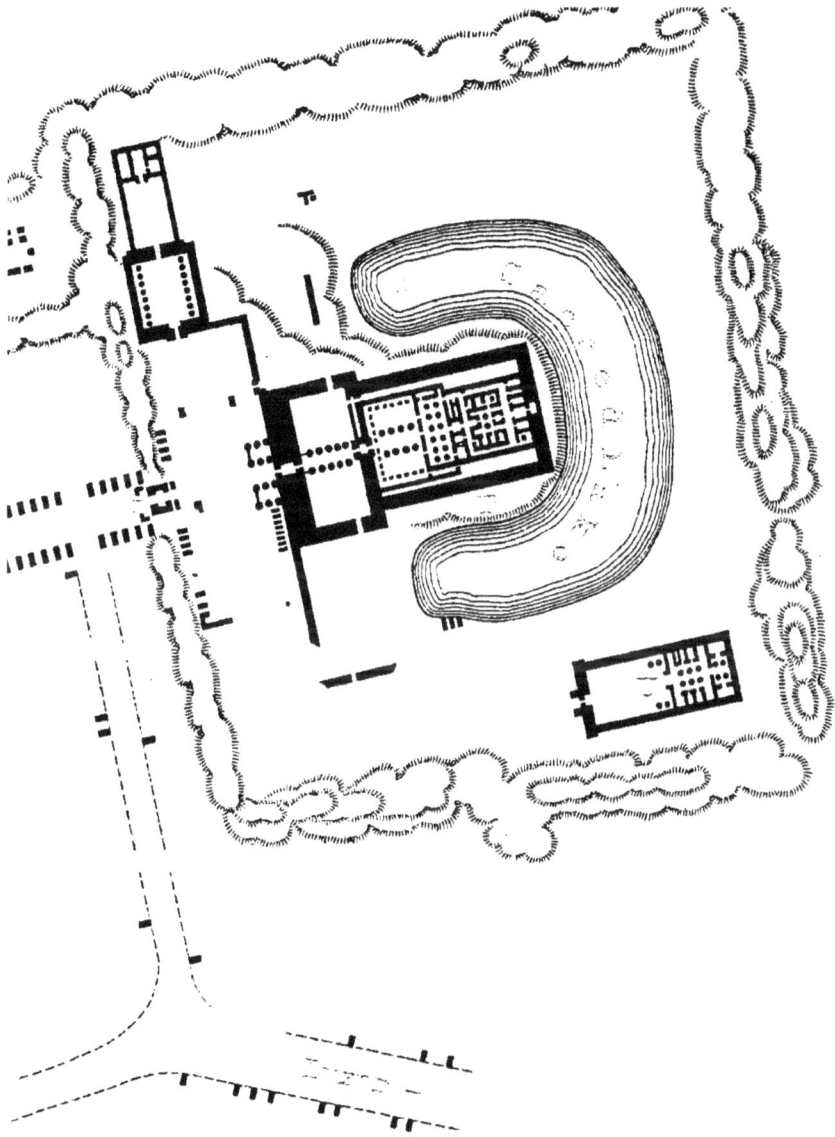

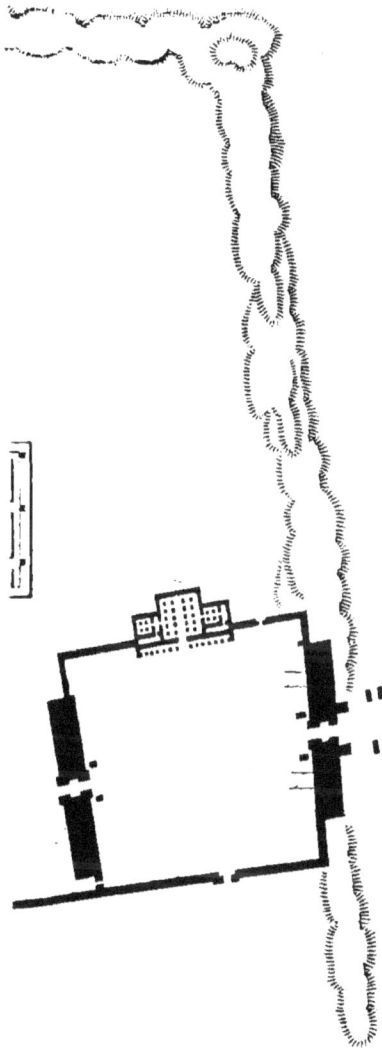

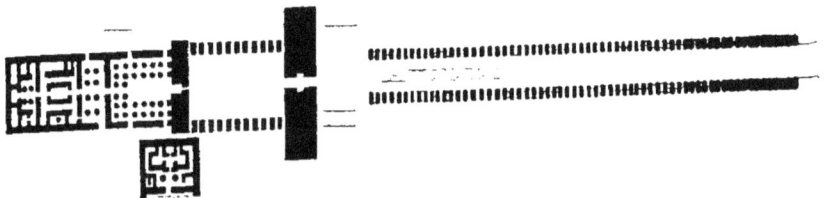

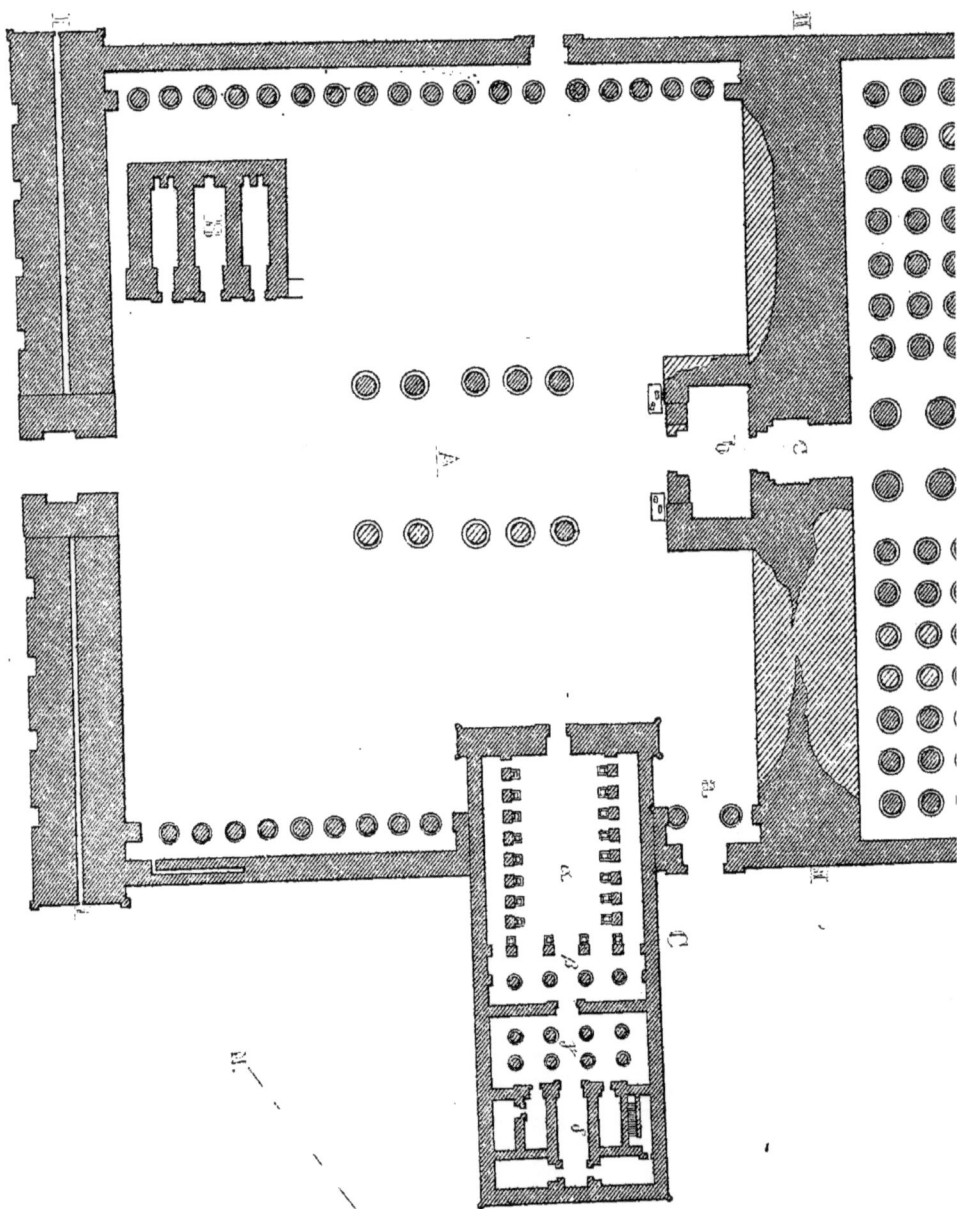

moved the long processions which left the temple of Ammon to visit
the W. parts of Thebes. State-barges, glittering with gold and
brilliant colours, waited here to receive the priests and the sacred
images. On the river-steps were ranged choirs, which, at least on
the five great festival days of Ammon, greeted the pilgrims from the
opposite bank with songs. The ancient constructions on the banks
have long been washed away. In January and February, the months
in which most travellers visit Karnak, the stream is only 100-200
paces from the procession-avenue; while during the inundation the
water penetrates into the interior of the temple, which in ancient
times it was prevented from doing by huge embankments Ramses II. constructed this route to the river, yet most of the Kriosphinxes that adorn it have statuettes of Seti II. Merenptah
between their legs, and two small broken obelisks also bear the
name of Seti who reigned towards the close of the 19th Dynasty.
In 1883 a small temple with the name of king *Psammuthis*, of the
29th Dyn., was discovered at the S.W. corner of the pylon to
the right.

The *First Main Pylon (Pl. I) is of enormous size. It is still
124 yds. wide, with walls 16 ft. thick and $142^1/_2$ ft. high. This
gigantic portal, which probably dates from the Ptolemies, although
no record of the fact is known, is destitute of inscriptions. Possibly
it was covered with stucco and adorned with paintings, as its decoration with reliefs would have demanded enormous toil and time.
No one should omit to make the *Ascent of this pylon. This may
be done most easily, and without any danger or special difficulty,
on the N. side, till we are about half way up, and thence by means
of a steep and narrow stair in the interior. The top is so broad that
even those who are subject to giddiness need not fear to trust themselves upon it. After enjoying the extraordinary view of the immense
ruins from this point of vantage, it is useful and interesting to seek
to identify, with the aid of the accompanying plan, the various columns, obelisks, and pillars which at first present themselves in
apparently inextricable confusion. This is comparatively easy as
regards the nearer (W.) portion of the temple; but the more distant
portions, from among which obelisks tower, are partly out of sight,
and are partly so foreshortened by distance, that they appear to
form one confused system of ruins. The view by moonlight is in-
describably fine. But on the whole the result is a general though
ineffaceable impression, rather than a clear idea of the arrangement
of the various parts of the building. The latter is only to be obtained
by wandering, plan in hand, through the ruins. It must, however,
never be forgotten that the temple of Karnak, so far from having
one single uniform plan, grew up gradually, and that many of its
parts owe their character not to any artistic calculation, but to
such accidental considerations as the space at the disposal of the
architect, the means and length of life of the builder, and the like.

The building is at once a temple of the gods and a temple of fame; dedicated 'à tóutes les gloires' of the empire of the Pharaohs, it was compelled to receive additions, often in most unsuitable places, whenever it was the will of the king to recognize the favours of Ammon by new buildings which should record for posterity what the god had done for him, and through him for Egypt.

Before we enter the peristyle court, an inscription on the door of the pylon, to our right as we enter, merits notice. This was placed here by the savants who accompanied the army of Napoleon to Egypt, and records the latitude and longitude of the chief temples of the Pharaohs, as calculated by them.

République Française. An VIII. Géographie des monuments.

Temples	Longitude	Latitude
Dendera	30° 21 0	26° 10 0
Thèbes { Carnac . .	30° 20 4	25° 44 15
{ Luqsor . .	30° 19 16	25° 42 55
Esneh	30° 14 19	25° 49 39
Edfou	30° 33 4	25° 0 0
Ombos	30° 38 39	24° 28 0
Syène	30° 34 19	24° 8 6
Isle Philae . . .	30° 33 46	24° 3 45

This monument of untiring and successful diligence deserves to be greeted with respect; it contrasts with the execrable taste of the idle tourists who have scribbled over and defaced inscriptions within the temple, with their own insignificant names. Opposite the French table an Italian learned society (Feb. 9, 1841) have erected another showing the variation of the compass (declinazione dell' ago magnetico) as 10'56''. The inscription is signed 'Marina genio' etc.

b. The Great Peristyle Court and its Additions.

The great *Peristyle Court (Pl. A) is believed by important authorities to have been built by the rulers of the 22nd Dynasty. The oldest part of the temple is the sanctuary (p. 134), situated much farther to the E. Probably the clearest view of the growth and historical development of the great house of Ammon would be obtained by beginning there and thence visiting the later portions in the order of their erection; but in following out this plan we should be obliged to diverge irregularly hither and thither from the main lines, and so would miss much of the effect designed by the builders. The influence of the god was supposed to radiate from within outwards; while the procession of his adorers advanced slowly towards Ammon from without inwards. The sanctuary was the final, unapproachable goal of the pious, few of whom were permitted to penetrate farther than the peristyle court. The hypostyle hall was indeed open to certain privileged worshippers, but only the 'initiated' were allowed to approach any nearer to the holy of holies. That sacred chamber itself might only be entered by the high-priest and the king, the representative of the god upon earth. The arrangement of the peristyle and succeeding chambers indicate in the clearest manner the nature of the services celebrated within them.

The *Architectonic Features* of the court must be noticed before we proceed to examine its uses. It is 275 ft. deep and 338 ft. wide, and covers an area of 9755 sq.yds. On each side a kind of colonnade or stoa is formed by a row of columns and the exterior wall. Eighteen columns still stand on the left side, but the row on the right was interrupted by Ramses III., who has here placed a temple (Pl. C), projecting considerably beyond the S. wall, and at right angles to it. Both rows of columns are unsculptured. Another small temple (Pl. B) was built in the N.E. angle of the court by Seti II. Merenptah. Both of these smaller temples are later additions, with no reference to the purpose of the court, and they interfere with the effect designed by the original builder. The double row of huge columns in front of the doorway of the second pylon was, on the other hand, part of the original plan. The lofty shafts, which were terminated by calyx-capitals of gigantic proportions, taper towards the top, and contract rapidly immediately above the convex bases on which they stand. The calyx of the capitals was surrounded with petals, from amidst which slender marsh-plants sprang. In the centre of each was a cubical abacus, serving as a pedestal for an image of a god. Mariette conjectured that a small hypæthral temple (like that at Philae) stood in front of the second pylon, and that not only was there an additional (sixth) pair of columns adjoining the others but that the vaulting of the whole was rendered possible by two central columns between the pairs at each end which are about 36 ft. apart. As, however, there is not the faintest trace of these conjectural six columns, it is perhaps more probable that this colonnade represents a processional or triumphal avenue, formerly covered only by a velarium, and that the continuation of it is to be recognized in the elevated central row of columns in the hypostyle hall (p. 125). Of the original columns only five can now be traced on the left side, and one on the right, close to the second pylon, which terminates the peristyle on the E. Three still show about $1/3$ of the original height, one about $1/4$, and another about $1/2$; the only complete column is on the right. Upon this last Psammetikh I., of the 26th Dyn., has placed his name over that of the Ethiopian Taharka, of the 25th Dyn.; above, on the abacus, is the name of Ptolemy IV. Philopator, which also appears on the recently excavated base of one of the broken columns. The shaft is composed of 36 courses of carefully hewn stone, the capital of 5 courses. The height is 69 ft.; the greatest breadth of the capital 16 ft., the circumference at the top 49 ft. — The above-mentioned second pylon, on the E. side of the court, is mostly in ruins. Before the doorway is an antechamber (Pl. b), the entrance to which was flanked by two statues of Ramses II. The figure on the left side has fallen down; that on the right, broken at the top, displays excellent workmanship, especially in the legs, and recalls the Daedalian figures of the earliest periods of Greek art.

We may mention here in anticipation that the roof of the following hypostyle hall was supported by a perfect forest of papyrus-bud columns, through the midst of which a broad passage was marked by calyx-columns, closely resembling the detached pairs of columns in the first court (comp. p. 126). At this point we first obtain a clear idea of the arrangement of this portion of the temple, and the same remark applies also to all the rooms between it and the sanctuary. It should also be remembered that the number of those privileged to follow and behold the procession gradually decreased from room to room as the sanctuary was approached. Headed by the king or chief priest, the crowd of priests, bearing the standards, symbols, and images of the gods, passed through the doorway of the first pylon into the peristyle court. The double row of calyx-capitals served at once to indicate their passage and to mark the limits beyond which the pious spectators must not press. The sacred procession rolled on slowly beneath the shade of the velarium and entered the hypostyle hall through the second pylon. Many of those who were permitted to enter the first court had there to quit the procession and to take up their positions to the right and left of the calyx-columns. Others again were not permitted to advance farther than the hypostyle, and so with each room until the sanctuary was reached. To this day the clearly defined passage thither may be traced, and it will be observed that at each successive stage the place appointed for those who had to quit the procession is smaller than the preceding.

LATER ADDITIONS IN THE PERISTYLE COURT.

1. The **Small Temple** of Seti II. **Merenptah** (Pl. B), in the N.E. angle of the court, to our left as we enter by the first pylon. This building, which has only recently been made partly accessible, is built of grey sandstone, except beside the three doors, where a reddish quartzose sandstone has been used. The figure of the god Seth has everywhere been erased from the name of the builder. Only a small portion of the walls is entirely sculptured; and the representations that are still extant show that the temple was dedicated to the Theban triad, Ammon, Muth, and Khunsu. In the chamber entered by the W. (left) door appears the sacred boat of the goddess Muth, to whom Seti Merenptah, accompanied by his son, offers a libation. The richly dressed boy is called 'royal prince' and 'heir to the crown'. Adjacent is the figure of the helmeted Pharaoh, presenting the image of the goddess of truth to Ammon and Khunsu.

2. The **Temple of Ramses III.** (Pl. C), dedicated to Ammon, interrupting the S. wall of the peristyle court.

The great *Harris Papyrus*, which is chiefly concerned with the erection and equipment of temples, details no fewer than six buildings and five estates in the vicinity of Thebes, distinguished by the terms Hat (temple), Pa (house), Menmenu (pasture), adding after each one of the two names of the king and frequently also an additional name, such as 'thy victory thou makest abiding for all eternity'. The personnel assigned to these foundations is reckoned at 86,486 individuals, of which 62,626 belonged to the largest temple (at Medinet-Habu). The above-mentioned Temple C. bore the name *Pa Ramses hak an* (House of Ramses, prince of Heliopolis) and had 2623 priests and attendants.

The building is in form a complete temple, but in view of the enormous dimensions of its surroundings can claim only the character of a chapel. Its total length is 170 ft. The *Pylon* with the entrance door is much injured, especially at the top. Beyond it is a *Peristyle Court* (Pl. α), with eight Osiris-pillars on each side, and at the end four caryatide pillars forming a *Passage* (Pl. β), whence a door leads to a small *Hypostyle* (Pl. γ), with eight papyrus-bud capitals. Finally come the chambers of the *Sanctuary* (Pl. δ). Sculpture is not wanting in this temple, which owes its origin to the wealthy founder of the Memnonium at Medinet Habu (p. 174). This most lavish of Egyptian kings had already founded within the limits of the temple of Ammon the temple of Khunsu (p. 148) as a worthy symbol of his liberality to the gods; and that fact explains the comparative smallness of the temple before us. The exterior of the pylons was adorned with representations expressing the gratitude of the Pharaoh to the god for victory in battle. On the *Left Wing*

(E.) Ramses III., wearing the crown of Upper Egypt, holds a band of prisoners by the hair and raises his sword for a blow which must strike off all their heads at once. Ammon, standing in front of him, hands him the sword of victory, and delivers to him chained together the representatives of the vanquished peoples, who appear in three rows. In the first two rows are the conquered nations of the south, in the third row those of the north. On the *Right Wing* are similar representations, the king here wearing the crown of Lower Egypt. In the doorway, Ramses III. receives from Ammon the symbol of life, etc. On the right side-wall of the pylons are representations of battles and captives, which were concealed by the colonnade, a conclusive proof that the circumference of the court cannot date from Ramses II.

In the peristyle court (Pl. α) the following inscription occurs on the architrave of the caryatid passage on the right. (We omit the lengthy introductory titles of the king.) 'Ramses, king of Upper and Lower Egypt, prince of Heliopolis (*i.e.* Ramses III.), the living and beneficent god, who resembles Ra that lightens the world with his beams on the E. and W. horizon, the lord of beams, like the sun's disc in the heavens. Men extol him, when they behold Ramses III., the king of Upper and Lower Egypt, the son of the sun, the lord of the diadems, Ramses the prince of Heliopolis, who built this monument for his father Ammon-Ra, the king of the gods. He erected anew (m maui) the building known as Pa Ramses hak an (princes of Heliopolis), as a house for Ammon, of white and well-hewn stone, finishing it with everlasting work'. The inscription (injured) goes on to describe the king as a darling of Ammon, a victory-bringing Horus, who is as rich in years as Tum, a king and protector of Egypt, who overthrows the alien peoples, etc.

The lower parts, especially in the sanctuary-chambers, are covered with rubbish. A long *List of Offerings* on the left (E.) exterior wall is of some interest. It records that Ramses III., in the month Payni in the 16th year of his reign, decreed that gifts for his father Ammon-Ra, the king of the gods, should be laid upon the silver altar, such as provisions, sacrificial cakes, etc. Then follow some details (injured) as to the amount of the offerings.

3. The Portique des Bubastites (*Portico of the Bubastites;* Pl. a), so called by Champollion, is the part of the court between the left (E.) wall of the temple just described and the S. part (*i.e.* the far- thost to the right) of the second pylon. This space, only 43 ft. wide, had a door admitting to the temple from the S., and is to be regarded as the E. end of the colonnade which lined the S. wall of the court. Two unsculptured papyrus-bud columns divide it from the rest of the court. Numerous inscriptions dating from the 22nd Dyn., which originated in Bubastis, cover the walls, and contain impor- tant material for the history of that period. This dynasty succeeded the inglorious line of priest-kings, who seized the throne of Thebes after the self-indulgent rulers of the 20th dynasty. Their names are rather Semitic than Egyptian, a circumstance that need cause no surprise when we remember that Bubastis is named as their home, a city in the E. part of the Delta which was settled by Semitic tribes. As their names appear to be of Aramaic origin it is not impossible that they were placed upon the throne of the Pharaohs by the Assyrian conquerors who are mentioned in the cuneiform inscriptions of Mesopotamia, though the Egyptian hieroglyphics ignore them. Like their predecessors of the 21st Dyn., they retained the chief priesthood in their own control, apparently by committing this office to their heirs. In the hall in which we now are the king appears several times with the crown-prince, who is named 'first prophet of Ammon-Ra'; and the crown-prince occurs also without his father. Sheshenk I. probably began the decoration of the building, for his name appears in the usual place for the de- dication-inscription, *i.e.* on the architrave above the columns. The names of Osorkon I. and Takelut I. also occur. The last-named king appears before Ammon-Ra accompanied by his son Osorkon, clad in the priestly panther-skin; and Osorkon also occurs alone offering sacrifice to Ammon. On the E. wall is a double painting representing Ammon to the right and left, wearing the feather- crown and seated on a throne, while the deceased son of the same Osorkon approaches in priestly garb to offer sacrifice. Beneath is a long but unfortunately damaged *Inscription,* dating from the 12th year of Takelut II., which mentions a remarkable event said to have occurred in the reign of the father of that prince (probably Sheshenk II.). The passage in question is not absolutely clear, but this much may be gathered with certainty, viz. that on the 25th Mesori in the 15th year of the father of Takelut II., something un-

usual happened to the moon, which plunged all Egypt in alarm. This was probably a lunar eclipse †. In the left wing, on the N. wall, Ammon appears presenting Osorkon I. with the notched staff of years and the sword of victory; beneath, the king drinks the milk of life from the breast of Hathor; and adjacent is Osorkon as a youth with the crown, to whom Khnum hands the symbol of life.

Before proceeding on our way towards the sanctuary, we must inspect a most important historical monument which owes its origin to Sheshenk I. (the *Shishak* of the Bible), founder of the dynasty of the Bubastites. This is on the outside of the *S. Wall* of the temple of Ammon, and is easily found. Issuing from the doorway of the Portico of the Bubastites, we turn to the left, and immediately find ourselves in front of this important representation. The massive form of the king, wearing the double crown, appears brandishing his weapon over a band of foes with pointed beards, who raise their arms in supplication. Farther to the left is the large figure of Ammon, with the double feather on his head, grasping in his right hand the sword of victory and in his left cords binding five rows of captives with name-labels. Foes with pointed beards kneel before him and beg for mercy with uplifte hands. The portrait of King Sheshenk was left unfinished, the outline drawing of the crown being still visible on the stone. His cartouche and the inscriptions placed in his and Ammon's mouth are more distinct. Beneath Ammon appears the goddess of Thebes with the symbol of the nome of the city of Ammon 𓉺 upon her head. In her left hand she holds a bow and arrow, in her right a battle-axe and six papyrus cords, which unite five rows of names of towns, surmounted by busts. These are the names of places besieged and captured by Sheshenk in his campaign against Rehoboam, and we have thus a collateral corroboration of the Biblical narrative, such as has not been found for any other portion of the Old Testament.

The Biblical passages are as follows: 1 Kings XIV., 25-26: 'And it came to pass in the fifth year of king Rehoboam, that Shishak king of Egypt came up against Jerusalem: And he took away the treasures of the house of the Lord. and the treasures of the king's house; he even took away all; and he took away all the shields of gold which Solomon had made'. 2nd Chron. XII., 2-4 & 9: 'And it came to pass, that, in the fifth year of Rehoboam, Shishak king of Egypt came up against Jerusalem because they had transgressed against the Lord, With twelve hundred chariots, and threescore thousand horsemen; and the people were without number

---

† It reads thus: 'In the year etc. .... the heavens did *not* swallow the moon'. This may possibly refer to the appearance of a new moon on the night immediately succeeding the last appearance of the old moon, without the usual intervention of a moonless night — a phenomenon which is possible in certain exceptional circumstances. But if, as Goodwin suggests, instead of ⌒ *not*, ⊢ *s* is to be taken, it would read "In the year etc. ... the heavens swallowed the moon", and we should have a direct mention of a lunar eclipse.

that came with him out of Egypt; the Lubim, the Sukkiim, and the Ethiopians. And he took the fenced cities which pertained to Judah, and came to Jerusalem'. Verse 9 is the same as the above passage from Kings. — The conquered people named in the representation are the Amu, Kenus (Nubians), Menti, and Sakti (Asiatics).

Champollion, the great decipherer of hieroglyphics, was the first to perceive that the names in the inscription belonged to the above-mentioned 'fenced cities', and that Sheshenk, called by the Greeks Sesonchis, was identical with the Shishak of the Bible. The third name in the third row from the top, attracted his attention especially; it reads 'Judah (Juda) Malek', and may be translated king of Judah. The heads of the busts above the name-labels, with their characteristic Semitic features, are sufficient by themselves to prove that only places could be here signified that were inhabited by peoples related to the Jews. Of the 120 name-labels only a few can be identified with certainty with otherwise known names of places in Palestine, such as Rabbath (last ring of the first row), Taanach, Shunem, Rehob, Hapharaïm, Adullam, Mahanaïm, Gibeon, Beth-Horon, Kedemoth, Ajalon (in the second row). Several symbols have recently been obliterated by the whitewash used to preserve the wall, and some of the name-labels have also been destroyed, as *e.g.* Megiddo at the beginning of the third row. The rest of the inscriptions, which are couched in the usual emphatic style, give no farther information as to the campaign.

We return to the peristyle court and proceed to the **Second Pylon** (Pl. II). The left or N. side has fallen and the right side is sadly damaged. The colossi of Ramses II., which guarded the projecting entrance, have already been mentioned on p. 119. But neither Ramses II., as appearances might suggest, nor even his father Seti I. built this pylon, but the predecessor and father of the latter, Ramses I., who also planned the hypostyle hall, afterwards adorned by Seti I. and Ramses the Great. The cartouches of Ramses II. frequently occur sunk instead of being embossed, because they have been placed on spots previously occupied by the older cartouches of Ramses I. or Seti I. The same is the case on the back of the N. pylon, whereas on the back of the S. pylon, which was erected by Ramses II., his name appears in genuine bas-relief. In the doorway (Pl. c), where the cartouches of Ramses I., Seti I., and Ramses II. are found, an intervening door was erected by Ptolemy VII.

Philometor and Ptolemy IX. Euergetes II., during their joint-reign (170-165 B.C.). The lintel and upper parts of this latter doorway are wanting, but the jambs are in good preservation, with expressions of homage to Ammon and his fellow-gods. On the inner side (to the left) of the earlier doorway appears Ramses II. kneeling before Ammon and receiving the symbol of kingship. Behind him stands the goddess Muth, and Khunsu, with the moon's disc on his head, conducts Ptolemy VII. Philometor to behold the god Ammon. Probably the representation is a restoration by Philometor of an older work on the same spot.

c. The Great Hypostyle Hall.

The ****Hypostyle Hall** of Karnak (Pl. D) was commenced under the 18th Dyn. by Ramses I., completed by Seti I. (19th Dyn.), and enriched with new sculptures wherever there was room by Seti's son Ramses II. Its breadth (inside measurement) is 338 ft., its depth 170 ft., and its area 5450 square yards, an area spacious enough to accommodate the entire church of Notre Dame at Paris. The roof is supported by 134 columns, of which the central row is higher than the others. Each of the 12 columns in this row is $11^3/_5$ ft. in diameter and upwards of 32 ft. in circumference, *i.e.* as

Hypostyle Hall of Karnak. (From Maspero's Archéologie égyptienne.)

large as Trajan's Column in Rome or the Vendôme Column in Paris. It requires six men with outstretched arms to span one of these huge columns. Their height is 69 ft., that of the capitals 11 ft. The remaining 122 columns are each $42^1/_2$ ft. in height and $27^1/_2$ ft. in circumference, and have papyrus-bud capitals. 'It is impossible', says Lepsius, 'to describe the impression experienced by everyone who enters this forest of columns for the first time, and passes from row to row, amidst the lofty figures of gods and kings, projecting, some in full relief, some in half relief, from the columns on which

they are represented'. Many of the columns are prostrate, others
lean as though on the verge of falling, and architrave and roof-
slabs have either fallen or seem on the point of doing so. Yet the
whole is so well-preserved that we never forget that we are in a
colonnaded hall, and the ruinous appearance so far from destroying the general impression adds a picturesque charm to it. The
enormous proportions of this structure are perhaps best appreciated,
if we place ourselves in the wide doorway of the second pylon and
look through the double row of huge calyx-columns towards the
sanctuary, *i.e.* towards the E. The magic influence of the place is
fully felt in the morning or evening, or by moonlight, when the
columns cast intense black shadows on each other.

Roof. The processional route (p. 119) was distinguished by
placing on each side of it higher columns than in the rest of the
temple. These higher columns have calyx-capitals, on which rest
cubical abaci, supporting the massive architraves which run parallel
with the main axis of the temple. Above the architrave another
small erection is visible. The lower columns immediately adjacent
on both sides were connected with this inner row, by erecting upon
them square pillars, separated by windows, and united with each
other by means of a long architrave, above which another smaller
erection is observed. Only one of the windows is now extant, and
that in imperfect preservation. The union of these four rows under
a common roof thus provided a lighted passage, about 78 ft. high
(about 32 ft. higher than the rest of the hall), through the centre
of the colonnaded hall. The shape of the columns in the outer rows
is shown in Vol. I., p. 164 b; the calyx-capitals of the two inner
rows in Vol. I., p. 165 a. — The *Columns* are not monolithic, but
are built, like huge watch-towers, of hewn stones. The central
rows have smooth shafts and enormous calyx-capitals with curved
edges. Five bands at the neck of the column fasten the striped
petals and slender water-plants, which, mingled with royal
cartouches and other decorations, cling to the calyx. Each capital
resembles a gigantic goblet. Unfortunately the minuteness of the
ornamentation, especially on the upper parts, is not very suitable
for the huge proportions of the columns. All the columns, both in
the inner and in the outer row, are adorned with the name of
Ramses II. and various embellishments. The shafts in every case
bore sunk reliefs ('en creux'), the former painting in which is still
traceable at places. The inscriptions and representations present,
on the whole, but little variety; but in a few considerable differences may be noted as regards the persons of the gods and the
gifts which they received or bestowed. This is specially the case
with the columns. Those in the first six rows to the N. have,
towards the top, the cartouche of Seti I., and farther down that
of Ramses IV.; the remaining rows have Ramses II. at the top and
Ramses IV. below. Ramses III., Ramses VI., and Ramses XIII.

have also recorded their names, sometimes filling in vacant spaces and sometimes scratching out older names. On the capitals the cartouches of Ramses II. or of his more immediate successors are found; on the border of the extreme top of the shaft, this same Pharoah is usually named king of Upper and Lower Egypt, lord of both worlds, son of the sun, lord of the diadems, etc. The broader field beneath exhibits almost universally vertical cartouches, surmounted with the feathers 〔symbol〕, and standing upon the symbol of gold 〔symbol〕. On the largest field, still lower, the king appears twice; once sacrificing to the god, and once with the celestials offering him emblems, generally symbolizing in some familiar way one of the higher blessings of life. The simple inscriptions repeat each other over and over again. They begin: 'I give thee', or, 'I grant thee', or else mention a visit of the king to the temple. The carvings and hieroglyphics placed by Ramses II. are much inferior to those dating from the reign of his father Seti I., a fact we have already noticed at Abydos.

By far the most important place among the gods here is filled by Ammon, Muth, and Khunsu, the Theban triad (Vol. I., p. 138). At Karnak Ammon was conceived of in two capacities, which must be distinguished from each other; he was in the first place Ammon Generator, in the second place Ammon-Ra, the king of the gods. Ammon may be identified by his feather-crown, Khunsu by the crescent on his head and the lock on his temples, and Muth by the vulture-cap. The other gods that appear with them may be easily identified with the help of the introduction on the Religion of Ancient Egypt (Vol. I., p. 124). On the architrave are some clearly cut inscriptions, of which a few deviate from the usual formulae. One of these, dating from Seti I., on the architrave above the bud-columns in the first cross-row to the E. (right), is as follows: 'He is a king, mounting his horse like the son of Isis (Horus). He is an archer of a mighty arm and like the (god of war) Mentu a great wall of brass. He is the protector of his soldiers, when they thirst in the hollow way, on the day of battle. No opposition is offered to him from the hundred thousand brave hearts that are united in one place'. In the inscriptions the king usually boasts of having erected an eternal and magnificent building in the house of his father Ammon, of founding festivals, or of offering great treasures.

d. The North Exterior Wall of the Hypostyle.

We turn to the left (N.) from the entrance to the Hypostyle Hall, and in the N. wall, between the 4th and 5th rows of columns from the pylon, reach a door (Pl. d), through which we pass. The outside of the temple-wall is covered with inscriptions and martial representations. These begin on the N. part of the E. wall of the

temple, which we reach by proceeding at once to the right (E.),
afterwards returning to the N. wall in following the description
below. On the *E. Wall* the reliefs are in two divisions, an upper
and a lower. The series begins at the top, to the left of the beholder.
Here we see King Seti alighting from his chariot, in a well-wooded
country belonging to the tribes of the Remenon (Armenians) and
Retennu (Syrians). These are compelled to fell trees, which are
leafy and seem to be tall and slender; and were probably to be used
for ship-building (as Solomon used the trees felled by the people
of Hiram) or for flag-staffs. The physiognomies of the Asiatics are
distinctly characterized. The fortress appearing behind the horse
is named 'Katbar to the N. of Henuma'. In the representation below
the king is shown driving in his chariot above the slain. Beside
the horses, which drew the king on state occasions, are their names;
the king's favourite horse is here called 'Victory in Thebes'. — The
Tema en pa Kanana, the fortress Kanana, is overcome. This was
Seti's first great exploit, which he performed, as the inscription
informs us, in the first year of his reign, when he overthrew the
Shasu, the Semitic neighbours of Egypt from Zar (Pelusium) to
the fortress of Kanana (Canaan). 'His majesty was towards them
as a furious lion. They were transformed to corpses, hewn down
in their blood within their valleys'. Confused heaps of slain appear
below the fortress (to the left). An Asiatic, with a hat, prays with
upraised hands for mercy; several fall pierced with arrows. Only
one escapes from among ten thousand to proclaim in distant lands
the bravery of the king. — We now reach the *N. Wall*, where also
there is an upper and a lower series of representations. In the first
scene (to the extreme left), above, the army has penetrated far
enough to storm the fortress of Ninûa (Nineveh), in the land of the
Chaldaeans. The stream which washes the stronghold is the Tigris.
The inhabitants of the country, who are represented full face somewhat awkwardly and contrary to the usual Egyptian method,
conceal themselves among trees. The king, advancing to the attack
in his chariot (his head and that of his galloping horse have been
broken off) seizes two of them standing in their chariot, and
shoots arrows against the mounted foes. In the adjoining scene
(nearly obliterated) the king is binding captives with his own hand,
and drags others behind his chariot; to the right he appears dragging four captives with him and drawing others in two rows behind
him. A single line inscription between the rows names these
prisoners the mighty princes of the Retennu (Syrians or Assyrians).
In the representation higher up, beyond a damaged portion of the
wall, the king appears in his chariot, with his right hand raised
and holding in his left his bow and the cords to which other two
rows of prisoners (described as Retennu hart, or Upper Syrians)
are fastened. The scene takes place before the Theban triad, Ammon, Muth, and Khunsu, to whom the king also presents costly

vessels of silver, gold, khesbet (lapis-lazuli), and mafek (malachite.)

In the corresponding scenes in the lower row the king appears in his chariot (at the left end of the N. wall), with his back turned to the great ones of the Khara (Syrians). He drives past several castles, built by himself, some of them described as water-stations; beside the lower ones is a small fresh-water lake. In the second scene the king is shown in his chariot, shooting arrows against his foes, who are named 'Shasu' (Beduins). Fortified water-stations appear here also and a beacon or watch-tower of King Ramenma.

The following representation is one of the most remarkable in Egypt, for it clearly proves that a kind of *Suez Canal, i.e.* a canal dividing Africa from Egypt, existed as early as the time of Seti I. The relief represents the king on his homeward journey. His spirited horses prance along before the light chariot, which carries only the Pharoah and the heads of his slain enemies. (The king's favourite horse is named 'Ammon gives the sword'.) In his left hand the king holds the reins and his bow, and in his right the sword of victory, the scourge, and a number of cords to which pinioned enemies are fastened. Three of the latter he drags after him, and three rows of Asiatics fastened together by the neck precede the horses. The bastions with reservoirs which the procession has to pass are represented at the foot of the relief, in accordance with the peculiar Egyptian system of perspective. The desert-station immediately beside the hind hoofs of the king's horses is called Migdol of King Ramenma. (Migdol is a Semitic word meaning a fortified tower generally.) Between the hind and forelegs of the horses appears another fortress, called the castle of the lions. The train of returning warriors is separated from their Egyptian fatherland by a canal full of crocodiles. That this is not merely an arm of the Nile is indicated by an inscription above the bridge, to the right, which names it *Ta tenat, i.e.* literally 'the cutting'. The crocodiles, which do not live in salt water, show that this canal was supplied from the Nile; and the two groups of figures on the farther bank show that it marked the boundary of Egypt. In the upper group are priests and grandees, with curious nosegays in their hands, who await the Pharaoh with low obeisances; in the lower group the women raise their hands in greeting to the returning king, who brings with him their husbands and sons. The inscription runs: 'The priests, the great ones, and the princes of Upper and Lower Egypt approach to welcome the good god (*i.e.* the king) on his return from the Syrian land, with enormous booty. Never has the like happened since the time of the god', *i.e.* probably since the time of Ra. — The 'cutting' which thus divided Asia and Africa can only be the canal by means of which the early Pharaohs endeavoured to unite the Nile with the Red Sea (comp. Vol. I., p. 427), the through communication from the Red Sea to the Mediterranean being then completed by the Pelusiac arm of the Nile. The canal, frequently suffered to fall into disuse, was restored by Nekho (7th cent. B. C.) and at a later period by Darius I. Communication between the Nile and the Red Sea was maintained even under the Arabs, but it was afterwards interrupted, and not restored until the construction of the present fresh-water canal by Lesseps. The bastions which defended it are those that compelled the Jews during the Exodus to change their N.E. route at Etham or Etam, *i.e.* the fortified places (khetem), and to turn towards the Red Sea on the S. The relief, which is gradually becoming more and more indistinct, deserves careful study. The conqueror of the Semites, who is here joyfully welcomed as he approaches in his chariot, is the ancestor of the Pharaoh of the Bible narrative who perished in the Red Sea.

The victorious monarch next appears, after his arrival at Thebes. As in the upper representation, he conducts to Ammon two rows of rebellious Asiatic princes, captured in the land of the Retennu, and presents to the god magnificent vessels.

We have now returned to the door by which we left the hypostyle hall. It is adorned with the name of Ramses the Great. To the right and left are two colossal companion reliefs, in which Ammon is represented holding several rows of captives by cords, and presenting the weapons of victory to King Seti, who raises his sword against a band of foes whom he holds by the hair. The name-rings on both sides refer to the conquered tribes. The legend on the relief to the left is noteworthy: 'He smites the great ones of the Annu Mentau (with the symbols of the shepherds), all the remote regions, all lands, the Fenekhu (Phœnicians) of the sea-region, the Sati, the great circle of the green ocean' (*i.e.* the Mediterranean Sea).

We turn next to the representation on the RIGHT (W.) SIDE of the door. To the extreme right, at the corner of Pylon II., above, we see the storming of Katesh in the land of Amara (the Amorites). This is the fortress which offered such serious resistance to the army of Tutmes III., and it was the greatest obstacle to the victorious progress of the Egyptian army in the wars of Seti and his son Ramses. The scene is depicted with great vividness. The Aramaic foes of the king (the Kheta) appear both on foot and in chariots; and Seti overcomes his foes fighting also on foot and in his chariot. The foes, who wear curious peaked hoods, flee in wild confusion. The Egyptian artist here shows some appreciation of landscape effects. A forest region is represented, though somewhat crudely, with six different kinds of trees and shrubs. A herd of cattle belonging to the Kheta, terrified by the approach of the king, fly from their pasture, accompanied by the herdsmen, who toss their arms in despair. Katesh is taken, and the defenders are thrown from the walls. This is the only relief that has been preserved in the upper row.

In the second row, to the right, the king in his chariot dashes against the discomfited foe, and aims a blow at a hostile leader, distinguished by a feather. Next the king on foot deals the finishing blow with his lance to an officer, who has been brought to his knees. To the left the victorious monarch fares homeward, 'preceded by two rows of prisoners, named 'ḥi anta en tahi'. The small figure behind the chariot is the crown-prince Ramses. Then follows the presentation of the prisoners, who are called Retennu and Tahennu (*i.e.* crystal-coloured, white), to Ammon, Muth, and Khunsu, who also receive the captured gold and vessels. — Similar representations occupy the lowest row. To the right is the pursuit of the Kheta in their chariots. The inscription above compares the king to Sutekh and *Baal*, to a wolf and a lion, that roams through the by-paths, to a bull that destroys the enemy in their blood. To the left is the homeward journey. The king leads captives on foot, and behind him is a chariot containing fettered prisoners, and preceded by two rows of the same. He brings his captives to the Theban triad, who are here accompanied by the goddess Mat. There also are Retennu, brought by the king from the land of Kheta 'to fill the lordly palace of Ammon'.

e. The older E. part of the Temple of Ammon.
1. *From the Hypostyle Hall to the Sanctuary.*

We now return to the central row of lofty columns with the calyx-capitals, and follow it eastwards to *Pylon III.*, which we pass through on our way towards the sanctuary, like the more highly privileged worshippers admitted to the temple in early times. This part of the temple has been terribly destroyed, but enough has been left standing to afford an idea of the general arrangement. The picturesque effect of the ruinous scene is enhanced by the variety of artistic forms employed, and by the tall and slender shape of the largest obelisk in Egypt, rising from the midst of the ruins, and testifying to the past proud splendour of this truly royal edifice, which has been ruthlessly trodden under foot by the monotonous cycle of years and shattered by war and earthquakes. — The nearer we approach to the sanctuary the older are the parts of the temple we traverse. The inscriptions afford materials for ascertaining the date of each different portion; while the practised eye will not find it difficult to support the conclusions thus arrived at by comparison of the successive styles of art. We here find the polygonal pillar-column and the finely carved bud-columns, bearing clear and unmistakeable evidence as to the idea, to which this order owed its origin. The third pylon seems to have marked the limit of the temple under the early empire, before the gigantic buildings of the 19th Dyn. were added. The W. side of this pylon, within the great hypostyle-hall, still shows the incisions made in the wall

9*

for the support of the flag-staves. The pylons lying to the S. were
built by the kings of the 18th Dyn., and were connected with the side
of the great temple of Ammon, whence they were reached by a door
between Pylon III and Pylon IV (p. 145).

On the rear of the left side of Pylon III is a long inscription
(unfortunately imperfect at the top), recording the gifts of Amenhotep III. to the god Ammon; and to the left is the representation
of several ships, recording a festival voyage instituted by the king
in honour of the god in his naos. The sanctuary existed before the
Hyksos period, certainly under the 12th Dyn., and the conquerors
and expellers of the intruders erected in honour of Ammon successive additions, increasing in size as they receded from the
sanctuary.

On passing through the third ruined pylon into the *Central
Court* (Pl. E), we come first upon two Obelisks, of which, however,
one has been destroyed, though Pococke saw them both erect in
1738. The standing obelisk (Pl. g) is, like most others, made of
granite from the quarries of Syene (Assuân). It is 76 ft. high and
stands upon a base 6 ft. square. Only the lower portions of the
inscriptions on its faces are seriously injured. The central rows are
in larger and finer hieroglyphics than the side-rows. The former
date from the time of Tutmes I., the latter contain the names of
later appropriators of this monument. The usual formulae occur in
these inscriptions; Tutmes I., among other titles, is named the
victory-bringing Horus, who fulfils the years and enlivens the hearts.
He, 'the lovely son of the sun, erected this monument in honour of
his father Ammon, lord of the throne of the world, who is worshipped in E. Thebes ('Apet')'. In front of this obelisk are the
remains of a cubical basis, which probably served to support a
colossus. The two obelisks and the colossus marked the entrance to
the temple in the reign of Tutmes I.

Next follows *Pylon IV*, in such a ruinous condition that its original form cannot be ascertained. It dates from the time of Tutmes I., who is represented by the Osiris-columns attached to its
inner (E.) side. Only the N. door-pillar is now standing. It bears an

expresssion of homage to Ammon from Tutmes IV. $\left(\odot \text{ⵑⵑⵑⵑⵑ} \; \bigcirc \atop \text{Ⅲ} \right)$,

but beneath the arm of the king is a short inscription, in which the
Ethiopian Sabako records a restoration of the temple by himself.
A similar reference to his campaigns appears in the inscription on
the left side. Seti II. has also placed his name upon this doorway.

The doorway closing the fourth pylon on the E. fell during the
inundation of 1865. Beyond its site are a few ruined fragments of
a structure, the original arrangement of which is only to be understood on the supposition that five couples of columns stood on the
left and six couples on the right, and that two couples were removed
from each side to make room for two imposing Obelisks. The

Right Obelisk has been overthrown, and the fragments of its shattered shaft are seen lying scattered around. The top has fallen some distance to the N. The *Left Obelisk* (Pl. h), still standing, is the largest obelisk in Egypt. The total height was estimated by the engineers of Napoleon's expedition at $97^1/_2$ ft., its diameter at the base $8^1/_2$ ft., its mass 4873 cubic ft., and its weight 3673 tons.† It is made of fine red granite, and the inscriptions upon it are among the finest specimens of the grand style, which flourished at the date of its erection. Queen Hatasu Khnumt-Amen, who was regent for her brother Tutmes III. during his minority, and who erected this monument, was a true child of the Egyptian 'age of chivalry' which did not close until the reign of Amenhotep IV., the sun-worshipper. Her name will frequently be met with again, especially in her terrace-temple at Dêr el-baḥri (p. 223). She was the half-sister of two kings (Tutmes II. and Tutmes III.), and was named queen by her father Tutmes I., probably because her mother was of purer royal blood than the mother of her half-brothers. After her father's death she reigned in her own name along with Tutmes II., whom she married, and on her husband's decease she ruled on behalf of Tutmes III., who appears also to have been her son-in-law. Masculine in disposition, she carried on important wars and reared large buildings. The less energetic Tutmes II. yielded to the guardianship of his sister and wife, but Tutmes III. appears to have early compelled her to relinquish to him the crown of Lower Egypt. After her death he caused her name to be chiselled out in some places and to be replaced by his own in others — an instance of the irreverent disfigurement of monuments only too common in ancient Egypt. Hatasu Khnumt-Amen, the royal Amazon, caused herself to be represented with the ornaments of the male Pharaohs, and even with a beard. The beautifully carved central inscription, formerly inlaid with electrum or silver-gilt, contains her name alone; though she permitted her brother's name to appear at the sides. Later usurpers have not entirely spared even this noble monument. The side-inscriptions contain short sentences with the formulae usually employed for the presentation of gifts and the bestowing of the blessings of life, while the central-inscriptions refer to the dedication of the obelisks. One of the inscriptions is as follows : 'The mistress of the diadems, whose years do not wither (literally 'are green or fresh'), the victory-bringing Horus, etc., Hatasu, erected this as a monument to her father Ammon, the lord of the thrones of both lands, while she reared two obelisks to him in front of the pylon of Ammon Arsaphes, adorned with statues, and inlaid it with a profusion of electrum (silver-gilt), in order that it might shine over both lands like the sun's disc. Never since the

---

† The tallest known obelisk is that in the piazza in front of the Lateran at Rome, which is 105 ft. high. The other obelisks at Rome are smaller than the one in the text.

creation of the world has anything been made like what has been erected by the child of the sun Khnumt-Amen Hatasu, who bestows life, eternal like the sun'. The queen is uniformly referred to by the feminine pronoun, though she is represented as a man and named 'a son of the sun'. On the rectangular base of the obelisk it is recorded (N. side) that the queen erected it in seven months in the 16th and 17th years of her reign, and (E. side) that it was overlaid with gold, that the queen herself weighed out the necessary gold in sacks and bars, so that (S. side) the people on both banks beheld it glittering at sunrise. — The obelisks are enclosed by a rectangular granite wall, 12-15 ft. in height.

As we proceed towards the E., we pass another *Pylon* (Pl. V), now completely ruined, and enter a Second Colonnade, with Osiris-figures representing Tutmes I. In each of the spaces to the right and left are five pairs of columns. Between them was a central space enclosed by Tutmes, with two of the Osiris-statues embedded in the wall. An inscription informs us that this surrounding wall was raised by Tutmes III. to cover the monuments of his father Tutmes I., 'so that the monuments of his father Usertesen (12th Dyn.) and the monuments of his fathers, kings of Upper and Lower Egypt, should not be seen in presence of his own'.

On the walls of this narrow room, and on the right and left of the gateway with granite pillars which forms the opening of Pylon V, are the name-labels of the peoples conquered by Tutmes III. The S. peoples are named on the right: 'List of the S. lands, of the Anu Kenes from Khent-hun-nefer, defeated by His Majesty, he wrought havoc among them, their multitude is not known, he brought all that belonged to them as living captives to Thebes, to fill the work-house of Ammon-Ra'. Beneath are 116 name-rings of conquered tribes of the S. lands; first those of Kush (Ethiopians; the Cush of Scripture), then those of Punt (Arabians), and lastly the Libu (Libyans). On the left are the names of N. peoples, above which is an inscription: 'List of the tribes of the upper Retennu, captured by His Majesty in Magda, the miserable place, their children brought by His Majesty as living captives to the fortified place in Apt-asu (Thebes) from his first campaign, as commanded him by Ammon, who has led him by good paths'. (Two similar lists of N. and S. tribes, one of them being still more complete, are to be found on Pylon VIII, lying to the S.; comp. p. 146.)

We now traverse a kind of pronaos and enter the **Sanctuary** (Pl. F), a chamber built of hard granite. The frequent repetition of the name of Philip Aridæus on its walls might lead one at first to suppose that this apartment is a comparatively recent structure, dating from the reign of this royal puppet under whom the power was really wielded by Ptolemy I., son of Lagus (Soter). But Philip is here named only as restorer, not as founder, and certain fragments of statues found farther to the E., afford a proof, as we shall see, that a temple must have stood upon this spot even before the epoch of the Hyksos. The building of every temple, without exception, began with the construction of the sanctuary; and beyond doubt, we are here standing in front of the most ancient part of the entire temple of Ammon. The granite pillars to the right and left, on which a large flower-calyx appears between two smaller ones, also date from Tutmes III. Beyond these pillars and a small ante-chamber we reach the space usually regarded as the *Sanctuary*. It is built entirely of pink granite, and is divided into two chambers, a very uncommon arrangement, although easily explained in the present case (see below). The front chamber, opening to the W., is 19 ft. long, the hinder one, opening to the E., over 25 ft. The roof has been completely destroyed; and a slab of granite, leaning obliquely downwards, seems as though on the point of falling. The latter was adorned with stars, and traces of colour are seen both upon it and upon the walls; but the sculptures were never fully completed, and the red outlines which served as a guide to the sculptor may still be made out here and there. The holes in which the door-hinges were fixed, still show traces of verdigris, a proof that the hinges were made of copper or bronze.

The entire double-chamber and the pillars at its entrance date from the reign of Tutmes III. Mariette believed, probably with justice, that the actual sanctuary, or at least the original sanctuary of the 12th Dyn., lay behind (*i.e.* to the E. of) the granite chamber, because that would alone explain the opening at the back of the chamber. A stele preserved in the museum at Gîzeh records that the temple of Karnak was in existence as early as the close of the 11th Dyn., though then of little importance. Wilkinson found the name of Amenemha I. (12th Dyn.) on a shattered pedestal to the S. of the sanctuary; and an inscription of the 21st Dyn., discovered by E. de Rougé in the southmost court of the temple (in the S.E. angle, to the right of the entrance by the pillars) contains an announcement by a certain Amenhotep, chief priest under Ramses IX., that the sanctuary of the temple of Ammon was built in the time of User-tesen I. and then restored by himself. Two steles in the quarries of Ma'ṣara near Cairo (Vol. I., p. 405) record that King Aahmes, the conqueror of the Hyksos, caused stones to be quarried for the temple of Ammon, in the 21st and 22nd year of his reign. At all events the ancient sanctuary stood near the site of the one now be-fore us, if not actually on the same spot. Tutmes entirely rebuilt it, providing it with two doors, a peculiarity commented upon above. The W. entrance must have existed before his time, for it was turned towards the portions of the temple built by his ancestors. When Tutmes, however, added the large new struc-ture farther to the E. (p. 138), he connected it with the more an-cient holy place, dividing the latter in two and adding a W. door-way, so that it became the goal for the processions from the E., as

well as from the W., and even for those advancing through the
series of pylons on the S. — It is improbable that Cambyses caused
the destruction of this 'heart' of the worship of Ammon, if we may
use that expression, and Nectanebus, who was a mighty builder
would certainly have restored it, had it been injured. On the other
hand, nothing is more likely than that one of the later Persian
kings selected this temple for destruction after some abortive insurrection on the part of the Egyptians, in order to punish the re-
bellions province in its most sensitive part. Ptolemy Soter, who
held the reins for Philip Aridæus, could have found no easier way
to win the hearts of his new subjects than to restore the holy places
destroyed by the Persians; while to do so was to imitate Alexander the Great. In this particular case the work was not difficult,
for though new sculptures had to be provided for the adytum, its
walls were for the most part still standing. In the dedication-
inscription in the interior of the sanctuary, Philip records merely
that he had restored with granite the sanctuary which was falling
to ruin, 'which was built in the time of Tutmes III., king of
Upper and Lower Egypt'; and a fragment of the older structure,
bearing on its upper side a representation of Tutmes offering gifts
to Ammon Generator, was used as a ceiling-slab in the restoration.

The inscriptions and carvings on the *Inner Walls* of the first
chamber are neither imposing nor specially interesting. They still
exhibit traces of colour, especially of the blue pigment, which was
lavishly used to make the figures stand out more distinctly from
the reddish stone. Ammon in both his main characters (Ammon
Generator and Ammon king of the gods) receives the homage of
Philip, or rather of the representative of the royal house of Macedon,
for it is certain that Philip never entered the valley of the Nile. *Muth*
of course also appears with Ammon, and once is depicted as
embracing him, an absolutely unique representation. The traveller
will see with surprise in this sacred spot a representation of the
king, under the auspices of Khnum, catching birds with a net, and
promising to bestow his booty upon Ammon.

The *Exterior Walls* of the holy of holies are covered with numerous low reliefs and inscriptions, not easily seen on account of the
smoothness and polish of the granite. On the right side (S.) the
Pharaoh is in one place sprinkled with the water of life by Hor Hut
(Vol. I., p. 133) and Thoth, and in another receives from them the
royal crown. Elsewhere we see the boat of Ammon being brought
in solemn procession to the sanctuary, and the king offering four
calves of different colours (perhaps symbolizing the nations of the
four quarters of the globe, over which he watched as shepherd of
the people). The inscription records that Ammon-Ra, the bull (husband) of his mother, is highly pleased with the beautiful monument
which Philip has erected to him, and that he promises all kinds of
gifts to the king in return. The foundation-ceremony is also men-

tioned on this wall; and on the other (N.) we see Philip offering to the god of Thebes at a step-altar. Various nomes of Upper and Lower Egypt took place in this ceremony. Mention should be made of a large flabellum or feather-screen, which appears to conceal the figure of Ammon, *i.e.* the hidden, the veiled. This symbolically indicates that the deeper conception of the essence of the god must remain hidden from the uninitiated.

Around the sanctuary lay a number of apartments (now all more or less destroyed) in which later kings, such as Seti II., Shesheuk, and the Ethiopians Sabako and Tabarka, have inscribed their names. The last placed their inscriptions upon walls which had been built much earlier, at the latest under Tutmes III. The last-named great warrior and builder caused a list of his acquisitions through war to be carved near the holy of holies, and this has proved of the greatest value for the history of his times. Part of this inscription was taken to Paris; what remains at Karnak is much injured, though still quite legible. It is to be found in the passage to the N. of the sanctuary (Pl. i), where it begins at the E. end, is continued beyond the door, and then at the point where the wall recedes to the W. First copied by Lepsius, it has been translated by S. Birch and H. Brugsch and several others, but it is too long to allow of more than an extract being here given.

Statement of the Acquisitions of Tutmes III. The first lines below, half destroyed, contain the royal commands to undertake the placing of the inscription. In the month Pharmuthi (the day is broken off) of the 22ud year of his reign the first campaign was undertaken, from Zar (Tanis). (The victorious king on his return in the following year seems to have got rid of the guardianship of his sister Hatasu.) The march of the Egyptian army leads at first through well-known towns, as the fortress of the land of Sharohanu (Sharon), which begins at Jeraza (Jericho?), etc. On the 4th day of the month Pakhon, in his 23rd year, the king encamped before the fortress of Gazatu (Gaza?), and entered it in triumph on the 5th. He brought the accursed prince thereof to ruin, that he might extend the borders of Egypt according to the commands of his father Ammon. On the 16th Pakhon in the same year (23rd) he proceeded against the fortress Ihero, for the prince of Katesh had marched to Magda (Megiddo), for the defence of which the princes from the river of Egypt (Wâdi el-'Arish) to Mesopotamia had united themselves together, and among them the Khar (Syrians) and Katu (Galilæans), on horseback and on foot . . . . There was a choice of two ways, and the king chose that viâ Aaluna (Ajalon?). On the 19th Pakhon of the 23rd year, the king encamped before the fortress of Aaluna, near which there must have been a navigable river as Tutmes made use of one. The army proceeded through the valley of Aaluna and at the seventh (*i.e.* an auspicious) hour reached the bank of the brook of Kina (Kanah) to the S. of Megiddo.

Here the king pitched his tent and delivered an inspiriting speech to his troops. The festival of the new moon, which was also the anniversary of the coronation, was celebrated on the 21st Pakhon. The king mounted his chariot, which was richly adorned with silver-gilt, and in his war-harness resembling Horus, Mentu, the god of battles, and his father Ammon, drew up his troops in two wings and a centre, which he himself commanded. The battle began in the plain of Megiddo and the enemy was defeated. Their horses were taken, and their golden chariots with silver-work, etc. The prince of Katesh and the prince of Megiddo were drawn up into the fortress by their garments and so escaped, while the Egyptian soldiers fell upon the goods that were left behind. Great booty was captured; and the slaughtered enemies 'lay in heaps, like fish upon the shore'. The hostile camp was taken, and Tutmes built a fort to restrain the rebellious city. The record of these deeds was inscribed in a leather-roll and deposited in the temple of Ammon, in the midst of which we are now standing. The great ones of the land came to beseech mercy and to bring tribute of silver, gold, lapis-lazuli, and malachite. They brought also corn and wine, etc. The prisoners numbered 340; 83 severed hands were reckoned up; and 2041 horses, 191 colts, and 6 bulls were captured. The defeated also lost a chariot inlaid with gold, a golden chariot-box, a chariot beautifully inlaid with gold belonging to one of the allied princes, and 892 war-chariots of their worthless warriors, in all 924; a beautiful suit of iron mail belonging to one of the kings, and the armour of the King of Megiddo; 200 other suits of armour, 502 bows, and 7 silver-mounted posts from the royal tent of the enemy. — The captured oxen numbered 1929, goats 2000, and sheep 20,500. Other prisoners, including king' sons, were captured in different strong places, and were led along behind the Pharaoh, to the number of 2503. Syrian metal vessels, and other metal-work including swords, were also among the booty, to a total weight of 1784 *ten* (10 *ket* = 1 *ten* = 3¹/₅ *oz*.). Of gold and silver ware there were 966 *ten* and 1 *ket*. There was also a statue, the head of which was of gold, ivory, ebony, and sesame-wood (probably cedar), inlaid with gold. The yield of corn was enormous, amounting to 208,000 *tena* (1 tena = nearly ¹/₂ bushel) of grain, 'besides what was cut down and borne off by the soldiers of the king'. The other details of the tribute we omit. — Then follows, probably for the sake of comparison, a description of the tribute brought to the king in the 40th (24th?) year of his reign from Syria and Assyria (Assur). — The next portions of the inscription have been removed and are now in the Louvre, having been acquired partly by purchase (from the Salt Collection in 1826), and partly by gift to Prince Napoleon (the portions re-excavated by Mariette, and published by Lepsius in his *Auswahl* and by Mariette in his *Karnak*). These refer to the capture of the towns of Tunep, in the 5th campaign and 29th year of the king's reign, and Aruthut, in the 6th campaign and 30th year, in the land of Ruten, with the list of the booty and captives, including the king's sons and brothers. They also contain lists of booty, of the 31st year, from the town of An-an-rut on the lake Nes-ro-an, and of the 33rd year, from the land of Ruten and Naharain (Mesopotamia) with the town of Ni; the tribute from inhabitants of Ramenen, Sangar (with real and artificial lapis-lazuli), of the Kheta, Punt, of the 34th year from the land of Zahi, captured towns, horses, chariots, golden utensils, etc., also from the king of Ruten. Asebi (Cyprus) and Kush had also to pay a high tribute, the latter chiefly in gold. In the 35th year, in his 10th campaign, the king met and defeated the Assyrian army near Ariana. The records of the remaining campaigns and the lists of booty are still in their original position. The 13th expedition (38th year) was against the town of Anaugas, and was followed by tribute from Zahi, Asebi, Arirekh, Punt, and Wawat (to the S. of Egypt); the 14th · campaign (39th year), against the Shasu and Ruten, was marked by the destruction of the towns of Arantu and Tunep. Finally appears the command to erect a memorial tablet of all these victories.

In the same corridor as the above inscriptions, appear representations of the gifts presented to the temple by Tutmes III., including the two obelisks mentioned at p. 133.

2. *Large Building of Tutmes III.*

Continuing our progress still towards the E. beyond the sanctuary, we reach first a flat open space (Pl. G), about 80 paces wide, in which, immediately behind the sanctuary, are a few scanty relics of the earliest recognizable buildings of the temple of the 12th Dynasty. Farther on, in the axis of the sanctuary, are two square granite bases, one behind the other, being the relics of sixteen-sided columns, with the name of Usertesen I. A little farther to the E. is the doorway of the —

Great Colonnade of Tutmes III. (Pl. H). The reports of the military success of this prince, which we have just perused, telling us of the enormous wealth at his disposal, and still more the reverence which we see him paying to Ammon at every turn, prepare us to find in this temple some important building reared by him to his divine patron. The space to the W. of the ancient sanctuary had already been occupied by the edifices of his ancestors, so that, as his new building was also to maintain connection with the holy place, he was forced to build on the site to the E. We have already seen how, contrary to the usual custom, he provided the sacred granite-chamber with a second doorway (opening to the E.). The form and appearance of the courts and chambers that lay between the sanctuary and the colonnade cannot now be determined, for they have been utterly destroyed. The ancient holy place built by the kings of the 12th Dyn. was probably surrounded by two concentric walls, separated by an archway or passage. The colonnaded hall, which we enter by the central door, is 144 ft. wide and 52 ft. deep. The roof was supported by 20 columns in two rows; while 32 square pillars (14 at the sides, 4 at the ends) formed four galleries with the walls of the hall. The pillars, though not so tall as the columns, were of the same height as the walls, and with the latter supported the roofing slabs. As the middle of the hall was also roofed, a small wall, with sloping exterior and decorated with the astragal and concave cornice, rose from the roof above the pillars and walls to the height of the columns in the centre. There was thus formed a kind of clerestory, which was provided with rectangular windows, broader than they were high, in order to admit light to the hall. The central columns belong to a peculiar order, the various parts of which on the shaft and capital were indicated only by painting. They have received the name of '*inverted calyx-capitals*', because the bells or calyces were placed inverted on the smooth shafts, which were painted a dark red and adorned with vertical inscriptions, recalling the similar decoration of the central panels of the fluted polygonal columns. As the edge of the flower-calyx rested upon the end of the shaft, the latter expanded at the top, with some abruptness; and the annuli had in consequence to be placed somewhat low down on the cylindrical shaft (below the beginning of the expansion), to save them from the appearance of slipping down. The capitals are adorned with calyx- or marsh-plants, the tips of which, of course, point downwards. In place of the fruit-germ, these inverted calyces support somewhat lofty abaci, on which rests an architrave adorned with fine hieroglyphics. The fourth abacus on the E. side (now in the Louvre) bears on its N. side an inscription of the king Takelut. The method of uniting capital and shaft gives evidence of genuine artistic feeling; but the general effect of this style of column was unattractive, and after its employment here it found no admirers and was given up. — This hall contains no inscriptions of general interest. The hieroglyphic characters on the architrave are carved in the large and handsome style of the 18th Dyn., but they merely announce in the usual formal way that Tutmes III. built the hall of fine limestone and sandstone in honour of his father Ammon.

The S. part of the rear-wall of this hall in adjoined by a chamber in which seven well-made polygonal columns are still standing. Two small doorways lead from the centre of the colonnaded hall into a SANCTUARY (Pl. I), on the front of which the name Alexander may be read. This, however, does not refer to the great conqueror of Darius, but to his and Roxana's son, Alexander II., a royal puppet for whom Ptolemy I. Soter ruled. Another inscription informs us that Tutmes built this sanctuary also. The latter was probably used for special cults, while, as we have seen, the granite room of Philip Aridæus (p. 134) must be regarded as the holy of holies proper, even for this temple. The colours on the walls of this room are in good preservation. In spite of the ruins and rubbish lying about here the traveller should not omit to glance into the chambers of the rear colonnaded hall. One of them contains an interesting representation. The god Seth (Vol. I., p. 132; here half defaced) of Nub (Kôm Ombo) teaches Tutmes II. to shoot with the bow, while Horus instructs him in the use of the lance. The hostile twin-brothers bestow upon the Pharaoh strength to win victory, which is symbolized by the vulture of victory hovering above the group.

The *Columns* which are still standing in the hinder portions of the temple are of interest as specimens of the favourite orders under the 18th Dynasty. Near the centre four beautifully sculptured papyrus-bud columns stand in a row from E. to W., and a few paces to the N.W. are two polygonal columns united by an architrave. In Room Y, excavated by Mariette, are some interesting representations of animals and plants, which, as the accompanying inscriptions inform us, were transplanted from Retennu (Assyria) to Egypt by Tutmes III., in the 25th year of his reign.

We now turn to the S., to the *Side-Building* of the temple of Ttmes III. (Pl. K), where there are 9 chambers adjoining each other, each opening to the N. The two at the E. end are halls, each with two columns to support the roof, while of the other seven chambers three are completely ruined. Opposite the westernmost of these lay the chamber which contained the celebrated *Karnak Tablet of the Kings* (Vol. I., p. 85), transferred to Paris by Prisse d'Avennes and now in the Bibliothèque Nationale. Only about 40 of the

60 cartouches which it included, are now legible. Besides the celebrated kings of the earliest dynasties, the series embraces especially the kings of the 11th Dyn. (the Antef) and of the 12th, 13th, and 17th (conquerors of the Hyksos) Dyn., who all probably resided at Thebes. The names, however, are not in chronological order.

Omitting for the present the lake (p. 144) to the S. of this row of chambers, we return to the middle of the building and quit it by the girdle-wall on the E. Immediately behind the wall Ramses II. built a *Hall* (Pl. L), adorned with caryatides, now completely ruined. About 45 paces farther E., and connected with this hall, is a small *Temple* (Pl. M), built by the same Pharaoh, but so ruined as to present little of interest. Caryatides were employed here also; and two papyrus-bud columns may be mentioned, on which the place of the usual cubical abaci is occupied by tolerably high fragments of earlier polygonal shafts, utilized in the same manner as the Arabs used the fragments of Greek and Roman temples. Beyond these ruins, and still farther to the E., is the well-preserved *Pylon VI.* (62 ft. high), which must be regarded as the main entrance to the great temple of Ammon for those approaching from the E. Outside it traces of the girdle-wall of the temple, built of bricks of Nile clay, may still be found. This eastmost pylon has few sculptures, but the inscriptions indicate that it was erected by Nekht-nebf, *i.e.* Nectanebus II., who had not time to finish its decoration. This prince, who ascended the throne of the Pharaohs during the Persian era and waged successful wars, especially in Upper Egypt against the satraps of the Asiatic invaders, found both courage and means, hard pressed and threatened as he was, to erect important buildings not only here but also on the island of Philae and elsewhere. Thus the pylon which limited the temple of Ammon to the E. may be regarded as a tangible proof of the obstinate independence of the Egyptians. — This pylon is 510 yds. distant from the first (W.) pylon.

If we turn to the right (S.) outside the E. pylon of Nectanebus II. we soon reach a small building bearing the cartouches of Ramses III. and Ramses IV. To the N. of the pylon lies a recently-excavated small *Temple*, in which occur the names of Ameniritis, sister of Sabako I. (25th Dyn.) and consort of King Piankhi, and of their daughter Shep-en-apt, who married Psammetikh I. of the 26th Dynasty.

f. The S. Side of the Temple of Ammon.

We now return towards the W., re-enter the hypostyle court of the great temple by the door (Pl. d) mentioned at p. 127, traverse the court from N. to S. between the 4th and 5th rows of columns (reckoned from the second pylon), and quit it by the door at Pl. e. If we turn and face the outside of the S. wall of the temple, we find, to the left, representations of the towns of Palestine captured by Sheshenk (described on p. 123), and, to the right, various military representations, referring to the campaigns of Ramses II. against the Kheta (Aramæans). The Epic of Pentaur, referring to the same

campaigns, which we have already met with on the pylon at Luxor
(p. 112) and which will be mentioned again when we visit the
Ramesseum (p. 161), occurs also here in long but not easily accessible lines of hieroglyphics. About 40 ft. to the right (E.) of the
door through which we quitted the hypostyle, a short wall projects
at right angles from the wall of the great temple, bearing a most
interesting and important inscription, containing the *Treaty of Peace*
destined to put an end to the wars between the Egyptians and the
Asiatics.

This is the most ancient international treaty extant in the world, and it is
as remarkable for its contents as for its form, which is so conceived in the
essential points that modern documents of a similar aim differ from it
only in the greater conciseness of their expressions. The bottom of the
inscription is at present concealed by rubbish. The treaty is dated the
21st Tybi in the 21st year of King Ramses II. Miamun, in the town of
Tanis, *i.e.* the Ramsestown. The Kheta prince caused the treaty to be
engraved on a silver table and sent an ambassador to seek peace. The
document proper, divided into paragraphs and translated by the eminent
French Egyptologist F. Chabas, begins as follows: 'Formerly and for a
long period the mighty king of Egypt and the prince of the Kheta lived
in good understanding (God grant that hostility never again exist between
them). Nevertheless he declared war against the great king (Seti I.) of
Egypt, in the time of Mautnur, my brother, prince of the Kheta. But
from to-day and from this day Khetasar, prince of the Kheta, makes a
treaty in order to arrive at a lasting understanding. May Ra, may Seth
lend them endurance, as well for Egypt as for the land of the Kheta
(Aramæa), so that hostility may never again arise between them. — The
following points were agreed upon: Khetasar, prince of the Kheta, unites
with Ramses Miamun, the mighty king of Egypt, to cause to exist between
them good peace and good alliance from this day onwards forever. He
shall be allied with me, he shall be at peace with me; and I, I shall be
allied with him, and I, I shall be at peace with him forever'. After a
brief historical retrospect, the treaty goes on: 'The prince of the Kheta
will never again invade Egypt to carry off anything whatever out of it,
and Ramses Miamun, the mighty king of Egypt, will never invade the
land of the Kheta, to carry off anything whatever out of it'. Then, after
another historical retrospect: 'When enemies turn against the land of
Ramses Miamun, the mighty king of Egypt, he will send to the prince of
the Kheta the message, 'Come and unite thyself with my might against
them'. The prince of the Kheta will be at the disposal of the king of Egypt
and will smite his enemies. If the prince of the Kheta does not take the
field in person, he will send his foot-soldiers and war chariots to smite
the enemies of the king of Egypt .... and vice versâ (with repetition
of the above paragraph). — Then follows a remarkable convention by
which the parties to the treaty bind themselves not to use force in preventing
skilled workmen from passing from one country into the other. The gods
and goddesses, the Baalim of the land of the Kheta (translated 'Seth'),
Astarte, and a 'thousand' local deities, mountains, and rivers are invoked
as witnesses by the Asiatics, while the Egyptians invoke Ammon Ra, Seth,
the warlike gods and goddesses, the mountains and rivers of Egypt, the
shore of the Mediterranean, the wind, and the clouds. These powers are
to punish the breaker of the treaty; while to him who keeps it they shall
grant life, to him and to his house, his estate, and his servants. Next
follow two remarkable articles in which the contracting parties bind
themselves mutually to extradite criminals; though, by a condition which
speaks highly for the civilization reached by both nations, his crime
'shall not be permitted to raise itself' against the extradited criminal, *i.e.*
the criminal process against him shall be suspended, and no harm shall
be done to his house, or to his wife, or to his children; he shall
also not be punished in the eye, mouth, or foot, and moreover no

accusation of crime shall be brought against him. The last legible lines of the inscription are as follows: 'On the front of the silver table is the figure of the statue of Seth, embracing the statue of the prince of the Kheta'. The encircling inscription runs: 'O figure of Seth, king of heaven and earth, grant that the treaty which Khetasar, prince of the Kheta etc.....'

II. The Northern Buildings.

A visit to the ruins to the N. of the temple of Ammon need not detain the traveller for any long time, unless his object be to decipher the inscriptions and to gather from them philological or historical information. They are in bad preservation; and the N.E. group, the temple of the war-god Mentu, is in especial so completely ruined that it is difficult to reconstruct its ground-plan, although in size it was originally as large as the temple of Khunsu (p. 148). The traveller who has little time at his disposal, or who must proceed with the steamer, may content himself with a glance at the great N. girdle-wall of Nile-bricks, and at the gate of the Ptolemies.

Beginning at the E. Pylon of Nectanebus (p. 141), we skirt the girdle-wall of the great temple of Ammon, first to the N. and then to the W. (left), until we see upon the right or N. side of our path another girdle-wall of Nile-bricks. Within this lies a ruined *Temple* (Pl. N), the axis of which lies S.W. and N.E. Like the N. pylon (see below) it was dedicated to *Mentu*, the god of war, and is frequently mentioned on demotic tiles (ostraca). Stretching N.E. from this building is an avenue of sphinxes, which we reach on passing through the door of a well-preserved pylon. Little now remains of the temple, which dates from the time of Amenhotep III. of the 18th Dyn. (who also erected two obelisks, as appears from a fragmentary inscription found here), though it was subsequently several times enlarged between the reign of Ramses IV. and the epoch of the Ptolemies, especially by Ptolemy IV. Philopator. Ptolemy II. Philadelphus and Ptolemy III. Euergetes have recorded their names here, and there is also a stone bearing the name of 'Ramses'. The earlier sculptures and architectural fragments are of great beauty; and columns with Hathor capitals were also employed. The above-mentioned *Pylon* (Pl. VII), the most N. part of the edifice now remaining, was founded by Ptolemy II. At its foot is a list of nomes, and higher up are numerous other inscriptions. The fellâhin boys are shy of accompanying travellers to this spot towards evening, as it is said to be haunted by an 'Afrit or devil. It is called by the natives *Bâb el-'Abîd*, or gate of the negro-slaves, probably on account of some of the representations on its walls.

From the pylon we proceed to the S.W., passing the remains of a Ptolemaic temple (Pl. O), of which the staircase is still to be seen, to another *Temple*, consisting of six small chambers (Pl. k to p). The second from the W. (Pl. l) contains the name of Ameniritis, with that of her brother Sabako. The fine alabaster statue of the queen, now in the museum at Gizeh, was found here. The temple *n* shows the rare name of Nepherites (29th Dyn.); *o* dates from the 22nd Dynasty. The names of Taharka, Osorkon II., and

queen Karomat, and on the wall of the second chamber, of Takelut II. and his consort Koromama, may be read here. The last
chamber (Pl. p) dates from Nectanebus I.

'.. On the other side of the girdle-wall, *i.e.* over the hill, is another.
Building (Pl. P), erected by Tutmes III., but where also are found
the names of King Horus, Sabako, Tabarka, and several of the Ptolemies, including Philometor and Neos Dionysus. This temple was
dedicated to *Ptah* and *Hathor*, whose priests are represented. In a
chamber, which may be described as the *Pronaos*, are traces of the
staircase leading to the roof, now fallen in. Here also are two polygonal columns, which, taken in connection with dedicatory inscription, indicate that the erection of the temple was begun under the
18th Dynasty. As we again approach the N. wall of the hypostyle
of the great temple and the door by which we issued to view the
battle-reliefs of Seti I. (p. 127), we pass, a little to the N. of the
latter, two small ruined temples (Pl. Q) of the 26th Dynasty. The
princes of this illustrious line were less able to rear elaborate buildings at Thebes in proportion as they devoted the means at their
disposal to building magnificent temples in honour of the gods of
Memphis and still more of Saïs, their residences in Lower Egypt.
These little temples, now surrounded by the ruined huts of a deserted Arab village, were, according to the inscriptions, built by
Queen Ankhnes, who here appears with Psammetikh III. (perhaps
her son?) and with her husband Aahmes. Ankhnes was the daughter
of Psammetikh II. To the right of the entrance and in the doorway
to the left of the smaller temple is the queen accompanied by her
young chamberlain Sheshonk, ascion of the Bubastites of the 22nd
Dyn., in whose veins flowed royal blood. Nitocris, wife of Psammetikh II., also appears in the second doorway of the interior. Her
magnificent sarcophagus is now in the museum at Gîzeh, while that
of Queen Ankhnes is in the British Museum.

III. The Southern Buildings.

The short projecting wall, on which is the treaty mentioned at
p. 142, is part of the series of courts and pylons which connected
the temple of Ammon with that of Muth, lying to the S. Before
inspecting this remarkable part of the great temple, we find our way
through the ruins to the somewhat more distant **Lake**. The Arabs
name this *Birket el-Mallâheh* or *Lake of the Salt-pit*, as the water has
become saline and undrinkable through infiltration. It is known
that each temple formerly possessed a *Sacred Lake*, and there is no
doubt that in antiquity the golden boat of the god used to float upon
the water of this pond, kept pure and fresh. The banks were anciently faced with hewn stones, and traces of these are still to be
seen on the W., S., and especially on the N. or nearest side, though
at most points they were covered by rubbish in the course of ages.
Between this lake and the part of the main temple that enclosed the

granite sanctuary (p. 134) are a few half-ruined chambers forming
a kind of annexe to the S. wall of the temple, and partly constructed
of alabaster, a substance rarely used for building. The ruins
nearest the lake date from the reign of Tutmes III., those immediately adjoining the temple-wall from the reign of the Ethiopian
Tabarka. A square apartment, decorated with paintings of which
the colours are still vivid, displays some curious deities, probably
Ethiopian, but only the upper parts of the paintings are now visible.

We now return to the doorway opening to the S., between the
third and fourth pylons (p. 132), upon which is the cartouche of
Ramses IX. ☉ ⌙ *Ra nefer ka.* To the S.W. of this point, in an
irregular line and at varying distances from each other, are *Pylons
VIII, IX, X,* and *XI.* From the last of these an avenue of sphinxes
(now concealed by a small wood) stretches to the temple of Muth.
Pylon XI is turned towards this avenue, but the pylons X, IX, and
VIII, succeeding each other towards the N., gradually effect the
transition to the great temple of Ammon by their position and the
angle they stand at with reference to the S. wall of the great temple;
for, as will be seen from the Plan, none of them is exactly parallel
with that wall. The four pylons are connected with each other by
side-walls running at irregular angles, and thus enclosing four
courts, which, however, are no longer clearly defined owing to gaps
in the walls. Through these four gateways passed the ancient processional route, which began at the temple of Muth, in which were
the statues of Sekhet (p. 148), and ended at the temple of Ammon
in the space with the two obelisks (p. 132), which may be regarded
as the vestibule of the sanctuary.

The series of four *Courts* between the pylons, which we now
visit, had an aggregate length of 310 yds. (not reckoning the sphinx-
avenue). It was begun in the early times of the 18th Dyn. (Tutmes I.), and was afterwards several times enlarged and adorned.
Beginning at the gateway of Ramses IX. (see above), we have on
our right the fragment of wall (probably dating from Seti I.) on
the W. side of which is the famous treaty (p. 142), and on the
left the wall running to meet Pylon VIII, and probably dating like
that pylon from Tutmes III. On the front of this latter wall king
Merenptah, son of Ramses II., caused an inscription of great interest to be carved.

From this we learn that the king victoriously opposed the Libyans
and their allies, the islanders of the Mediterranean, whose later expeditions
against Egypt are recorded in the inscriptions at Medinet Habu (p. 177).
Under his father the Egyptians had advanced into Asia; now, the peoples
to the W. and N. of the Nile valley, the Libyans and Maxyans, and with
them Lycians, Sardinians, Sicilians, Achæans, and a tribe named Pulesta
(more probably Philistines than Pelasgians), dare to invade the Delta and
to dwell there 'like previous kings' (*i.e.* probably the Hyksos). Merenptah
assembles an army, and encouraged by a dream, defeats the allies. The
number of the slain and the most valuable portions of the booty are de-

tailed. The triumphant king does not forget his father Ammon, in whose temple he causes the record of his victory to be inscribed.

Though Tutmes III. erected *Pylon VIII*, Merenptah afterwards appropriated it to himself. On the side to the left of the beholder the S. tribes, and on the right side, the N. tribes are depioted as captives, with their name-rings.

The lists seem to have been edited three times. At first there were on the left only 47 names, written from left to right, and on the right 52 names, written from right to left. Subsequently three rows, written in the opposite direction, were added to the three lowest rows — on the left the name-rings 48-70, 71-94, 95-117, and on the right the name-rings 53-74, 75-97, 98-119 — so that 117 S. tribes and 119 N. tribes were recorded, corresponding with the two other long lists of tribes by Tutmes III. on Pylon VI, in the great temple of Ammon, and on the S. side of Pylon VII. At a still later date (possibly not till Merenptah's reign) 152 name-rings were added at the ends on the left (S. tribes) and 240 name-rings on the ends on the right (N. tribes).

On the right (N.) end of the N. wing of Pylon VIII is a short inscription of the 21st Dyn., relating to the restoration of the rights of a Princess Ramaka. The other (S.) side of the pylon consists of two portions, some distance apart, representing Tutmes III. seizing prisoners in presence of Ammon. On the left (W. side) are the N. tribes, described as the great ones of the Retennu, of all the remote (seta) lands, of the Fenekhu (Phœnicians). On the right (E.) side are the peoples of the S. Before the centre of the pylon are remains of statues of Tutmes III.

The next court is much smaller than the courts between the pylons farther to the S. The well-preserved *Second Pylon* (Pl. IX) is interesting as the most ancient part of the entire building. It was founded by Tutmes I., and its gateway was provided with inscriptions by his sons, Tutmes II. and Tutmes III. Tutmes I. is seen on the N. side (left) worshipping the triad of Thebes; and beside this representation is an interesting poetic inscription (damaged) extolling the might and the victories of this prince. Above is the boat of Ammon Ra borne by priests, in front of which is Tutmes II. receiving the symbol of life from the lion-headed Uarthekau (the great sorceress), behind whom is the goddess Hathor of Denderah, pouring water from a vessel. To the left of this King Seti I. appears twice before Ammon Ra, who is followed by fifteen deities in three rows of five. On the right side of the pylon, towards the top, is a similar boat, beneath which are representations of Ramses III. Hak an. On the S. side of the pylon, to the right, is Amenhotep II., smiting a band of enemies. As this king was unable to complete the inscriptions on the left side, Seti I. took advantage of the vacant space to commemorate his name. *Four Colossi* originally stood before this pylon. Those to the right have disappeared, but those still extant to the left are highly interesting. The huge yellowish torso immediately to the left of the door has the name of Tutmes II. on the girdle; and in an inscription on its back Tutmes III. announces that he erected the statue in the

42nd year of his reign in honour of his father Tutmes I. The
skill shown in the working of the sandstone conglomerate used for
the statue is noteworthy. Pebbles as large as bullets occur in the
stone, yet the surface has a wonderfully smooth polish. The other
colossus, which belongs to Amenhotep II., is made of white limestone of a fine grain. The head is still *in situ* but the face is dis-
figured. An adjoining *Stele*, with a much defaced inscription, records that Amenhotep II. led the Egyptian army as far as Niniveh.
On the E. side of Pylon IX is an invocation of some length to Ammon
from the high-priests Roma and Roi, in the reign of Seti II. On
the outside of the E. wall between Pylons VIII and IX and on Pylon IX next to the small doorway, are inscriptions by Amenhotep,
high priest of Thebes in the time of Ramses IX. (Neferkara), in
which he speaks of the restoration of a then ruined building that
had been erected by Usertesen I. (12th Dyn.). Close to Pylon VIII
is a small *Chapel* (Pl. q).

The next *Pylon* (Pl. X) has collapsed, leaving fragments of walls
standing to the extreme right and left, separated by a saddle-shaped
depression. From the shattered inscriptions we learn that King
Horus founded this pylon, though Ramses II. afterwards unjustly
placed his own name upon it and upon two granite statues no longer
extant. The names of Ramses IV. (Hak ma) and above it Ramses VI.
(Nefer hak an) are also found, on the horizontal band on the N. side
of the pylon. King Horus and Ramses VI. are represented on the
W. side of the connecting wall. The ruins are most easily skirted
on the W. side, and beyond them is a spacious *Court*, bounded on
the S. by the *Last Pylon* (Pl. XI). The wings of this huge edifice,
constructed of hewn sandstone, have collapsed, but the central doorway of granite is still standing. Four blocks of granite, on the right
of the doorway and facing the court, are decorated with a *Relief*,
representing with remarkable vivacity King Horus approaching the
god with two libation-vessels. An inscription within the granite
portal informs us that this king, who ruled at the close of the 18th
Dyn., built the pylon, using for that purpose some hewn stones
bearing the name of Amenhotep IV. (Khu-en-aten), the strange
sun-worshipper whom we met at Tell el-Amarnah (p. 23). From this
it has been concluded that a building erected at Karnak by the
schismatic was destroyed soon after his death. In front of the N.
side of the pylon are two headless limestone colossi. Ramses II.
placed his name upon these as well as upon the pylon; and some
priests of Ammon of the 21st Dyn. have also commemorated themselves upon the latter. — On the *W. Wall*, uniting Pylons XI and
X is a representation, restored by Horus, of the *Sacred Boat
of Ammon*, which must have been carried in solemn procession
through the series of pylons now engaging our attention. The *E.
Wall*, which bears an inscription to the effect that King Horus conquered Punt (Arabia), is interrupted by a building (Pl. S) in which

square pillars are used in place of the more usual columns. These simple artistic forms themselves suggest an early origin for the edifice, and the inscriptions record that it was built by Amenhotep II. and III. A gallery is adjoined by a hall with 20 pillars, and that again by several apartments arranged in a manner not elsewhere found. On several of the pillars, whose unadorned capitals are striking, the king appears before Ammon. It is not easy to determine the purpose of this building. It cannot have been a palace. Perhaps it contained stables for the sacred animals of the different deities, or was the depository for the sacrificial gifts presented within the first pylon. Perhaps Ammon's guard of honour, which is frequently mentioned and which had to watch over the temple, was quartered here; or it may have been used by the priests on duty for the day as a temporary resort. Various reasons prevent us from regarding it as the actual abode either of the kings or of the attendants on the gods. — To the S. of Pylon XI is the base of a *Statue of King Horus*, the lower part of which dates from Amenhotep III.

Beyond the pylon, ·which we skirt rather than pass through, is the *Avenue of Sphinxes*, bounding the processional route that led to the S. buildings. To the E. of the avenue two *Chambers*, painted in bright colours, were excavated by Mariette. They belong to a temple of Osiris-Ptah, who is here represented as worshipped by Tabarka and by Amontanut, apparently a contemporary king (the Urdamani of Assyrian inscriptions).

The avenue leads to the temple of Muth (see below), while it is connected by a branch with the sphinx-avenue leading from the temple of Khunsu to Luxor (comp. p. 116). In a straight direction the first-mentioned avenue is terminated by a *Gate* (Pl. r), built by the Ptolemies, in the N. side of a girdle-wall enclosing a horse-shoe shaped lake. In front of this lake stood the **Temple of Muth** (Pl. T), built by Amenhotep III., and now so completely ruined that it is difficult to determine its original arrangement. To the right and left of the gate of Ptolemy Philadelphus (which bears a beautiful hymn to the goddess Muth), and both without and within the girdle-wall, were numerous lion-headed *Figures of Sekhet*, many of which have already found their way to European museums (*e.g.* at Turin). A second gate bears the cartouches of Seti II. and Set-nekht. In a small *Apartment* on the E. side of the temple is a record of a restoration of the temple by Mentuemhat, priest of Ammon, in the time of Tabarka. To the W. of the horse-shoe lake are the remains of a small *Temple* (Pl. U), built by Ramses III., who here recorded his victory over the land of Tahi and the animals and other rich booty which he thereby obtained.

IV. The Temple of Khunsu.

About 150 paces to the W. of the last pylon (p. 147) passed in our way towards the S., lies the beautiful and interesting *Temple

of Khunsu (Pl. V), the portal of which we have already seen on our
way from Luxor to the river-front of the great temple of Ammon.
An avenue of sphinxes, approximately parallel with the above-mentioned avenue between Pylon XI and the temple of Muth, leads to
the slender Ptolemaic Pylon XII and beyond it to the temple of
Khunsu proper, which lies a little farther N. The temple is beautifully proportioned, in many places adorned with remarkable care,
and in various respects of great interest. It was erected by Ramses III. in honour of *Khunsu*, *i.e.* the god who represents, so to
speak, the youthful Ammon in the triad of Thebes. Elsewhere, it
may here be noted, Khunsu is conceived of almost as the moon-god
(with the child's lock of hair on his temple and the crescent-moon
on his head), and thus identified with Thoth - Hermes. Just as
Ammon is called the soul of Ra, so Khunsu is to be regarded as the
spiritual quintessence of the earlier moon-god, and may be named,
like Thoth, 'the representative of the spirit, the *ratio interna* of all
things'. As *Pa ar sekher* or 'plan-maker' he guides the deliberations
of mortals, and he becomes also the divine physician (*Khunsu nefer
hotep*, 'the good helper'), who considerately restores the sick to
health. Cynocephali, sacred to Khunsu as well as to Thoth, were
kept here. — In the great *Harris Papyrus* Ramses III. says of this
temple : 'I built a house in Thebes for thy son Khunsu, of good hewn
stone, of sandstone, black stone, its doors covered with gold, adorned
with electrum like the celestial horizon'. In the same document it is
named *Pa* (house) *Ramses hak an* in *Pa Khunsu* with 264 persons;
and afterwards : 'Persons whom he (Ramses III.) gave to *Pa Khunsu
in Uas Neferhotep, Hor lord of the wide heart,* 249'. There thus
appear to have been two different temples erected to Khunsu. The
inscriptions inform us that he had not time to finish the 'House
of Khunsu', but was obliged to leave later rulers to complete the
Peristyle Court and the *Pylon*. The last was erected by the priest-
king Pinozem, son of Piankhi, of the 21st Dyn.; but Alexander II.
is also commemorated in the doorway to the peristyle court. This
court itself has on three sides a double row of papyrus-bud columns,
six in each row. From the inscriptions we gather that after portions of this building were built by various Ramses of the 20th Dyn.,
the priest-king Horhor, predecessor and perhaps grandfather of Pinozem, contributed to its decoration. Most of what we know of the
kings of the 21st Dyn. is derived from the inscriptions here.

The close connection which must at that time have existed between
Asia and the Nile valley is proved by a *Stele*, found in the temple of
Khunsu and now preserved in the Bibliothèque Nationale at Paris. Upon
this one of the last kings of the 20th Dyn. records that he married the
daughter of a tributary prince, made her his queen, and in order to cure
her younger sister who was possessed by devils (*i.e.* insane) sent first a
physician and then a statue of Khunsu to Bekhten. After the healing god had
done what was expected of him, the father-in-law of the Pharoah detained
the statue until he was warned in a dream to send it back to Egypt in
its sacred boat.

The peristyle court is succeeded by a narrow *Hall*, extending

across the entire breadth of the temple and having its roof supported
by eight columns in two rows with calyx-capitals. This was at least
adorned, if not built, by Ramses XIII.; while the door bears the
cartouche of Nekhnebf I. The calyx-capitals are comparatively low,
and their edges are bent out to a remarkable extent. Beyond this
hall are the rooms of the *Sanctuary.* Here, especially in the rooms
to the E., are a series of deeply carved inscriptions, some of which
are of great scientific importance though of little general interest.
Ramses IV. (Ḥak mā) and Ramses XIII. occur here, and several
Ptolemaic princes have carved their names. Various Greeks, of
late date, have also left their names in longer or short inscriptions,
placed beside representations of foot-prints (indicating that they
had visited the spot as pilgrims), a habit illustrated also at Philae
and elsewhere (*e.g.* Lesbos). Isis and Khunsu (besides Thoth)

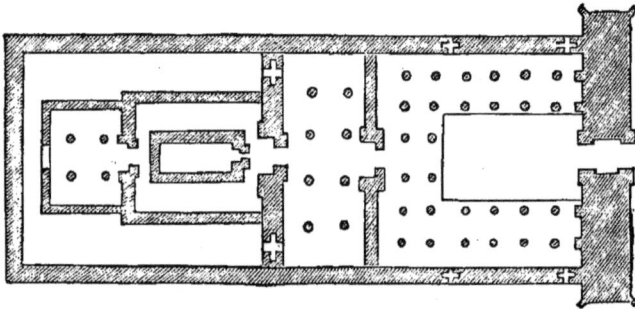

were the gods to whose shrines pilgrimages were most frequently
made in search of health. It is worth noting that the temple of
Khunsu contains the only representation of circumcision yet discovered in Egypt. Not only Khunsu, but also the other gods of the
triad to which he belonged were worshipped in this temple; both
Muth, called 'the great' and the 'mistress of Ashru', and Ammon-
Ra, 'lord of the throne of both worlds in E. Thebes, ruler of
heaven, and king of all gods'. Of the dedication-inscriptions,
which abound in wearisome profusion on the architraves and elsewhere, one, of the time of Ramses XIII., will serve as an example:
'The living good god (*i.e.* the Pharaoh) raised this building in the
house of his father Khunsu, the lord of Thebes, and built this temple
of good limestone and sandstone in workmanship for long duration'.

V. The Small Temple of Apet.

The *Temple of Apet* (Pl. W), once occupied by Champollion as
a dwelling, lies close to the W. wall of the temple of Khunsu. It
is now used as a depository for the smaller monuments found at
Karnak, the best of which are periodically transferred to the Egyptian museum at Gîzeh. *Diab Timsah,* who lives opposite (a boy
will summon him), opens the temple on request. Among less interesting objects a beautifully executed torso of Tutmes III. is

preserved here. The roof of the *First Room* is supported by two
Ptolemaic columns, with Hathor-masks on the abacus. To the right
and left of this wide hall are two rooms, and behind are three
others, the middle one of which gives access to the *Sanctuary*. The
inscriptions on the walls owe their origin to the Ptolemies; the
earliest, as the dedication-inscription also informs us, to Ptolemy IX.
Euergetes II., and to Cleopatra, his sister and wife. The pregnant
hippopotamus-goddess Apet was the goddess of births. Her finely
executed statue of serpentine, found in the ruins of the ancient
city, is now in the museum at Gizeh. It dates from the 26th Dynasty. The inscriptions and representations refer largely to Osiris,
whose birth was commemorated here, and to the gods associated
with him. On the outside of the temple-wall and on the walls adjoining it are found the names of Ptolemy Auletes and the emperor
Augustus. A list of nomes, also found here, is unfortunately much
damaged.

EXCURSION TO MEDAMÛT, only to be undertaken when there is abundance of time; 4-5 hrs. are necessary. The site is reached after 1½ hr.'s
rapid riding. We proceed first to the E. sphinx-avenue of Karnak, where
the road diverges to the right, along a large embankment. It then turns
to the left and runs mostly along the edge of ditches, frequented, especially
in December, by wild fowl.

The Temple of Medamût, at one time a large and beautiful edifice, is
now so completely ruined that even its ground-plan cannot be traced. The
village, a kind of suburb of Thebes, was called *Tèman* and lay to the N.
of the temple. Month of Thebes was the god chiefly worshipped here, but
Buto (uazi) and Apet were also revered. The erection of this temple dates
from the time of Amenhotep II., of the 18th Dynasty. His name occurs
on the large granite pillars which are still standing and which probably
formed part of the *Sanctuary*. Numerous blocks of granite lie scattered
around. The sanctuary was adjoined by a large edifice, lying approximately from E. to W. Much farther to the W. was a *Pylon*, facing the
river, but now destroyed, leaving nothing but a heap of blocks of sandstone. Various fragmentary inscriptions in a good style inform us that
it was built by Seti I. and Ramses II. Under the Ptolemies an addition
was made to the earlier temple, including the *Colonnade*, which is now
the most conspicuous and most interesting feature of the ruins. Five
columns are still standing. Four of these, on which still rests the stone
architrave, appear to have bounded a now destroyed peristyle court and
to have formed the first row of columns in a hypostyle hall, which cannot
have existed before the time of the Ptolemies. The other column is the
only relic of the second row. Both this and the two bud-columns (to the
left) in the first row appear to belong to the 18th Dyn.; the two latter
certainly did, for their sculptured shafts and capitals clearly indicate that
the artistic idea which dictated their form still retained a vigorous
freshness at the time of their erection. On the other hand the late elaborate plastic decoration of the calyx-capitals of the other two columns
more to the right, the curious closing of the intercolumniations by means
of barrier-like walls, half as high as the shafts, and crowned with a concave
cornice, and the treatment of the doors, whose absent covering was merely
indicated on both sides by erections with concave cornices, would in themselves be proofs that the building was not erected before the epoch of the
Ptolemies, even if the inscriptions did not contain the same information.
Bees have built their nests in many of the deep hieroglyphics which com-
pose the inscriptions, but we can still distinguish the names of Ptolemy IX.
Euergetes II., the captor and destroyer of Thebes, and those of Lathyrus

and Auletes. Antoninus Pius bestowed some attention on the decoration of this edifice, the picturesque remains of which show that even in the age of the Ptolemies the practice of using ancient columns for new buildings was well understood, a practice which became very common under the Arabs. The use of other ancient fragments of buildings (especially hewn blocks of stone) was frequent even in very early times.

As we return, we may once more walk through the temple of Karnak, a digression which will not add more than $^1\!/_2$ hr. to the day's expedition. If the traveller have made an early start, he may lunch in the hypostyle hall of Karnak, under the shadow of the largest columns in the world, where the destroyers of the temple and previous travellers have provided seats in the shape of blocks of stone.

B. THE WEST BANK AT THEBES.

Passengers by the three-weeks' tourist-steamers devote the 1st and 3rd (Cook) or 2nd and 3rd (Gaze) day of their stay at Thebes to the West Bank; those by the four-week's steamers the 2ud and 4th (Cook) or 3rd and 4th (Gaze) day; arranging in each case to spend the first day in a visit to the sepulchral temple of Seti I. and the Tombs of the Kings (RR. 19, 20), and the second in visiting the Ramesseum, Shêkh 'Abd el-Kurnah, Dêr el-Medineh, and Medînet Habu (RR. 13-18). A different arrangement is recommended on p. 102, for a three day's stay at Thebes, according to which the first day's visit to the W. bank is devoted to the Colossi of Memnon, Medinet Habu, Dêr el-Medineh, Shêkh 'Abd el-Kurnah (RR. 12-18), and the next day to the sepulchral temple of Seti I. and the Tombs of the Kings (RR. 19, 20). If five days are spent at Thebes, three should be devoted to the W. bank, the first being occupied by the Colossi of Memnon, the temple of Medinet Habu, and Dêr el-Medineh (RR. 12, 15, 17), the second by the Ramesseum, the tombs of Shêkh 'Abdel-Kurnah, the temple of Dêr el-baḥri, etc. (RR. 13, 18, 21), and the third by the Temple of Seti I. and the Tombs of the Kings (RR. 19, 20), with which Cook's and Gaze's tourists begin.

The ensuing description follows the distribution of time suggested on p. 102 for a three day's visit to Thebes.

The following points may be visited in a *single* day (the 2nd of our stay in Thebes), though not without considerable fatigue: 1. *Colossi of Memnon; 2. *Ramesseum; 3. Tombs of Kurnet Murraï; 4. *Medinet Habu; 5. Tombs of the Queens and Dêr el-Medineh; 6. Tombs of Shêkh 'Abd el-Kurnah. A little time may be saved by beginning at the Ramesseum, and thence proceeding to the Colossi of Memnon, Medînet Habu, etc.; but it is better to visit the Colossi first, for they are at no time so impressive as when seen in the early morning.

An *early* start should be made. *Guides, donkeys,* etc., see p. 103. If the dhahabîyeh has been anchored at Luxor and not beside the W. bank (p. 101), it will be necessary to cross in a boat to the island opposite Luxor. Donkeys are usually found here, but a large party is recommended to order them the night before. The island, which is dotted with bushes and at places well-cultivated, is crossed in about 10 min., and the donkeys then ford a shallow arm of the river. If the river is high, however, travellers must row round the island. We pass the village, pleasantly shaded by trees, and cross a very frail bridge over a water-course descending to the Nile. On the bank is a handsome farm. — A *Ferry* ($^1\!/_2$ piastre) also crosses from Luxor and lands its passengers a little higher up, a convenience if they are bound for the temple of Kurnah and the Tombs of the Kings.

We have already seen that the streets of Thebes with the palaces and the dwellings of the citizens lay near the great temple of Ammon, on the E. bank. between the river and the Arabian moun-

N

Tombs of the Kings
(West Valley)

24 25

22

8
12 9 7
14 13
Tombs of t
15 11 10 6 5
16
17
18
Kings
21
19

Kings

bs of the
Queens

Shêkh 'Abd
el-Kurnah

Dêr el-Medineh

Tomb of Hui

Kurnet Murraï

Southn. Asasif

Ramesseu

of Ramses III
Medinet Habu

T. of Tutmes III.

Agiz

Kom el-Hêtân

(T. of Amenophis III)

Colossi of Memnon

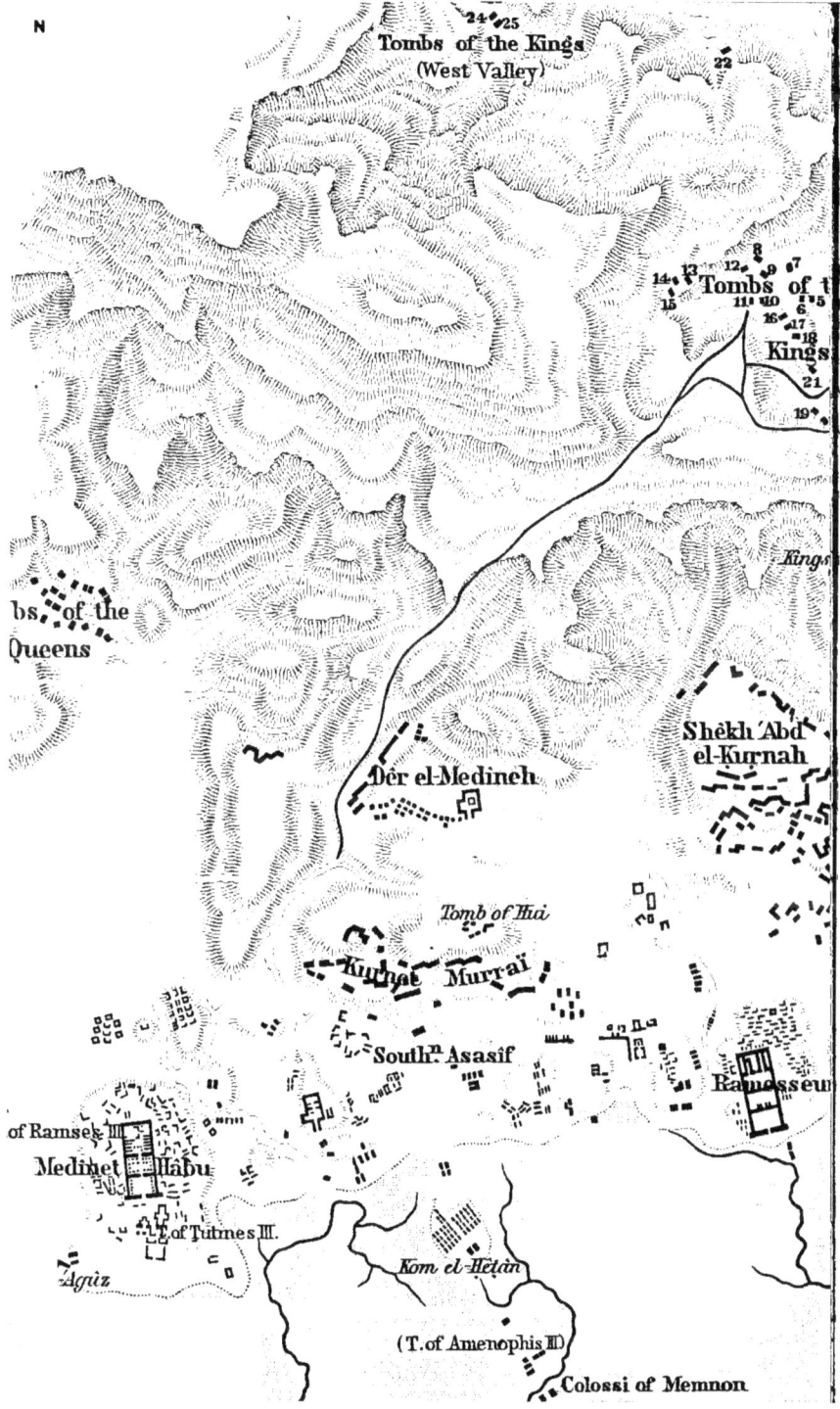

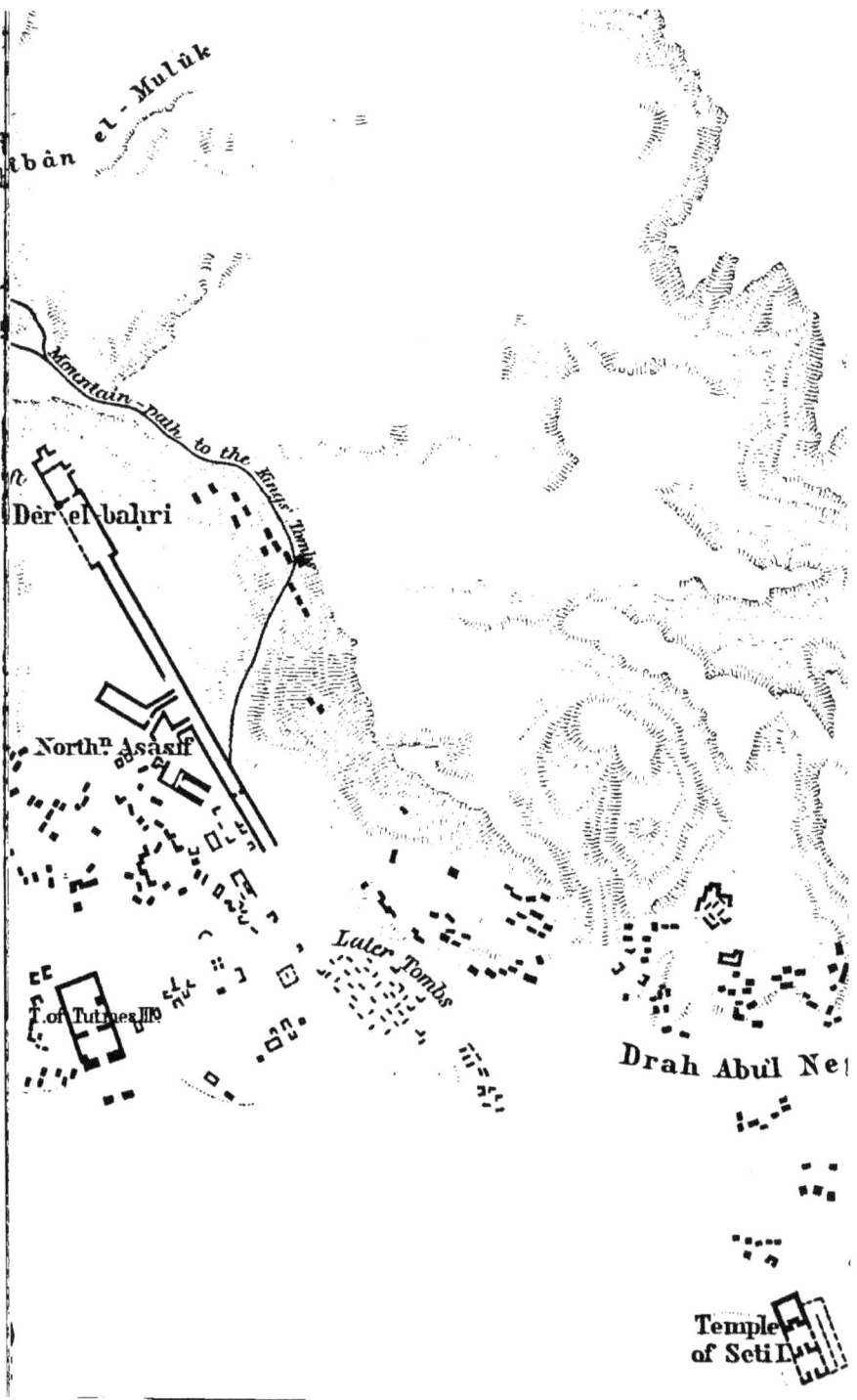

bân el - Mulûk

Mountain-path to the Kings' Tombs

Dêr el bahri

North.ⁿ Asasîf

Later Tombs

T. of Tutmes III

Drah Abûl Ne

Temple
of Seti I

tains. On the *West Bank* lay the **Necropolis** or *City of the Dead*, connected with which were a large number of temples. These latter are called *Memnonia*, because they were dedicated to the memory of the lives and deeds of the great Pharaohs, and because they were regarded as the abodes of the dead monarchs, and sacrifices were offered within them to the royal manes and to the gods, to whom the kings owed their might. Built on the verge of the necropolis, they stood in close relation to the worship of the dead. Just as scientific institutions etc. were maintained in connection with the Serapea adjoining the cemeteries of Memphis and Alexandria, so the temples here were adjoined by various other establishments. These included libraries, schools, dwellings for the priests, medical colleges, embalming-houses, stables and pastures for the sacred animals, and lodgings for pilgrims, while near the sacred ponds and groves were entire streets, containing not only barracks for the temple-guards and dwellings for the ecclesiastical and lay officials, but also shops and houses of private citizens who carried on trade in the various articles used at burials or brought as offerings to the deceased. The guild of Kolchytes or embalmers is frequently mentioned (especially at a late date) as a numerous and by no means harmonious society. Public works of various kinds are mentioned in the demotic and Greek commercial contracts which have been found here and are dated from this place. Among these a canal, a sacred lake, a large street, etc. are named. There were many other temples besides those whose ruins are now traceable, and round each were grouped houses of various kinds, so that Strabo and other Greek writers were justified in describing Thebes as sporadically inhabited. The last-named reliable geographer writes: 'Thebes is now sporadically inhabited. Part of it lies in Arabia (E. bank of the Nile), including the city proper, and part on the opposite bank, where the Memnonium is situated'. Strabo, like all his countrymen, was especially attracted by the so-called *Colossi of Memnon*, which he considered as repaying in themselves the trouble of the journey to Thebes.

12. The Colossi of Memnon.

The *Colossi of Memnon, which are visible from a great distance, are reached on donkey-back in 20-25 min. after crossing the W. arm of the Nile. The route, which leads through well-cultivated lands, cannot be mistaken, for the goal is in view all the way. These two colossal statues have suffered severely from the hand of time and have lost their artistic value, but they still exert all their old attraction in virtue of the innumerable associations that cling to them. They are surpassed in size and in beauty of material only by the shattered colossus in the Ramesseum. The two immense figures and the cubical thrones on which they are seated are carved out of a pebbly and quartzose sandstone-conglomerate, of a yellowish-brown colour and very difficult to work.

The *S. Colossus* is in better preservation than the N. one, but there is little difference between them in point of size. The dimensions of the former, in which the original form is more easily seen, are as follows: height of the figure, 52 ft., height of the pedestal on which the feet rest, 13 ft., height of the entire monument, 64 ft. But when the figure was adorned with the long-since vanished crown, the original height may have reached 69 ft. The legs from the sole to the knee measure $19^1/_2$ ft., and each foot is $10^1/_2$ ft. long. The breadth of the shoulders is $19^3/_4$ ft.; the middle finger on one hand is $4^1/_2$ ft. long; and the arm from the tip of the finger to the elbow measures $15^1/_2$ ft. The entire colossus, including the throne and pedestal, weighs 1175 tons.

Both statues face E.S.E. and stand parallel to the course of the Nile, though they are no longer perpendicular, as one inclines a little towards the other and both are canted slightly backwards. The S. colossus is a little in front of the N. one, from which it is 22 paces distant. Both are seamed with cracks, and such large fragments have fallen from them, that one could imagine that an attempt has been made to destroy them by fire. The Arabs call the N. colossus *Tama*, the S. one *Shama*, and both together *Salamât*, or 'the greetings'. †

When the Nile is at its highest, its waters reach the soles of the feet of the colossi and sometimes the upper surface of the pedestal on which they rest. As this pedestal is 13 ft. high and as the statues must have been beyond the reach of inundations in the time of the Pharaohs, Lepsius is correct in assuming from his observations of the nilometer at Semueh (p. 342) that the bed of the Nile at that point must have been considerably raised within historical times. He estimates the total rise at 25 ft. In winter, however, the traveller reaches the statues dry-shod. These colossi were not always solitary monuments, remote from all other buildings. On the contrary they originally stood on either side of a gigantic *Pylon*, which rose behind them and formed the entrance to a *Memnonium*, of which extensive relics still remain, though for the most part covered with earth. This temple, now completely annihilated, was founded by Amenhotep III., who is represented by the colossi. Neither this monarch nor his statues have any connection whatever with the Greek Memnon, who was the son of Eos (the dawn) and Tithonus, became one of the allies of Priam, and slew Antilochus, the brave son of Nestor, for which he was himself slain by Achilles. Homer mentions this Memnon twice in the Odyssey:

'For he thought in his mind of the likeness of the noble Antilochus'
'Whom the lordly *son of the brightening dawn* slew'.

And of Neoptolemus, the son of Achilles, it is said:

'No one handsomer than he have I seen, next to the godlike *Memnon*'.

This Memnon was an Asiatic hero, who is said also to have built the fortresses of Susa and Ecbatana. When the Greeks became acquainted with the Nile valley and its monuments, they imagined that they had found sumptuous buildings of the Homeric hero in the commemorative monuments named 'mennu' by the Egyptians (p. 55). The colossi before us were also called 'mennu' by the inhabitants of Thebes, and soon came to be described by the Hellenes as statues of Memnon, though the Egyptians even to a late period knew that they represented Amenhotep III., a king of the 18th Dynasty. Pausanias was informed of this fact, and Greek inscriptions on the legs of the statues also mention it. When it afterwards

---

† That at least is the present name. Lepsius states that they were named in his time *Ṣanamât*, or the 'idols', which seems more in keeping with Arab conceptions.

became known that the N. colossus emitted a musical note at sunrise, a new and beautiful myth arose among the Greeks who were always ready to invent a legend in order to explain a fact. The hero of this myth was a Memnon, hailing from Ethiopia, who fell at Troy. Appearing as a stone image at Thebes, he greeted his mother Eos with a sweet and plaintive note when she appeared at dawn. The goddess heard the sound, and the morning dews are the tears which she shed upon her beloved child.

The enormous size of the colossi and the legends that clustered round them, rendered them so attractive to the Greeks and Romans, that Tacitus mentions them among the chief marvels (*praecipua miracula*) of Egypt; and under the Roman empire travellers to the Nile considered that the object of their journey was attained when they had seen the pyramids and heard the musical note of Memnon.

The *Northern Colossus* is the famous **Vocal Statue of Memnon.** This is distinctly indicated by the effusions of early tourists, varying both in length and excellence, which are inscribed on the legs. The statue is composed of two parts. The lower and older part consists of a single block of sandstone-conglomerate, and reaches to the middle of the arm resting on the knee and, behind, to above the girdle. The upper part was broken off by an earthquake in the year 27 B.C., and was not restored until the reign of Septimius Severus, many years later. The restoration was not very happily managed, for instead of being made out of a single block, the body and head were built up of thirteen blocks of common sandstone in five courses. The care with which the lower part (now much injured) was executed offers a great contrast to the crudeness of this newer part. To the right and left and between the legs stand female statues leaning against the throne, representing the mother and wife of Amenhotep III., *Mut em ua* and *Tii.* On each side of the seat two Nile-gods were represented in sunk relief, holding papyrus plants wound round the symbol of the union of Upper and Lower Egypt. The inscriptions on the S. colossus enable us to supply what is here broken off; but these, and the hieroglyphics on the back of the statue, contain nothing beyond the high-sounding titles of Amenhotep III. and the information that he erected these palatial buildings and colossal statues of sandstone in honour of his father Ammon. The king, whom we have elsewhere found mentioned as a great warrior-prince, is also named a destroyer of foreign peoples, a Horus (who conquered the enemies of his father), and the beloved of Ammon.

After the breaking of the colossus by the earthquake of 27 B.C., attention began to be directed to the *musical phenomenon* connected with it. Strabo says: 'Of two gigantic monolithic statues situated close to each other, one is entire, while the upper portions of the other, from the waist upwards, are said to have been thrown down by an earthquake. It is popularly believed that a sound, as though caused by a gentle blow, is heard once a day proceeding from the remaining portion on the throne and pedestal. I myself, when I was on the spot along with Aelius Gallus and numerous other friends

and soldiers, heard the sound about the first hour; but I was unable
to decide whether it proceeded from the base or from the statue, or
indeed whether it was deliberately produced by one of those standing round the pedestal. For as I do not know the cause, anything
appears to me much more credible than that the sound issued from
the stone thus placed'. Doubts as to the genuineness of the phenomenon ceased soon after Strabo's time, and while that famous
geographer mentions only an inarticulate sound (ψόφος), Pausanias
speaks of a musical note and Juvenal refers to the 'resonance from
the magic strings of the shattered Memnon'. By later observers the
sound is compared to that of a stroke upon metal, or even of a trum-
pet-blast and of human voices singing. The sound was heard only at
or soon after sunrise, though by no means invariably then; and some
of the most distinguished visitors were disappointed of hearing it.
Among these was Septimius Severus, who caused the restoration of
the upper portions, perhaps with a view to propitiate the angry god.
Thereafter the phenomenon ceased, and the colossus, abhorred by
the Christians as a pagan idol, fell rapidly into oblivion as the new
religion spread.

Letronne has proved that the resonance of the stone is on no account
to be explained as a mere priestly trick, and in the opinion of eminent
physicists, it is perfectly possible that a hard resonant stone, heated by
the warm sunlight suddenly following upon the cold nights in Egypt,
might emit a sound in the early morning. A similar phenomenon has
been observed elsewhere, as by Professor Ebers under the porphyry
cliffs of the Sinai mountains, and by the savants of the French Expedition near the granite-sanctuary at Karnak and in the granite quarries
of Assuân (Syene). An English traveller near the Maladetta in the Pyre-
nees heard a sound issuing from the rocks, not unlike the note of an
Aeolian harp, and the name given to it by the natives, 'the matins of the
damned', seems to prove that it was ·of frequent if not regular occurrence. The 'music-stones' of the Orinoco are well-known. In the Gova
valley, to the S. of Lake Nyassa, Livingstone observed the thunderous
sound of splitting stones, ascribed by the natives to the agency of Mohesi
or evil spirits. And the German consul, Dr. Wetzstein, reports similar
phenomena in the volcanic region discovered by him to the E. of Da-
mascus. Possibly the extensive broken and sloping surface of the colossus, wet with the dews of early morning, was exposed unusually directly
to the rays of the rising sun, and the famous sound may have been produced by a current of air, generated by this sudden change of temperature,
passing over the rough and pebbly surface. In that case the phenomenon
would naturally cease when the upper part of the figure was replaced.

The numerous Greek and Latin inscriptions, in prose and verse, inscribed upon the legs of the figure by travellers under the Roman empire,
are peculiarly interesting. These are more numerous on the left than on
the right leg, and none are beyond the reach of a man standing at the
foot of the statue. The earliest were carved in the reign of Nero, the
latest in those of Septimius Severus and Caracalla, and the most numerous (27) in that of Hadrian. Only one Egyptian (who is responsible for
a short demotic inscription) is found among these scribblers, who show
both more reverence for antiquity and more wit than their modern representatives. At the same time it must be acknowledged that the writings on the
colossus of Memnon are not without scientific value. They were for the
most part the work of men of some eminence, including 8 governors of Egypt,
3 epistrateges of the Thebaïd, 2 procurators, etc. Many, though not all, are
dated. Nearly all of them afford proof that only the N. colossus emitted the

famous sound. The oldest inscription dates from the 11th year of Nero's reign. — Many of the great officials who visited the marvels of Thebes were accompanied by their wives. Thus Lucius Junius Calvinus and his wife Minicia Rustica, in the 4th year of Vespasian, heard the phenomenon at the second hour, though most other visitors heard it at the morning-hour, *i.e.* at or soon after sunrise. The colossus was frequently dumb, in which case the visitor usually waited until a more favourable occasion. Many were so struck with the phenomenon that they were not content till they had heard it three or four times. Hadrian, who journeyed through Egypt in 130 A.D., spent several days here along with his wife Sabina and a large retinue. In his reign a perfect flood of verses spread over the legs of the colossus, most of them by the vain court-poetess *Balbilla*, the descendant of a noble house, as she is careful to mention. One of her effusions (on the left leg) relates in 16 hexameters, that Memnon greeted Hadrian, as well as he could (ὡς δυνατόν) when he perceived the emperor before sunrise, but that a clearer note, like that caused by a blow on an instrument of copper, was emitted at the second hour, and that even a third sound was heard. Hadrian greeted Memnon as often, and all the world could see how dear the emperor was to the god.

'Balbilla, by an inward impulse stirred'
'Has written all she saw and all she heard'.

By far the best verses are those on the front of the pedestal by *Asklepiodotus*, who calls himself imperial procurator and poet. They may be translated as follows: —

'Sea-born Thetis, learn that Memnon suffered never pangs of dying'.
'Still, where Libyan mountains rise, sounds the voice of his loud crying' —
'(Mountains which the Nile-stream, laving, parts from Thebes, the hundred-gated)' —
'When he glows, through rays maternal with warm light illuminated'.
'But thy son who, never-sated, dreadful battle still was seeking',
'Dumb in Troy and Thessaly, rests now, never speaking'.

On the right leg of the colossus is a curious 'Homeric' poem, inscribed by a certain *Areies*, and made up of four lines from the Iliad and Odyssey, pieced together by the poet so as to express his meaning:

'Alas, a mighty wonder I there behold with mine eyes'
(Il. xiii, 99)
'Truly a god is here, a noble inhabitant of heaven!'
(Od. xix, 40)
'Loud he raises his voice, and stays the assembled multitude'.
(Od. xxiv, 530)
'Never could a mortal man accomplish such a thing as this'.
(Od. xvi, 196).

The ruins in the neighbourhood of the colossi are unimportant. About 3 min. beyond them is another *Statue* of great size, now, however, almost completely covered by arable land. Farther to the N.W. are very numerous smaller statues. The ruined *Amenophium*, at the gates of which the above-mentioned statues stood, has left an important memorial in the shape of a conspicuous colossal *Sandstone Stele*, erected by Amenhotep III. It now has its broadest surface uppermost, and is covered with hieroglyphics in the grand style, which, with the representations, refer to the dedication of the temple. In the rounded pediment the Pharaoh appears receiving the symbol of life from Ammon on the right, and from Sokar-Osiris on the left; above are the winged sun-disc and the name of Amenhotep III. Behind the Pharaoh in each case is his consort Tii, adorned with the feather-crown. The first line of the inscription contains the pompous titles of the king; the second begins as follows:

'He speaks : come to me Ammon Ra, lord of the throne of the world of E. Thebes. Look upon thy dwelling, which has been prepared for thee in the excellent site of Thebes, whose beauty is united with the region of the dead'. The inscription is continued in the style of a hymn, extolling what had been done for this temple, and expressing the god's approval of the work that was here dedicated to him. — In the neighbourhood of this stele are numerous blocks of stone and architectural fragments, which belonged to the rich temple of Amenhotep mentioned in the inscription. There is no possibility of reconstructing the ground-plan of this building, and the half-buried sphinx-columns and broken statues present little interest. — Still farther to the N.W., at the foot of the Libyan mountains, two fragments of an ancient brick-building, known as *Kôm el-Hêtân*, project like huge horns from the ground, and at a distance may easily be taken for the colossi of Memnon.

13. The Ramesseum.

The *Ramesseum, better known as the **Memnonium of Ramses II.**, lies about ¼ hr. to the N.N.E. of Kôm el-Hêtân. The route skirts the fertile land, and the ruin soon appears conspicuously on our right, as we look towards the Libyan mountains. We pass a small canal with a water-wheel worked by a buffalo, which waters the well-cultivated fields near the Ramesseum, as well as a small grove of ṣuṇt and tamarisk-trees to the E. of it. Whether it is approached from the N. or from the S., the Ramesseum presents a most picturesque appearance. As almost all the side-walls have fallen, it is possible to obtain a comprehensive view of the well-proportioned arrangement of this beautiful temple and to grasp its general architectural idea. Though time has destroyed much, it is still possible to realize the form of its main portions. — So far as the *Purpose* of the Ramesseum is concerned, it may be asserted with absolute certainty that it was dedicated to the worship of the manes of Ramses II., and stood in the same relation to the tomb of that prince, as the chapels at the entrance of the rock-tombs of wealthy private citizens to the adjoining mummy-shafts (Vol I., p. 170). This is clearly indicated by the position of the monument, by the procession with images of ancestors at the festival of the staircase, on the N. part of the W. side of the second pylon, by the list of the sons of the Pharaoh, and by the ceiling-carvings in the last rooms of this Memnonium. Finally several inscriptions inform us that the Ramesseum resembled the temple which Ramses the Great vowed in gratitude for his rescue out of the hands of the Kheta who had surrounded him (p. 161).

The question has been much discussed whether the Ramesseum is to be identified with the *Tomb of Osymandyas*, minutely described by Diodorus. The affirmative view has been stoutly advocated by Jollois and Devilliers in the report of the French Expedition, and is now generally adopted in spite of Letronne's protest. It is true that while many points in Diodorus's description tally with the Ramesseum (*e.g.* the colossal sitting statues, the

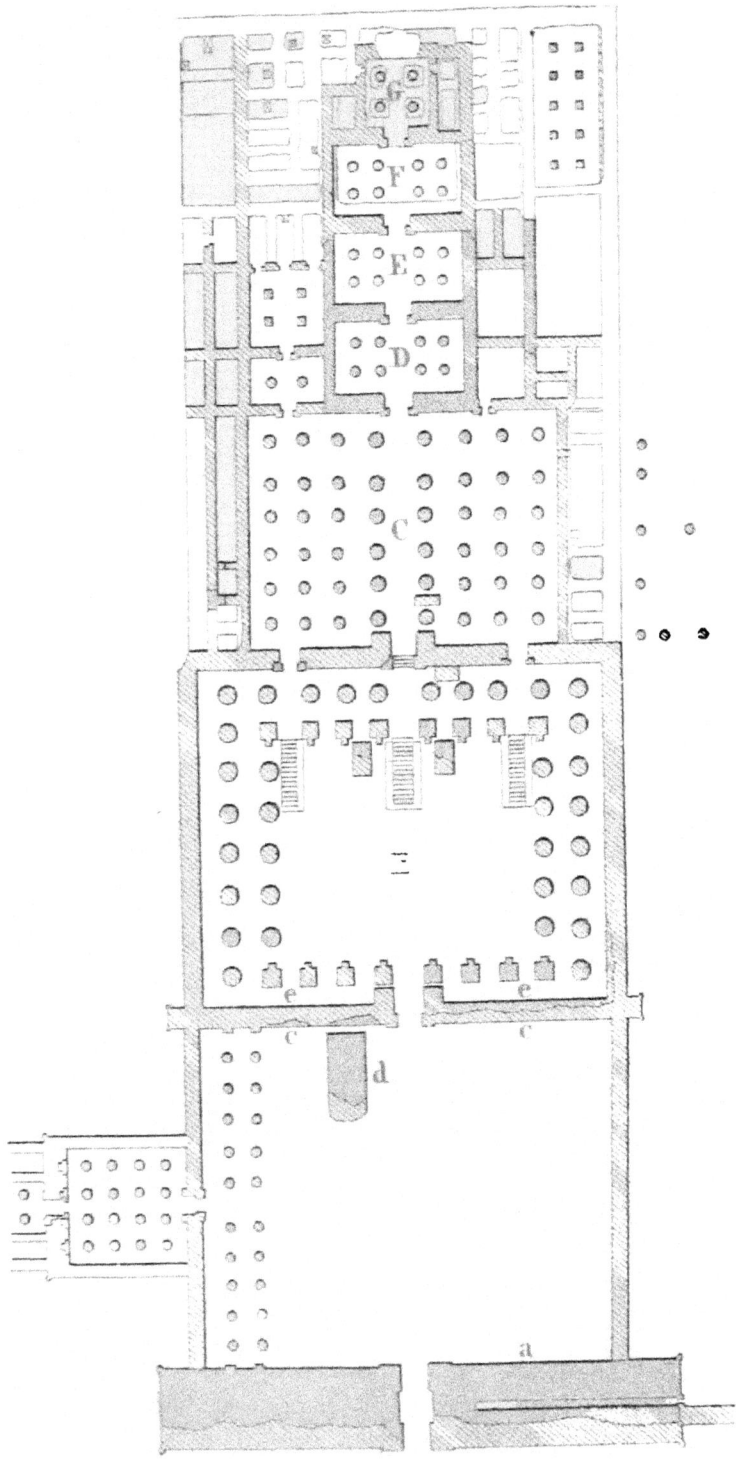

G

F

E

D

C

e   e

c   c

d

a

astronomical representations etc.), others seem to apply much more closely to the temple at Medinet Habu, built by Ramses II. who bore the name *Usermara meramon* (Osymandyas) as well as Ramses III. Among these latter points are the lion-hunt on the N. side of the temple, the treasury, the severed limbs, and perhaps also the temple-library (p. 167). Possibly the explanation is that Diodorus wrote his description from memory after leaving Thebes and mingled features of both temples in his account.

The traveller will be assisted to form a judgment on the question for himself by the following main points from the description by Diodorus. 'At the entrance is a pylon of coloured stone (probably granite is intended, though erroneously), 2 plethra long (202 ft.) and 45 ells high. Then follows a square peristyle, with sides measuring 4 plethra (404 ft.). The roof is supported, not by columns, but by 16 figures of living beings, each carved in an antique style out of a single stone. The entire roof is 2 orgyia (11½ ft.) broad, and is formed of solid stone, decorated with stars on a blue ground. Beyond the peristyle are another entrance and a pylon, differing from the first only in having various figures carved upon it. Beside the entrance are 3 monolithic figures of the Memnon of Syene (or, according to a better reading 'of stone from Syene'). One of these, a sitting figure, exceeds in size all other statues in Egypt; at its foot (footstool) it measures more than 7 ells. The others, to the right and left respectively of the knees of this statue, represent the sister and mother, and are smaller than the first. This work is not only noteworthy for its size, but deserves admiration also for its artistic beauty. It is also remarkable for the character of the stone, in which neither a crack nor a flaw is to be seen in spite of its unusual size. — This pylon is succeeded by a peristyle court which seems even more worthy of remark than the preceding. It contains various sculptures carved in the stone, representing the wars carried on by him (*i.e.* the king) against the Bactrians, who had revolted against him'. Diodorus farther informs us that the army consisted of 400,000 foot soldiers and 20,000 cavalry, in four divisions commanded by the king's sons. On the first wall the king was represented storming a fortress surrounded by a river, and hurling himself against the enemy, along with a fierce lion which accompanied him in battle ... "In front of the last wall were two monolithic sitting statues, 27 ells in height, and beside these were three exits from the peristyle, admitting to a hypostyle, which had the form of an odeum (music-room), and was 2 plethra (202 ft.) long on each side". According to Diodorus this building also possessed a library. The last part of the temple and its upper story are too completely ruined to be satisfactorily compared with the report of the Sicilian geographer.

We are able to recognize the first pylon, the caryatides in the second peristyle court, the largest colossus in Egypt, the battle-sculptures with the lion and the fortress surrounded by water, the hypostyle odeum, and traces of the library. Diodorus describes them in tolerably correct order, but as vaguely as hasty travellers usually do who are unable to take notes on the spot.

We enter the temple by the most easterly of the three extant *Pylons*. This was originally 220 ft. broad, but its ruined exterior is now more like a quarry than a building. Many representations are still recognizable, though much defaced, on the broad surface of its W. *Side*, next the first court. Beginning our inspection with the N. *Wing* (Pl. a), to the extreme left (N.E.) of the beholder, we first notice the slender representations of pinnacled Asiatic fortresses, in six rows, the two highest of which have been destroyed. Fourteen of the original eighteen are still recognizable, each with an inscription containing its name, and in some cases also the year in which it was taken by Ramses II. The isolated inscription at the top, to the left, is translated by Burton, Champollion, and Brugsch as follows: 'The fortress, captured by His Majesty in the 8th year; Shalma (its name)'. Lepsius suggests a different translation. Shalma is perhaps Salem (or possibly Σόλυμα = Hierosolyma?). The inscription referring to the second fortress from the top in the third row to the right, reads: 'Fortress captured by His Majesty in the land of the Amāur; Tapur its name'. The mention of Amāur and the names of the other fortresses seem to refer Tapur to Palestine (a fortress on Mount Tabor), in spite of the natural temptation to connect Tapur with the ancient name of the Tapurs, a people dwelling in the Margiana between Bactria and Hyrcania, and to recall Diodorus's statement that the warlike representations on the tomb of Osymandyas referred to the campaigns of the builder against the Bactrians. Between the fortresses Egyptian youths appear leading the captured Asiatic princes, most of whom are chained by the neck, though some of them have their hands tied together above their heads. The conquerors accelerate the steps of their unhappy victims with staves, and in the second row from the foot, a young officer is shown plucking the beard of an aged Asiatic. Farther to the right, and reaching to the fallen and more or less severely injured summit of the pylon, are some very varied military representations, some of which are unfortunately much defaced. To the right is a realistic battle-scene. The Egyptian chariots have overwhelmed those of the Asiatics; and below appear fresh regiments of Egyptian infantry, marching in step. Each soldier is armed with a lance, a short or curved sword, and a large shield. Before every four soldiers is a non-commissioned officer with a staff. The command to pitch the camp has already been given, and below and to the left of the combatants are men and animals enjoying their well-earned rest. Weapons and booty lie in heaps; soldiers are drinking from leather-bottles; and others are foddering the horses and asses. The war-chariots are drawn up in two long lines, and the veterinary surgeon is operating with a pointed instrument on the hoof of an ass. The camp-police are using their staves, not in jest merely, for beside a man drinking from a wine-skin are some drunken and roystering soldiers. Immediately above the horizontal surface, whence the broken part of the pylon rises in steps, we see the war-horses beside the chariots, and the recumbent fighting-lion of the Pharaoh guarding the royal tent. The chariots approach in good order like the infantry; in the lowest row the wheels pass over slaughtered enemies. The five extant rows of chariots excellently illustrate the passage in Exodus xiv, 7: 'And he took six hundred chariots, and all the chariots of Egypt, and captains over every one of them'.

The representations on the *S. Half of the W. side* (Pl. b) of the first pylon, also representing scenes from the war with the Kheta, are even more realistic. (Other similar scenes from the Kheta campaign are to be seen on the pylon at Luxor, p. 112, and in the temple of Abu-Simbel, p. 335.) To the left is the storming of Katesh, a fortress on the Orontes, probably situated on an island near Hums (Emesa). Nearer the centre, the king hurries to the fight, with bended bow. Above the rearing and spirited horses in his chariot are the words: 'The most excellent horse of his majesty Miamun from the stable of Ramses II., the beloved of Ammon'. In the inscription within the bent bow the Pharaoh is named the beloved of Mentu, god of war. The royal leader overwhelms his foes with his impetuous attack and hurls them with their horses and chariots into the stream. Some of the Egyptians are put to flight, and a legion of archers hasten in chariots to the aid of the Pharaoh. Among the slain are various noble Aramaic warriors considered worthy of being specially mentioned, for their names are inscribed above them. One of these was Khirapasor, historiographer of the Kheta prince, whose dead body is represented beside the hind legs of the king's horses, between two lines of hieroglyphics. A short 12-line inscription in front of the elaborately decorated heads of the king's horses (the bridle is surmounted with lion's heads and feathers) explains the exact episode here depicted. It is the famous scene that forms the culminating point of the *Epic of Pentaur*, that Egyptian Iliad, which we have already met with on the pylon at Luxor (p. 112) and on the S. wall of the temple of Karnak (p. 141). 'He (*i.e.* Ramses) halted and encamped to the N.W. of Katesh. Then he pressed against the worthless foe, the Kheta. *He was alone and no other was with him.* He found himself surrounded by 2500 war-chariots, etc.' The escape of the king from his imminent danger by the help of the gods and his own right arm forms the subject of the epic, which has been preserved not only upon the walls of temples but also in a papyrus-roll. Its chief contents have been given elsewhere (p. 112). The relief before us represents this eventful moment in the warlike career of Ramses, while a repetition of the same subject on the W. side of the second pylon and the inscription on the architrave in the second court of the temple, inform us that the Ramesseum was erected by Ramses II. as a *Votive Building* in gratitude for his deliverance out of the hands of 2500 enemies.

To the extreme right, in front of the horses of the king, appears first the confused mass of men and horses overthrown by the royal hero. Beside three Egyptians who hold an Asiatic head downward, is the inscription: 'The miserable lord of Khileb (Khalybon-Aleppo). His soldiers pull him out of the water into which His Majesty had cast him'. At the end of the relief the prince of the Kheta is shown in his chariot, surrounded by unarmed followers, with the accompanying words: 'He stands still beside his foot-soldiers and cavalry. His face turned backwards. He advanced no more into the battle from fear of His Majesty, when he had seen His Majesty'.—Here as elsewhere the king and his chariot are on a larger scale than the other figures; the Kheta prince is smaller than the Pharaoh but

larger than the other soldiers. — The limestone blocks forming the
Doorway of this sandstone pylon display various sculptures and inscriptions, the latter containing the usual dedicatory formulae.
The Theban triad (Ammon, Muth, and Khunsu) and another triad
consisting of Ptah, Sekhet, and Hathor are among the divinities
which here received sacrifices and bestowed gifts.

On entering the **First Court** (Pl. A) we observe that it had on
its right and left sides a double row of columns, of which, however,
only a few scanty remains are to be found on the S. To the W.
this space is bounded by the *Second Pylon*, now in ruins. On the
left (S.) stood the **Colossus of Ramses II.** (Pl. d), the material of
which was justly admired by Diodorus (p. 159), and which really
may be termed the hugest statue in Egypt. The remarkable granite
statue (not sandstone like the colossi of Memnon) was probably
floated down the river on rafts from Assuân to Thebes. It has been
deliberately destroyed (apparently, from the marks at the fractures,
by means of damp wedges), though to do so must have cost its
enormous pains. In the time of Diodorus, who visited Egypt about
60 A.D., it appears to have been still uninjured; and we may conclude, therefore, that it was destroyed in consequence of the edict
of Theodosius, as one of the principal pagan idols. The name of
Ramses II. appears in well-preserved hieroglyphics on the upper
arm and on the seat of the statue, which lies close by in shattered
fragments. It cannot now be put together, as the inhabitants of 'Abd
el-Kurnah have broken off slabs of granite and smoothed them for
the purpose of husking their corn. The face is unfortunately completely destroyed. The remains (breast, upper arm, one foot, etc.)
still testify to the care with which this gigantic monument was
chiselled and polished. The savants of the French Expedition carefully measured the various parts, as follows: length of ear $3^1/_2$ ft.,
surface of face from ear to ear $6^3/_4$ ft., surface of breast from
shoulder to shoulder $23^1/_3$ ft., from one shoulder to the other in a
straight line $21^1/_2$ ft., circumference of the arm at the elbow
$17^1/_2$ ft., diameter of the arm between the elbow and shoulder
$4^3/_4$ ft., length of the index finger $3^1/_5$ ft., length of the nail on the
middle finger $7^1/_2$ inches, breadth of ditto 6 inches, breadth of the
foot across the toes, $4^1/_2$ ft. The total height seems to have been
$57^1/_2$ ft., and its total weight over two million pounds.

The colossal head of another *Statue of Ramses II.* was found on the
S. side of the temple farther back, and was conveyed to the Nile by
Belzoni in 1816, and thence to Alexandria. It is now one of the chief
treasures in the Egyptian Gallery of the British Museum.

The **Second Peristyle Court** (Pl. B) is in much better preservation than the first court, and is mentioned with its caryatides
in Diodorus's description of the tomb of Osymandyas (p. 159). Its
general arrangement is easily understood. On all four sides were
colonnades, those to the right and left (N. and S.) having two rows
of papyrus-bud columns and that on the E. (front) side pillars with

statues of Osiris, while on the W. (rear) side, the roof of the colonnaded passage was supported by Osiris-caryatides (facing the court) and papyrus-bud columns. The N. and S. colonnades have almost completely disappeared, but four caryatide-pillars still stand on the E. and as many on the W. Towards the W. end, in the direction of the entrance to the hypostyle hall, afterwards to be described, a number of steps ascend from the pavement of the court to the doorway. Standing in the doorway of the second pylon and looking westward through the central door of the hypostyle hall and through the smaller doorway in its farther (W.) side, we command an architectural perspective of great charm. The builder has succeeded in producing the effect of distance and size by raising the floor-level of the temple towards the W. and by gradually diminishing the size of the doorways that succeed each other in the same axis.

In the second court the representations on the **W. Wall of the Second Pylon** (Pl. e), in front of which rose the E. row of caryatides, are of special interest. The S. side of the wall has completely collapsed. In the midst of the ruins project two blocks of stone, which bear a representation of the fortress of Katesh, surrounded by a blue stream (to the right of the beholder in the second court). To the extreme left, the Pharaoh, much larger than the other warriors, dashes along in his chariot with his bow bent. This is one of the most vigorous of the numerous battle-scenes that have been preserved on Egyptian pylons. The leaping lion beside the king's chariot is part of its adornment merely, though at the first glance it is apt to be taken for the king's battle-companion preparing for a mighty leap. Diodorus perhaps had this in his mind when he described the relief of a fortress surrounded by water, and the Pharaoh dashing against the foe along with a fierce lion that used to accompany him in battle. The Asiatics fall before the onset of the king like ears of corn before a hail-storm. Huddled pell-mell in confused heaps, pierced by arrows or trodden down by the horses, the Kheta fall a prey to death. The Orontes flows by the side of the combatants and crowds of Kheta are hurled into it; warriors, horses, and chariots sink beneath the waves. We are irresistibly reminded of the crossing of the Red Sea by the Israelites, that took place only half a century later. 'Pharaoh's chariots and his host hath he cast into the sea: his chosen captains also are drowned in the Red sea. The depths have covered them: they sank into the bottom as a stone' (Exod. xv, 4, 5). Farther to the right, beneath the fortress, some soldiers hold out a rescuing hand to the drowning. Everything indicates that we have here a free repetition of the battle-scene on the first pylon. The battle rages near Katesh, among the slain here also are Khirapasor, the historiographer of the Kheta prince, Kerebatusa his charioteer, Titure, chief of his attendants, Pisa his master of the horse (Kazen), Tarḳanunasa, etc.

Here also appear long rows of chariots, hastening to the fight. Most decisive of all, however, is the inscription beside the heads of the king's heises, which contains once more the passage from the epic of Pentaur, telling us what event in the life of Ramses was commemorated by the erection of the Ramesseum. Once more occur the words: '*He was alone and no other was with him. He found himself surrounded by 2500 chariots*', etc.

It may be mentioned here that a series of monuments of the Hittites (Kheta) with picture-writing (differing from hieroglyphics) has recently been discovered, including several blocks in a bridge at *Hamâh* (now in Constantinople) and a silver plate (also found at Hamâh) with the name of *Tarriktimma* (Tarkondêmos) in cuneiform and Kheta characters. In 1888 Dr. Humann excavated one of the chief cities of the Kheta, near *Sinjerli*, to the N.E. of Antioch. The highly important inscribed stones found there are now in the New Museum at Berlin.

On the *Upper Part* of this pylon we observe the procession of the *Festival of the Staircase*, in honour of the god Khem (represented in detail at Medinet Habu and described on p. 178). The figures which bear the statues of the king's ancestors, should be noticed. The names besides the ancestral images are those of Mena, first king of Egypt, and of the Pharaohs of the 18th Dynasty. From this representation we perceive that the monument is sepulchral. Adjacent are priests letting fly the birds into which the four children of Horus (Amset, Hapi, etc.) have changed themselves, for the purpose of carrying tidings to the four quarters of the globe that the Pharaoh has attained the crown of both worlds. Each bird is told whither it must fly. 'Haste, Amset, to the S. and bring tidings to the gods of the S. that Horus, the son of Osiris, has obtained possession of the crowns of Lower and Upper Egypt'. In the next line this is repeated with the substitution of Ramses for Horus. The other birds are despatched in similar terms to the N., E., and W. Farther to the right the king appears cutting a sheaf with a sickle, thus discharging the second coronation-ceremony usual at the festival of the staircase.

Proceeding now to examine the rest of the court, we observe that on the *Architrave of the W. Colonnade* the space usually devoted to the dedicatory inscription is occupied by fine hieroglyphics. After what has already been said, it is scarcely surprising to meet once more the famous passage from the epic of Pentaur: — 'The king, who abounds in strength, who chastises the barbarians and the world of alien lands, striking them to the earth. *He was alone and no other was with him.* Ramses II., the life-giver, king of Upper and Lower Egypt'. Statues of the king adorned this peristyle court, as is indicated by the extant pedestals. Fragments of one of these, in beautiful grey granite, lie upon the ground. The *Head*, with down-cast eyes, is a master-piece.

We ascend to the W. colonnade by means of the shallow steps mentioned at p. 163. Behind the Osiris-columns stood finely designed papyrus-bud columns, in which, however, the artistic ground-idea was indicated merely by lightly carved root-leaves on the lower part of the shafts. Beyond this colonnade is a *Hypostyle Hall (Pl. C), which can hardly, however, be identified with the odeum-shaped hall mentioned by Diodorus in his description of the tomb of Osymandyas (p. 159). The inscriptions call it the 'Hall of the Appearance' (comp. p. 85). Diodorus describes his hall as square, whereas the one before us is 98 ft. deep and 196 ft. broad. The three *Entrances* mentioned by Diodorus still exist, and are framed with sculptured blocks of granite. The artistic forms displayed in this hall are so extraordinarily congruous with each other, the dimensions so skilfully calculated, and the proportions so harmonious, that we do not hesitate to describe it as the most beautiful hall extant in any Egyptian temple. In its arrangement it resembled the great colonnaded hall at Karnak. In the centre a passage was marked out by six couples of higher columns with calyx-capitals, on each side of which were three rows of lower papyrus-bud columns. Upon the latter a wall rose as high as the calyx-columns, with which it shared the weight of the roof, while a subdued but sufficient light was admitted to the beautiful hall through openings in this wall. On the outside of the still standing S.E. wall of this hypostyle hall appears the kneeling king doing *Homage* to Ammon, Muth, and Khunsu, farther to the left Thoth writing the cartouche of the king, and to the extreme left the king between Mentu and Tum. Beneath is a procession of the sons of Ramses II., only some of whom, with their names, have been preserved. They are found in better preservation to the right and left of the door in the W. wall of the hall. Diodorus mentions that the odeum contained numerous wooden statues, representing persons before a tribunal and gazing upon the judges. Reliefs of judges, 30 in number, are said to have been seen on one of the walls (but this has possibly arisen from a confusion with the sons of Ramses). In the midst of the judges appeared a presiding judge, from whose neck hung the image of truth with closed eyes, and by whose side lay numerous books. These statues were said to intimate by their attitudes (διὰ τοῦ σχήματος) that the judges might accept no gifts and that the president could look only to the truth. — That statues actually did stand in this hall is indicated by pedestals found between the first and second columns in the central row. It is also by no means impossible that a trial-scene (like the Judgment of the Dead at Dêr el-Medineh, p. 189) may have occupied the wall of one of the adjoining chambers; and it is easily conceivable that the hypostyle of the Ramesseum, with which a library and a famous school of scribes were connected, may have been used as a court by the supreme college of justice.

The representations which have remained are concerned with other subjects, while the fine inscription on the *S.E. Wall* returns to the war with the Kheta. The relief accompanying the latter is

distinguished for the beautiful modelling of the kings horses dashing into the fight, and for the representation of the Asiatic fortress
of Tapura, which is stormed by the Egyptians on scaling-ladders,
while the defenders are hurled headlong from the battlements. Several sons of the Pharaoh, the names of whom are given, distinguish
themselves in the battle. Two of these (towards the left) are depicted on a larger scale than the others, viz. Kha-em-us, the favourite son of Ramses, and Menth, prince of the blood, each of whom
is in the act of slaying an enemy. The younger princes, Meri-Amen,
Amen-em-ua, Seti, and Setep-en-Ra, covered with their shields,
take part in the attack (below the fortress). Diodorus apparently
had this scene in his mind when he described the Egyptian army as
commanded by the sons of the king.

The reliefs at the side of and above the portal (adorned with
the concave cornice) in the *Rear Wall* are in good preservation.
Each pillar is divided into four fields. In the first (top) fields the
king is shown offering to Sokar-Osiris (on the left) and to Ptah (on
the right); in both the second fields he offers sacrifice to Ammon
Generator; and in the third to Ammon-Ra as king of the gods (left)
and to the same god as lord of heaven (right). From the fourth
fields we learn the use to which the following rooms were put; on
the left is enthroned the ibis-headed Thoth-Hermes, god of wisdom
and of writings; on the right (opposite) is Safekh, goddess of history
(recognizable by the ⌐⅄⌐ above her head), named here 'the king's
mother Safekh, the great mistress of book-writing'. At the foot is
the dedicatory inscription, informing us that the king erected this
palatial building to his father Ammon, king of the gods and lord
of heaven, prince of Thebes. — On each side of the door is a procession of youthful forms, with the look of hair hanging to the side,
peculiar to the royal children. Their left hands are raised, and their
right hands hold the herdsman's crook ⌐, the symbol of princely
dignity, and the fan ⅄, the symbol of court-rank. The list to the
right is the more complete; but at the end of the procession on the
left two princesses appear, who are wanting in the other. Over the
first figures but applying equally to the others appear the full titles
of Egyptian royal princes. The first is as follows: 'The fan-bearer
at the right hand of the king, the prince and royal scribe, the leader
of the army, the great (Ur) son of the king, the first-born of his
body, his beloved Amen-hi-khopeshf'. While this son is named the
(great) son of the *king*, the next one, Ramessu, is called the (great)
son of the *lord of both worlds*. The third prince, Ra-hi-uanemif
(Ra at his right hand) is named master of the horse and charioteer.
Fourth comes the king's favourite son, Kha-em-us (see above), whose

mummy was found in the region of the Apis-graves of Sakkârah. There are in all 23 princes, of whom only the thirteenth need still be mentioned. After the death of 12 brothers he ascended the throne at a ripe age. As we may gather from the list to the left, this is *Merenptah*, frequently though inaccurately named the *Pharaoh of the Exodus*, whose name as king was afterwards added in the cartouche above him. A similar honour naturally could not fall to any of the other princes. On the columns appears Ramses II. offering sacrifices to and receiving gifts from the 'gods worshipped in the Ramesseum', conspicuous among whom are Ammon in his various forms, Seth, Thoth, Isis, Mā, Nut, Sekhet, etc.

The **Second Smaller Colonnaded Hall** (Pl. D), with four couple of papyrus-bud columns, is remarkable for two features. The first is the roof richly decorated with astronomical representations, proving that the Ramesseum was a monument dedicated to the worship of the dead. The second is a representation on the N. part of the rear-wall (the S. part is ruined), which seems to support the statement of Diodorus that a sacred library was deposited in the tomb of Osymandyas, with the legend 'Hospital for the soul' (ψυχῆς ἰατρεῖον). The Pharaoh, with all the royal attributes, sits upon his throne. At his side rises the leafy persea-tree, with heart-shaped fruit, upon which the king's name is being written by three deities, viz. to the left Tum on a lofty throne, to the right the goddess of history, and behind her Thoth-Hermes. Behind Tum are the words: 'Address of Ammon-Tum, lord of the great hall (of Heliopolis), in the Ramesseum to his son Ramses, the beloved of Ammon. Up, for the distinguishing of thy name to all eternity, that it may be preserved on the sacred persea-tree'. In this hall also, on either side of the door, is a procession with the sacred boats of Muth, Khunsu, the deified king, and his consort.

The following *Room* (Pl. E) is much injured, though four columns are still standing. It contains lists of offerings, and a few not uninteresting sculptures (chiefly on the door-pillars), which seem still farther to support the belief that we are now in the rooms of a *Library*. The figures of the Theban triad are not unusual; but the forms of Safekh, mistress of libraries, and Thoth-Hermes, the celestial scribe (both facing the room we have now entered) are noticeable. The god is accompanied by a form representing the personified sense of sight, with an eye as his symbol; the goddess by the personified sense of hearing, with an ear above his head. Thoth writes down the resolutions and thoughts of the god, while Safekh, the goddess of history, causes the fame of the great deeds of the past to ring in the ears of posterity. The dedicatory inscription states that this door was overlaid with silver-gilt (electrum), and Champollion found that the very low relief was formerly covered with a cloth coated with stucco, and was then probably gilded. No traces of the gilding is now to be found. — The side-rooms adjoining this W.

portion of the Ramesseum are in a very ruinous condition, but their arrangement may be partly made out.

Behind the Ramesseum, especially towards the N.W., are the remains of a number of extensive *Brick Buildings*, some of which were erected in the time of Ramses II., as we learn from the stamps on the bricks. Among the rest are some well-constructed vaults. As the tomb of Ramses II. has been discovered at Bibân el-Mulûk (p. 207), there can be no question of his grave being here. On the other hand we learn from the papyrus-rolls that a celebrated university and a seminary for scholars, comparable to the Museum at Alexandria, were connected with the Ramesseum, and stood at the zenith of their prosperity under Ramses and his son Meren-ptah. The light-coloured soil, strewn with fragments of bricks and tiles, between the Ramesseum and Shêkh 'Abd el-Kurnah, covers a multitude of graves, whose existence is undreamed of by those who walk over them. One of these, belonging to a certain *Mesra*, contains some interesting representations, the style of which indicates (for no king is named) that it dates probably from the early empire, and is certainly not later than the beginning of the 18th Dynasty. We may therefore conclude that Ramses II. built his votive Memnonium on an ancient portion of the Theban necropolis.

About 500 paces to the N. of the Memnonium we observe the remains of an extensive wall built of Nile bricks. The name of *Tutmes III.* found here on many tiles renders it probable that a temple built by this king or dedicated to him stood on this site.

14. The Tombs of Kurnet-Murraï.

Travellers who are not pressed for time should visit one of the tombs of Kurnet-Murraï (viz. that of *Hui*), on the way to Medinet-Habu. On reaching the fields of W. Thebes, if we look towards the Libyan mountains, our eye falls upon numerous tomb-entrances. The vaults of the Diospolites of the zenith of the ancient empire are hewn in the limestone hills that bound the plain of Thebes to the W. They have recently been classified in groups, bearing the names of the fellâh-villages in whose domain they lie. The tombs on the slopes behind the Ramesseum are called those of Shêkh 'Abd el-Kurnah. Following thence the undulating desert region at the foot of the Libyan hills in a S.W. direction towards Medinet Habu, we soon pass, on the right, the gorge of Dêr el-Medineh, and then direct our way towards the mountain-slope, projecting between the Ramessoum and Medinet Habu. This slope, on which stand some fellâh huts is known to the guides as **Kurnet Murraï.** Several of the tombs here date from the 18th Dyn., but the majority are of no interest to the ordinary traveller. Only one, to which the guides conduct travellers at once, is of exceptional interest (though recently much injured), on account partly of the subject and partly of the vivid colours of the representations it contains. Near the village (the dogs of which are cross-grained though cowardly) is a tomb partly converted into a stable by the fellâhin. In the adjoining tomb of *Hora-Khemti* are some hieroglyphics, of interest only to the scientific traveller. — Then follows the finest tomb in the necro-polis, belonging to a certain **Hui,** who held the high rank of a prince of Kush (Ethiopia) and was governor of the Sûdân. One of the sons of the Pharaoh used to be called prince of Kush, just as the heir-apparent to the British throne bears the title 'prince of Wales'. *Amenhotep*, a brother of Hui, who appears to have shared the same grave, is frequently named along with him. The accessible part of the grave is shaped as in the accompanying cut.

We enter by the door at *T*. The inscriptions are in good preservation only in the transverse chamber, *i.e.* the sepulchral chapel, and there especially on the rear-wall to the right (c) and left *(b)*. On wall *b* appears a much defaced figure of a king, belonging to the later 18th Dyn., viz. the not altogether legitimate Ra-kheperu-neb, whose throne-name was Tut-ank-amen-ḥak-an-nes, *i.e.* 'Living representative of Ammon, prince of the S. An'.' Hui, who was not only prince of Ethiopia but also chief of the S. house at the king's right hand, stands before him and addresses him. In his right hand is the fan, the symbol of his rank, in his left the crooked staff. Behind him, on a table covered with costly stuffs and panther skins, are golden vases and table-services, and imitations of the most striking phenomena of the Sûdân. Among the latter are the conical hut of the characteristically represented negroes, and inhabitants of the interior of Africa represented gathering their harvest from the dûm-palms that grow in thick woods, and driving giraffes among them. Higher up are various precious articles; red and blue gems in cups, rings of gold, sacks of gold-dust, shields covered with golden plates and gay skins, foot-stools, chairs, benches, and head-rests of ebony, a costly chariot, red jasper (Khenemt), lapis-lazuli, green stone, etc. Five divisions of men bearing tribute are received by Hui and Amenhotep in the king's name. Brown and coal-black people from the Sûdân are represented in the top row. Their princess, shaded by an umbrella, approaches in a chariot drawn by oxen, and is followed by chiefs wearing ostrich-feathers in their hair which is plaited into a kind of hood (as is the custom to this day among these tribes). The procession is closed by a brown and a black Ethiopian woman, with pendant breasts. The former carries a child in a basket on her back, and each woman leads a nude boy behind her. The

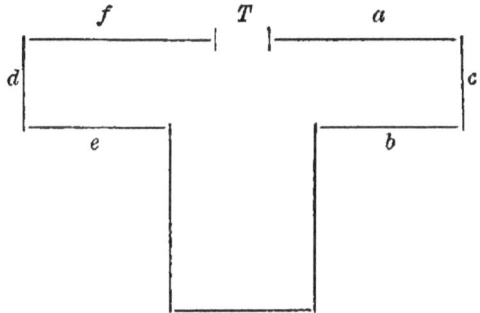

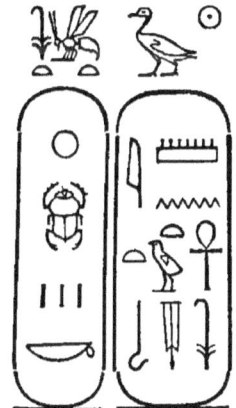

second row begins with kneeling chiefs from the Sûdân, who are
followed by white-clad Ethiopians with rings of gold, panther-skins,
a giraffe, and oxen. The last have unusually variegated hides, and
each has a brown and a black human hand most singularly fixed on
the points of its horns. The inscription above this procession runs:
'the great ones of Kush (Ethiopia) speak, Hail to thee, king of
Egypt, sun of the foreign peoples. We shall breathe as thou per-
mittest and shall live according to thy pleasure'. In the third row
brown and black chiefs from Kush bring gold and precious stones,
and semicircular fans of ostrich-feathers, of exactly the same shape
as the flabellum which now shades the pope on certain solemn
occasions and which was formerly used by the Pharaohs. An ox
with artificially bent horns, between which is a pond with fish
and bushes, should be noticed. The fourth and fifth divisions are
much injured. They show bright red persons (Erythræans who
dwelt between the Nile and the Red Sea), Egyptians, and very light
coloured Egyptian women with nosegays, earthen vessels, gazelles,
etc. Hui appears again on the same wall. Above and beneath may
be seen the ships which brought to Egypt the choice tribute of the
south. The two richly adorned and brightly painted dhahabîyehs
(above) resemble the craft (the ornamentation of course excepted)
in which the products of the Sûdân are to this day transported to
the north. Five Ethiopian princes kneel upon the deck of the second
boat. Cattle and other goods are being brought to Egypt in the
smaller vessels below.

On wall c appears the deceased, with the jackal-headed Anubis
on his right and Osiris on his left, while between him and the gods
are offerings to the dead. On wall *a*, near the door, stands the
deceased, with his domestics, singers, etc., and two richly adorned
Nile boats behind him; still farther back is the prince of Kush again,
surrounded by his treasures — earthen vessels, skins of wild animals,
bright coloured boxes, etc. Rings of gold are being received and
are weighed by a treasurer named Hornefer.

On the rear wall to the right *(e)* appears the king (near the
corner pillar), with Hui before him. — Amenhotep, another prince
of Kush, is bringing pieces of lapis-lazuli on a dish. By his right
hand hangs a breast-plate, set with precious stones, like that worn
by the high priest of the Jews. Behind Hui are several of those
gold and silver vessels, which at that time were manufactured by
the Phœnicians and Syrians with extraordinary artistic skill. Here
also are lapis-lazuli, red cornelians, and priestly breast-plates. An
inscription extols the Pharaoh in emphatic terms and informs us that
Syria pays this tribute. Their appearance alone is quite sufficient to
enable us to decide with certainty as to the origin of the men here represented, casting themselves in the dust before the king, or standing
and offering him homage and tribute. Some of them are light-
coloured, others of a reddish hue; their profile is unmistakably

Semitic. All of them have pointed beards, and several have long ringleted hair in fillets; while those of higher rank wear long robes and short cloaks of a fine-woven, richly patterned cloth, dyed a bright blue and red. Their feet are naked but their legs are covered to the ankle. Nude slaves, wearing only aprons, appear among them carrying the tribute. Besides costly vessels, lapis-lazuli, and cornelians, they also bring a lion and two splendid light-coloured horses.

On wall *f*, to the right of the entrance, is a representation of an offering of flowers.

15. Medînet Habu.

To the S.W. of Kurnet Murraï, and at no great distance, appears an extensive temple-group. This bears the name of *Medînet Habu*, a Christian village which arose around and even within the ancient sanctuary as early as the 5th cent., and of which considerable traces still remain. On the N. side of the temple-ruins rise heaps of rubbish, which we follow in the direction of the river, until we reach the main façade, which fronts the S.E. and is as imposing as it is curious. The traveller of experience will at once perceive that here we have not to do with a monument erected, like the Ramesseum, under the influence of a single continuous impulse, but with a building begun in early times and not completed until the epoch of the Ptolemies. The entire edifice may be divided into three easily distinguished portions. The earliest of these is the small oblong temple (Pl. N), lying parallel with the N. girdle-wall, and founded under the 18th Dynasty. The most recent is the pylon (Pl. K) adjoining this, with a beautiful and richly adorned portal, seen to especial advantage by those who approach the temple from the plain. A glance at the capitals of the two large columns rising in front of the gateway and at the style of the inscriptions informs the expert that this edifice dates from the epoch of the Ptolemies. Reserving these for later inspection, we proceed first to the third portion, the main temple.

The MAIN TEMPLE OF MEDÎNET HABU was erected as a Memnonium by Ramses III. of the 20th Dyn., without any reference to the previously existing temple of the 18th Dynasty. Though this temple is beautiful and finely proportioned in many of its parts, its architect has displayed no skill in incorporating what already existed with the new edifice. The erroneous opinion that the temple of Medinet Habu was a royal palace must be most emphatically contradicted. It was no more a palace than was the Ramesseum or any of the other buildings in W. Thebes. It was a Memnonium devoted to ancestor-worship, and its principal part was intended for the worship of the manes of Ramses III., and to remind posterity of his fame and his exploits. The temple served also for the celebration of festivals, including a specially important one for whose adequate

observance the Pharoah made enormous grants and gifts, in gratitude
to the gods who had favoured him.

For Ramses III. and his time, see Vol. I., p. 90. Here it may be
briefly noted that after the reigns of Ramses II. and his weaker son
Merenptah (under or more probably after whom the Exodus of the Israelites took place), rebels and [revolutionists reduced the house of the
Pharaohs to the verge of destruction and inflicted great injury on the
valley of the Nile, until Setnekht, a ruler allied to the legitimate line,
restored order with a firm hand. After a reign of seven years he died,
leaving the once more prosperous kingdom to his son Ramses III. The
temple which we are on the point of inspecting is a biographical authority
of the greatest value, for its inscriptions and representations not only
inform us of the warlike achievements of Ramses IH., but enable also
the attentive beholder to form a distinct picture of the peculiarities of
the public and private life of this prince. Ramses III. is the wealthy
Rhampsinitus of Herodotus, the most splendour-loving of all the Pharaohs,
a timid favourite of the gods, whom he endeavoured to propitiate by
overwhelming the temples and priestly colleges with gifts, while in the
building of Medinet Habu he shows himself to have been a ruler given
over to self-indulgence. The victories won under him were important,
and it almost seems as though this luxurious ancestor of a degenerate
race recovered the manhood of his forefathers amid the tumult of battle.

a. Pavilion of Ramses III.

We first enter a kind of FORE-COURT (Pl. A), with two small
buildings, which were probably the *Porters' Lodges.* Both these
and the girdle-wall stretching towards the S. are surmounted by
round pinnacles, resembling those already noted in the pictures of
Asiatic strongholds stormed by the Egyptian armies (*e.g.* on the 1st
pylon of the Ramesseum). These small buildings bear (behind,
above the lintel) the cartouches of Ramses II., Ramses III., and
Ramses IV. Passing between the porters' lodges, we are confronted
with another building almost in the 'shape of a horse-shoe, which
differs considerably from the pylons of other temples. It consists of
truncated pyramids, with almost imperceptibly sloping walls, and
a slightly receding central edifice. An excellent survey of this peculiar structure, which contains numerous apartments, may be obtained from without, as there is an open space of about 35 ft. between
it and the entrance between the porters' houses. The French explorers have given this edifice the name of **Pavilion,** and it is now
generally regarded as the dwelling of Ramses III., chiefly on account of the reliefs in the interior representing scenes from the
private life of the Pharaoh (comp. p. 174). The apartments were
probably designed for the reception of the king when engaged
in festal celebrations and in ancestor-worship. As has been said
before, there were no regular royal palaces on this bank of the Nile.
The royal dwellings looked very different from the temple of Medinet
Habu, and were never built of hewn stone. — To the W. opens the
Gate a, of lesser height. This led from the pavilion to the temple
proper, and affords a view of the first court.

The CENTRAL EDIFICE has windows and doors in every direction.
On the exterior walls of the pavilion-wings, which stand close to

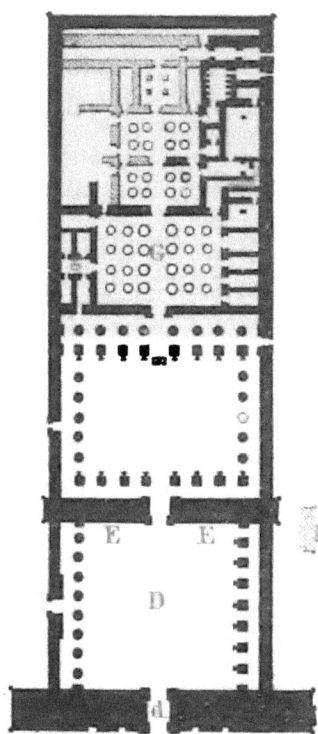

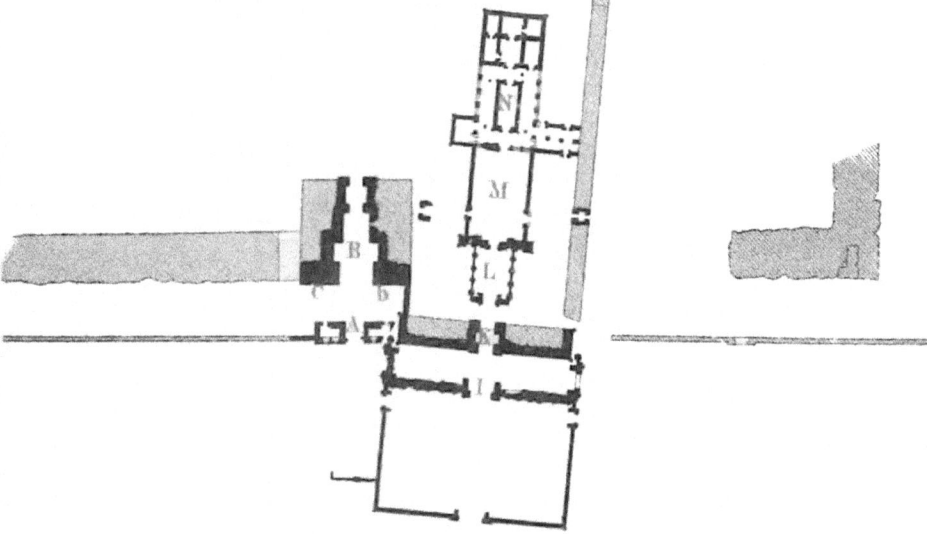

and opposite each other, are some curious projecting heads. These are, as is still clearly visible, representations of foreign peoples conquered by the Pharaoh, and probably served to support a balcony, or to fasten the velaria which shaded the entrance to the temple. The reliefs on the exterior walls of the pavilion are much mutilated. On the walls facing us as we approach, of the wings *b* and *c*, we may recognize (towards the top) the Pharaoh, holding a number of enemies by the hair and raising his battle-axe to strike, while Ammon Ra, on the left, and Harmachis, on the right, offer him the sword of victory ⨍. Low down, immediately above the sloping substructure, are the captive princes of the conquered peoples. In these, as in all representations of foreign tribes at Medinet Habu, careful attention is paid to the race-type and the costumes and weapons of the various conquered peoples. Even those who are not Egyptologists will at once perceive that here we have to do for the most part with tribes entirely different from those against whom the kings of the 18th and 19th Dyn. warred. The present pictures represent especially the western neighbours of the Nile valley, the Libyans and the allied (and apparently related) islanders of the Mediterranean, who even in the time of Merenptah made an expedition against Egypt, and who after their repulse returned with new and stronger forces in the reign of Ramses III. All are depicted with light complexions, a circumstance as natural in the case of the islanders as it seems strange in the case of the Libyans. The latter, however, must be regarded as immigrants from the north, among whom the Mashuasha played an important part. Along with the Pelasgians, Etruscans, Danai, Sicilians, Sardinians, Oscans, etc., they were first conquered by Ramses III., and then permitted to take service under the Pharaohs, at whose court, especially under the 22nd Dyn., they were destined to play an important part. On the lower part of the *E. Wall of Wing c* we perceive their captive representatives beside those of the Libyans and of two other western peoples, whose banner the Ethiopians also followed. On the *E. Wall of Wing b* are captive princes of the islanders, among whom specially to be noted are the leader of the Zekkari, with a curious hood, the prince of the 'Sardinians from the sea', and of the 'Tursha (Etruscans) from the sea', whose head is adorned with a fisher's cap.

Other representations occur to the right and left in the *Narrow Court*, over which the above-mentioned velaria probably extended. As in all other parts of this temple, the deeds of Ramses III. are here celebrated. To the left as we enter, the king, bow in hand, presents to Ammon the conquered tribes, arranged in two columns and bound with lotus-bands. On the right (N.) wall Ramses III. receives the weapons of victory from Ammon. In the narrow *Gateway* to the first court (Pl. a) is the portrait of the Pharaoh as the overcomer of his enemies. To the left, he again receives the sceptre and leads behind him captive island-princes.

The INTERIOR of the pavilion can only be gained from one of the walls of the court to our left as we enter. The attempt is not without difficulty; and some of the rooms are not accessible at all. In several of the apartments are well-preserved wall-sculptures of no little interest; *e.g.* in the apartment above the passage and in the right wing. Ramses III. is here represented in his harem. The nude maidens with whom he is playing chess (the scene in the ruined N. entrance-room to the right is well seen from before the façade of the building), or who hand to him one a fig, another a pomegranate, another a melon, another a flower which he smells, appear from the shape of their faces and from the arrangement of their hair to be captive princesses rather than his own children. This supposition is farther strengthened by the occurrence here of several representations of a distinctly immodest character.

The vicious propensities of this king are gibbeted with biting scorn on other monuments. He himself appears to have looked with peculiar pride upon his harem, which was rich in beauty of all kinds, and to have immortalized its memory in his Memnonium. At all events his reign marks the beginning of an epoch of luxury and immorality, upon which decay followed close.

After passing through the gateway a, we traverse an open *Space* between the pavilion and the first pylon. Before we reach the pylon, 210 ft. wide, which conceals the first peristyle court, we pass a number of ruined walls of baked and unbaked bricks, which belonged to the Coptic village built within the temple. In front, to the left, is a small *Temple of Ameniritis* (26th Dyn.), to the right a block with the cartouche of Nectanebus II. Behind is the temple founded under the 18th Dyn., which we visit later (p. 184). Standing on the rubbish heap in front of the first pylon and looking through the gateway into the temple, our view penetrates to the last court. There is no more remarkable perspective in Egypt.

b. Large Temple of Ramses III.

The large **First Pylon** (Pl. C) is covered with representations and inscriptions. First to the right we see the Pharaoh as the conqueror of his enemies, and opposite is Ammou-Ra, the king of the gods, holding in his right hand the curved sword, in his left the sceptre, and several wall-rings surmounted by busts of their princes. In the first we read the name of Punt or Arabia, which, however, must be here interpreted in a narrow sense, as equivalent to the coastlands of the Red Sea. Between the king and the group of his enemies is the inscription: 'He strikes to the earth the princes of all lands', beneath which is a horizontal row of figures of some tribes (partly damaged). Beneath that again is the chief *Inscription*, from the 11th year of the king, relating his great deeds.

All the inscriptions in Medinet Habu differ from the reports of victories under the 18th and 19th Dyn., by their extravagant titles of honour, immoderate flattery, and the absence of fact. The names of the conquered nations are here recorded, but we learn few particulars of the course of the wars. The value of the booty is here and there indicated, but it by no means corresponds to the gigantic achievements performed by Ramses III. according to the exaggerated representations of his priestly flatterers. There can be little doubt that he successfully opposed a league of several peoples, who attacked his kingdom by land and sea; but he did not penetrate into the heart of Asia as his great ancestors did, and the critic cannot avoid regarding the paeans of Medinet Habu as exaggerated and unreliable. The report on the first pylon, referring to the victory of the 7th day of the month Mekhir in the year 11, contains some passages of considerable poetic force. After relating that the enemy had intended to settle in Egypt and to till the land as his own, the account goes on: 'Death lurked in Tamer (Egypt) for those, who had come on their own feet to the furnace, in which fire consumed impurity under the glow of the heroism of his majesty, who inspired terror like Baal on high. All his limbs are filled with the power of victory . . . His right hand grasps multitudes, and over those who place themselves against him his left hand is stretched out like missiles directed against them to slay them. His battle-scythe (mows) mightily, like his father Month. — Kapur (prince of the Libyans), who came as one smitten with blindness to receive homage, laid down his weapons on the ground with his warriors, and cried aloud to heaven to beseech grace (r ṭebh). His son held his foot and his hand and remained standing in his place. But the God, who knew what was passing in his inmost mind (what was in his intestines), fell upon their heads like a mountain of granite . . . Their blood mingled with the earth like the overflowing river', etc.

On the S. or *Left Pylon* are similar representations. Between the two flag-staffs the king appears with his fettered enemies before the god Ptah, who aims a blow at two enemies. Beneath is another horizontal row of ten conquered peeples, and a stele of the 12th year of the king (imitated from a stele of the 35th year of Ramses II. at Abu-Simbel), containing a dialogue between Ptah and the king. To the left (S.) is a colossal figure of Ammon-Ra, handing the sword of victory to the king, beside six rows of fettered enemies.

Within the gateway (Pl. d) leading to the next court is the name of Ramses III., engraved unusually deeply in the stone. The Fore-court (Pl. D), forming an approximate square of 115 ft., is enclosed on all sides, and is not destitute of shade even at midday. On the left (S.) are calyx-columns and on the right (N.) are Osiris-statues placed against pillars, which form galleries with the outer walls. If we can imagine this space cleared of rubbish and ruined walls, we can form some idea of its pristine effect. Even as it is it impresses the beholder, with its pylons to the E. and W. to shut out the uninitiated, its colonnades to the N. and S., and its magnificent decoration in carvings and inscriptions. Here and elsewhere at Medinet Habu we notice that want of symmetry, which is frequently made a reproach to the Egyptian artists; but there is no doubt that the priestly architects deliberately here placed columns of different forms opposite each other, with the intention of disguising or relieving the uniformity dictated by the hieratic canon.

We now turn to the *Inner Side* of the first pylon. To the right we see a long hieroglyphic inscription; below, to the left, the Pharaoh with his bow bent dashing against the foe, in a chariot drawn by beautiful horses. The slaughter which he causes is immense, and, so far as the vividness of the representation goes, may well be compared with the similar subjects at Karnak and the Ramesseum, though it is inferior in point of style.

Higher up is an inscription from the 11th year of the king; and here also the long rows of hieroglyphics are more concerned with extolling the king than with relating events. The war is once more against the western peoples, the Libyans, Maxyans (Mashauasha), etc. The leaders of the foe are the Libyan prince Kapur and his son Māshashar. The opponents of Pharaoh were (according to the inscription on the N. Pylon) utterly routed, and lost miserably both property and life, 'while the whole earth rejoiced as it beheld the heroism of King Ramses III.' The world bowed before the king, who is compared to Baal, who punishes the impious. The conquered are compared to a flock of goats attacked by a lion. The endless pictorial laudations of the victor are positively wearisome, while the representations of the defeat, impotence, and overthrow of the conquered are almost equally abundant. Finally the king harangues the leaders of his foot-soldiers and charioteers, not forgetting to celebrate in swelling words the deeds that he himself has done. The number of prisoners and slain (the latter with their hands, etc., cut off) is recorded. One of the lists accompanying the inscription includes one prince of the Mashauasha, 5 superior officers, 1205 common soldiers, 152 inferior officers, 131 young men, 1494 in all. Also 342 women, 65 young women, 151 girls, 558 in all. These figures give a total of 2052 persons. Besides these 2175 Mashauasha were slain by the king in their ranks. The total loss of the enemy was thus not more than 4227 persons. The number of captured swords, bows, chariots, etc., corresponds: 115 large swords, 124 smaller, 603 bows, etc.

Another series occupies the back-wall of the colonnade on the right (N.) side of the court, supported by seven pillars with the Osiris-figures of the king. The uppermost row contains sacrificial scenes. The first of these depicts the king, who has alighted from his chariot, shooting his arrows against a hostile fortress occupied by warriors (the town *Amaro,* recalling the Amorites). In the next scene the king drags three rows of prisoners behind his chariot. He is congratulated by the grandees. Finally he presents the captives to Ammon, Muth, and Khunsu.

The inscriptions and sculptures on the **Second Pylon** (Pl. E), enclosing the rear of the court, are still more interesting. To the left are Ammon Ra and Muth, the great queen of heaven, to whom Pharaoh, wearing a richly decorated crown, leads three rows of captives chained together. The two upper rows have distinctly European features, and wear embroidered aprons and low helmets. Over the first row no name appears, but according to the inscription before Pharaoh, they are Shakalsha, *i.e.* probably Sicilians. The captives in the second row are called Tanauna or Danauna, a name in which we are probably correct in recognizing the 'Danai', or Hellenes of the Trojan era. The third row, in which the individual figures resemble those of the other two, is accompanied by the following inscription: 'Provide breath for our nostrils, O king, son of Ammon, say the foes from Pulasata'. In these Pulasata we must recognize the Philistines, new and no contemptible foes of Egypt.

On the *Right Wing* of the second pylon is another long inscription devoted to the deeds of the king in the 8th year of his reign.

Here also facts are obscured by empty titles and elaborate trifles, recited in praise of the king. 'His form, his limbs', runs the fifth line, 'have been weighed in the balances of Baal; he commands the multitude;

and there is none like to him'. Of the enemy, through whose discomfiture he won so much praise, it is said that they worshipped him as soon as they heard of his bravery, that they threw themselves on the ground at his feet, etc. He is compared with Ptah, Osiris, Shu, and Ra. In line 13 the king addresses his faithful followers, telling them that Ammon has lent him his throne, power, strength, and victory. In line 16 the nations that were unable to resist the attack of the islanders are named. Of the latter it is said: 'No people made head against their arms, from the land of Kheta to Kati, Kirkamasha (Karkhemish), Aratu (Arados), and Arasa (Assyria). They assembled in the land of Amara (Amorites?), they overcame the people and the land as though they did not exist. They came, and a fire was prepared beforehand for those who had turned their faces towards Egypt'. Among these foes, as line 18 recounts, were the Pulasata (Philistines), Zekkari (Teucrians?), Shakalsha (Sicilians), Dananna (Danai), and Uashasha (? Oscans according to Chabas). Their hearts were high, and they were filled with their plans'. But the king of Egypt laid a snare for them. God stood by him. He firmly maintained Zaha (Northern Syria) as his frontier. The battle must have taken place in Egypt itself. The king barred the mouth of the Nile as with a wall with well-manned ships, and attacked the enemy with land-forces and chariots, treading them to the ground. The king boasts that he had fought like Month at the head of his troops, acting like a champion (ustennu), that knows his strength, like a brave warrior, that saves his people in the day of battle. 'Those who reached my borders reaped no more harvests on earth'. He strewed their corpses along the bank; their ships and goods sank in the waters. 'I made the lands go back, to remember the land of Egypt, chanting my name in their lands'. In line 25 he extols himself and claims to have taken their lands from the barbarians, to have made their borders his own, and to have received the homage of their princes. He orders general rejoicing, calms the hearts of his followers, and extols his own strength. At this point the inscription is interrupted by a gap in the fourth, fifth, sixth, and seventh courses of masonry from the top. The remainder contains nothing of interest.

The granite gateway of the second pylon admits to the **Colonnaded Hall** (Pl. F), which presents a curious appearance owing to the prostrate columns of a Christian church, erected here at an early period and destroyed after the spread of Islam in Upper Egypt. This second court is a specially retired enclosure, in which the slightly projecting concave cornice, running round the entire open space of the square hall, produces the finest effect. It is 125 ft. long and 138 ft. broad. On all four sides is a colonnade.

The roof is supported on the N. and S. by columns, on the E. by a row of caryatides, while on the W. the rear is closed by a passage, with eight caryatide-pillars in front and eight columns behind. An inscription at the top of the inner side of the left (S.) pylon informs us that this was the *Festal Hall* proper; while the same fact is to be gathered from the sculptures on the back-walls of the colonnades. Turning first to the right we see in the upper row a series of *Representations*, beginning at the N.W. angle of the hall and running all along the N. side and on the E. side as far as the entrance. This illustrates the beautiful Festival of the Staircase, which was celebrated in honour of the god Khem. It took place in the month Pakhon, *i.e.* the first harvest-month, and at the new moon. The course of the moon was represented as a staircase with fourteen steps (days), hence the name of the festival. It was sacred to *Khem, i.e.* Ammon during the process of his self-pro-creation, and may be regarded as one of the greatest of the Egyptian festivals, as even among the representations in the Ramesseum and elsewhere a conspicuous placé is given to it. It might well be solemn-izod in a Memnonium, for Khem caused the new birth of the dead god, and the soul separated from the body arose to new lifè, as the vanished orb of night returns at the new moon. As the inscription of Ammon-en-heb says, the heir to the throne succeeded the dead Pharaoh on the following day, just as one moon succeeds another after a moonless night. The inscription above the reliefs would still preserve for us their subject even if the latter had disappeared. It runs as follows: 'In the month Pakhon, at the festival of the god Khem, at the appearance of the light of the Moon-god. The king, crowned with his helmet, comes in his litter. The body-guard goes before him. Each bears at his side shield, spear, and sword. The lords of his retinue, the higher and lower officers, come behind him, and after them the princes and warriors. The chief orator of festi-vals (kherheb) conducts the festival of his father Khem, while the king presents to his father Khem great offerings of bread, beer, cattle, geese, and all good things. Khem, the lord of Sen, is brought forward, and his son Ramses III. advances before him. The god wears the double feather on his head, and about his neck a finely-worked chain from which at his left arm hangs the portrait of the goddess Ma. The kherheb strikes up a dance, the choir-master (chief singer) does his duty, and the Arabian negro praise the god. Then also appear before the god his vowed servants, with por-traits of the kings of Upper and Lower Egypt, as the divine an-cestors. No more follows, for the god places himself down upon his staircase, and His Majesty offers a great sacrifice to his father Khem, the consort (bull) of his mother. Behold, there also is the white bull before His Majesty, etc.' ... In presence of the living king and of the royal ancestral images an attendant brings the black blade of a sickle inlaid with gold, and a sheaf of corn, and presents them to the king. Then the reaper (mamit), walking round the king seven times, says 'The king has reaped with the sickle that is in his hand, he raises it to his nose, he lays it down before Khem, who gives the king the harvest'. The king quits the staircase, turns to the N., and walks round the staircase, etc. — We shall now see how this description is illustrated by the reliefs.

Procession at the beautiful Festival of the Staircase. This very interesting series begins to the left (W.), on the rear-wall of the N. colonnade. First appears the Pharoah, on a throne-shaped litter adorned with figures of lions, borne by 12 grandees, of whom four are princes of the blood. Attendants wave fans; and three smaller figures with feather-fans are supposed to be marching by the side of the litter. Behind the Pharoah are the two goddesses of rewarding and punishing justice, with out-spread wings, and with

the feather of truth on their head. In two rows before and behind
the king appears the rest of the procession. In the upper row (before the king), a drummer and a trumpeter turn towards the grandees of the kingdom, who wear the double feather on their heads
and carry in their hands the symbols of their power. The last of
these, a bald priest, with a censer turns towards the king. A
short inscription explains that he is offering incense to the Pharaoh,
and names him the fan-bearer at the right hand of the prince, the
royal scribe, general, and crown-prince, whom he (Ramses) loves.
In the lower row are various dignitaries, preceded by two young
princes. These, according to the inscription above, are 'the royal
relatives of the king, young and old, great and worthy, all (who
have appeared) to march before his majesty as he proceeds in his
litter, in order to cause his father Khem to be carried in procession,
at his beautiful festival of the staircase'. Immediately before the
king is a priest, turning towards him and offering incense, and then
the orator of festivals (kherheb), 'who performs all his customary
ceremonies before the king at his solemn procession'. Behind the
king, the procession is also arranged in two rows. In the upper
row are dignitaries, with the symbols of their rank, and armed
warriors; in the lower, royal princes, fan-bearers, and *pastophori*
with portions of the sacred staircase and cases containing sacred
vessels. At the end of the relief is a kind of grated door, with
a vertical inscription in front of it, to the effect that 'His Majesty
arises solemnly, like the sun's disc, from his dwelling of life, constancy, and power (in other words, his palace). The king betakes
himself in his litter to the abode of his father Khem, to gaze upon
his beauties'. Then follows the main object of the procession, *i.e.*
the image of the ithyphallic Khem, who here stands beneath a
canopy crowned with Uræus-snakes. Farther on towards the E.
wall, the image appears borne by priests on a stand covered with
a gaily-coloured carpet and adorned with enormous wreaths of
flowers. The priests, who wave aloft fans of different shapes, are
completely covered by the carpet, with the exception of their heads
and feet. Behind and a little above, two priests spread out a sail,
the emblem of breath, freshness, and joy, and beneath them four
others bear a chest with five ornamental trees. Before the former
figure of the god the king, offering incense and drink-offering,
wears the helmet of the ruler of Upper Egypt; while before the
image on the covered stand the Pharaoh, bearing a staff and sceptre
and following a white bull, wears the crown of Lower Egypt. Above
him hovers the vulture of victory (as in nearly every place where
the king appears in the present series), bearing in its talons the
symbol of the innumerable periods, which (according to the inscription beneath) Ammon-Khem has bestowed upon the Pharaoh
for his appearance at the festival. An inscription in front of the
sacred bull names it 'the white bull'. Its horns are shaped like

12*

the crescent moon and enclose the disc adorned with the double feather of the goddess of truth. Above the bull and the following procession are two hieroglyphic inscriptions, between which are the portraits of the first favourite and queen (whose name, however, is not given in the cartouche in front of her), and of the kherheb, with an open volume, who is called the president of the singers and the chief of the festival orators, etc. The hieroglyphics above the bull contain a hymn, in which the kherheb extols the god Khem. And in the inscription turned towards the singer, the praise of the god and of the bull symbolizing him is also sung in words placed in the mouth of the god Thoth. — A long train of standard-bearers precedes the bull. Between these and the bull a priest facing the latter, with the censer (the Horus-hand), and the festival-orator in the act of reciting. The series on the N. wall ends at the tenth standard-bearer, but it is continued without interruption on the *E. Wall.* Besides the usual emblems, sacrificial vessels, and ancestral statues, images of sacred animals on standards are borne along. The bearers of the hawk, vulture, dog-headed ape, and bull are clad in curious sleeveless garments, covering them from neck to foot. The procession advances towards the Pharaoh, who awaits it, wearing the double crown of Upper and Lower Egypt, and holding in his hands a staff, arrow, and sceptre. On a table in front of him stands a staff with the double feather, and the sacred wreaths; and before his eyes takes place the ceremony of letting four geese fly, usual at the coronation of the kings of Egypt. The geese, which here, as in the Ramesseum, have the names of Amset, Hapi, etc., the children of Horus, attached to them, are to announce in all quarters of the globe the accession of the new Pharaoh. The kherheb here appears, declaring that the geese must hasten to the N., S., E., and W., and announce to the gods of those regions that Horus, the son of Isis and Osiris, that the king etc. Ramses III., has assumed the great crowns of Upper and Lower Egypt. Behind the orator four, and below him three priests carry the images of the predecessors of Ramses III., each with its name. Above the first of the men bearing standards with the jackal stands a figure clapping its hands, which is named the Nehos en Punt, *i.e.* the Negro of Arabia, and which is regarded as the personification of the moonless night preceding the new moon. This curious figure greets the god Khem, lord of Senu, etc., at whose approach every heart expands with joy. Farther to the right we see the Pharaoh, who (as in the Ramesseum, p. 164) cuts with a sickle the sheaf held out to him by a priest. Behind stands the kherheb and his hymn, relating to Khem. Almost above the sheaf is the queen, then before the Pharaoh the white bull again, and beneath it a row of images of ancestors. Finally the king offers incense to the god Khem, who stands beneath a canopy, and presents to the ithyphallic Khem the image of justice, the goddess Mā.

The lower series of representations on the N. and E. walls are less interesting. Several boats appear in them, and beneath them (to the extreme left) the festal-barge of Ammon. A dialogue between the king and the god Ammon, in which the building of the temple is extolled, also occurs here.

Corresponding to the festival of Khem on the N. and E. walls, a *Festival of Ptah-Sokar-Osiris* is displayed in the upper row of the S. and S.E. side of the colonnade. It begins to the left of the door with a train of priests of various forms, bearing standards and arranged in two rows. Next appears the king, to whom incense is offered, and above whom hovers a vulture. Then follow dignitaries, succeeded by a colossal symbol of the god Nefer Tum, borne by 18 priests. The kherheb reads 16 formulae of invocation. After him come 16 exalted personages, including the king's sons holding a cord which reaches to the hands of the king. Then follow 16 priests bearing the barge of Ptah-Sokar-Osiris; and finally the king before Khnum and Ptah-Sokar-Osiris.

More interesting than these festal representations are the *Warlike Reliefs*, in the lower division on the S. and E. walls. The inscriptions relate the conquest of the Libyans and the annihilation of the N. tribes of the Philistines and Zekkari, who had penetrated into the Nile delta and were there captured by the king. One of the reliefs on the exterior of the N. wall represents this occurrence. The inscription contains 75 lines and covers a considerable part of the S. wall. The *1st Scene* to the left of it depicts in four rows the captured Libu, conducted by the king's sons and other notabilities. One counts and another notes upon a leaf the number of hands and phalli cut off, which in both cases is given as 3000. The king seated in his chariot and turning his body, addresses his sons and officials. — *2nd Scene* (to the left of the first). The king standing in his chariot shoots an arrow against the falling foe: 'He sees defeat like a flame beneath them; he holds the bow in his right hand and looses the arrow with his left; he goes against them, knowing his own strength. Face to face, he smites a hundred thousand. The hearts of the Temhu, their life, their soul have ceased'. — *3rd Scene*. The king drives, with his enemies in fetters. Beneath marches a row of his soldiers, armed with spear, shield, and knife. — *4th Scene* (next the door in the E. wall). The king, standing, brings three rows of captives into the presence of Ammon and Muth. In the four lines between him and the gods the captives are described as Temhu and Mashauasha (Maxyans); and in the small inscription above the top row as Rabu or Libu (Libyans). — On the W. or *Rear-Wall* of Hall F, to the right and left of the door to the next hall, are portraits of the king's sons, with their names; on each side the same number (10). Those who afterwards came to the throne have the royal cartouche.

We now enter the **Second Hypostyle Hall** (Pl. G). The roof was formerly supported by 24 columns in 4 rows of six, of which the central row was considerably thicker than the others. The roof, however, has long fallen in, and nothing remains of the columns save the plinths and the lower part of the shafts. Two smaller chambers follow, with four couples of columns, and then a *Central Apartment* with four pillars. On both sides these are adjoined by a series of rooms (comp. Pl.), of which those to the N. are accessible, those to the S. covered with rubbish except the two front apartments (Pl. g). A special door leads from the colonnaded hall to the latter, which are arranged differently from those on the N. These rooms have been carefully examined by Prof. Dümichen; and from the inscriptions in and near them they are now known as the TREASURY of this Memnonium of Ramses III. Even on the external walls of these apartments are artistic representations of vases, jars, and other vessels in the precious metals.

The INTERIOR of the treasury consists of a hall turned towards the N., adjoined on each side by two chambers. The inscriptions without exception relate to the gifts of gold, silver, electrum, lapis-lazuli, malachite and other stones which Ramses III. extravagantly heaped upon Ammon, so that 'the offering of his gifts found no end'. Even those visitors who do not understand the inscriptions will at once recognize that they are in a treasure-house, from the representations which adorn all the walls, especially those of the chambers on the right. The hieroglyphic ⌐⌐⌐ nub means

gold and ⌐⌐⌐ nub hez *white gold* or *silver*. Whole heaps of these metals are seen lying in grains or nuggets. Sacks of gold from different lands and all kinds of precious vessels meet the eye. Pieces of lapis-lazuli and malachite shaped like bricks are built up in stepped masses, each in three rows. Arabian indiarubber (Kami) and the tree whence it is obtained are also depicted. In the chambers on the right appear also sheets of silver, and plates of brass and lead. The Pharoah boasted ceaselessly that he had filled the treasure-house of his father Ammon; and the god Thoth (in the second chamber to the right) writing reckons it by the countless hundreds of thousands and tens of thousands (a million altogether) in silver, gold, brass, lapis-lazuli, malachite from Reshata (Sinai Peninsula), etc., which he has offered to his venerable father Ammon-Ra, king of the gods, who on his side has accorded to the king the periods of Ra and the years of Tum. — It is impossible not to recall the passage in Diodorus's description of the tomb of Osymandyas (p. 159), in which the king is represented as offering to the divinity gold and silver to the value of 32 million minae.

Ramses III. was no other than the rich Rhampsinitus of Herodotus (II, 121); and it is not impossible that we here stand before the very *Treasure-house of Rhampsinitus* which figures in the pleasant tale narrated by the Father of History.

Rhampsinitus the Pharaoh was possessed of such vast treasures that he commanded a builder to erect for their safe custody a stone building beside the palace. The architect coveted the treasures, and being a cunning man so arranged a stone in the wall that two men, or indeed one, could easily withdraw it. Before his death he imparted the secret to his sons. These immediately on the death of their father betook themselves to the treasure-house, removed the stone, and favoured by the darkness of night, succeeded in carrying off a large amount of treasure. They repeated their visits, until the king remarked that his treasure was decreasing, without, however, being able to accuse anyone of the theft, as he invariably found the seals unbroken and the doors fast locked. He accordingly had a trap constructed and placed it beside the chests containing the gold. The thieves once more came, and the one who entered first was caught in the trap. Perceiving what had happened to him, he conjured his brother to cut off his head lest he should be recognized, and so bring his accomplice into trouble. The advice was followed, and the brother departed with the head, closing the opening behind him. The next morning the amazed king discovered the headless corpse in the securely fastened room. He resolved to expose the body in public, under the care of a guard who had orders to observe the passers-by very closely and to arrest immediately anyone who shewed signs of grief at the mournful spectacle. The architect's widow, who had learned the occurrence, was, as a true Egyptian, beside herself at the dishonourable treatment of her son's body, and threatened to reveal all to the king unless the surviving brother contrived to bring the corpse to her. The crafty youth soon hit upon a plan. He loaded an ass with wine-skins, three of which he opened just as he was about to pass the soldiers guarding the headless trunk. When the wine began to escape, he broke into loud lamentation which soon attracted the soldiers. They hastened to catch the wine in cups, and drank it up in spite of his pretended opposition. Finally the hypocrite appeared to reconcile himself to his fate, and pressed the soldiers to drink until they fell helpless in a drunken sleep. He then shaved off the right side of each man's beard, and taking possession of his brother's body, brought it to his mother. — The king though enraged, was now devoured with curiosity to discover the author of this trick. He accordingly commanded his daughter to suffer the love of anyone who consented to relate to her his craftiest and wickedest deed. If any of her wooers should relate the above incident, she was to seize him and cause his arrest. The adroit thief, no whit alarmed, procured the arm of a corpse, placed it under his cloak, and going to the princess, related his adventures with the treasure and the soldiers. When the princess sought to seize him, he thrust the dead arm into her hands, and escaped. The king, astonished by such cunning and boldness, caused a proclamation to be made that he would not only pardon the thief but reward him if he revealed himself. Upon this the architect's son presented himself. 'Rhampsinitus expressed his admiration and gave the princess as wife to him as the craftiest among men; for, said the king, 'the Egyptians excel all other men in craft, and he all the Egyptians'.

The immense wealth of Ramses III. is a historical fact. We have seen representations of it in the rooms which we have just quitted; and this Pharoah records in the great *Harris Papyrus* his donations to the temples of Egypt, donations so enormous that we are justified in describing the giver as the wealthiest prince that ever sat on the throne of the Pharoahs.

At the N. side of the hypostyle we emerge into the open air and examine the interesting representations on the outside of the *N. Wall* (Pl. c). Between the N.W. angle and the second pylon, there are *Ten Reliefs*, which are described and illustrated in the works of Champollion and Rosellini. At present the three first (to the W.) are covered with rubbish.

1st Scene. Procession of Pharaoh, besides whose chariot a lion advances. In another chariot before that of the king is the standard of Ammon-Ra with the ram's head. — *2nd Scene.* Fierce battle, the Mashauasha turn to flee. — *3rd Scene.* The king harangues five rows of soldiers, who bring captive Mashauasha and Libu. The severed hands etc. are counted, amounting to 12,535. — *4th Scene* (the first uncovered, from the right). Standards are brought out and weapons distributed to the soldiers. The king orders the archers to shoot so as to destroy the enemy. — *5th Scene.* The king starts for Zeh (N.E. borderland); before him march soldiers with lances and bows. A small doorway, above which are Coptic crosses, made through the horse, conducts to the hall behind. — *6th Scene.* The king, standing in his chariot, shoots arrows against the enemy, who are identified as Zekkari (Teucrians) from the curious striped caps, not unlike an Indian headdress. In the middle, among the latter, are ox-waggons with children in them. Some of the Egyptian soldiers are Shardana, distinguished by the conical ornaments on their helmets. These, at first enemies of Egypt, afterwards took service under the Pharaohs. — *7th Scene* (beyond a gap in the wall). The king at a lion-hunt. One of the lions, concealed in a thicket, has been pierced by the king's spear and arrows; another lies dying beneath the horse's feet; and the king turns to transfix a third, of which only the claws are shown. Beneath is a procession of the Egyptian army with allies (Shardana and Kehak). — *8th Scene.* The king, having alighted from his chariot, shoots against the hostile fleet. The painting illustrates the occurrence mentioned in the inscription of the 8th year, on the second pylon (p. 176) as well as in the long inscription in the colonnaded room. The hostile Shardana and Zekkari (Sardinians and Teucrians) had penetrated into the Nile delta, where they were held fast, like birds in a net, by the Egyptian army, until they fell beneath the arrows of the king and his followers. We may clearly distinguish the Teucrians by their caps resembling tufts of feathers, the Shardana by their horned helmets, and the Egyptians by their laced head-cloths. The representation is exceedingly animated, though not very distinct in the oblique light. One of the ships has capsized. The Egyptian vessels are denoted by the lion's head on the prow. The ship below to the right is steered by two men with large oars, while the rest of the crew are rowers seated upon benches. Archers standing up ply their bows. In the interior of the ship are a number of bound Teucrians, and others appear in the lower row. The king himself is treading upon a captive foe. In front of him are some archers, and above him, the protecting vulture Uazi. — *9th Scene.* The king, having alighted from his chariot, graciously receives the grandees who conduct the prisoners. In the lower row the severed hands are being counted and the number noted. Above the horses a fortress is represented, named *Makatiro* (Migdol castle) of King Ramses. — *10th Scene.* The king presents two rows of captives, described as Zekkari (Teucrians) and Rabu (Libyans), to Ammon, Muth, and Khunsu, the Theban triad.

We have now reached the second pylon, between which and the first pylon are two more *Reliefs.* One represents the king attacking a hostile fortress, whose defenders, many of whom are pierced with arrows, beg for mercy. The other depicts the king, waving his sword, at the head of his charioteers, as he attacks a fortress. Some of his soldiers are beating in the doors, while others ascend by ladders. Trees are being felled in the vicinity.

On the outside of the *S. Wall* (Pl. f) of the temple is a long *Festival Calendar*, which contains a list of the appointed sacrifices for the period between the 26th Pakhon (the day of Ramses III.'s accession) and the 19th Tybi. The mention of the rising of Sothis (Sirius) on the 1st Thoth (beginning of the year) has led to the probably erroneous assumption that under Ramses III. the Sothis-year of $365\frac{1}{4}$ days coincided with the Egyptian civil year of 365 days, and has thus provided a fixed era for Egyptian chronology.

c. The Small Temple of Medinet Habu.

We now quit the large temple, beside which we note the considerable ruins of the Christian village, whose church stood in the second court (p. 177). We retrace our steps between the pylons, and to the left we see the smaller temple, founded under the 18th Dyn., the oldest part of the remains at Medinet Habu. Even if the inscriptions had been defaced, the architectonic forms here used would have told us in what epoch of Egyptian history the building was erected. Its axis is not exactly parallel with that of the temple of Ramses. The small temple was entered from the E. It is an open

question how the courts were originally arranged, which preceded
the actual sanctuary. Little of them remained, and the later Pharaohs.
and even the Ptolemies and Roman emperors (notably Antoninus
Pius) extended the old building. The following description begins
at the E. façade, which faces us when we turn to the left (N.) after
returning through the gate of the so-called pavilion.

The visitor approaching from the Nile is confronted with a handsome *Pylon* (Pl. K), to the N. of the entrance to the temple
of Ramses. In the centre is a beautiful gateway, with a well-
executed winged disc of the sun in the deep concave cornice. The
narrow fore-court in front was enclosed under the Ptolemies with
columns, of which only the two at the entrance have been preserved
(beside Pl. I). In the broader fore-court outside (Pl. H) the cartouche of the emperor Antoninus Pius occurs several times. The
large *Pylon* (Pl. K) dates from the late Ptolemaic epoch, for it exhibits Ptolemy Soter II. Lathyrus worshipping the gods; but it includes stones from an earlier edifice, some of which are upside down
and some show detached fragments of inscriptions (*e.g.* sacrificial
lists, with the names of Ramses II.). Beyond the pylon is a *Chapel*
(Pl. L), only 30 ft. long, dating from the reign of Nectanebus II.,
who was acknowledged as king by the Egyptians in the middle of
the Persian epoch. The roof was supported by eight columns which,
however, have disappeared, leaving only the low walls which connected them like screens. Immediately adjoining the chapel is a
Second Pylon, 50 ft. wide, which was erected under Taharka the
Ethiopian (25th Dyn.) and renewed and provided with inscriptions
by Ptolemy Lathyrus. On the front of this pylon appears Nectanebus II., on the back Taharka. Beyond this is a ruined *Court*
(Pl. M), with (to the right) the granite lintels of a gateway, built by
Petamenap, a noble living under the 26th Dyn., to whom the
large tomb at el-Asasif (p. 222) belongs. We now at last reach the
OLDEST TEMPLE BUILDINGS, begun under Amenhotep I. and Tutmes I., completed under Ramaka, Tutmes II., and Tutmes III., and
restored by later kings, including even Ptolemy Physkon. These
late restorations were of trifling importance; as a whole the building is beyond doubt a work of the 18th Dynasty. It consists of a
Sanctuary (Pl. N), like the cella of a Greek temple, forming the
kernel of the entire edifice, surrounded on three sides by pillars,
while on the rear it is adjoined by *Six Apartments*. Between the
rows of pillars to the right and left and the cella, and also behind the
latter, were polygonal columns, resembling those which are to be
found at Benihasan and the oldest parts of Karnak. Those in
front have been destroyed, but one has remained erect behind
the cella. The inscriptions are written for the most part in the
beautiful style of the 18th Dyn., but contain nothing of importance.

The *Builders' Inscriptions*, found on various parts of the temple, are
interesting as throwing light on the HISTORY of the edifice. Over each
of the rows of pillars to the right and left of the cella are two long two-

line inscriptions which meet in the middle, dating from the time of Tutmes III. In front of the second door occurs a mention of the restoration
of the building by Horemheb (18th Dyn.); within the cella Seti I. is
named as a restorer; and in another place the second year of Merenptah I.
is mentioned. The name of Ramses III. also occurs in the rooms behind.
Inside the cella we should note the tree on which the god Ammon is
writing the name of Seti I. In the adjoining building on the N., the roof
of which includes remains of the old building of Ramses II., not only is
the priest-king Pinozem, son of Piankhi, of the 21st Dyn. represented, but
also Hakoris of the 29th Dynasty. Ptolemy Euergetes II. occurs in the
upper inscription running round the cella.

The building, though small, is distinguished by its harmonious
forms. About 65 paces to the N.E. is the well-known *Fresh Water
Spring*, a pool to which a subterranean passage leads. It is a remarkable fact that the freshness of the water remains entirely un-
affected by the saline exudations from the ground, even in the necropolis at Thebes.

To the S. of the temples of Medinet Habu are traces of a *Sacred
Lake* of considerable extent, formerly taken for a hippodrome. At
its N.W. angle is a small temple, now known as *Kaṣr el-ʿAgûz*,
erected by Ptolemy Euergetes II. to his ancestors. It consists of
a wide vestibule and three rooms, one behind another. Still farther
to the S., at the S.W. angle of the former lake, stood a small sanctuary dating from the Roman period. It was erected by Hadrian
and Antoninus Pius, while the ruined pylon bears the names of
Vespasian, Domitian, and Otho, the last of exceedingly rare occurrence owing to the emperor's short reign (69 A.D.). The temple
consists of a cella surrounded by apartments. A staircase leads to
the roof from a space to the extreme left of the entrance. The inscriptions announce that the sanctuary no longer belongs to the
Diospolitan district, but to the district of Hermonthis; and it was
specially dedicated to the Isis of the W. mountain of Hermonthis.
— Grebaut discovered in 1889 in the vicinity the remains of a *Palace of Amenhotep III.* and his consort *Tîi*.

16. Tombs of the Queens.

The *Tombs of the Queens* are in every way less important than those
of the Kings in Bibân el-Mulûk, which should in any case be seen; and
a visit to the former, for which at least 1¼ hr. is necessary, renders it
almost impossible to complete the first day's programme on the West
Bank. Those who, however, decide to visit them should proceed thither
direct from Medinet Habu, and visit Dêr el-Medineh on the way back.
From Medinet Habu to the Tombs ½ hr.

The road from Medinet-Habu to the Tombs of the Queens crosses
the desert to the W., and passes through a mountain valley with
bare and lofty sides of limestone, picturesquely formed and carved
with inscriptions of various lengths. The latter contain prayers to
the gods of the regions of the dead, and date from the 19th and
20th Dynasties. The **Tombs of the Queens** belong to the same
period, except a few which are of the 18th Dynasty. Altogether

20 have been discovered, many of them unfinished and entirely
without decoration, and in their rough and blackened condition,
resembling mere caves in the rocks. It is rare to find either inscriptions or representations carved in the stone; even in the finest
tombs the limestone walls were more often covered with plaster
which could be adorned with paintings without much difficulty.

Of the two tombs which we reach first, the second only (to the
W.), that of a queen of Ramses III., is preserved. Her name is no
longer legible, but only those of her husband and her son *Ra-ḥi-
anemi-f.* The tomb consists of an ante-
chamber and a large hall with 4 pillars,
in the midst of which is the broken sarcophagus.

The next three tombs, of which the
farthest belonged to a *Queen Sitra* of the
20th Dyn., need not be visited. But of
the four on the side of the valley next
reached, the second and the first deserve
notice. The former is the **Tomb of Queen
Tītī** . It lies on the
S. side of the valley and consists of the
usual antechamber (Pl. 1) open to the N.,
a long passage (Pl. 2), and a large chapel
(Pl. 3) with a small chamber on each of
its three sides. In this as in most of the
better preserved tombs of the Queens the
freshness of the colour is extraordinary. On the left wall (Pl. *a*) of
the *Passage 2* we see the queen before Ptah, Ra Harmachis, the genii
of the dead Amset and Tuamutef, and Isis; on the right (Pl. *b*)
Tītī with the sistrum stands before Thoth, Tum, Hapi, Kebsenuf
and Nephthys. Ptah is placed opposite to Thoth, Ra Harmachis,
i.e. the morning sun, to Tum, *i.e.* the evening sun, the two genii
of the dead Amset and Tuamutef to the two others Hapi and Kebsenuf, and lastly Isis to her sister Nephthys. As a border above the
figures runs an inscription from which we learn that Tītī was the
daughter of a king, the sister and the mother of a Pharaoh, and
queen of Upper and Lower Egypt, and that she received in the other
world a friendly welcome and all that is wished for the dead.

The name of the wife of Amenhotep IH., which often occurs on
scarabæi, is also mentioned on the cuneiform tablets recently discovered
at Tell el-Amarnah. She was perhaps the daughter of a Babylonish king.
This would account for the reddish skin and blue eyes with which she
is represented here.

In the passage leading to *Room 3* are at Pl. c the Goddess Isis
(Selk with the scorpion on her head), and at Pl. d Neith, 'the great
lady of Saïs, the mistress of heaven, and princess of all the gods, the

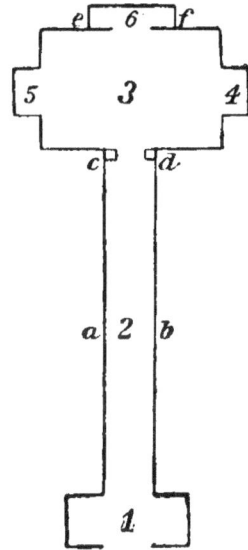

daughter of Ra; she has not her like'. In the *Side-chamber* 5 is the mummy-shaft. In the innermost *Chamber 6* Osiris sits enthroned as supreme judge to whom Selk conducts the queen. Behind him are Nephthys and Thoth. On the walls *e* and *f* are tables of offerings on which, by the side of distributions of bread etc., lie masses of flowers far larger than are found in the tombs of men. In the *Side-chamber 4* we see the Hathor cow, richly decorated and standing out of a background of radiance and flames of fire painted with dazzling colours. This painting, which meets us several times in the tombs of the Queens, represents Hathor as a goddess of heaven and especially of the horizon. She is the cow which in the lower world gives birth to the young Sun, who begins his active life with flame and light.

On the right close to the tomb of Titi lies that of **Queen Isis,**

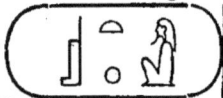

Ast, wife of Ramses IV. (Nefer-ḥak-an) of the 20th Dynasty. The entrance is filled up, and the inscriptions are much injured and covered with debris. In the inner room corresponding to room 3 in the tomb of Titī stands a broken granite sarcophagns.

On the W. side, running parallel to that just described, the first tomb approached from the N. is in ruins; close to it is that of a queen, whose name has been obliterated, and in its place another written with ink, apparently to be read *Tuattent Apt.* In this the first and third rooms were supported by pillars. The names are on the inner wall of the second room. The inscriptions were incised. The two tombs beyond were the resting-places of another princess, the favourite daughter of Ramses II., *Bant anṭa,* and of *Amen-meri,* *i.e.* the beloved of Ammon, the latter consisting of a principal hall with a chamber behind and on each side. Contrary to custom the shaft is on the left of the entrance in front of the principal hall.

17. Dêr el-Medîneh.

No one should miss seeing the beautiful small Ptolemaic temple of Dêr el-Medîneh lying to the N.W. of Medinet Habu. It lies on the way to Shêkh 'Abd el-Kurnah either from Medinet Habu or from the Tombs of the Queens. From Medinet Habu we reach Dêr el-Medinch in 20 minutes.

On the way from the Tombs of the Queens to Dêr el-Medîneh, we pass (1/4 hr.) a hillside with some remarkable historical steles of the 18th, 19th, and 20th Dynasties. On one appears King Ramses III. before Horus, and his father Set-nekht before Ammon. Another contains an account of the campaigns of the former king.

The graceful **Temple of Dêr el-Medîneh** was founded under the Ptolemies for the worship of the dead, and dedicated to the goddess Hathor. It lies in a barren hollow, in which several fragments of buildings are to be seen, and is surrounded by a lofty wall of dried bricks which are fitted together in waving lines. Through this a

Doorway of stone (on the S.E.), by which we have to pass, leads into
the temple, at the back of which (N.) are steep rocks. The sanctuary was founded by Ptolemy IV. Philopator I., and sculptures were
added by others of the house of the Lagidæ, and later also by the
Emperor Augustus. The traveller on passing through the doorway
in the outer wall sees on his left an archway of Nile bricks, and
before him the front of the temple of freestone, on which many
Greeks and Copts have written their names. In Christian times it
was used by the monks as a dwelling-place, and to this is due the
mutilation of many of the inscriptions and also its present name
(Dêr = monastery). We first come to a small hypæthral *Antechamber*
with 2 columns, and a few steps further reach the true Ptolemaic entrance of the *Naos*. This is ornamented by two pilasters with masks
of Hathor, and two columns with sculptured calyx-capitals in the
middle, which support the architrave and are connected by walls resembling screens (reaching half-way up). Between the pillars is a
semi-portal similar to the one at Medamût(p. 151). The pilasters are
brightly coloured and peculiarly ornamented, with a lotus flower and
a bud on slender stems at the side. Above are Uræus-serpents with the
crowns of both kingdoms. On the left side is an elegant window which
lights a staircase. The inner portion of the temple is in three parts.
Over the door of the middle room, the sanctuary, are placed 7 Hathor-
masks corresponding to the number of the Hathors. Euergetes II.
and his wife are named as beautifiers of the temple, and the four
sacred bulls, Hapi, Urmerti, Temur, and Abekur, are portrayed. In
the cell to the right is the king before the various gods of the lower
world, and also an astronomical painting, Sothis (Sirius) and Orion.
In the room to the left, on the left wall, is a remarkable representation of the *Judgment of the Dead.*

The valley of Dêr el-Medîneh is rich in **Tombs** of various periods,
some of them early and of great interest, with the colours of the
paintings marvellously preserved.

Here was discovered the well-known collection of *Papyri*, obtained
by *A. C. Harris* in 1855, containing the famous papyrus of Ramses III. (see
p. 120), the largest known, from the archives of the temple of Medinet Habu.

The earliest tombs here belong to the beginning of the New Empire and to the times of Aahmes I. and Amenhotep I. They belonged to great officials, especially to the *Sotem-as*, supreme judge
at the Seat of Truth, possibly a college which met at Dêr el-Medineh. We may mention the small brilliantly coloured chapel of the
royal scribe, *Mesrā*, the similar one of *Khā*, the tombs of *Amenmes*,
Zesken, and *Amenhotep*. In several tombs we find numerous fragments of mummies, damaged and ransacked by the fellâhin. Continuing farther into the valley we reach a tomb with a wide entrance
from which there is a fine view of Dêr el-Medîneh and of the fertile
plains to the E., traversed by the Nile and bounded by the distant
Arabian mountains. In the foreground are seen Medinet Habu, the

Colossi of Memnon, and the Ramesseum, and on the other side of the river the gigantic ruins of Karnak.

18. The Tombs of Shêkh 'Abd el-Ḳurnah.

With this part of the Necropolis of Thebes, which may be reached from Dêr el-Medineh in 25 min., we conclude our first day on the W. bank in our three days' plan. Gaze's tourists make it their second day, Cook's begin their third day with the Ramesseum (R. 13) and the tombs of 'Abd el-Kurnah, as in our five days plan. The tombs to be visited may be found without a guide. They are reached by ascending the E. side of the Libyan mountains in a direct line from the Ramesseum. Many of the tombs here are inhabited by fellâhin. The sepulchral chambers serve as dwelling-places, wooden doors are hung in the entrances, and the fore-court is often enclosed by a clay wall for the confinement of their live stock. In front of most of these cave-dwellings stand covered cylinders like gigantic mushrooms, of Nile mud and straw kneaded together. These are the primitive granaries of the inhabitants of 'Abd el-Ḳurnah, several of whom are well-to-do, with houses of Nile bricks, conspicuous from a considerable distance. Those who are desirous of staying any length of time should make arrangements with the wealthy and worthy Copt, *Todrus,* uncle of the German consular agent at Luxor. The erection of a house for travellers has been under consideration, and would be of especial benefit to scholars by sparing them the daily journey to and from Luxor. Shelter may be found in the house of Moḥammed 'Abd er-Rasûl, provisions being brought from Luxor. Several European scholars have chosen 'Abd-el-Ḳurnah as their centre for investigations on the W. bank, among them Champollion, Wilkinson, Lepsius (whose lodging in the tombs is still known by the fellâhin as the Ḳaṣr Lepsius), Prisse d'Avennes, and Ebers. The visitor to the tombs must first face some savage dogs, but he will be thoroughly repaid partly by the interest which some of the tombs afford, and partly by the magnificent *View* which is obtained from those in the higher positions, especially at sunset. In this part of the Necropolis of Thebes were buried the wealthy nobility of the 18th Dyn., upon whose tombs large sums of money must have been spent. The inscriptions record that the deceased were in their life-time invested with the highest spiritual and temporal dignities and that they enjoyed almost royal estates, their pride in which they show in sculptures and inscriptions. However death is not forgotten in these tombs, for there is no lack of funereal epitaphs. In almost all of them too we find genealogical tables, by which we learn that many of those buried here were related to each other.

The more important tombs were numbered by Wilkinson, but most of the figures have been obliterated. In 1885 Prof. Eisenlohr renumbered the tombs, in all 127, including those with no inscriptions. In the following description' of the tombs reference is made to these numbers, which appear in the adjoining small plan. If time is limited, it will be sufficient to visit the tombs of Kha-em-ḥāt, Ramses, Nekht, Sen-ncfer, Anna, Horemheb, and Ramenkheperseneb.

The traveller is recommended to begin with two tombs on the eastern side of the hill behind the Ramesseum. The one to the left is that of **Kha-em-ḥāt** (No. 120), superintendent of the royal granaries, of the time of Amenhotep III. The tomb has been long known, and in consequence is much injured. It lies behind a square court cut out of the hill, and has two other tombs near it.

The tomb of *Kha-em-ḥāt* consists of three halls lying one behind the other, the first and third of which are at right angles to its length. On the sides of the first and third were placed niches of which only one (on the left) is preserved in the first hall, and three in the third. There is a wide passage between halls 1 and 2. The third hall is adjoined by a fourth smaller room. On the left of the entrance is *Kha-em-hāt* offering a prayer to Ra with uplifted hands. In the niche to the left two statues of Kha-em-hāt and his relative, *Imhotep*, the treasurer (the neighbouring tomb 121 belonged to an Imhotep). On the right of the entrance is the deceased offering two dishes with two geese in each. On the left are four series; in the two upper, fowling scenes; below the king driving a four-horse chariot; and in the lowest, harvest scenes. A flute player encourages the reapers. On the inner wall to the left, Kha-em-hāt presents a report on

the harvest to King Amenhotep III. sitting beneath

a canopy. The nine captive tribes, at the foot of the canopy, among whom are Greeks *(Hanebu)*, should be noticed. On the right again the deceased with a peculiar head-dress delivers to the king the harvest report of the year 30. Behind him are two rows of his officials in humble attitude. The chess-board decoration of the ceiling is peculiar. In the entrance to the second hall on the right, there is a long 16 column inscription of deeply-cut hieroglyphics. In the second hall are several chapters of the Book of the Dead (110, 112). The sides of the third hall are destroyed, the fourth was entirely without inscriptions.

To the right at no great distance is a tomb first opened in 1882 (now No. 118), known as **Stuart's Tomb** from its discoverer Villiers Stuart. It belonged to *Ramses*, a mayor (mer nut zet) and his sister *Ptahmerit*, of the time of Amenhotep IV., the sun-worshipper, who, as Khu-en-aten (splendour of the sun) removed his residence to Tell el-Amarnah (see p. 22). Here as there the sun is represented with his rays spread out as hands protecting the king and queen. Proceeding a little farther to the N., we soon reach the tomb of *Nekht* (No. 125), first opened in 1889 (the door unlocked on request) with representations of fowling, wine-pressing, etc.; the drawing is rough but the colours fresh and well preserved. We then climb the somewhat steep hill and, passing the richly decorated tomb (No. 119) of *Amenuser*, who lived under Tutmes III., come to that marked No. 35. *Khamsatelâtîn*, by Wilkinson, at one time considered the most worth visiting of all. It consists of a vestibule, and a large chamber from the centre of which an unusually long passage of remarkable and gradually increasing height runs into the rock. It was laid out by a prince. governor. etc., named **Rekh-ma-rā**, who died in the time of Amenhotep II., the successor of Tutmes III., when the tributes of Asia were flowing into Egypt in exceptional abundance, to the benefit of the relations and favourites of the royal family.

The pictorial decoration of the walls can now be scarcely seen, and can be much better studied in the works of Wilkinson and Hoskins (Ethiopia). The tomb served as the abode of old Husên Barûr, the companion of Harris and Lepsius, and is a convenient room for luncheon. The opportunity should be taken of looking at the faded paintings of the left corridor, and of the passage into the rock. They represent payment of tribute by the Ethiopians (Punt, Kefa) and Asiatics (Retennu), various kinds of work such as brick-making for building, pottery, carpentry, joinery, glass-blowing, carving and polishing of statues, and a company of mourners with harpers and women playing musical instruments.

Mounting to the left of the tomb of Rekhmarā we reach (to the left of No. 48) a lately discovered tomb, rather difficult of access. The trouble of the ascent, however, is repaid· by the beauty and freshness of the paintings. It belonged to **Sen-nefer** (good brother), superintendent of the southern city, overseer of the granaries of Ammon, and superior of the flocks of Ammon, under Amenhotep II. Strangely enough the name of *Alexander* (Arkes antes) is also found here. To the right, immediately above the tomb of Rekhmarā, is that (now No. 51) of **Amuzeh,** superintendent of the palace under Tutmes III. and Amenhotep II. This also consists of a large vestibule with niches in the sides, and a rather long passage cut into the hill.

The representations on the inner wall of the vestibule are worth noticing. On the left are the African tribes bringing in their tribute consisting of gold, ivory, apes, panther-skins and the like. On the right is the tribute of the Asiatics, jars, a carriage, a white and a brown horse, and various weapons. In both corners of the vestibule were steles, of which only that on the right has been preserved containing a prayer to Ra in the name of the deceased. On the right-hand side of the long passage into the hill is a scene illustrating the chase of waterfowl.

To the right close to No. 51 is the tomb of **Amen-em-heb** (No. 36) known to Champollion and described by Ebers and Stern. It consists of two halls one behind the other, of which the length is at right angles to the passage between them, and of a chamber behind the second hall.

The historical *Inscription* on the left inner wall of the first hall painted in blue on white stucco, and discovered by Prof. Ebers, is of special interest. In it *Amen-em-heb* describes the part which he took in the campaigns of Tutmes IH., and gives¹ exact information of the length of that Pharaoh's reign, and the accession of his successor Amenhotep II. He does not forget to record the honours which the favour of his prince had heaped upon him. 'I was', he begins 'his lordship's great fidelity, the pride of the king of Lower Egypt, the half of the heart of the king of Upper Egypt. I followed my lord into the country of the north and of the south according to his will etc. 'Then he recounts how he took part in the victorious

expeditions to South Palestine ([hieroglyphs] Neḳeb נגב), Mesopotamia (Naharain), the well-wooded Uān westward of Khalyboņ (Aleppo), Karkhemish, beyond the river of Mesopotamia (the Euphrates), Tyre (²), Katesh, Niniveh, etc. Everywhere he obtained spoil and was rewarded with presents of rings and helmets, and decorated with necklaces, the badges of orders, including the 'Ornament of the Lion'. The following is an interesting passage: 'Another time the lord of both worlds performed a mighty deed before Niniveh, when he hunted 120 elephants for their tusks.' I killed the greatest among them, fighting in the sight of His Majesty, and cut off its trunk'. On returning to Egypt Amen-em-heb remained with King Tutmes IH., who died in the 54th year of his reign on the last day of the third winter month. 'He ascended to heaven at the going down of the sun, and the servant of God made himself one with his Maker. When it was morning and the earth became clear and the sun's face arose and the heavens were made bright, then did the king of Upper and Lower Egypt, Amenhotep II., ascend his father's throne'. Under this Pharaoh also the general enjoyed high honours. His skull is preserved in the anatomical museum of Leipsic. His biography was composed by another commander-in-chief, named Mah.

Below this inscription are seen Syrians bringing tribute, some rais-

ing their arms in prayer, others kissing the dust. Among them are eunuchs, easily recognized by the fatty swellings on their breasts. The garments of the Asiatics are peculiar, white with coloured stripes down the
seams even of the sleeves. Many of them wear white bands on their fore-
heads. Their profile is strongly Semitic; the red pointed beards and the
hooked noses being carried almost to the point of caricatures. Some
bring cattle, others finely worked vases. Amen-em-heb was a great
lover of flowers, as we learn from other inscriptions in the first chamber
of his tomb.

In the *Second Hall* on the left inner wall there is a remarkably interesting picture of Amen-em-heb on his chariot, the latter unfortunately
half obliterated. In his left hand he holds a long pointed staff, perhaps
for urging on his horses, in his right a golden necklace, with which he
has been decorated, his diploma (which is frequently mentioned), and the
reins. On the right hand side of the inner wall there is a curious representation of an Egyptian party. There is an abundant provision of food
and drink. The servants in attendance carry flowers on the arm as modern
waiters carry napkins. The wife of this lover of flowers has a green bud
in her hair. The guests, two of them on easy chairs and three on stools,
are offered refreshments. Below, in the second row, the ladies are seated.
An attendant holds in each hand a staff wreathed and crowned with flowers,
and all the lady guests have blossoms in the hair and round the neck,
and hold a lotus flower in the hand. In the lowest row is a band of
music in full activity. It consists of two harpers, a man sitting and a
woman standing, a flute-player and a lute-player, both of them women
standing. The women's faces, including those of the musicians, are exceedingly pretty. On the wall to the right are fowling-scenes.

In the *Third Room* the dwelling-house is represented, and its roof is
supported by a wooden pillar with a capital consisting of a rich variegated flower in red, white, and two shades of green, with two comparatively large buds on long stems projecting from the upper part of the
shaft. — Below is the sledge with the sarcophagus drawn by servants
and a white cow, and the arrival before Osiris. On the wall to the right
is Amen-em-heb's garden, in the centre of which, surrounded by plants, is
a pond with fish swimming in it. There is a plentiful supply of flowers and
fruit, which the gardeners are preparing to carry into the house.

We now ascend still further to No. 31, the tomb of **Pehsu-kher**
who was adjutant to the lord of both lands, colonel in the army,
and fan-bearer to the king. In this tomb which has been for a long
time known, the colours are particularly well preserved. A large
party of ladies and gentlemen is represented. On the large stele the
different festivals kept by the Egyptians are mentioned. If there is
time we may visit No. 39 (to the left), the tomb of **Piuar**, not to be
confounded with the mayor of the same name of the time of Seti I.,
at the foot of the hill. This Piuar was a companion of King Amenhotep II., and followed him, it is said, into all countries by land
and water, and was therefore honoured with gifts.

To the right and a little above the tomb of Pohsu-Kher (No. 31,
see above) there is a deep pit into which one can be let down with
ropes brought from the dhahabîyeh. The tomb of **Amen-em-hāt,**
who lies here, is remarkable for some hunting-scenes, and in the
inner chamber for copious extracts from the Book of the Dead,
written in black and red on white stucco. Ascending to the right
(N.) we reach the tomb (No. 26) of **Anna,** prince (erpa-hā) and
royal scribe, as well as overseer of the fruit-stores, who died after
a long life in the reign of Amenhotep III. (18th Dyn.). The roof

of the antechamber has fallen in, and the sun lights up its walls, which are covered with a variety of interesting representations.

On the fragment of wall to the left prince *Anna* is seen with his wife *Tuau* sitting under a light pavilion, supported by a pillar, which shows that the calyx-capital belonged originally to wooden buildings, and was only adopted later in stone architecture. The pavilion has a natural connexion with the picture of Anna's garden, as he was a zealous planter of trees. A number of the plants cultivated by him are named, and to this we owe our knowledge of the names and characters of several of the plants of ancient Egypt. On the long outer wall, on the left, we see the noble Anna again, this time standing upright, in full enjoyment of his rank, while receiving the different kinds of tributes for the storehouses of Ammon. There are scribes to take down the amount of each contribution, and even the number of strokes which are inflicted upon a debtor. From Ethiopia there is a variety of contributions to be received, including negress slaves carrying their children in baskets on their backs, ivory, ebony, apes, panther-skins, etc. The Asiatics bring lapis-lazuli, etc.

On the same outer wall but to the right of the spectator Anna is seen again, but this time in company with his united family. His hound is standing below his seat, while ostriches, wild asses, a kind of wild goat, and other goats and cattle of various kinds and colours are being brought to him. One man brings rows of pomegranates etc. on strings. The interior of the tomb is small, but is not without interest, especially from the abundant list of offerings on the right wall from which alone we learn the names of five kinds of wine and two kinds of beer. On the left wall is the country-house and garden of the deceased; two women are standing at the door, probably his wife and his mother. In the background Anna is sitting with his wife before a richly furnished table of offerings. Opposite to him is seen his coffin being drawn along, and the weeping women throwing dust on their heads, just as may be seen in Egypt at the present day. The innermost room of No. 26 together with the shaft has been filled up with stones, and all that can be recognized of its paintings is the back of an enormous Apep serpent, the enemy of the Sun-ship of Ra.

We notice the two long galleries to the left with numerous entrances but without any remarkable tombs, and ascend again to the right to No. 16, a tomb well worth seeing, belonging to **Horemheb**, who 'seems to have held a series of offices, especially that of overseer of the cattle, in the successive reigns of Tutmes II. and III., Amenhotep II. and III., and Tutmes IV., of the 18th Dynasty. Close to it is the tomb (No. 17) of **Tenuna**, a fan-bearer on the king's right hand, and adjoining this, but turned towards the N., the tomb of **Amenophis** (No. 102), second Prophet to Ammon, and of his wife *Roi*. The paintings in this contain a scale in which gold rings are being weighed, various workmen, one of whom is making a sphinx, clerks with tables writing out the crops, and a statue with a ram's head; on the right music and dancing.

A little higher to the right is the tomb of **Zanuni** (No. 104). Care should be taken at the entrance, to avoid falling into the deep shaft. The paintings represent Retennu bringing presents in gold, silver, lapis-lazuli, and emeralds.

We have now almost reached the summit of the hill, and can enjoy the magnificent *View including the Ramesseum, the Memnon statues, and on the other side of the Nile Luxor and Karnak; to the right below the hills is seen the temple of Dêr el-baḥri, and the path leading to the Tombs of the Kings. We now descend past

No. 26 (see above) to the tomb of **Ramenkheperseneb** (No. 34), which, having been opened only for a few years, is remarkably well preserved and is well worth a visit. For stout people, however, the entrance is almost too narrow. The deceased was chief architect to Tutmes III. The right hand inner wall of the large hall tells us of the important works which were entrusted to him, such as the carving of a statue of the king from a single stone, the erection of a hall of pillars, and of numerous obelisks. Here again we see tribute being brought by princes, of Keftu (the Phœnicians), of Kheta, Tunep, Kat, Katesh, etc. The arms and helmets of the foreigners, their carriages and handsome vases are remarkable. Near this, a little to the right, is the fine and well-preserved tomb (No. 54) of **Amenemha**, the scribe of the harvest, in which should be noticed the harper and the long list of relations of the deceased, whose father and mother were named Tutmes and Entef. In a passage there are represented barges with mummies of himself and his wife *Bekt*. In the last chamber there is a *Stele* of the 28th year of Tutmes III. The shaft in the tomb contains a large room covered with writings Still farther to the right is the tomb (No. 60) of a prince (erpa-hā) **Entefaker**, and on the N.E. slope that of **Amkhent**, the son of *Auta*, which was completely excavated in 1883. A descent should now be made to the gallery, in front of which is seen *Wilkinson's House*, and to the tomb (No. 88) of **Imaiseb**, who was scribe of the altars of sacrifice under Ramses IX. (Neferkara). The festal barges with the name of the king should be noticed, as well as the many golden utensils, and the money-bags, and also a series of kings, among whom appears King Raskenen, who fought against the Hyksos, and whose remarkable mummy is in the museum at Gizeh.

We now descend to the plain, where there are a few more tombs to be seen in the direction of el-Asasif, including that of **Neferhotep**, who lived under King Horus, the last of the 18th Dynasty. In this should be especially noticed the funeral processions by boat which have been copied by Wilkinson *(Manners and Customs)*. The funeral services are also recorded.

We have to crawl through the entrance which is choked up. The ceiling is decorated, and has a regularly recurring series of hieroglyphics, signifying 'First' and 'Prophet'; the deceased in fact held the office of Prophet of Ammon. The family scene in the first room explains itself; the 39 rows of hieroglyphics above record the names of the relations of the deceased, who on the left are paying homage to King Horus with whom they were closely connected. In the second room we see *Neferhotep*, sitting by the side of his sister who is adorned with flowers. Behind them is an °*Inscription* which indicates that distinguished Egyptian families kept private bands of music; and it may be that the special duty of the harper whose song has been handed down to posterity by this inscription, was to gladden the hearts of the family when they were assembled in their ancestor's tomb for the solemnities in his honour. The song is not in any way of a mournful character, and it is clear that in the time of the Pharaohs, it was a pleasure to be reminded in the tombs of the shortness of life, and the duty to enjoy it, so long as it lasted. The song is headed: 'The words of the harper, who tarries in the tomb of Osiris, of the righteous prophet of Ammon, Neferhotep'. After an introduction, wishing peace to the dead, and glorifying the sun-god, it continues literally as follows: 'Celebrate the great day, O prophet. Well is to thee, fragrant resin and ointments are laid before thee. Here are wreaths and flowers for the waist and shoulders of thy sister, who is pleasant to thine heart, as she rests beside thee. Let us then sing and strike the harp in thy presence. Leave all cares behind and think of the joys, until the day of the voyage comes when man casts anchor on the land which delights in silence'.

Near this is the once splendid tomb of another *Neferhotep*, overseer of the cattle of Ammon, but now in ruins and used as a magazine by the keeper of the Gizeh museum. There may also be visited in the neighbourhood the tombs of *Kherûf*, of the time of Amenhotep III., of *Moi*, and of an official in charge of the stables of Amenhotep II., the inner room of which is the resting place of *Mahu*, a writer of the treasury in the time of Ramses II.

If the dhahabîyeh is lying at Luxor, the small boat should be ordered to wait with some men on the left bank of the river at the E. end of the island.

19. The Mortuary Temple of Seti I. at Ḳurnah.

Second Day on the W. bank: 1. Temple of Ḳurnah; 2. Tombs of the Kings (Bibân el-Mulûk); 3. Necropolis of el-Aṡasif and of Drah Abu'l-Neggah; 4. Dêr el-baḥri.

To the W. bank as on the previous day, see p. 152. From the landing-place of the ferry we ride across the fields in a northerly direction and in $^3/_4$ hr. reach the handsome *Temple, the front of which with its columns is visible at a considerable distance. The original building (see the annexed plan) was of smaller dimensions than the Ramesseum and Medinet Habu, its complete length being 518 ft., and of this only the actual sanctuary with its halls and chambers, 153 ft. in depth remain, while there are only scanty remains to prove the former existence of two *Courts* and the *Pylons* which enclosed them. The *Sphinxes* which were placed like guardians to the right and left of the door leading into the first Court on the inside, are half covered with earth. They were placed there by Seti I., and on the bases were inscribed the names of all the nations which he had conquered. Of all the buildings in the Necropolis of Thebes, this one most reminds us of the Memnonium of Abydos (p. 54), and a closer inspection of the style of inscriptions and representations will both bring out and explain their similarity, for the temple of Ḳurnah was founded by Seti I., the builder of Abydos, and both the sanctuaries were restored and completed by Ramses II. They both served the same purpose, as a place where the manes of the founder might be remembered, and offerings made. At Abydos it is true that throughout attention was paid to the pilgrims to Osiris, while here it is the gods of Thebes that were prominent, and this was the centre of the festival of the mountain valley,

(the entrance to the neighbouring Bâb el-Mulûk was

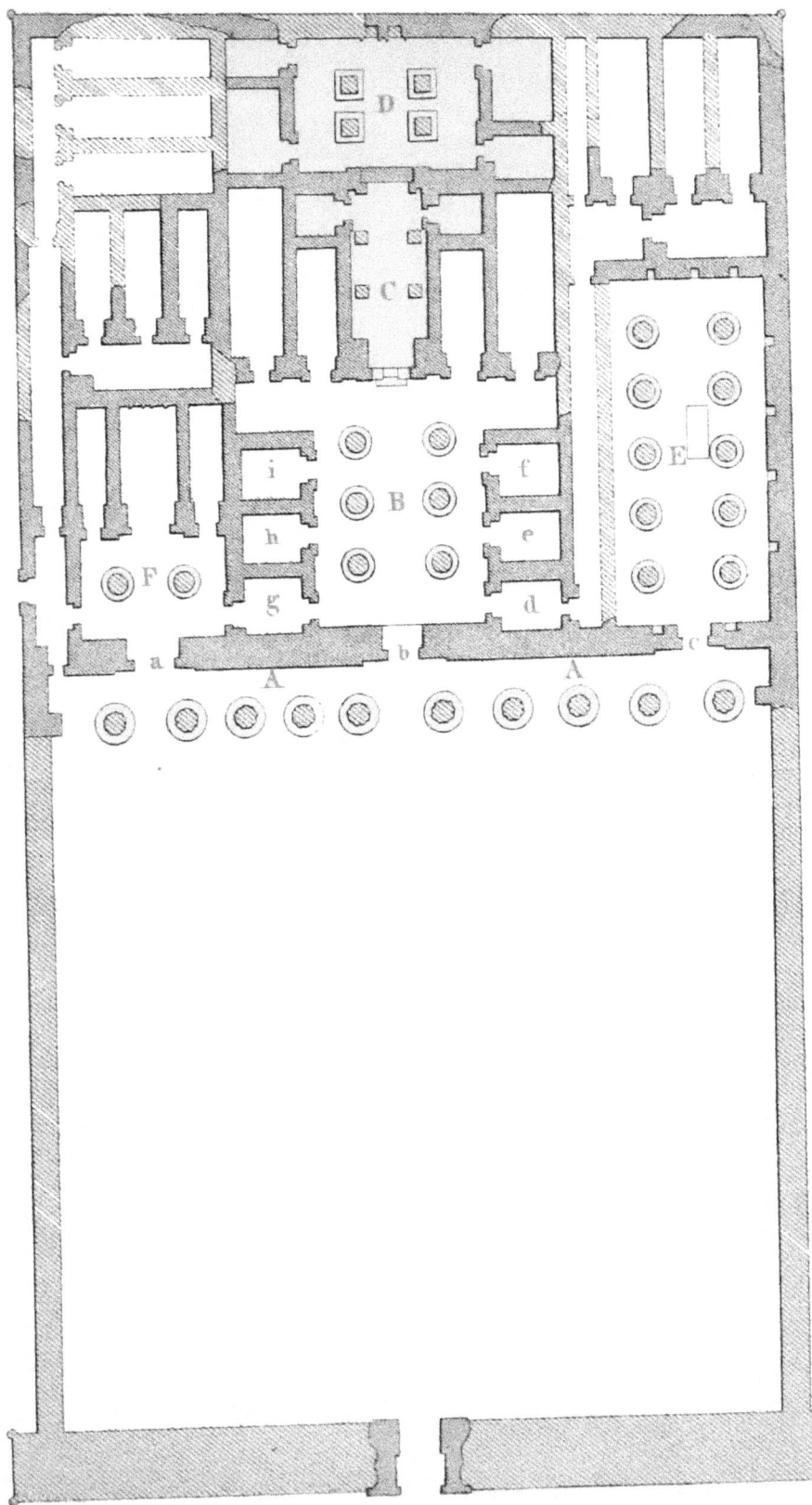

The Tombs of
SHÊKH 'ABD EL-ḲURNAH.

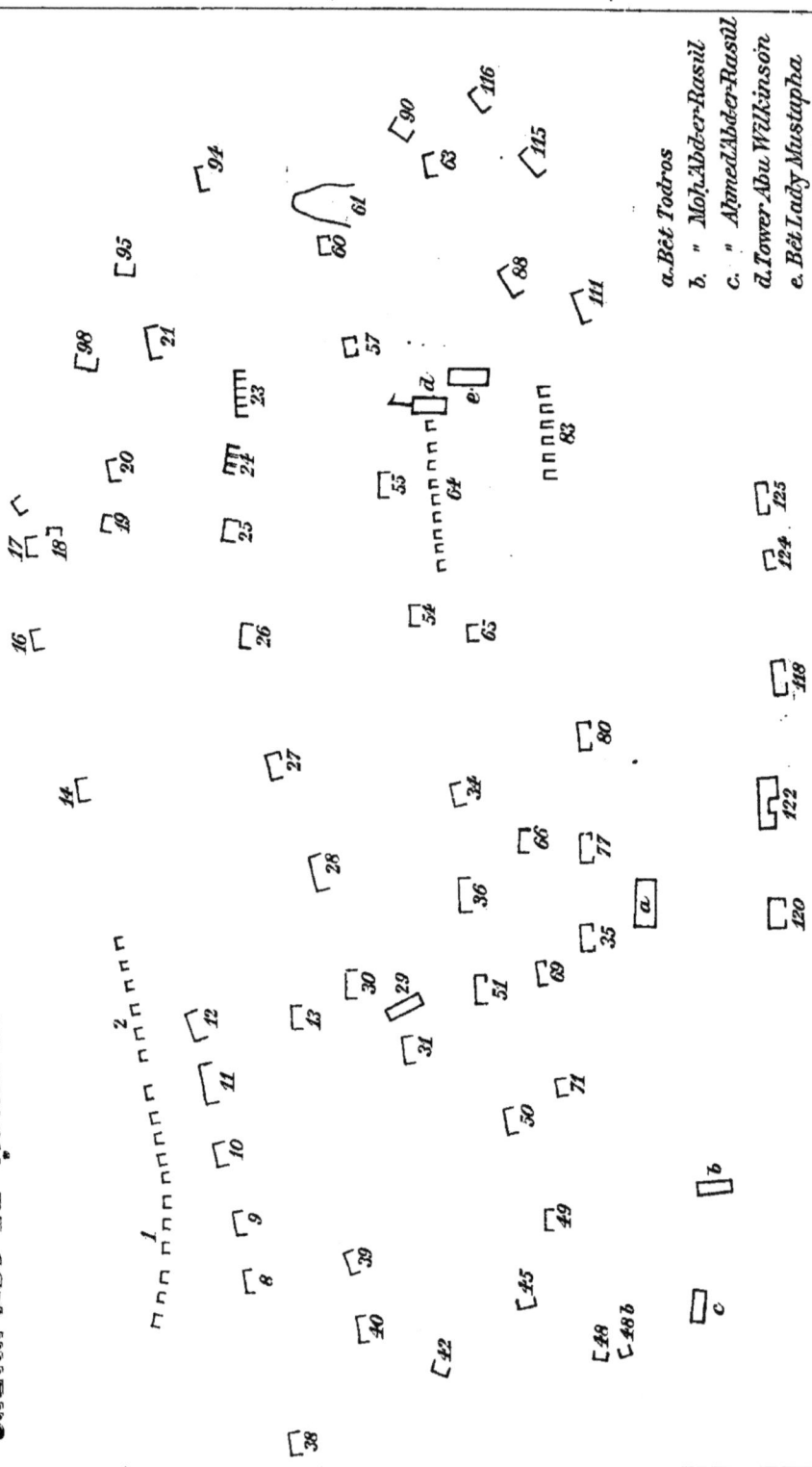

a. Bêt Todros
b. " Moḥ.Abder-Rasûl
c. " Aḥmed Abder-Rasûl
d. Tower Abu Wilkinson
e. Bêt Lady Mustapha.

probably the scene of the festival). Moreover in the Memnonium
also Seti I. with filial piety thought of his father Ramses I., the deceased Ramses Ra-men-pehti. To him are especially dedicated the
sculptures on a false door, which is reached by
passing through the left entrance door from the
colonnade on the last façade, and crossing the hall
with two columns and the long chamber lying behind it. On the inner wall of this last, on the right
and left panels of the false door referred to, Ramses I. is seen enthroned as 'King Osiris', and from
two inscriptions between these which are divided
by ornaments and two others which frame the whole,
we learn that Seti I. dedicated this portion of his
Memnonium to the memory of his father. His son
did for him what he had done for his father, while later kings,
Merenptah, Siptah, and Ramses III., had their names carved in
various places, but do not seem to have either restored or enlarged
the Memnonium. The traveller should especially notice the extraordinary beauty and purity in style of the inscriptions and paintings. The existing remains of the temple of Ḳurnah may be divided
into four parts: 1, the colonnade on the front of the temple facing
the E.; 2, 3 and 4, the three series of halls, chambers, and closets
separated by partition-walls, one in the centre, one on the left, and
one on the right.

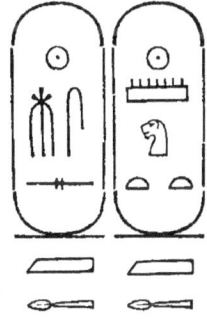

The **Colonnade** (Pl. A) originally displayed 10 fine columns
with papyrus-bud capitals, excellent specimens of this order, but
of these one on the S. side (left) has been destroyed. In its
inner wall, the eastern wall of the temple, are three doors (Pl. a
b, c), which lead into the three series of rooms mentioned above.
and the sculpture on it is of great interest, representing 12 pairs
of divinities, each a god and a goddess, eight of which may certainly be taken to represent branches of the Nile forming the Delta
On their heads they carry well-known geographical symbols. O:
each pair it is said that they come in order to bring gifts to Pharaoh
The dedicatory inscription reads: 'The saying of the gods and the
goddesses of the north to their son etc., Ramses II. We come to
thee, our arms are laden with choice goods and produce. We gathered for thee all good things from all that the earth brings forth
to place the temple of thy father in a festival of joy ... Thou hast
made good that which had fallen, and built up thy father's house
in that thou bringest it to an end with works of eternal standing
Thou didst cause to be shown by art his sacred boat of

....' This boat is often

represented, and was borne in procession at the feast of the mountain
valley. The Canopic arm of the Nile was considered the most im

portant, but otherwise the branches were reckoned from east to west.
More to the left, but not so well preserved, are the river-gods of the
southern Nile. Here the dedicatory inscription tells us that Seti I.
set this up to Ammon-Ra, the lord of the throne of the universe,
in the region of Ammon of the western Thebes for millions of years
etc., and that his son Ramses II. was the restorer of this building.
'Not all his works', it literally continues, 'were finished in writing
or in hollowing out. So his son, the lord of both worlds,

Ramses II., commanded to build up everlasting
buildings in his temple opposite to eastern Thebes' etc.

Passing through the middle door (Pl. b) of the colonnade, we enter
a kind of **Hypostyle** with 6 papyrus-bud columns (Pl. B). This is
bounded on each side by three chambers, and beyond the last pair
of these expands to their full depth. It is considerably smaller than
other similar halls, measuring only 50 ft. by 35 ft. A part of the
roof has fallen in, on the slabs which are preserved are the vulture forms of Hebent (Nekheb?) and two inscriptions. On the right
is the ordinary dedication of the building, on the left a special
mention of this hall, which like all similar ones is called '*The Hall
of Appearance*'. Everywhere we see on the walls Seti I. offering
incense to the gods of Thebes, and bringing the symbol of his
name, and flowers etc. On the right and left of the door Seti I.
meets us as a boy, with Muth on the one side, and Hathor on the
other giving him the mother's breast. The young prince already
wears the helmet and holds the symbol of princely rank ; Hathor
with the horns of a cow and the disc upon her head, supports with her
right hand the nourishing breast, and says: 'I am thy mother, who
fashions everything that is perfect. Feed thyself with my milk'.
Besides the Theban triad are mentioned Hathor as goddess of the
western horizon, Isis, Tum, Ptah, and Anubis. The *Frieze* of the
Hall of Appearance displays the name and surname of Séti I. constantly repeated. Several inscriptions show that Seti left this hall
unfinished, and that Ramses completed what his father had begun.
In the adjoining rooms there are several clear references to the
cultus of the dead which was celebrated here. In hall C, which is
supported by 4 pillars, we see Seti I. before a Naos with the boat
of Ammon-Ra.

The series of chambers to the left divides into two parts: a
Hall (Pl. F) with 2 pillars, into which three long rooms open, while
behind are three running parallel with the axis of the temple, and
three in a N. and S. direction, which are reached by a passage from
the extreme left of the inner wall of the colonnade. This part of
the building was dedicated to the memory of father, son, and grandfather, Seti I., Ramses II., and Ramses I. For the inscriptions to
the last see above.

The right hand portion of the temple consisted of a long *Hall* (Pl. E) with 10 columns (no longer standing), and of five rooms behind, three larger and two smaller, originally separated from it. The sculptures of this part are of the time of Ramses II., and far inferior to those of the central building and left hand portion of the sanctuary.

A little to the N. of the temple is a water-wheel and spring with some ṣunṭ trees, used as a watering-place for cattle. Passing this we leave to the left the side of the Libyan mountains with the Necropolis of *Drah Abu'l Neggah*, and continue directly by the lower path to the valley of the Tombs of the Kings.

Drah Abu'l Neggah is one of the oldest cemeteries of Thebes, and the treasures discovered by Mariette's excavations have been, of extra-ordinary value, but the tombs are now filled up, and the traveller will find nothing unless he excavates for himself. Tombs of the 11th, 17th, and 18th Dynasties were discovered here, and in one of them was the mummy of *Queen Aah-hotep*, whose precious ornaments are preserved in the Gizeh Museum (Vol. I., p. 302). In her time it was the custom to pay more attention to the decoration of the dead body than to that of the tomb. The Necropolis of Drah Abu'l Neggah was a source of plunder from a very early time. There are papyrus legal documents, preserved in London and Turin, which acquaint us with the proceedings taken against thieves, who had robbed the tombs at Drah Abu'l Neggah, and those of the queens during the 20th Dynasty.

20. Bîbân el-Mulûk. Tombs of the Kings.

The entrance to the valley of the Kings' Tombs may be reached in about 3/4 hr. from the landing-place of the ferry on the W. bank of the Nile, by the path indicated above viâ the temple of Kurnah. The moun-tain-track viâ *el-Asâsîf*, more fatiguing though shorter, is better followed on the return.

We enter this valley of the dead by an old road of the Pharaohs. Beyond a rocky ravine we reach an open space, whence two roads diverge. That to the left leads to the *Bîbân el-Mulûk* proper, visited by all travellers; that to the right to the W. cross-valley of the gorge of the Kings' Tombs. The latter route describes a wide curve round the greater part of the Bîbân el-Mulûk and leads past steep crags, on which hundreds of vultures perch in the afternoon, to two Kings' Tombs. We reach the valley of the Tomb of Ai (Arab. *Turbet el-Ḳurâd* or Tomb of the Apes) by the route leading to the right from the open space, or by a very difficult path (not recommended) over the mountain (between Nos. 8 and 9). — Visitors who are pressed for time may content themselves with inspecting Tombs Nos. *9, *11, *17, *6, 8, and 14; Cook's tourists visit Nos. 2, 6, 9, 11, 17, and lunch in No. 18. A visit to the W. tombs (see p. 202) will also be found interesting. The numbers have been inscribed on the entrances of the tombs by Sir Gardener Wilkinson. The name Bîbân el-Mulûk means 'gates of the kings' (bîbân pl. of bâb, the gate). The inhabitants of Thebes apply the name بَاب *Bâb* to every ancient tomb.

Strabo tells of 40 tombs 'worthy of a visit', the scholars of the

French Expedition mention 11, while at present 25 are accessible, to which a few more have quite recently been added. Pausanias, Ælian, Heliodorus, Ammianus Marcellinus, and other ancient authors refer to them as the *Syringes* (σύριγγες) of Thebes, which name also occurs in the Greek inscriptions within the tombs. The word 'Syrinx' meant first a shepherd's pipe formed of longish reeds, then it came to mean a hollow passage, and thus was applied to the long rock-hewn passages of Bibân el-Mulûk.

These tombs and the subjects represented in them require some words of explanation. The tombs which are in good condition and accessible are Nos. 1, 2, 6, 8, 9, 11, 14, 15, 17; the rest either contain only the name of a king, or are unsafe owing to snakes (*e.g.* No. 7) or are simple passages cut in the rock. *Plan and Arrangement.* Nos. 1 and 2 simply consist of a passage, a hall for the sarcophagus, and an inner room. Of the rest only Nos. 9 and 11 are completed. In the first the plan is most clearly seen: 1) three long halls, 2) a square hall, 3) first smaller hall with pillars, 4) one or two inclined oblong halls or passages, 5) a square room, 6) a second larger hall with pillars, the hall of the sarcophagus, in the corners of which are side-chambers, 7) at the end another square or several oblong rooms or passages. — The first hall with pillars has also a side-chamber to the right, as in Nos. 8 and 11, and with some variation, in No. 17. The roof of the second is supported by 8 pillars, and as in No. 17 may also have an adjoining room on the left. From the plan of No. 14 we conclude that this tomb was intended for several persons, as there are two sarcophagus-halls. The tombs of the 18th Dyn. were arranged quite differently from those of the 19th and 20th. In those a sloping passage leads into the square sarcophagus-hall, and adjoining this is a second hall with pillars, the entrance to which is placed six feet above the ground. — The oblong rooms usually contain niches, which were hewn in the stone at four to six feet above the ground, possibly for the keeping of sacrificial vessels. All the tombs slope downwards into the rock, except Nos. 1, 2, 4 and 14; in those of *Seti I.* (17) and of *Ai* we find a flight of well-worked steps at the entrance, while in the others the descent is made by inclined planes. Although the general plan is the same in all, and the difference in size seems to have depended only on the amount of time and money which each Pharaoh was able to give to the work, there is no similar arrangement of inscriptions and representations; in fact only a certain general resemblance can be observed, though the inscriptions vary not in sense or even in words, but only in quantity. The style is often enigmatical and the interpretation of both the signs and their meaning is extremely difficult. The following is a brief account of the inscriptions and representations. In the first place there is cut in the wall a long hymn to Ra in Amenthes or the lower world, which recounts the 74 forms of Ra with the invocation: 'Praise be to Ra, the Almighty!' Then it is said that the king knows the 74 forms of the god by name. The works of Ra are farther glorified, and his victories over his foes. In front of this hymn there is usually represented an antelope's head with a serpent beside it above the disc, and an antelope's head with a crocodile below. It is usually found in the first oblong hall, as in Nos. 2, 8, 11, 15 and 17. The texts are more or less injured or defective, and it has been the task of MM. Naville and Lefébure to collate and correct them. — The *Sun*, with which the worship of the Egyptians began, was conceived by them in various forms, as we have seen (Vol. I., p. 125). According to one conception, which is the prevailing one in Bibân el-Mulûk, is the god Ra, who in the golden age of the Egyptians ruled over the earth; he is dead and dwells in Amenthes; Khepera is light as the unchangeable being, constant in the midst of continual change, represented in the form of a

scarabæus , which therefore is placed in the dark grave; finally

Ammon-Ra is the lord and master of the throne of the universe, the living and acting God of heaven. These three form a trinity which is the deity of Bibân el-Mulûk, and is worshipped in Amenthes, as we find represented in every tomb. Here also Isis and Nephthys mourn for the dead, and worship those who have become Ra of Amenthes; for as the pilgrimage of human life is only an image of the daily and yearly pilgrimage of the sun, so the dead king, who once ruled over the land, becomes like a Ra of Amenthes, and every royal tomb an image of Amenthes itself.

The largest part of all the representations is occupied by the *Description of Life* in ☓ 𓅃 ⌂ *i.e.* Tua-t, or the depth of the grave. The centre of this life is Ra the blessed, who is here always called Afu-Ra, *i.e.* the body of Ra, in opposition to his soul which dwells not in Tua-t, but in heaven. He passes by in a boat, always accompanied by Sa and Hekau. Sometimes he is followed by other gods; he stands in a pavilion, round which a serpent coils. The gods of Tua-t draw his boat. By the side of this we are generally shown these deities worshipping him, and also Tum piercing with a lance the serpent which resists his boat. The serpent may be either good or evil. In No. 8, Room V, the Uræus-serpent 𓆓 , and the serpent of life are instances of good serpents. Those that place themselves before the boat are evil. They are called by various names: Nehebka, Neheb-Ashuheru, etc. Sometimes they are rearing up in combat, sometimes lying slothfully coiled up, and sometimes they appear with legs and wings, and scattering fire. The serpents at the doors apparently only held the post of Bôâb, or doorkeepers. Besides these we find mentioned a large number of other beings connected with Tua-t.

As to the *Nations* represented in Nos. 11 and 17, it need only be said that all are humbling themselves before Ra, after all his enemies have been conquered by Tum.

An active life prevails in Tua-t; there is driving, singing, fighting, reaping, etc. It should be noticed that the same representations of Afu-Ra are found in many of the papyrus-rolls.

The *Gods of the Dead* by whom the deceased are introduced into this world are almost all represented here. Most often it is the jackal-headed Anubis that is invoked as god of the dead by Isis and Nephthys in favour of the deceased. The infernal Hathor or Mersekhet also often appears. The worship of Osiris gives way to that of the blessed Ra, but still the king is represented as adoring him, usually over the door of the hall of the sarcophagus. Thoth and the Moon only occasionally appear.

Before the *King* can enter his last resting-place in peace, he must first be justified; and referring to this the 125th chapter of the Book of the Dead is usually found in the square room in front of the sarcophagus-hall, as in No. 9, VIII, and No. 2, IV. In No. 6 it is found on the left of the entrance.

The *Priestly Ceremonies* connected with the king's effigy, in which apparently his son took part, are most perfect in No. 14, less well preserved in No. 17, and most abridged in No. 11, in the passage leading down from the first hall of pillars.

The whole represents the *Fortunes of the Dead.* After Afu-Ra and with him the king have overcome the obstacles of evil, and he has justified himself from all his sins, he enters into the Most Holy Place, the Empyrean, the highest heaven or abode of the blessed, where the visible world of Ammon-Ra appears to touch the Tua-t of the blessed Ra. Here the songs of joy and hymns of praise resound, and Ammon-Ra spreads out his wings like a mighty bird. The gods move past in their barks, the stars rise and set, the hours, the days, the years pass by. The king is placed among the gods, he dwells among the stars, and the Divine Comedy is finished.

a. West Valley of the Tombs of the Kings.

The W. valley of the *Bîbân el-Mulûk* should be visited immediately after Tombs No. 9, 11, and 17 by those who are pressed for time. The first tomb here is that of **Amenhotep III.**

discovered by the French Expedition. We enter from the W.; the tomb soon bends at a right angle towards the N., but finally resumes the direction from W. to E.

The three first passages have either been destroyed or were never completed. The way to the fourth crosses a deep trench, which is not easily crossed without a ladder. It contains several representations of the reception of the king by the gods. The gods are making Nini

i.e. are pouring purifying water over the hands of the king. The countenances are all well-formed and even gentle and the colouring is unusually well-preserved, but the face of the Pharaoh has everywhere been obliterated, as his successor, Amenhotep IV. Khuen-aten (P. 23), discouraged the worship of Ammon, which Amenhotep III. favoured. Some of the pictures have been only sketched in, and the field divided into squares. Portions of the Book of the Dead are painted in red upon stucco. The sarcophagus has been broken; and beside it lie human bones (no skull), perhaps belonging to the king, whose mummy was not found in the shaft of Dêr el-baḥri. Fragments of the coffin of Amenhotep III., found in this tomb, are now in the museum at Gizeh. The *Astronomical Ceiling-paintings* in the chamber with the sarcophagus are noteworthy. The chambers beyond this room have no inscriptions and are full of bats.

The second tomb, called by the Arabs *Turbet el-Ḳurûd* (Tomb of the Apes) is in a very retired spot. It belongs to **Ai**

, a priest-king of the 18th Dynasty.

A staircase descends to an apartment, with coloured inscriptions, and containing the magnificent sarcophagus. To the right is a portrait of the king, with the serpent-sceptre and birds, and beside him is that of his wife, whose name, like the king's, is scratched out wherever it occurs. To the left are twelve sacred apes, with double names. The king before the dark-green Osiris, and again before the goddess Mersekhet, who performs the 'nini' (see above) and places the symbol of life ⸸ in his mouth; four white-clad genii of death, sitting opposite each other in pairs, Kebsenuf and Ṭuamutef with the crown of Upper Egypt,

Amset and Hapi with that of Lower Egypt . In a boat named

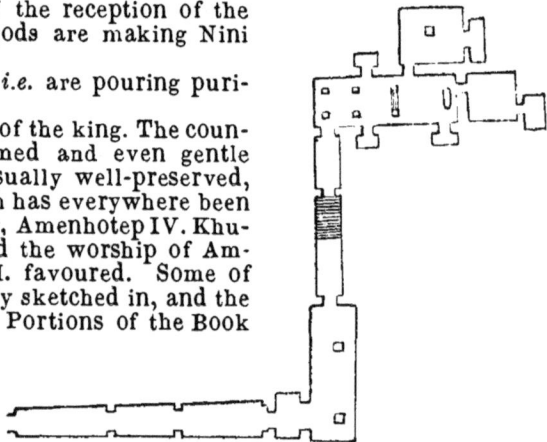

are Harmachis, Tum, lord of An (Heliopolis), Shu, Tefnut, Seb, Nut, Osiris, Isis, and Horus. Behind the boat is Nephthys. Adjoining are sepulchral inscriptions.

On the steep cliff near this tomb is a ruined hut in which a Coptic hermit is said to have sought a retreat from the world. Here, as elsewhere in the Bibân el-Mulûk, names have been inscribed by Egyptian scribes, Greek travellers, and anchoretic Christians. The still undiscovered *Tombs of the Kings of the 18th Dynasty* (Amenhotep II., Tutmes IV., and Horus) will perhaps one day be found in in this W. valley.

b. East Valley of the Tombs of the Kings.

The E. valley, usually the first visited, contains the tombs of kings of the 19th and 20th Dynasties. On the right (W.) of the path:

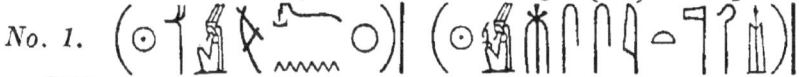

No. 1.

Ramses VII.

1. Chamber. To the left the king sacrifices to Ra-Harmachis or is being greeted as justified; to the right he sacrifices to Ptah-Sokar-Osiris, enthroned as the beneficent god of the deep, who addresses the king: 'Thy name remains fresh, according to the judgment of Sokar Osiris, while thy body rests in the coffin. But thy heart appears daily in thy disc'. The union of the king with the sun is indicated by these words. To the left is a boat with a disc, round which a serpent winds, and two companions ⌐ and ⌐ symbols of 'that great god Khnum'; above, worshipping figures and serpents rearing themselves aloft. To the right, a seven-line inscription to the goddess of the deep and of the tomb. To the left, 18 figures who 'extol Ra, bewitch the serpent Apep (Apophis), and present their sacrifices'; beneath is the boat of the god, who sits in a tent, round which a serpent winds; Hekau and Sa appear as his companions here, as in numerous other paintings. Four figures, preceded by a guide, drag the boat, and other gods accompany it. Adjacent are the words: 'this great god travelling on the path of the deep, and the gods of the deep drawing him'. Beneath are about a score of recumbent or fettered enemies. The inscription runs: 'Tum accomplishing a noble deed, bringing destruction upon his enemies; I vindicate my father Ra against you', etc. To the right are curious figures, 9 serpents, 7 genii with bulls'-heads, and numerous others, standing, reclining, and enclosed with serpents as in a frame; also five women with arms hanging down, on the sign ⌣, the meaning of which is still undetermined. — In the corner of Room I, the high-priest, clad in a panther-skin, offers upon an altar a sacrifice to Osiris. Below the roof the goddesses Hebent and Uaz, with vultures' or serpents' heads, spread their protecting wings over the king's cartouches. — *II. Chamber*, containing the sarcophagus. To the right and left of the entrance are represented the tutelary deities of the dead, Ur-heka, with a flower, and Sekhet Bast, who bestows 'the duration of life'. On the left wall: Various scenes of worship of Osiris, who appears as a mummy, or lies in his coffin, or is represented as the *Body of Ra*, with the head of a bull or of a crocodile. Beneath are four worshippers, then Osiris and Nephthys, tearing their hair as a sign of grief, and then gods with heads of animals or men. On the right wall are other curious figures: the worship of the sun-god with a ram's head, Tatunen and Seb worshipping Osiris, who stands beneath an awning. Tum destroying his enemies with a lance. An officer of those appointed to bind the worthless (enemies) may also be distinguished. The entire room is surrounded with a border of bound captives 🜨. — On the rear-wall is the king and the disc of the sun.

— *III. Chamber.* The king, bearing the symbol of truth on his hand, appears before Osiris. — A kind of standard, composed of the various signs of power and protection; sacrificial table; boat with two discs, in the midst of which stands a pig. — A *Greek Inscription* proves that the tomb was known and accessible in Greek times.

No. 2. (⊙ 𓀀𓏤𓈖) (𓀀𓏤═𓏤𓏤), the some-

what larger tomb of **Ramses IV**. To the right, before the entrance, is a Coptic inscription with a cross and a corpulent bishop raising his arms in prayer. Above the door are Isis and Nephthys, worshipping the solar disc with Khnum and 🪲.

To the left, in the *First Corridor*, appear the king worshipping Harmachis, and the large solar disc (Vol. I., p. 133). Behind, in good preservation, begins the 'Book of the praise of Ra in Amenthes' (45 lines). The continuation of this inscription in the second corridor and on the right wall of the first corridor is not so well preserved. The *Second Corridor* contains two other inscriptions: 'Worship of the infernal gods, when Ra perishes in life'; the other, 'O Ra, come to thy son'. Above are numerous demons. In the *Third Corridor* are serpents and praying men and women, like those in Tomb 1. Farther on are other worshippers, before the coffin and the ram's-headed Khnum (Kneph), and then an inscription: 'O ye gods of the deep and of the tomb of Amenthes, who guard the doors', etc. *Room IV*, a smaller square apartment, has an inscription from *Chapters 123-125 and 127 of the Book of the Dead, which contain the Justification of the Dead. Room V*, the main chamber: Boat of Afu-Ra, who stands beneath a canopy, encircled by a serpent; in front is the king, kneeling, with the symbol of truth 𓀀 in his hand.

Hekau and Sa also appear in the boat. The inscription runs: 'Thus this great god traverses the path of the deep'. (The god is uniformly named 𓂝𓂝𓂝 ⊙, the *Limbs* or rather the *Body of Ra*, in these inscriptions.) Farther down is Horus, with the words, 'The deed of Horus for his father; he makes him noble; he rewards him'. Opposite is an exactly similar representation, except that Horus is replaced by Tum with a lance in front of the coiled Apep serpent, while the inscription runs: 'The deed of Tum for Ra, for he made the god noble, smiting his enemy'. The boat with Afu-Ra and the king advances in

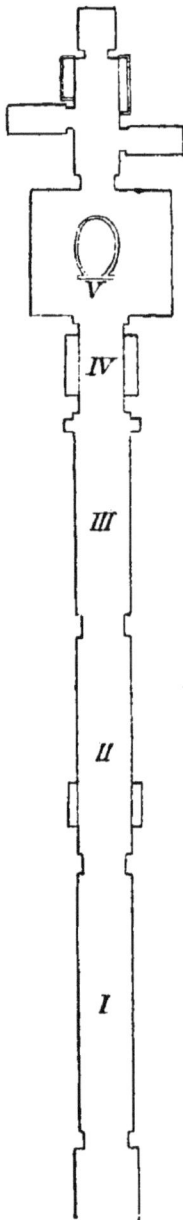

victory, for the enemies are bound or lie upon the ground. — Beneath the roof extends the double body of Nut, apparently supported on the left by Shu. The visitor should observe the constellations on the body of the goddess of the sky, the demons of the constellations, the three crocodiles (one sitting on the back of another) and, farther down, the tables of the hours. The goddesses of the hours have distorted (too broad) faces. The roof is vaulted. The sarcophagus is 10 ft. long, 6 ft. broad and $7^{1}/_{2}$ ft. high, and is adorned with representations. In the next corridor are inscriptions: 'O ye gods of the deep', and 'Doorkeepers of the tomb', etc. Then follows a representation of the boat of Khnum above the double lion. To the left of the praying king are the words 'May the coming in and the going out be blessed', recalling a similar Christian wish. In the room

behind is a representation of the mummy of the king ⏾, repeated 17

and then 23 times; finally comes a bier, beneath which stand canopi.

A representation of the tomb of Ramses IV., giving the dimensions, occurs in one of the papyri in the museum at Turin, published by Lepsius.

No. 3, to the left of the path, is filled with rubbish; but it is known to have belonged to another *Ramses*.

No. 4. Tomb of **Ramses XIII.** (or according to Maspero Ramses XII.).

This tomb is not quite finished. Even in the *First Chamber* are outline drawings upon the stucco, most of which, however, has been scratched away. To the right and left the king sacrifices to the god of the wind, who has four rams' heads, to the sun-god, and to Mersekhet. In the last chamber is a wide and deep shaft, in which perhaps coffins still are to be found though probably already plundered by the fellâhin. In the *Second Corridor*, as in many other tombs, above ground, are niches sunk in the rock, and generally bearing a long series of gods or demons. They served probably as depositories for vessels, canopi, etc.

No. 5, farther on, to the left, is a hole without inscription.

*No. 6.

Ramses IX. (according to Maspero Ramses X.), a finely executed tomb. Before the door is the disc, with the king on both sides worshipping it. Behind the latter are Isis and Nephthys, who exclaim 'Praise be to this god when he comes forth from his mother, to lighten the earth with his beams'.

1a. Chapel, in which the king stands before Ra-Harmachis and Osiris. — *b.* Inscription from the 125th chapter of the Book of the Dead. — *c.* Chapel, with the king standing before Ammon and the goddess Mersekhet, *i.e.* the subterranean Hathor and Hecate. — *d.* Worshippers with heads of jackals and bulls. The scattered stones in the side-chambers are a serious hindrance to the visitor. — In Chamber *II.*, at the entrance *e*, is the large serpent, rearing itself, with the words 'O thou great serpent in the tomb, who there watchest the door of him who dwells there, that he do not escape his watchers in the darkness'. At *f* is another serpent, with the address 'O ye serpents in the hidden place, who watch the gates of

Osiris'. In the niches are represented gods with curious names (*e.g.* 'the great cat'). — At *g* is a fine figure of the king with an inscription containing the chapter on the Entering of the Great House. Thereafter the king appears again, and at his head Hebent, of whom it is said that she bestows the kingdom of Ra in ⟨hieroglyphs⟩, *i.e.* the city of the thousand gates, hovers in the guise of a protecting vulture. Farther on we observe the king praying before Khunsu, 'he who is beautifully united with Shu, separating the earth from heaven, who raises himself millions (of miles?) above the ground, the great god, who has powerful wings, and who dwells in the fire-pool in Antset of Memphis'. This god says to the praying king, 'I give thee my dignity, my lifetime, my seat, my throne upon earth, to become a shadow in the Amenthes'; and farther on 'I give thy soul to heaven, but thy body to the deep ⟨hieroglyphs⟩ for ever'. Above are goddesses with peculiar names. — To the right *(h)* are serpents, Osiris-figures, veiled forms, etc., before Afu-Ra. There are also symbolic signs and the annihilated soul ⟨hieroglyphs⟩. The representation of Osiris in his Secrets is very remarkable: Isis and Nephthys bend over the moon-shaped Osiris-mummy, above which floats the disc. Under the roof are tables of the hours. — At *III* we again see the rearing serpents to the right and left. — *k.* The king with the sun-disc worships before seated deities bearing swords, Horus, Benti (dog-headed) apes, a demon with heads of Seth and Horus and even limbs of Osiris. Beneath is the boat of Khnum, with Sa, Apheru, etc., and some curious symbols. — *i.* Demon with ⟨symbol⟩ in his hand; others with knives.

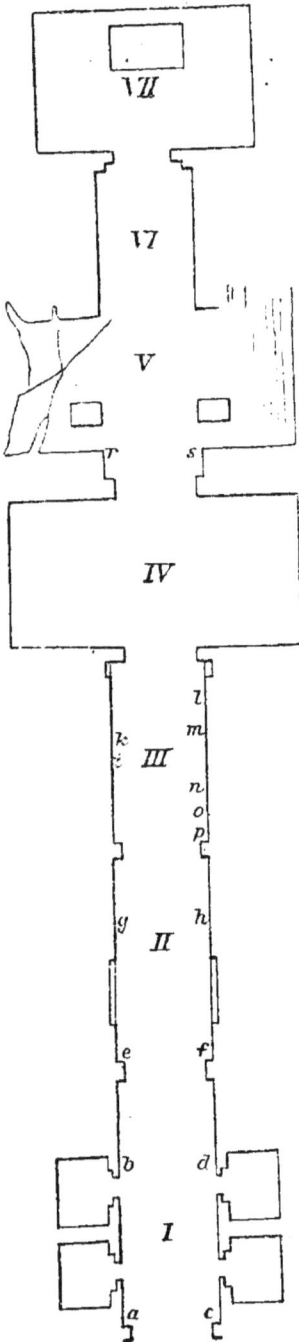

Behind the seated Osiris appears the god Khnum. — *p.* The king hands the symbol of truth to Ptah, 'the lord of heaven, the king of the north and the south, with the beautiful countenance', in front of whom is a small figure of the goddess Ma. — o. The black mummy of the king lies stretched out over a constellation. The disc and scarabæus float above it. — *l.* The back-view of a man with extended arms and legs, eight times repeated. — At *m* appears a boat gliding over the coils of the snake 𓆓𓆓 , with the scarabæus and the two Uza-eyes 𓂀 , and in front of it a series of serpents being killed with poisoned arrows. — At *n* are four figures bent backwards, taking the seed in their mouths, and spitting it out as a young child. Beneath is a border of bound enemies and, under the roof a number of persons with no inscription. — *IV.*, defaced except at *s*, where a priest, clad in a panther-skin, sacrifices before a standard. — *V.* is completely destroyed. — *VI.* Disc with worshippers. The refrain of the inscription here is 'Ah, I have penetrated into the deep, and the enemies of Osiris are destroyed'. Room VII, with much defaced astronomical pictures, in all probability represented heaven, the *Holy of Holies.* The dead entered it after he had overcome the various obstacles and had been justified. The 125th chapter of the book of the Dead, relating to the justification, must have occupied Room V. Above the entrance of Room VII, the disc with Khnum is worshipped by the Benti-apes, and under the roof stretches the long double body of Nut, the goddess of heaven.

Opposite, on the right side of the path, is *Tomb 7*, half filled up with rubbish. Visitors are warned against the snakes in this tomb. This large and spacious tomb, difficult of access, belonged to

Ramses **II.** or **XII.** The coffin of Ramses II. was found in the shaft of Dêr el-baḥri in 1881; and the remarkable mummy of a man over eighty years old was unrolled. Papyrus-rolls now in London and Liverpool describe the plundering of this tomb (see p. 199).

No. 8. lies in a side-gorge, a little to the right of the path. Near it, to the left, is a rock with hieroglyphic inscriptions, preserving for us the names of several of the writers. This tomb belongs to

Merenptah I., the supposed Pharaoh of Scripture, who endeavoured to hinder the Exodus of the Children of Israel, and is said to have been drowned in the Red Sea.

Above the entrance are Isis and Nephthys, worshipping the disc with Khnum and 𓎛. In the adjoining inscription, Harmachis and Osiris grant the deceased a seat in Amenthes. — *I.* Corridor: to the left, *a.* The king before Harmachis. The former wears the

high feather-crown ⫛ , 'he praises Ra, he extols Harmachis'; the
latter bears the sceptre ⌐ and ☥ in his hands, and says 'I give
thee the beginning of Ra'. Farther on *(b)* is an inscription containing the '*Book of the praise of Ra and of Temt in Amenthes*'.
This rubric occurs only here and in the
tomb of Teti II.; it is followed by the text
of the Ḥakennu (praising), continued at *c*
on the right in tolerable preservation. This
is the most important inscription in the
Tombs of the Kings, and it is here more
perfect than in No. 6. Beneath the roof
are the goddesses Hebent, with the vulture's
head, and Uzi, with the snake's head, extending their wings over the cartouches of
the king. — *II. d*, in the recess are gods
and demons; beneath is the soul of Ra,
a mystic form, also frequently represented
as a talisman. The side *e*, to the right, is
destroyed. Then above, to the left, are
other gods, with the great cat beneath. At
f and *g* appears Anubis, god of tombs, and
before him Isis or Nephthys. The goddess
speaks: 'I come, I extend my protection
to thee, I give thee breath for thy nostrils
and the north wind which proceeds from
Tum, and I praise thee'. At *h* three gods
are represented, with three crocodiles below (and the Uar-tesiu
[hieroglyphs]). At *i.* and *k.* is an inscription, 'A prayer to this
great god of the tomb'. — *III. l*, Boat of Afu-Ra (flesh of Ra), in
which are Horus and Seth (Typhon); beside it, the snake Nehebka,
with three heads, four legs, two wings, etc., and other gods, apparently sidereal. — At *m*, Boat of Afu-Ra, with Apheru, Horheben,
Nehes, Hu, and other gods. The inscription is 'He approaches
hither, this great god, while they draw him to this tomb'. Above
are the standards ⌐ of the cycle of the nine gods, to which belong
Khepra, Shu, Tefnut, Seb, Nut, Osiris, Isis, Nephthys, and Meht
netert. — *IV.* is a small ante-chamber. At *n*, to the left, the king
is received by the demons Amset, Ṭuamutef, Anubis, Kher-Keb,
Isis, Neith, and to the right, Hapi, Ḳebsenuf, Anubis, Hor, Nephthys, and Selk. Below is Anubis, with Ṭuamutef before him; to
the right is Horus, with Kebsenuf before him. — *V.* Large chamber

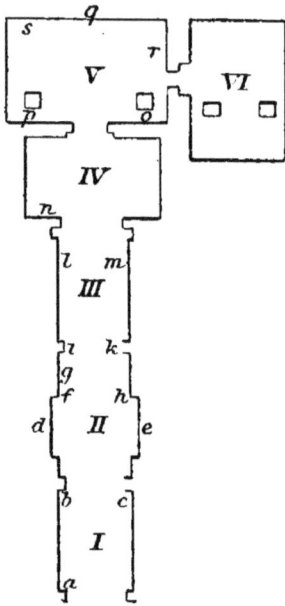

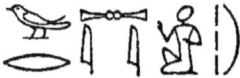

The pillars usually bear representations of the king standing before a god, sacrificing to him, worshipping him, being touched by him with the symbol ⚲, etc. To the right, at *o*, are two kinds of serpents in ponds, first the Uræus-serpents 𓄿𓅱𓏏𓅱 *Aū rutu*, and second the serpents of life 𓋹𓈖𓐍𓏏 *Ankhtu*. To the left, at *p*, is a long row of persons *(Heniu)*, worshipping the god of the under-world. On the rear-wall, at *q*, where there is a descending passage, are representations of a double shrine and of the king worshipping Osiris, with the inscription : 'He is surrendered to the lord to all eternity'. There are no inscriptions in the passage, as the tomb was never completed. — At *r* is an inscription: 'They gaze at the view of Ra, they enter following him', etc. To the right is the boat of Afu-Ra: 'this great god being drawn by the gods of the deep'. Above are many figures, like 𓀾 *i.e.* the 'bearers of the Metau', etc., a large serpent, and other forms, of which the last is 'the leader in his corner, who commands men in the under-world'. At *s*, in the rear wall, to the left, is the boat of Afu-Ra, with Hekau and Sa. Throughout the chamber are inscriptions from the *Am ṭuat*, the Book of the Under-world. — The side-chamber *VI* has only a few paintings in a recess in the left wall.

*No. 9. (⊙𓏤𓏤𓏤) (⊙𓏤𓏤𓏤𓏤) **Ramses VI.**

This tomb was named by the French Expedition *La Tombe de la Métempsychose*, and by British scholars, following the groundless traditions of the Romans, the *Tomb of Memnon*. This large tomb is characterized by an abundance of mystic representations and inscriptions, of which, however, none are executed in a good style. Coptic and Greek inscriptions are most numerous in this tomb; among them one to the effect that 'Hermogenes of Amasa has seen and admired the Syringes; but this tomb of Memnon, after he had examined it, he more than admired' (or admired more than the others, ὑπερεθαύμασα). — It is a remarkable fact that the cartouches of Ramses VI. are superimposed upon others, which either represent the earlier name of Ramses VI., or probably of his predecessor Ramses V.

Before the doors are representations like those before No. 8. — *I.* To the right is the king before Harmachis, to the left, before Osiris, then the serpent Apep, demons with heads of bulls and serpents, chained captives, etc. — *II.* Representation like those in Room v. of No. 8: 'the beniu of the deep', 'the bearers of the cord in the fields of the deep', etc. In a chapel with steps appears Osiris, and on the steps are men with a guide. Above is a boat, out of which an ape is driving a pig

. Another ape stands in front of the boat, and a third approaches with an axe, perhaps to lend emphasis to the expulsion of the pig.

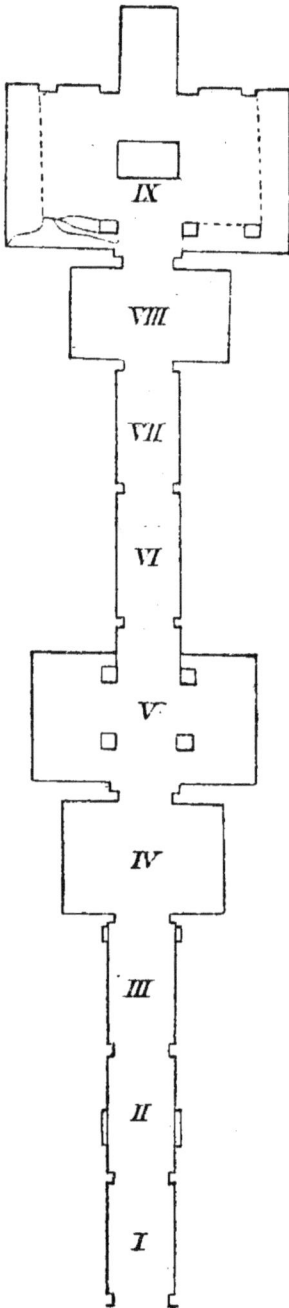

— To the right are long inscriptions and black forms standing on their heads (the annihilated) before Khnum. Coptic inscription. — *III. Corridor*, to the left. The bearers of the , the feather of Ma or the 'truthful', and beneath, the boat with two attendants, then a bearer of the sceptre , and beside him pictures of the gods Tum, Seb, Shu, Hur, and Her shef. Beneath is the 'lord of satisfaction' *Neb fut āb*, 'the chosen who harvest the grain in the fields of the under-world', and the 'bearers of the sickle' . Farther on are the bearers of the measuring-lines that measure length and breadth, and the bearers of a line that measures depth. At this point is a Greek inscription, which can scarcely be anterior to Constantine the Great: Νεκτάριος Νεικομηδεὺς ὁ λαμπρότατος καθολικὸς (?) Αἰγύπτου εἰδῶν ἐθαύμασα. I, Nectarius of Nicomedia, the august catholicus (chief of the exchequer) of Egypt, saw and admired this'. Next is a boat, in front of which is a band of twelve 'sceptre-bearers in Amenthes', and four mummy-forms. — III., to the right: defeated enemies, beside which are the sun's disc and serpent. Here also is represented the double lion of the horizon Aker, with human face, and above him the disc and scarabæus, and Seth bending down upon him. Emerging from the Aker, to the right are Sebti, Afni (sic) and Tum; to the left Tefnut, Nut, Isis, and Nephthys. — Next follows a long inscription, then chained captives standing on their heads, beside whom is a cat-headed god Maufti. The captives are indicated as the groaning, the weeping, the shrieking, and the lamenting. Beneath is Osiris in his Secrets, as in No. 6, II. The ceiling, from the third corridor to the first main chamber with four pillars, is occupied by a continuous representation of the vault of heaven, embraced by the long extended figure of Nut, with the twelve hours of the day (☉) and those of the night (✳). At the end are two celestial charts, and tables of the culmination of stars during the hours of night, from fortnight to fortnight throughout the year. (Similar tables are found in Tomb 6.) The results are arranged on the different parts of a human figure. Biot, the French astronomer, used these tables in calculating the date of their formation. — *IV. First small antechamber.* To the left: picture of the serpent Kheti, darting fire against fettered forms; demons stand upon it. In the second row are persons 'bathing and swimming' in Nun, *i.e.* the ocean, and also souls praying. To the right: Disc, serpent, and at the left angle a curious representation of Seb; then (in the left angle) the serpent rearing up, and 'this great god' in ithyphallic representation. *V. First Room with Pillars*, considerably deeper than the preceding. In the corner to the right, the boat of the sun upon the hands of Nut; above the door (twice) Osiris and the king offering sacrifice. Under the roof, Nut. — The bodies of two gigantic winged serpents with crowns stretch hence down into the following room; to the left is Hebent, with the double crown, to the right, Mersekhet, princess of Amenthes, with the crown of Lower Egypt. — VI. and VII. are two farther corridors. The representations in the former are so mystic as to defy description. The latter contains gods, serpents, boats, the moon ◯, and, above the door, a hitherto unexplained figure. — *VIII. Second small antechamber*, with inscriptions: the king before Ma, the goddess of Truth, and Chap. 125 of the Book of the Dead. — *IX. Room*, a large hall, of which the corner pillars remain unfinished. The sarcophagus placed in the centre is destroyed. On the pillars appears the king praying to various gods. This has been called the *Hall of Astronomy*, on account of the representations on the roof, which have been executed with the greatest skill and with incredible labour and trouble. We here see, twice, the goddess Nut, with stars and gods, who sail in boats on the lake of the heavens. The deities of the hours also appear, with curious symbols beside them. Next the entrance is the sky by day, towards the back wall, the sky by night. The imagination of the artist who designed this ceiling-painting was licentious, as the immodest representations in the left angle indicate. On the long wall to the right, above, are the *Hours*, looking behind them, and each casting on the one preceding a ray from the disc on her head. Then follow the most varied forms of the light-god, the solar-disc, the stars, etc.; and finally an interesting *Representation of the boat of the 𓊽, accompanied by Khepra and Tum, being drawn on the waters of Nun or the celestial ocean over the eastern Aker or lion of the horizon, and sinking from the western, being received by Tatunen. The Arabs call this the Shellâl

or Cataract. The remaining figures are repetitions of those seen
elsewhere. On the left wall the paintings representing the punishment of enemies and evil-doers are particularly interesting. In the
last room, the names of the hours appear to the side; straight in
front are the sun's disc and a divine figure. The last is held by a
form, beside which the king sits, saying: 'Praise be to Ammon-Ra,
Harmachis, to the great fire-disc, to the light-god Khepra in the
boat of Seti, Tum, when he perishes, to the beloved soul of heaven,
· the venerable Sekhem, who there causes fruitfulness' †.

No. 10 destroyed. The stucco has been torn from the walls,
and the shaft filled with rubbish. It belongs to a king **Amonmeses,**
whose position in the 19th Dynasty is uncertain. It is, however,
certain that he preceded Ramses III., for the tomb of the latter (see
below) has had to curve to the right to avoid impinging upon this
tomb of Amonmeses.

**No. 11.

Ramses III. This imposing tomb, usually called '*Bruce's Tomb*' or
'*The Harper's Tomb*', owes its existence to the lavish builder of
Medinet Habû (p. 172). Inferior in size only to No. 17 and No. 14,
this tomb with the former of these, most deserves careful examination. The style of the sculptures is not the best, but the variety
and richness of the representations are unexcelled. This tomb possesses a unique peculiarity in the ten side-chambers, one on each
side of the first corridor, and four on each side of the second corridor.

Above the door appear Isis and Nephthys praying on their knees
to the sun-disc, as at No. 8. At the entrance here the cartouche
of Ramses III. has been chiseled over that of his predecessor Seti-
nekht , who rests in Tomb No. 14 (p. 215). At each
side is a pillar, with a bull's head in bas-relief at the top. — *I.* (to
the left): the king before Harmachis; then the 'Book of the extolling of Ra in Amenthes'; in poor preservation. Of the two side-
chambers in this corridor, that to the left (*No. 1*) is devoted to the
Festival. Oxen are being slaughtered, their flesh cut in pieces, and
thrown into cauldrons. A servant is blowing the fire, while another
wields a ladle. A second group attends to the wine. All kinds of
eatables, cakes, and implements are at hand, and the cooks are busy.
Two dancers enliven the scene with their performances. In side-
chamber *No. 2* (to the right) a dhahabîyeh in full sail is ascending
the Nile, and another, with sweeps, is descending it. — *II.* In the
recesses is a long series of demons, including the 'great cat', the
'lamenting one', with hair hanging down, etc. To the right, the

---

† A large number of the pictures and inscriptions in this tomb have
been published by Champollion in his Notices (vol. II., pp. 400 seq.); the
rest by Lefébure in his Hypogées Royaux (vol. II).

wicked of Amenthes, with arms tied together. Eight side-chambers adjoin this hall. No. 3 (to the left) is dedicated to the gods of harvest, the inundation, riches, and food, who are represented in human guise with an ear of corn on their heads, but in the second row, also as serpents. No. 4 (to the right) is the royal *Armoury* or *Arsenal*. Sacred standards, bows, arrows, huge swords, helmets, scourges, shirts of mail, etc. are here represented, and are peculiarly interesting and instructive on account of the admirable preservation of the colours. To the right of the door and on the same wall is the black cow Hesi, from the N. basin, and to the left the black bull from the S. basin, with a red caparison. No. 5 (to the left): 'May the blessed king by the good god receive all pure and beautiful things'. And in fact all kinds of things are represented as being presented. A man (the Nile) bears flowers, a woman (An, the northern Heliopolis) brings flowers, fruit, and partridges, Ta-mehi (an arm of the Nile) brings flowers and fruit, Sekhet (the fields) plants and sheaves, a man fruit, a woman (Saïs) geese, another woman ducks and sheaves, Memphis, sheaves and fruit. Nine other districts besides the Nile bring their produce to the king. A kind of list of nomes or domains is here presented to us. Four gods of wealth are also here depicted: Hapi, Hu, Ra, and Zefa, each with

on his head. No. 6, to the right, *Domestic Furniture* of the king: jars, pots, baskets with the royal arms; bottles, trinkets, bows, the panther-skin worn by the Pharaoh as high-priest, couches ascended by steps, head-rests

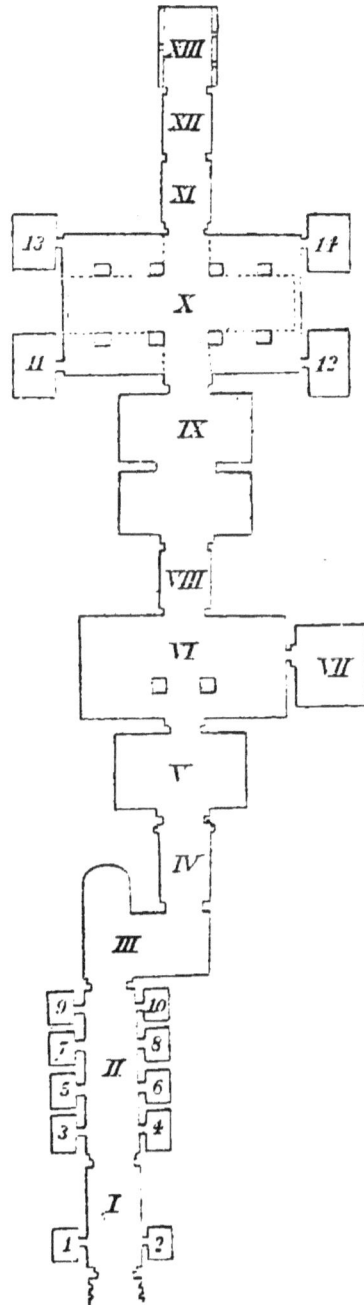

⚱, and sofas of great beauty and splendour. No. 7, to the left, the yellow bull (Mnevis) standing and the black bull (Apis) lying, both richly adorned. Also two serpents, one with the crown of Upper Egypt, the other with the crown of Lower Egypt. At No. 8 (to the right) a landscape is represented, on the banks of the Nile, with men ploughing, sowing, and mowing. Other men are filling the granaries ⌂, the celestial deities approach, and the boat of the sun-god appears on the horizon. At No. 9 (to the left), are two *Harpers*, one, to the left, before Anhur and Harmachis, the other, to the right, before Shu ´and Tum, with the inscription 'these are the two harpers who play to the infernal deities'. By the door is the refrain of the song they are singing: 'Receive the blessed king Ramses'. No. 10, to the right, is the *Osiris Room*, in which Osiris, with whom the king is now united, appears under 12 different forms and names. — *III.* The Pharaoh offering to Tum and Ptah, on the *left*, and to Ptah-Sokar-Osiris in a coffin, to the *right*. In the right corner, Osiris, lord of the under-world. Towards Room IV, the king surrendering the symbols of his power to Anubis. The tomb here makes a slight bend to the right in order to avoid the adjoining tomb of Amonmeses (p. 212). — *IV.* At the entrance are prayers to the infernal deities, and two-headed and three-headed serpents, etc. In the recesses, Khopra. — *V.* The king standing before gods. — *VI.* Chamber with two pillars. Serpents and figures bearing symbols, bearers of Amu (serpents), and, to the left, bearers of Nennuḥ. In the left corner are representatives of the four races (p. 219) subject to Pharaoh, conducted by Horus. This same subject appears also in Tomb 27.

Tmehu, with pointed beards, light brown (Libyans).		Amu, yellow (Semites).
Neḥesu, black (Negroes).		Rotu, dark (Egyptians).

VII. (much blackened by time). At the entrance, Neith and Selk; to the right, the king with one hand ǀgrasped by Harmachis, before whom he stands, while he stretches the other to Thoth, represented as the moon-god. In the other paintings are spirits engaged in mowing and reaping. — Passage *VIII.* contains a representation of the ceremony of erecting the image, in which the crown-prince, the high priest with the panther-skin, the Kherheb with the book, and other spiritual dignitaries take part. The inscription contains the ritual used on this occasion. — *IX.* The king confesses his sins in presence of several gods. — X. This large chamber, supported by eight pillars, was found by the French Expedition to contain a sarcophagus, now in the Louvre. The lid, which was wanting, is now in Cambridge. The mummy of the king from the shaft of Dèr el-baḥri was discovered in a large coffin of queen Nofretari, along with a female mummy, which fell to pieces. This is the 'astronomical' room. On the wall to the right, Ammon-Ra spreads wings like a bird; while elsewhere there are numerous representations of stars, the hours, etc., and other curious figures. The paintings in the small rooms at the corners also refer to the sidereal bodies; *e.g.* stars in No. 11, the cow in No. 14, etc. — *XI.* At the entrance is a green ape with a bow. Then, to the right, men with lizards in their hands, probably indicating length of years, for *ash* means 'many' or 'numerous'. — *XII.* The last rooms and recesses are devoted to Anubis-headed gods, *i.e.* with jackals' heads, and especially to gods of the dead.

No. 12. Cave, without inscriptions.

No. 13. Very low, and largely filled up, shows the cartouche of *Seti II.*

No. 14.

Siptah and his wife   Tanser.

Also

Seti Nekht.

This tomb originally belonged to an anti-king *Siptah* and his wife *Tauser*, but it was afterwards appropriated by *Seti-Nekht*, father and immediate predecessor of Ramses III., and suppressor of a rebellion in his kingdom (p. 172). Whether the tomb also contained the names of Seti II., who rests in the adjoining tomb, is exceedingly doubtful; they are not now visible. The queen Tauser is more conspicuous in the paintings here than her husband, whence it has been justly inferred that Siptah founded his claim to the throne on rights vested in his wife.

I., to the left: The queen before Harmachis, and before Anubis; King Siptah before Isis, and before Horus; the queen before Nefertum-Hor. Then a Ḥekennu inscription. To the right: The queen before Ptah and Ma, Siptah and his consort before a god, the queen before Harmachis, Hathor, and Nephthys, Hathor with flowers. — *II.* King Seti Nekht before Somti. Champollion believed that he had here discovered the cartouche of Seti Nekht engraved above that of Seti II. , and the latter above those of Tauser and Siptah. Now, however, there is no visible trace of this superposition, which would assign to Siptah a date anterior to Seti II. — *III.* Anubis and other genii, armed with knives, watch in front of a chapel, 'to keep off the evil ones'. Hathor again appears in the doorway at *a.* — *IV.* Large representation of Anubis and the genii of the dead; and also of Isis and Nephthys. At *b b* is the king, at *c c*, the high-priest with the panther-skin. — *V.* Above the door Anubis and Horus sacrifice to Osiris; figures with knives in front of chapels; beneath, the king. In the doorway the winged Ma, for only truth may find admittance here. — *VI.* The *Ha nub* or *Hall of Gold.* 'The act of the opening of the mouth by the royal likeness in the Hall of Gold. 'The high priest (Sem) is represented with the staff and panther-skin, the Kherheb with the book, and there are priests of inferior rank who take part in the ceremony. Besides these there are people introduced and named as 'Those who come to the tomb', 'One who enters that he may see it' etc. They appear to make offerings. A peculiar kind of incense (*bet)* is used. The columns of text below this representation contain a ritual consisting of versicles and responses by the priests and the son who has set up the likeness of his father. A special birth-day festival is also referred to, and mention made of another ceremony which occurs elsewhere, 'the opening of the eyes' with a hook. — *VII.* Anubis by the bier and the canopi beside him. — *VIII.* Antechamber. Representations of the gods: Osiris enthroned, Isis, Nephthys, Horus, Seb, Ptah, embracing Ma, offerings brought to Harmachis and Ma, Thoth with the moon ◯ upon his head; on the door to the next principal room, Ma with wings. — *IX.* In this large hall a second sarcophagus may have been placed, and the representations of coffins and seats render it very probable. On the right hand wall is Ammon-Ra as a bird with outspread wings, on the left the serpent, at *e* the boat. A god with the head of Seth and Horus spreads his hands over the double lion, at *d* is a swimmer in the ocean. — The corner room and the succeeding side-wings remain unfinished. — X and *XI* are empty. — *XII.* The colouring of the carved stone ends here. The serpent Ashu-heru is seen with many heads, also the boat. — *XIII.* A chained serpent with knives in its back and captive foes. — *XIV.* The hall of the sarcophagus

is damaged in many places, the pillars being entirely destroyed.
The sarcophagus of Queen Tanser bears her likeness between Isis
and Nephthys.

No. 15.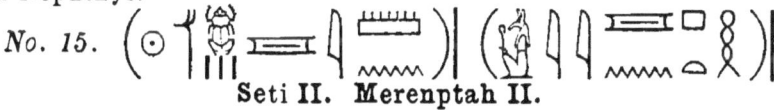
Seti II. Merenptah II.

This scarcely completed tomb lies farthest up the valley. The
king in addition to the ordinary titles is called 'Sun of the earth'
and 'Sokaris'.

I. To the right and left of the entrance is the winged Ma. On the
right the king makes offerings to the Ra of Merenptah, he presents Ma
to the god Sokaris of Merenptah: then begins the book of praise of Ra
in Amenthes, the first part of which is carved and painted, but the end
merely sketched in red. On the left is the worship of the god Ptah,
well preserved. Farther on, the disc with the crocodile, and the 75 He-
kennu or invocations to Ra the almighty. The stone of this tomb is
dazzling white like marble. — *II.* Outline sketches for the picture of the
boat, etc. — In *III* are sketches which are barely visible. — *IV.* *a* the king
in a small boat, *b* Isis and Nephthys. Also symbols and banners. — *V.*
Over the door two offerings are made to Osiris, there are also the boat,
and the heniu, the bearers of the measuring line, of the Metau, and of
the Secret. A sloping passage leads downwards from the hall with pillars;
all the rest is destroyed. The torso of a broken statue of Isis lies on
the ground.

No. 16 has no inscriptions.

****No. 17.*  Seti I.,

usually known as *Belzoni's Tomb* from its discoverer in Oct. 1817
In beauty of execution it far surpasses all the other tombs of Bîbân
el-Mulûk, and the sculptures on its walls appear to have been
executed by the same artists whose works we had the opportunity
of admiring at Abydos. In size it resembles Nos. 11 and 14; its
length is 330 ft. The descent is made by a steep flight of steps,
in which it resembles only the tomb of Aï.

I. On the left begins 'The book of the praise of Ra in Amenthes',
which has been edited by *Naville*. It says: 'When this book is read,
the figures of clay are upon the ground at the going down of the
sun, *i.e.* the lordship of Ra over his enemies in Amenthes; who is
wise on earth is wise also after death'. This paragraph of the book is
followed by a picture divided into three compartments, in the
middle a scarabæus with Khnum, below a crocodile with an antelope's head, above a serpent with an antelope's head reversed. The
first chapter begins in the first corridor on the left, and runs straight on,
occupying only a part of the wall. In the second corridor on the left
begins the second chapter, while the upper part is covered with the
15 forms of Ra in long niches. The two sides of the second corridor
contain the 2nd, 3rd, and part of the 4th chapters. At the end some
passages were omitted, and the rest of the 4th chapter was placed
on the part of the right hand wall of the first corridor that was yet
unused. — *II.* Here the process of the work may be followed, a part

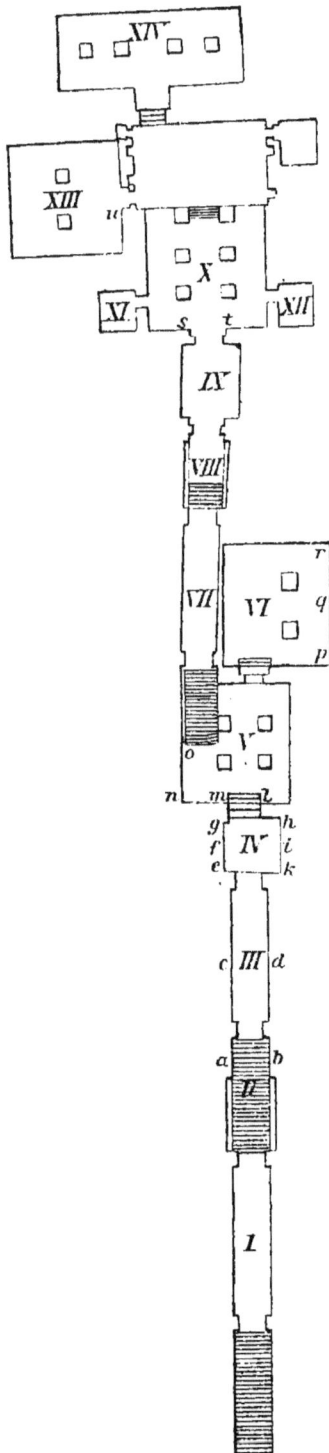

being sketched, and another part
still uncoloured. In several places
the artist had to lay down his chisel
or pencil when in the midst of his
work. The roof is painted with
vultures and the cartouches of Seti I.
The wide passage slopes downwards
with a double flight of steps of dif-
fferent width. At *a* is Isis, at *b*
Nephthys represented as kneeling
before Anubis. — *III.* At *c* the boat
of Afu-Ra is being drawn along by
gods on the ocean; his foes are also
seen and before them a goddess, of
whom it is said that she lives upon
their blood, close by is Horus, standing upon and holding the wings of
a serpent stretching itself over the
lion. At *d* the twelve-headed serpent Nehebka, another winged serpent, etc. — *IV.* The king before
several gods. To the left, *e*, he is
brought before Isis by Horus. At *f*
he makes offerings to Hathor of
Thebes, the Heniu of heaven, and
the princess of all gods in the region of Amenthes who says to him:
'I give thee the throne of Osiris'.
g The king before the mummy of
Osiris. By the side is written: 'I
grant thee the ascent into heaven'.
h Osiris, Anubis and Horus. *i* The
king before the mistress of the
worlds in the land of Manun. *k* is
similar to *f*. This room seems to
bear the name of *Hall of the Gods.*
A shaft was found here, and it was
considered to be the end of the
tomb, until the hollow sound of the
wall betrayed to Belzoni that there
were more rooms beyond. — *V.* Hall
with 4 pillars. To the right and
left of the door at *l* and *m* are represented two great serpents rearing their heads, from the Book of
the Lower World (IV, V). One is
called Set-m-ar-tef, or fire-eyed,

the other Teka-her, or torch-faced. 'They illumine', the text by
the side tells us, 'the hidden dwelling, they close the door after
the entrance of this great god'. Near them is seen a double door,
in which are represented nine mummies one upon the other,
guarded by two fire-breathing serpents. At *n* we see the heniu, ihe
worshippers, the 'cycle of the god' in the boat, and the god being
drawn along, and lower down Tum (?) destroying his enemies with the
lance. All these scenes are taken from the Book of the Lower
World. Here also are to be seen the four nations which we met in
Tomb 11, Room *VI*. The Libyans and Egyptians are fairer here. At o
are the bearers of the measuring-line, the bearers of the serpent, the
souls (bau; mummies with heads of birds), the people of the lower
world, and the bearers of the *Hau* ; at *u* the bearers of the Metau,
of the Amu serpent, of the Manenu ✳, a chain which comes from
the neck of Osiris. On the entrance-wall to the right in the second
row is the boat of Afu-Ra with Sa and Hekau, drawn by the dwellers
below, and lastly the mysterious bearers of the Secret. In the third
row is Tuti on a serpent Neheb, on which twelve mummies rest,
'they who tarry with Osiris, who have travelled hither and are
weary'. — From this hall on the left a flight of 18 steps leads into
the long *Passage VII*, and so to the other rooms. At the back of Room V
a small flight of steps leads to *Hall VI*. The inscriptions in this are
merely written on stucco. In one place we see serpents which spit fire
at figures lying upon the ground, in another we see them roasted
in an oven, scenes suggesting the Inferno of Dante. — *p* Demons
carrying a serpent before the boat. *q* Others with bows and spears.
r A cow standing on the symbol of sovereignty, a ram, and a bird
with a human head ⌣, all scenes of the 9-12th hours of the
Am-tuat. The outline sketches of some of the unfinished figures
are most remarkable, and some of the greatest modern artists have
expressed their astonishment at the master-hand which they display.
— *From VII* other steps lead down to *VIII*, the *Hall of Gold*, of the
priestly ceremonies of the 'opening of the mouth' (ap-ro). Unfortunately it has not remained uninjured, though on the whole in
better preservation than the hall of gold in No. 14. — *IX*. The king
before the infernal Hathor, Anubis, Isis, Horus, Hathor and Osiris,
twice repeated; then Ptah in his shrine. — *X*. Large hall with six
pillars. Unfortunately some of the reliefs on the pillars have
been removed, and in consequence, this, the finest hall in the
tomb, threatens to fall in. *s t* On the door to the right is seen the
serpent Akebi, to the left the serpent Saā-set, and passages from
the Book of the Lower World. The dwellers below praise Ra, and
offering is made by 'those in the depths' by the side of 24 figures
who drop their hands in prayer, below is the boat of Afu-Ra with

Sa and Hekau, drawn by 'those who are in the depths'. To meet
those represented here come other gods 'who have already found
admission'. Below all is Tum, the conqueror of the foes, who lie
bound on the ground before him. Again we see the boat, the heniu,
and the men or people of the lower world; also the members of the
household of Ra, to which belong (1) nine apes which sing when Ra

enters the depths, (2) fire-breathing serpents ⟨glyph⟩ which illumine

the darkness in the depths, (3) nine men with arms upraised,
who praise Ra on the ninth of the month, (4) twelve women who
do homage to Ra, when he enters the Atur uarnes, or Ocean. The
roof contains astrological figures, lists of decani, constellations and
the like, below is Api etc. The magnificent sarcophagus of alabaster,
together with the fragments of the lid, discovered here by Belzoni
(Oct. 19th 1817), is now at the Soane Museum in London. It was
empty, and the splendid mummy of Seti I. was discovered in 1881
in the shaft at Dêr el-baḥri (see p. 229) in a sarcophagus borrowed
from the high-priests of the 21st Dynasty. — *XI.* Serpents at the
door, boat, recumbent Osiris, etc. — *XII.* Astronomical figures.
The cow, supporting Shu, and surrounded by worshippers. — *XIII.*
Larger square room, with one of the pillars supporting the roof
destroyed. Round it runs a parapet on which statuettes, vases,
amulets etc., probably stood. The astronomical figures are exceedingly difficult to understand; below is a serpent with the heads
of the four genïi of the dead. *n* The boat of Afu-Ra with his usual
companions. At their head Isis, with hands outstretched, exorcises
a serpent, which has many knives sticking in its body, and is held
by the neck and throttled by a goddess. — *XIV* remains unfinished.
The rudely constructed passage which slopes downwards some
70 yds. farther offers nothing more, and the traveller may now return
satisfied with what he has seen, and astonished at the labour which
it must have cost.

No. 18. ⟨cartouche⟩ **Ramses X.** The name which is
half destroyed can have belonged to no one else. The tomb contains nothing worth a visit, but is a convenient place for luncheon.

No. 19 is not a king's tomb, but was made for a prince of the
19th or 20th Dynasty, a royal scribe and commander-in-chief, named

Ra-meses Mentu-her-khopesh-f ⟨cartouche⟩.
The inner part of the tomb is filled up. The portrait of the deceased
should be noticed. In 1885 several ornaments, fragments of a garment of many colours and with gold buttons, etc. were discovered
in the tomb.

Near the above is a passage sloping downwards for 80 yds., first
in a westerly and then in a southerly direction, which may possibly

have been connected with the shaft of Dêr el-baḥri, in which the royal mummies were discovered.

21. From Bîbân el-Mulûk to el-Asasîf and Dêr el-bahri.

From Bâb el-Mulûk we need not return by the way we came, but may take the path over the hill which separates the Tombs of the Kings from Dêr el-baḥri and el-Asasif. The path, which cannot be missed, begins at tomb 16; from tomb 17 which every one will visit, it is reached by going a few steps to the west. Persons not equal to the climb may ride to the top, but it is a great strain upon the donkeys. Riding down the hill is by no means to be recommended. The donkey-boys usually lead the animals by a narrow path over the ridge, and await the travellers at the foot. The zigzag path is fatiguing but safe, and is easily accomplished in $^3/_4$ hr. The *View* is most remarkable; first into the desolate valley of the Tombs of the Kings, then from the summit and as we descend into the peculiar ravine of Dêr el-baḥri; we see the steep projecting mountain side with its tombs, and buildings old and new, with the rich green of the fertile plain below spread out on both sides of the Nile, and here and there its groups of palms and gigantic temples, as far as Karnak and Luxor on the E. bank.

Those who are interested in the prehistoric stone-age, and the flint implements of the childhood of the world, may notice at the beginning of the path as well as on the top of the hill, and as they descend to Dêr el-baḥri, several open spaces covered with fragments of flint. Lenormant and Hamy considered these to be prehistoric knife-manufactories, and the myriads of fragments lying about to be the work of man; but Lepsius has proved that they are nothing more than the fragments of flint nodules such as may now be seen lying about, which split owing to the rapid changes of temperature. The traveller will in fact find thousands of fragments resembling knives and scrapers. And this is only natural, for whether the splitting is due to nature or to art, the same shapes are likely to be constantly produced. The calcareous limestone of these hills is full of crystals of silex. The walls of the tombs may be remembered with the dark broken nodules which stand out against the light-coloured limestone. What Hamy and Lenormant took for flint manufactories at the entrance of Bibân el-Mulûk are only heaps of stone, cut out of the rock with metal tools at the making of the tomb. The fragments of limestone and flint were necessarily removed from the excavations and were thrown down on the sides of the valley. On the other hand Virchow assumes a prehistoric Egyptian stone period, and considers the stone-fragments of Dêr el-baḥri to be to some extent artificial productions.

Before turning to the temple of Dêr el-baḥri which is seen, with the tower of clay-bricks, as we descend the hill, a visit should be paid to the Necropolis lying between Shêkh 'Abd el-Ḳurnah (p. 190) and Drah Abu'l-Neggah (p. 199) known as —

El-Asasîf. The part to be visited is known by the Arabs as *el-Asasîf el-baḥrîyeh* or the northern Asasif. Numerous tombs of various periods lie here in the series of low hills, which form the back as it were of the steep rocky range rising behind Dêr el-baḥri. Only a few tombs at el-Asasif are usually visited by the ordinary traveller. Some belong to the 18th and 19th Dyn., but the most important are of the 26th. Broken walls seem to indicate that the cemetery was divided into sections. We also find here various brick buildings and a large arched doorway. During Mariette's excavations many mummies were found, not in regular tombs, but either in the earth itself, or in small vaults 3 to 6 ft. below the surface. In some of them, papyrus-rolls of great value were discovered. The tomb of **Petamenap** ( ) is larger than Nos. 14 and 17 at Bîbân el-Mulûk, and is worth a visit on account of its great size. Petamenap was a prince of the empire and an official of the 26th Dyn., whose remarkable position entitled him to the unusual honour of completing buildings at the temple of Medinet-Habu, and of placing his name upon them. The tomb is cut out of remarkably beautiful limestone; and its inscriptions display the neatness of finish which is peculiar to the sculptures of the Egyptian renaissance. It has become the home of thousands of bats, which render the attempt to copy the inscriptions in the inner rooms very difficult by constantly extinguishing the light. The smell, moreover, which they cause is so strong and offensive that a thorough inspection of the tomb is recommended only to those who can overcome the feeling of nausea. Any one who is subject to giddiness should avoid going far into the tomb, as in the middle it is necessary to balance oneself, though only for a few steps, along a narrow path on the edge of a deep shaft. Sir Gardner Wilkinson undertook the measurement of the tomb, and the inscriptions have been almost completely copied and partly published by Dümichen. These are important chiefly for the details of the funeral ceremonies.

The entrance, as in almost all the tombs in this part of the necropolis, is by an open courtyard without walls, 103 ft. wide and 76 ft. deep, which leads to a hall in the rock (the mortuary chapel), with side-chambers and passages. This is 67 ft. wide by 53 ft. deep, and its roof is supported by two rows of pillars. All the walls are ornamented with inscriptions and reliefs carefully executed, but now unfortunately much injured and blackened. These, almost without exception, refer to the fate of the soul in the lower world. — A vaulted *Corridor* leads into a second large *Room* (53 ft. by 37 ft.) in which 8 pillars remain to prevent the roof from falling, while in the *Room* adjoining it, 32½ ft. square, only 4 have been spared. A *Chamber* with niches (21 ft. by 12 ft.) concludes this series of rooms, the total length of which together with the courtyard is 312 ft. The nature of the stone having apparently prevented further advance into the rock in this direction, the masons turned to the left and dug out a wide *Hall*, and also to the right, where six successive *Passages* were made at right angles leading to a small room. These not being on the same level were connected by flights of respectively 9, 23, and 9 steps. In the small room mentioned is a shaft 45 ft. deep with a chamber. Caution is necessary here. This series of passages is 177 ft. in length. From the room containing the shaft a *Corridor* runs again to the right, and leads to a transverse *Chamber*, making 60 ft. in this direction. However, before reaching the steps on the second line, we find leading to a second shaft a fourth set of passages to the right, 125 ft. long in a straight direction. Adjoining this on the left is a large *Gallery*, 58 ft.

square, in the decoration of which the central block is treated as if it
were an enormous sarcophagus. In fact the *Sarcophagus* of the deceased
lies below the centre of this block, and is reached by means of a perpendicular shaft, 18 ft. in depth, at the end of a *Corridor* to the right of
the main passage. By descending the shaft, a room 19¹/₂ ft. deep is reached,
and from the roof of this there is an entrance to the sarcophagus-hall,
which is exactly beneath the square block above described. The length
of this private tomb without the side-chambers is 862 ft., and its super-
ficial area 2470 sq. yds. or with the shaft-chambers 2660 sq. yds.

To the N. of this huge tomb are several smaller ones of the
same period, with finely worked antechambers, and false doors, and
carefully executed inscriptions. Some of these, especially those of
the royal ladies and priestesses of Ammon, *Shep-en-apt* and *Neit-*

akert or *Nitocris* [cartouche], contain valuable contributions to the knowledge of the family of Pharaohs which formed
the 26th Dynasty. A queen Nitocris of the 6th Dyn., known as a
pyramid-builder, is said to have been beautiful and light-haired.
With her may have been confounded the princess of the 26th Dyn.
with the same name, who was buried at el-Asasif, and lived shortly
before the famous courtezan of Naucratis, named *Rhodopis* or the
rosy-cheeked. Nitocris the elder and Rhodopis were probably called
by the same name, *i.e.* the fair one, in the mouths of the Egyptians,
and Herodotus hearing that the 'Fair one' had lived shortly before
Amasis, confused the two, and reported that the courtezan Rhodopis
was considered the builder of pyramids. See Vol. I., p. 346.

The Terrace-Temple of Dêr el-baḥri.

This temple derives its name, meaning the *North Church* or
North Monastery, from an ecclesiastical brick building of the Christian period, the remains of which are mentioned on p. 227. Dêr
el-baḥri is reached from el-Asasif in 10 minutes. Its situation is
remarkably fine, its terraces which we ascend, being framed by a
semicircle of high and rugged rocks, of a light brown and golden
colour. If Thebes had been in Greece, this is where its citizens
would have placed their theatre. The Egyptians whose thoughts
were fuller of death than of life, founded a sanctuary for the
worship of the dead. Apparently an avenue of sphinxes, of which
some traces remain, connected this with the landing-stage, where
boats coming from Karnak on the W. bank were anchored. This
magnificent work was carried out during the rise of the New Empire, and the numerous processions of pilgrims began in the
16th cent. B.C. The laying out of the terraces was begun by Tutmes I., and completed by his daughter, Queen Hatshepsu, or Hatasu-Ramaka, familiar to us as the raiser of the great obelisk of
Karnak (p. 133). Here too her brothers, Tutmes II. and III.,
although their names are mentioned, fall into the background
when compared with their energetic and ambitious sister. After-

wards Tutmes III. erased in many places the name of his obnoxious guardian, who seems also to have been the wife of his elder
brother Tutmes II. The great monarchs of the 19th Dyn., Seti I.
and Ramses II., Merenptah, son of the latter, Ramses III., Pinozem,
one of the priest-kings of the 21st Dyn., Taharka, the Ethiopian,
of the 25th Dyn., Psammetikh II. and Nitocris of the 26th Dyn.,
Ptolemy IX. Euergetes II. and his wife Cleopatra, and Ptolemy X.
Lathyrus, all contributed by works of restoration to prevent the
building which had been completed under Hatasu, from falling
into decay. Both the style, and the inscriptions tell us that Dér el-
baḥri is to be considered completely a work of the beginning of the
New Empire. The size and simplicity of its parts, and especially
the polygonal columns are a sign to those who are familiar with
the development of Egyptian architecture, that the Hyksos period
must be considered to have been a time of stagnation in Egyptian
art, and that exactly the same forms and arrangements of columns
were common to the architects of the |12th and to those of the
18th Dynasties. In Thebes, and not least at Dêr el-baḥri, the observer is tempted to regard the New Empire as an immediate continuation of the Old, although between them lies a period of five
hundred years.

The plan of this terrace-temple is remarkable, and cannot be
compared with any other in Egypt. The arrangement in four
terraces rising from the level ground up the steep side of the Libyan mountains is quite unique. The stages were cut out of the
E. slope of the mountain, and support was given to the outer and
inner walls by means of blocks of the finest sandstone. At the S.
end of the terraces we can best see the care taken to support the
earth-works. The outer wall consists here of finely polished blocks
of limestone with simple but effective ornamentation. Broad pilasters, but only 3 in. deep, placed some distance apart, project
from the wall with which they are connected. Above each is
enthroned a gigantic hawk with the crown of Upper and Lower
Egypt, standing upon an Uræus-serpent, and above it is the symbol
of life supported by an Uræus-serpent.

A long *Avenue of Sphinxes*, probably beginning with a pylon,
near the entrance to the tomb of Petamenap (p. 222) led up to the
series of terraces, the successive stages being reached by steps
placed in the middle.

The *First Terrace* (beginning from below) is almost entirely
destroyed, but we can make out the pathway which led from the
bottom to the top, and divided the whole into two equal parts. Below the *Second Terrace* (Mariette's *Terrasse de l'Est*) are the ruins
of a *Hall*, supported by columns of 16 sides, which in this form
were used only under the 17th and 19th Dynasties. The pressure
of the earth is sustained by a lofty inner wall on which are some
well preserved inscriptions, and representations of ships, soldiers

with axes, olive-branches, etc. Lying on the ground is a peculiar capital, such as may be seen also in other parts of the temple, consisting of a cube, with the mask of the goddess Hathor carved on the front and back. The upright broken shafts should also be noticed; one half was treated as a pillar, the other as a polygonal column with 7 sides, and an inscription was placed on the surface of the pillar.

The *Third Terrace* (Mariette's *Terrasse du Centre*) deserves especial notice. Underneath there were on each side, left and right, two rows of 11 square pillars which together formed two halls, 88 ft. long, open to the east. Of these the pillars of the left hall still stand, only two remaining in that on the right. These halls supported a roof, of which all that remains is a fragment of the architrave and a broad slab on the 11 pillars in the back row. The scenes represented on the inner wall and on the left side are of great interest.

Disregarding for the present the part of the temple to the left (*Speos of Hathor*, p. 227) we begin with the right side of the inner wall below the third terrace. The first scenes are somewhat damaged, but those which follow are in a good state of preservation, and refer chiefly to the expedition on which Queen Hatasu-Ramaka sent her ships to Arabia (⬚ ∿∿∿ Punt). 1. Ramaka represented as king, with the double crown on her head, and the staff in her hand, before Ammon-Ra. There is a long but obliterated inscription. 2. The queen with two bowls full of grains of incense, and with the helmet on her head, before the sacred boat of Ammon-Ra. The boat with a ram's head at each end is carried by priests, of whom the two in the centre are high-priests, clad in leopard-skins. Next we see 7 Neha-trees in tubs, probably incense-bearing trees imported to Egypt from the East; men with tubs are piling up the incense in heaps. Above are the weighing and measuring of precious metals, as may be seen elsewhere. The weights used for weighing the gold rings are in the form of oxen lying down. The goddess Safekh marks the result on a tablet. Next are 3 Neha-trees. Below is seen a group of 8 cattle, two eating the reed-grass on the river-side. The scene reminds us vividly of Pharoah's dream (Gen. XLI. 1). 'And it came to pass at the end of two full years, that Pharaoh dreamed: and, behold, he stood by the river. And, behold, there came up out of the river seven well-favoured kine and fat-fleshed; and they fed in the reed-grass'. Near this are sacks with cosmetics *(mestem)*. Again we find the king with the insignia of power. Then 2 rows of ships belonging to the fleet which Ramaka-Hatasu sent to Arabia. The shape of the vessels, their rigging, oars, and rudders should be noticed, as well as the cargo which can be seen on board, and the loading by means of a small boat. The necessary explanations are given by small inscriptions above the pictures. To the left,

below, is an inscription of 13 lines, of which the 8th and 9th
were destroyed by Ramses II., for the purpose of inserting his own
name in honour of Ammon-Ra, the lord of heaven, etc. It speaks
of 'the voyage on the sea, the beginning of the great journey to
Ta neter, i.e. the holy land, the happy arrival in Arabia of
the soldiers of Pharaoh, the lord of the world, according to the
command of Ammon, the lord of the gods', etc. — Another inscription between the trees, to which the boat is fastened, tells us
that Punt as well as Arabia Petræa was dedicated to the goddess
Hathor. To the left of the two ships are 10 lines describing by name
the different kinds of wares which sailors are carrying on board along
narrow planks. 'Loading of the ships with untold quantity of
valuables from Arabia, precious kinds of wood from the holy land,
heaps of the grains of incense-gum (kemi-ent-anta)†, Nehut trees
of fresh incense-grains (ānta), ebony (hebni) for sacred vessels with
gold and silver from of the land Amu (Asia), Deas††, and Khesit-
wood, possibly cassia-bark, grains of Ahem†††, incense and cosmetics (antimony), Anau and Kefu apes, Desem beasts or greyhounds, coloured panther-skins from the south, natives and children'.
The inscription concludes with the statement that nothing like it had
been done under any king before, and it speaks the truth. Hatasu
showed her people the way to the land whose products were later
to fill the treasuries not only of the Paraohs, but also of the Phœnicians and the Jews. — These pictures are of special interest as
exactly illustrating I Kings x. 22: 'Once in three years came the navy
of Tarshish, bringing gold and silver, ivory, and apes, and peacocks'.
Except these last named birds all the treasures may be seen on the
vessels of Hatasu. Her expedition must have been accompanied by
some nature-loving priests, as below the ships we see the water-line
in which are swimming various kinds of the most remarkable
fish of the Red Sea. The drawings of these are so characteristic that
Prof. Doenitz has been able to determine their species. Among them
are Naseus unicornis, Xiphias gladius, Platax Teira, Balistes assasi,
Acanthurus velifer, Chaetodon strigangulus, Scarus viridescens, etc.
In a sole 'one eye was drawn larger than the other, showing a fine
observation of nature'.

On the wall adjoining the right-hand corner there was to be seen
until a few years ago the transport of the incense-trees, 9 soldiers with
officers, and in two places, one above the other, the prince of Punt, named
Pirahu, coming from the left, and followed by his wife, remarkable for her

---

† From the Egyptian ⟨hieroglyphs⟩ ḳemi, resinous exudations from
various trees, comes our word gum.

†† From the fruit of the Deas tree a sacred ointment was obtained.

††† These belong to the mineral kingdom.

obese appearance, a son and a daughter, as well as a donkey, to carry the princess on her travels. Unfortunately this piece of wall has been destroyed by tourists, and only a small fragment showing the princess and her husband is preserved in the museum at Gizeh.

The representation ends with a settlement of the inhabitants of Punt. It lies close to the water which is populated by fish, turtles, and crayfish, and it would seem as if the inhabitants were lake-dwellers. At all events their conical houses rest upon piles. The door could only be reached by a ladder, which the artist has not forgotten to represent. Palms and incense-trees give shade to the village. In this southern landscape appear, or rather used to appear, on the right a cow reclining, and on the left a long-tailed bird flying through the air.

The third terrace was formed by the roof of this hall, on the inner wall of which were the above-described paintings, together with a *Temple*, placed in the centre and supported by round columns and by the ground behind. From this terrace a well-preserved granite doorway leads to the burial chambers lying behind (see below).

At the end of this terrace to the left there is a remarkable small *Sanctuary* dedicated to the goddess Hathor, and built by Hatasu and her husband-brother Tutmes II., which should not be left unvisited. The two outer rooms are in ruins, so that even the partition-walls betweeen the halls lying one behind the other are scarcely recognizable. Some of the pillars and bases of the columns, however, are still upright. We turn to the right and find the remains of a *Hathor Cow*. There are also some more paintings of ships, but very faint. On the outer wall of the temple built into the mountain, is an ox licking the hand of king, *i.e.* queen Ramaka. As the adjoining text says, 'She licks Horus to whom she gave birth'. To the right of the door is Tutmes III. (Ra-men-kheper-ka), and within Tutmes II. who built the door and gave his name to it.

The *Burial Chambers* lying behind are reached through an antechamber with two small niches on each side. This is succeeded by another long room with a flat blue ceiling, ornamented with red stars at one time probably gilt. On each side of this funeral chamber are niches. Next is a narrow room with two niches. At the back of this last on the two side-walls above the shaft is an exceedingly interesting *Representation* of Queen Hatasu, drinking the milk of life from the udders of the *Hathor Cow*. The cow is the finest piece of animal painting which has come down to us from Egyptian antiquity. The cartouche of the queen was erased, probably by order of her indignant ward Tutmes III. when he became independent. All the inscriptions and paintings in this room (cynocephali, lions, etc.) are perfect in style; those in the niches tell us that these were used for the storing of offerings.

The last or *Fourth Terrace* is badly preserved. We first come to a granite doorway built by Tutmes III. on the central path, on the left hand side of which we see an inscription of the 3rd year of Merenptah I. Next we reach the tower and fragments of wall, both of rough Nile bricks, belonging to the monastery or church, which

15*

has given its name to the place. To the left are the remains of
other rooms. The name of Ramses II., inserted by himself as a
correction, should be noticed; behind are offerings for the dead. The
fine roof is not a true vault, the stones lying horizontally and being
cut out. The colours are fresh ; to the right and left of the door
are Tutmes III. and Tutmes II. ; over the door 4 bulls. — Ascending 34 steps further we reach another granite doorway also built
by Tutmes III., through which we enter a vault sprinkled with stars.
This last rests against the wall of rock which rises above Dêr el-
baḥri, without being cut into it. A second archway with 2 side-
niches leads deeper into the mountain, and there is a third unvaulted
room which was constructed under Tutmes I. of the 18th Dynasty,
but appropriated by a distinguished official named Amenhotep,
under Ptolemy Euergetes II., and his wife Cleopatra. The inscriptions of this later period compare very disadvantageously with
those of the time of the Tutmes kings.

From the N. side of the third terrace it is possible to creep into the
Burial Chapel, half filled with rubbish, which is supported by 12 eighteen-
sided columns in four rows, and contains two empty sarcophagus-chests.
On the inner wall are Anubis and offerings for the dead. This is followed
by a vaulted *Chamber* the arch of which is pointed, and from this a similarly vaulted *Passage* runs off at a right angle, to the W. of which is a
very small *Room*, also vaulted in the same way. We thus find three vaulted
rooms, each smaller than the preceding. In front of this arrangement of
tombs there was a building of which there now remains (on the right
as we leave the tombs) a *Colonnade* with 7 eighteen-sided columns, bearing an architrave, the astragal, and the concave cornice. These rooms are
much choked up, and full of fragments of mummies, and linen rags. In
later times they were used as a common burial ground. The same fate
from the 26th Dyn. onwards befel the rooms at the end of which is the
fine picture of the Hathor Cow (p. 227); but these are now kept clean and
easily accessible.

On the fourth terrace also pictures of a procession have been preserved. Of the row of ships nothing is left but the water-lines below them,
but it is from here that a picture of a ship now in the Berlin Museum
was taken, with an accompanying inscription telling us that the *Procession*
was arranged by Tutmes III. in honour of Tutmes II.

At no great distance from Dêr el-baḥri there is a roughly worked
passage cut, only about 3 ft. high and scarcely accessible, which was ex-
plored by Ebers. It leads into a sepulchral chamber, entirely covered
with semi-hieratic inscriptions, in which was buried a princess named
Nefru, a favourite, and perhaps the mother of a princess Hatasu belonging
to the early period of the New Empire or, according to Naville, to the
11th or 12th Dynasty.

_____

This neighbourhood should not be quitted without a visit to the shaft
from which the famous royal mummies were obtained. In order to reach
it we walk over the heaps of sand to the right at the foot of Dêr el-baḥri
(or we may take an easier path from the village and tombs of Shêkh
'Abd el-Kurnah down the slope to the west). In scarcely 10 min. we are
in front of a narrow chasm in the rock, up which there is a steep climb
for 5 minutes. Above is the Shaft, 6 ft. square, descending perpendicularly
for 38 ft. A strong rope and great caution are necessary in order to be
let down. At the bottom is an entrance 5 ft. wide and 3 ft. high which
leads in a straight direction for 24 ft. This passage then turns to the right
in a N.E. direction for the length of more than 195 ft., its height varying from 6 to 13 ft. To the right five or six rude steps lead to a niche.

Straight on is a room about 25 ft. long. Here on July 5th 1881 *Emil Brugsch* discovered the famous royal mummies, now in the Gizeh Museum. Since January 1876 Ushabtis, tablets, and large funereal papyrus rolls, all coming from this spot, had been sold to wealthy tourists through the medium of Mustapha Aga, the English consular agent at Luxor. Attention was aroused by the *Papyrus of Notemit*, a queen of the 21st Dyn. which was produced in several pieces, one of which is now in the Louvre, another in the British Museum, having been presented to the Prince of Wales, and a third in the possession of a Belgian lady. Enquiries showed that there were several brothers 'Abd er-Rasûl who were especially concerned in the sale of these antiquities. The arrest and trial of Aḥmed, one of the brothers, followed by flogging, led to no result. However partly from fear of punishment, and partly for a promised reward the secret was betrayed by Ahmed's elder brother Mohammed, to the Mudîr of Keneh, who gave information to the Khedive. Brugsch describes the discovery as follows: 'Every inch of the subterranean passage was covered with coffins and antiquities of all kinds. My astonishment was so overpowering that I scarcely knew whether I was awake or whether it was only a mocking dream. Resting on a coffin, in order to recover from my intense excitement, I mechanically cast my eyes over the coffin-lid, and distinctly saw the name of King *Seti I.*, the father of Ramses II., both belonging to the 19th Dynasty. A few steps further on, in a simple wooden coffin, with his hands crossed on his breast, lay *Ramses II.*, the great *Sesostris* himself. The farther I advanced, the greater was the wealth displayed, here *Amenophis I.*, there *Amosis*, the three *Tutmes*, Queen *Ahmes nofertari*, Queen *Aahhotep*, all the mummies well preserved; in all 36 coffins, belonging to kings and their wives or to princes and princesses. . . . .

By the evening of July 11th all the mummies and coffins had been carefully packed at Luxor. Three days later the Museum steamer came to carry the precious burdens to Bûlâk. From Luxor to Koptos on both sides of the Nile, the fellâhin women followed the boat with loosened hair and uttering plaintive cries, while the men fired off guns, as at a funeral. The coffins were taken to the museum at Bûlâk, and thence removed to the new museum at Gîzeh. — The discovery included King *Rasekenen*, of the 17th Dyn., the opponent of the Hyksos; of the 18th Dyn. King *Aahmes*, queens *Aahmes nofertari* and *Aahhotep*, kings *Amenhotep I.*, *Tutmes I., II.,* and *III.,* prince *Sitamon*, princesses *Sitamon* and *Meritamon*, *Nebseni* a priest, and others; of the 19th Dyn. *Ramses I., Seti I.,* and *Ramses II. Ramses III.* of the 20th dyn. was also afterwards found. Of the priest-kings of the 21st Dyn. *Pinozem, Nozemit, Ramaka* with her daughter, a second *Pinozem*, queen *Hathorhont'aui, Masahirta* a priest, two princesses *Ast-em-kheb* and *Nesikhonsu*, and others. There were also found a large leather tent in red, green, yellow, and white for *Ast-em-kheb*, the daughter of King *Pinozem*, 40 canopi, 3700 statuettes of Osiris, 12 to 15 ceremonial wigs, and 46 wooden chests together with inscriptions, bronze stools, papyrus rolls, and the like. The inscriptions found on the older mummy-chests, *e.g.* that of Seti I. and on the wrappings, were of great importance, recording that the mummies had been taken from their tombs by the priest-kings of the 21st Dyn. (Herhor, Sitamon, Pinozem, and Masahirta the priest) and removed to that of a lady named *An keb* or *An hapu*, in which also lay Amenhotep I. In the *Abbott Papyrus*, which is a judicial enquiry into the robbery of the tombs, the passage 120 ells long in the tomb of Amenhotep I., which was to the N. of the temple of Amenhotep, is mentioned. This corresponds to the passage in the Dêr el-baḥri pit. The colours of the garlands of flowers were marvellously well preserved. The plants have been named by Prof. Schweinfurth.

On June 1st 1886 by the wish of the Khedive the unrolling of the mummies, a somewhat bold proceeding, was taken in hand, beginning with the grey-haired Ramses the Great, whose sharp features and curved nose are remarkably striking. In the coffin of Nefertari the mummy of Ramses III. was strangely found. Then followed Seti I. with his mild features, Rasekenen with his fierce look and broken skull, having perhaps fallen in battle with the Kheta, Aahmes I., and the priest-kings of Thebes. A mummy unknown showed terribly distorted painful features, as if it had died by poison. In the course of a month all the mummies were unrolled, measured, described, and covered up again, though whether they will long survive the process remains to be seen. Excellent photographs of the mummies unrolled were taken by Emil Brugsch, the conservator of the museum.

In Feb. 1891 another large rock-tomb was discovered to the E. of the temple of Dêr el-baḥri, containing 163 mummies of priests and dignitaries of the 19th, 20th, and 21st Dyn., besides a large number of papyri, Osiris-statuettes, chests and boxes, baskets of flowers, funereal offerings, etc. Several of the sarcophagi are elaborately adorned with religious scenes. Judging from the manner in which the sarcophagi were piled upon each other, and from the fact that several of the mummies are damaged, it is probable that, like the royal mummies, they were hastily removed from their original tombs to preserve them from spoliation. The contents of the tomb are now at Gizeh, where the deciphering of the papyri will be undertaken.

22. From Thebes to Edfu.

Comp. Map p. 98.

67 M. *Steamer*, up in 11¹/₂, down in 7¹/₂ hrs.; *Dhahabîyeh* in 3-5 days, according to the wind.

The picturesque forms of the Arabian side of the Nile remain long in view, Kôm el-Ḥêṭân being the last of the Memnonia to disappear. In 2 hrs. the steamer reaches —

9 M. (W. bank) **Erment,** the ancient *Hermonthis,* with an important sugar factory belonging to the Khedive.

The place contains nothing else worth seeing. as the temple buildings distant about ¹/₂ hr. from the town have been almost entirely destroyed, or built into the factory. It was a *Mameisi* or birth-place dedicated to ꜣꜤ ≋ the goddess *Ratati,* who as mother of the young Horus is compared to Cleopatra, and contained pictures of the famous Cleopatra VI., and of Cæsarion the son of Julius Cæsar and that queen. The *Temple* consisted of a court with columns, about 55 ft. wide by 65 ft. deep. This was followed by a long room, surrounded by columns, in the centre of which was the cella in several divisions. The length of the whole temple was 190 ft.; the front faced south-west. Until a few years ago the cella, and 5 columns on the left, and 2 on the right of the fore-court were standing; scarcely anything now remains.

To distinguish it from the northern *An* or Heliopolis (Vol. I., p. 333) *Hermonthis* was known in hieroglyphics as [hieroglyphs] *i.e.* the An or On of the god Month, or [hieroglyphs] *i.e.* An Kemat, or the southern An, a name which probably applied to the whole district of Thebes, to which it belonged in earlier times. Later it is mentioned as the capital of a special district or nome, and large portions of Thebes were included in it. Under the Ptolemies an important royal excise-office had its seat here. — A *Christian Church,* now in ruins, must at one time have been a building of considerable size.

Travellers who have abundance of time, should land. The bank is shaded with stately sycamore trees. Close by are a clean *Bazaar* and a shop kept by a Frenchman. Donkeys for hire. A good road, bordered with trees and traversing a well-cultivated district, leads in less than half-an-hour to the village, among the houses of which lie prostrate columns. The inhabitants cherish the curious belief that Moses was born here. Near the cemetery are some ancient sub-structures, with fragments of inscriptions recording that Hermon-this, which must have existed even under the old monarchy, was adorned under the 18th Dyn. with fine buildings for the deity of the city. Strabo relates that Zeus and Apollo were worshipped and that a sacred bull was kept here. As a matter of fact the monu-ments, besides mentioning several female deities, name Month (Zeus) and seven forms of Horus (Apollo) as the chief gods at Her-monthis, while the coins of the Nomos Hermonthites bear the figure of a bull turned towards the right, and preparing to fight, with lowered horns and extended tail. The Pharaoh is described as fall-ing upon his foes, like 'Month, the bull raising himself to combat'. — At *Rizagât*, 4½ M. to the S.W. of Erment, a stele of the 18th Dyn. was found, in which this place is named *Aimatiru*.

On the right bank, facing the curve which the Nile describes at the village of *Senâd*, lies the village of *Tûd*, the ancient *Tuphium*, with a ruinous chamber, the sole relic of a small temple of the Ptolemies. Maspero recently discovered here a granite sacrificial table, with a dedication by Usertesen I. to the god Month. Steles of the 12th and 13th Dyn. (now at Gizeh) were found at *Salamîyeh*, 1¾ M. to the W. of Tûd. — At *Mealâh*, on the E. bank, are frag-ments of a sphinx with the name of Amenhotep I.

On the W. bank, 13 M. above Erment, and opposite a large is-land, rise two rocky heights, known as **Gebelên,** *i.e.* the 'two moun-tains', on one of which is the tomb of a *Shêkh Mûsah*, probably confounded with Moses (see above). Here, on the site of the ancient *Ánti*, probably once stood the ancient *Aphrodito-polis*, which, according to Strabo, must be looked for between Her-monthis (Erment) and Latopolis (Esneh). Extensive excavations carried on at this spot by Maspero yielded sarcophagi of the 12th Dyn. and also numerous domestic articles, etc., appropriate to per-sons of comparative poverty.

On the W. bank, 13½ M. farther up, lies **Esneh,** the ancient *Latopolis*, a town of 9000 inhab., where the tourist-steamers halt for 3 hrs., while the mail-steamer on the downward voyage stops all night. The profane name of this place under the Pharaohs was *Sen,* whence came the Coptic CHH *(Sne)* and the Arabic Esneh. Esneh has large grain and cattle markets, at which prices are lower than at Assuân. The town, in which there are numerous coffee-houses and ghawâzi, is somewhat notorious for the dissolute disposition of the otherwise industrious inhabitants, many of whom are employed in wool-weaving. The *Bazaar*, at the entrance to which is a kind of *Market-Place*, is tolerably well furnished. The streets are well built and some of the shops are European in cha-racter. There is also a *Druggist's Shop*. Passengers usually land

either near the former Mudîrîyeh (now removed to Ķeneh), beside which are some ancient riparian constructions dating from the Roman imperial times, or near the post-office, a little to the N., where the steamers lie. The chief object of interest is the *Temple;* and if time permit the garden of the Khedive to the N. of the town (p. 235) and the old Coptic church (p. 235) may also be visited. The former lies 10-15 min. from the landing-place (see above), and is reached by passing through part of the town. The old temple-site is at present used by the Excise Office for storing the grain, beans, and other tribute paid in kind, but travellers will have no difficulty in inducing one of the by-standers to fetch the keeper who will unlock the door. Cards empowering a visit to the antiquities must not be forgotten (see p. xiv).

The so-called *Temple* is in reality only a *Hypostyle*, which evidently from its size must have belonged to an unusually large sanctuary. The ground-level of the town has been raised by accumulations of rubbish etc. to the height of the capitals of the columns, so that travellers descend by steps into the interior of the building. Above the rest of the temple now pass streets, the removal of which would probably bring to the light of day many monuments of antiquity. The savants of the French Expedition were profoundly impressed by the sight of this huge colonnaded hall; and as the traveller standing in front of the steps leading to it, gazes down into the mysterious twilight of the ancient sanctuary, he cannot but be struck by the air of solemnity that pervades it.

The remarkable ****Hypostyle of Esneh** is built throughout of excellent sandstone, and remains in perfect preservation with the exception of the lower part of the rear wall, which has been somewhat corroded by the saline exudations of the soil. The noble hall is kept clean by government. The roof is borne by 24 columns (in 6 rows), the first six of which are connected by balustrades; and a dim light penetrates to the remotest corner of the hall between the columns. The façade is 120 ft. wide and almost 50 ft. high; the rectangular hall is $52^1/_2$ ft. deep and 108 ft. broad. Each column is 37 ft. high and $17^3/_4$ ft. in circumference. The intercolumniation is $1^1/_2$ times the diameter of the columns, except in the central passage, where it is nearly 3 times the diameter. Upon the somewhat lofty abaci of the columns rests a massive architrave, which supports roofing-slabs, 22-26 ft. long and $6^1/_2$ ft. wide. It has been calculated that about 110,000 cubic feet of sandstone have been used for this one hall alone. The enormous wall-space, the entire ceiling, the shafts, the antæ (on the façade), and the architrave are covered to the last inch with inscriptions. Though these last fall short of the dignity of style which claims admiration in the earlier works of Egyptian art, yet they display that remarkable care in the representation of details and that elaborate variety of form which at once distinguishes the inscriptions of the time of the Ptolemies and of the Romans, and renders their interpretation more difficult.

The temple of Esneh was founded not later than the 18th Dyn. under Tutmes III., according to one of the inscriptions; and prob-

ably the sanctuary founded by that prince still lies beneath the
houses of the town. The hypostyle, however, must have been ruined
and rebuilt under the Ptolemies, for the adornment of the hall begun by these princes was continued by the early Roman emperors
and completed by their successors. The inscriptions on the rear-
wall were begun by Ptolemy VII. Philometor. The *Dedication Inscription* above the entrance celebrates the 'autocrats' Tiberius,
Claudius, Germanicus, and Vespasian as the builders, while a share
in the decoration of the interior was taken not only by these princes, but also by Titus, Domitian, Nerva, Trajan, Hadrian, Antoninus Pius, Marcus Aurelius, Commodus, Septimius Severus,
Caracalla, Geta, Julius Philippus, and Decius (249-251). The name
of Decius is specially noteworthy as being the latest imperial name
that appears in hieroglyphics on any Egyptian monument.
It appears in the following capricious form: —

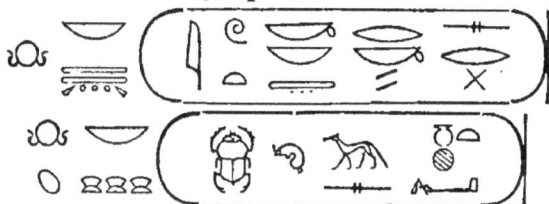

i.e. the sun, the lord of both worlds, the autocrat Caesar, son of the
sun, and lord of the diadems, *Tekis ente-khu*, i.e. Δέκιος σεβάστος. The
emperor offers a fire-altar to Khnum. On the main architrave is *Vespasian;*
on the abacus and entrance-door *Titus;* on the lower side of the main
architrave *Domitian;* on the columns *Nerva* and *Trajan.* Nerva occurs here
only once and is found nowhere else. *Antoninus Pius, Marcus Aurelius,*
and *Commodus,* occur on the exterior wall; and the last also on the N.
half of the W. wall and on the N. wall. *Septimius Severus, Caracalla,* and
Geta appear on the N. and S. walls; *Caracalla* and *Julius Philippus* on the
left half of the rear-wall; and *Decius* at the foot of the rear-wall.
The building, referred to several times in the inscriptions, as
the 'House of Khnum', was dedicated to the ram-headed *Khnum-
Ra,* with whom, forming a triad, appear an *Isis-Neith* under the name

 (Nebuut), and a peculiar Horus-form, named *Hirka.*
There was also a special cycle of gods of Esneh, at the head of
which was *Khnum,* followed by Ra, Tum, Khepera, Shu, Osiris,
Horus the son of Isis, Thoth, and Khunsu. Strabo narrates that
Athena and the fish *Latus* were worshipped here in Latopolis; and
he was not misinformed. We not only find the latter mentioned in
the inscriptions of the hypostyle, but the latus gave the town its
name under the Greeks, while the coins of the *Latopolitan Nome*
bore the figure of a fish, and finally an inscription at Edfu informs
us that the people of Latopolis were forbidden to eat fish. Athena
(Nebuut) frequently appears, as we have seen; and as Strabo makes
no mention of Khnum, who was undoubtedly the chief of all the
gods of this sanctuary, it must be concluded that he was for some
reason led to assign to the latus the place of this deity. Probably

this fish, which appears not only on the coins, but is also repro-
sented with the disc between the horns, was used as a symbolical
representation of Khnum-Ra, especially as we actually find Khnum

united with the fish on the rear-wall of the temple 𓄿𓏏 𓅓 𓋹 .

The SIDE WALLS are entirely covered with paintings and inscriptions. The former show the king making offerings to various
divinities of the temple, who promise him in return the good things
of life. At the foot of the wall to the right of the entrance is the
emperor Commodus with Aruëris and Khnum capturing with a net
the various products of the Nile (birds, fishes, plants, etc.). On the
other side of the net is Safekh. This symbolical representation possibly refers to the legend according to which Horus fighting against
Seth-Typhon fell dead into the water and was drawn out of it
again living, — a legend, which is connected with the course of
the moon. A main door and two side portals are seen in the rear-
wall of the temple. The latter probably gave admittance to a corridor surrounding the *Sanctuary*, which was entered by the central
portal. Recent excavations in this direction have hitherto remained
without result.

On the pieces of wall between the pillars on the *Front* are several highly important inscriptions, of which by far the most
valuable is the celebrated *Calendar of Festivals* on the wall-pillars
to the right and left. A specimen of the eccentricities and freaks
indulged in by the hierogrammatists under the Romans, may be
seen in the crowd of crocodiles on the pillar at the extreme left of
the E. or entrance wall.

The 24 *Columns* of the portico are specially noteworthy on account of the shapes of their capitals, some of which are overladen
with ornament. Of the columns, 18 stand detached, while 6, towards the front, are built into the outer wall. All the columns have
flat plinths, and shafts most elaborately adorned with inscriptions.
The *Capitals* are of various shapes and of unequal height, but this
irregularity does not offend the eye owing to the fact that the annuli
of all the columns are arranged so as to lie in the same horizontal
plane. Most of them belong to the calyx order, and are not adorned
merely with painting as at Karnak or the Ramessoum, but with
richly carved ornaments from the vegetable kingdom.

We begin with the front row, reckoned from the right (N.). Columns
1-6: Four petals, separated at the top, surround the calyx, which is ornamented with marsh-plants and mushrooms. — 7-12 (second row): calyces
with circular horizontal section, adorned with palm-twigs and other foliage. — 13 (beginning of third row, to the right), Calyx with palm-twigs.
— 14-17: Calyx with foliage. — 18. Smooth calyx-capital, in circular horizontal section, adorned with palm-twigs amongst which appear a lavish
profusion of all kinds of fruit, especially grapes and dates. — 19, 20 (two
first to the right, at the rear wall): Calyx-capitals, with marsh-plants. —
21-23: Calyces at the base of which are fruits in flat work, interrupted
by leaves, towards the top, a network of slender plant-fronds. — 24: The
base of the capital is formed of luxuriant vegetable forms in exaggerated

lavishness, the stems of which, of considerable thickness, surround the top of the shaft. The leaves lying against the upper part of the calyx are of an exaggerated coarseness.

In connection with the whole of which they form a part, these capitals produce an impression of great richness; while regarded separately they may be taken as specimens of the rococo period in Egyptian art, if the phrase may be permitted. — The *Ornament* on the front and back walls is sunk into the wall ('relief en creux'); the side-walls and columns were on the other hand adorned with bas-reliefs. — The *Ceiling* is occupied with a rich profusion of astronomical representations.

The small *Coptic Church* in the town contains little of interest. As in most Jacobite churches, the *Nave* is divided into two parts by three arches. Behind the wooden screens, which are tastefully inlaid with ivory and mother-of-pearl, lies the sanctuary, in four parts. The figures of the saints are poor and comparatively modern. They represent St. George and the dragon, St. Michael, the Madonna and Child, and an Ascension.

The *Palace of the Khedive (Ḳaṣr Efendînah),* built by Moḥammed 'Ali, lies near the Nile, to the N. of the town. The buildings, including a handsome rotunda, are much neglected, but the gardens, with their profusion of roses, lemon-trees, and orange-trees, are very attractive. The gardener, who usually presents the visitor with a nosegay, expects a small gratuity (about 4 piastres).

The *Quay* on the right bank of the Nile, near the Mudîrîyeh, also contains some fragmentary inscriptions of the Roman imperial epoch.

A *Temple*, which formerly stood about $2^1/_4$ M. to the N. of Esneh, is now represented only by a few fragments of columns, which bear the name of one of the emperors; and with it have disappeared also the beautiful zodiac and the lists of peoples, among which Macedonians and Persians were mentioned. This temple too was dedicated to Khnum. — Another temple, dating from the later Ptolemies, stood on the W. bank opposite Esneh *(Contra Latopolis)*; but this was demolished before 1880 and has left not a trace behind.

Numerous memorials of an early Christian civilization are still to be traced in the Convent of **Ammonius**, which is considered the oldest convent in Egypt and which was certainly founded at a very early date, possibly by the Empress Helena. The route thence from the town follows at first an embankment towards the S., and then strikes off to the W. across the fields. The *Convent Library* still contains numerous Coptic liturgical writings, some of them lying on the floor in a locked room. A visit to the now abandoned convent, the key of which is kept by one of the fellâhîn, is not without interest, for the sake both of the curious MSS. and of the ancient paintings and Coptic inscriptions. A cruel persecution of the Christians is said to have taken place at Esneh under Diocletian at the beginning of the 4th cent.; and the convent is said to have been founded in honour of the martyrs who suffered here. According to other accounts the Christians expelled from Medinet Habu by the Arabs were massacred here.

About $7^1/_2$ M. to the N.W. of Esneh, on the road to el-Khârgeh (p. 348), lies the large ruined *Convent of Pachomius,* with numerous elegant mausolea.

Esneh is sometimes selected as a starting-point for journeys to the W. oases of *Dâkhel* and *Khârgeh;* see R. 35.

El-Ken'ân, $13^1/_2$ M. to the S. of Esneh on the W. bank, where there are ancient river-embankments, is perhaps the ancient *Khnu-*

bis. On the W. bank stretches a broad and fertile plain, on the E. is the finely shaped *Gebel Sheroneh*. At *el-Hawi*, on the E. bank, appears the first sandstone.

On the W. bank, about 3/4 hr. farther to the S., is the pyramid of el-Kulah, which now presents the aspect of a step-pyramid, owing to the decay of the filling-in material. The entrance was on the W. side. In spite of its ruinous condition it is still about 30 ft. high, while its base occupies an area about 55 ft. square. Maspero recently carried on excavations here, which injured the building without yielding any important result. As there are no inscriptions it is difficult to determine the date of its construction.

18 M. **El-Kâb,** on the E. bank, the ancient *Eileithyia*. — The station of the four week steamers (from 9 a.m. to 2 p.m.) and of the mail-steamer is at *Başalîyeh*, properly *eṣ-Şulêhîyeh*.

An old fellâh appears to proffer his services as soon as a dhahabiyeh lands. He is well-informed and provides donkeys, though with very poor saddle-cloths.

Half-a-day suffices for a flying visit to the following: 1. the **Ruins* of the ancient town; 2. the *Rock Inscriptions;* 3. the **Chapel of Amenhotep III.;* 4. the *Rock Tempel* of the Ptolemies; and 5. the **Tombs.* If so much time cannot be spared, the last should at least be visited. The various monuments may be visited in the above order as follows. We skirt the boundary wall of the ancient town, which is distinctly visible, then turn to the E. to (3/4 hr.) an isolated hill, rising from the plain, on the right side of which are most of the rock-inscriptions. At the end of this valley we turn a little to the left to reach the chapel of Amenhotep III., with four columns in the interior. We here turn round, and following the S. wall of the more northerly chain of hills, reach the steps which lead to the rock-temple. We may then visit the small temple of Thoth (called by the Arabs *el-Ḥammâm,* 'the bath'), or proceed to the tombs, about 1 M. from the river.

The now vanished town of *Hebent* was called by the Greeks *Eileithyia* or *Leucothea* (Pliny), and in the inscriptions the *Fortress*

Hebent ⸥, often with the surname of ⸥ '*the white town*'.

The interpretation of the name of the city and its goddess as *Nekheb* and *Suben* is probably wrong. The **Girdle Wall* is in excellent preservation, and encloses a square the sides of which are 700 yds. long, with a total circumference of 2800 yds. The wall itself is of immense thickness, 37 ft. or as wide as a considerable street, and is built of huge sun-dried Nile-bricks. The savants of the French Expedition estimated that the ancient town accommodated 10,000 inhabitants. Visitors should not omit to mount the broad ascent to the top of the wall on the W. side, from which a good survey of the tombs on the N. hill-chain is also obtained. Apparently only the temples and public buildings, the 'inner city', stood within the walls, while various suburbs stretched beyond them; though in times of danger the entire population found refuge within the ramparts. The temple was destroyed only a few months before Champollion's arrival at el-Kâb in 1829, and only a few scanty traces of it (a basin, some faint hieroglyphics, etc.) are now left. The sanctuary, which stood within the wall, was dedicated to Sebek and Hebent and existed even under the 18th Dynasty. Champollion saw here the cartouches of Tutmes II., Ramaka, Amenhotep III., two scenes in which Ramses II. did homage to Sebek and Hebent, and Hakoris and Nectanebus I. from later times. The town itself was founded at a much earlier date, and in fact is, as we shall see, one of the very oldest in Egypt. It existed even under the ancient empire. During the period of the Hyksos it was scarcely less conspicuously than Thebes the residence of the legitimate Pharaohs who had been driven towards the S. The most important monuments for the history of the freeing of Egypt from the foreign domination are to be found here.

Rock Inscriptions. — The route leads due E. from the E. gateway in the girdle-wall, and crosses the dazzlingly white sand, past a small ruined *Temple* close to the wall. In rather more than ½ hr. we reach the small temple of Thoth, known to the Arabs as *el-Hammâm* (p. 239). We keep straight on, leaving the larger temple of the Ptolemies on the left, and soon reach two *Rocks* projecting from the plain, at the point where the road turns N. towards the desert, halfway between el-Hammâm and the E. temple of Amenhotep III. Both rocks bear numerous inscriptions, most of which use the hieratic contractions. The royal names of Pepi and Teta refer these to the 6th Dynasty. The inscriptions are chiefly names of priests and their sons, who probably selected this spot for the consummation of the sacrifices to the after-world. At all events there are but few representations of offerings to the local goddess

Hebent-Eileithyia. There are also some brief prayers. On the S.W. side of the larger rock is a very interesting *Figure of an Ancient King*, with bare head, above which hovers the disc with the Uræus-serpent.

The small temple or Chapel of Amenhotep III. lies fully ¼ hr. to the E. It may be reached direct in about an hour from the Nile, though the shadeless route, especially at midday, is somewhat fatiguing. The little temple which is nearly 50 ft. deep is of considerable interest from the artistic forms which it displays. The small *Cella* (22⅓ by 19 ft.) stands upon a paved platform, which was at one time surrounded by a wall of freestone. The gateway still stands, and was formerly connected with the sanctuary proper by a passage, at the sides of which stood smooth columns with calyx-capitals.

The Interior of the cella forms a single octagonal chamber, the roof of which is supported by four sixteen-sided columns. An attempt was made, as we have already noted at Dêr el-baḥri, to continue this column-form of the ancient monarchy, along with the plastic demands of the architecture of the new monarchy; and we here see, in place of the capital next the central passage, the mask of the goddess Hathor, with her cows' ears and head-dress. The front of a small portable temple with handles, which rested on the head of the goddess, was placed on the abacus, and upon this rested the architrave. The mask of Hathor here appears only on one side of the capital; at Dêr el-baḥri it appears on two sides. This artistic form was afterwards abandoned, but was again revived by Nekhtneb-f (Nectanebus II.), a rival king to the Persians, belonging to the 30th Dyn., who loved to compare himself to the expellers of the Hyksos, and who therefore reverted to the art-forms introduced by them. Finally under the Ptolemies this form was developed into a capital in the fullest sense of the term. The masks are here united with the plinths by means of a vertical *Ornamental Stripe*, covering two of the sides of the polygonal shafts and adorned with inscriptions. As each of the sixteen sides or faces of the columns measures 5 inches in breadth, the stripe is 10 inches in breadth. — On the walls at the height of the architraves, beneath the roof, appear other Hathor masks, alternating with the names of the royal builders. *Amenhotep III.* dedicated to his father *Tutmes IV.* the chapel of the goddess *Hebent*, who here appears beside Ammon-Ra in place of Muth. Both hieroglyphics and pictures retain the freshness of their colours. The former represent the making of offerings. On the side with the door appear two lions, like door-keepers, beside lucubrations of later travellers in demotic characters.

On the *Façade* of this chapel, *Kha-em-us*, chief-priest of Ptah

, and Ramses II's favourite son, whose mummy was found in the Serapeum at Memphis, has commemorated himself. He came hither in the 41st year of his father's reign, to attend the fifth great festival held in honour of Hebent. On the rear door-posts, *Seti I.* — Another *Inscription* in clear hieroglyphics must be mentioned here. It is certainly the latest found in Egypt, and was dedicated to Hebent, 'in the 13th year of his majesty, lord of both worlds, Napoleon III.'

It was engraved in the rock by a celebrated young French Egyptologist, whose name we suppress.

At this chapel we turn, direct our steps towards the Nile, and in ¼ hr. reach the ROCK TEMPLE, on the right side of the valley, recognizable from a distance by the *Stair* leading up to it. The latter consists of 41 steps hewn in the rock, with a massive balustrade on each side. The temple was constructed under Ptolemy IX. Euergetes II. (Physkon), and subsequently provided with new inscriptions by Ptolemy X. Soter II. The site was regarded as holy even before the building was erected, as we are informed by an inscription of the reign of Ramses VI., cut in the rock on the E. side of the door leading into the mountain.

The *Rock Chamber* has a vaulted ceiling covered with stucco, and, being the sanctuary of the temple, was constructed earlier than the preceding chambers to which the stair leads. The latter form two parts. On reaching the top of the stair, we pass through a doorway to a *Fore-Court*, not quite 33 ft. wide, the exterior sides of which were bounded by low walls built between columns. Two rows of columns in the centre led to the door of a smaller *Hall* (only 19 ft. wide) of curious construction, being bounded on the right and left by four low walls, of which each was built in between a pillar and a column. The door leading to the rock-chamber opened at the back of this hall. This sanctuary also was especially dedicated to Hebent.

The SMALL TEMPLE below, farther to the S.W. in the valley, is in good preservation, but it is only 16 ft. high and 27 ft. deep. The Arabs call it *el-Hammâm, i.e.* the Bath.

As the walls are about 3 ft. thick the *Interior* is very small. On the left and back walls is a small window, at some height from the ground. Thoth, Hebent, and Horus, the gods here worshipped, are represented as forming a triad. In the doorway is the Pharaoh offering sacrifice, below; and a cynocephalus with the moon-sickle 'and disc on his head, above. It was to be expected that the sacred animals that symbolize the qualities of Thoth should be found represented here along with the moon-goddess Hebent.

*ROCK-TOMBS. A donkey is not necessary for a visit to these. They are reached in about $1/4$ hr. from the usual landing-place of the Nile boats; and the last few minutes' climb up the hill-slope on which the tombs lie, must be accomplished on foot. The *Shafts*, found both outside and inside the tombs, require caution.

These *Tombs*, hewn side by side in the rock, are, like all the monuments at el-Kâb, of small dimensions, but their distinct pictures of ancient Egyptian domestic life will interest even those travellers who have already seen the tombs of Benihasan and 'Abd el-Kurnah. One of the *Inscriptions* (in the tomb of the ship-captain Aahmes, see p. 241) is of the greatest scientific importance, partly on account of the contemporary narrative of the expulsion of the Hyksos which it contains, partly on account of the simple and intelligible style in which it is expressed. It has been critically translated and analysed (by E. de Rougé) as the *first* of all the larger inscriptions. — Most of the tombs were constructed before, during, or shortly after the rule of the Hyksos, for male and female members of noble families, who discharged the peaceful duties of chief priests of Hebent or of tutors and nurses to the royal princes. There are 31 tombs in all, but only 13 have inscriptions and only 6 repay a visit.

We first enter the third inscribed tomb, counting from the E., which is conspicuous by its wide opening. This belonged to the overseer ( ), of el-Kâb, the scribe (*i.e.* savant) *Pihari* grandson (daughter's son) of the ship-master Aahmes, son of *Abna*, whose tomb lies farther to the left (W.). It is distinguished by a series of representations from the life and burial of the deceased, on both sides of the tomb.

To the left (W.) of the entrance appears the deceased with his staff of office in his right hand and a long stick in his left; behind him stand three servants. The accompanying inscription is: 'The inspection of the labours of all seasons of the year, which take place in the fields, by the overseer of Hebent (el-Kâb) by the manager of Anit (Esneh)'. — The *Labours of the Field* are next represented in three registers, beginning from beneath. In the lowest row: a cart drawn by two horses, showing that horses were used by the Egyptians as early as the beginning of the 18th Dyn.; tilling the ground with hoe and plough, ploughing and sowing. — Middle row: Reaping, the grain being cut not close to the ground but one-third or one-half way up the stalk; vessels with refreshments for the workers are represented, and kept cool by a screen; binding the sheaves; reaping or pressing the fruits of the earth. — Top row: Ears of corn carried away in baskets; threshing by means of oxen; piling up the fruits of the earth; packing them in sacks or storing them in granaries. Above the oxen treading out the corn is the following song, inscribed also in the tombs of Benihasan (p. 12) and Sakkârah : —

Thresh for yourselves,
Thresh for yourselves,
Oxen thresh
For yourselves. Thresh
For yourselves. The straw
Remains for you to eat.
The grain is for your masters.
Do not let weari-
Ness steal over your heart. There is abundance to drink!

In the series below these, *Pihari* is seen with a book in which he is writing, before him a large writing apparatus. The accompanying inscription is: 'Recording the number of cattle by the overseer of Anit, the director of the fields of the S. district, from the temple of Hathor (Aphroditopolis, p. 231) to el-Kâb.' — Then follow cattle of various kinds, calves, oxen, asses; several of these being prepared for the table or for sacrifice; a fire-place. Next appears Pihari, seated and inspecting the weighing and shipping of gold which is mostly made into rings. Farther to the right, the catching and preparing of fish and also of poultry, Pihari standing and looking on. — Above Pibari bears on his lap the young prince Uazmes, second son of king Aahmes (1680 B.C.), whose nurse (*i.e.* tutor) he is named. Pihari with his wife *At renheh*, in a bower, receiving fruit. Grapes are being gathered, and trodden out in a wine-press by nude figures, holding cords as they work.

The remaining paintings illustrate the *Burial* of Pihari, whose coffin is drawn upon a sledge. On the right wall Pihari and his wife receive an offering made by their son *Amonmes*, who is clad in a leopard's-skin. Beneath the chair is a cynocephalus. Behind Amonmes the mourning friends are seated in two divisions. At the head of each division is a seated married couple, and then two rows of relatives, father, mother, grandfather, grandmother, brothers, sisters, and aunts; above is the ship-master Aahmes, son of Abna, with his wife; below is *Ateftera* the nurse of King Uazmes, and at the foot, female musicians and a female harper.

Of the tombs to the right that of *Aahmes* surnamed *Pen heben* or *Pen suben* is noteworthy, not only because two stones from the base of a statue with historical inscriptions (now in the Louvre) were found here and because a statue of Aahmes was discovered in 1883 in the ruins of el-Kâb, but also because the services rendered by the deceased to the kings of the 18th Dyn. and the rewards he received are recorded on the right and left of the entrance, as well as on the stones above-mentioned. The kings mentioned are Aahmes, Amen-hotep I., Tutmes I., II., and III., and Queen Ramaka, with her son and daughter. See Lepsius's Denkmäler III, 436.

From these inscriptions we learn that *Aahmes*, surnamed *Pen heben*, followed the kings of the 18th Dyn. from Aahmes to Tutmes III. on their various campaigns to Zahi, Kush, Naharina, and against the Shasu, and that he captured men, horses, and chariots, for which he received rich gifts. In this tomb is also commemorated the royal prince *Amenhotep*, sur-named *Hapu*, chief (tep) of El Keb, whose father, grandfather, and great-grandfather also held the same dignity. Probably this Amen-hotep reposed also in this tomb.

To the left of the tomb of Pihari, which we inspected first, is that of *Setau*, whose daughter's husband *Ramses Nekhtu* in a leopard's skin brings to him the offerings of the high-priests. A crowd of relatives, including Hui, another son-in-law, is also represented. In this tomb mention is made of the 4th year of a king Ra-neferka..., whose name also occurs with Aahmes, Binpu, and a king Suazen on the pedestal of a statuette of Harpocrates, now in the museum at Gizeh. Those, with the exception, of course, of Aahmes, were probably provincial or local kings. Above some ships in the left part of the tomb a festival of Ramses III. is mentioned, probably a later addition. According to Maspero this tomb dates from the 20th Dynasty.

Farther to the left lies the tomb of *Aahmes, Chief of the Sailors*, the son of *Abna* and her husband *Baba*, who was the maternal grandfather of Pihari. The *Funereal Inscription* is carved in the rock instead of being painted on stucco, a fact which lends great importance to this tomb.

The inscription covers nearly the whole wall to the right, as we enter, sharing it with the figure of the deceased. Aahmes appears with *Aipu* his wife, seated in a chair beneath which cowers a pet monkey; before them stand their daughter's son Pibari, who caused this tomb to be adorned for his gallant grandfather. Beneath is another *Pihar*, offering sacrifice to his father *Harari* and his wife, and beneath him again are three sons, including yet another *Pihar*. Beside the door to the side-chamber is another dedication to Aahmes, the chief of the sailors, from his grandson Pibari (p. 239), to keep his memory green in this spot. The biography of Aahmes thus begins: 'Aahmes (Amasis), commander of the sailors, son of the late Abna, speaks: I speak to you, all ye people. Learn the marks of honour which fell to my share; for I was distinguished seven times with the golden necklace, in the presence of the whole country ... Male and female slaves were my own (the names of the slaves presented to Aahmes are inscribed on the outside of the tomb), and I received many fields. The name of a great hero which he (the speaker) won for himself, will nevermore be obscured in this land. He speaks: I was born in the town of Hebent (Eileithyia); my father was a colonel under the late king Rasekenen (Vol. I., p. 89), and was named Baba, son of Roan; then I served in his stead as captain on board the ship 'The Young Ox', in the reign of Ra-neb-pehti (*i.e.* Aahmes I.). I was young and unmarried and slept on the couch of the Khennu (perhaps those excluded from the dwelling of the married, *i.e.* bachelors). But after I had founded a household (taken a wife), I betook myself to fight in the N. fleet. Then I followed the king on foot, when he mounted his war-chariot. When the fortress of Ha-war (Abaris, a stronghold of the Hyksos, Vol. I., p. 89) was besieged, I had to fight on foot before the king. Then I was appointed to the ship 'Kha em Mennefer' (Ascent in Memphis); we fought in the arm of the river at Abaris and I acquired booty and won a hand (of a slaughtered enemy). This was reported to the officer of the king, and I received the golden necklace for valour. Another contest took place on the same spot and I was again awarded the golden necklace for valour'. Aahmes was decorated a third time at Takemi, to the S. of the fortress. 'Abaris was taken and I captured there in all 4 persons, a man and 3 women; His Majesty assigned them to me as slaves'. — The next lines inform us that after the king had captured the fortress of the Hyksos and overcome the nomadic tribes, he carried on war with the tribes of the S., in which Aahmes took part and won fresh laurels. He served also under Amenhotep I. and Tutmes I. Under the last-named prince the Egyptian army penetrated far into Asia. The inscription goes on: 'Thereupon his majesty set out for Syria (Ruten), in order to reduce the peoples to his good pleasure. He reached Mesopotamia (Naharina). His Majesty, the living, sound, and strong one, met this wretched one (the prince of Mesopotamia), and undertook the attack. The king wrought terrible butchery among them; and the prisoners taken alive by His Majesty were innumerable. I was present as colonel of my soldiers, and His Majesty praised my bravery. I captured a war-chariot, with its horses, and him who stood in it; I led them as living captives to His Majesty, and once more was awarded the golden necklace. I have become great, I have reached old age ... I shall 'rest in the vault, which I have prepared for myself'.

The tomb of *Renni*, still farther to the left (W.), contains numerous representations of interest. The deceased, a son of a lady named Aahmes and father of another Aahmes, was a prince (erpa ha) and a large landed proprietor. Two obelisks seem to have stood at the entrance to this vault; and the statue of the deceased is to be seen in its recess.

The roof of the chapel is vaulted, and covered like the walls with a thin coat of stucco, on which the representations and inscriptions were painted. On the right wall are the funeral of Renni and other scenes connected with his death, while on the left wall are scenes from the life of the deceased, who accompanied by his dog, surveys his possessions. Here appear his carriage, his serfs busied in tilling the ground, and his family in friendly union. Beside each of the persons waited on by the servants of the deceased appears his name and his relationship to the head of the family. Among the livestock belonging to Renni 1500 swine are mentioned, a circumstance which appears somewhat surprising at first, for the flesh of swine was an article of diet as strictly forbidden to the Egyptians as to the Jews. Renni, however, was a prophet of Hebent, and had to provide swine to be sacrificed to this goddess, which accounts for his possession of the otherwise abhorred animals. This remarkable circumstance did not escape the notice of Herodotus, who writes: 'They sacrifice swine to no gods except Selene (goddess of the moon, *i.e.* Hebent) and Dionysus; making this sacrifice to the moon always at full moon, at which time they also eat swine's flesh. The Egyptians assign a particular reason for abhorring swine at other festivals and offering them at this one, but!although I know it I am not permitted to reveal it'. Herodotus was bound by an oath not to reveal the mystery, from which, however, we may be able to lift the veil by a study of the monuments. It is related that Typhon (Seth), while hunting by moonlight, fell in with the coffin of Osiris, and hewed the corpse into 14 parts, *i.e.* the 14 n'ghts of the waxing and waning moon. This orb is called the left eye of Horus, and, as the inscriptions explain, it·was in jeopardy on the 15th night, *i.e.* the time of the full moon. It had been observed that eclipses of the moon affected the light only of the full moon, and thus arose the myth that Seth Typhon, in the form of a swine, attacks the orb of night at the full moon and endeavours to swallow it. The desire of injuring the enemy of the moon and of assisting the latter in her contest against the animal that seeks to devour her, finds symbolical expression in the slaughter of swine at the time of the new moon. Many other Egyptian customs are also to be explained by reference to the contest betwixt Horus and Seth.

The last three tombs farther to the left (W.) appear to date from the 13th Dyn., and are therefore much more ancient than those just described, unless we regard the 14-17th Dyn. as ruling in Upper Egypt contemporaneously with the Hyksos in Lower Egypt. The first was erected to a lady named *Sebeknefru*, by her father *Beba*, who possibly himself is buried here too. Sebeknefru was

suten am, i.e. belonging to the king's court.

Brugsch has published the contents of a *Stele* from the rear-wall of this tomb, in which Beba records the great size of his household, and also his distribution of grain during a long-continued famine. To recognize in this, however, a reference to the famine that brought Joseph's brethren to Egypt, is entirely gratuitous. In the last tomb to the left, belonging to the prince *Sebekhi* there occurs an actual mention of a king

of the 13th Dyn., viz ⟨ cartouche ⟩   *Ra-sekhem-suaz-lati.*

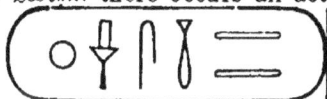

The tomb between the two last-mentioned belongs to a lady named *Sebekhi*, perhaps a wife of Beba.

On the W. bank opposite el-Kâb, on a hill about 3 M. from the Nile, are the partly destroyed rock-tombs of **Kôm el-Ahmar** ('Red Hill'), dating from the time of Tutmes I. Landing at *Ghemawîyeh*, we procede thence due E. through the field viâ (20 min.) *Monisât*. In 20 min. more we reach *Kôm el-Ahmar*, on the site of the ancient town (mentioned by Strabo) of *Hieraconpolis* ('City of hawks'), Egypt. *Kamhesu*, with the town *Nekhen* ⊗ ⊗

or ⊗. The three hawks are Horus, Ṭuamutef, and Kebsenuf. A hawk is also named in the tombs as a local god. The name of User-tesen was not found on the heaps of rubbish in 1885 by Professor Eisen-lohr. — About $^1/_4$ M. farther to the E. begins the desert, and $^1/_4$ M. farther is the ancient Roman fort of *Sefian*, on which large vultures frequently perch. In 20 min. more we begin to mount the hill with the tombs. There are altogether eight tombs, of which only the first to the right *(Tut)* and the first to the left *(Horanes*, chief priest of Hieraconpolis) repay a visit. The former contains a well-preserved stele of the time of Tutmes I.; outside the latter, to the right, dancing-girls were painted. Not long ago three black granite statues were found here, with the names of Kings Pepi (6th Dyn.), Ra-kha-kheper (Usertesen II.), and Ra-en-mat (Amenemha III., 12th Dyn.). These are now in the museum at Gizeh.

$13^1/_2$ M. from el-Kâb is *Edfu*, on the W. bank.

23. Edfu.

Edfu is a steamboat-station. The *Mail Steamers* arriving on Tues. and Frid. at 8.30 a.m. halt here for $2^1/_2$ hrs.; the *Tourist Steamers* spend a night here on their upward journey. Tourists on a three-weeks tour visit the temple on the evening of their arrival (11th day, Frid.); those on a four-weeks tour visit it the next morning. Steamers do not stop here on the downward voyage. The halt of the mail-steamers gives hardly time even for a hasty visit to the temple, especially as the latter lies 20 min. from the landing-place.

Those who travel in their own dhahabîyeh should spend two days at Edfu, bringing their provisions from the boat to the temple. Egyptologists, who may find material to occupy them here for days and weeks, will obtain, if necessary, poor lodging and scanty fare in the *Post House*, $^1/_4$ M. to the E. of the temple. Insect-powder should in this case not be forgotten; and wine and preserved meat should be brought from Luxor.

Donkeys and horses are to be had at the *Landing-place.* Camels may also be obtained. Riders unaccustomed to the latter animals must be careful not to fall forward when the camel kneels down.

The way to the temple leads almost due W. from the landing-place, then, turning to the N. (right), skirts the *Canal of Edfu* and crosses it by a good new bridge. It then proceeds to the W. through several streets and finally turns N. again for a short distance. — Another route leads straight on from the landing-place, bends to the right through fields, and then traverses the streets of the town without crossing the canal.

A flight of steps descends to the massive *Pylons* of the temple (p. 249). As at Esneh (p. 232) the accumulated rubbish of cen-

turies has heaped itself around the temple; and later dwellings
have been erected on the top of earlier ones. This alone can explain
·how the temple is now at a much lower level than the surrounding
village.

The building presented a very different appearance only thirty years
ago. Arab houses stood upon the temple itself·and were built against
its walls. The interior was filled with rubbish almost up to the capitals
of the columns, and the outside was equally deeply buried. A picture of
the edifice as it then was may be seen in plates 49 and 55 in the first
volume of the Antiquités in the *Description de l'Egypte*. In the beginning
of the sixties, however, the entire temple was laid bare by Mariette under
the auspices of the Khedive, and the buildings clustering upon and around
it were removed. Now the temple of Edfu is seen in wonderful, almost
perfect preservation, exceeding that of any other Egyptian temple or even
of any antique building in .the world, in spite of the 2000 years that
have passed over it. From top to bottom it is covered with representations and remarkable inscriptions, the interpretation of which was
·reserved for the present century, so rich in discoveries of every kind.

The **Temple of Edfu** is superior to the temple at Denderah in
the much greater distinctness of its sculptured reliefs and inscriptions, due probably to the use of better sandstone than that of
Denderah which contains more lime. It is also much more complete,
for in addition to chambers corresponding to those found at Denderah, there are at Edfu a passage running round the temple and
a lofty wall enclosing the latter, besides a spacious fore-court and
two massive pylons. (Comp. the accompanying Plan with that of
Denderah at p. 80.)

The inscriptions in the, temple at Edfu have been published in
Dümichen's *Altägyptische Tempelinschriften* (113 plates; 1867), the geographical inscriptions in his *Recueil de monuments égyptiens*, and in J. de
Rouge's *Edfu*, from notes by his father E. de Rougé (1880). The last-
named work, however, has many errors. The important *Builders' Inscriptions* are to be found in the *Ägyptische Zeitschrift* for 1870-71-73-75,
and in Brugsch's *Kalenderinschriften* (Thesaurus II.). Mons. *Naville* of
Geneva has published the text of the battles of Horus at Edfu, and *Lepsius* the first three of the field-texts.

The modern Arabic name of the village of *Edfu* is derived from
the Coptic ⲁⲧⲃⲱ, formed in its turn from the old-Egyptian
Tebu, the name given in the inscriptions to the metropolis
of the second district of Upper Egypt. This district, named *Tes-
Hor*, i.e. the district of the raising of Horus,† the *Apollinopolites*
of Greek coins, was bounded on the S. by the *Nomos Nubia*, the
capital of which was Elephantine, and on the N. by *Latopolites*,
the capital of which was *Seni*, the modern *Esneh*. In the great war
of the gods waged by Ra-Helios and his companions against the
evil Seth-Typhon and his allied demons, the principal champion is
the great Horus-Apollo, who destroys the enemies of Ra. The
scene of the first meeting of the hostile gods, of their first great

---

† 'Because the goddess Isis has raised (tes) her Horus in the town
of the raising (tes), its. chief name has become town of the raising of
Horus (tes-her)'. — From an inscription on the N. girdle-wall.

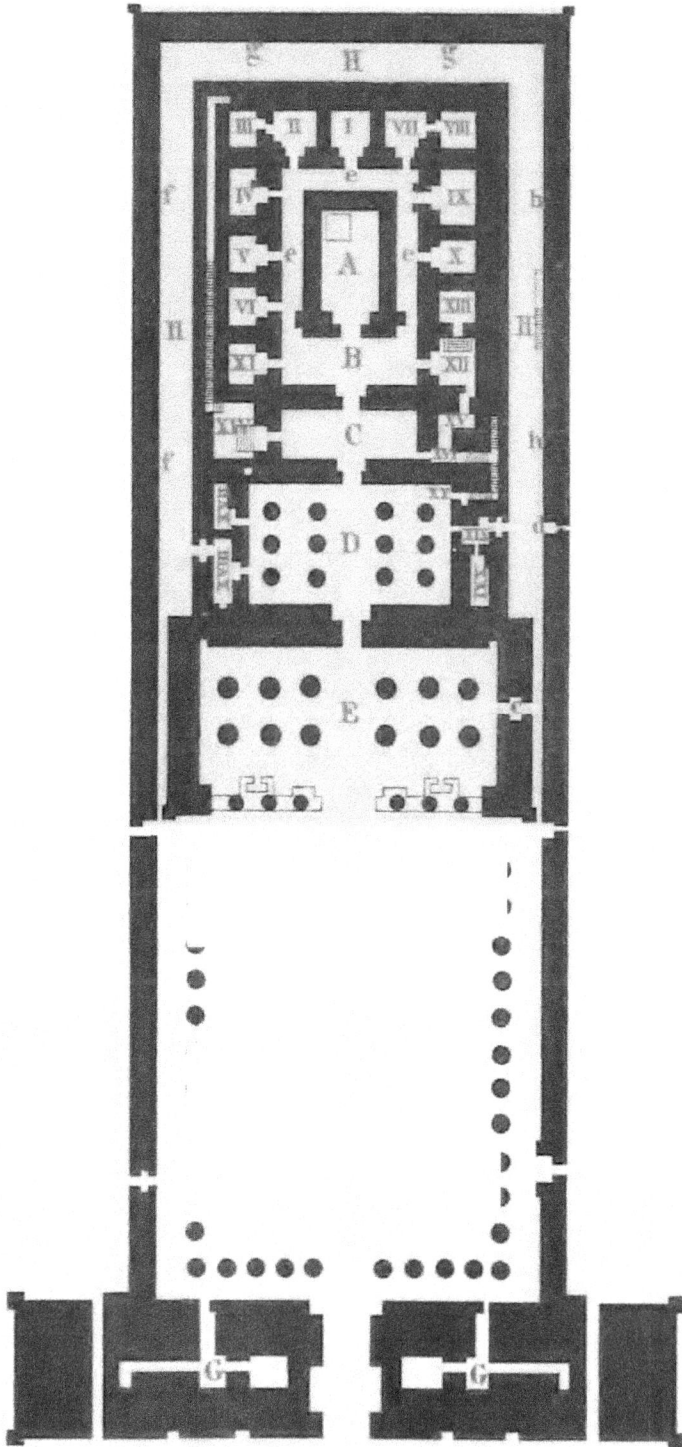

HORUS TEMPLE AT EDFU.

battle, is traditionally laid in the nome of Apollinopolis. An inscription relating to the Horus myth, on the inside of the W.
girdle-wall, states that 'they reached Seth-Typhon and his companions in the nome of Apollinopolis'.

Horus emerged victorious from this battle, and the evil Seth-
Typhon was pierced by him (ṭebu). 'Piercer thereupon became his
name, and 'place of the piercing' the name of his district and town.
This name is clearly preserved in the modern name *Edfu.* Another name, that occurs most frequently next to this one and has
also reference to the chief deity of the temple at Edfu, is *Hut* or
Behut. Thus the winged sun-disc, which was placed over the entrance to every Egyptian temple, was named

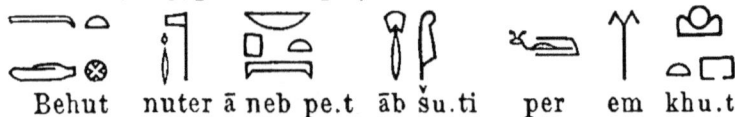

Behut   nuter ā neb pe.t   āb šu.ti   per   em khu.t

'Hut, the great god, the lord of heaven, who, clad in bright plumage, comes forth from the sun-mountain'.

Another name for the winged sun-disc is *Api,* which means
'flying' and 'wings'.

At the head of the gods worshipped at Edfu stood, as is apparent from what has already been said, 'Horus, who spreads his
wings, the great god, the lord of heaven, who, clad in bright plumage, comes forth out of the sun-mountain'. Next to him rank the
Hathor of Denderah, who undertook a special festal journey to Edfu,
Ahi, son of Hathor, *Osiris, Isis, Nephthys, Shu,* and *Tefnut.*

History of the Temple. The representations and inscriptions
that cover the walls of the great temple of Horus at Edfu place it
beyond doubt that the building in its present form dates from the
period of the Ptolemies. Yet like the sanctuary of Hathor at Denderah, it is not an architectonic creation of that period, but merely
a splendid restoration of an earlier temple carried out under the
Lagidae. The *Temple* proper, *i.e.* the sacred apartments exclu-
sive of the later hypostyle with its 18 columns (Pl. E) and of the
fore-court with its 32 columns (Pl. *F*), as well as of the still later
pylons and girdle-wall, was begun by *Ptolemy III. Euergetes I.* in
the 10th year of his reign. It was finished 95 years later, in the
28th year of the reign of *Ptolemy IX. Euergetes II.,* and the 18th
Mesori in that year was fixed by the priests for its consecration,
as an important festival took place upon that day. The image of
Horus was carried in solemn procession into the temple, and the
author of the builders' inscriptions at Edfu, in describing this solemn entry, introduces the god as astonished by the magnificence
that greeted him, and moved by joy, as addressing his surroundings. In his speech the god expressly states that 'the halls were
renewed in their building', and that 'commands went forth from
their majesties to rebuild his house, an edifice of ancient times, and

his sanctuary, which had been raised by their ancestors, and to make it more magnificent than before'.

An inscription (on the outside of the E. girdle-wall) states that this beautiful monument (the present temple) lay behind (*i.e.* probably to the S. of) the building of his father; another (on the inside of the same wall) records that the foundation-stone was laid in the time of Ptah in the holy place of Tes Hor for the God Ra; and a third (on the inside of the N. girdle-wall) informs us (on the left) that the building was carried out 'as it was in the plan of the great writing that fell from heaven to the N. of Memphis', and (on the right) that 'this great wall was built according to the book of the arrangement of temples, written by the *Kherheb Imhotep*, son of the god Ptah'.

An inscription in one of the crypts at Denderah (Mariette III, 78) mentions a festal journey of Hathor from Denderah (P. 80) to the temple of Horus at Edfu. This festival, which was established by Tutmes III. (1600 B.C.) took place at the new moon of the month Epiphi.

The Naos, still to be found in the holy of holies (p. 252), bears the name-rings of Nectanebus I. (378-360 B.C.) and probably dates from the original temple. The document, inscribed on the outside of the E. wall of the temple, relating to the gifts of lands, mentions King Darius as well as Nectanebus I. and Nectanebus II. as benefactors of the temple.

Two accounts of the building of the present temple have come down to us. The shorter of these occurs on the outside of the W. wall of the temple proper, in the second line of the lower marginal inscription, dating from the time of Ptolemy IX. Euergetes II.; the other, at greater detail, in the one-line lower *Marginal Inscription*, on the outside of the W. girdle-wall. In the second inscription we read as follows:

'On this beautiful day of the opening of the building in the 10th year (supplied from the shorter inscription), on the 7th Epiphi (*i.e.* Aug. 23, 237 B.C.), in the time of King Ptolemy III. Euergetes I. It was a festival of the Sixth, when the interior of the ground was opened, the first of all the festivals of the Sixth of the ceremony of laying the foundation.

The king himself, along with the goddess Safekh, was engaged in fulfilling the ceremony of laying the foundation of the adytum, the starting-point for determining its halls. Its side-chambers (were erected) in their places, carefully arranged by the wise (zasu). The sacred architects built with the lord of the papyrus-writing. The great hall of the temple was finished, the sanctuary (mesen) of the golden hawk was prepared, by the 10th year, on the 7th Epiphi, in the reign of King *Ptolemy IV. Philopator*' (a date corresponding to Aug. 17, 212 B.C.). Thus 25 years (237 B.C. to 212 B.C.) were spent in erecting the walls of the temple.

The decoration of the walls with hieroglyphics and reliefs and the completion of the great gateway and of the two doors to one of the halls are noted as follows:

'The inscribing of its walls with well-executed sculpture of the names, the great ones, of His Majesty, and with the figures of the gods and goddesses, the dignified ones of the shining city (one of the many names of Edfu), and the finishing of its great door, and of the two wings of the door of its hall (lasted) till the 16th year of His Majesty. (The first year of ¡Ptolemy IV. was the 103rd| of the Lagidæ = 222 B.C., so that his 16th year corresponds to 207 B.C.) Then a revolution broke out, and it came to pass that the instigator of the rebels in the outlying lands had his secret retreat from the city of the throne of the gods to the place . . . . in the S. (One of the chambers of the temple, viz. Pl. V, was called 'city of the throne of the gods', but the phrase is here used to describe the town of Edfu.) That ended (nefr) in the year 79 in the reign of the late King Ptolemy V. Epiphanes, after the king had suppressed the revolution in the land; behold, his name is officially placed in it' (the temple).

The inscription continues: 'In the 5th year, 1/30 of the Shaftbet (*i.e.* on the 1st of the month Tybi) of his beloved son, the late King Ptolemy VII. Philometor, were erected the great wooden door in the Hall of the Strong Victor (one of the names of the temple of Edfu), and the two wings of the door of the Hai-hall (the name of Hall D, with the 12 columns). Similarly what had been made in work in the interior of the Chamber of Victory (*i.e.* Room I, behind the adytum) in the 30th year of this king was restored. The finishing of the hieroglyphics, carved with the graving tool, the decoration of the walls with a covering of gold, the application of the colours, the finishing of the top-ornament of its wooden doors, the making of the door-stands of good brass, with the metal hinges and locks, the fixing of gold plates on the wings of its doors, the finishing of the interior of the temple-proper with perfect work by the best artists of the time — these operations lasted until the 28th year, on the 18th day of the month Mesori, under the *late* King Ptolemy IX. Euergetes II. and his consort, the regent Cleopatra III. This makes a period of 95 years from the ceremony of the first hammer-stroke to the festal entry, the festival of the consecration of the ancestral abode by His Majesty to his divine lord, Horus of Edfu, god Ahi, the lord of heaven, which is the great festival of Tekhu, and has been equalled by nothing since the creation of the world to the present day'.

The dates given above as to the progress of the work are as follows : —
1. 1st Tybi, 5th year of Ptol. VII. Philom.   = 3rd Feb. 176 B.C.
2. The 30th year of the same king   = 152-151 B.C.
3. 18th Mesori, 28th year of Ptol. IX. Euerg. = 10th Sept. 142 B.C.

Finally from the foundation-festival on 23rd Aug. 237 B.C. to the festal entry on 10th Sept. 142 B.C. is a period of 95 years.

The inscription next devotes some space to the description of the festival of the solemn entry of the god, and then goes on: In this beautiful 30th year, month Payni, 9th day, festival of the union of the moon-god Osiris with the sun-god Ra, again the festival of a 6th of Payni, the foundation was laid of the *Khent Hall* (Pl. E, the 18-columned hypostyle), which has two side-chapels within it (referring probably to the small chambers to the right and left of the portal, in the front wall), and the roof of the sun-god who commands in heaven was completed in the 46th year, month Mesori, 18th day (*i.e.* Sept. 5, 122 B.C.), which is 16 years, 2 months, 10 days from the foundation of the hall of the sun-mountain (another name for Hall E), which was laid on the 9th Payni in the 30th year of Ptolemy IX. (*i.e.* July 2, 140 B.C.). Thus from the founding of the hall to the completion of the roof there elapsed, as the inscription correctly states, a space of 17 years, 2 months, 10 days, reckoning to the dedicatory festival of the noble Kheut hall, which took place on the day of the Tekhu festival.

Fifteen definite dates are given in this important inscription detailing the history of the temple of Edfu, beginning with the foundation-ceremony on the 7th Epiphi in the 10th year of Ptolemy III. (23rd Aug. 237 B.C.), and ending with the year of Ptolemy X. Soter II.'s second assumption of the government, viz. the 236th year of the Lagidæ = 89-88 B.C. To these we may add a sixteenth, dating the final completion of the huge building. From an inscription given thrice inside the portal of the pylons and the colonnade of the fore-court, we learn that the two brass-mounted wings of the door of the great pylons were erected on the 1st Khoiak in the 25th year of Ptolemy XIII. Neos Dionysus, and of his sister and wife Cleopatra Tryphæna, *i.e.* on December 5th, 57 B.C. Thus the complete rebuilding of the temple at Edfu was accomplished within the period of 180 years, 3 months, and 14 days.

As a kind of pendant or companion-piece to this long historical inscription of the W. girdle-wall, there appears another no less interesting *Inscription* at the foot of the *E. Girdle Wall* (Pl. k). This second inscription, which has a total length of 240 ancient Egyptian ells, contains a summary account of the whole temple, followed by a detailed description of each of its rooms. Like all dedicatory inscriptions of the kind, it begins with the name of the monarch under whom the monument it refers to (in the present case, the girdle-wall) was completed.

The inscription begins as follows: 'The golden Horus, who shows himself in heaven as the wing-spreading god of Edfu, clad in bright plumage, he has taken possession of his abode ... prepared by ... Ptolemy XI. Alexander I.'

'This beautiful large wall, behind his temple at the side of his father's building, its length 240 ells, its breadth 90 ells, its height to the summit 20, the thickness of its foundation 5 ells. This monument, which was erected by His Majesty and his father, is formed like the sun-mountain of heaven.' These dimensions correspond with measurements made by the writer. The length of the girdle-wall to the pylons was found to be 414¹/₂ ft., which reckoning the ancient Egyptian ell at 1³/₄ ft., is equal to 240.₅₈ ells; breadth 133³/₄ ft. = 89.₇₂ ells; height 33¹/₂ ft. = 19.₅ ells; thickness 6¹/₂ ft., *i.e.* not quite 4 (instead of 5) ells.

We may now bestow a glance on the general arrangement of the temple as a whole. The main axis lies W. and S., as is repeatedly mentioned in the inscriptions referring to this point

, 'from Orion (the S. star) to the Great Bear (the N. constellation)'. The early Egyptian architects seem to have been guided by these two constellations in determining the orientation of any new temple, as appears to be indicated with some certainty by inscriptions at Edfu. The laying of the foundation-stone of an early Egyptian temple was a ceremony of peculiar solemnity, in which the king himself, as has been observed in the account of Denderah (p. 86), took part; and even in the case of temples built at a time when the rulers of Egypt had ceased to share personally in these ceremonies (as *e.g.* under the Roman emperors who did not live in Egypt at all), the inscriptions still sometimes speak in the old-fashioned style as though the monarch had duly performed his part. An inscription along the foot of the wall in Hall D states that 'His Majesty in his proper person, with his hand on the wooden peg and holding the line in his grasp, along with the goddess Safekh, is to be found beside his measuring-instrument to determine the four corners of the temple at Edfu'. This N. and S. axis divides the entire building into a right and a left (or W. and E.) half, reckoned from Room I (p. 252), which occupies the exact centre of the rear-wall of the temple, and is named in the inscriptions 'divider of the middle'. All the walls and rooms to the right of this line (as we look S.) are described in the inscrip-

tions as lying on the right or W. side, and all to the left as lying
on the left or E. side.

The **Pylon-Portal** (Pl. G) forms a worthy introduction to the
temple, flanked on either side by a tower with sloping walls, about
100 ft. high. This is usually named ⟨hieroglyphs⟩ *Mahet,*
i.e. 'portal-building', 'entrance-hall', in the inscriptions, a designation which is not unfrequently employed to include the entire
gatehouse and the two towers, though the most usual term for the
entire entrance-structure was ⟨hieroglyphs⟩ *Bekhen, i.e.*
'tower', 'watch-tower'.

This passage was formerly closed with a massive door with two
wings. The entire lofty gatehouse is covered from top to bottom
and on all sides with reliefs and inscriptions, amongst which,
especially on the right and left, the colossal *Figure of the King* (Neos
Dionysus) is conspicuous, smiting his foes, whom he holds by the
hair, in presence of Horus and Hathor. In two rows, above, the
king appears praying and offering sacrifices before the gods of Edfu.
— Below, on the left (W.) pylon, the king and queen conduct a
procession of representatives of the districts that yield gold, silver,
other metals, precious stones, cosmetics, etc., and furnish them to
the temple. On the front of the pylon towers are four wide incisions,
two on each side of the central portal. These were intended to
support the huge copper-mounted wooden poles with gilded tips,
which are illustrated in Vol. I., p. 168. One of the lower marginal
inscriptions states that these poles were intended at Edfu to avert
the storms of heaven, and that they were adorned with gay flags at
the top.

The pitch-dark lower *Pylon Chambers* on each side are entered
from the court by doors to the right and left of the portal, and from
each of them an easy *Staircase* of 242 steps in 14 flights ascends to
the *Platforms* of the towers. One of the towers should certainly be
ascended, in spite of the numerous steps. The view from the top
is unusually attractive, commanding not only the most imposing
survey of the temple-buildings, but also ranging over the surrounding country. The plain through which the Nile flows, with its
verdant crops and its villages fringed with palms and mimosas,
framed by the desert-mountains in the distance, presents a scene
of surprising beauty, especially when seen under the evening light
that renders the Egyptian landscape so wonderfully distinct.

The **Fore-Court** (Pl. *F*), which is bounded in front by the
pylons, at the back by the hypostyle hall (Pl. E), and on the right
and left by the great girdle-wall, is a spacious court, paved with
broad flags, and surrounded on its E., W., and S. sides with a covered colonnade of 32 columns. The inscriptions call it variously

'*Usekht uten* or court of the offerings, *usekht khā en Sa-Hor* or court of the appearance of the protecting Horus, *usekht en bekhen* or court of the pylons, and *usekht en tesnefru Ra-Khuti* or court of the sacred boat of the god of the sun-mountain. *Ptolemy X. Soter II.* is named in the marginal inscriptions as the builder and finisher of this court, in harmony with the great inscription on the W. girdle-wall.

The lower marginal inscription on Wall a of the court says of this king: 'He has built the Court of the Appearance of the protecting Horus (usekht khā en Sa-Hor), the lord of the gods, as a copy of the building of the sun-mountain with the god of the sun-mountain, completed in his building in excellent work in good sandstone; offerings are made to his divine image in it'. An inscription on the opposite wall (Pl. b) says of the same king, that he built the Court of Offerings (usekht utent) 'in order to sacrifice to the sun-god thrice a day'.

Detailed information is given in the inscriptions as to the size of this fore-court, the height and thickness of its walls, the number and shape of the columns, and the side-doors and main-portal. The length is repeatedly given as 90 Egyptian ells, the breadth as 80, the height of the walls as 20, and their thickness as 5; measurements, which taking the ell as $1^3/_4$ ft. correspond tolerably closely with measurements made on the spot (length 155 ft., breadth 138 ft., height of wall $34^1/_2$ ft., thickness $8^1/_2$ ft.). The number of the 'columns, the great ones, erected in it' is correctly given as 32; their beauty and strength is extolled; and the capitals and shafts minutely described. The doors are also described in order, details being sometimes given as to whether they had one or two wings, of what wood they were made, and whether they opened inwards or outwards. Besides the four side-doors of the court and the main portal between the pylons, the two doors leading from the court to the gate-towers are also described, as well as the door (Pl. d) in the N. half of the E. girdle-wall and another smaller door, nearer the N. end of the same wall, leading to the *Temple-Well.*

The *Back* of this court, forms, as has already been remarked, the front of the **Temple Proper,** which differs but slightly from the temple of Denderah. Here, as at Denderah, the first chamber is a —

Hypostyle Hall (Pl. E), open in front. The roof is borne by 18 columns, while at Denderah there are 24; and the two small chapels in front have nothing corresponding to them at Denderah. The chapel to the left as we enter is called ⌐⌐ *Patua, i.e.* 'incense-chamber', and was used by the monarch, in his capacity as high-priest, when performing the ceremonies of purifying himself on his entrance into the temple, with holy water and incense. The small room on the right was called ⌐⌐⌐, *Pa-hotep* (?), *i.e.* 'room of the written rolls' and appears from the inscriptions to have been used to contain all the written documents referring to the temple-service: 'many boxes with papyrus-rolls (hotepu) and great leather-rolls (aru-uru-en-mesek)'. A very interesting *Catalogue* on the walls of this room gives the names of the books preserved here. — A *Side-door* (Pl. c) in the E. wall of the hypostyle admits to the open passage between the temple and the girdle-wall.

The *Ceiling* of this hall, which, like that at Denderah, is named *Khent*, 'the front room' or *Khent ur*, 'the great antechamber', is completely covered with astronomical representations.

To the left are the first six *Hours of Night*, to the right the second six (Champollion, Mon. II. pp. 123 seq.). Above the door to the following Hall D is a curious representation. The *Sun Disc* appears with the figure of a crowned beetle ascending from the horizon into a boat guided by *Hor mai* and *Hor khent khrud*. Next the sun, on the left, is *Thoth*, on the right *Neith*, and also *Apheru* (Anubis), *Mat*, and *Hathor*. In an attitude of worship, at the sides, are *Four Senses;* to the right the eye and ear (*i.e.* sight and hearing), to the left taste (symbolized by a tongue) and reason. At the top of this wall is a long astronomical frieze. First appear figures of the 36 '*Decani*', at the end of which are the chief constellations of the S. (*Orion* and the *Sothis Cow* or *Sirius*) and of the N. (the bull's leg fettered by *Ape*), then come the *Planets*, the *Stair with the Fourteen Steps* of the waxing moon, the gods corresponding to those lunar days, representatives of the *30 Days of the Month*, the *Gods of the 12 Months*, and finally three *Female Figures* with raised hands†.

On the *N. Wall* of this hall, on either side of the door to Hall D, are scenes from the *Founding of the Temple* by the king, similar to those at Denderah. They are continued along the W. wall of the hall.

Next, as at Denderah, follow three **Prosekos Halls**, with their side-chambers, and here also the first of these, the *Hai* or *Festal Hall* (Pl. D) is much the largest. This hall is the only one of the three that has columns, of which there are 12 arranged in three rows, while the corresponding hall at Denderah had only 6 columns. The side-chambers, however, are more numerous at Denderah, where there were six, three on each side, while here there are but four, viz. the *Laboratory* (Pl. xvii) and a *Passage Room* (Pl. xviii) in front of it, on the W. side, and on the E. side another *Passage Room* (Pl. xix), in the S. wall of which is a door leading to a *Corner Room* (Pl. xxi). The next of the prosekos halls is the *Hall of the Altar* (Pl. C), with two side-chambers (Pl. xiv on the W. and Pl. xvi on the E.), whence we reach the two great staircases leading to the roof of the temple. Both the structure of the staircases and their plastic adornment closely resemble those at Denderah. From the third and last Prosekos hall, the '*Hall of the Centre*' or of the '*Repose of the Gods*' (Pl. B), we enter on the right the two connected '*Rooms for the Offering of what is necessary*' (Pl. xii & xiii), and on the left the '*Room of Khem*' (Pl. xi). We now reach the **Sekos Rooms**. The *Sanctuary* (Pl. A) in the centre is, like the sanctuary at Denderah, surrounded on all sides but the front by a *Corridor* (Pl. e), from which *10 Side-Chambers* open (Pl. i-vi on the left or W., vii-x on the right or E. side). On the inside wall of the corridor, *i.e.* on the outside of the sanctuary, are represented the gods of the districts or nomes. — All these rooms, their size and use, their plastic decorations, the painting, gilding, etc. are fully described in the inscriptions and in the reliefs.

---

† See Brugsch, Monuments de l'Égypte, plates vii-x.

Two important and specially instructive *Inscriptions* describe the various rooms in order in the course of a summary review. One of these forms the lower marginal inscription on the outside of the E. girdle-wall; †† the other is on the outside of the W. wall of the temple proper. ††

The inscriptions at Edfu begin their account of the different rooms with Room I., at the centre of the rear-wall of the temple, which they name 'Divider of the Middle' (comp. p. 248). Thence they proceed to the rooms lying to the right and left, and then to the Adytum (Pl. A) and the Prosekos rooms in front of it. Those who desire to follow the description in order begin at Room I. Of this *e.g.* it is said: 'The apartment *Mesen* (No. I) is in its (the temple's) centre as the chief apartment, with the great throne of the dispenser of rays; the goddess Ma is with him, as Hathor the great, in his shrine, the very secret place, in it (*i.e.* the room), whose breadth is 8¹/₃ ells and its depth 6²/₃. Its wall is painted with the cycle of the gods of the true Mesen-chamber, their forms according to their prototypes'. The word *Mesen* means here probably dwelling of the helpers of Horus. In the second inscription this room is also named *Ha-ken*, 'chamber of the victor', and it is stated that 'the figure of the protecting Horus, in his noble shape as a perching hawk, an ell high, with the scourge (is there to be seen). The goddess Ma is before him; she does not separate herself from him, who is ever united with her. As Hathor, the great, she is with him in the shrine within the mysterious cella of dark granite'. Room II. is named 'the right chamber' and the 'west chamber' or 'dedicated to the god of the west' (Osiris); Room III, 'the chamber of the great' (Osiris); Room IV, 'the inner-room of the tomb-chamber'. These three are the *Osiris Rooms.* Room V is called the 'room of the throne of the gods'; Room VI, the 'cloth-chamber'; then on the E. side, Room VII, 'the Sebek-chamber' of the moon-god Khunsu; Room VIII, the sanctuary of Hathor; and Room IX, the 'throne-room of Ra'. Of Room X we read: 'the *Room of the Spreader of Wings* (No. x) contains on its E. wall the divine image of the lion-headed goddess of the north, and of the cycle of gods, that watch over Osiris. There is the god Shu as the representative of the N. wind, inflating his nostrils, as is his wont in the kingdom of eternity (*i.e.* the under-world), and the lion-headed goddess Tefnut, as the representative of devouring fire, in the act of burning his (Osiris's) enemies, as she does it in the place that is the goal of millions (another name for the under-world). There also are the goddess Ment, daughter of the sun, with her backward glance, and the great Sekhet-Artemis, the mistress of the goddesses of vengeance'.

The *Adytum* or *Holy of Holies* (Pl. A) is next described: 'The room of the great throne (*i.e.* the adytum) in the centre, round which the passage runs, is in ells 19²/₃ + ¹/₆ by 10¹/₃. A door leading into the passage is found on its right and on its left side, in order to reach the closed rooms lying round it. The sacred boat of Tesneferu the bright-coloured and his sacred shrine are placed there; his great cella, of dark granite, it is a wonder to behold it'. This *Cella* of dark granite, erected by King Nectanebus, stands to this day in the adytum (p. 246).

With reference to the *Staircases* the inscription states that the E. stair was ascended on New Year's Day, in order to unite the god with his soul, and that the W. stair was ascended to offer sacrifice in the morning. Of the *Doors* in Hall D the inscription says: 'The door upon its W. side is for the bringing of refreshing water, and that on its E. side for the bringing of meat-offerings'.

We now betake ourselves to the passage round the temple proper (Pl. H). Special attention should be bestowed on the inscriptions and reliefs on the *Inside of the W. Girdle-wall* (Pl. f f), representing

---

† Published by Dümichen and Brugsch in the Ægyptische Zeitschrift for 1873 and 1875.

†† Published by Dümichen in his Tempelinschriften, plates 91-94, and De Rougé, in his Edfou, 74-77.

the contests of the god Horus with his enemies who are depicted as crocodiles and hippopotami. Perhaps the overthrow of the foes of King Ptolemy X. Soter II. is symbolically represented in these compositions. The cartouches on this wall probably belong to this king; one of them contains the name of *Ptulmis*, while the other is vacant. The name of Ptolemy XI. Alexander I. does not appear until near the left extremity of the wall, towards the end of the list of nomes.

The **Representations**, ranged in two registers, are 22 in number. The chief are the following: 1st Scene (below, to the right). The king, standing on shore, attempts to transfix a hippopotamus, that bends its head aside. *Horus*, who is accompanied by his mother *Isis*, does the same; in his left hand he holds a chain, and in his right a javelin; beside the helm is a small *Horus.*—2nd Scene. The king appears on land, before two ships, in each of which are a *Horus* and an assistant with a boar's head. *Horus* holds the hippopotamus with a chain and pierces its head with a javelin; the assistant carries a javelin in his right hand and a knife in his left.—5th Scene. The hippopotamus lies on its back, with a chain fastened to its hind feet.—7th Scene (the finest of all). *Horus*, in a ship with expanded sail, aims a blow with his right hand at the head of a hippopotamus, whose hind foot is caught in a line held in the god's left hand. *Isis* kneeling in the bow of the boat holds the head of the animal by a cord. The king, standing on the bank with two attendants armed with javelin and knife, seeks to pierce the skull of the hippopotamus.

On the inside of the N. *Girdle-wall* (Pl. g g) are several long hymns to the god of Edfu. — The traveller is recommended to walk round the outside of the girdle-wall, which is also completely covered with representations and inscriptions. The above-mentioned important inscription relating to the history of the temple is to be seen on the outside of the W. *Wall* (Pl. i), and the description of the various rooms outside the E. *Wall* (Pl. k). The eight *Records of Donations of Fields* are also on the E. wall. These inscriptions and the decoration of the entire external face of the girdle-wall date from the reign of Ptolemy XI. Alexander I. (106-87 B.C.).

The half-buried **Birth House** (*Mameisi*), lying to the left of the entrance to the great temple of Horus, is less worthy of a visit. It was built by Ptolemy IX. Euergetes II., while the interior decorations date from Soter II. In the *Interior* are seven representations of Hathor, who facilitate the birth of the young Horus and nourish him.

24. From Edfu to Gebel Silsileh.

Comp. the Map, p. 98.

26 M. *Steamboat* in 4 hrs. Only the four-weeks tourist steamer spends the night at Silsileh and affords time for a visit; the three-weeks steamer and the mail-steamer go on to Kôm Ombo.

On the E. bank, about 5 M. above Edfu, is the village of **Redêsiyeh,** after which a *Temple of Seti I.*, lying 37 M. to the E., has been named, because the ancient desert-route from Redêsiyeh to the emerald-mines of *Mt. Zubârah* leads viâ the temple.

The Arab name of the place is *Wâdi 'Abbâs.* The temple is in the district of the *'Abâbdeh Beduins*, who are independent of the dwellers in the Nile valley and assume a hostile attitude both towards them and to the Egyptian government. They also have a language of their own. Their domain extends to the Red Sea. It is therefore necessary before beginning this desert-expedition (1½ day; camel and tent necessary) to secure the protection of the shêkh of the 'Abâbdeh. — The route leads through a sandstone region, with many small seyal-acacias. Passing a (4 hrs.) *Well* and then the *Tomb* of a saint, we reach the (3 hrs.) *First Station* on the desert-route, consisting of two rectangular spaces 45-50 ft. long surrounded by walls. The *Second Station*, on the route leading to the Red Sea (comp. R. 6, p. 78), is 6 hrs. farther on. Near it lies the temple, beautifully situated at the foot of an isolated hill. The road to Ḳoṣer (p. 77) diverges to the N., at a valley planted with acacias.

The **Temple** was discovered in 1816 by *Cailliaud*, on his first journey to the mines of *Mt. Zabârah*, where he found old emerald-mines instead of the sulphur that he expected. It is about 40 ft. long, and the front portion is occupied by a Vestibule, about 22 ft. wide, with 4 columns, of which the first pair form the entrance. The representations here are familiar to us from other Egyptian temples. King *Seti I.* appears before *Ammon-Ra*, who hands to him the sword of victory. 'He smites the princes of the miserable Kush' (Ethiopia). Behind Ammon are 10 names of fettered tribes. Ammon speaks: 'Receive the sword, Oh King, lord of the peoples, to smite down the princes of Kush and to cut off their heads. Fear of thee penetrates their limbs like Sekhet in her wrath.' On the other wall the king appears before *Horbehet* (Hut), once more smiting his foes. — At the rear-wall of this vestibule and in two niches to the right and left of the entrance to the next hall are *Osiris Statues*. The next Hall, about 16½ ft. square, is, like the back-wall of the preceding, entirely hewn out of the rock. It contains 4 pillars. At the back are three niches each with a triad of gods; in the centre is *Ramenma* (Seti I.) himself. The interesting *Inscriptions* here record, among other things, that the king came hither in the 9th year of his reign on his way to the gold-mines, accompanied by a large retinue and by architects, and caused wells to be sunk, etc. — On an adjoining rock are three steles. On one of these is the goddess *Aasit* on horseback, with a shield in her left hand; the second is dedicated to the official entrusted by Seti with the sinking of the well; and on the third is the kneeling figure of Ani, king's son of Kush and commander of the Mazai (police). Higher up on the rock are figures of gazelles, Greek graffiti, and the prænomen of Amenhotep III. preceded by the statement: 'made by prince Mermes'.

Farther along the E. bank (12 M. from Edfu), on the mountain-slopes approaching close to the river near the hill *es-Serâg*, are the picturesque remains of an ancient Arab fortress with a mosque. This is sometimes identified with the ancient *Thmuis*, which, however, more probably lay farther to the S.

Near the village of **el-Ḥôsh** beside the *Gebel Abu Shegah*, on the W. bank, a great number of inscriptions and drawings of very various dates have been found scratched on the rocks.

The oldest *King's Name* met with is that of an Usertesen (12th Dyn.), but most of the devices are of a very much later date. Greek names are not wanting, and most of the inscriptions appear to have been carved by masons who worked in the large quarries, which are still to be found beside the village of el-Ḥôsh. The signature of a builder's foreman,

Amam, and numerous stonemasons' marks ⬆, ⬆ ⊖ ⬆, ⊖, ✕, seem to support this conclusion.

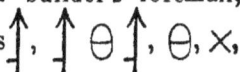

We here find giraffes, horses, gazelles, boats, fighters, etc., closely resembling those at Wâdi Mokatteb (Vol. I., p. 493); and there is also the picture of a man with an ox, an elephant, an ostrich, and a capitally executed dog. Among *Egyptian Names* are those of Amenhotep, Asarhotep, a military colonel 𓅓 𓀀 , Kab Ranseneb, overseer of the temple of Koptos, and Rebtan, overseer of granaries. In few cases, unfortunately, are the reigns mentioned in which they were written. The *Greeks* generally wrote merely their names, some of them suggesting a Christian date, *e.g.* ΠΑΧΟΥΜΙΟΣ (Pachumios), ΠΕΤΡΟΣ (Petros). We also find a ΦΙΛΉΜΟΝ (Philemon), ΕΥΕΝΟΣ (Euenos), and other names, besids which not more than the common τό προσκύνημα, an act of reverence or worship, stood. The inscriptions are found for miles, scratched on the rocks and crags of the low hills skirting the river; they are most numerous to the N. of the village.†

A little to the N. are several *Greek Inscriptions*, first discovered by A. C. Harris. These date from the 11th year of the emperor Antoninus Pius (149 A.D.), and record that a master-engineer (ἀρχιμηχανικός) quarried huge blocks of 11 ells (16 ft.) for the gate (πύλη) of Apollo (at Edfu?).

On the W. bank, ¼ hr. above el-Ḥôsh and about ¾ hr. below Silsileh, is a gorge known as Shaṭṭ er-Regâl, 'Shore of the Men', or *es- sab'a regâl*, 'the seven men'. On the left side of a cliff here, a few paces from the river-bank, is a most interesting relief (also discovered by Harris) representing the *Homage* of an inferior king (𓀀) *Entef* before *Mentuhotep III.* (⊙ ◡ 𓏸) *Ra neb* kher, the uniter of the two lands, and before the king's mother *Aah* (moon). Behind Entef is a chamberlain named *Kheti.*

This Mentuhotep, with the staff of empire in his hand, was an important king at the close of the 11th Dyn., and his name is mentioned in all the extant lists of kings. A stele (now at Turin) dating from the 46th year of his reign attests his long and prosperous rule. He seems to have been the first monarch after a long interval (6th-11th Dyn.) to unite the whole kingdom under a single sceptre,, and he is thus a worthy predecessor of the Amenemhas and Usertesens of the 12th Dynasty.

On the right site of the cliff is the name of *Penati*, an architect who worked under Amenhotep I., Tutmes I., and Tutmes II. Farther up in the same valley occur the signatures of other royal officials, and also (according to Petrie) the joint cartouches of Hatasu and Tutmes III., with another mention of Penati below them. —

A second *Scene of Homage* before King Rasankhha (⊙ 𓊽 𓏤), the successor of Ranebkher or Mentubotep, is reported by Petrie, who also discovered other kings' names, some hitherto unknown, on these rocks.

26 M. **Gebel Silsileh** *(Mountain of the Chain).* Though we land on the W. bank on which the most interesting monuments lie, we should not omit to visit also the E. bank, where there are larger quarries than on the Libyan side.

At *Gebel Silsileh* begins the *Sandstone Zone* of the Nile valley (Vol I., d. 56). The rocky hills which here confine the bed of the river supplied the material for most of the gigantic buildings we have already visited, for where monuments exposed to the air were to be erected the Egyptians

---

† They are published in Flinders Petrie's 'A Season in Egypt' (London, 1888).

preferred sandstone to limestone and even to the harder but more easily disintegrating granite. For substructures, however, and for walls surrounded with earth :they wisely gave the preference to limestone. — The hills on the two banks of the river approach so close together at Gebel Silsileh that they have justly been compared to the pillars of a .gigantic [gateway. The legend of the chain that once barred the passage of the river here is probably pure invention, taking its rise from the Coptic name of the city of quarries, which in the hieroglyphics isn amed *Pa Khennu*. The later Egyptians named the town ⲭⲟⲗ ⲭⲟⲗ *i.e. sae-pes*, *claustrum*, barrier, probably in reference to the gorge of the river. The Romans, who maintained a garrison here, converted the T'el t'el of the Egyptians into *Silsili*, which was confounded by the Arabs with *Silsileh*, the Arabic for 'chain'. The people, seeking meanings for every name and preferring those that come in the guise of a legend, thereupon invented the story of a chain, that once barred the gorge at Gebel Silsileh. By and by the very place where this mythical chain had been fastened came to be pointed out.

The dhahabîyehs generally halt in the very midst of the monuments. We turn first to the N., ascend a well-beaten track, and then gradually descend the rocky hill. On the slope beside the river are some tomb-like *Recesses*, belonging to officials of the 18th Dyn., with the names of Tutmes III. and his sister Hatasu over the entrance. In one of these, the surface of which is divided into squares, some of the figures are sketched but left unfinished. Farther on is a cave with a painted ceiling. Beside it are inscriptions of the time of Ramses III., builder of Medînet Habu, who is represented before Ammon, Muth, and Khunsu. There is also a larger memorial tablet of the 21st year of Sheshenk I. (22nd Dyn.). Sheshenk had commanded his architect Horemsat to quarry stones at Silsileh for the gateway erected by the king on the S. side of the first court of the temple of Ammon at Karnak. Immediately to the N. is a *Stele* bearing various conventional phrases and dating from Ramses V. ( ), whose name seldom occurs on the monuments. Finally we reach the broad façade of the shallow —

*Rock Chapel *(Speos)*, which may be reckoned among the most important monuments in the Nile valley, on account of its reliefs and inscriptions. This chapel, hewn in the rock close to the summit of a hill, dates from the 18th Dyn. In front are five doorways, separated from each other by pillars at varying distance, and crowned with the astragal and concave cornice. Numerous gods are named in it. Sebek, who forms a triad with Ammon-Ra and Muth, takes the first place; Ptah of Memphis is also mentioned. King Horus is here spoken of as the beloved of the Anka-t (Onka), 'Mistress of Asia', and this Egyptian-Phœnician goddess is represented with a head-dress, elsewhere only found on the heads of Asiatic warriors.

The *Interior* consists of a broad but shallow vaulted chamber, at the back of which is an oblong room. All the walls are covered with carving and inscriptions. On the S. wall is the Uræus goddess, offering the breast to the infant king Horus, while above her head hovers the vulture of

Hebent. On the back-wall, to our left as we enter, King Horus is depicted
returning in triumph from his campaign in Ethiopia.

This *Relief*, of great artistic value, shows the Pharaoh seated on
his throne which is borne by 12 nobles adorned with feathers. The throne
has lions' feet and its back also consists of lions. The king wears the
war-helmet and carries the staff of empire in his left hand. Behind
and before him are court-officials, warding off the sun's rays with the
long-handled flabellum. The Kherheb precedes the litter, offering incense,
and a train of captured Ethiopians is led along by the victor. Vanquished
blacks are lying on the ground and others are being rapidly marched off
by Egyptian soldiers. Above the captives are the words: 'Leading of the
captives of the miserable Kush by Horus, king of Upper and Lower
Egypt, etc. His majesty came out of the land of Kush (Ethiopia) with
the booty which his sword had made, as his father Ammon had commanded him'. Before the priests, who stand in a reverential attitude, is
written: 'The good god approaches, he celebrates his victory over the great
ones of all lands. When he grasps the bow in his right hand he is like
the lord of Thebes (*i.e.* Month, the god of war), as king of the strength
of heroes. Above the prisoners is the inscription: 'Hail to thee, king of
Egypt, sun of the barbarians! Thy name is extolled in the land of the
Ethiopians. Thy battle-cry resounds over their seats. Thy heroic strength,
O thou perfect prince, converts the alien lands into tombs. Pharaoh, long
life and health, O my sun-god' (Shu).

Farther to the right and also on the back-wall is a recess with King
Siptah Khuenra before Ammon, with Bai, an official (overseer of the
whole land). Next is a *Stele of Panehesi*, of the second year of Merenptah I. and his consort Astnefert; then a stele of the time of Ramses I.,
and upon it the first tablet of the *Festival* instituted by the king's son
Khaemus in honour of his father Ramses II. The first tablet dates from
the 30th year, the second from the 34th, the third from the 37th, and the
fourth from the 40th.

Beside the pillar is the small *Sanctuary* of Ramses II. To the left of
the entrance is King Horus (who built the sanctuary), before Harmachis
and the goddess Jusas, and the same king before Ammon-Ra and Muth.
At the back of the very dark recess is a god, with three forms on each
side. Numerous figures of gods. To the right of the entrance to the
sanctuary is a reproduction of the *Festival Stele* mentioned above. Adjoining is the stele of the high-priest *Moi*, who instituted a festival in
the third year of Merenptah I. Farther on is another *Festival Stele*, with
Ramses II. before Harmachis and Muth, Ptah, and Sebek. The date is
the same as on the preceding, but the marshal of the festival is here the
Erpa Ha (prince) and mayor *Shai*. The same official appears also in the
same stele of the 46th year of Ramses II. as marshal of the 6th festival
in the whole land (Khaemus had probably died in the interval).

The numerous reliefs above and below the five doors and in the recesses outside should also be noticed. Over the central door: King *Horus*,
here called the beloved of Ammon and Muth, of Khnum, of Abu, and of
Ank, mistress of Sati (Asia). Over the second door (from the left):
Ramses III. with the commander of his cavalry. Between the fourth and
fifth this king presents Ma to Anhur. Last relief on the right: Ramses II.
brings Ma to Ptah in his shrine and to Sebek. Within the adjacent fifth

door is the small chapel of *Pa war* ( ), in which Ramses II.

appears with his consort Astnefert and a princess (Bainut aant) before
Ptah and Nefertum. There is also a small figure of Khaemus. On the
inside of the front wall is a *Hieratic Inscription* of the 6th year of Ramses III., containing a command to *Setemheb*, overseer of the palace, to
build in the house of eternity in the W. of Thebes (*i.e.* the tomb of
Ramses III. in Bibàn el-Mulùk. The number of workmen under him
(2000), ships (40), and boats (4) are detailed. Two other hieratic *Inscriptions*, of a similar purport, are to be found on the central doorway, to the
right and left.

The *Monuments to the South are as interesting as those just described, from which they are reached in about $1/4$ hr. The route leads to the S., sometimes skirting the river-bank, sometimes leading through the ancient quarries. We first reach *Two Chambers*, with the openings facing the river, and recesses at the back. At the first are two, and at the second are three unnamed sitting statues, hewn out of the rock. The chambers belonged to officials of Tutmes III., whose name occurs over the entrance along with those of Ammon Harmachis and Sebek. The first cave belonged to *Khem nekht*, overseer of granaries, who is here represented along with his wife. The second, to the N., belonged to the mayor *Amatu* and his wife, and contains a series of figures. To the S. occurs the name of Amenhotep II. $\overline{A}a$ *kheperu*; with two small *Steles* in bad preservation on the left, and two others, better preserved, on the right. Farther to the S. near the river is a brightly painted *Cave*, with painted ceiling. A relief here depicts Amonemhat, a high priest of Ammon (probably, from his name, under the 12th Dyn.) sacrificing to his parents and those of his wife Mimi.

The guides point out large square holes in the lofty rocks as having been used to fasten the above-mentioned mythical chain of Silsileh. Skirting the bushy river-bank we presently reach three *Inscribed Tablets*, offering a picturesque appearance as seen from the Nile. Two of them, adorned with concave cornices and with doors, lie close beside each other. The architrave is borne by sculptured bud-columns, the shafts of which represented stems of plants bound together by a band. Both of these brightly painted façades act as frames for large *Steles*, placed at the back of small chapels about 6 ft. deep. That to the S. (left) was erected by Ramses II. in the first year of his reign, that to the N. (right) by Merenptah I. (Hotep-hi-ma) in his first year. Each is formed of three parts. At the top is the triad to which it was dedicated, next is a *Hymn* to the *Nile*, and below is a list of sacrifices. In the one case the divine triad consists of Ammon, Muth, and Khunsu, the chief triad of Upper Egypt. in the other of Ra Harmachis, Ptah, and Hapi, recalling Lower Egypt. A third, similar *Stele*, dating from the 6th year of Ramses III., is to be seen on an isolated rock to the right. All are more or less damaged; but a restoration of the text, which is the same on all three, with a few trifling variations, is rendered possible by collation.

L. Stern has published a German *Translation* of the corrected inscription on the stele of the first year of Ramses II. (the oldest and best given preserved), with a collation of the other two. A few extracts are here from this thrice-repeated *Hymn to the Nile*, the god to whom Egypt owed her very origin, and upon whom she was dependent for the conditions of continued existence from year to year. Similar hymns to the same god have come down to us in a papyrus from the hand of *Anna*, one of the most famous authors of the period of the Pharaohs; and these are clearly connected with the hymn now before us. The inscription begins: 'In the

1st year, on the 10th Epiphi, in the reign of His Majesty etc. .... Ramses-Miamun, who loves the Nile, the father of the gods, his creator. Long may he live, possessing firmness and might, eternally. Long live the beneficent god, the Nile that loves the primæval waters (*Nun*), the father of the gods, who form the cycle of the nine deities, which belong to the floods, the blessing, the abundance, the support of Egypt, who blesses all the world with life by his rich abundance, who is dignified in his course and distributes blessings with his fingers. The elect are rejoiced at his approach. Thou art one that hast created thyself, and no man knows whence thou art. On the day that thou comest out of thy surroundings, all the world rejoices. Thou art a lord of many fishes and gifts, who bestowest nourishment upon Egypt. Even the nine deities know not whence thou art. Thou art their life. Therefore when thou approachest they redouble their offerings; they furnish the altars richly and raise their voices in exultation when thou appearest. Thou metest rich measure to us, to nourish the elect, like Ra when he ruled this land. Strong and wakeful is he at all times, to seek nourishment for the living, to make the corn abundant like the sand of the seashore, and to load the granaries with gifts. Behold, therefore His Majesty sought how he might exalt the father of all gods, the prince and ruler of the flood, and meditated like the god Tehuti (Thoth) to find out what was adequate to his love (*i.e.* how he might give most adequate expression to his love). No king has done so since thy time, Oh Ra! And His Majesty spoke: 'Whereas the Nile nourishes the world, and blessing and abundance follow upon his rising, and behold each one lives in his dwelling, enriched through his command; and seeing that I know what stands in the book-store that is preserved in the library; therefore when the Nile comes forth from his two sources, then let the offerings to the gods be increased; but if the holy stream is at Silsileh (Khennu-t), at the right time, King Ramses H. will redouble the offerings to it there'.

This king appointed two festivals to be kept at Silsileh in honour of the Nile, as the following portion of the inscription records. One was to be observed at the beginning of its gradual rise (the 15th Epiphi), the other on the 15th Thoth, when the rapid rise set in. L. Stern compares these appropriately to the two main festivals of the modern Egyptians, the *Night of the Drop*, and the *Cutting of the Dam*, which are also two months apart (Vol. I., p. 239). Merenptah I. and Ramses III. confirmed the grants made by Ramses II. for the purposes of these festivals, and erected the above-mentioned steles in commemoration of the fact. The nature of the grants (sacrificial bread and cakes, antelopes, beef, veal, six kinds of wine, honey, oil, beer, milk, essences, etc.) is recorded in the lists below the inscriptions, from which we also learn that the king offered fowls to the river-gods and as much corn as a granary could contain to Ammon of Thebes. — The side-walls of the two chapels are also occupied with scenes of sacrifice and worship.

Various opinions have been expressed as to the reason of the special reverence paid to the Nile at this particular defile. The narrows of Silsileh were perhaps difficult or even impossible to pass in earliest antiquity, and so probably came to be regarded as the second entrance of the river into Egypt, the first being at the cataract at Assuân. This is the more probable as Kôm Ombo was certainly reckoned as belonging to Nubia.

Between the above-mentioned chapels of Ramses II. and Merenptah, is a small *Stele* erected by the mayor *Panchesi* (p. 257), who appears here along with a son of the king accompanying the king before Ammon. The prayer is addressed not only to Ammon, but also to the 'holy water' (mu ab, see above) and to the god Sebek.

17 *

A few paces farther to the S., and at a lower level than the steles, is a small *Chapel*, which in spite of its very ruinous condition, we can recognize as having been founded by the great builder *Seti I.* The inscriptions on the stele are completely obliterated. — To the right of this chapel is a carefully hewn but empty *Recess*, and in the same cliff but facing N. in the direction of the two steles, is a *Tablet* of a chief-priest of Ammon named *Roi*, who here appears with Merenptah I. before the god.

The *Quarries* on the W. bank of the Nile are of enormous size, but few traces of inscriptions are now to be found. An *Inscription of Amenhotep III.*, however, records the transport of stones by the Nile for a temple of Ptah (at Memphis?). There are two *Posts* of the time of Seti I., and *Demotic Inscriptions* from Roman times. An unfinished colossal *Sphinx*, nearly opposite the usual landing-place of the dhahabiyehs, is also not without interest. Even if all the monuments of Egypt had disappeared, these huge quarries would serve as a proof that building operations of unsurpassed extent had once been carried on here. The town of *Khennu* appears to have stood here, not on the E. bank. A few unimportant ruins may be traced.

According to papyri now in Turin, the residence of the kings of the 12th Dyn., the Amenemhas and Userteseus, was transferred to *Khennu*. Under the 19th and 20th Dyn. this town possessed a *University*. A papyrus, now in the British Museum, contains a warning to the students of this institution against excessive beer-drinking and idleness.

25. From Gebel Silsileh to Kôm Ombo.

Comp. the Map at p. 98.

15 M. (39½ M. from Edfu). Kôm Ombo is a *Steamer Station*, at which the three-weeks tourist-steamer halts ½ hr., the four-weeks steamer 1 hr., both on the upward voyage; while the mail-steamer passes a night here on the downward voyage.

The mountains recede from the river immediately above the defile of Gebel Silsileh (p. 255), giving space to the desert which appears grey on the Arabian side and yellow on the Libyan side. The narrow cultivable strip is tilled by peasants of a distinctly darker complexion than the fellâhin of the Thebaïd. Both land and people approach gradually nearer to the Nubian type. At the village of *Menîyeh* (E. bank) we enter the E. branch of the stream, which here forms the island of *Mansûrîyeh*, with a village of the same name. On the W. bank of the Nile, opposite the lower end of this island, lies *Abu Mangar*, where Arcelin claims to have discovered stone implements in a deposit of gravel containing marine mussels, which was overlaid by more recent deposits of the river.

On a hill on the E. bank next appears the beautiful *Temple of Kôm Ombo*, conspicuous from a considerable distance. Somewhat nearer the river is another temple, now almost entirely destroyed. The double door of the hypostyle of the higher temple presents an imposing appearance; but the nearer we approach the temple, the more clearly we perceive that the stream has already washed away the pylons and colonnade, and that in no long time the whole of the handsome building will be undermined, like the temple of Ḳâu el-Kebir (p. 48). Large fragments of the building are even now to be seen sunk beneath the stream, near its edge. On one of these is the dedication inscription, recording that the building had been founded as 'a work to endure for eternity'. The high-lying ruins of Kôm Ombo are especially picturesque by the light of the full moon.

A single glance is enough to reveal to the practised eye that a comparatively late monument lies before the traveller. Ptolemy VII. Philometor founded the temple:

Ast en neteru pir ptah kheper sotep en amon ar ma ra, Epiphanes son of the gods, begotten by Ptah, chosen by Ammon, making the truth of Ra. Euergetes II., Ptolemy XIII. Neos Dionysus, his wife Cleopatra V., and at a later date Tiberius enlarged the building. It belonged to the Egyptian town ⟨hieroglyph⟩ *Nubi* (Coptic Mbô), called by the Greeks *Ombos*, as capital of the district *Ombites*, which formerly was part of the Nubian nomos, while from the Egyptian Nubi they formed the names Unbi-Ombi and Omboi (᾽Ομβοι).

It would be a great error to dispute, in face of the present building, the existence of an earlier temple on this site. A gateway which existed on the E. side of the girdle-wall down to 1870 showed on its jambs the figure of Tutmes IH., builder of the temple, which was named Pa Sebek (temple of the crocodile-headed Sebek) in the inscription of Ramaka beneath. According to Champollion the door-posts were provided by one of the Ptolemies with a new lintel; the old lintel, dating from Tutmes IH., was found on the river-bank in 1833 by Maspero, along with a door-post bearing the name of Amenhotep I., and a block of stone with the cartouche of Ramses the Great. The old temple of Tutmes III. probably faced the east.

Corresponding to the double division of this temple, two different triads were especially worshipped within it. The chief of the first was Sebek-Ra with the crocodile-head, along with whom were Hathor and Khunsu; at the head of the second was Har-war, the elder Horus (Arueris), with whom were associated Tasentnefert (the good sister) and her son Pinebtati, lord of both lands. The entire left half of the temple was dedicated to the triad of Arueris, the right half to that of Sebek. The coins of Ombos display a warrior, with a lance in one hand and a crocodile in the other; figures which represent Horus and Sebek in the Roman style. The 'memory of the worship of the two divine brothers in the same temple seems to have lingered in the following legend, related to the writer by a boatman at Kôm Ombo.

'Once upon a time two brothers reigned as princes of Ombo. One was wicked and strong, the other was good. The latter, who loved his fellow-men, was expelled by his wicked brother, and when he departed towards the N., all the inhabitants of Ombo went with him as his companions, leaving the town by night. It was then the season for sowing. When the wicked prince awoke, his vizier said to him, 'All thy subjects have left the country along with thy brother; who will now plough the fields?' The wicked prince was very angry when he heard that; but as he was a great magician he said, 'Then the dead must help me'. So he summoned the dead from their graves; and in the morning he beheld from his castle (the temple) the dead at work, ploughing and sowing. But when the harvest came, not a blade grew in the fields, for the dead had carried the ploughs in the air above the earth, and had sowed sand instead of grain. Then the wicked prince once more was angry and descended from his castle to convince himself with his own eyes of the failure of the harvest. When he saw not only that no blade of corn grew green, but also that the former fields were now covered with sand, he uttered a terrible curse, so fearful that his castle fell to the earth, and a block of stone crushed him to death'.

The temple of Kôm Ombo is a *Double Temple*, and it is the only one in Egypt that is divided along its longer axis into two distinctly defined parts. Even the entrance has two portals. In the interior the various chambers are not approached as usual by one door each; everywhere two doorways are seen, separated by broad pillars each of which is a point in the imaginary line indicating the division between the two portions of the temple. The plan of the whole may be made out with perfect certainty, though many of the rooms, especially those towards the rear, are largely sanded up. The temple moreover contained two sanctuaries, a fact which is scarcely surprising after what has been said of the two chief deities, Arueris and Sebek.

The **Hypostyle Pronaos.** — The *Double Portal* of the main temple consists of two doors, framed by three columns and each displaying a concave cornice and a winged sun-disc. The floor of the hypostyle is encumbered with sand. Thirteen columns are still standing, each of which measures no less than 20 ft. round the middle of the shaft. The two corner columns in front are apparently wanting; there were in all three rows of five or perhaps three rows of seven. The capitals, of great variety of form, belong to the Ptolemaic-Egyptian order; but they differ in various points from those to be seen at Denderah, Esneh, and Edfu. The middle column in the back row has a calyx-capital, with a foliage-cup displaying a unique ornamentation, with three flowers and three buds springing from it. The unfinished calyx-capital of the most northerly column in the same (rear) row has, at its base, a wreath of flowers with serrated edges, between which are arranged pairs of buds, each pair surmounted by a six-pointed star, though elsewhere the Egyptian star is always five-pointed ✖.

This hypostyle was built by Ptolemy XIII. Neos Dionysus and his wife Cleopatra V., whose surname Tryphaena is of frequent occurrence among the Ptolemies. The name of the builder

Aa n pi neter nti nehem, son of Soter, is to be found on the abacus beneath the two-line entrance-inscription, part of which lies on the ground, and also on the interior columns. The rear-wall of the hypostyle, *i.e.* the entrance-wall of the adjoining hall with ten columns, dates from Ptolemy IX. Euergetes II. and his two wives, Cleopatra II. and Cleopatra III. — Above the door of the right (Sebek) side of the temple this king appears with his first wife and sister, presenting the figure of Ma to Sebek, Hathor, and Khunsu; above the left door he appears with his second wife, before Arueris, Tasentnefert, and Pinebtati. Between the cornice and frieze are the dedicatory inscriptions, on the left to Harwar, on the right to Sebek. To the right and left of the two doors to the next (first) room in the direction of the Pronaos, are other two rows of • *Dedication Scenes.* To the right (Sebek side): in the lower row, is King Euergetes II. presenting wine to Shu and Tefnut, farther to the right, the king with two nosegays before Seb, the first born of the gods, and Sebek Nubti; then the king before the celestial goddess Nut, mother of the gods, and Hathor, mistress of Nubt; and finally before Osiris, Isis, and Nephthys (partly broken). In the upper row, the king presents Sebek with two wine-vessels, upon which is a basket . In a third scene, the king appears before the wife (Tasentnefert) and son (Pinebtati) of Sebek. — To the left (Arueris side) : in the upper row, to the left, is the king before Sebek, Hathor, and Khunsu, Har neb fuāb (Horus. the broad-hearted), and then the same with two *Uza* eyes before a moon-god (called Harwar by Champollion) and another god (Pinebtati?). The presentation of the two eyes *(Uza)* refers to the united lands of Lower and Upper Egypt, or perhaps to Nubia and Egypt, of which the temple of Ombos was a representation. The name of *City of the two Uza*, moreover, is frequently bestowed upon Ombos, and was perhaps its sacred name. — In a third scene, in the upper row, the king presents two vessels to Harwar and Hathor. — In the lower row, the king presents the seated figure of Ma to Harwar, Tasentnefert, and Pinebtati.

The traveller's attention may now be directed to the *Astronomical Representations*, some of which are only outlined in red and left unfinished. The constellations in boats floating over the heavens, on the ceiling-side of the architrave, are the most important. The squares into which the surfaces were divided to guide the artist in drawing the figures are still visible, and prove that the recognized proportions of the various parts of the human body to each other were here not identical with those regarded by the artists of earlier epochs.

Lepsius, who had already established the existence of two canons of proportion, here discovered a third, and demonstrated that in the epoch of the Ptolemies the human body was no longer divided into 18 parts from the crown of the head to the soles of the feet, but into 21¼, as Diodorus states. 'The central point between brow and sole falls in all three divisions beneath the hips. Thence downwards the proportions according to the second and third canons are the same; but those of the upper part of the body differ very essentially. The head is larger, the chest recedes farther, the abdomen is higher. The contours become in general fuller, and abandon that early beautiful simplicity and tenderness of form, on which depended their imposing and specially Egyptian character, in favour of an imperfect imitation of an unassimilated style of art. The proportion of the foot to the total length of the body still remains, but the foot is no longer the fundamental unit of measurement'.

The smaller **Colonnaded Hall** (two rows of 4 and 2 central columns), lying behind the hypostyle, is filled with sand, but access may be gained by creeping through one of the half-choked doorways. Within is the hieroglyphic *Dedication Inscription* of Euergetes II. and of his two consorts, one of whom is called his sister ⚲ ◐, the second his wife ⚬ ◐. On the back-wall of this hall, beneath the cornice, is the hieroglyphic dedication of Ptolemy XIII. Neos Dionysus to the two chief deities of the temple, and beneath it the Greek *Dedication Inscription*, written in unusually fine uncial characters. †

The translation is as follows: — 'In honour of King Ptolemy and Queen Cleopatra, his sister, the godlike Philometores and their children, the foot-soldiers, cavalry, and others stationed in the Ombitian district (erected) this temple to Aroeris, the great god, Apollo, and the gods worshipped with him in the same temple (χαὶ τοῖς συνναοις θεοῖς), in consequence of their (the gods') goodwill towards them'. From this inscription it appears that the garrison and officials of the Nubian district, which included Ombos, undertook an adornment of the temple of the gods, to whom they applied the Egyptian name Aroeris (Harwar) and the Greek name Apollo, in gratitude for some special mark of favour shown to them by the gods.

Beside the door of the next room, the second in the direction of the Pronaos, is a seven-lined *Calendar of Festivals*. The hall itself was built by Euergetes II. The third room is the first that shows Ptolemy VII. Philometor offering homage (cartouche see p. 261). Here we see that king before Harwar and Tasentnefert, and before Sebek and Hathor. A fallen block of stone exhibits all the cartouches of the king. The entrance to the last *Double Chamber* or *Sanctuary*, and the reliefs within it (including astronomical scenes), also date from Philometer.

The **Small Temple** in front of the larger one is now largely overwhelmed by the Nile, but the *Pylon* on the S., a few columns,

---

† The following copy, discriminating the words and showing the accents, will assist the traveller to decipher this fine inscription.
Ὑπὲρ βασιλέως Πτολεμαίου χαὶ βασιλίσσης Κλεοπά-
τρας τῆς ἀδελφῆς θεῶν Φιλομητόρων, χαὶ τῶν
τούτων τέχνων Ἀροήρει θεῷ μεγάλῳ,
Ἀπόλλωνι χαὶ τοῖς συνναοις θεοῖς τὸν σηχὸν
οἱ ἐν τῷ Ὀμβίτῃ τασσόμενοι πεζοὶ χαὶ
ἱππεῖς χαὶ οἱ ἄλλοι, εὐνοίας ἕνεχεν τῆς εἰς
αὐτούς.

and some fragments of the walls of the temple proper still remain.
The temple stood from N. to S. On the pylon appears Ptolemy XIII.
Neos Dionysus sacrificing to the gods of Ombos. The same families
of gods are found here as in the larger temple: Horus on one side,
Sebek and Hathor on the other. There is also an altar. From the
frequently repeated figures of *Ape*, goddess of births, the remaining
walls of the temple proper seem to have belonged to a *Pa mes* or
Birth-house . Dates are recorded, including the 5 Epago-
menæ or intercalated days, as the birth-day of Osiris and Horus.
On the wall facing the N. are Euergetes II. and his wife fowling in
presence of Khem Ammon-Ra. Remains of topographical maps of
the nomes are also distinguishable.

The names of Tiberius and several other Roman emperors may
be read on the scattered columns and fragments of walls.

Many blocks bearing interesting inscriptions may be found
between the temple and the Nile. Among them is one, unfortunately damaged, with a *Sacred Inscription*, specially composed for
Ombos, commencing: 'Beginning of the chapter of the book of
sacred knowledge, composed for the house of the venerable god, the
lord of Ombos ,' etc.

26. From Kôm Ombo to Assuân.

Comp. the Map, p. 98.

26½ M. Steamboat in about 6 hours.

The W. side of the narrow river-channel is barren, while on the
E. side there is only a narrow strip of cultivated land. Dark-skinned,
nude Arabs of the tribe of the ʿAbábdeh (p. 253) here and there
work a water-wheel. Occasionally a crocodile may be seen on the
bank; but travellers who ascend only to Philæ are rarely gratified
with a sight of one of these reptiles. — *Darâwi*, a station of the
mail-steamer, on the E. bank, marks the limit of Arabic. Here
begins the Ethiopian dialect known as *Kenûs*, which differs essentially from the dialects spoken farther to the S. by the *Mahas* and
the *Dongolah* (comp. p. 304). Even in ancient Egypt, as we learn
from a papyrus, the inhabitants of the Delta did not understand the
speech of Elephantine.

The scenery becomes tamer after the village of *Kubánîyeh*, on
the W. bank. At *el-ʿAtárah*, opposite, granite appears for the first
time. Before we reach Assuân the scenery assumes entirely new
aspects. As we approach the city, the scene presented to us is one
of great and peculiar beauty. In front of us lies the S. extremity
of the island of *Elephantine* (p. 271), with its houses shining from
between the palm trees; the scarlet uniforms of British soldiers and
their white tents, conspicuous at a considerable distance, form a

strange feature in the landscape; and sandstone now gives place to
masses of granite on the banks and in the channel of the stream.
Farther towards the S. this rock forms the natural fortress known
as the first cataract, which consists of innumerable cliffs of dark
parti-coloured granite, among which the Nile pursues its rapid
course towards Egypt by means of many narrow channels.

26¹/₂ M. (580 M. from Cairo) *Assuân.*

When the stream is low the steamers are compelled to anchor below
Assuân, but at other times they touch near the bazaar. Dhahabiyehs anchor
at various points, sometimes beside the island of !Elephantine opposite.
— The mail-steamers remain here from Sun. or Wed. morning till Mon.
or Thurs. afternoon at 3 p.m.; the three-weeks steamer halts 2 days (Sun.
and Mon.) for a visit to Assuân and Philæ; and the four-weeks steamer
2¹/₂ days. Those who wish to proceed to Wâdi Halfah (p. 299) must
quit the steamer on Mon. morning and take the train to Shellâl (Philæ).
— In 1890 a dhahabîyeh belonging to Messrs. Cook and Son, near the
station, provided board and lodging for 1*l*. per day.

Assuân, Coptic *Suan* (Arabic, with the article, *Al-Suân, Assuân*),
the steamboat terminus for the lower Nile, with a post and telegraph
office, lies on the E. bank, partly on the plain and partly on a hill,
in N. lat. 24° 5′ 30″. The fertile strip here is narrow, but supports
numerous date-palms, the fruit of which still enjoys a high reputation. The native inhabitants have increased under the British
occupation to about 10,000; but that number is only a fraction of
its former population, when according to Arabian authors, no less
than 20,000 died of the plague at one time. Some of the houses
are elegant, but the mosques do not repay a visit. The howling
dervishes have a house here in which they meet on Fridays for
prayer. A considerable trade is carried on in the products of the
Sûdân and Abyssinia, brought hither on camels, and shipped northwards by the Nile to Keneh, Assiût, or Cairo. Among the chief ex-
ports are ostrich feathers, ivory, india-rubber, senna, tamarinds,
wax, skins, horns, and dried dates. The steamers and dhahabiyehs
are here boarded by negroes, Nubians, and handsome Beduins,
with artistically dressed curly hair, who offer for sale ostrich feathers
and fans, silver rings and armlets, ivory hoops, weapons from Central Africa, small monkeys, amulets, beautiful basket-work, and
aprons of leather fringe, the costume of the women of the Sûdân,
which they oddly call 'Madama Nubia'. Grey and black ostrich
feathers are comparatively cheap (8 piastres = 2 fr. each), larger
and perfect white feathers cost 10-20 fr. apiece and upward. Travellers who desire to buy in quantity should betake themselves to
one of the wholesale dealers in the town. The bazaar is like the
bazaars of all Nile towns, but is distinguished for its excellent local
pottery of great beauty of form. Candles, porter, ale, and even
tolerable Dutch cigars may be obtained at a Turkish 'bakkal'. —
Copper money is, curiously enough, accepted very unwillingly in
Assuân and the rest of Nubia; the traveller should provide himself
beforehand with silver piastres.

HISTORY. The ancient Egyptian name of the town of Assuân was *Sun*

, that of the whole cataract-district was *Senem* .

The name *Sun* means 'the place affording an opening or entrance', because here the threshold of Egypt was crossed. The name seldom occurs in hieroglyphic inscriptions, because the metropolis or chief town of the nome to which Sun belonged, was Elephantine, on the island of that name. The place, however, is very ancient, for even under the 6th Dyn., the granite required by the builders of Lower Egypt was furnished by the quarries in its neighbourhood. In later times the city of the cataracts was frequently referred to by Greek and Roman writers under the name of **Syene**. It acquired special fame on account of its well (see below), and as the place of banishment of *Juvenal* in his old age.

The *Well* of Syene, in which there was no shadow at midday, and which thus seemed to prove that Syene was situated under the tropic, has disappeared. The report of its existence led the learned Athenian *Eratosthenes* (276–196 B.C.), attached to the Museum at Alexandria, to the discovery of the method of measuring the size of the earth that is still employed. 'He selected the arc of the earth between Alexandria and Syene (Assuân) on the Nile, of which place he assumed that it was in the same meridian. Since he knew that the midday sun at the summer solstice cast no shadow within a radius of 300 stadia from Syene, and that in Alexandria at the same time the angle determined by the shadow of the sun-gnomon was equal to one-fiftieth of a circle, he correctly concluded that the distance between Alexandria and Syene must equal the fiftieth part of a meridian circle, or 7° 12'. † The distance from Alexandria to Syene was taken by Eratosthenes simply at the popular estimate of 5300 stadia, equal to 593 M. (Lepsius) or 518 M. (Hultsch). *Peschel.* — A glance at the map shows that Assuân no longer lies under the tropic of Cancer, but somewhat to the N. of it, so that no shadowless well can exist there at present; but it has been calculated that in the 4th cent. B.C. Syene *actually lay exactly under the tropic*, whence we may gather that the Egyptians must have noticed the shadowless well long before Eratosthenes and must have known the true situation of the tropic.

Juvenal was still living under Hadrian; but it is not quite certain whether, as is usually assumed, he was sent to Egypt by Domitian. The rhetorician and satirist, while living in Rome, had fiercely attacked the actor Paris, who was a court-favourite, and he was on that account removed from the capital. He was not exactly banished but appointed prefect of the garrison at Syene, on the most remote frontier of the empire. His trenchant muse found abundant material on the banks of the Nile. His 15th Satire describes the contest between the inhabitants of Ombos and Tentyra (Denderah) at a festival at Koptos. The two hostile nomes, whom he erroneously calls neighbours ('vicinos'), had long cherished a mutual enmity on account of the gods they worshipped. At Tentyra the crocodile was persecuted, while it was held sacred at Tentyra for the sake of Sebek who was worshipped there. Thus arose a strife resembling that mentioned on p. 7. The Tentyritians even slew a man of Ombos and devoured him. Juvenal is indignant, and indicates that his residence on the Nile had by no means taught him to love the Egyptians. If he composed the 15th satire at Syene, that town has the honour of being the birth-place of the following fine verses: —

'That nature gave the noble man a feeling heart'
'She proves herself, by giving him tears!'
'This is the noblest part of all human nature'.

The 16th Satire, in which Egypt is again mentioned, seems to be erroneously ascribed to Juvenal. Doubts also attach to the authenticity of a frequently quoted edict of the emperor Diocletian, ordering the Christian

---

† The actual difference between Alexandria (31° 12') and Assuân (24° 5' 30") is only 7° 6' 30".

churches on the Nile as far as Syene to be torn down and the temples to be restored.

The place suffered greatly at the hands of the Blemmyes, but became the seat of a Christian bishop, and appears to have rapidly regained its prosperity under the Khalifs. *Leo Africanus* (14th cent.) saw here some towers of unusual height, which can only be regarded as the pylons of some large temple, as they were named *Barba* by the natives, a name easily traced from the Egyptian '*pa erpe*' i.e. the temple.

After the close of the 12th cent. Assuân suffered still more severely from the incursions of plundering Arab tribes, finally put a stop to by a Turkish garrison stationed here by the sultan Selim, after the conquest of Egypt in 1517. Many of the present inhabitants claim descent from these Turks.

To the S. and N. of the landing-place, at which various craft are always lying, two edifices project into the river. One of these is a ruined Arabian fort, the other a ruined building, probably a bath, for which stones of earlier buildings have been used, and dating more probably from the Khalifs than from Roman times. The upper part of the town presents large clay walls with few windows towards the stream; the lower part is screened by palm-groves, through whose green foliage gleam the outlines of crags, heaps of rubbish, a dark gray clay wall, and a pure white minaret. Huge granite cliffs rise from the stream. To the W. lies the green and fertile island of Elephantine, shaped like the head of a lance, and still farther to the W., on the Libyan bank, rises a ruined Arab castle, projecting darkly from the yellow sand-slopes of the range of hills across which the telegraph-wires are conducted. To the E. the prospect is bounded by the Arabian hills, in which, more to the S., are some huge empty graves of saints. Everywhere the eye finds rest. The Nile, with its divided channel, appears small; but it still preserves its venerable aspect, for everywhere, even on the rocks by the stream, are inscriptions and numerous memorials of the grand old times, especially as we look towards the island.

In *Antiquities*, Assuân is not very rich. Besides the small *Ptolemaic Temple* beside the land-route to Philæ (p. 274), only a few *Rock Inscriptions* on the river-bank call for mention.† One dates from Rameren of the 6th Dyn.; several from the 12th Dyn., from Usertesen I., from the 35th year of Amenemha II. coinciding with the 3rd year of his adopted successor Usertesen II., and one from the 5th year of the same king. In both the latter a certain Mentuhotep is mentioned. There is also a stele of the 10th year of Usertesen III. and one with the name Neferhotep, of the 13th Dynasty. Another important stele, dating from the first year of Tutmes II. (⊙ 🪲), contains a detailed report of the conquest

† The remains of two other temples are described in the Description de l'Egypte, but both have now disappeared. One was a tetrastyle *Portico*, the other a *Hall*, dedicated by the emperor Nerva to the gods of Assûan, Khnum, Sati, Anuke, and Nephthys, and to Osiris, Isis, Sebek, and Hathor. Champollion saw the latter in 1829.

of some rebellious S. tribes in the land of Kush and the district
of Kenes. Some inscriptions of a certain Senmut before Hatasu
and her daughter Raneferu record the quarrying and despatch of
two large obelisks; another is from the 9th year of Seti I.; others
are by a Mes (Moses) under Merenptah I.; and another is by a certain
Seti, a loyal son of Kush and president of the gold-land of Siptah,
and his minister Bai.

In 1885-86 some important **Tombs** of the 6th and 12th Dyn.
were opened on the hills ('*Mount Grenfell*') lying to the W. opposite Assuàn, first by Mustafah Shakir, British consular agent at Assuân, and then by Major-general *Sir F. Grenfell*. They lie about
1/4 hr. to the N. of the W. convent (*Dêr el-gharbîyeh*). We cross
the river in the small boat and land at a ruined stone quay, whence
an ancient staircase, hewn in the rock, ascends for about 150 ft.,
flanked on either side by a wall of more recent date. The stairs
are in three flights, from the top of each of which inclined planes
lead towards the tombs, evidently intended for the transport of the
sarcophagi. At the summit of the staircase is a platform with
tombs of the 6th and 12th Dynasties.† *Tomb No. 26*, with a curious
door placed one-third up the height of another door, belongs to a
court-official named **Saben** ⌐⌐⌐, who flourished under Neferkara Pepi II. (6th Dyn.) and was employed on the pyramid of
that king ⌐⌐⌐ Men-ankh (see Plan, Vol. I., p. 378).
The tomb consists of an oblong hall (69 ft. by 26 ft.), with a ceiling supported by 14 square pillars. Close to the entrance, beside
the first pillar on the right, is the standing figure of Saben, with
red complexion and black hair. On the back-wall the deceased
appears spearing fish from a boat, with a companion engaged in
catching birds that rise from a bed of papyrus-plants. To the left
is a passage, leading to a winding mummy-shaft. On the left side
of this tomb, and not separated from it by any partition wall, lies
Tomb. No. 25, belonging to a certain **Mekhu** ⌐⌐⌐. This
contains eighteen columns in three rows, resembling the so-called
proto-Doric columns in the tombs at Benihasan (p. 12). Between the first two rows stands a square stone, probably used as an
altar. To the right of the entrance are a few paintings. Mekhu
leans upon a staff, being perhaps lame, while offerings are presented to him (one of his sons was also named Mekhu, his wife
Aba was a priestess of Hathor, while another son, called Saben, was
possibly the owner of tomb 26). In the adjoining paintings Mekhu
is shown making an offering himself and ploughing with oxen and

---

† Described by *Budge* in the Proceedings of the Soc. for Bibl. Arch.
for November 1887, and by *Bouriant* in the Recueil X, p. 181.

reaping. Good representations of Egyptian donkeys. From the point where the two tombs touch, another passage leads to a mummy-shaft, at the back of which is a square chamber.

Climbing up to the right from this double tomb we find several other tombs, most of which have no inscriptions. One belongs to *Hek-ab*, son of *Apt* and of *Penatmai*. A four-line inscription over the entrance mentions festivals of the dead.

Another important tomb is No. 31, belonging to **Ranub-kaunekht** , who appears from his name to have been a high official under Amenemha I. It seems also to be the sepulchre of his son (?) *Si Renput* (son of Satihotep), whose portrait is of frequent occurrence in this tomb and who is named commander of the light troops in the S. frontier districts. Beyond a narrow passage follows a hall with 6 square columns, and then another passage with three recesses on each side, the first on the left containing a bearded figure of Osiris. At the end of the second passage is a small chamber with four columns, whence a long passage leads to the right to a quadruple shaft.

Farther on, at the top of another ascent, is a tomb, named after the Prince of Naples who was present at its opening, and belonging to *Baikhenu*, a priest at the pyramid of Pepi II. (p. 269). Then the large sepulchres of *Khunes* and *Semnes*. Finally on the N. side of the same hill is the interesting tomb (No. 32) of another **Si Renput** (son of Tena), who served under Usertesen I., and was grandfather or great-grandfather of the above-named *Si Renput* through his daughter *Satihotep*. To the right and left of the entrance are some half-defaced inscriptions. The antechamber has seven pillars, on one of which (to the right) reference is made to a campaign undertaken by the king for the subjection of a hostile tribe (Kat?). Another important inscription (unfortunately damaged), over the entrance to the rock-tomb proper, treats of the influential position enjoyed by Si Renput under the king and in the campaign against Kush (Ethiopia). To the left scenes of fish-spearing and fowling, and cattle. In the interior are a small tetrastyle hall, a long passage, and then another tetrastyle hall, at the back of which is a recess. We may descend direct from this tomb to the bank of the river.

Among the other points to be visited hence are *Elephantine*, the small *Temple of the Ptolemies*, the old *Cemeteries*, and the *Quarries* on the way to Philæ.

27. The Island of Elephantine.

This island is reached by small boat in a few minutes from the landing-place. Cook's tourists are first transported in comfortable boats to Elephantine and then to the bazaar at Assuân (small gratuity). A row round the island is recommended (¹/₂ hr.). The entire visit takes barely an hour.

Elephantine was a place of great sanctity from a very early period among the ancient Egyptians. It formed a nome by itself with a capital, named like the entire island 𓉐𓊖 *Ab* and also 𓃰𓊖. *Ab* was the Egyptian for elephant, so that Elephantine is merely the Greek translation of a native name. The Arabs call it simply *Gezîreh, i.e.* island, or *Gezîret Assûan;* and it is also said to be named *ez-Zâhir* or 'the blooming'. Though the vegetation is luxuriant in many spots, the writer never heard the last-given name applied to it.

The Egyptian priests described the *Source of the Nile* as a mystery, that would only be revealed to the soul at the twelfth gate of the underworld; yet at the same time, they pointed out the 'symbolical sources of the Nile', so to speak, in the eddies among the rocks of the cataracts to the S. of Elephantine. They named these ⟨hieroglyphs⟩, *i.e.* the *Kerti* or sources of Elephantine. Herodotus heard of these from a scribe in the treasury of the temple of Athena at Saïs. The Halicarnassian thought that the priest was but jesting when he told him that between Syene and Elephantine lay two lofty peaked mountains, Krophi and Mophi, from the midst of which gushed the bottomless sources of the Nile, one half of which flowed to the N. to Egypt, the other half to the S. to Ethiopia. — However foolish this opinion, which Seneca also reports, may appear, it was not pure invention, for the monuments inform us that the people were really taught to believe that the Egyptian Nile had his abode among the rapids to the S. of Elephantine. Some located it to the N. of the island of Bigeh-Senem (P. 297). Khnum, the god of cataracts, was revered before all other gods on this island; and next to him ranked Sati (a form of Isis-Sothis), because the beginning of the inundation coincided with the early rising of this constellation, and the cataract may be regarded as the threshold of the swollen Nile entering Egypt.

In the year 1822 Mohammed 'Ali, in order to build a palace for himself at Assuân, caused the destruction of the *Temple of Khnum*, built under Amenhotep III. of the 18. Dyn. near the S. end of the island, and also of a smaller *Temple of Tutmes III.*, lying more to the N.W., and known as the N. temple. Travellers pass the latter on their way to the city, in whose N. outskirts it lay. The savants of the French Expedition saw this temple before its destruction and published views of it. Now all that is to be seen on the island are some huge heaps of ruins, a granite doorway of the time of Alexander I., and a granite *Statue of Merenptah I.* Blocks of stone and sculptured fragments lie around.

The inhabitants of the two villages on the island, many of whom understand nothing but Nubian, offer coins, small antiquities (many imitations), and fragments of pottery with inscriptions (ostraca) for sale. The last-named are sometimes valuable; the inscriptions are written with ink in Demotic, Greek, or Coptic characters. A roll containing poems by Homer was also discovered here.

By far the most interesting object on the island is the *Nilo-meter, on the W. side facing Assuân, known to the Arabs as *Mikyâs*. The learned court-astronomer of the Khedive, Mahmûd Bey, restored this well-preserved monument to use in 1870. Strabo gives the following excellent description, which is interesting to compare with the monument as it now exists. 'The Nilometer is a well built of regular hewn stones, on the bank of the Nile, in which is recorded the rise of the stream, not only the maximum but also the minimum and average rise, for the water in the well rises and falls with the stream. On the side of the well are marks, measuring the complete rise of the water and all the other degrees of its rising. These are observed and published for general information'. Readers are referred to our account of the Mikyâs at Cairo (Vol. I., p. 319). The Nilometer at Elephantine consists of a narrow roofless chamber, connected with the stream, and is reached by 52 steps in 6 flights. The lowest landing is reckoned as 4 Arabian ells or about 7 ft. above the lowest water level (the dir'a or Arabian ell being equal to 54 centimètres or about $21^{1}/_{3}$ inches). Above that point 13 ells are marked, so that the highest point marked is 30 ft. (17 Arab. ells) above the minimum water-level. Each ell is divided on the side of the well into 6 parts and 24 *kirat*. The 13 old Egyptian ells, each divided into 7 spans and 28 fingers, have a total length of $6{,}_{895}$ mètres (about 20 ft.), from which Mahmûd Bey obtained 53 centimètres as the equivalent for an ell instead of the previously accepted $52^{1}/_{2}$ centimètres. The water-level fluctuates actually between the top of the first ell and the seventeenth, *i.e.* has a range at Assuân of 16 ells of 54 centimètres each. The old and new marks are placed on every third step. From the surface of the water upwards are 11 marks, of which, however, only the half are necessary, as the Nile no longer rises higher.

Close beside the river, farther to the N., lies a massive *Roman Structure*, built of hewn blocks from earlier edifices. Many of these blocks are covered with inscriptions of different dates, including fragmentary lists of offerings and festival calendars and a portion of a Nilometer. The rock-inscriptions close to the stream should also be noticed. They include inscriptions by Neferkara (Pepi), Unas, Antef aa, with one by Amenemha on the other side.

The higher parts of the island command a fine *View of the black and brown, rough and smooth rocks of the cataract, among which the Nile, split up into many small branches, sometimes dashes in foaming energy, sometimes flows in unruffled calmness.

28. From Assuân to Philae.

a. Passage of the First Cataract.

The *First Cataract* (Arab. *Shellâl*, from the earlier form *Djéndal*) lies between Assuân and Philæ. It must be passed by all who desire to proceed in their own dhahabîyeh to Wâdi Halfah and the second cataract. When the river is high the passage is quite without danger, and though it is more difficult at later periods of the year, nothing more serious need be feared than some slight damage to the boat. A considerable amount of time, however, is consumed by the passage, except under favourable circumstances and when the river is at its highest. Including the necessary preparations, 2-3 days must be set aside for the passage; and a carefully drawn-up contract (p. xxii) will be found here especially useful. Travellers who have previously arranged with their dragoman to be conveyed to and from Wâdi Halfah for a fixed sum including the passage of the cataract, will come off best. Those who have no such arrangement must come to terms with one of the shêkhs of the Shellâl or chiefs of the cataracts. With a reliable dragoman the matter may be arranged in ten minutes, but otherwise (too frequently the case) difficulties are sure to arise. The boat will be objected to as too high, too weak, or two large, the water will be described as too low, or the wind (which must certainly be taken into the calculation) as too gentle; but none of these objections should be listened to, if the dhahabîyeh has been originally hired to ascend beyond the cataract. Energy and bakshish will overcome difficulties. If the dragoman prove too recalcitrant, the traveller should threaten to proceed to Wâdi Halfah by camel or by a dhahabîyeh from Philæ, and to bring an action for damages against the dragoman on his return to Cairo. That will generally produce an effect; but the action for damages should not, in the interest of future travellers, be allowed to remain an empty threat. Dhahabîyehs may be hired above the cataract, but they are inferior and dear. The cost of ascending the rapids varies from 4 to 6*l*., according to the size of the boat, to which a bakshîsh of at least 2-3*l*. must be added. This amount of bakshish must be paid because as many as 50 or 60, or even, when the vessel is large and the water low, 100 men are required to tow a dhahabîyeh up the rapids. Travellers may remain on board during the operation if they choose, but as the passage takes several hours, they lose much time.

Since the construction of the railway from Assuân to Philæ, and owing to the disturbances caused by the Beduins, the journey between the cataracts is now very seldom made by dhahabîyeh; and the ascent of the rapids by a passenger-boat is quite exceptional.

The descent of the foaming rapids is much more interesting. Those who are very cautious may perhaps cause their more precious possessions to be transported past the cataract by land; but serious accidents almost never occur, though the wrecks of some dhahabîyehs on the banks prove that the descent is not absolutely without danger. An excellent view of the passage may be obtained from a rock on the bank (*Baò esh-Shellâl*, p. 278).

Passengers by Cook's steamers are conveyed down the rapids to Assuân in a rowing-boat for 4*s*. a head, an interesting trip, not wholly devoid of danger. A halt is made before the chief rapid, in order to view the natives descending it on trunks of trees. As usual the visitor is harassed by demands for bakshish. The voyage is then continued through smaller channels, and at dangerous points, the boat is secured by ropes. See description of a trip of this kind on p. 279.

The dhahabîyeh ascends in untroubled· water as far as the island of *Sehêl*. There it is surrounded by the dark, sinewy, and generally most symmetrical forms of the Arabs who are to tow it through the rapids. Some come on board under the direction of a shêkh, while others remain on the bank. At first the dhahabîyeh passes the beginning of the rapids comparatively easily, but by-and-by, ropes are fastened to the mast, and the severe struggle with the descending current begins. Some haul on the ropes from the bank, others guide the course of the vessel with poles from on board, and others in the water keep it upright or ward it off from striking on sharp rocks in the river-bed. Old men, young men, and boys rival each other in the most exhausting activity, that seems almost frantic, from its never-ceasing accompaniment of shouts, cries, and chants. Every saint in the calendar is invoked, especially the beneficent Sa'id, who is believed to render especially effective aid in sudden dangers. At the most difficult point, the *Bab el-Kebîr* (p. 278) boys, for a small fee, will plunge head-first into the stream, to reappear astride pieces of wood below the boiling surf, through which they swim with marvellous skill. If the work is not accomplished before sun-set, it is left unfinished till next morning. — It may be remarked that the Egyptian government contemplates widening the channel and introducing fixed regulations for the passage. — The time occupied in taking the dhahabîyeh through the rapids may be advantageously turned to account by the traveller by first inspecting the cataract from the bank and then, by proceeding by land to Philae, where he should pitch his tent or take up his abode in the Osiris room (p. 295). The most necessary articles can easily be transported through the rapids by a few of the sailors in the small boat. The dragoman will arrange the new household with the assistance of the cook and the camp-servant. A few days spent at Philæ, especially at full moon, will not easily be forgotten. — It is not advisable to bring the dhahabîyeh as far as the island of Sehêl and to visit Philæ thence, because there are no donkeys to be there obtained.

b. From Assuân to Philæ by land.

Railway in 1/2 hr., fare 5 piastres; one train daily (1891) to Shellâl at 8.30 a.m., returning at 11 a.m. — The *Ride* to Philæ takes 1½ hr.; excellent donkeys at the landing-place. Rich inhabitants of Assuân spend large sums upon their riding-asses; spirited Abyssinian donkeys, if they are also handsome, cost from 30*l.* upwards. — The inspection of the objects of interest of Assuân occupies 3-4 hrs.

The route leads past the *Post Office* into the town, then turns to the right (leaving the Bazaar on the left) and follows the telegraph-wires across a (5 min.) bridge over the railway to Philæ (Shellâl). The *Ptolemaic Temple* lies a few minutes to the left, below (see below). Thence we proceed straight on to the *Mohammedan Tombs*, passing on the way the graves of an Austrian and of a sailor of the British ship 'Monarch' (Dawe; d. 1884). The *Quarries* are reached from the Ptolemaic temple by continning straight on for a few minutes, then turning abruptly into the desert path, which soon brings us in sight of tall blocks of stone, behind which is the quarry (p. 276). The obelisk lies 10 min. to the right of the above-mentioned European graves.

1. The Ptolemaic Temple.

The attentive observer will notice many blocks and slabs with hieroglyphic inscriptions built into the houses of Assuân. In the

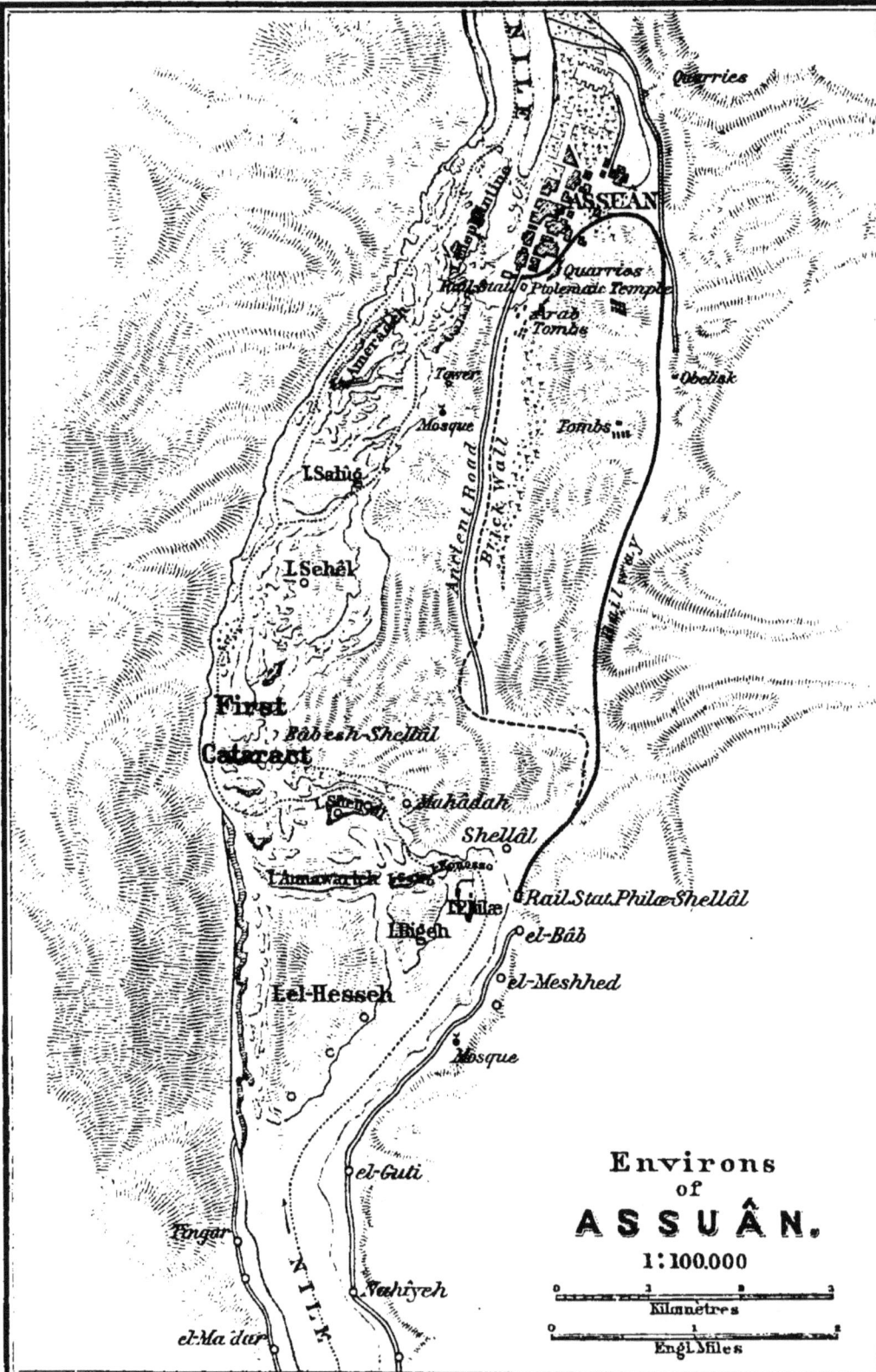

NILE

Quarries

ASSUÂN

Quarries

Rail.Stat. Ptolemaic Temple

Arab Tombs

Obelisk

Tower

Mosque

Tombs

Ancient Road

Brick Wall

Rail way

I. Salug

I. Sehêl

First Cataract

Bâb esh-Shellâl

I. Suhêl Mahâdah

Shellâl

I. Amawartek I. Sem.

I. Konosso

Philae

Rail.Stat. Philae-Shellâl

I. Bigeh

el-Bâb

I. el-Hesseh

el-Meshhed

Mosque

el-Guti

NILE

Tingar

Nahîyeh

el-Ma'dar

Environs
of
ASSUÂN.
1:100.000

Kilomètres

Engl.Miles

Geograph. Anstalt von

station also there is a block of granite with the name of Tutmes III., possibly dating from a temple at Syene, on which Khnum, lord of *Kebu*

(hieroglyphs), within *Abu* (Elephantine) is named. Several attractive houses, one belonging to a wealthy Jew, form a kind of suburb here.

To the left of the road lies the small TEMPLE, founded by Ptolemy III. Euergetes and adorned by Ptolemy IV. Philopator, but never entirely completed. On the left of the *Façade* is Euergetes I. and his wife Berenice II., before Isis in Sun (Syene). Isis is named conductress of the soldiers, because the frontier-town and its neighbourhood were strongly garrisoned from very early times as well as under the Romans. (Under the Romans the Cohors Quinta Suenensium was stationed at *Contra Syene*, the Cohors Sexta Saginarum in the *Castra Lapidariorum*, on the E. bank to the S. of Syene, the Cohors Prima Felix Theodosiana on *Elephantine*, and the Legio Prima Maximiana on *Philæ*.) Next appears Ptulmis, son of Euergetes, otherwise Philopator, before Khnum, Sati, and Anuke, who each wears his special head-dress. On the right side of the façade is Euergetes I., before Sebek and Hathor, and offering incense before Osiris Unnofer (the good), Isis, and the child Horus.

On the inner sides of the two doors leading to the antechamber with its two square columns, and on the inner side of the door to the adytum, are inscribed stirring *Hymns to Isis-Sothis*, to whom apparently the little temple was dedicated. To the left, on the latter door, are e.g. the words: 'Thou hurlest forth (sati) the Nile, that he may fertilize the land in thy name of Sothis, thou embracest (ank) the fields to make them fertile in thy name of Ankht. All beings on earth exist through thee, through thy name of Ankht ('the living').

Unusually thick pillars in the first and largest chamber of the temple support flat Greek abaci, upon which rests a broad but flat architrave. Completed inscriptions are to be found only on the partition-wall between the sanctuary and the preceding hall, on the entrance door, and at a few points on the inner walls.

Near the temple is a rock-inscription of the time of Khu-en-aten. To the left appears the sculptor *Men*, before a sitting figure of Amenhotep III. perhaps carved by himself, to the right is a son of Men named *Bek*, making an offering. Bek is also a master-sculptor of the sun, whose beams radiate in the form of hands. The cartouches of Khu-en-aten are defaced.

2. THE ARAB CEMETERIES.

A brief ride brings us to an immense number of Arab graves, lying in the midst of the desert, each marked by a rectangle of unhewn stones, and a slab bearing an engraved inscription. Many are covered with a pall of yellow sand. The earliest of the hundreds of *Epitaphs* exhibit the venerable Cufic character and date mostly from the 9th and 10th cent. A.D. A few are older and many are more recent. The inscriptions usually give the name of the deceased and the date of death. Texts from the Korân are not uncommon, in spite of the Prophet's express command that the name of God and passages from the Korân should never be placed upon tombstones. The tombs of the richer dead are small domed erections. On the summit of the hill to the right of the road are some large mosque-like *Cenotaphs*, dedicated to famous saints, such as the Shêkh Maḥmûd, the Shêkh.'Ali, our lady (sitte) Zeinab, etc., whose memory is celebrated by festivals on their birthdays, etc.

3. The Quarries (Arabic *Ma'adîn*).

About 1/4 hr. beyond Assuân we quit the road and turn to the E. (left). In a few minutes more we reach the verge of a hill, on which blocks of granite are scattered both singly and in heaps. A moderately lofty cliff beyond shows manifold traces of the industry of the ancient builders, who, from the erection of the pyramids to the time of the Ptolemies, drew their supplies of granite from the quarries of Syene. Almost all the granite pillars, columns, architraves, roof-slabs, obelisks, and statues that we have hitherto seen in Egypt, hail from this spot.

Syenite owes its name to the early Greek form of the name of Assuân *(Syene)*, although the stone here found is far too poor in hornblende to be reckoned true syenite at all. † *Hartmann* describes it as follows: — The granite, which interrupts the sandstone at the cataracts of Assuân, is of a reddish hue, caused by bright rose-coloured orthoclase. It contains a large proportion of translucent quartz, yellow, brownish, pink, and black mica, and only a little hornblende. Huge coarse-grained masses of this composition are here found and also hard fine-grained masses, containing much red felspar, but little quartz and very little mica. Veins also occur rich in dark mica and greenish oligoclase, and containing a little pinite; and finally veins of a dark green diorite, in which the proportion of hornblende is much greater than that of albite'. The glaze on the rocks of the cataracts is noticed on p. 279.

The diligent hands of the stone-cutters of the Pharaohs have left distinct traces behind them. The method in which the blocks were quarried in tiers may still be distinctly seen on a cliff facing the N., about 8 min. to the N.E. of the town. The skill with which huge masses were handled and detached without injury from the cliff to which they belonged, is absolutely marvellous. The certainty of the process adopted is amply vouched for by the fact that obelisks were completely finished on three sides before they were finally detached

---

† This curious fact is explained by Prof. Zirkel as follows. The term *Syenite*, which occurs in Pliny, was first employed in a scientific sense by Werner in 1788, who applied it to the characteristic stone formed of orthoclase felspar and black hornblende, found in the Plauensche Grund, in Saxony. Thenceforth that mineral was accepted as the typical syenite. Wad subsequently proved that the stone quarried at Syene was not syenite at all, *i.e.* that its formation was quite different from that of the rocks in the Plauensche Grund. When Rozière discovered true syenite on Mount Sinai he proposed to alter its name slightly and to call it *Sinaite*, a suggestion, however, which has never been adopted.

from their native rock, this final operation being probably accomplished with the aid of wet wedges. Such an *Obelisk*, still attached to the rock, may be seen about ¹/₂ M. to the S. of the town and about as far to the E. of the Nile. It is not easily found, as it is frequently more than half-covered with sand. At its broadest part this obelisk measures 10¹/₂ ft.; its length is 92 ft. (72 ft. cut out), not reckoning the pyramidal top, which has already been hewn. The economy of material on the part of the stone-cutters is noteworthy. In the quarry near the road and visited by all travellers, is a huge *Block of Rock*, from which the mason has begun to hew both a roofing-slab and a column. Here we clearly perceive that the ancients well understood how to disintegrate the granite with borers and to split it with wedges. Numerous holes were made in a fixed line (probably with the help of draw-boring), the damp wooden wedges were driven in, and in this manner tolerably even fractures were obtained. The art of splitting the stone by heat was also understood.

The *Chapel* transported from Elephantine (*i.e.* Assuân) to *Sais* by Aahmes (26th Dyn.) was especially celebrated, and is mentioned by Herodotus (II, 175). It consisted of a single block and its transport occupied 2000 men for 3 years. It is said to have been 21 ells long, 14 broad, and 8 high, outside measurement; and 18⁵/₆ ells long, 12 broad, and 5 high, inside measurement. It had to remain outside the temple at Sais, on account of its size and weight. Still more striking, in point of weight at least, were the *Statue of Ramses II.* transported hence to the Ramesseum (p. 162), and a stone *Chapel*, seen by Herodotus (I, 155) at Buto. The latter was cubical in form and measured 40 ells each way; and it has been estimated that its weight must have been about 7000 shipping-tons, or more than twice the burden of a large East Indiaman.

4. The Ancient Road and the Brick Wall.

We turn to the right (W.) from the quarries and follow the broad sandy road leading S. to Philæ. The desert has a wonderful preserving virtue. If the road along which the traveller now rides were practicable for carriages, Strabo's description would still fit it in every point. 'We drove', writes the ancient geographer, 'from Syene (Assuân) to Philæ, through a very flat plain about 50 stadia long. At many points all along the road, and on both sides, we saw the rounded, smooth, and almost conical blocks of dark, hard rock, resembling Hermes-towers, from which mortars are made. Smaller blocks lie upon larger ones, and support others in their turn; here and there were isolated blocks', etc. — To this we need only add that pious pilgrims and wayfarers have chiselled their *Names and short Inscriptions* on many of the above-mentioned blocks. Princes, dignified priests, and warriors, have travelled this way, as far back as the times of the Amenembas and Usertesens. Down to a late period pilgrims were in the habit of placing inscriptions on these stones, accompanied with the representation of the soles of the feet. Among the more noteworthy of these *Inscriptions* are a short one of the fourth year of Usertesen I. , and a longer one of the fifth year of Amenhotep III., in which the king is likened to a fierce lion that seizes the Kushites in his claws. A *Stele* also, of the second year of Ramses the Great, shows on the left Ammon and on the right Khnum presenting the *shopesh* or sword of victory to the king, who grasps a negro by the hair. Many other ancient reliefs and inscriptions will be found by the careful seeker, both along this road and beside the Nile in the direction of and beside Assuân. †

By-and-by we perceive considerable fragments of a high *Brick Wall*, built to protect the road from the attacks of the Blemmyes (p. 302) and also perhaps from the shifting sand. Strabo, curiously enough, does not mention it. It first appears to the right (W.) of the road, crosses it twice, remains then on the E. side, and ends on the flat bank opposite Philæ. It is 6 ft. broad, and at some places 13 ft. high.

As this curious erection is almost entirely destroyed or covered with sand in the neighbourhood of Assuân, and as there are also other points of interest on the land-route to Philæ (the inscriptions are most numerous near the island), no one who has a reasonable time to devote to the region of the first cataract, should fail to traverse this route once at least. The view of Philæ, as the traveller approaches the end of his journey, will never be forgotten.

c. Route partly through the Desert, partly beside the Cataract.

This route is recommended to those who have arrived by steamer and have time to go to Philæ and back once only. The return to Assuân is usually made (when there is moonlight invariably) after sunset, in which case, however, the traveller follows the desert-route all the way and sees nothing of the cataract. The rocky nature of the river-bank renders it impossible to skirt the stream during the first half of the distance from Assuân to Philæ. After visiting the quarries, therefore, we follow the above-described desert-route for about 1/2 hr. towards the S., then enter a path diverging to the right (W.), which brings us in about an hour after quitting Assuân to the rocky bank of the river, whose hoarse roar is heard for some time before. Hence we are conducted to the rocks known as the **Bîbân esh-Shellâl**, or 'gates of the cataracts', that with the largest fall being known as *Bâb el-Kebîr* or 'great gate'. Here we may be fortunate enough to see a boat guided through the rapids; but in any case there are always naked young Nubians ready to plunge into the river and allow themselves to be carried down by the foaming stream, either astride of a tree-trunk or floating unsupported in the water, in the manner described long ago by Strabo. The air of course resounds with shouts and requests for bakshish. Those who expect to see a cascade like the falls of the Rhine at Schaffhausen will be disappointed. The foaming and impetuous stream makes noise enough as it dashes through its rocky bed, but there is nothing here in the shape of a regular waterfall. Yet all

---

† These have been copied by *Flinders Petrie* and *Griffith*, and published by the former in his 'Season in Egypt' (1883).

the same, especially when one beholds the placid surface of the
river to the S. of Philæ, one can sympathize with the question of
the linen-clad Achoreus in Lucan: 'Who would have supposed that
thou, Oh gently-flowing Nile, wouldst burst forth with violent
whirlpools into such wild rage?' When the river is high all the
rocks in the bed of the stream are under water; but in February
and March even the smaller rocks are visible: *Inscriptions* are found
on many of these, and on all the cataract-islands, twenty in number.
The smooth glaze, like a dark enamel, which covers the granite-
rocks between this point and Philæ will not escape notice.

A similar effect was noticed by Alexander von Humboldt at the
cataracts of the Orinoco. 'The granite of Assuân', says R. Hartmann,
'like that at the southern cataracts, etc., is distinguished by the remarkably rounded shape of the blocks. These have surfaces as smooth as
glass, and are of a black hue, glistening in the sun, like the flat surface
of a well-used smoothing-iron. The almost spherical shape seems to be
due to the attrition of the detritus washed down by the stream. The
dark colour, which only penetrates a few lines, as is easily seen in detached fragments, is caused by protoxide of iron according to Russegger,
or by silica according to Delesse, precipitated on the stone by the Nile-
water'.

A few yards to the S. of the cataract lie the pleasant villages
of **Mahâdah** and **Shellâl**, shaded by palms and sycamores. In Mahâdah huge piles of dried dates lie in the open air, brought hither
from Nubia for transport to Egypt. At this point begins the passage
of the rapids downstream; and boats (or dhahabîyehs for large parties) may be hired here, if desired, for the safe voyage to Philæ
through a picturesque rocky landscape. A bargain should be struck
before the boat is entered. A small boat costs 10 piastres by tariff;
a dhahabîyeh not less than 10 fr. The boatmen demand much larger
sums at first.

DESCENT OF THE CATARACT IN A SMALL BOAT. This expedition can
hardly be recommended, for even when the river is full it is not un-
attended with danger. H. Brugsch and Ebers both accomplished it. The
latter records that he looks back upon the experience not without pleasure,
especially on account of the extraordinary skill and presence of mind of
the cataract-re'is who steered. He describes the trip as follows. 'I had
two of our own sailors on board, one able-bodied, the other a Nubian
little more than a boy. The old cataract-re'îs was at the helm. The
roar of the cataract was heard beyond the village of Shellâl, and became
louder every minute as we proceeded. The rocks and stones in the river-
bed are reddish brown, but wherever they have been washed by the
stream and then dried by the scorching sun of this latitude, they glisten
like the black surface of an evaporating pond. Behind and before, to
the right and left, above and below, I saw nothing but rocks, little pools,
and the blue sky; while my sense of hearing was as though spell-bound by
the roar of the waters, which as soon as the keel of the boat approached
the rapids proper, lifted up their voice as loud as surf lashing against a
rocky coast in a storm. Then followed some minutes of the most intense
exertion for the crew, who cheered and encouraged themselves by continual invocations to helpful saints, especially to the holy Said, the
rescuer from sudden dangers. With each stroke of the oars broke forth
a 'ya Said' (O Said) or 'ya Mohammed' or 'God is gracious'; while the
arms wielding the oars dared not relax their strength, at it was essential
to keep in the middle of the rapids in order to avoid being hurled against
the rocks. The Arab, who guided the boat, was a sinewy old man over

sixty years of age, who sat with his long neck craning forward so long
as we hovered in danger, and who, with his eyes sparkling with intense
excitement and his lean bird-like face, looked like an eagle on the look
out for prey. All went well at first. Only a man and boy, however,
were rowing on the left side, while two men were rowing on the right.
As we quitted the second rapid and were entering a different channel,
the sailors on the left side had to row with all their strength; that,
however, proved inadequate and the stream swept the boat round, so that
the stern was foremost. This was the culminating point of the passage.
The re'is without losing his presence of mind for an instant, guided the
helm with his foot, while he assisted the rowers with his arms, turned
the boat round once more, brought it into the right channel, and finally
into the less rapid part of the Nile, and so to Assuân. The entire passage
lasted 42 minutes.

FROM MAHÂDAH TO PHILÆ the crooked road skirts the bank of
the river. The village-children pursue the traveller, begging for
bakshîsh. When the path, covered with granite-dust, grows narrower
and begins to lead over smooth granite, the traveller should dismount. The curiously-shaped rocks in the bed and on the bank of the
Nile bear numerous inscriptions. Some of them look as though they
had been built up out of artificially rounded blocks. These forms
seem to have struck the ancient Egyptians most forcibly, for in the
relief of the Source of the Nile at Philæ (p. 294) — one of the few
representations of landscape in Egypt — the river-god crouches
under a pile of blocks like these. In 25 min. we reach a small plain
and obtain a charming view of *Philæ*, the most beautiful spot on
the Nile, and the goal of travellers who do not wish to go on to the
second cataract. The small plain above-mentioned, to the E. of the
island, is shaded with handsome sycamore trees, near which is a
long low building of a semi-European appearance, with battlemented
roof. This is the deserted station of the Roman Catholic missionaries,
who hence founded settlements in Central Africa, all of which, however, including finally that at Kharṭûm, have been
abandoned. The walled island, surrounded by clear
smooth water, presents, with its imposing temple,
graceful kiosque, and flourishing vegetation, a
beautiful contrast to the rugged, bare and precipitous rocks that bound it, especially on the N. and
W. To the N. a massive double rock, with the name
of Psammetikh II. conspicuous upon it, towers
above the rest; to the W. rises the rocky island of
Bigeh (p. 297), with numerous monuments and inscriptions. The ferry-boat is to be found at the
village of Shellâl. Between the railway-station of Shellâl and the
Nile is a fine palm-grove, with the tents of the Egyptian troops
under British command. The handsome dhahabîyeh near the bank
is the residence of the commandant. Breakfast may be obtained on
board, but those who come by rail are recommended to bring their
provisions with them from Assûan.

29. The Island of Philæ.

Both the tourist-steamers and the mail-steamers allow one day for a visit to Philæ. Tourists by the four-weeks steamer may visit the island twice, and they are recommended to do so. Travellers to Nubia who are unable to find time to visit Philæ on the outward journey, should not fail to devote to it at least a few hours on the return, either on the evening of reaching Shellâl, or on the next morning, after spending the night on board the steamer. When more than one visit is paid the traveller should come once by rail, once by land returning by boat. Accommodation at Philæ can only be obtained if a dhahabîyeh happens to be there.

The name of *Philæ* is derived from the old Egyptian, in which it is called, with the article, *Pa-alek* , or usually merely *Alek* 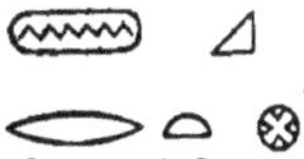. This name occurs thousands of times on the island itself, with many variations, and probably means the island of *Lek, i.e.* of *Ceasing* or of the *End* †, referring to the Nile-voyage hither from the N. The Copts called it *Pilak* or *Pelak*, and the Arabs used to call it *Bilak*. Now-a-days none of these names are known to the natives, who usually call the island *Anas el-Wogûd*, after the hero of one of the tales in the Thousand and One Nights, which has undergone considerable change in the Egyptian version and has its scene transferred to Philæ.

The boatmen relate it as follows. 'Once upon a time there was a king, who had a handsome favourite named *Anas el-Wogûd*, and a vizier, whose daughter was named *Zahr el-Ward*, *i.e.* Flower of the Rose. The two young people saw and fell in love with each other, and found opportunities of meeting secretly, until they were discovered through the imprudence of the maiden's attendant. The vizier was violently enraged and, in order to secure his daughter from the farther pursuit of the young man, despatched her to the island of Philæ, where he caused her to be imprisoned in a strong castle (the temple of Isis) and closely guarded. But Anas el-Wogûd could not forget his love. He forsook the court and wandered far and wide in search of her, and in the course of his travels showed kindness to various animals in the desert and elsewhere. At last a hermit told him that he would find Zahr el-Ward on the island of Philæ. He arrived on the bank of the river and beheld the walls of the castle, but was unable to reach the island, for the water all around it was alive with crocodiles. As he stood lamenting his fate one of the dangerous monsters offered to convey him to the island on his back, out of gratitude for the young man's previous kindness to animals. The lover was thus able to reach the prison of his mistress, and the guards suffered him to remain on the island, as he represented himself to be a persecuted merchant from a distant land. Birds belonging to Zahr el-Ward assured him that she was on the island, but he could never obtain sight of her. Meanwhile the lady also became unable longer to endure her fate. Letting herself down from her prison-window by means of a rope made of her clothes, she found a compassionate ship-master, who conveyed her from the island in which the lover she sought then was. Then followed another period of search and finally the meeting of the lovers. A marriage, with the consent of the father, ends the tale. — The *Osiris Room* on Philæ (p. 295) is regarded by the Arabs as the bridal-chamber. The tale in the

† This meaning belongs to the old Egyptian root *lek*, which is preserved in the Coptic λωϫ.

Arabian Nights ends as follows: 'So they lived in the bosom of happiness to the advanced age, in which the roses of enjoyment shed their leaves and tender friendship must take the place of passion'. †

It seems as though this legend had arisen on Egypt soil, and as though it contained some echoes of the ancient mythology of Philæ, *e.g.* the search of Isis for her beloved Osiris and the disposal of the goddess on an island in the Nile. It is even more remarkable that Anas el-Wogûd reached the island on a crocodile and that on the W. side of the temple of Isis is a relief (p. 294) representing the mummy of Osiris borne by a crocodile.

The rocky island of *Bigeh*, opposite Philæ, seems to have been an even earlier pilgrim-resort than the latter; yet there was probably a temple also on Philæ in comparatively early times. In the 4th cent. B.C. this must have been either unimportant or in ruins, for

the name of *Nekht nebf* Nectanebus II.,

is the oldest name occurring as that of a builder, and that prince reigned as a rival king to the Persian Achæmenides and recognized only by his countrymen, at the date mentioned. The work that he began was zealously continued by the Ptolemies, who had greater resources at command, but even they left ample room for additional buildings and farther decorations at the hands of the Roman emperors down to Diocletian.

The principal temple, like the island itself, was sacred to *Isis*, whose priests resided here down to comparatively late times as a learned college. As one of the graves of Osiris was situated here, it early became a pilgrimage resort for the Egyptians, one of whose solemn oaths also was by the Osiris of Philæ. When the cult of Isis as well as that of Serapis became known to the Hellenes and afterwards to the Romans, many Greek and Italian pilgrims flocked to the shrine of the mysterious, benign, and healing goddess. Even under Ptolemy Physkon the priests were compelled to petition the king to check the superabundant stream of pilgrims, who consumed the temple-stores and threatened to reduce the priests to the necessity of withholding from the gods their bounden offerings (comp. p. 284). On all the walls and columns of the temple are inscriptions, placed there by Greek or Roman officials, tourists, and pilgrims. They are most numerous in the S. part of the temple and in

---

† In the Thousand and One Nights this tale occupies the 371st to the 380th nights. It differs considerably from the versions of the sailors, which moreover vary very much among themselves. The tale of *Anas el-Wogûd* and his mistress *El-Ward* ('the Rose') is the title of a lithographed pamphlet of 34 leaves in which the above story is narrated in verse in the fellâhin dialect (not the literary Arabic). With several other pieces, *e.g.* the 'Cat and the Rats', it supplies the usual material for recitations in the Arab coffee-houses, and is thus universally known. It begins 'I shall build for thee a castle in the midst of the sea (*i.e.* water) of *Kenûs*', *i.e.* Nubia.

THE ISLAND OF PHILÆ.

1 : 3030

Yards

0   100   200   300

Wagner & Debes, Leipzig

Geograph. Inst. von

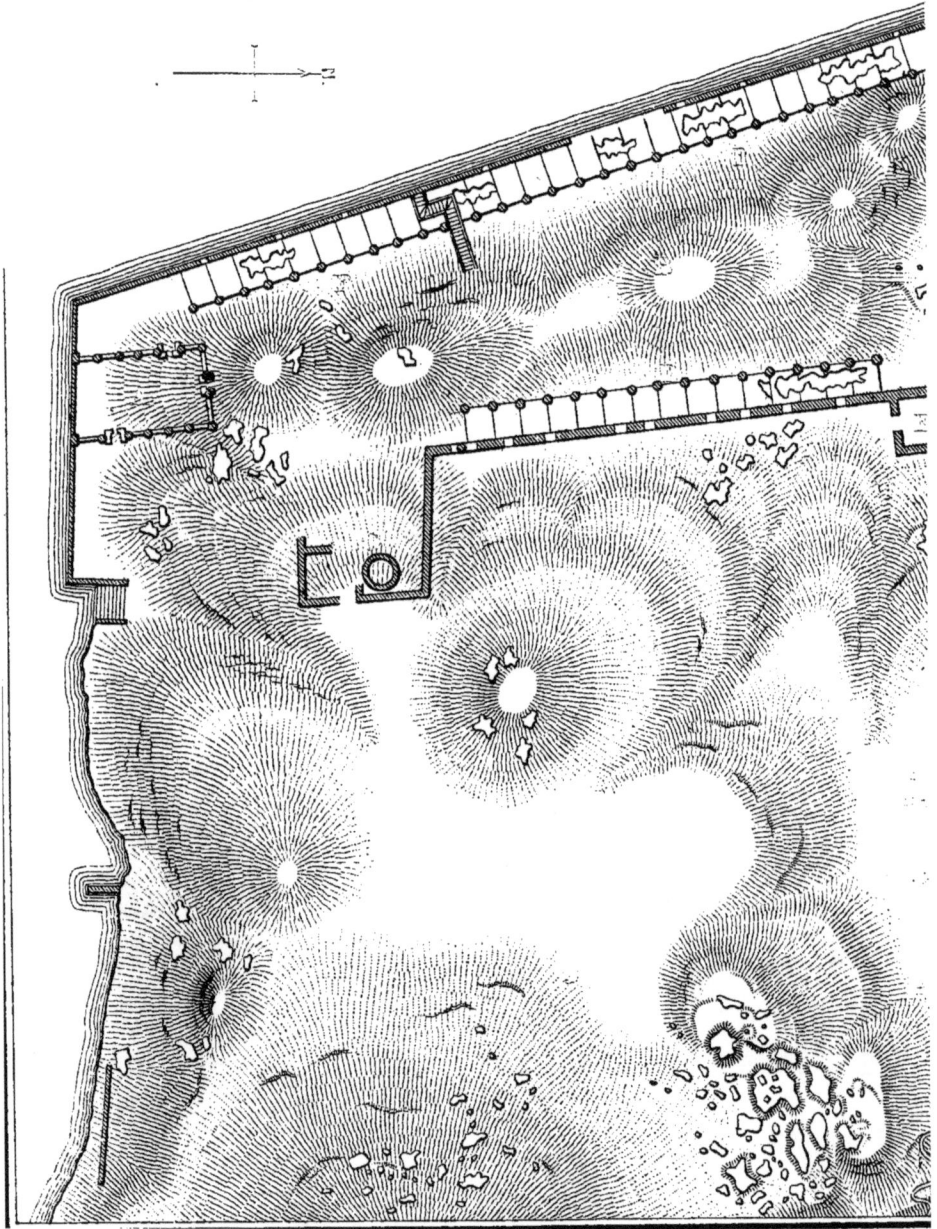

the oldest part, dating from Nectanebus. We know also that the goddess of Philæ was worshipped by the *Blemmyes* (p. 302), who maintained the custom of human sacrifices until the time of Justinian. After Diocletian, who personally visited the island, had conquered these restless children of the desert, he destroyed the fortifications of Philæ, and new temples were erected in which priests of the Blemmyes and *Nobades* were permitted to offer sacrifices to Isis along with the Egyptian priests. And these tribes even obtained the right of removing the miraculous image of the mighty goddess from the island at certain solemn festivals and of retaining it for some time. Even after all Egypt had long been christianized and the Thebaïd was crowded with monks, the ancient pagan-worship still held sway in Nubia, in spite of the Edicts of Theodosius. The Nohades were converted to Christianity about 540 A.D. under the auspices of the Empress Theodora, and shortly afterwards Narses, sent by Justinian to Egypt, closed the temple of Isis on Philæ, and sent its sacred contents to Constantinople. At first the people of Philæ adopted the orthodox creed, but when Egypt was conquered by Islâm, they exchanged this for the monophysite heresy. Although an inscription has been found in the pronaos in praise of a Bishop Theodorus (577 A.D.), who dedicated a portion at least of the temple of Isis to St. Stephen, it is doubtful whether Philæ was ever an episcopal seat. It is certain, however, that Christian services were held in the hypostyle. The inscriptions and reliefs were plastered over with Nile-mud or had crosses carved upon them, so as to spare the feelings of the faithful and to exorcise the evil spirits. — Like Christianity, Islâm was late in finding its way to Philæ, and there is not a trace of a mosque or anything of that nature on the entire island. Nubia was effectually conquered in the 13th cent. by the Egyptian sultans, who included the cataract-region in their private domains, and thus secured the temples from destruction. — Philæ was described in 1737 by *Norden* and *Pococke*, though at that time the natives were as hostile to strangers as they are now friendly and obliging.

Isis, the chief deity of the island, is usually represented in the triad completed by Osiris and Horus, but she frequently also appears alone. Everywhere, in her various forms, she occupies the foremost place, just as Hathor does at Denderah. The deities of Philæ include Ra and Menth, the twin-gods Shu and Tefnut, Seb and Nut, Osiris-Unnofer (Agathodæmon) and Isis, Khnum and Sati, the gods of the cataracts, Horus the son of Isis, Hathor, and the child Horus. Thoth, Safekh, and other deities also frequently appear.

Philæ is the pearl of Egypt, and those who have several days to spend at the cataract, should certainly take up their abode upon it. It is 420 yds. long, 150 yds. wide at the broadest part, and has a circumference of 980 yds. It is uninhabited, but an old watchman,

who lives with his children and grandchildren on Bigeh, willingly
assists travellers. The view of Philæ from the river-bank is un-
expectedly beautiful, especially to those who have just quitted the
rugged rocks of the cataract or the arid desert; while, on the other
hand, the views from the island, especially from its rocky S. end,
are imposing and sometimes peculiarly wild.

The buildings on the island which demand a visit are: 1. The
* *Temple of Isis;* 2. The *Chapel of Hathor;* 3. The *Ruins* and the
Portal of Diocletian, in the N.W.; and 4. The **Kiosque. — Bigeh*
and the *Cataract Islands* also repay a visit.

The Temple of Isis.

This beautiful structure dates from various periods, and its
different parts show an almost capricious irregularity in their positions with reference to each other. The traveller is recommended
to visit the various portions in the following order, but he is warned
against lingering too long over any of them, if his time be limited
or if his inspection have no special scientific aim. It is better to
obtain a good general impression from the whole, than to examine
the details minutely. In order to understand the arrangement of
the temple, it must not be forgotten that it was preëminently a
pilgrim-resort. The processions of pilgrims, whether they approached from Egypt or from Nubia, were compelled to steer for
the S. end of the island, for the rocks to the N. of it prevented
anything like a ceremonial approach. The portals of the temple
therefore faced the S., and the festal boats disembarked their passengers on the S. coast. We likewise begin our visit from the S.,
or more exactly from the extreme S.W., to which we proceed
direct from the landing-place. Our attention is first attracted by
the strong erection of hewn stones facing the stream. The steps of
a *Stone Staircase* within the quay-wall are still to be seen on the
S.W. coast; and there was another staircase on the S. coast, to the
E. of the building of Nectanebus.

a. The **Building of Nectanebus** (Pl. A). Two *Obelisks* flanked
the entrance to the hypæthral *Fore-Court,* which the pilgrim entered
first, and where he was received, and perhaps also examined and
taxed. With the exception of the central portion of the first pylon
(p. 287), dating from this same king, Nectanebus II., this is the
oldest part of the whole temple. The obelisks, made of sandstone,
instead of the usual granite, were small and stood upon stone chests.
The W. obelisk is still standing, but the E. obelisk is represented
by its chest merely.

The E. obelisk itself was found prostrate by Bankes in 1815, and at
his request removed to Alexandria by Belzoni, despite the protests of
Drovetti who regarded it as his private property. From Alexandria it
was taken to England, where it now stands at Kingston Hall in Dorset-
shire. On the lowest part of the pedestal is a long Greek inscription
containing a petition addressed by the priests of Isis to King Euergetes II.

and his two wives, against the expense caused by the too frequent visits
of royal officials and their retinues, which impoverished the temple.
Above this are two other inscriptions, only fragments of which are preserved, in which the granting of the petition by the king and the con-
sequent royal decree are announced.

This obelisk has been of the greatest importance for the interpretation
of the Egyptian hieroglyphics. The names of Ptolemy Euergetes and
Cleopatra, which occur in Greek on the pedestal, were discovered by
Champollion in 1822 on the obelisk itself, and from the latter name he
was enabled to add a few more alphabetical signs to those already ascertained from the Rosetta decree (Vol. I., p. 111).

The *W. Obelisk*, as we have said, remains *in situ* though it has
lost its point. Upon it is inscribed, in Greek, a petition from Theo-
dotos, son of Agesiphon, to Isis and her fellow-gods, dating from the
time of Neos Dionysus. There are also some Arabic inscriptions.

The hypæthral vestibule was bounded on each side (E. and W.)
by six columns and one of the obelisks. The six W. columns are
still standing, but only three stumps of the E. row remain. Between
the columns were screen-walls, half as high as the shafts, and
adorned with concave cornices and balustrades of Uræus-serpents.
The columns, only $2^1/_6$ ft. in thickness, are $15^1/_3$ ft. high, and have
calyx-capitals supporting an abacus decorated with the Hathor-
mask, on which rests a small chapel. These capitals, which resemble those of the Ptolemaic epoch, are specially remarkable, as
they were erected by Nectanebus *before* the period of the Lagidæ.
Nectanebus who maintained himself for some time in opposition to
the Persian kings, appears to have delighted in comparing himself
to the ancient Pharaohs, as we may gather from his first name *Ra-
kheper-ka*, which was also that of Usertesen I. of the 12th Dyn.;
and it is possible that he adopted, in the same spirit, old and forgotten artistic forms in his erections. It is certain that the Hathor-
mask at the top of the columns is only found earlier than his time
on the monuments of the 18th Dyn. at Dér el-baḥri (p. 223) and
el-Kâb (p. 236). The architects of the Ptolemies were afterwards attracted by the abacus adorned with the countenance of the goddess
of Denderah, adopted it, and farther developed the sculptured calyx-
capital, here first introduced by Nectanebus. — On the W. and E.
sides of each of the six standing columns are dedication-inscriptions.
On the outer (W.) side of the most southerly column (next to the
obelisk) is the inscription: 'The good god, lord of both worlds,
Ra-kheper-ka, son of the sun and lord of the diadems, Nectanebus,
the ever-living, erected this sumptuous building for his mother
Isis, the bestower of life, in order to enlarge her dwelling with excellent work, for time and for eternity'. — On the outer side of the
third column the name of Philæ appears as *Alek* (with the
article, *P-alek*), a form found at many other places, and the mistress
of the island is named as ,

Isis, the life giving goddess of *Aab*, *i.e.* of *Abaton* or the holy island. The last name deserves mention here, for the spot known to
the ancients as Abaton, which must have been peculiarly holy in
their eyes, is named innumerable times in the inscriptions of the
temple of Isis. It must therefore be looked for on Philæ itself. The
inscription on the *Architrave* of the outer or *West Side* states that
the king erected this building for his mother Isis, and that he rebuilt the hall for her of good white hewn stone, surrounded with
columns, with inscriptions throughout its whole extent, and, as the
line below the architrave adds, painted in colours. The inner side
of the architrave bears an invocation to Isis, mother of the gods.

This little temple had doors on the E. and W. sides, not,
however, opposite to each other, and another on the N. side, next
the main temple. The last leads into a spacious *Fore-Court*
(Pl. B), enclosed on the right and left by covered *Colonnades*. The
W. colonnade (Pl. F) follows the bank of the river, while that to
the E. or right (Pl. D) runs in the direction of the centre of the
first great pylon, but not at right angles to it, affording an example
of the variety of axial direction exhibited throughout the temple.

When we remember that a portion of the first pylon and the
hypæthral space, which we have just quitted, were built by Nectanebus, and that all the other parts of the temple are of later data,
we have an adequate explanation of the great irregularity displayed
in its plan. It is quite certain that the structures that now bear
the name of Nectanebus (a portal and a vestibule) were not the
only buildings on Philæ under that king, for the construction of
every temple, without exception, began with the sanctuary and
ended with the doors. We may assume that an extensive temple
stood here before its removal by the Persians; and that the latter
largely destroyed the works of their rival. The parts that were
spared were then incorporated by the Ptolemaic builders, while the
Romans united the work of the Lagidæ with the ancient vestibule
of Nectanebus by means of the tapering peristyle court.

b. **The Colonnaded Court.** This space is bounded on the W.
side by a long wall, pierced here and there with windows, which,
based on a firm substructure on the river-bank, forms the back of
a narrow, but unusually long *Colonnade* (Pl. F; 100 yds.). The
latter, built under the Romans, has a row of 31 (formerly 32) columns, each 16 ft. high, on its E. side, and has a roof of good cas-
setted work. The colour of the hieroglyphics and representations
is still remarkably vivid in various places, especially in the S. portion near the vestibule of Nectanebus. There appear Nero with his
cartouches, Claudius Cæsar and Germanicus Autocrator before
Horus, Tasentnefert and Pinebtati (who also appears at Ombos,
p. 261) worshipping the lord of Ombos. Farther to the N., on the
back wall of the colonnade are the name of Tiberius and a fine
Greek inscription, beginning Ἀμμώνιος Διονυσίου εὐχὴν ἐποί-

ησε, etc. The translation of the latter is as follows: 'Ammonius, son of Dionysius, fulfilled a vow made to Isis, Serapis, and the gods worshipped along with them, by presenting to them the worship of his brother Protas and his children, of his brother Niger, his wife Klidemas, and his children Dionysius and Anubas. On the 12th Payni of the 31st year of Cæsar'. — This Cæsar is Cæsar Augustus, in whose reign therefore the wall, though furnished with inscriptions by later emperors, must have existed at least in a rough state. The other inscriptions are of similar purport.

At the S. end of the *E. Colonnade* (Pl. D) was a large *Hall* (Pl. C), of which only fragments of the N. and E. walls remain. It bears the name of Tiberius. The colonnade, which adjoins its N. wall, was never entirely completed. Only three of the capitals of the columns (including a very fine palm-capital) are finished; the rest are merely roughly blocked out, but they are of interest as showing us that the more elaborate carving was not taken in hand until after the capitals had been placed in position upon the shafts. The E. colonnade does not extend as far as the first pylons, but is separated from them by a small *Temple of Æsculapius*, the Egyptian Imhotep, son of Ptah (Pl. E), consisting of two chambers, and facing the S. The Greek inscription over the entrance dates from Ptolemy V. Epiphanes, his wife, and son, the Egyptian cartouches on the door itself from Ptolemy IV. Philopator.

— The W. colonnade which skirts the river, is joined on the N. by a narrow passage (Pl. a), which leads past the pylons at some distance to the left (W.). The peristyle court, for which fore-court would be a more accurate name, is thus by no means enclosed by the pylons.

c. The **First Pylon** (Pl. H) turned towards the approaching processions two lofty and broad *Towers*, with a narrow *Portal* between them. This portal, built and adorned by Nectanebus II., is the oldest part of the pylon. The smaller portal, to the left, like the temple behind it (*Birth-house*, see p. 289), which stands in relation with it, dates from Ptolemy VII. Philometor ; while the decoration of the façade was added by Ptolemy XIII. Neos Dionysus. Within the chief portal appears also Ptolemy X. Soter II., with his mother and wife, presenting to Isis the symbol of a field. The entire imposing erection is 150 ft. broad and 60 ft. high. The S. façade, fronting the processions advancing from the Nile, is covered with *Reliefs en creux*.

At each side of the *Central Doorway* (Pl. b) is a figure of Isis. On the upper part of the left tower is the *Pharaoh* sacrificing to Osiris and Isis, and to Isis and Horus; on the corresponding part of the right tower, he appears before Horus and Nephthys, and before Isis and Horus. The lower parts of the towers are devoted as usual to military scenes. The Pharaoh (Neos Dionysus, 59 B.C.) appears as the smiter of his enemies;

to the right, Isis with Hor-hut presents him with the staff of victory. Half of the figures have been deliberately defaced.

The *Ascent of the Pylons*, commanding an excellent view of the whole island and its surrounding, is made from the peristyle court entered by the central portal. Within this portal, to the right, is the following *Inscription*: 'L'an 6 de la république, le 13 messidor. Une armée française commandée par Bonaparte est descendue à Alexandrie. L'armée ayant mis 20 jours après les mammelouks en fuite *aux Pyramides*, Desaix commandant la première division les a poursuivies au delà des cataractes où il est arrivé le 13 ventose de l'an 7'. (*i.e.* March 3, 1799). Then follow the names of the brigadier-generals. — The staircase leading to the top of the *East Tower* begins in the small chamber (Pl. c), in the S.E. corner of the peristyle court. It ascends gradually, round a square newel. Several unadorned chambers, probably used for the storing of astronomical instruments and for the use of astrologers, are to be found within the tower. They are feebly lighted by window-openings, decreasing in size towards the outside wall. — The *West Tower* can only be reached from the E. tower. The crosses on the stones of the roof formerly held braces of wood or iron.

Two *Obelisks* and two *Lions*, all of granite, formerly stood before the entrance. The foot of the W. obelisk is all that remains of the former; the latter lie much damaged on the ground. Numerous *Greek Inscriptions* have been carved here by pilgrims. — Adjoining the S.E. side of the pylon is the beautiful *Gateway* (Pl. G) of Ptolemy II. Philadelphus, who appears on its E. side. On its W. wall, to the right and left, is the emperor Tiberius, above, Philadelphus.

d. **The Inner Peristyle** (Pl. I), bounded on the S. by Pylon H., is bounded on the N. by another *Pylon* (Pl. K). These, however, are by no means parallel to each other, while the edifices to the E. and W. of the peristyle are so entirely different, that it is at once apparent that the court was not constructed according to any preconceived plan. The requirements of the moment and the available space were taken into account, not any artistic considerations. Nevertheless this court, entirely enclosed by buildings of the most varied forms, must be described as unusually effective. On the E. and W. are two oblong edifices, each with columns on the side next the court. That to the W. (left) is a distinct temple, forming a kind of peripteros; that to the E. was used by the priests. This court, which is mostly uneven, contains one spot excellently adapted for the pitching of a tent. Cook's parties usually lunch here; if there are more than one party at the same time, the second lunches in the kiosque (Pl. R).

e. **The Temple** to **the W. of the Peristyle** (Pl. L) stands immediately behind the left (W.) wing of the first pylon, and a doorway in the latter (p. 287) lies exactly opposite the S. *Entrance Door* (Pl. d) of the temple, from which it is separated only by a narrow open passage. At the N. end of the colonnade on the side of the temple next the court is a side-entrance. The S. door admits to a *Pronaos* with 4 columns, of which two are engaged in the portal. Beyond lies a *Cella* with three chambers, surrounded on three sides by a colonnade. This temple was founded by Pto-

lemy VII. Philometor, and most of its decorations were due to Ptolemy IX. Euergetes II., though the later Lagidæ and Tiberius also
contributed a share.

The vestibule here is loftier than the other rooms of the cella. The
entrance was adorned by Philometor, but the numerous interior reliefs
represent Tiberius before the different deities of the temple. The carefully
elaborated doorway at the back of the pronaos dates from Euergetes II.
The first room is quite unadorned. Above the door to the second room
is a window, bordered on each side by two Hathor-masks. Tiberius is
named several times on the walls, which have been partly plastered over
with mud. The early Christians, who perhaps used the second room for
purposes connected with their services, have entirely plastered over the
heathen *Inscriptions* there; while the highly interesting *Representations* in
the third room have been left quite untouched. From these we learn that
the temple was intended to represent the **Birth-House** or *Meshen*, in
which the infant Horus first saw the light (similar buildings at Denderah,
Edfu, etc., pp. 80, 253). The reliefs on the rear wall are in two sections.
The lower series represents the *Birth of Horus*, who is introduced into
life by Ammon, Thoth, and other gods. In the upper row we see Horus
ascending from a huge bunch of lotus-flowers, and beside him the serpent
coiling round a column adorned with lotus-flowers, beneath which kneel
two forms, covered with the Uræus-hood. The allegorical meaning of
this latter composition is obscure. On the W. wall of the chamber is
a *Goddess* (head destroyed), offering the breast to the new-born child, and
close by is *Hathor*, the good fairy of Egyptian nurseries, placing her
left hand in benediction on the head of Horus, and holding his arm
with her right. King Ptolemy IX. Euergetes II. is depicted handing
to her two metal-mirrors 'to rejoice the golden one with the sight of her
beautiful form'. — These representations do not only celebrate the mystic
birth of the god, they refer also to the most beautiful and most responsible
duties of motherhood, which Isis, Hathor, and Nephthys undertake. Their
nursling appears indeed to be the infant Horus, but it is evident from
many allusions, that the young Pharaoh, the heir to the throne of Ra,
was considered as the incarnation in human form of the young god, and
that these representations were meant to convey to the Ptolemies that a deity
had borne and suckled them or their first-born, and that the immortals
had guided their upbringing with invisible hands. Cleopatra I., the mother
of the two brothers who caused the placing of this inscription, had acted
as guardian and regent especially during the childhood of Philometor, the
elder. She was the Isis of the young Horus. On the E. outside wall of
the cella a relief shows us Horus learning from the goddess of the N.
to play on the nine-stringed lute, while Isis superintends the lesson. The
shape of the instrument is Greek, and by the goddess of the north is
perhaps meant Hellenic music, which was cultivated even by the earlier
Lagidae.

All the *Inscriptions* here date from Tiberius, who is named 'Autokrator
Kisres' on the E. side and 'Tiberius' on the W. side. A double votive-
inscription of the same date proves that the former phrase applies to
Tiberius.

The columns of the *Colonnades* on the W. and N. sides of the
cella exhibit genuine Ptolemaic capitals with a very high abacus.
On the N. side (Pl. f) is the peculiar but elegant capital, found
only on Philæ, consisting of a bunch of papyrus-buds, supporting
the abacus on their tips. Screen-walls, more than half as high as
the shafts, connect the columns. The most conspicuous columns are
the seven on the side of the temple next the court. These have
finely sculptured Ptolemaic capitals, surmounted by a cubical aᵣ
cus with Hathor-masks and chapels. The *Architrave* above, adorᵣ

with the concave cornice and astragal, exhibits an unusually fine inscription, carved in the grand style, of which a duplicate occurs on the architrave of the E. colonnade opposite. This *Dedication-Inscription* records that Ptolemy IX. Euergetes II. Physkon (with numerous titles) and his wife Cleopatra, princess and mistress of both worlds, the Euergetæ (divine benefactors), loved the life-giving Isis, the mistress of Abaton, the queen of the island of Philæ and the mistress of the S. lands. The king and the queen, Philadelphi (divine brothers), Euergetæ, Philopatores, Epiphanes, Eupatores, and Philometores, erected and restored this beautiful monument, that it might be a festal hall for his (the king's) mother Usert-Hathor, etc., and a scene of joyful excitement, *Tekh*, for the mistress of Philæ, that she might settle in it, etc. The above list of Ptolemaic surnames is especially important.

At the top of the left colonnade, next the first pylon, are some demotic and hieroglyphic *Decrees*, of the 21st year of Ptolemy Epiphanes, one relating to the celebration of the suppression of a revolt and the punishment of the rebels, the other in honour of Cleopatra, wife of Epiphanes. These inscriptions, of great scientific value though extremely lightly and almost illegibly carved, were discovered by Lepsius in 1843. Unfortunately they have been much injured by figures carved over them under Neos Dionysus. An upper story of Nile bricks, now in ruins, was built at some later period on the roof of this peripteral temple. It is entirely out of place and should be removed.

f. **The Building on the E. side of the Peristyle** (Pl. M), mentioned on p. 288, lies opposite the birth-house, and presents a long *Colonnade* of 10 columns, with elaborate capitals, towards the court. In the rear-wall of this colonnade is first, to the left, a large doorway, leading through a vestibule to the outside of the temple, and then three lesser doors leading into three small chambers, partly devoted to scientific purposes. At the S. end, close to the pylon, is a fifth door, admitting to a room now half in ruins. To the left of this room is another chamber (Pl. 1; see below), and straight on is the *Staircase* (Pl. m) leading to the rooms on the upper story. Some of the latter are tolerably spacious, but have no inscriptions; whereas the lower story and the columns were adorned with hieroglyphics by Ptolemy XIII. Neos Dionysus. The *Inscriptions* in the various rooms are due to Tiberius, to whom Philæ in general is much indebted.

The most interesting rooms on the E. side of the peristyle court are first that into which the door nearest the pylon and leading to the staircase admits us, and secondly that to the right of the large doorway. Both are without windows. Inscriptions on the door-posts inform us of the purpose of these rooms. The first (Pl. l) was the *Laboratory*, in which was prepared the excellent incense known as **Kyphi**, which must have been used in great quantities for the services of the gods. The names and the proportionate quantities (in figures) of the drugs used in its preparation are recorded on the door-posts. The interior has no inscriptions. The other (entered by the fourth door from the pylon) is, on the other hand, very rich in inscriptions. This small room, extremely elegantly adorned with sculptures by the orders of Tiberius (here named 'Autokrator Kisres'), was the *Library* (Pl. h); and on the right door-post is the legend: 'This is the library-room ⬚⟋ of the gracious Sa-fekh, goddess of history, the room for preserving the writings of the life-bestowing Isis'.

The representations over the door must have been specially objection-able to the Christians, for they have all been carefully chiselled out. On the left side of the chamber itself is a recess like a wall-cupboard, in which perhaps the most precious rolls were preserved. Beneath is a life-like relief of a cynocephalus (the sacred animal of Thoth-Hermes) writing a papyrus-scroll. Here as usual the Pharaoh (Tiberius) is depicted receiving the blessings of life in symbols from the deities upon whom he had be-stowed gifts; on the right wall he appears before Isis and Horus, on the back-wall before Isis. Between the emperor and the goddess in the latter scene stands an altar, beneath which are two swine, as the sacrificial animals. On the left wall, over the above-mentioned recess, are the sacred ibis of Thoth, Ma, the goddess of truth with the palette and the chisel in her hand, Tefnut, and Safekh; on the door-wall is Khunsu, here named the 'sacred ibis of Philæ' and thus placed entirely on an equality with Thoth. On the right wall, opposite, is the cow-headed Hest, mother of the gods, with two vessels with handles, before Osiris, Isis, and Horus.

The next door to the left, higher than the others, leads into a room (Pl. g), named '*Chambre de Tibère*' by Champollion, because Tiberius is represented sacrificing to the gods on both the side-walls and over the door, on the outside, while in the second row on the right he appears again before the Nubian god ⟨⟩ Arhesnefer. Above are dedicatory inscriptions by Euergetes II. and Cleopatra his wife, who appear on the door entering from the colonnade.

Returning once more to the colonnade, we find another door at its N. end (Pl. n). Here, an inscription informs us, stood the door-keepers entrusted with the purification of those entering the temple. The lions on the outside wall were also named in an in-scription 'temple-guards', though symbolically only. — Outside the temple M., in the direction of Bigeh, a *Nilometer* was discovered by Capt. Handcock in 1886.

g. The Second Pylon (Pl. k), standing at an obtuse angle with the E. colonnade, encloses the peristyle court on the N. It is smaller (105 ft. wide, 40 ft. high) and in poorer preservation than the first pylon. An inner staircase ascends to the W. pylon, whence we proceed across the ruined roof to the E. pylon. To reach the top of the W. pylon, we ascend the staircase to the Osiris-rooms (p. 295), and then proceed leaving these on the right. The ascent of the first pylon (p. 288) is, however, preferable in every respect. On the front of the E. wing facing the peristyle court is a semi-circular *Stele* of reddish brown granite, erected to commemorate a lavish grant of lands, by which Ptolemy VII. Philometor (94 B.C.) enriched the temple. It was inscribed on the polished rear-wall of a monolithic chapel built into the pylon. The king, however, seems merely to have granted to the priests a new lease of the ancient property of the goddess. On the pylon are some *Colossal Figures.* To the right is King Neos Dionysus holding his enemies by the hair, before Horsiisi and Hathor; beneath, smaller representations. To the left the king appears before Osiris and Isis. The grooves for the flag-staffs should also be noted. The *Portal* (Pl. p) to the temple proper, approached by a shallow flight of steps, was built by Euergetes II. in imitation of the portal of Nectanebus in the first pylon. Within it the predecessors of the builder are recounted.

The **Temple of Isis** proper, entered by this portal, was built according to an independent plan, embracing a hypostyle, a pronáos with various divisions, and a sanctuary, with two side-rooms. Ptolemy II. Philadelphus was the founder of this temple, to whose decoration the hostile brothers Philometor and Euergetes II. (Physkon) contributed most largely. It was only natural that both the weak but amiable Philometor and the vicious but energetic Physkon should interest themselves in the sanctuary of Isis, for both were much interested in retaining Nubia. We are aware that the former maintained a military station to the S. of Philæ, which afterwards grew into the town of *Parembole* (p. 305). Later Ptolemies are also named here. We refrain from a closer examination of the reliefs and inscriptions in this temple, though they are not uninteresting from a mythological point of view, contenting ourselves with a reference to the detailed p n ' of the Ptolemaic temples at Denderah (p. 80) and Edfu (p. 24)scri tio s

h. The **Hypostyle** (Pl. N) contains ten columns arranged in three rows. The second and third rows contain each two columns to the right and two to the left; while the first row has only the two corner-columns, the space between them being left uncovered for the sake of light. The hall thus consists properly speaking of two portions: an uncovered fore-court with two doors, on the right and left, leading to the outside of the temple, and a covered part behind. The columns are $24\frac{1}{2}$ ft. high and $13\frac{3}{4}$ ft. in circumference. The uncovered portion could be shaded from the sun by means of a velarium; the holes for the cords are still visible in the upper part of the concave cornice turned towards the second pylon. The colouring of this hall, which has been preserved on the ceiling and the columns, must have been very brilliant. The *Capitals* are the most instructive of all the specimens that have come down to us of the manner in which the Egyptians coloured their columns.

Sky-blue, light-green, and a light and a dark shade of red are the prevailing colours; but these were distributed according to conventional rules. Although vegetable forms are imitated with admirable fidelity, the artists did not shrink from colouring them with complete disregard to nature, simply because ancient convention demanded it. Light-green palm-twigs receive blue ribs, and blue flowers have blue, red, or yellow petals. Below the annuli on the shaft is a kind of band (found also elsewhere), indicating that the vegetable forms surrounding the core of the capital were supposed to be firmly bound to the top of the shaft. The height and ornamentation of the lower parts of the shafts are the same in all the columns; but the capitals, some of which are beautiful palm-capitals, are varied.

On the *Ceiling* are astronomical representations. The entire hall bears the inscriptions of Ptolemy IX. Euergetes II.—Above the door in the back wall leading to the pronaos is a long *Inscription*, carved over the hieroglyphics by the Italian Expedition of 1841. The Christian successors of the priests of Isis have cut numerous Coptic crosses in the walls to signalize their appropriation of the temple and to guard against the cunning malice of the heathen deities. Christian services were celebrated in this hall. A Greek inscription in the doorway to the pronaos, on the right, records that the good work (probably the plastering up of the reliefs and the preparation of the hall for Christian worship) took place under the abbot Theodorus. This was in the reign of Justinian.

i. The Chambers of the Pronaos. The three successive rooms of the pronaos date from Ptolemy II. Philadelphus. The *First Room* (Pl. r) was adjoined on each side by others. That on the right, now destroyed, was connected with a *Second Room* (Pl. s), on the E. wall of which Philadelphus is shewn presenting a great offering to his mother Isis. In the room to the left (Pl. t), in which the staircase to the roof starts, Philadelphus appears before Isis and before Hathor. The next room to the left is a dark chamber. Right round the foot of the wall in the following wide *Third Room* (Pl. u), immediately before the sanctuary, runs a list of nomes. The doors on the right and left of this room admit to long, narrow, dark apartments, perhaps used as *Treasure-Chambers*. The entrance to that on the left (Pl. w) is about 2 ft. from the ground. The visitor should enter, strike a light, and inspect the sculptures in this chamber which resembles a huge stone chest. The lower part of the wall is smooth, as it was concealed by the treasures stored here; but higher up Ptolemy II. Philadelphus caused the walls to be adorned with elegant reliefs and inscriptions.

On the rear-wall is represented Ra enthroned on the symbol of gold . At the S. end of the W. wall Ptolemy Philadelphus appears kneeling and holding in his arms the large chest of gold, which he presented to the temple of Isis; and the same scene is repeated on the W. wall. In the former case the king wears the crown of Lower Egypt , in the latter that of Upper Egypt .—The inscriptions explain that the Pharaoh came to the goddess bringing to her gold to her content, and that the mistress of Philæ granted him superabundance of everything, all gifts of plants and fruits that the earth produces, and placed the whole world in contentment. — Similar representations (offerings of bags of gold and bright-coloured garments) occur in the chamber to the right (Pl. *v*), which is in communication with Room *s.*

In the ADYTUM (Pl. O) is a small *Chapel* formed of a single stone, with the names of Euergetes I. and Berenice II. (which also occur in the room on the left). But as the inscriptions on the walls attest, this, the oldest part of the inner temple, dates from the time of Ptolemy II. Philadelphus. In the rear-wall of the cella is a crypt. In the room to the right of the adytum is a subterranean floor, with Nile gods and the young prince; above, Philadelphus before Isis and Harpocrates (Horpekhrud).

k. **The Building to the W. of the Hypostyle** (Pl. P) is reached by quitting the hypostyle by the first door on the W., (to our left as we enter). It consists of a ruined *Cella* and a chamber, in fairly good preservation, facing the river. On the S. wall are some remarkable representations. Horus receives the water of life from Isis and Nephthys. The goddess of history behind Isis, and Thoth behind Nephthys write the name of the royal builder on a palm-branch, at the end of which waves the sign of festivals, composed of the hieroglyphs of life, endurance, and power.

Ma holds in her hand the sail, the symbol of new life. Here also is an *Isis*, who has been converted into a St. Mary. — The handsome *Portal* (Pl. x), built by Hadrian, bears on the right and left, the secret symbols of Osiris. Over the door, to the left, is a small representation of the *Island of Philæ*. On one side appear the cliffs of Bigeh, on the other the pylons of Philæ. In a square between these is a highly remarkable relief. At the bottom is a Croco*dile bearing on its back the mummy of Osiris*, from which flowers spring (comp. the legend of Anas el-Wogûd, p. 281). Above appears the risen Osiris,

Source of the Nile.

enthroned with the young Harpocrates, in a disc before which stands Isis. Above the whole the sun appears on the left and the moon to the right, with stars between them; adjacent are a large and two smaller pylons. On the N. wall, close to the room lying nearest the river, is the famous *Representation of the Source of the Nile*, already mentioned in Vol. I., p. 135. Bigeh (Senem), one of the cataract islands, is here depicted, with a cave in its lowest part. In this crouches the Nile, guarded by a serpent, and

pouring water from two vases. On the summit of the rocky source
of the waters are a vulture (Muth) and a hawk (Horus), gazing into
the distance and keeping watch. This is almost the only landscape
hitherto discovered on any Egyptian monument. The inscription
is in these words: 'the very remote and very sacred, who rises in
Bigeh (Senem)'.

On the front of this little temple, to the left, is a *Demotic Inscription*
in red letters, in which Aurelius Antoninus Pius and Lucius Verus are
mentioned with their titles derived from conquered provinces. The
Cartouches of these late emperors occur also on the walls of the temple;
and on the outside of the W. wall are numerous inscriptions, chiefly
demotic.

1. The great **Outside Walls of the Temple** are covered with
Inscriptions; to the left (W.) by Tiberius, to the right (E.) by
Autokrator Kisres (perhaps Augustus or even Tiberius again). The
most noteworthy is a *List of Nomes,* of great importance for the
geography of the ancient Egyptians (Vol. I., p. 31). On the W. wall
are the nomes of Lower Egypt, on the E. wall, near the foot, those
of Upper Egypt. Other lists are found within the temple.

m. The *Osiris Room, remarkably interesting on account of
the sculptures which cover its walls, is found as follows. Returning
to the second room (Pl. t) of the pronaos we pass through the door
on its W. side (next the Nile), and immediately to the right see
a *Portal* (still in the temple), leading to a *Staircase* which we ascend. A second staircase then leads to the roof of the cella. Here
we turn towards the S. and finally descend some stone steps to a
doorway built over with Nile bricks. The *Vestibule* is interesting.
Hapi (the Nile) lets milk trickle from his breast and Horus pours
the water of life, ⎯⊙⎯⊙⎯⊙ , over Osiris, who lies in the
shape of a mummy upon a bier. Twenty-eight lotus-plants sprout
from him, referring perhaps to the 28 days of the month, or the
28 ells of the maximum height of the Nile at Elephantine, or to
the 14 scattered and reunited parts of his body.

The 'sprouting' of the dead into new life is a conception frequently
made use of, even with regard to the passing away of mankind. In the
Book of the Dead are the passages 'I have accomplished the great path
(in the boat of the sun), my flesh sprouts', 'He has become a god forever,
after his flesh acquired quickening power in the underworld'.

At the resurrection of Osiris all the spirits are present who play a
part in the Egyptian doctrine of immortality. They here appear in long
rows on the walls of the sacred chamber. The risen Osiris is adorned
with all the insignia of his dignity as a ruler of the underworld.

On the left door-post of the Osiris room are three *Greek Inscriptions,*
of which the longest dates from the 165th year of Diocletian (449 A.D.)
and another (very short) from the 169th year of Diocletian (453 A.D.).
From these it is evident that the pagan worship of Isis and Osiris was
practised here down to a late period. The votive inscriptions were composed by the proto-stolistes Smetkhen and his brother Smet.

A few smaller edifices still remain to be visited. To the N. are
the ruins of a *Christian Church,* into which have been built fragments of an earlier structure of Tiberius. Here also is an inverted

Naos, dating from Ptolemy and Cleopatra.—If we quit the hypostyle of the temple of Isis proper by the small portal in its E. wall between the first row of columns and the second pylon, we see about 50 paces in front of us the **Chapel of Hathor** (Pl. Q), the smallest temple on the island. That it was especially dedicated to Hathor we learn from hieroglyphic inscriptions

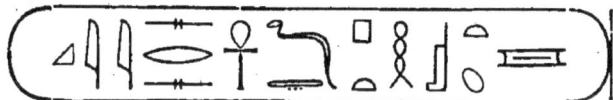

of the time of the emperor Augustus, and from the Greek inscription ΙΕΡΤΙΑ ΕΠΟΙΗϹΕΝ — ΤΗ — ΑΦΡΩΔΕΙΤΗ, 'Hiertia directed (a prayer) to Aphrodite (Hathor)'.† The fact that the rear wall of this chapel has no inscriptions and the ruins behind it indicate that it was once joined to some larger edifice. At the entrance stand two Ptolemaic columns, with a doorway between them, the side-posts of which, unconnected with each other at the top, reach to the bands below the capitals. This doorway is built up, and it is probable that the single apartment within the temple was used as a dwelling, as its walls are much blackened.

Within appear Ptolemy VII. Philometor and Euergetes II. with Cleopatra; and also over the entrance. On the S. side is the emperor before Hathor and Horsamtaui, and before Khnum and Hathor; ou the N. side before Osiris and Isis. Beneath was a geographical inscription.

The Kiosque.

A few minutes bring us from the chapel of Hathor to the elegant and airy *Pavilion* (Pl. R), frequently called '*Pharaoh's Bed*', one of the chief decorations of the island, which may be easily recognized by the lofti abaci, or rather imposts, that support the architrave. Passengers are usually landed immediately below it. It is situated on the E. coast of Philæ, which is here bounded by a carefully built wall. The builder of this beautiful temple, dedicated likewise to *Isis*, was Nerva Trajanus; but its ornamentation with sculptures and inscriptions was never quite completed. The inscriptions contain little of importance, so that the visitor may resign himself at once to the pleasure of rest and luncheon on this beautiful spot. The Kiosque of Philæ has been depicted a thousand times, and the slender and graceful form, that greets the eyes of the travellers as they approach the island, well deserves the honour. The architect who designed it was no stranger to Greek art, and this pavilion, standing among the purely Egyptian temples around it, produces the effect of a line of Homer among hieroglyphic inscriptions, or of a naturally growing tree among artificially trimmed hedges. We here perceive that a beautiful fundamental idea has power to distract the attention from deficiencies in the details by which it is carried

---

† After ἐποίησεν the word εὐχήν is probably to be inserted.

out. Although exception may be taken to the height of the abaci
and to many other points, no one who has visited Philæ will forget
this little temple, least of all if he have seen it by moonlight.

In the N.E. of the island are the ruins of a village and of buildings
of various kinds. In the extreme N.E. is a *Roman Triumphal Arch* (Pl. S),
with a lofty middle portal flanked by lower wings. The structure, which
has also been taken for a city-gate, faces the E., *i.e.* the well-fortified
bank of the Nile. The S. wing is in good preservation but is somewhat
clumsy. Above it is a brick dome supported on sandstone consoles. It
is possible that Diocletian passed beneath the central arch when he
visited the sacred island of Philæ. His name, at all events, is to be
found on the blocks of sandstone scattered on the ground †.

The huge heaps of ruins scattered over the island defy description,
and contain little of interest. On the other hand study may well be
devoted to the numerous *Inscriptions* in demotic, Greek, Latin, Coptic,
and Arabic. Some of the Greek inscriptions are elegant. The *Verses
of Catilius* surnamed Nicanor, son of Nicanor, who lived 7 B.C., are excellent; and his acrostics display considerable skill.

The Cataract Islands.

The islands in the neighbourhood of Philæ are picturesque, but
a visit to them can be recommended only to Ægyptologists and geo-
logists, for they contain nothing but rocks with a few inscriptions
carved upon them.

Bigeh, called by the ancient Egyptians 〰〰 ◠ *Senem-t*, lying
opposite Philæ, is the most easily accessible. It is reached in about
two minutes from Philæ, of which it commands a picturesque view,
as Philæ does of it, with its bare rocks and ruined buildings. Bigeh
enjoyed a very early reputation for peculiar sanctity, and we have
already seen (p. 294) that one of the symbolical sources of the Nile
was located here. Various *Rock Inscriptions* and also the hieroglyphics on a granite *Statue of Osiris* found here record that as
early as the 18th Dyn., under Amenhotep II. and Amenhotep III.,
this island was visited by pilgrims and was provided with temples.
The deities chiefly worshipped in the latter were the ram's-headed
Khnum, god of the cataracts, and a Hathor. Senem was not regarded
as belonging to Egypt but to *Kush*, *i.e.* Ethiopia, or *Ta-kens*, with
which the modern *Kenûs* may be compared. Among the pilgrims,
whose names are found on Bigeh, were several governors of Ethiopia, who were usually royal princes. The ruins of the *Temple*
visible from Philæ, in which the name of Ptolemy Neos Dionysus
is of most frequent occurrence, are now inhabited by an obliging
Nubian family, only a few of whose members understand anything
but Kenûs. The most interesting remains here are *Two Columns*,
with unsculptured Ptolemaic capitals and a *Portal* with a carefully
built arch, adorned with a Greek ornament. Adjoining the latter is
a *House* built of bricks, Nile-mud, and broken stones, in which is

---

† The following words have been deciphered:
ΔΙΟΚΛΗΤΙΑΝΟΝΕΡΛΟΝΚѠΝΣΤΑΝΤΙ

a stele with figures of Horus and Isis, Khnum and Sekhet. Behind
the temple is a well executed *Colossus of Amenhotep II.* (18th Dyn.),
'the beloved of the mistress of Senem (Bigeh)', treading upon the
nine bows, *i.e.* the barbarous tribes. Kha-em-us, the favourite son
of Ramses II., visited this island and recorded the festivals of his
father. Dignified officials of the 26th Dyn. celebrated themselves
and their princes (Psammetikh II., Hophra, Aahmes) in brief inscriptions cut in the hard stone. At a later date Philæ superseded
the rocky Bigeh as a pilgrim-resort.

The island of **Konosso** (called by the ancients

Keb-t), whose name seems to be connected with *Kush* and *Kenûs*,
also contains numerous *Rock Inscriptions*, some dating as far back
as the 11th and 12th Dynasties. Several long inscriptions of the
18th Dyn. have been preserved. One of 13 lines celebrates the
victory of Amenhotep III., represented in the colossi of Memnon,
over the Kushites or Ethiopians. Konosso was also visited by pilgrims down to the 26th Dynasty.

The island of **Sehêl,** which contains many peculiar kinds of
stone, may be reached by the dhahabîyehs. Its rugged rocks abound
with inscriptions, mostly of the 18th and 19th Dyn., though the
earliest date from the 13th, while a few were inscribed under the
20th and 21st. This island was specially dedicated to the cataract-
god Khnum and to the goddesses Anuke and Sati.

LOWER NUBIA

from Philæ to Wâdi Ḥalfah.

217 M. The voyage from *Philæ* to *Wâdi Halfah* was until about ten years ago easily accomplished and formed an agreeable continuation of the Nile-route. Travellers either caused their own dhahabîyehs to be towed up the rapids (p. 273) or proceeded in Cook's fortnightly tourist-steamer. Circumstances were, however, completely altered by the war in the Sûdân and by the giving up of the region above Wâdi Ḥalfah in 1885. After that date the only means of ascending the Nile to Nubia was offered by the weekly government steamer which conveyed the mails and military stores, and performed the entire journey without stopping sufficiently long at any intermediate point to allow of a visit to the monuments. In 1890, however, Messrs. Cook and Son again started a weekly service of steamers between the first and second cataract. These 'stern-wheelers' (*Semneh*, *Aksheh*) are small (12-14 passengers) and not very comfortable, especially when there is a large party on board. The dining-saloon is over the stern-paddle, the cabins are confined, and the commissariat limited. Halts are made at comparatively few points, though it is possible to increase these by arrangement with the engineer, if the passengers are unanimous. Zaptîyeh or gens d'armes accompany the steamer to protect it. The voyage lasts for 7 days, *i.e.* Philæ is usually reached again on the afternoon of the 7th day. The inclusive fare is 30*l.*, or 21*l.* for those who have ascended the Nile to Assuân as Cook's tourists.

1st Day (Monday). Start at 10 a.m. Viâ Debôt, Kertassi, and Bab-el-Kalabsheh to Kalabsheh. Visit the two temples there.

2nd Day. Viâ Dendûr and Gerf Huṣên (Kirsh) to Dakkeh, where the temple is visited; thence to Sebûʿah (temple).

3rd Day. To Korusko and ʿAmâdah, where the temple is inspected. If time permit, also the temple of Derr. Ibrim.

4th Day. Toshkeh; Abu-Simbel; Wâdi Ḥalfah.

5th Day. Excursion by land to Abusîr on the 2nd cataract. The steamer starts at noon for the return to Abu-Simbel, where the temple is visited.

6th Day. Start at 10 a.m. from Abu-Simbel for Korusko, arriving in time to ascend the hill Awas el-Guarâni.

7th Day. Return to Kalabsheh. — *8th Day* (Monday). Philæ is reached early in the morning and passengers and luggage are transferred to the tourist-steamer leaving Assuân on Tues. morning.

When the halts are multiplied at the request of the passengers, a different distribution of time may be adopted; *e.g.* 1st day: Debôt, Kertassi, Tafeh, and Kalabsheh; 2nd day: Dakkeh (4 hrs. halt), Ofedînah, and Korusko; 3rd day: ʿAmâdah and Abu-Simbel; 4th day: Wâdi Ḥalfah; 5th day: Visit to the second cataract; return in the afternoon to Abu-Simbel; 6th day: Korusko (1/2 hr's. halt) and Sebûʿah, where the temple is visited; 7th day: After short halts at Dendûr and Kalabsheh, reach Philæ at 5 p.m.

It is to be hoped that the region of the Upper Nile will soon be safe enough to permit the voyage to be made by dhahabîyehs once more. The writer accomplished such a voyage in 1870, visiting all the important monuments both going and coming. The cost, including the towing of the dhahabîyeh up the first cataract, may be reckoned at about 170*l.* for a party of 4-5, which added to the cost of the journey (2 months) to Assuân 420*l.* gives a total of 620*l.* for the 3 months journey; for 6 pers. 700*l.*, for 8 pers. 800*l.*, for 10 pers. 1000*l.* (comp. the Introduction, p. xix). Some dhahabîyehs are not adapted to ascend beyond the first cataract; travellers therefore who desire to proceed to the second cataract should stipulate in their contract (p. xxii), for a boat able to perform the entire voyage.

Nubia extends from the first cataract to Khartûm, *i.e.* to N. lat. 16°, and is divided into *Lower Nubia*, between the first two cataracts, and *Upper Nubia*, above the second cataract. Upper Nubia, which with the Sûdân and Dârfûr was formerly subject to Egypt, is at present independent, and is not accessible for tourists. Lower Nubia belongs to the mudîrîyeh of Keneh, from which it is governed, so far as it is not under military (British) rule. It extends to about N. lat. 22°.

The cultivable strip, even in Lower Nubia, is seldom more than a few hundred yards wide, while it is generally much narrower, so that the desert approaches close up to the banks of the Nile. As a natural consequence the population is scanty; it is estimated to be not more than 40,000 between the first and second cataracts. The Nile flows for the first half of the distance between the cataracts from S. to N., for the second half from S.E. to N.W., and in Upper Nubia from N. to S. The *Monuments* of Lower Nubia are nearly all on the W. bank, where they were less exposed to hostile attack. The most interesting is the temple of *Abu-Simbel*, the last station before Wâdi Halfah. The monuments in Upper Nubia are rarer but not less remarkable, as *e.g.* those at Gebel Barkal.

History. The first cataract forms the natural boundary of Egypt. But in early times, when the Egyptian monarchy was at its zenith, it extended its power much farther to the S., at first as far as *Ta-kompso.* The district of 12 *Ar* (Greek, *Dodekaschoinos*), assigned by the Egyptian rulers to the Isis of Philæ, stretched upon both banks as far as this point, as is attested not only by Herodotus (II, 29) but also by inscriptions in the temple of Philæ. If *Ta-kompso* (Egypt. , with many variations) be correctly identified with *Hierasykaminos* (Holy Sycamore), which lay near the modern village of Maharakah (p. 322), the length of these 12 schoinoi was, according to measurements by Prokesch, equal to $36^{1}/_{2}$ hrs. journey or 100 M., giving about $12^{1}/_{3}$ M. per ar or schoinos. The inscriptions speak of the entire region above Ombos, including the Dodekaschoinos, as being in the first nome of Upper Egypt, which they name *Ta khent* (?), 'frontier land' or 'bow-land', because the natives were armed with bows. To the S. of this lay *Kush* or *Cush* , the כּוּשׁ of the Bible. The names *Khent hon nefer* and *Ta nehesi* 'negro-land', also occur. The kings of the 6th Dyn. carried on

war against the Beduins (amu herusä), having as allies various
negro-tribes, from the lands of *Arth*, *Meza*, *Amam*, *Wawa*, and
Kaau, as we learn from the inscription of *Una* (now in the museum
at Gîzeh). The *Wawa* especially are often mentioned in the inscriptions as having been fought against and subdued by the Egyptians. — The powerful monarchs of the 12th Dyn. continued the
conquest of the S. Amenemha defeated the *Wawa;* and a son of
Usertesen I., as a stele now in Florence records, overthrew seven
negro-tribes. Usertesen III. advanced the boundary of Egypt to
Semneh; and we hear of a campaign directed against Kush in the
19th year of this king. His successor Amenemha III. recorded at
Semneh and at Kummeh, lying opposite, the height of the Nile,
which was then 25 ft. higher (p. 272) than at present. A king of

the 13th Dyn., $\left(\odot \ominus \ \stackrel{\dagger}{\underset{0}{|}} \right)$ *Ra kha nefer*, is mentioned on the is-

land of Argo. The kings of the 18th Dyn., however, did most of
all to extend the Egyptian might in Upper Nubia. Amenhotep III.
led a prosperous expedition into the land of *Abhet* and took many
prisoners. He built a large temple at *Napata*, near the fourth
cataract, and adorned the temple of Tutmes III. at *Soleb*. Both
there and on a statue of this king in the Louvre are recorded the
names of many conquered tribes of the S. The Egyptian governors
of these provinces now received the title of princes of Kush. The
victorious campaign of Ramses II. against the Ethiopians, and the
tribute paid by them in ebony, gold, and ivory, are not only described by Herodotus (II, 110), but in the temple of Abu-Simbel
and in numerous tombs at Ḳurnah are depicted negroes as prisoners
and paying tribute. While Egypt was embroiled in internal dis-
cords, an independent priestly monarchy established itself at *Napata* beside the holy mountain *(Gebel Barkal)*, where Ammon,
Muth, and Khunsu, the triad of Thebes, were worshipped. Numerous buildings were reared of which traces remain to the present
day. We are unfortunately not yet able to decipher either the
peculiar hieroglyphics or the demotic writing of the Kushites, found
side by side with Egyptian hieroglyphics on these monuments.
Some important steles brought by Mariette from Gebel Barkal record
the victorious advance of the Ethiopian prince Piankhi into Lower
Egypt, his defeat of several local kings (Tafnekht, Nimrod, Osorkon, etc.) probably set up by the Assyrians, and his capture of the
city of Memphis. *Shabako* and *Taharka*, the successors of Piankhi,
repeated his exploits, to the extent at least of making themselves
masters of Upper Egypt. They founded the 25th Dyn., and in that
way united the whole of Nubia with Egypt proper. Taharka, however, was defeated by the Assyrian kings *Esarhaddon* and *Assur-
banipal (Sardanapalus)*, though after his death his sister's son *Urdamani (Nut-Amen)* maintained himself for some time in Thebes
and even besieged Memphis. An end was put to the independence

of the petty Egyptian kings by Psammetikh I. (664-610). In his reign, according to the somewhat incredible story of Herodotus (II, 30), 240,000 soldiers, discontented with the severity of their service, emigrated to Ethiopia, where they settled near Meroë under the name of Automoles or Sembrites, and did much to refine the manners of the Ethiopians. Psammetikh II. undertook an expedition against the Ethiopians (Herod. II, 160), to which references are made in Greek and Phoenician inscriptions in the temple of Abu-Simbel (p. 334). The steles at Barkal mention two other Ethiopian kings, *Hor-si-atef* and *Nastosenen*, whose reigns cannot be accurately dated. The former reigned for forty years, warred against the *Rehrera* and *Madia*, African tribes of Dârfûr and Abyssinia, and erected temples; of the latter we learn that he was solemnly crowned in the temple of Napata.

The early royal residence Napata now began to decay, and *Berua* (Meroë) near Begerawîyeh became the capital of the Ethiopians. From *Diodorus* (III, 6) we learn that under Ptolemy Philadelphus a king of the name of *Ergamenes* shook himself free of the influence of the priests and caused them to be massacred in the golden temple. This can hardly be the same Ergamenes whom we meet at Dakkeh (p. 316), for the latter does not seem to have flourished until the time of the Roman emperors. During the Roman period, an Ethiopian invasion of the Thebaïd led to the campaign of Petronius (25 B.C.), in which Napata was destroyed. Queen Candace made peace with the Roman general (Strabo XVII, 54).

Towards the close of the 3rd cent. A.D. the country above Philæ was devastated by the *Blemmyes*, a fierce Nubian tribe dwelling between the Nile and the Red Sea, who carried their depredations even into the Roman territory beyond Assuân. To restrain them the emperor Diocletian summoned the tribe of the *Nobades* from the oasis of el-Khârgeh (p. 348) to the Nile valley, and settled them in the district from Elephantine upwards, while the temples of Philæ were assigned as common sanctuaries to them and to the Blemmyes. In spite of the aid of the Nobades, the five towns of the *Commilitium Romanum* (Prima, Phœnicon, Khiris, Taphis, and Talmis) fell into the hands of the barbarians, who made Talmis (Kalabsheh, see p. 307) their capital. In the 4th and 5th cent. they ravaged the Thebaïd, so that in 451 A.D. *Maximinus*, the general of the emperor *Marcian*, was forced to conclude a peace on unfavourable terms for 100 years, which, however, only lasted until the death of the general. Between 530 and 550 the Nobades were converted to Christianity; and *Silko*, one of their kings, defeated the Blemmyes. His victory is recorded in a Greek inscription found in the temple of Kalabsheh (p. 308). Christianity gradually invaded the temples of Nubia; and the Nobad king *Eirpanomos* and *Bishop Theodorus* (p. 283) of Philæ exterminated paganism. But not long afterwards Ethiopia, like Egypt, fell into the hands of the Moḥammedans. *ʿAmru ibn el-ʿAṣ* conquered Nubia in the year of the Hegira 20, Dongolah was captured, and a tribute of slaves imposed upon the Nubians. When Egypt became an independent Moḥammedan kingdom under the Fâṭimite Muʿizz in 969, the Nubians recovered their freedom. In the year of the Hegira 568 (1172 A.D.) Saladin's brother captured the citadel of *Ibrîm* and plundered the church. Similar disasters followed, and the people only escaped compulsory conversion to Islâm by heavy sacrifices, the loss of the provinces nearest to Assuân, and the payment of a poll-tax. The Nubian kingdom now split up into various petty states, among which *Sennâr*, founded in 1484 by the negro-tribe of the Fungis, rose to importance and held sway over the provinces of Shendi, Berber, and Dongolah. This, however, was of no long duration. Dongolah was frequently invaded by the robber tribe of the Shêgîyeh. — *Ismaʿîl Pasha*, son of *Mohammed ʿAli*, made himself master of all these provinces in 1821. He conquered Dongolah without opposition, defeated the Shêgîyeh at Korti, and acquired Sennâr also. This conquest, however, cost Ismaʿil his life. At a festival given by him at Shendi, a hut in which he had been secured was set on fire, and he and his companions perished in the flames. But this incident did not prevent the complete subjugation of the Sûdân, which was converted into an Egyptian province, with the newly-founded Kharṭûm as its capital. Dârfûr, too, was conquered and annexed in 1874. But the war with Abyssinia (1875-76), a revolt in Dârfûr, the rotten state of the Egyptian finances, the rebellion of Arabi Pasha, the victorious advance of the Mahdi, and the death of the devoted General Gordon (Jan. 1885) led to the loss of all the Egyptian possessions to the S. of Wâdi Ḥalfah, in spite of the British occupation of Egypt (1882) and the belated expeditions to Dongolah and to Kharṭûm (1884-85). It is but too probable that these districts will remain beyond the influence of Egypt or of European civilization for a long time to come.

POPULATION AND LANGUAGE. † The inhabitants of the upper valley of the Nile, even from below the first cataract, are called *Barâbra* (Berbers) by the Arab population of Egypt. A more accurate name for them is *Nubians*, and as the aboriginal inhabitants of Africa they must be distinguished from the *Kushite* tribes who immigrated from Asia at a very early period, partly to the N. viâ the isthmus of Suez, and partly to the S., across the straits of Bâb el-Mandeb into N.E. Africa. Of these immigrants the former became the inhabitants of what is now modern Egypt, the latter (also Kushites according to Lepsius) were the ancestors of the *Beyah* tribes, who settled to the E. of the Nile between that river and the Red Sea. The Begab tribes also include the *ʿAbâbdeh* on the N.,

---

† See also the introductory remarks on the Modern Egyptians, Vol. I. pp. 39 seq., especially paragraphs 3 and 5, on the Beduins and Berbers.,

the *Bishárîn*, adjoining these, and the *Hadendoah* farther to the S.
These tribes inhabit the region known as the *Etbai*. Lepsius ascribes·
to the ancestors of the *Begah* the numerous inscriptions that are
found as far up as Meroë, both in picture-writing resembling
Egyptian hieroglyphics and in a demotic alphabetic writing, which
suggests an independent literature. A different view is held by
H. Brugsch, who has made within the last few years the first attempt.
to decipher these Meroïtic-Ethiopian inscriptions, as they are called.·
He inclines to the opinion that they have some connection with
the Nubian tongue.† Three Nubian dialects are recognized, according to their geographical distribution, the *Kenûs*, *Mahas*, and
Dongolah. The first is spoken in the district between Assuân and
Sebû'ah, where it is succeeded by an *Arabic* strip, at the beginning
of the desert-routes to Abu Hamed on the S. and to Wâdi 'Olâ̩ki
on the E. Thence to Hannek, above the third cataract, the *Mahas*
idiom prevails, while the *Dongolah* dialect is spoken from Hannek
throughout the province of Dongolah to Gebel Dēgah. The most N.
and the most S. of these dialects have a closer affinity with each
other than either has to the central Mahas, a fact explained by
Diocletian's transference of the Dongolese inhabitants of the oasis
of el-Khârgeh to the district above Assuân (p. 302). The Mahas
apply the name *Oshkir* to both the N. and S. dialects.

30. From Philæ to Kalabsheh.

Comp. the Map at p. 98.

38½ M. The MAIL STEAMER stops only at the stations of *Umm Barakat*
(5 min. halt), *Kalabsheh* (1 hr.'s halt), and *Abu Hor* (where the night is
spent).

As we leave *Philæ* (*Shellâl*, p. 279), we have a fine view of the
pylons of the temple of Isis and the other buildings, and of the
rocks of the island of *Bigeh*. On both sides of the river rise lofty
granite cliffs. To the left, the ruins of *el-Meshhed* and then the
tomb of a shêkh. Beyond Bigeh lies the island of *el-Hesseh*, separated from the W. bank by a rocky channel. At *el-Guti* our
course bends to the S.W., afterwards returning to its S. direction.
The scenery becomes less wild, and a narrow strip of verdure appears on each bank. — To the W. is the *Gebel Shemt-el-Wah*.

12 M. **Debôt**, on the ·W. bank. A paved route, 230 paces long,
leads from the Nile to the gate in the girdle-wall of the *Temple.*.
On the bank of the stream several large blocks have been built into

---

† Two elaborate works have appeared on the Nubian language: one
by *Reinisch*, Die Nuba-Sprache, I. Theil, Grammatik und Texte, II. Theil,
Nubisch-Deutsches und Deutsch-Nubisches Wörterbuch. Vienna. 1879
(not absolutely reliable for pronunciation and quantities); the other, by
R. Lepsius, Nubische Grammatik, with an introduction on the peoples
and languages of Africa, Berlin, 1880. To the latter important book, a
most instructive and valuable work, our description is considerably indebted.

THE NILE

from

Demhîd to the Second Cataract.

1:1.000.000

0   5   10   15   20
English Miles

Mirian
Demhîd
Demhîd el-gharb
Kertassi
Temple ruins
Sehdâb
Umm Barakât
Tindau
Tafeh (TAPHIS)
Temple ruins
Darmût
Nezleh
Kalabsheh (TALMIS)
Temple ruins
esh-Shekik
Abu Hôr
Dendûr esh-Shark
Kueshâb
Dendûr el-gharb
Temple ruins
Meriet esh-Shark
Meriet el-gharb
Gerf Husén
Ru. Sabagûrah
Temple ruins (TUTZIS)
Kirsh
Koshtamneh
Dakkeh (PSELKHIS)
Kobbân
'Alâķi
Korti
I. Derâr
Ofedînah
Temple ruins
Temple ruins HIERASYCAMINOS
Maharraķah
Roman Castle Mehendi
Shêkh Sheraf
Seyûleh
Za'meh
Bârideh
Gokân
Medik
Medik el-Gharb
Sebu'ah
Tagireh
Ru. Shaturmah
Husâyah
Ru. Begrash
sirsirrah
'mâdah
Tomâs
Derr
Emârîyeh
'arabah
'Aiseh
Shakket
'arekah
Katas
Sonkâri
Korusko

Tropic of Cancer

N.
S.

Wâdi el-'Arab
Wâdi Derr

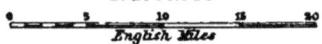

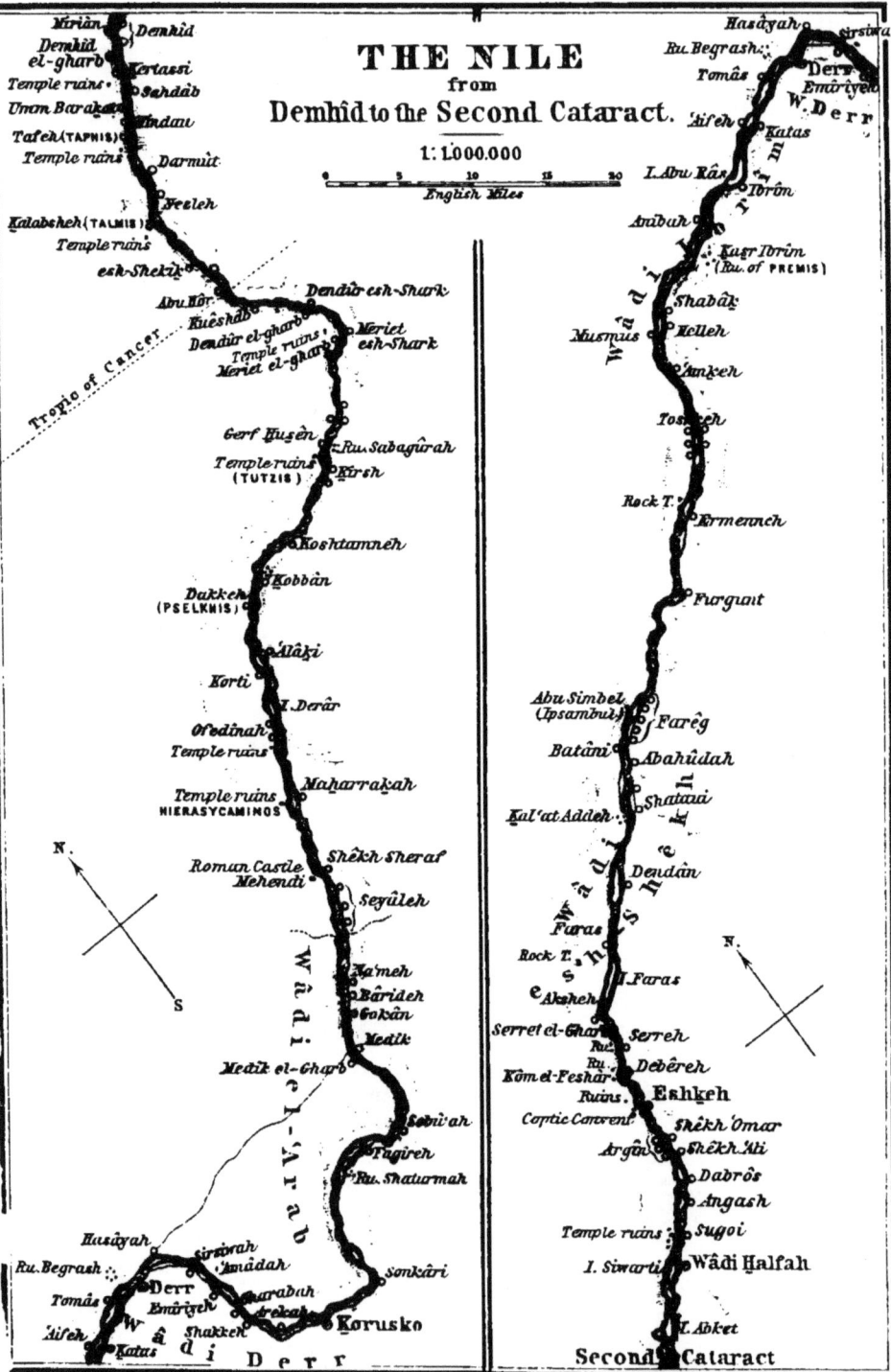

Drawn by H.Kiepert.

Hasâyah
sirsirra
Ru. Begrash
Derr
Tomâs
Emârîyeh
'Aiseh
W. Derr
Katas
I. Abu Râs
Ibrîm
Anibah
Ķaṣr Ibrîm (Ru. of PREMIS)
Shabâk
Musmus
Helleh
Amkeh
Toskeh
Rock T.
Ermennch
Furgunt
Abu Simbel (Ipsambul)
Farêg
Batâni
Abahûdah
Shataui
Ķal'at Addeh
Dendân
Faras
Rock T.
I. Faras
Aksheh
Serret el-Gharb
Serreh
Ru.
Kôm el-Feshar
Debêreh
Ruins
Eshķeh
Coptic Convent
Shêkh 'Omar
Argîn
Shêkh 'Ali
Dabrôs
Angash
Temple ruins
Sugoi
I. Siwarti
Wâdi Halfah
I. Abķet
Second Cataract

Wâdi shesh Kaïn

N.

Engraved by Wagner & Debes, Leipzig.

a wall. The first doorway, about 25 ft. high, has no sculptures; on the second doorway, about 50 ft. farther back, appears the winged sun-disc. The second pylon shows a much damaged Greek inscription of Ptolemy Philometor and his consort. In a straight line, 24 ft. farther, is a third pylon; and 42 ft. beyond that is the small temple proper (65 ft. deep and 40 ft. broad), with a side-chamber on the left (S.) side. The temple-façade, with its four columns, was thrown down in 1868 by earthquake, which also destroyed the first room. The latter contained a dedication from the Emperor Tiberius (*Tibrīs*), and the Autokrator Kisres (Augustus?) to the gods of Debôt *Ta-bet* (comp. the Hebrew בדרה *bet*, house). The names of the Roman emperors also appear on the door to the main chamber of the temple, though at the top of the inner side of this door is the dedication inscription of a native king *At en neteru,* *sotep en ra At'-kheramon ankh* *t'eta mer ast.* This *At'kheramon*, like the *Ergamenes* occurring at Dakkeh (p. 316), was one of the dynasty of native kings who reigned in Nubia during the period of the Ptolemies and the Roman emperors. On each of the sides (right and left) of this apartment are eight scenes in two rows one above the other, representing King At'kheramon making offerings to the gods of the place, Osiris, Isis, and Horus, and to the gods of the region of the cataracts. The sanctuary behind contains a granite naos, broken in two, dating from Euergetes II. Physkon and Cleopatra.

A stele of the 12th dyn. (Ranubkau Amenemha II.), found here and now in the Berlin museum, proves that Debôt must have been a very early settlement. The Roman *Parembole* (fortified camp; p. 292) must have been situated in this neighbourhood, for in the Itinerarium Antonini, a list of Roman military stations, the distance from (Contra) Syene to Parembole is given at 16 Roman miles or about 12 Eng. miles. As a matter of fact, the remains of an ancient fortification are found near Debôt.

At *Dimri* (W. bank) is an ancient wall; and on the E. bank farther on is the substructure of a temple. The island of *Morgos* *(Markos)*, next passed, has some unimportant ruins.

To the right (W. bank) next appears the (15½ M.) small temple of **Kertassi**, an attractive building, recalling the hypæthral temple at Philæ (p. 285). At the entrance, which faces N., only two columns are now standing, with the cow-headed Isis and Hathor and a house surmounted by a Uræus-serpent (Hat-hor, house of

Horus) as at Denderah (p. 80) and Philæ. Four columns are also left on each side, united by means of a building between them, which has a semi-portal on the W. side, farthest from the Nile. The capitals of the side-columns resemble those of the front columns of the hypæthral temple on Philæ. They are lotus-calyx capitals, framed at the top with leaves springing from buds, while beneath are the usual five annuli or rings. Only a single cross-beam now rests upon the beams running lengthwise in this little temple, which cannot have been more than about 25 ft. square.

About 10 min. to the S. is a double girdle-wall of large hewn stones, stretching to the Nile, and furnished with a gateway. A flight of steps leads down to the river. The pylon-like gateway appears to have been faced by another of the same kind. The wall has been taken for the remains of a Roman permanent camp. An ancient road leads thence to the S.W. to some *Sandstone Quarries*, which contain about 50 Greek votive inscriptions (and one demotic) dating from the Roman imperial epoch (Septimius Severus, Caracalla to Gordian). There are also two busts and a carefully constructed niche, with the winged sun-disc above it, apparently intended to hold a statue. The inscriptions have been carved mostly by priests of the *Gomos* (ἱερεύς γόμου, also ἀρχιερεύς, πρόστατης, etc.), a word which Franz explains (Corp. Inscrip. Graec. III, 460) to mean the carriage of stones under priestly management from the quarries for the purpose of building temples.

At all events in the inscription to the left of the head of the bust (in Lepsius 373) a priest of the *Gomos*, named Orsēs, son of Psentauax, records that he had despatched 110 stones for the work of *Isis of Philæ*, *i.e.* probably for one of the later temples (perhaps the one next the stream on the W. side). Considerable sums were paid for the privilege of holding this probably lucrative office. Eight tablets (the four earlier beside the left bust, the four later beside the right bust) record that a certain *Gaius Dioscuros (Julius) Macrinus*, who is probably represented by both the busts, held this office eight times, for which first and last be expended no less than 300 pieces of gold (χρυσοῦς), equal to about 275 l. in modern currency. The years of his office are given: the 18th and 22nd years (of Septimius Severus and his co-regent Caracalla), the 2nd of Heliogabalus or Alexander Severus, the 12th (of the last named emperor), the 1st (of Maximinus), the 3rd (of Gordian), and the 2nd and 5th of Philippus Arabus, *i.e.* in all a period of about 50 years, between 200 and 249 A.D.

A tablet of the 19th year of Caracalla (198 A.D.) records that a priest of the Gomos (erected) the gnomon (sun-dial) on the pylons περί τοῦ γόμου, *i.e.* probably to determine the right time for sending off the stones. *Gau* found a sun-dial in the quarries of Kertassi.

Among the deities worshipped here besides Isis, were a goddess named Σρουπτιγις *(Sruptichis)* and a god named Πουρσεπμοῦνις *(Pursepmunis)*, probably native Ethiopian gods.

On the right (W.) bank lies the considerable village of *Umm-Barakat*.

4½ M. (W. bank) **Tafeh** occupies the site of *Taphis*, mentioned in the Itinerarium Antonini. Two temples are mentioned by earlier travellers as being here, but in 1890 Prof. Eisenlohr was able to discover one only, at the N.E. end of the village. The entrance, facing the S., consists of a central portal (closed) and smaller adjoining door. Its only sculptured ornament is the winged sun-disc above the central door. In the interior of the temple, which has a substructure of dressed masonry, are four standing columns, with tastefully carved capitals, and farther on are various ruinous chambers. To the W. are the remains of some large and solid structures. — At the foot of the mountains to the S. of the village, not far from the river, are some scanty remains of enclosures and the angle of a wall, in which perhaps are to be identified the traces of the other and larger temple, which was still standing in 1870. On the hill above is a castellated building to which climbers may ascend. On the opposite (E.) bank lay *Contra Taphis*, which has left no remains of importance.

Beyond Tafeh the dark shining rocks advance close to the river-bank, forming a gloomy gorge, known as *Bâb el-Kalabsheh*, in the middle of which, on the E. bank, are some houses with plantations of palms. The navigation of this reach is somewhat dangerous, owing to the frequent bends of the river and the numerous islands. On one of the islands are some ruins. On the right (W.), beyond the gorge, appears the large —

7 M. **Temple of Kalabsheh,** situated a little below the tropic of Cancer (N. lat. 23°31′3″). The magnificent constellation of the Southern Cross may be seen hence onwards (best between 2 and 4 a.m. in Jan. and Feb.). Cook's tourist-steamers spend the first night here, and the traveller has time to visit one if not both of the temples in the evening. The ancient name of Kalabsheh was *Talmis*, written ☒☒☒ and ☒☒☒ *Termes*, in hieroglyphics. It existed as early as the 18th Dyn. and was perhaps founded by Amenhotep II. (☒☒☒) *Ra āā kheperu*, who is represented on the inner E. wall of the second court, before Khem, presenting wine and milk to the local deity *Mandulis* (☒☒☒), a son of Horus. Beside him appears one of the Ptolemies handing the sign of the possession of a field to Isis, Mandulis, and another goddess (perhaps Neith?). Although this representation dates from a late Roman period, it shows that Amenhotep was regarded as the founder and one of the Ptolemies as the restorer of the temple. The cartouche also of Tutmes III., the predecessor of Amenhotep II., is found on a granite statue lying before the entrance of the temple. The above-mentioned Ptolemy is probably *Soter II.*, who appears in several reliefs in the small temple in the N.E. angle of the passage round the outside of the large temple. *Talmis* was long the capital of the *Blemmyes* (p. 302),

who were, about 540 A.D., defeated by Silko, the Christian king of
the Nobades (p. 302) who celebrated his victory in an inscription
on one of the pillars of the temple at Kalabsheh (see below).

The extant *Large Temple* was built under the Roman emperor
Augustus and his successors. The numerous inscriptions (in Greek,
with the exception of one in Latin hexameters) date from the reigns
of Domitian, Trajan, Hadrian, and Antoninus Pius, and of the later
emperors Alexander Severus and Philippus; they express the reverence of the soldiers of the Spanish, Iturean, and Theban cohorts
for the great god Mandulis.

Including the inner girdle-wall the temple is 235 ft. long and
117$^{1}/_{2}$ ft. broad. There is also an outer girdle-wall, with small
temples at the N.E. and S.W. angles. Before the last stand five
columns one behind the other. The inner girdle-wall joins the
massive pylon, forming a continuous building with it. In front of
the pylon is a narrow platform, reached by a flight of steps beginning at the Nile, then by a paved passage about 100 ft. long and
25 ft. broad, leading to a second flight of 20 steps. The entrance to
the temple is blocked by fallen stones and the dwellings of natives,
who have settled all about the entire temple. In the interior of the
pylon are stairs and chambers, as at Edfu (p. 244). On passing
through the door of the pylon, which is not in a straight line with
the rest of the building but at a slight angle with the axis of the
temple, we find ourselves in a fore-court, 65 ft. long, the floor of
which is quite covered with fallen blocks of masonry. Of the double
row of columns which once stood here, probably in 4 couples on each
side, only a single column, on the left side, is now erect. On each
side of this court four narrow chambers have been constructed in
the wall; and a door on the right communicates with the exterior
passage round the temple. The walls of the entrance to the next
room retire towards the top in the manner of a pylon. Here on the
right the above-mentioned decree of Silko is inscribed in bad Greek.
On the nearest column is a long inscription in the Ethiopian demotic character, hitherto undeciphered, which may perhaps be a replica
or repetition of the decree.

The English translation of Silko's important Greek inscription is as
follows. 'I, Silko, sub-king (βασιλίσκος) of the Nobades and all Ethiopians,
came twice to Talmis (Kalabsheh) and Taphis (Tafeh). I fought against
the Blemmyes and God gave me the victory over them, three to one.
Again I conquered and took possession of their cities, I fortified myself
there the first time with my troops. I overcame them and they sued to
me. I made peace with them and they swore to me by the images of
their gods, and I trusted their oath, for they were brave men. I ascended
once more into the upper districts. Since I became sub-king, I go no
longer after the other kings but before them. And those who seek to
strive with me, I do not allow to remain in their land unless they beg for
pardon from me. For in the lower districts I am a lion, and in the upper
districts a bear. — I fought again with the Blemmyes from Primis to
Talmis. And I laid waste the other districts, the upper Nobad regions,
when they sought to strive with me. The rulers of the other peoples,
who seek to strive with me, I do not allow to seat themselves in the

shade, if they do not bow before me; and they may not drink wine in their house. For whosoever raise themselves against me, them I deprive of their wives and children'.

On the pillar between the two columns to the right of the entrance to the main temple is another Greek inscription. This is a decree of Aurelius Besarion, also named Amonius, military governor of Ombos and Elephantine, ordering the owners of swine to remove their animals from the holy Talmis. It probably dates from the year 248-9 A.D. — On the left side of the elegant entrance-door appears the Pharaoh ⌐⌐⌐ (probably Augustus), over whom Thoth and Horus *hut* (or *behat*) pour the symbols of a peaceful life ☥ ⎨. Beside him stands Hor-si-isi (Horus, son of Isis), the lord of Talmis. Leaving now the entrance-wall with its four columns behind us, we find ourselves in the main building of the temple, the portico preper, which is 40 ft. deep and 66 ft. broad. This portico is considerably higher than the three rooms behind it, from which a double staircase ascends to the roof (now fallen) of the portico. It has four, or including those of the entrance wall six, elegant columns on each side, with varying capitals. Only two, on the left, are now standing in the interior. On the E. wall the emperor appears sacrificing to the gods of Talmis, and adjoining this scene is the above-mentioned relief of Amenhotep II. presenting wine and milk to Khem-Ammon. — The next three rooms are small ($17^{1}/_{2}$ ft. deep and 40 ft. wide), and have sacrificial scenes on their walls. Each probably contained two columns, those in the second room being still preserved. The staircase to the roof ascended to the left from the first room. On the outside of the W. back-wall of the temple are various well-preserved representations, including the goddess Isis with Ptolemy Caesarion, son of Julius Caesar and Cleopatra. The temple, like that of Edfu, is surrounded by a passage, widening towards the rear and entered from the fore-court by doors on both sides; and, as mentioned above, there is also a second and wider passage outside the first one, with which it has communication by means of a door on the left side. This outer passage could be closed by means of doors. The whole structure is a faithful reproduction of an early Egyptian temple, but dates from Roman times.

The little **Temple* of Bêt el-Walli, situated upon a hill about 20 min. to the N., is much more noteworthy than the large Roman erection at Ḳalabsheh. The way to it leads along the verge of the mountain, level at first, but finally ascends steeply. The temple consists of a vestibule, of which only the side walls are now standing, a main chamber, entered by a central and two side doors, and a small adytum, adjoining the latter. In the vestibule our interest is excited by the warlike scenes on the side-walls. These indicate

th'at the temple was dedicated not only to the worship of the gods
Ammon-Ra, lord of Nubia, Horus, Isis, and the gods of thè cataracts
Khnum, Anuke, and Sati, but also to the memory of the victories
gained by Ramses the Great over the tribes of the N. (Tehennu) and
of the S. (Kushites). The victories over the N. tribes are depicted
on the N. wall; those over the S. tribes on the S. wall.

We turn first to the right (N. wall). The *Tehennu*, a tribe of the Libyan stock, had settled to the W. of Egypt. They wore pointed beards,
and were distinguished by having the hair cut smooth across the brows,
with long pendant side-locks. We begin our inspection of the reliefs
at the end to the left. Here appears the Pharaoh, seated in a naos,
holding in one hand a long staff bent at the top, and in the other the

symbol of rule ⌐ ḥak, while on his head he wears a crown of bull's

horns ⨾, to which eight serpent-diadems are attached. At his feet
is a lion. In the upper row, *Amonhianemif* ('Ammon at his right hand'),
one of his sons, armed with a bow, leads three bound prisoners to him.
In the lower row is a fan-bearer followed by a band of soldiers. Adjacent
is the inscription: 'The prince speaks, who is before His Majesty, Hail
to thee, Oh good and beloved prince, son of Ammon, having proceeded
from his limbs. Thou goest out into the country. Thou art like Ra above,
who travels on the horizon. Thou taxest the inhabitants of Egypt. Thou
art in the body of thy contemporaries. Thou wearest the different helmets.
Thou art an annihilator of the ill-doers in the body of thy mother Isis. Thou
causest both halves of Horus to become green. Years like Tum, prince
of both lands, like Ptah ta tenen, red Egypt under thy feet, Khara (Syria), Kushi (Ethiopia) in thy hand. The land of *Mera* (Egypt) rejoices, O
prince, because thou hast widened its boundaries'. — The following scene
shows us the king on the point of cutting off the hair, or perhaps even
the head, of one of the Tehennu, with a sickle-shaped knife. His dog
(antha em nekh) springs upon the kneeling foe. The king is here called
a 'strong lion, the lord of the sword, who binds the rebellious lands of
the Tehennu, and cuts the nine alien peoples in pieces with his sword
and casts them under his feet. — In the third relief, the king in his
chariot aims a blow at two foes whom he holds by their hair, and presses
hard upon his enemies who are armed with spears. He is compared to
the war-god Mentu, lord of Thebes. He next appears on foot before a
fortress, and on the battlements above is the prince *(abkher)*, whom
Ramses seizes by the hair to kill him. On the lower battlements stand
men and women suing to the Pharaoh, of whom an inscription says,
'there is no other like Baal, O prince, his true son to all eternity'. A
woman is letting a child down from the castle to save it from death, a
man throws himself headlong down, while one of Ramses' followers is
beating in the doors with an axe. — In the last scene on this side the
king appears with fettered enemies, some led to him by cords.

The reliefs on the *S. Side*, no less interesting, relate to the subjugation of the Kushites, although the inscription beside the king reads 'the
ruler of Egypt, who has subdued the nations, and made the borders as
he chose among the Retennu (Syrians and Assyrians)'. Here again we
see the king's sons in two rows bringing the captured booty to the Pharaoh. In the upper row, *Amonhianemif*, the king's eldest son, points to a
stand adorned with flowers and leaves on which men kneel in supplication, while rings (of gold?) and skins hang from it; next is *Amenemapt*,
the king's son of Kusu, and behind him rings. bags, weapons, panther-
skins, shields, chairs, fans, and many other articles. The lower row is

introduced by three officials, carrying the ⨾ and ⌐ , and among them is again the king's son *Amenemapt.* Au Egyptian bears a pole with rings and skins, and then in both rows approach negroes, some bound and others free, with all kinds of animals — monkeys, a giraffe, antelopes, a lion, cows with twisted horns, greyhounds, ostriches, and panthers. The negroes are unmistakable, not only on account of the swarthy hue of their skins but also on account of their excellently reproduced facial characteristics. Another scene shows us the king in his chariot, followed by his sons, among whom *Khaemus* appears (lower row), launching an arrow against the fleeing negroes, some of whom are already prostrate on the ground. The wounded father is brought back to his wife and children, and a meal is cooked for him. A monkey sits upon one of the trees peculiar to this region, with heart-shaped leaves and fascicular fruit.

These scenes serve as excellent illustrations to the life of king Sesoōsis (Ramses II.), as related by Diederus (I. 53 seq.) Sesoosis was first sent by his father with an army into Arabia, and succeeded in subduing the people of that land, hitherto invincible. He was then despatched to the W. regions and made himself master of the greater part of Libya, while still but a youth. On his father's death he assumed the kingdom. He prepared a mighty armament and marched first (I. 55) to the S. against the Ethiopians. He conquered the country and imposed upon it a tribute of ebony, gold, and ivory.

The temple proper, hewn in the rock, is entered by three doors. The central and highest, is rounded at the top; the smaller doors to the right were obviously not made until after the wall had been covered with sculptures. On the inner side of both of these side doors is Ramses represented as a traveller, with a long staff, and saying 'I come to thee, Ammon-Ra, I am thy son, etc.' On the back of the two entrance-pillars is the king receiving the symbols of life from *Horus,* lord of 〖𓏏𓃀𓉐〗 *Mam* (the name of a temple near Dakkeh), and on the right from *Tum.* The two representations on the right and left of the entrance-wall are unusually fine; on the left the king holds a negro (Kush), and on the right a Tehennu, by the hair, and smites them with his weapon. In each case the single enemy symbolizes the entire nation; so that the inscription beside the right scene reads: *pet pet ment mehet,* 'he smites the people of the N.' The architrave supported by two columns has a fine effect. The Doric columns are fluted, and the abacus bears the name of Ramses II. (similar columns at the tombs of Benihasan, see p. 12). The builder's inscription is on the architrave. In the right half the king is called a son of Khnum, who formed himself on the potter's wheel with his own hand (Khnum is the creator of men). In the left half are the words: 'The king of the Unmanez-nez, the true defender (Gr. *Soter*), who sacrifices to the cycle of the gods, built the temple for his father's father, and renewed the buildings of the temple'. By 'father's father' the god Khnum may be meant or the king's actual grandfather Ramses I. On the right side-wall Ramses II., conducted by Anuke, proffers wine to Khnum and Sati, the gods of the cataracts; and on the left wall he offers incense to Horus, lord of Beheni (opposite Wâdi Halfah, p. 341), and to Isis-Selk with the scorpion on her head. On the back-wall similar homage is paid to Ammon-Ra. In the recess on the right

the king sits between Khnum and Anuke, and in that on the left
between Horus, lord of Bek, and the cow-headed Isis. The colours
of these pictures are well-preserved. The doors to the little sanctuary, which bore the name *Rauserma sehotep neteru*, *i.e.* 'Ramses
offering to the gods', and the sanctuary itself are decorated with
various inscriptions. The king, staff in hand, is conducted, on the
right by Sati, on the left by Maket. On the wall to the right of the
door, Anuke, mistress of Abu, offers her breast to the king, on the
left Isis, mistress of the land of Khent ⸺ , does the
same. Each calls herself his mother. Isis says that she bestows
upon him firmness along with her milk, so that he is said to have
been destined from his mother's breast to long life and mighty
deeds. [Diodorus relates that Hephæstus appeared to the king's
father, announcing to him that the new-born babe would subdue
the whole world; and in the long inscription at Abydos Ramses is
said to have done great deeds while still a child.] On the side-
walls are scenes of homage to the king, with offerings piled up
upon tables bearing the cartouches of Ramses II. At the back is a
recess with three obscure figures, perhaps Ptah, Ammon, and
the king.

31. From Ķalabsheh to Dakkeh.

Comp. the Map, p. 304.

23¹/₂ M. On the voyage to (7 M.) *Abu Hor* (W. bank) we pass
between low rocky banks, causing rapids. The mail-steamer spends
the first night after Shellâl at Abu Hor, starting next morning at
4 a.m. Above this point vegetation almost ceases and the scenery
becomes desert. To the right appears the —

6 M. **Temple of Dendûr,** dating entirely from Roman times. It
consists of a handsome pylon and of the temple proper, supported
by two columns, about 30 ft. farther back. The pylon stands upon
a solid platform of masonry, 14 ft. high and 95 ft. broad. The
portal, single instead of double as at Edfu and Philæ, rises at the
back of this platform, surrounded by a low wall. At the top is the
winged sun-disc, and within and on the front (E.) and back (W.)
the pylon is adorned with representations of the emperor sacrificing to various gods. The emperor, here called simply
Pir-āā, Pharaoh, though within the temple he is named *Autokrator
Kisres*, is probably *Augustus*, as Tiberius, Nero, and other succeeding emperors are usually designated by their names.

These sacrificial scenes are particularly interesting because
they make known to us not only some of the native gods, whose
names may be of importance for our knowledge of the native language, but also the names of various native princes. such as the

Nobad king *Silko* met at Ḳalabsheh (p. 303), who continued to rule subject to Roman supremacy. Thus in the first scene under the door-lintel the Pharaoh is seen before two personages, of whom the first, an Osiris [hieroglyphs] *Petàst* ('he who belongs to Isis'), is described as *ma-kheru*, *i.e.* as dead, and is named [hieroglyphs] *Si* and elsewhere [hieroglyphs] *Sĕr* (the Nubian word for prince) [hieroglyphs] *nte ḥet*, which is perhaps the ancient name of Dendûr, and with the [hieroglyph] *Hor* (nte ḥet hor) added in the lowest representation to the right, approaches also the modern name. Petàst was probably a deceased native prince; and *Pihar* [hieroglyphs], his brother, who stands behind him wearing a Uræus-fillet and no crown, was probably another. The latter stands in the recess at the back of the cella before Isis, mistress of Abaton and Pilak. Like Petàst he is called the son of *Kupar*, with the addition of [hieroglyphs] *Hest* or *Hesi* in the holy mountain [hieroglyphs], which perhaps means 'interred' or may be a title. A *Pihar* is mentioned twice as *Phripahor* in the demotic inscription in the temple at Dendûr, as deciphered by Revillout.

In the second (middle) scene to the left on the front of the pylon a god [hieroglyphs] *Arpesnefer* (perhaps pronounced arḥesnefer, see below), with bulls' horns like Khnum, stands before Tefnut. Perhaps Arpesnefer is the native name for Khnum (or for Osiris Unnofer, árpes = un). — We pass through the pylon and find ourselves in front of the elegant façade of the temple, only 13 ft. wide, and crowned with the winged sun-disc *(beḥet)* and the symbols of endurance [hieroglyph] and fertility [hieroglyph]. Uza (eyes) are represented on the abaci of the two columns with palm-capitals. To the right and left of the central entrance (at the sides of which were once probably balustrades, now destroyed) are crowned snakes coiling round a staff, flowers, etc. The pillars to the right and left exhibit sacrificial scenes (three on each side): above, to the right, is the emperor *(Autokrator Kisres)* before Petàst, son of Kupar; below, to the right, the same before [hieroglyphs] *Arḥesnefer*, to the left, before Horus, and before Thoth and Isis. — The temple is divided into three apartments. A door leads to the outside from each side of the first apartment. Behind the temple proper, which is only 42 ft. long, is a small recess hewn in the rock, and adorned on the outside. The N. and S. outside walls of the temple are also sculptured.

Beyond Dendûr the banks of the Nile become flatter and are partly cultivated.

8¹/₂ M. **Gerf Ḥuṣên** has a *Rock Temple*, formerly called the *Temple of Kirsh* after the opposite˳village (p. 316).

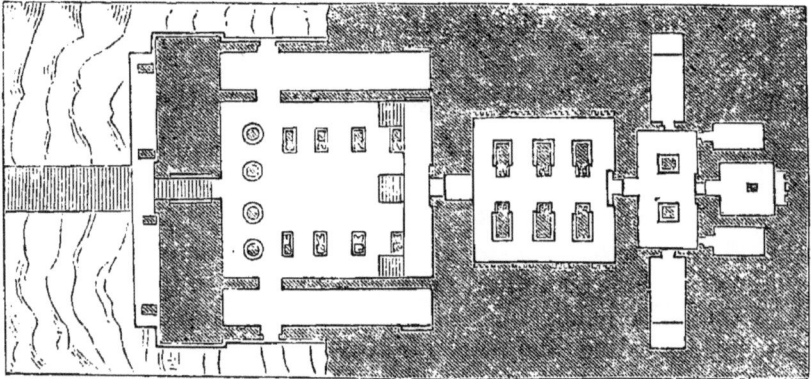

The village of Gerf Ḥuṣên occupies the site of *Tutzis*, a place mentioned in the Itinerarium Antonini, 20 Roman miles, *i.e.* 18 Engl. M., above Talmis (Ḳalabsheh). The sacred name of this place was ⌐⌐ 𓁗 *Pa Ptah*, the House of Ptah. The pylon, of which Gau and Champollion saw traces in front of the rock-temple, has disappeared, having been washed away by the stream. The word *gerf* جرف means, in fact, a bank washed away by a stream. Several sphinxes, with small statues of the king, still remain, forming an avenue from the river-bank to the temple. Next to the pylon was a *Vestibule*, built outside the hill, while the temple proper is hewn in the rock. In this vestibule two columns to the left are still standing (the two to the right have disappeared), and seven of the original eight pillars, with somewhat clumsy Osiris-statues. The last bear on their shoulders the name of Ramses II., who built this temple and is the only king mentioned in it. He appears not only as the founder, but also as one of the deities to be worshipped here. On the beams of the architrave he is named with both his names as lord of the festivals like his father Ptah, as the ruler of Egypt and conqueror of his foes (expressed pictorially). The next room (45 ft. square), hewn out of the rock, requires artificial light; it produces a serious and gloomy effect. The ceiling is supported by six Osiris-pillars, 28 ft. high, representing the king as Osiris, with the crown on his head, his crossed arms bearing the signs of rule (the crook and the scourge), and wearing an apron with a lion's head. The figures of Osiris, especially the lower parts, are somewhat roughly executed. On each side of the chamber are four recesses, each with the king, variously clad, standing between two deities. The wall-spaces above and between these recesses are occupied with representations of the king making offerings, the king being depicted alone in the lower row, and the god to whom he offers worship in the upper row.

Left (S.) Side from the entrance: 1. The king with incense before Ammon-Ra; 2. before Ra with the hawk's head and sun-disc; 3. before Tum; 4. offering incense before Ptah in his naos; 5. before Ra with the crown; 6. before Thoth, with the ibis's head. In the four recesses below: 1. The king between Ammon-Ra and Muth; 2. between Horus, lord of Bek, and Horus, lord of Beheni; 3. between Ptah and Hathor; 4. between Ptah and Sekhet, the lion-headed loved one of Ptah. Here and elsewhere in this temple two forms of Ptah are distinguished; one shows him bareheaded, the other with the headdress 〰 .

The upper scenes on the *Right (N.) Wall* are partly destroyed, but we can make out the king before Ra, Tum, Mentu, and Khnum. In the recesses (right) is the king between Harmachis and Jusas; between Horus, lord of Mam (Abu-Simbel?) and Isis, mother of the gods; between Nefertum and Sati; between Khnum and Anuke.

On the back-wall, to the right and left of the entrance to the next room, are two large scenes. To the left is the king before Ptah, before Ramses himself and the goddess Hathor, with the cow's head, with erect horns, between which are two feathers as in the headdress of Ptah (see above). To the right, the king appears before Ptah in the form of a mummy, before the deified Ramses, and Sekhet seated on a throne.

The following room, the *Sekos*, about 36 ft. wide though only 17 ft. deep, is entered by a proportionately small door, on the left side of which is the king before Ptah. The ceiling is supported by two square pillars. To the right and left two oblong recesses (see Pl. p. 314) run off from this chamber, and at the back are three other recesses, the central and largest of which is the *Sanctuary*. On the pillars the king appears worshipping various deities. On the N. side of the right pillar he is named 'Beloved of Ra-Harmachis in the land of *Wawa'* 𓅃𓏤𓏤𓏤, a name for Nubia already met with (p. 301). At various places the temple is spoken of as 𓉐 *Pa Ptah*, 'House of Ptah', *e.g.* on the door of the sanctuary, to the right of which the king is called the beloved of seven gods, Ammon, Ptah, 𓁲 Shu, Mentu, Khnum, Sekhet, and Hathor. At the back of the sanctuary is a recess with four seated figures, representing (from the left) Ptah, the deified Ramses, Ptah with the headdress (see above), and Hathor with the cow's head.

On the left bank of the Nile, above Gerf Ḥusên, are the considerable ruins of *Sabagûrah*. The village of *Kirsh* (E. bank), opposite Gerf Ḥusên, has been conjecturally identified with *Kerkis*, mentioned in the Greek inscription of the officers of Psammetikh at Abu-Simbel (p. 334). At the village of *Kostamneh*, on the E. bank, are some ancient walls. Our course bends to the W. and leads past granite crags to —

10¹/₂ M. **Dakkeh,** on the W. bank. [Cook's steamer halts long enough to permit a visit to the temple.] Dakkeh is the ancient *Pselchis*, hierog. *P-serket*, the 'House of Selk' or of the 'Scorpion', an animal that is here remarkably common. The Roman general Petronius defeated the Ethiopians at Pselchis in 23 A.D., on his campaign to Napata (p. 302). Dakkeh early became the site of a temple; Prof. Eisenlohr found a stone here with the name of *Amenemha* (now at Heidelberg). In the embankment leading to the N. from the pylon, in the axis of the present temple, stones of earlier buildings have been used, several with the cartouche of Tutmes III. (which occurs also on a column) and Seti I. Gau's theory that there was formerly another edifice to the right, almost as large as the present one to the left, seems insufficiently supported, though suggested by existing remains. The present temple was built by the native king Ergamenes (the inner temple C, comp. Pl. p. 317), Ptolemy IV. Philopator (Sekos B), and Ptolemy IX. Euergetes II. (the pronaos A), and it was completed by a Roman emperor *Pirāā* (Pharaoh), by which name Augustus is usually understood. It has already been related (p. 302) that the Nubian sub-king Ergamenes, in the reign of Ptolemy II. Philadelphus freed himself from the priests at Napata, causing them to be murdered in the temple there. Names of such Nubian sub-kings, especially under the Roman empire, are found on the Ethiopian buildings and in the demotic inscriptions at Philæ, Kalabsheh, and Dakkeh. It is somewhat improbable that this same Ergamenes was the builder of the temple of Dakkeh, for the Ergamenes of the temple is represented before *Pirāā* (Pharoah) and Anuke, and the title of 'Pirāā' is usually employed only by the Roman emperors (Augustus, Tiberius?), and often along with 'Autokrator Ḳisres', as in the innermost chamber D as well as in the front chamber A at Dakkeh. On the other side, there are proofs that the chamber D must be more ancient than the two front rooms, which existed even under Ptolemy Philopator and Euergetes II.

The present *Temple Buildings* of Dakkeh embrace the massive pylons and the temple proper, lying 40 ft. behind them, both facing the N. (30° E. deviation). The whole stands upon a substantial

terrace of masonry, in a barren and stony district. The temple
is dedicated to the god *Thoth* of Penubs (Ethiopia), the Hermes
Trismegistus of the Greeks. He is the chief deity of the temple,
and to him are addressed the numerous prayers in the demotic and
Greek inscriptions that cover the temple. He is frequently represented with a snake coiled round a staff, like the Hermes of the
Greeks. Along with him Tefnut usually appears, but Hathor, Isis,
and the gods of the cataracts also occur. On both sides of the Pylons, which are about 80 ft. broad, staircases (93 steps) ascend to

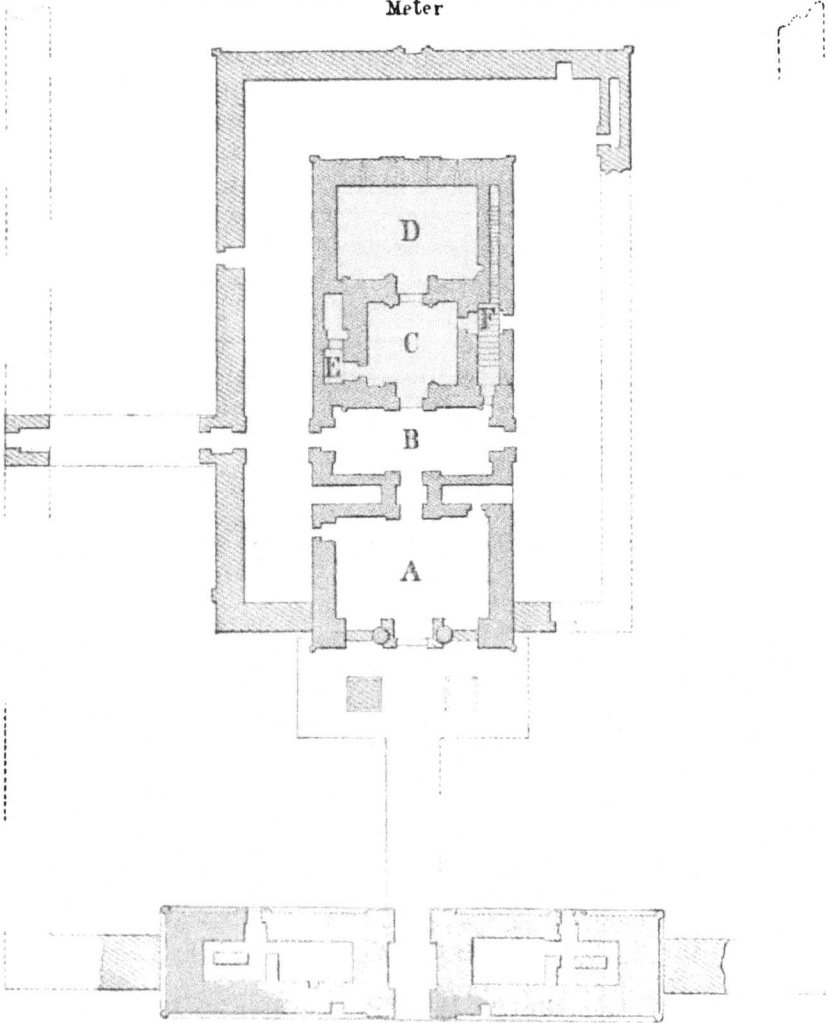

1: 317

the roof, and there are interior chambers as at Edfu (p. 249). A
small door in the gateway between the pylons also admits to the
pylon on the right. There are no hieroglyphics on the outside
of the pylons, the only place in which they are found being the
inner walls of the central gateway. On the left side here is an unnamed king making offerings to the god Thoth with the quadruple
crown, and to Tefnut and Hathor, while Isis appears below. The
sculptures on the right side are destroyed. Numerous inscriptions,
chiefly Greek though some are demotic, are found both on the outside of the pylons and in the central gateway.

The entrance of the **Temple** has two columns with palm-capitals. The portal has been partly destroyed, and the partition walls
crowned with serpents, which connect the columns with the sloping
buttresses, have been broken through the middle, and the representations upon them defaced. On the left (E.) side the temple-wall
adjoins a wall of dressed masonry, which formerly enclosed the entire temple, forming a kind of court; while another wider girdle-
wall, now disappeared, seems to have begun at the pylons. A path
constructed of ancient hewn stones led from the pylon to the temple,
but this has been destroyed except close to the temple, so that we
have to climb up to the platform. The first portion of the temple,
the *Pronaos* (Pl. A), 24½ ft. broad and 17 ft. deep, is covered
with huge flagstones, placed lengthwise in the direction of the
temple axis. The frieze beneath this roof bears the dedication-
inscriptions of the pronaos, that in the middle being a much damaged Greek inscription between two winged serpents with royal
crowns. The following words are still legible: —

ὑπερ βασιλεως πτολε ΄. . . . . . . ελφης
θεων εὑεργετων . . . . ι και
παοτπνουφι . . . . λ ε

From this we gather that the pronaos was dedicated to Hermes
Paotnuphis in the 35th year of Euergetes II. (136 B.C.), by that king
and his wife and sister Cleopatra. Paotnuphis occurs as Pautnuphis
in another inscription, placed by Saturninus Veteranus Aquila,
who executed the gilding in the temple. The two-line hieroglyphic
inscription, on each side of the Greek, corresponds with the latter:
to the left, 'Horhut (referring to the adjoining protecting vulture
with outspread wings), the great god, ... protect thy beloved son
Ptulmis Euergetes and his sister and his wife Cleopatra, the divine
Euergetes, beloved of Thoth Penubs'; to the right the last phrase
is altered to 'beloved of Isis, mistress of Pilak and the southern
gods'. On the right Horhut is described as dwelling in the northern

house [glyph], and on the left as dwelling in the southern

house. The side-pillars on the right and left bear scenes of worship,
on the left addressed to Shu and Tefnut, Thoth and Nehemaaut,
Khnum, and Hathor; on the right to Ammon-Ra and Muth, Horus

and Hathor, and Osiris and Isis. Attention should be paid to the two lowest representations, which are double scenes showing the king with lotus and papyrus-plants, the queen with bouquets of flowers, followed by the Nile-god *Hapu* and by *Sekhet* 𓁹𓁹𓁹 , goddess of the fields, who carries sacrificial cakes and fowls of various kinds and is accompanied by a small bull. On the partition-wall, now partly destroyed, to the left, the king stood before Thoth Penubs, whose figure is still visible. He is here named lord of Pselk ▭ ⬭ 𓏏𓏏 . To the right stood the king and queen worshipping before Isis, daughter of Seb and Nut. Behind Isis is her cartouche, like that of a queen; 'may she protect King Euergetes'. On the front of the two columns are not only the names of the founders of the pronaos, but also those of their ancestors, the divine Adelphi, Euergetæ, Philopatores, Epiphanes, and the divine Philometor; while one of them is dedicated to the memory of Thoth of Penubs, the other to that of Isis, mistress of Pilak (Philæ). The representations on the back of these columns are very remarkable. On the right side is a cynocephalus (symbol of Thoth), with an object like a sistrum 𓏲 in its hands; on the left side is an entirely un-Egyptian seated figure of a dark bearded man, with a quintuple headdress, playing upon the harp. This is the figure of the Ethiopian god 𓏌𓏲 *Sopt* or *Bes*, who smites the enemy. The interior decoration of this hall dates from Augustus, who is here distinguished by the cartouches of *Autokrator Kisres* (*e.g.* on the back of the partition-wall) as well as by the name 𓊽 (*e.g.* on the side-walls).

On the left side-wall is an interesting picture, representing the Pharaoh proffering to the god of writing (Thoth) a palette, which is borne by figures of Isis and Nephthys.

On the right wall the emperor stands before the crowned ram's-headed Khnum, before Osiris and Isis, before Horus and Hathor, and before Arhesnefer and Tefnut. A scene on the back wall of the pronaos shows the king handing wine to the god Thoth, who holds iu his hand a staff 𓌪 beside which two serpents and a scorpion are placed. Some figures of Christian saints have been depicted on this wall.

The doorway to the next room (Pl. B), which dates from Ptolemy IV. Philopator, was erected as the door of a pylon, as is indicated on the Plan (p. 317). There is an exit from the pronaos through the right wing of this pylon, and another exit to the left leads into the court outside the temple. The rear-wall of the pronaos, *i.e.* the front wall of the *Sekos* or Room B, exhibits Ptolemy

Philopator ⟨𓉐𓏤𓉐𓏤⟩, *Son of*
the divine Euergetes, chosen by Ptah, strong in the highness of Ra,
living image of Ammon. On the left he brings offerings to Ra, then
to Khnum and Isis, on the right, to Ammon-Ra and to Horus,
avenger of his father, and presents the field to Isis. Within the
portal, Augustus offers the figure of Ma to the god Thoth of Penubs
and to the lion-headed Tefnut. Above the doorway, on the inside,
is a double scene; both right and left Isis presents the symbols of
life to a crowned hawk, the symbol of the king. Behind the hawk
on the left are the cartouches of King Philopator and his wife
Arsinoë, and behind these, the cartouches of King Philadelphus and
his wife who also was named Arsinoë. On the right side, behind
the cartouches of Philopator and his wife, are those of the king's
father Euergetes I. and his wife Berenice.

The back-wall of this narrow chamber, whose side-walls fell
some years ago, is at the same time the entrance-wall of the most
ancient portion of the temple, viz. the *Sanctuary* (Pl. C), built by
the above-mentioned native king, *Ergamenes.* This king appears
with his full cartouches on the right wall

⟨hieroglyphs⟩ *Ámen ṭeta ankh át ra,*
'Living hand of Ammon, Part of Ra',

⟨hieroglyphs⟩ *Árk ámen ankh t'et ast mer,*
'Ergamenes, ever living, beloved of Isis'. He makes offerings to
Osiris, Isis, and Horus, then proffers wine to Ammon-Ra, Muth,

and Khnum, and finally appears with 𓏌 before Osiris, Thoth

Penubs, lord of Pselk, and Tefnut. · At the foot are Nile-gods.
Similar representations occur on the left side, where the king makes
offerings to Thoth, the lion of the south, to Shu and Arhesnefer,
and then to Khnum, Hathor, and various other deities.

The door of the sanctuary appears to have been gilded. Above
it is a double dedication-inscription of Ergamenes, arranged in
two parts, like the later inscription of Euergetes II. on the outer
portal. On one side the king calls himself the son of Osiris and
Isis, suckled by Nephthys, and son of Khnum and Sati, suckled
by Anuke; on the other side he styles himself son of Ammon, beloved of Osiris and Isis, and again, beloved of Arhesnefer

⟨hieroglyphs⟩ and of Thoth Penubs. The inner walls of this chamber
were also adorned with the most varied sacrificial scenes arranged
in rows one above the other. One of these, in the second row on

the wall to the right, shows the king (Ergamenes) pouring out wine for a god described as ⊏⊐ *Pir-āā* of Senem. In another the king appears before *Imhotep*, son of Ptah, kherheb and overseer of the royal writings.

A small door in the E. (left) wall admits to a richly decorated *Cell* (Pl. E). Two lions depicted on the back-wall recall the Gate of the Lions at Mycenæ. Above them is an allegorical composition: Thoth in the figure of a baboon stands before a lion (Tefnut), above which is the sun-disc and a vulture with a curved sword: this is *Tefnut*, daughter of Ra on the holy island (of Philæ). Another door on the right of the sanctuary leads to the staircase (Pl. F) ascending to the roof of the temple. — The innermost room *(*Pl. D), named the 'Roman sanctuary' by Champollion, was entirely built by the emperor designated (cartouche) *Pir-āā*, and contains scenes of worship to the same gods as appear in the preceding chambers. One of the scenes represents the emperor bestowing upon the goddess Isis a headdress decorated with the Hathor-mask.

Of the *Outside Walls* only the W. wall is adorned. Above the door to the outside was placed a four-line hieroglyphic inscription, with a demotic inscription below. The former is said to read: 'May his name remain before Thoth of Penubs, the great god, the lord of the town of scorpions *(P-selk)*, before Tefnut, before the great gods of the temple of the house of scorpions'. Prof. Eisenlohr was unable to discover this inscription in 1890.

On the E. bank, nearly opposite Dakkeh, lies the village of **Kubbân,** on the site of *Contra Pselchis*, mentioned in the Itinerarium Antonini as 24 Roman M. (22 Eng. M.) from Contra Talmis (Kalabsheh), though in reality it is 32 Eng. M. The ruins here are those of an ancient Egyptian fortress, defended by ditches and towers. To the S. are blocks with the names of Tutmes III., Horus, Ramses II., and later Ramessides; and still farther to the S., a stele of Amenemha III. and the foundations of a small temple. Prisse d'Avennes discovered here the well-known stele describing the route to the gold-mines in the *Wâdi 'Olâki* and the method of supplying these with water. This stele, dating from the 3rd year of Ramses II., which was taken by Count St. Ferriol to his château at Uriage, prompted Chabas to the composition of his interesting treatise on 'Les Inscriptions des Mines d'Or' (Châlon, 1862). The numerous gold-mines, worked until the Middle Ages, were reached by a route a little above Kubbân leading through the extensive Wâdi 'Olâki. Granite mortars and mills and other articles used in the search for gold are still to be seen, especially in tho *Wâdi Khawanîb.* Diodorus (III. 12-14) gives a detailed account of the working of the metal by convicts.

32. From Dakkeh to Abu-Simbel.

Comp. the Map, p. 304.

97 M. — Above Dakkeh the Nile expands. At (3 M.) *Korti*, in hierog. ⊔◯⌢ ⌢, on the W. bank, are the ruins of a small temple of the Roman period, dedicated to Isis and Horus. The name of Tutmes III. appears here on some blocks built into the walls. Straight in front of us rises an isolated mountain. The island of *Derâr* (3 M. from Korti), which we pass on our right, is the ancient *Takompso*, hierog. ⎡▱⎤ ℮℮℮⌢ / ℮℮℮⊗ *Ta-kem-so* (600), described by Herodotus (II. 29). Here ended the territory of 12 schoinoi above Elephantine belonging to Isis of Philæ, of which mention is made on the stele of Philometor in the temple-court of Philæ (comp. p. 300).

On the W. bank, opposite a dark mountain-peak, lies the *Temple of Ofedînah*, also called *Temple of Maharakah*, after the village of **Maharakah**, which lies a little higher up on the E. bank. Dating from the Roman period, its Greek and demotic inscriptions show it to have been dedicated to Serapis and Isis. It consisted of an entrance-hall (now destroyed) approached by a broad flight of 14 steps, and of a main colonnaded building, 40 ft. long and 50 ft. broad. Part of the walls has fallen; but 3 columns to the right and 2 to the left of the entrance still stand, besides 8 columns in the interior. In the innermost corner, to the right, are traces of a staircase leading to the roof. A wall connects this temple with a smaller square structure to the E., on which is a curious representation: beneath a fig-tree (ἱερασυκάμινος, whence the Greek name of the place, which was perhaps named *Penubs* in early Egyptian antiquity) sits a goddess with cow's horns (Isis-Hathor), before whom is a boy with a jug in his hands; above are three other gods. To the left of this scene is Thoth with the ell; beneath is Isis.

The route now lies between monotonous hills. At *Seyâleh* we reach the boundary between Wâdi Kenûs and the *Wâdi el-'Arab*, which extends to Ibrim. At *Mehendi*, on the W. bank, are the ruins of a Roman settlement. The mountains, especially on the E., become higher. At *Medîk* is a picturesque group of hills with groves of palms. The river makes a wide bend to the W., and we soon come in sight of the temple of Sebû'ah, 27 M. from Dakkeh.

The **Temple of Sebû'ah.** — *Es-Sebû'ah* or *Sebû'ah* (the lions) or *Wâdi Sebû'ah* is the site of a temple dedicated to Ammon and Ptah by Ramses II., and constructed like the temple at Gerf Ḥuṣên, partly by excavation in the rock, partly by building. The name is apparently derived from the avenue of *Lions* or *Sphinxes* in front of the temple. Eight of these lions with human faces are supposed to have been ranged on each side, though only the two first have retained their heads. A

few without heads lie behind. Beside the two first are two colossal
statues of Ramses II., 10½ ft. high, placed against pillars, bearing
the cartouches of the king, 'beloved of Harmachis and Ptah' on the
right, and 'beloved of Ammon-Ra and Ptah', on the left. The king's
name appears on the girdles of both figures and on the chests
of the sphinxes. Statues of the king, probably four in number (now
destroyed), also stood in front of the pylon, which is 32 ft. high
and 42 ft. broad. On the back of one of these statues it is recorded
that the king erected this noble pillar in *Pa-Amon* (apparently the
holy name of the temple) in memory of his father Ammon-Ra and
adorned it with costly gems. On the outside of the pylon, as in
various other Egyptian temples, are two colossal figures, which,
however, are difficult to identify owing to the weatherworn state
of the sandstone, of which the temple is built. On the right the
king holds eight foes by the hair, menacing them with his weapon
while they raise their hands in supplication: 'he smites the great
ones of all lands'. The god Harmachis hands him the sword of
victory. To the left is a similar scene, in presence of Ammon-Ra,
who promises to the king victory over all alien lands. The large
fore-court, which we now enter, is 65 ft. square. The interior is
very interesting. To the right and left are corridors, each with 5
Osiris-pillars supporting an architrave. On the left (S.) side the
roof of slabs is still extant, but on the N. side it is wanting, so that
the drift-sand has found entrance and now covers a considerable
portion of the court. At the top of the back of the pylon occur the
varying cartouches of Ramses II., and beneath the cornice his name
occurs again, in anaglyphic characters. On the left (S.) wing of the
pylon, the king presents a sphinx to Ammon-Ra and Muth, to the
right he offers bread to Harmachis and Jusās. Round the court in
the row nearest the ground appears a procession of the children of

the king, each with the name appended, the sons bearing fans,

the daughters bearing sistra. There are two series, both beginning on the W. or back-wall of the court and running respectively
to the right and left from the W. entrance to the main temple. On
the W. wall, to the right of the temple-door, are 19 men (mostly
concealed by the sand), on the N. wall 40 men and 8 women, and
on the E. wall, to the N. of the entrance to the court 27 women,
i.e. in this series 59 sons and 35 daughters. On the W. wall to the
left of the temple-door are 19 men and 20 women, on the S. wall
33 men and 12 women, *i.e.* 52 sons and 32 daughters. If the
names are not repeated, as at Medinet Habu, Abydos, etc., 111
sons and 67 daughters are thus attributed to Ramses the Great.
— The following room is the first in the rock-hewn portion of
the temple. The examination of this and the following rooms

is rendered difficult by the accumulations of sand. The first room contained six large and six small pillars, the former being meant to support the central beams. The following narrow room is adjoined by two side-chambers and three other chambers in the back-wall. In this room appears Ramses II. worshipping and presenting offerings to various deities. Under a canopy are four gods. The foremost is Ptah, bare-headed and in his usual mummy-form, with [𓊽] and [𓋴]. He is named the *Ptah of King Ramses in Pa-amon.* Then, as at Dakkeh, follows the seated figure of a second Ptah, wearing as a headdress the bull's horns with two feathers between them [𓋽]. This Ptah is described as 'lofty with the two feathers and the horns'. Next is a female figure with the moon-disc (perhaps *Rat-tati*), and finally comes Hathor, goddess of the southern Nchet (sycamore tree), with horns turned upwards enclosing two feathers and the sun-disc. The colouring of the sacrificial scenes in the side-chambers is well-preserved; and this is still more the case in the adytum, the central of the three chambers at the back. Both to the right and left in this room the king is represented sacrificing before a richly adorned dhahabîyeh. The dhahabîyeh on the right has the hawk's head of Harmachis as its emblem, that on the left the ram's head of Khnum-Ra. Both stand on ornamented tables. On the left the king is offering incense above an altar, on the right he is offering flowers. A large fan is borne beside him, and behind are standards with the heads of the two gods and of the king. — The central picture exhibits Khnum-Ra seated in a boat beneath a canopy, with the kneeling king to the left and three cynocephali to the right. Beneath is a recess, in which the outlines of three gods may still be made out, although a figure of St. Peter, with a halo und a large key, has been painted over them. The king, who appears on the right and left, with flowers, has now the appearance of offering them to the saint. Beneath is an inscription, running both to the right and to the left and extending on to the side walls: 'The living Hor-Ra, the strong, the beloved of Ma, lord of the festivals, like his father Ptah, king of both lands, Ramses the Great, he has made it in memory of his father Ammon-Ra, king of the gods'.

Beyond Sebû'ah the scenery assumes a regularly desert character, which it retains until near Ḳorusko. Rocky isolated peaks rise on the left. At *Malki* the Nile makes a sudden bend, and beyond this point the banks are once more cultivated, while dense palm-groves appear on the left (E.), with scattered huts and many sâḳiyehs.

11½ M. **Ḳorusko.** The weekly mail-steamer spends the night here, and Cook's tourist-steamer touches here both on the way up and the way down, if the passengers desire to visit the Awas el-

Guarâni. Until a few years ago Korusko was the chief emporium and port of shipment for the caravans crossing the desert to or from *Abu Ḥamed*, which lies 8-10 long days' journey distant (see below). This road avoided the three upper cataracts, which are not navigable when the river is low, and it also shortened the journey considerably by cutting off the windings of the Nile. Russegger, Lepsius, and finally Gordon (1884) selected it on their way to Kharṭûm. A short excursion along this desert-route, between the hills, black with iron-scale, is not uninteresting; or the traveller may ascend ($^{1}/_{2}$ hr.; steep and stony) the hill of *Awas el-Guarâni*, close to Korusko. On the summit is the tomb of the saint to whom the hill owes its name, a frequented pilgrim-resort. The view extends over the Nile valley as far as Derr. A fort has recently been erected by the British at Korusko. On the bank of the river is a coffee-house.

The desert route from Korusko to (227 M.) Abu Hamed and Berber is described in Lepsius's Letters from Egypt and Ethiopia (see p. xxv). From Abu Hamed to Berber the hire of camels was formerly 60 piasters each, afterwards increased to 80 and 90 p. Among the stages on this route are *el-Bâb*, a range of sandstone hills extending for two days' journey; *Bahr belâh mâh* with its greenish fine-grained rocks continuing the preceding; *Bahr Hatab;* and *Wâdi Delah*, where dûm-palms are found. The route intersects the *Gebel Roft* by means of the *Wâdi es-Sufr*, with a few india-rubber and sunt-trees, and then the *Gebel Seneyât* by means of the *Wâdi Mûrat*. The last, the half-way point, contains some brackish water, the only water met with on the entire route, and a few huts. Next follows the wide plain of *el-Münderah*, bounded by the lofty hills of *Abu Sihah*, then the stony hills of *Adar Auîb*, and the boundless plain of *Adererâd*, which extends to Abu Hamed, with the low *Gebel Farût* on the left, and the *Gebel Mokran* on the right. Mirages, called by the Arabs *Bahr Sheitân* or 'waters of Satan', are frequently seen on the way. *Abu Ḥamed* on the Nile is reached on the 8th, or at latest on the 10th day.

A little beyond Korusko the Nile valley trends to the N.W., so that the N. wind which prevails in winter frequently retards navigation. On the left bank rises a picturesque chain of hills. In this reach travellers have a chance of seeing crocodiles, which frequent the sandbanks and lay their eggs in the clefts of the shore. Recently, however, they have become somewhat rare. On the W. bank the inconspicuous *Temple of 'Amâdah*, 8 M. from Korusko, comes in sight. It lies deeply sunk in the desert-sand, while on the opposite bank a cultivated strip with many trees stretches between the river and the hills. Passengers by Cook's steamers have an opportunity of visiting this temple.

The **Temple** of **'Amâdah** has a very unpretending exterior and seems at first hardly worthy of a visit. Yet it is in reality of great interest both for scientific and ordinary travellers as an excellent example of the graceful and elegant architecture of the 18th Dyn., under which it was built. Nothing is left of the front of the entrance-hall except the doorway; and the structure of Nile bricks adjoining the latter indicates that the temple has been used as a mosque or as the tomb of a saint. (A Mohammedan cupola, removed only a few years ago, was an additional proof.) On the right side of the door-

way appears Tutmes III., to the left, his son and successor Amen-
hotep II. $\left(\odot \longleftarrow \text{🪲} \; \middle| \; \right)$ *Ra āū kheperu*, with the god Harmachis.
On the inside of the doorway is the name of Seti I. (19th Dyn.).
Also in the doorway appears the praying figure of *Setau*, royal prince
of Kush, who according to the royal cartouche above, served under
Ramses II. The *Antechamber* itself consists of three rows of pillars,
arranged in three couples on each side, and behind is a row of
proto-Doric (p. 12) columns. The side-pillars on the right and left
are connected with the side-walls. Most of the pillars exhibit the
cartouches of Tutmes IV., distinguished from that of Tutmes III.
by the three strokes signifying the plural. On the first engaged
pillar to the left Tutmes IV. is mentioned as 'beloved by *Ra kha
kau* $\left(\odot \; \ominus \; \text{LJLJLJ} \right)$, Usertesen III., lord of Sekhem', a king of
the 12th Dynasty. On the outer and inner sides of the two archi-
traves over the central pillars are dedication-inscriptions by Tutmes IV. On the N. side of the architrave on the right, we read:
'The living good god of the *Unma* (genuine), who defeated Ethiopia,
brought the boundaries like him who was not created (Ptah), a
brave king with his sword, like Mentu, of a steady heart above many,
he makes the mountains quake'. On the S. side of the left architrave
are the words: 'Thoth, lord of divine words, speaks to the great
cycle of gods in Pa Ra (probably the home of the gods): Come,
behold the great and holy monument, carefully hewn, the divine
temple of millions of years, made by King Ra-men-kheperu (Tutmes IV.) for his father *Ra-tum*, the great god, who made him'. The
inscriptions on the other architraves are similar. On the two columns to the left are the names of Tutmes III. and Amenhotep II., so
that the columns seem to be older than the pillars and architrave.

The *Sekos*, beyond the antechamber, is broad but shallow
($24^{1}/_{2}$ ft. by $6^{1}/_{2}$). On the outside of the doorway here also
Amenhotep II. is commemorated; on the inside Seti I. is named as
the restorer $\left(\text{🦅} \; sma \right)$ of this monument meant for Ammon-
Ra and Harmachis; and over the door on the inside, Tutmes III.
To the right on the inside of the entrance-wall is Tutmes III. embraced by Isis, and then Amenhotep II. offering drink-offerings to
Ammon-Ra. On the left Thoth and Hor-Hut strew the symbols of
life over Amenhotep II. Three doors in the back-wall of this Sekos
lead into other apartments. The central one enters the *Sanctuary*,
which occupies the whole of the remaining length of the temple
(about 16 ft.). The doors to the right and left each admit into two
chambers, one behind the other, the front chamber in each case
being the larger. Tutmes III. styles himself 'beloved by Harmachis
and Ammon-Ra' in a three-line inscription over the door of the
sanctuary'; it is therefore evident that the temple of 'Amâdah was

dedicated to these two deities, as is also indicated by the representations to the right and left of the entrance-door. Above the small door on the right are the dedications of Tutmes III. and Amonhotep II. The three apartments contained scenes of worship, scenes from the founding of the temple,and sacrificial scenes. The traveller should notice the carefully executed portraits of the three kings who took part in the erection of the temple, Tutmes III., Amenhotep II., and Tutmes IV.

On the back-wall of the sanctuary is a stele of great historical importance. At the top is a relief of Amenhotep II. presenting two vessels of wine to Harmachis and Amon-Ra; beneath is an inscription of 20 lines, from the 3rd year of the reign of Amenhotep II. After a flattering account of the king and his achievements (repeated on a stele found at Erment and now in Vienna), the completion of the temple begun by Tutmes III. is mentioned.

Line 12. 'Behold, the king adorned the house of the god (which had been erected by) his father, King Tutmes IH., for all 'the divine fathers, built of stone as an enduring work, with a protecting wall of bricks around it. The doors were of the finest acacia-wood, the gateways of enduring stone, with the object of commemorating for ever the great name of his father Tutmes III. in this temple. King Amenhotep II. celebrated the festival of the laying of the foundation-stone in honour of all his ancestors, while he dedicated to him a massive gate-tower of hard stone in front of the protecting-wall of this splendid dwelling of the gods, a colonnade round it of hard stone as a lasting work, many sacrificial vessels and utensils of silver and brass, stands, altars, a bronze caldron, brasiers, dishes, and censers. Thereupon the king caused this stele to be prepared and placed in this temple in the place where (stands) the statue of the great Horus, the king, and he caused to be graven on it the mighty name of Amenhotep II. in the house of 'his divine fathers, after he returned from the land of Upper Syria, where he overthrew all his adversaries, in order to widen the boundaries of Egypt on his first compaign.

Still more remarkable is the narrative at the end of this inscription:

'The king had returned home, with his heart full of gratitude to his father Ammon. With his own hand he had struck down with his club seven kings, who were in the region of the land of Takhis. They lay pinioned on the fore-deck of the royal ship, the name of which was 'Ship of Amenhotep II., maintainer of the land'. Six of these enemies were hanged on the walls of Thebes, and their hands the same. The remaining enemy was carried up the stream to Nubia, and hanged on the walls of the town of *Napata*, in order to make the victory of the king manifest for ever among all the tribes of the land of the negroes, since he has taken possession of the tribes of the S., and tamed the tribes of the N., even to the ends of the whole earth, upon which the sun shines, without finding any opposition, according to the command of his father Ammon-Ra, lord of the throne of both lands. Such things has King Amenhotep II. done'. From *Brugsch*, History of Egypt, pp. 390, 391.

Those who ascend to the roof of the temple will find a memorial of **Herodotus**, the 'father of history', not, however, inscribed by himself, for he himself informs us (II.29) that he came no farther than Elephantine. The worn aspect of the letters indicates that the inscription (as follows) is of considerable antiquity.

ΗΡΟΔΟΤΟΣ ΑΛΙΚΑΡΝΑΣΣΟΥ
ΕΙΔΕΝ ΚΑΙ ΕΦΑΥΜΑ

'Herodotus of Halicarnassus beheld and admired'. Beneath, in a
later style of writing, is the word ΟΥΔΑΜΩΣ 'not at all', indicating
the unauthentic character of the inscription above.

3½ M. **Derr,** on the E. bank, prettily situated beneath sycamores and date-palms, contains mud-houses. The one brick-building is the residence of the Kâshef, who was formerly independent
ruler of Lower Nubia and owned a large harem. Outside the town,
about half-way to the hill, lies the mosque of a saint. The top of
the hill commands an attractive view of the town and the Nile. Near
its foot lies the small and unfortunately much injured *Rock Temple
of Derr.* The vestibule, the sides of which were formed by the
smoothed rocks of the hill, and which was 42½ ft. deep by 46 ft.
broad in the open air, contained a triple row of pillars, of which the
hindmost alone is standing. This row has Osiris-figures against the
pillars (as at Medinet-Habu, p. 175, etc.). The two front rows and
the gateway are now represented only by fragments a few feet in
height. On the back of the left side of the gateway are some traces
of a warlike scene, with chariots and warriors. The right side-wall
of the vestibule was covered with warlike representations, now much
damaged, in three rows. In the topmost row only the legs of the
figures are now left. In the second row Ramses II., founder of this
temple, can be distinguished in his chariot accompanied by a lion,
before a group of prisoners. The lowest row showed the king
launching arrows against his fleeing foes. We see the fugitives conveying their wounded to the mountains, where a herdsman's family,
surrounded by their domestic animals, wait in grief and anxiety for
their son. On the left wall also are remains of three scenes, including one in which the king leads two rows of captives to Harmachis.
The third row of pillars, hewn out of the rock and still standing,
bore dedications from the king to various gods. The representations
on the back wall of this hall, to the right and left of the entrance
into the dark excavated part of the temple (lights necessary), are
specially effective.

On the right side the king holds by the hair some foes, bending
in presence of Ammon-Ra, while between the king's legs is his
lion, here said to follow the king and to slay his enemies. The
heads of the king and the god are unfortunately destroyed. To the
left of this scene are two smaller ones showing the king before Ptah
and (Sekhet) before Thoth. Beneath is a row of the king's daughters
with sistra, corresponding to a row of his sons, with fans, headed
by *Amenhikhopeshf*, on the left wall. The chief scene on the left
wall, above the king's sons, shows the king fighting against his foes
in presence of the hawk-headed Harmachis, with the lion biting the
leg of one of the foes. In the small adjoining scene, Ramses presents
the ram's-headed Khnum with a figure of Ma, goddess of truth.

The next room, almost square, is entirely hewn out of the rock, six square pillars being left in two rows in the centre. The architrave above the pillars contains the customary dedication-inscription. On the right we read: 'The living Hor-Ra, the strong lord of both lands beloved by Ma, who rules Egypt and has conquered the nations, the gold-hawk, rich in years, great in victories, the king of Upper and Lower Egypt, Ramses II., has reared in memory of his father Harmachis the *Hat Ramessu meramon* in *Pa Ra*. 'Pa Ra' is thus the holy name of the spot and 'temple of Ramses Meramon' the name of the sanctuary. On the left architrave *Ammon-Ra* is mentioned instead of Harmachis, as lord of the throne of both lands, so that the temple must be regarded as dedicated to both deities. On the six pillars are figures of the king before Tum, Ptah, Khnum, and other gods. On the right side-wall is the boat of Harmachis borne by 12 priests and conducted by the king; on the left side-wall the king, in a boat, offering incense. From this chamber a large door, surmounted by the winged sun-disc, leads into the sanctuary, and doors to the right and left admit to smaller apartments. Four seated figures occupy the rear-wall of the sanctuary, viz. (beginning to the left) Ptah, Ammon-Ra, the king, and Harmachis with the hawk's head. They are all represented full face, and would be difficult to identify were it not for the inscriptions adjoining. — Not far from the temple is a small rock-stele, dedicated to the king's son *Amenemheb*, with the figure of a temple.

Beyond Derr the Nile valley again turns to the S.W. To the right is the island of *Tomâs*. Crocodiles now become more numerous, looking from a distance like tree-trunks or like huge frogs. A nearer view is only to be obtained by rowing on ahead of the dhahabiyeh in the felukeh or small boat. At *Ellesîyeh* (E. bank), also called *ed-Duknesrah*, is a rock-tomb of the 18th Dynasty. On a stele here, dating from the 43rd year of Tutmes III., the king presents offerings to Horus, lord of *Mâm* ⌐⌐⌐ , and to Sati, mistress of Abu. The wall-paintings represent the king seated between Muth and Uaz; then offering to Horus, lord of the land of Kheut, to Horus of Mam, and to Thoth and Hathor.

On the W. bank, opposite *Ketteh*, we next see an ancient ruined fort. Then to the right is the verdant island of *Abu Râs*, and to the left the village of —

13 M. Ibrim. To the E. rises a considerable chain of hills, and to the W. (left) is a narrow strip of palms and castor-oil plants, beyond which is the desert. On the W. bank, a little inland from the village of *Anibeh*, and hidden behind a palm-grove, lies an interesting rock-tomb of the reign of Ramses VI. (⌐⌐⌐⌐⌐), *Amen hi-khopesh ramses neterhik an*. It belonged to *Pennut*, son of Ha-

runefer, governor ([hieroglyphs] ten) of the land of Wawa. On the
E. part of the S. wall is inscribed a record of the presentation of
lands for the maintenance of the statues of the king in the town of
[hieroglyphs] *Emād*, which was apparently the name of this place
or of 'Amâdah.

On the E. wall is a royal prince of Kush, standing, fan in hand, before
Ramses VI., and announcing to him the gift of *Pennut*, who presented.
the adjacent statues of the king and two silver anointing-vessels. In the
lower row, Pennut and *Ta Kha*, his wife, the singer of Ammon, present
an offering before their deceased relations, the men being represented
above, the women below. These family scenes are continued on the E.
part of the N. Wall; above is the worship of Harmachis, below that of
Osiris. On the W. part of the N. wall and continued on the W. wall
and half of the S. wall are scenes relating to the worship of the dead.
Pennut appears on his knees before a mountain, from which the head of
Hathor, a goddess of the under-world, projects among lotus-flowers.
Within the mountain is a chapel with a tapering roof, and in front of
the mountain is the goddess Ape, holding a frog in her hand. On the
W. wall is the preparation of the mummy of the deceased, and the pre-
sentation of the deceased and his wife to Osiris, by Horus, son of Isis.
Beneath, the fields of *Aalura* are being tilled; and Harmachis, Tum, and
Khepera, seated upon a pedestal, are receiving homage. On the W. half
of the S. wall are the balances of the dead, the entrance to the grave,
and the laying of the deceased in the vault by a long train of mourning
relations.

A little above Anibeh (p. 329) a flat-topped hill of some size
rises steeply from the Nile on the E. Upon this stands the partly
ruined fort of **Kaṣr Ibrim**, dating from Roman times. A visit to it
is interesting. The ascent is made on the N. At the top are some
blocks with the name of Taharka of the 25th Dyn., and a basilica
with Byzantine capitals of granite. Kaṣr Ibrîm is identified with
the Roman *Primis Parva* or *Premis*, a fortress stormed by Petronius
(p. 302), who afterwards restored it and garrisoned it with 400 men,
with provisions for two years. At the beginning of the 16th cent.
the sultan Selîm placed a garrison of Bosnians here, whose descendants were defeated in 1811 by the fleeing Mamelukes. Finally
Ibrahîm Pasha captured the fortress.

In the S. slope of the mountain, not far above the river-bank,
are five grottoes hewn in the rock, all of which except the most
northerly, bear inscriptions. The first (on the S.) shows over the
entrance the cartouches of Tutmes III., 'beloved by Horus, lord of
Mām [hieroglyphs], and by Sati, mistress of the land of *Khent*'. This
grotto belonged to *Nehi*, overseer of the palace and royal son
(probably only a title), and overseer of the S. land. Beside a much
damaged relief of Nehi presenting booty or tribute from the S. land
to the king, is the inscription: 'Bringing of the tribute of the S.
lands in gold, ivory, and ebony, by the gracious overseer, the privy
councillor . . . . ., the royal son, and president of the S. land

Nehi'. In the recess at the end of the cave Tutmes III. sits between
Horus and Sati. Immediately to the left is the second cave (about
10 ft. deep), much less skilfully executed, in which appear ten
persons before Ramses. Among these are *Setau*, prince of Kush
(whose name is found elsewhere in Nubia), and a number of scribes
and officials.

The third cave, which lies a little higher up, also shows the
cartouche of Tutmes III. The recess contains the somewhat roughly
executed figures of four seated personages; to the right the king
and Sati, to the left the king and Horus, lord of Mām. — The fourth
cave (from the S.) is the most important. It belongs to Amenhotep II., who appears conducted by Horus, lord of Beheni, to a
row of gods including Khnum, Sati, and Anuke, the gods of the
cataracts, and Horus, Hathor, and Heben. — To the S. of Ḳaṣr
Ibrim a few steles are found, one showing a victorious king in his
war-chariot.

The mountains presently retire, leaving room for a strip of cultivated land. Numerous *Sâkîyehs* or water-wheels are seen. To the
left (E.) appears the village of *Djimeneh*, beside a pretty wood.
Farther on, on the same bank, lies *Toshkeh* (Nubian 'Three Mountains'), a small place among palms, with a somewhat uncivilized
population. At *Toshkeh el-Gharb*, on the W. bank, 7 M. from the
river, a large force of dervishes was defeated with the loss of their
cannon by the British on Aug. 3rd 1889; several thousand slain
were left on the battle-field, and their weapons and clothing were
sold by the neighbouring natives. Cook's tourists may visit the
battle-field if they desire it.

The district we next enter upon is very monotonous and almost
uninhabited; and navigation is rendered difficult by rocks. To the
left lie *Gurgundi* and three shêkhs' tombs; then the villages of *Debüt*
and *Feraig*. The river-bed becomes very wide at places. On the
right we catch sight of the colossi that guard the temple of Abu-
Simbel.

33½ M. *Abu-Simbel*, on the W. bank.

35. The Rock-Temples of Abu-Simbel.

Cook's tourist-steamers usually reach Abu-Simbel in the evening of
the third day, in time to permit of a visit to the temples before night.
Next morning they proceed to Wâdi Ḥalfah. On the return-voyage they
again spend the night at Abu-Simbel, starting next morning at 9 or
10 o'clock.

The two temples of **Abu-Simbel** ('Father of the Ear of Corn')
lie a short distance apart at the foot of a precipitous cliff close to the
W. bank of the Nile. No other temple in Egypt produces so unex-
pectedly grand an effect as the great rock temple of Ramses II.,
especially by moonlight. By itself it would repay the trouble of
the ascent from Philæ. both by the dignity of its sculptures and by

the gorgeously coloured representations in the interior. Although the smaller temple also has its attractions, and though the appropriate order of visiting the temples would be to proceed from the smaller to the larger, yet it is probable that the traveller will be

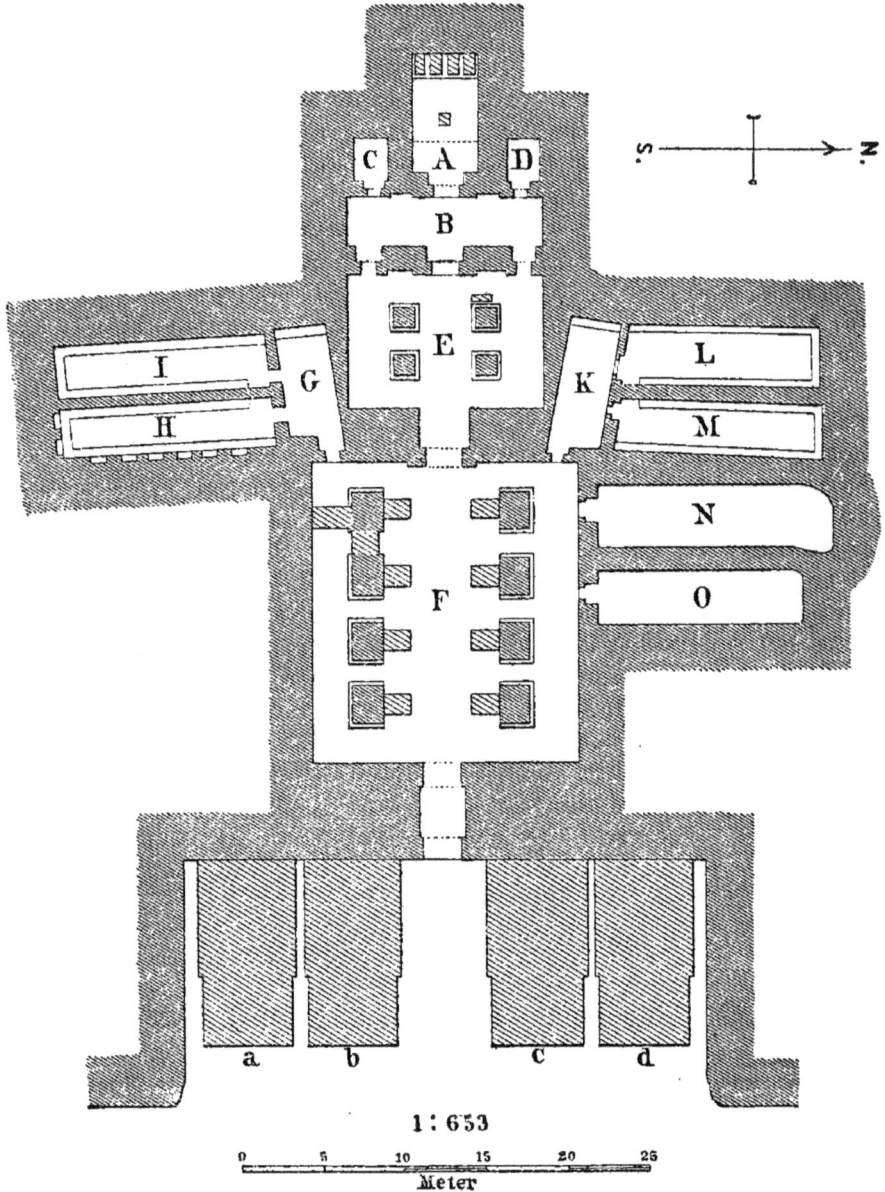

1 : 653

drawn by the magic charm of the great temple to visit it first. Boats and steamers moreover usually land their passengers in front of the latter.

The **Great Temple of Abu-Simbel.** The cliff has been hewn away and smoothed for a breadth of 119 ft. and a height of nearly

105 ft., in order to form the imposing rock-façade of this temple. At the top we see a row of 22 cynocephali (some destroyed), which we learn from other Egyptian temples to recognize as worshippers of the sun-god. Below these are the cartouches of the king, surrounded with Uræus-serpents. Then follows the short dedication inscription of Ramses the Great, which begins in the middle and runs in both directions; on the right it styles the king 'beloved by Harmachis', on the left 'beloved by Ammon, king of the gods'. Still lower, in a recess in the centre of the temple-wall, is a full-relief statue of Horus (Harmachis), with the sun on his head and the symbols of life in his hands, while below, to the right, is the goddess Ma, to the left the symbol $\bigdownarrow$ *user*, thus expressing the king's name in picture-writing. To the right and left is the king again, presenting figures which also express his name, and worshipping the god. Below, and somewhat indistinct, are the double cartouches of the king.

Our attention is most forcibly attracted to the four seated *Colossi* (Pl. a, b, c, d), hewn out of the rock, with their backs against the cliff. That to the left of the entrance (Pl. b) has unfortunately been violently deprived of its head and arms', which now lie on the ground in front. The colossus on the other side of the door (Pl. c) was restored by Seti II. Each of those figures is not less than 65 ft. high, their various limbs being in proportion. In spite of the enormous scale the general effect is successful, and the countenances have a pleasant and intelligent expression. All four represent Ramses the Great, as is testified by the cartouches on the breast and arms and between the legs. To the right and left of each are standing figures, mostly of women; to the right and left of the entrance, *Nofertari Meri-en-mut*, consort of Ramses; between the legs of the injured colossus, prince *Amenhikhopeshf* ('Ammon in his sword'), who is introduced in the temple of Derr as the oldest son (semes) of Ramses II.; to the left of this colossus *Tua*, the king's mother. Beside the colossus farthest to the left are two daughters of the king, viz. *Nebt-tati*, on the left, and *Bant-anta* on the right; between the legs is an unnamed female figure. The figures at the sides of the colossus to the extreme right, the names of which arc concealed by the sand, probably correspond to these. In 1817 Belzoni spent 14 days in freeing the temple from the sand that had drifted into it from the desert behind. Burckhardt, however, had mentioned it previously. It was again laid bare by Lepsius in 1844 and by Mariette in 1869, but the sand has already covered great part of it to a considerable depth.

Before we enter the temple our attention is claimed by a *G*reek inscription which is found on the left leg of the injured colossus, along with various other Greek, Carian, and Phœnician inscriptions. It runs as follows: —

Βασιλέος ἐλθόντος ἐς Ἐλεφαντίναν Ψαμματίχο
ταῦτα ἔγραψαντ οἱ σὺν Ψαμματίχοι τοὶ Θεόκλος
ἔπλεον ἦλθον δὲ Κέρκιος κατυπερθένισσο ποταμὸς
ἀνίη ἀλόγλοσος Δηχεποτάσιμτο Αἰγύπτιος δὲ Ἄμασις
ἔγραφε Δαμεραρχον Ἀμοιβίχου καὶ Πέλεχος Οὐδάμου.

In English : When King Psammetichus came to Elephantine, the companions of Psammetichus, son of Theokles, wrote this. They came by ship viâ Kerkis (p. 316) to where the river rises, the differently speaking Dechepotasimto (*i.e.* a foreigner, perhaps a Carian) and Amasis speaking Egyptian. Demerarchon, son of Amoibichos, and Pelekos, son of Udamos, wrote.

The leader of this company is here named Psammetikh; in a Phoenician inscription on the same spot one of the mercenaries is spoken of as a servant of *Hor, the general.* The writers of the other Greek inscriptions were partly Ionians from Teos and Kolophon, partly Dorians from Rhodes, a Sidonian, and a Carian.

Providing ourselves with candles, or still better with a magnesium lamp, we now enter the rock-temple, the interior of which, with its still vividly coloured pictorial decorations, is no less remarkable than the exterior. The walls of the first hall (Pl. F), which is 58 ft. long by 54 ft. broad, are covered all round with representations, which were first chiselled in the stone, then covered with a thin coating of stucco and painted. The ceiling is supported by eight square pillars, against which stand Osiris-figures of the king, with the scourge and the crook in his crossed hands. The ceiling itself is adorned with vultures and the names of the king. Above the entrance is the remarkably simple dedication-inscription, on the right to Harmachis, lord of the land of Kheut, on the left to Ammon-Ra, king of the gods. The pictorial scenes in this hall are symmetrically arranged, so that those referring to events in the N. of Egypt are placed on the N. (right) side, those to events in the S., on the S. (left) side. A similar arrangement was adopted in the exterior hall of the temple of Bêt el-Walli (p. 310).

On each side of the entrance-wall within are representations, such as are commonly found on the pylons of more recent temples; as *e.g.* at Edfu and Philæ. The king aims a blow with his club at a number of foes, whom he holds by the hair, while they raise their hands in supplication. On the left are represented N. tribes, on the right S. tribes, easily distinguished by their facial characteristics. Harmachis stands before the king on the left, and Ammon, handing him the sword of victory, on the right. Hovering above the king is a protecting vulture. On a standard behind him is the name *Ka nekht meri ma,* 'the strong bull, beloved of the goddess Ma'. In his right hand is an ostrich feather, in his left a head with the *Suten Ka,* the person of the king, with the legend 'the living royal Ka, lord of both lands in the grave, in the house of the deep'. Beneath are the children of the king; to the right his sons, to the left his daughters, with sistra.

We now turn to the S. wall, on the left. At the top are five religious pictures: sacrificial scenes before Ammon, Harmachis, the king in the tree of life kneeling upon the symbol of the festival,

〇〒 *heb*, before Ptah, before a ram's-headed deity (*Mer nut-f*, loving his mother), lord of Khāit, and before Apt. Beneath are three large warlike scenes. The first represents the king in his chariot at the storm of a fortress. The horses with handsome harness are galloping, while the king launches an arrow against the fortress. Above him is the guardian vulture, and behind him are his three sons *Amenḥikhopeshf*, *Ramses*, and *Raḥiuanemif*, with their shield-bearers in chariots. The defenders of the well-drawn fortress are pierced by arrows; one is falling from the walls. A herdsman takes to flight with his herd.

Beside the king's horses are the words, referring to the king: 'The good god, son of Ammon, the advancing lord of the sword, protector of his soldiers, shield of the fighters, bravely knowing the place of his hand, firm in his war-chariot like the lord of Thebes, a lord of victory he slays hundreds of thousands, one bull against numberless (foes), he sweeps away the confederates, he defeats the rebels on the summit of their mountains, he penetrates into their valleys like the grasshoppers. Thou causest them to be cut off in their dwellings. Thou destroyest their seed with the royal sickle'.

A second picture exhibits the king on foot, treading upon a prostrate enemy, and piercing a Syrian with a lance so that his blood gushes forth. The king is represented as a young man of vigorous frame, probably as at the beginning of his warlike career.

The inscription runs: 'The good god who breaks in pieces the nine tribes of the bow, who exterminates the lands of the N., a strong hero against the nations, with a brave sword like Mentu. He leads the land of the negroes to the N. land, the Amu to the land of Khent (Nubia). He transplants the people of the Shasu to the land of . . ., he places the land of Tehen at the mountain-ridge. He fills with his victories the temples that he has built with the booty which he won when he overthrew the land of Syria, and annihilated the land of Retennu, thrown down upon its back'.

The third picture exhibits the triumphal return of the king from battle. His chariot is preceded by two rows of fettered captives — black and brown people from the S. (*i.e.* Nubians and Sûdânese) — clad in skins and wearing caps of straw or reeds. The king follows calmly in his chariot; his horse, named *Nekhtu em was* (Victorious in Thebes), paces proudly along; and beneath the horse is the king's lion, which accompanied him in battle.

The inscription is as follows: 'The living and good god, who tames the rebellious, smites the land of the S., and annihilates the land of the N. A brave king with his sword he drives far back those who have crossed his borders. His majesty comes to (distant) lands, he places many in terror'. Farther on we read 'He slays their chiefs, he causes the negroes of Wawa to say 'he is like a flame in its uprising, he (spares) not the Retennu'.

A large picture on the opposite (N. wall) deals with the warlike events connected with the storming of the fortress of *Katesh*, on the Orontes (Aranuta), with which we have already become acquainted in the Ramesseum (p. 161), and at Luxor, Karnak, and Abydos.

In the upper half of the picture the besieged fortress is depicted, with the king, bending his bow, attacking it on the left. The Egyptian chariots surround that of the king. Beneath the fortress are the divisions of the army of the Kheta (Hittites) and their allies, of which one is stated at

6000, the other at 9000 men. The Egyptian chariots meet those of the Kheta and their allies, who ride three in a chariot. Many of the enemy, both Kheta and Libyans, have fallen into the water. To the extreme right, above the blue-painted river, is the king in his chariot, addressing gracious words to his officers, who count the severed hands and limbs of the Kheta and Naharina before him and bring fettered prisoners. A narrow strip below represents the chariot-fight. Beneath, to the left, is the stockaded camp, into which, according to the adjoining inscription, the enemy forced their way but were repulsed by the single legion of Ammon, commanded by the king, who had been lulled into security by the false reports of two spies, and had despatched several of his regiments in another direction. In the picture to the right the king sits upon his throne, among his courtiers. To the right and left of the royal person is the account of an event in the 5th year of his reign, already known to us from the Ramesseum (p. 161). It relates that two Arabs (Shasu) entered the Egyptian camp, pretending to be refugees from the Kheta, and seeking service under the Pharaoh. They stated that the Kheta lay at Khirabu (Helbon *i.e.* Aleppo) to the N. of Thunep, and were in terror of the Egyptians. This information was false, and the two spies were flogged (in the lowest scene to the right), in order, as the inscription says, that they might say where the miserable Kheta lurked. The spies were next brought before the king on his golden throne, and cross-examined, and finally confessed that the Kheta, with numerous allies, lay behind Katesh. The king assembles his generals, relates what the spies have told, chides his officers for being so imperfectly informed, and orders the recall of the troops that had been sent elsewhere. He himself puts on his armour, attacks the enemy, slays them, and throws them into the river.

Two pictures on the back (W.) wall of this main hall show the king presenting the enemies in fetters to the gods. On the left are two rows of negroes and Nubians before Ammon-Ra, the deified image of the king, and Muth; on the right the Asiatics (Hittites) before Harmachis, the figure of the king, and a lion-headed goddess (Sekhet). The adjoining inscription runs: 'Bringing of the tribute by the good god (*i.e.* the king) for his father Ra, when he came out of the land Kheta, annihilating the rebellious lands and smiting the enemies in their dwellings, with silver, gold, khesbet (lapis-lazuli), mafek (malachite), and precious stones, as the conquest of every land had been commanded him'. Between the two last pillars in this hall is a stele of the 35th year of Ramses II., on which, beneath a relief, is a long decree in favour of King Ramses, issued by the god Ptah Totunen. This decree was repeated almost word for word by Ramses III. on the pylon of the temple of Medinet Habu.

The other chambers of this temple are less interesting, and their examination is rendered troublesome by the swarms of bats that fly against the lights. They contain only the usual scenes of offerings, most of them unfinished. As the accompanying plan (p. 332) shows, two parallel chambers (Pl. O, N) run off from the N. side of the main hall, while from the ends of the back wall lead two oblique passages (Pl. K, G), from each of which run two parallel chambers (Pl. L, M, and Pl. H, I). Round the walls of these latter chambers run stone benches, less than 3 ft. high. In the S.W. chamber (Pl. I) is the picture of an altar with a hieratic inscription. Directly behind the main hall (Pl. F) is a smaller hall (Pl. E; 36 ft. broad, 25 ft. deep), with four pillars. On the N. and S. walls are depicted the boats with the shrines of Harmachis and Ammon, borne in each case by 20 priests. Three doors lead hence to a long narrow chamber (Pl. B), at the back of which are three recesses (Pl. A, C, D). In the central recess, the sanctuary, stands an altar, behind which are painted four figures, viz. Ptah (to the left), Ammon in blue, King Ramses, and Harmachis. No one should omit to enjoy the mysterious effect of the interior view of this temple, with its eight Osiris-statues, as seen by the light of torches or a magnesium-lamp.

We now climb over fallen stones and heaps of sand to the smaller temple, which lies a little to the N.

The *Smaller Rock Temple of Abu-Simbel lies close to the river. The cliff has here been smoothed for a breadth of 90 ft. to make room for the façade of this attractive temple of Hathor, which in modest contrast to Ramses's huge monument, will not fail to produce a satisfactory impression. The six statues on the façade do not project boldly like the colossi of the great temple, but stand in niches supported on projecting pillars. Moreover it is not only the king that is here represented; to the right and left of him stand female figures equally large in which we recognize his consort *Nofertari Merienmut*. The latter holds a sistrum in her hand and wears a double headdress with horns twisted round a disc, such as is worn by Hathor, goddess of love, whose representative the queen is. The figures at the corners represent Ramses again; on the left in his usual form with a dagger in his girdle, and on the right as a deified king, with a crown consisting of the double feather springing

from the sun, and the twisted horns ⟨symbol⟩ . Besides the six co-

lossi there are a number of much smaller statues of the children of the king and queen. Beside the colossi on the right and left of the door are the two eldest sons of the king, viz. (on the right) *Amenhikhopeshf* (Ammon in his sword) and (on the left) *Rahiuanemif* (Ra at his left hand); beside the outer colossi are the princes *Meritum* (right) and *Merira* (left); and beside each of the colossi of the queen are statues of the princesses *Meritamon* (right) and *Honttaui* (left), with sistra in their hands. The first and third pillars on the right bear interesting inscriptions: 'He (the king) has made the temple

in an excavation ⟨cartouche symbol⟩ *shet* ⟩ in the mountain, in everlasting

work, in the land of *Khent'* ⟨symbol⟩ , 'Frontier-land' or 'Bow-land',

and 'His Majesty has commanded to make a temple in the land of Khent, in an excavation in the mountain: never was such a thing done before'. A narrow portal admits to the temple, which, to judge from a relief and inscription beside the door, was dedicated also to Ammon and a Horus (em heb).

The *Main Hall* is practically the only one in this temple, as the rooms behind are merely its dependencies. It is 34 ft. deep and 27 ft. broad, and has six pillars in two rows, each decorated with the head of Hathor with the cow's ears ⟨symbol⟩, and bearing the car-

touches of Ramses II. and his queen Nofertari. On the architrave
above is the inscription (to the left): 'The living and good god
punishes the Hannu (Nubians), conquers the land of Nehesi, smites
the S. lands, ploughs the N. lands. King Ramses and his great
consort Nofertari Mer-en-mut, they have made the temple on the
holy mountain *Tu ab'* (the name of the moun-
tain of Abu-Simbel). On the right, 'the living and good god, great
in terror, the brave lion, lord of the sword, has overcome the rebellious lands' etc.

The pictures on the E. wall (entrance-wall) of this hall resemble
those in the great temple; to the left, the king, before Horus who
hands him the sword of victory, seizes an overthrown Tehennu (N.
tribesman) by the hair to slay him; to the right standing before
Ammon, he slays a negro. The legends are almost word for word the
same as those on the architrave. But in both the pictures in this
temple, there appears behind the king the form of his consort Nofertari, who is named the *Erpat uart*, the great princess, of every
grace in her heart, the beloved palm, mistress of both lands, beloved of the king, and united with the ruler. Several portraits on
the pillars (to the right) show her to have been of great beauty.
She is represented wearing the fan-crown, the disc and horn crown,
and the serpent-diadem, holding in her right hand a sistrum with
the head of Hathor, and a flower-stem in her left.

On the S. wall the king appears between the deities Horus, lord
of *Maha*, and Seth, who bear long toothed
staves, with the notches for the years, and the symbols of eternity.
Here also appears Hathor with a harp, generally called mistress of
Abshek, which perhaps was a name for Abu-Sim-
bel. Three doors lead hence into a narrow apartment, which contains a picture of the queen between Isis and Hathor. On each side
of this room is a recess, and another at the back. In the last is a
remarkable figure of Hathor standing in a temple, with a human
head and above it a cow's head with horns surmounted by the disc
and two fans. The king stands outside the temple, offering flowers.

To the N. of the small temple and still on the smoothed part of
the cliff, we observe a tablet on which a prince of Kush, Ani by
name, a man of Khinensu, appears with the fan and princely staff
before Ramses the Great; beside it is a finely executed stele, containing the homage of a grandee to the king. To the S. of the great
temple is a passage with a somewhat weather-worn stele facing the
N., dating from the 34th year of the king. This is more especially
interesting from the fact that above, to the right of the king who
sits beneath a canopy between two gods, appears the beautiful

daughter of the Kheta prince, followed by her father. Since her
name *(Ra-ma-uarneferu)* is enclosed in a royal cartouche, it is
probable that she became the legal wife of Ramses. Friendly relations with the Kheta prince *Khetasar* were established in the 21st
year of the king's reign by the peace mentioned at p. 142. Beside
it is a small tablet of the general *Amenhi*, with the prince *Seti*, the
king's mother *Tua*, and the princess *Bant-anta*. Farther back (towards the E.) is another large stele, with the winged sun-disc beneath which Ramses the Great is shewn before Ammon with the
double crown, before Harmachis (*Hor akhuti*, Horus of the two
horizons), and before Horus, lord of *Ha* 𓏏𓏏 𓅃 𓈗, the great
god. In the following 23-line inscription the king, who spreads
abroad fear and terror, annihilated the land of Kush, and subdued
the land of Kheta, is compared to the gods Horus, Mentu, and Seth.

Immediately to the left of this passage a rock-chamber was discovered in 1874 by a party of travellers including Miss Amelia
B. Edwards, the well-known writer, who has described it in her
interesting *Thousand Miles up the Nile*. The first chamber, 25 ft.
deep, is adjoined by another rock-cave, 15 ft. deep and 21 ft.
broad. This little *Temple* was dedicated by Ramses to Thoth and
Harmachis, the former of whom is here called lord of Khmunu
(Hermopolis Magna) in Amonhari (perhaps a name for Abu-Simbel). Both gods are represented in golden coloured dhahabîyehs,
before which the king stands worshipping (to the left the boat of
Thoth, to the right that of Ammon-Ra). The name of Usertesen II.

☉ ⬦ 𓍼 *Ra-kha-kheper* (12th Dyn.), a king celebrated in Nubia,
is also found here. The theory that this was the library of the king,
of which Thoth was president, is unfounded. Still farther to the left
are a number of steles incised in the rock, some of which are difficult to reach. One of them dates from Seti II. The farthest to the
left is a double stele of the 38th year of Ramses II., inscribed by a
prince of Kush named Setau.

34. From Abu-Simbel to the Second Cataract.

Comp. the Map, p. 304.

38½ M. About 3 M. above Abu-Simbel, near **Feraig** on the E.
bank, is a small rock-temple, dating from the reign of King Horus
(Hor em heb), the last king of the 18th Dynasty. This temple, which
faces the W., was once used as a Christian church; a figure of Christ
may be seen on the ceiling and one of St. George on the wall of the
main chamber. The structure is also sometimes called the *Temple
of Gebel Addeh* (Champollion), and sometimes the *Temple of Abu-
hudah* (Prokesch), after a village lying farther to the S. The main
chamber (25 ft. square, 10 ft. high) is adjoined on each side (N. and

S.) by a smaller side-room, while at the back several steps lead into a third room, the cella. The four clustered columns which support the ceiling of the main chamber recall the proto-Doric columns of Benihasan (p. 12). A stone bench runs round the walls. On the W. wall is Anuke suckling the infant King Horus, with the words: 'I am thy mother, I give thee milk, it brings to thee peaceful life, youth for thy limbs and strength for thy arms.' Beside her stands the ram's-headed Khnum, lord of the fresh water in *Tu-ab.* On the N. wall (left) King Horus appears before the ibis-headed Thoth and four different forms of the god Horus, viz. as lord of Mām, of Beheni, of Bek, and of Maha — all names of places in Nubia. Over the door into the left side-chamber is the cartouche of the king, 'beloved of Ammon-Ra and of Thoth'. On the N. wall the king is led by the hand by Seth, with the ass's head and the god Horus, with the symbol of life. Some of the pictures are now scarcely recognizable. On the W. wall, to the right of the entrance, is the king before Thoth, who promises him strength, health, and victory. The two side-rooms have neither pictures nor sculptures.

The Saracen fortress of *Addeh* (W. bank), sometimes called *Shataui*, is named *Mashakit* by Champollion. In the mountains to the S. of it are some almost inaccessible steles and a rock-cave, which is wider than it is deep. The cave belonged to the scribe *Pa-uar*, prince of Kush and president of the S. lands, fan-bearer at the king's left hand. Two-thirds of it are occupied by a broken seated figure of a god. On the inner side of the entrance is the kneeling figure of *Pa-uar* before Anuke, mistress of Amonhari. On the walls we see one of the sun-worshipping kings (p. 23), viz.

King *Ai* (⊙ 🪲 🪲 | 𓀠 👁 ─) || *Ra kheperu ar māt*

(⚱ 🏺 🐍 𓏏 𓏏 𓂋 𓏏 𓏏) || *Netera ai neter hak uas,* the predecessor of King Horus, with sacrificial vessels before Ammon, Ptah, and three different forms of Horus. Then prince Pa-uar appears again before Anubis, Sebek, and King *Ra kha ka* (⊙ 🪲 ⊔) || Usertesen III. (12th Dyn.). Part of the inscription with the name of Ammon is defaced.

On the rocky slope to the right of the entrance to the grotto is a proskynema dedicated to the gods of the district, by Kaza, son of a Tutmes.

The hill of Shataui is the last spur on the E. bank of the range of hills running close to the Nile from Ibrim, and presenting some curious pyramidal formations. At this point the chain bends eastwards towards the desert. On the W. bank, however, the river is still skirted by hills for a short distance farther. On this bank lies *Faras*, probably the *Phthuris* of Pliny, round which are numerous

Roman remains and sculptures. Farther to the S. on the same bank, above the island of *Kargiu*, is the village of *Aksheh*, with a few sepulchral vaults and a small temple, in which Ramses II. worships the god Ammon in *Pa-Rauserma* as well as his own deified person. Opposite *Serreh* (E. bank), lie the ruins of a walled village, a little beyond which, near *Dibereh* (E. bank), occurs a fine palm-grove. Above *Eshkeh* (E. bank) are the tombs of the shékhs 'Omar and 'Ali. We next pass the island of *Dabros*, with a village of the same name on the E. bank, and finally reach **Wâdi Halfah,** consisting of several settlements, and named after a kind of grass (Ḥalfah) which is here common. The present military station and stopping-place of the steamboat is named *Ankish.* A permanent garrison has been stationed here since the war in the Sûdân, consisting of native regiments (mainly negroes) under British officers. An introduction to the commandant is convenient and ensures a friendly welcome. A railway, constructed for military purposes to avoid the second cataract, extended hence to (35 M.) *Sarras*, 10 M. from Semueh, but it has been partly destroyed by the dervishes and trains run now only to (23 M.) *Sigajah* (trains start on Mon. and Thurs. at 8 a.m., returning the same day at 4 p.m.; fare 1*l.*; special trains may be obtained for 5*l.*). The village of *Wâdi Halfah* proper lies 1¹/₄ M. farther to the S. On the bank opposite Wâdi Halfah the remains of two temples were found close together, and were described by Champollion. The *North Temple*, now no longer visible and either entirely destroyed or buried, was dedicated to Khem-Ammon in Beheni (Wâdi Halfah). It contained pillars with the name of Amenhotep II., and also a stele of Ramses I. (now in the Louvre); and in the sanctuary was found a stele of Usertesen I. (12. Dyn.), with a list of conquered tribes (now in Florence). The *Southern Temple* has recently been exhumed by Col. Smith, and may be conveniently visited in connection with the excursion to the rocks of *Abusîr* (see below), as it lies on the way thither, ¹/₄ hr. to the S. of the ferry. It was dedicated by Tutmes II. and Tutmes III. to the *Horus* of *Beheni*. To the left of the entrance is a stele of the 23rd year of Tutmes III., in which the victories of that king over the Fenekhu (Phœnicians), Retennu, and Tehennu are mentioned. The columns and pillars are covered with well-preserved sculptures.

Some alterations require to be made in the dhahabiyeh to prepare it for the return-voyage downstream. The long yard is unshipped and stowed on the top of the cabin, the large lateen-sail is replaced by a smaller one, and the planks of the fore-deck are removed to make room for rowing-thwarts. While the sailors are thus engaged the traveller should not omit to visit the **Second Cataract** and to ascend the rocks of **Abusîr** (W. bank) which may be reached in 1-2 hrs. The latter not only command the best view of the broad and rushing cataract, but also enable the visitor to see far to the S. The expedition may be made either by boat, passing

the island of *Kenisab*, at the beginning of the rapids, or more safely
on land by donkey or the quicker and more agreeable camel. Travellers by land must cross to the opposite bank. The British commandant will on request kindly telephone to the fort opposite to
have the necessary camels in readiness; but donkeys must be taken
from the E. bank. The route at first skirts the stream, passing the
above-mentioned temple of Horus of Beheni, then turns inland
towards the mountain ridge, finally ascending with considerable
steepness to a plateau, where the donkeys or camels are left. The
summit of the hill is reached on foot in about 5 min. more after a
somewhat steep climb. A rock on the stop bears the names of some
famous travellers, including that of Champollion. The view of the
broken cataract, which extends for 5 M., is very interesting. The
stream here forces its way through ferreous sandstone, not through
granite as at Assuân. The boulders at the foot of the rock are
coated with dark ferreous Nile mud. The view southwards to the
blue hills of New Dongolah is not less attractive, and kindles the
desire to visit Upper Nubia, which contains numerous most interesting antiquities between this point and Khartûm. We think of
the temples of *Soleb* and *Sesebi*, the temples and pyramids of *Gebel
Barkal*, the fifteen pyramids of *Nuri*, *Meroë* with its group of pyramids, and the temples of *Nagah* and *el-Meṣaurât*. All these, however, are at present forbidden regions for the tourist. At most he
may visit the ancient fortresses of **Semneh** and **Kummeh**, situated
in the *Baṭn el-Hager* (belly of stones), 37 M. from Wâdi Halfah.
These contain buildings of the 12th Dyn. and the remains of two
temples built by Tutmes III.; and they are interesting also for the
records of the height of the Nile under the 12th Dyn., which show
that 2600 years before Christ the Nile rose about 25 ft. higher than
it does to-day.

To visit these spots we take the railway to (23 M.) *Sigaja* (2 hrs.;
see p. 341), thence proceed by donkey to (12 M.) *Sarras* and (10 M.) *Kummeh*. *Semneh*, on the opposite bank, is reached by boat or by one of the
native rafts made of palm-logs. The expedition from Wâdi Halfah and
back takes 2-3 days. Permission from the military authorities is necessary, and is somewhat unwillingly granted as Semueh lies beyond the lines.

It is much to be hoped that the time will soon come when the
way will be open as far as Khartûm, which fell into the hands of
the Mahdists on Jan. 27th 1885, when the brave Gordon met his
death. The possession of Khartûm and the security not only of the
Nile-route thither but also of the desert-route from Berber to Suâ-
kim are the necessary conditions for the gradual civilization of the
Sûdân.

35. The Western Oases.

By the term Oasis (old Egypt. ⟨hieroglyphs⟩ *Ut*, Arab. الواح *el-wah*), Copt.

ⲟⲩⲁϩⲉ from the old Egypt. ⟨hieroglyph⟩ *Uah*, Greek αὔασις (Strabo XVII,791),
is understood a fertile and inhabited spot in the midst of the desert. The
oases owe their fertility to the springs which rise in them, frequently
thermal and containing iron, sulphur, or other mineral ingredients. The
most abundant trees in the oases are the date-palm, acacias of various
kinds (Acacia Nilotica or ṣunṭ-tree), apricots, and other fruit-trees; the
chief grain-crops are wheat, barley, and rice, with a little dura (*Sorghum
vulgare*) and dukhn (*Penicillaria spicata*); and indigo, tobacco, and cotton
are also grown (see Vol. I., pp. 63 seq.).

Seven oases are mentioned in the Ptolemaic inscriptions in the temple
at Edfu. According to Dümichen the first of these, ⟨hieroglyphs⟩ *Kenem*, corresponds to the oasis of el-Khârgeh, the second, ⟨hieroglyphs⟩ *Zeszes*, to Dâkhel,
the third, ⟨hieroglyphs⟩ *Ahe*, to Farâfrah, the fifth, the N. oasis, to Bahrîyeh, the
sixth, ⟨hieroglyphs⟩ *Sekhet kemam i.e.* 'Salt-field', to the region
of the natron lakes, the seventh ⟨hieroglyphs⟩ *Sekhet amu*, to Siwah. —
A simpler arrangement, recognized as early as Tutmes III., divides them
into *Northern* and *Southern Oases*, the first signifying probably *Bahrîyeh*,
the latter *Khârgeh* and *Dâkhel*. The two last were also united under the
name *Great Oasis* (ὄασις μεγάλη)!, distinguished at the same time as the
Outer (اخرج, الخا الواح El-wâh el-kharigeh) and the *Inner Oasis*
(الداخله الواح El-wâh ed-dakhileh). The oasis of Bahrîyeh, the *Northern Oasis* was also called the *Small Oasis* (ὄασις μικρά), and frequently
also *El-wâh el-behnesah*, because the route to it diverged at *Behnesah* on the
Nile. Most travellers who wish to see an oasis will be satisfied with a
visit to Khârgeh and perhaps also to Dâkhel, for the visit to Siwah involves a long and fatiguing journey. The latter, however, is also described below on account of its great historical interest.

For a visit to the oases a caravan of riding and sumpter-camels is
necessary. *Riding Camels* or dromedaries travel about 28 M. in 12 hrs.,
or considerably more if pressed (comp. p. 75); ordinary camels only about
19 miles. The camels should be divided into convenient groups, and the
traveller should make sure that he has a comfortable saddle for his ride
of eight days or more. A tent, a generous supply of tinned provisions,
and water must also be provided. Water may be carried either in casks
(*bermil*), leather skins (which, however, impart a disagreeable flavour to
their contents after a day or two), or still better in iron coffers lined
with enamel (*safiha*). The services of a trustworthy caravan-leader should
be secured by application to a consular agent or other reliable authority;
and guns, powder and shot, and a supply of money in small coins and
Maria Theresa thalers should be provided. The traveller should avoid
displaying large sums of money before the Arabs, and he should be strict
in maintaining the discipline of the caravan.

I. Oasis of Jupiter Ammon, now Sîwah.

Authorities. *Browne,* W. G.,'Travels in Africa, Egypt, and Syria from 1792 to 1798.
Hornemann (1797-1798). London 1802.
Cailliaud, Fr., Voyage à Meroë etc. Syouah (Nov. 1819) et 5 autres oasis. Paris 1823 seq. (Siwah in Vol. I.) 150 plates. Pl. II., 43 is the best plan of Umm el-bêdah.
Minutoli, Reise zum Tempel des Jupiter Ammon 1820-21. Berlin 1824. With atlas.
Hamilton, J., Wanderings in North Africa (1853). London 1856.
Parthey, G., Das Orakel und die Oase des Ammon. Berlin 1862.
Rohlfs, G., Von Tripoli nach Alexandrien (1869). 2 vols. Bremen 1871. Containing a good plan of Siwah on a small scale.
Rohlfs, G., Drei Monate in der libyschen Wüste (1873-74). Cassel 1875.

Two main routes lead to the oasis of Siwah. One, beginning at Alexandria, leads to the W. along the Mediterranean coast viâ the '*Akabet eṣ-Ṣoghêr* (Katabathmus Parvus) to *Medjed* near *Baraṭûn* (the ancient Parætonium), in 80-90 hr.'s. travel spread over 10-11 days, and there turning to the S. reaches Siwah in 5 days or 62 hrs. more. This was Alexander the Great's route, and was also taken by *Browne* (see above) in 1792. Or the traveller may follow the Mediterranean coast for 4 days more to the '*Akabet el-Kebîr* (Katabathmus Major) near *Bir el-Kor*, and there turning S., reach Siwah in 5 days or 64 hrs. more. This was *Minutoli's* route in 1820. The second main route, starting from *Terâneh* or from *Cairo*, leads viâ the Natron Convents to Siwah, in about 13 days (Hornemann 1798), while the first route takes 15-20 days. One route is usually taken for the journey out, the other for the return. *Fr. Cailliaud* reached Siwah in 1819 from the Fayûm in 16 days, viâ *Rayân*, *el-Fereîs*, and *el-Karah*, but the hostile natives permitted him to pay but one visit to the monuments. In the following year (1820) Moḥammed 'Ali despatched a military force with artillery, which reduced the hitherto independent Siwah under the authority of the pasha of Egypt. *Drovetti* and *Ricci* accompanied this expedition. *Gerhard Rohlfs* has twice visited the oasis; in 18:9 on his journey from Tripoli to Alexandria; and in Feb. 1874 in the course of an expedition undertaken along with *Jordan, Zittel,* and *Ascherson,* at the expense of Isma'il Pasha. This expedition starting from Assiût proceeded viâ *Farâfrah* and *Dâkhel,* then struck W. to 27°40', where they turned to the N., reaching Siwah in 14 days. The return was made viâ Farâfrah, Dâkhel, and *el-Khârgeh* to the Nile. Unfortunately this costly expedition had not secured the services of an Egyptologist, and even their photographer *Remelé* was left behind at Dâkhel, so that it has contributed little or nothing to our knowledge of the inscriptions at Siwah. We have on the other hand very full information concerning the temples at el-Khârgeh from *Cailliaud, Robt. Hay,* and *H. Brugsch* (1875), to which also the photographs taken by M. Remelé at Dâkhel and Khârgeh have largely added. The inhabitants of the oasis of Siwah speak a peculiar dialect, of which Minutoli has communicated 400 words. Herodotus (II, 42) mentions that the Ammonites are colonists from Egypt and Ethiopia and speak a dialect midway between the languages of these lands. They understand a little Arabic, but their own speech is a dialect of *Tamasirht*, a *Berber* tongue, understood in the Atlas and elsewhere in N. Africa.

The deity worshipped in the temple of the oasis was a ram's-headed and ram's-horned *Ammon*, such as appears on some Theban monuments (*e.g.* the N. wall of Medinet Habu), and also on coins of the Ptolemies. He was supposed to have been identified with *Hor-shaf*, who was worshipped in , a place-name formerly read as *Sutensinen* and referred by Chabas to the oasis of Siwah until H. Brugsch discovered the correct reading, *Khinensu,* and recognized in it *Khenes* (Heracleopolis Magna), the capital of the 20th nome of Upper Egypt. As practically nothing is known of the Egyptian inscriptions in the oasis of Ammon itself, we give it the name recognized by Dümichen, *i.e.* [hieroglyphs]

Sekhet Amu, *i.e.* 'field of trees', 'field of date-palms'.

The Oasis and the Oracle of Ammon were celebrated from a remote antiquity. Bacchus is said to have been the first to consult the oracle; and in the legend of Perseus and Andromeda, the latter was said to have been offered to the sea-monster to save her country, in obedience to a response of this god. Hercules presented a great offering to Ammon. Semiramis consulted the Oracle on her expedition to Egypt. The law-giver Bocchoris (Bek-eu-ranf; 28th Dyn.; 8th cent. B.C.) expelled the Jews from the land at the bidding of the god. Psammetikh I. enrolled the Carians with plumes of cock's feathers in obedience to his response. Herodotus relates (III, 25, 26) that Cambyses sent 50,000 men to take the Ammonites slaves and to destroy their oracle with fire. This force reached the city of *Oasis*, also called the *Island of the Blessed*, after 7 days march, and then vanished into space, apparently being overwhelmed by a whirlwind. The oasis and its oracle are, however, best known from the visit of *Alexander the Great*, recorded by *Diodorus* (XVII, 49), *Quintus Curtius*, and *Arrian* after Aristobulus. After Alexander had made himself master of Phœnicia by the battle of Issus, he marched to Egypt which submitted without resistance. Desiring to consult the famous *Oracle of Ammon*, he undertook the adventurous march through the desert. Ambassadors from Cyrene met him with a valuable gift of war-horses. His supply of water came to an end after four days, and he was only saved from perishing by an unexpected fall of rain. The way was pointed out to him by crows, flying on the right side of the army. He passed the Bitter Lakes, then 100 stadia (about 10 M.) farther the so-called *Cities of Ammon*, and another day's journey brought him to the vicinity of the temple. Diodorus thus describes the place. 'The Ammonites dwell in villages, but in the midst of their land is a castle defended by a triple wall. The first (*i.e.* innermost) wall encloses the palace of the ruler; the second the women's apartments, with the dwellings of the women and children and the palladia of the place, with the temple of the god and the sacred spring; the third encloses the abode of the spearmen, etc. A little beyond the castle another temple of Ammon has been erected under the shade of numerous large trees. Near it is a spring, called *Spring of the Sun* on account of its peculiar properties. It is warm in the morning, cold at midday, and hot at midnight. The image of the god is encrusted with emeralds and other gems, and gives its oracular responses in a curious way. It is carried in a golden boat on the shoulders of eighty priests, who direct their course according to signs from the god. Women and girls accompany the god with songs'.

When Alexander entered the temple he was hidden welcome by the oldest priest in the name of the god. Alexander accepted the welcome and promised to worship the god, if he gave him the lordship of the whole earth. The king then asked whether all the murderers of his father had been punished. The Oracle replied that no one could aim at the life of him that had made him (*i.e.* of the god); but that the murderers of Philip were punished

The *Oasis of Siwah*, formerly called also *Santaria* (after Iskander, Alexander the Great) lies, according to Jordan's calculations, 95 ft. below the sea-level, in N. lat. 29° 12' and long. 25° 31' E. of Greenwich. Browne estimated the length of the oasis at 7½ M., its breadth at 6 M. Rohlfs estimates the length from *Maragi* in the W. to *Muley Yus* in the E. at about 18½ M., in a line running first N.W. and S.E. and beyond Siwah S.W. and N.E. The breadth varies from a few yards to 1¼ M. It is situated on the S. verge of the steep so-called Libyan coast-plateau, which consists of limestone, and on the S. it is bounded by sand-hills.

Several steep rocks are found in the oasis; *e.g.* the *Amelal* and *Djari* in the W., the *Gebel Mûtâh*, ½ M. to the N. of Siwah, the rocks of *Siwah* and *Akermi*, *Gebel Sidi Hamed* to the S., and *Gebel Brik* to the S.E. of the capital. Of the numerous warm springs (upwards of 30) in the oasis, the strongest are those of *Khamisah*, and the most famous *'Ain Hammâm* (see below), with a little salt (· 1615 %), *Ain Mûsah* (spring of Moses) to the N. of Sîwah, and *'Ain ben Lif* to the S. The climate is unhealthy only towards the end of summer, when the evaporation of the numerous marshes induces fevers. These marshes *(sebkhah)* add largely ·to the difficulty of travelling about the oasis. The mean temperature is 77° Fahr. — The oasis contains about 300,000 date-palms; and about 3000 tons (9000 camel-loads) of dates are annually exported to North Egypt by the Beduin tribe of the *Waled-'Ali.* The olive tree also flourishes here, oranges and le-mons in *Khamisah*, and throughout the oasis grapes, pomegranates, apri-cots, peaches, plums, and a kind of dwarf apple. — Live stock is not numerous, owing to a dangerous fly, about as large as a bee, whose sting is fatal to cattle and camels. Wild pigeons abound. — Salt is procured by evaporation in an almost pure state. Sal ammoniac is prepared by artificial distillation from camels' dung. Minutoli estimated the number of the inhabitants at 8000, Rohlfs at 5600. The two principal tribes, the *Lifayah* and the *Rharbyin*, both of which include numerous sub-tribes, are hostile to each other. — The annual tribute to the Egyptian government is 10,000 Maria Theresa thalers, equal to about 2000*l.* An Egyptian go-vernor presides over the oasis. Strangers are quartered in the Kaṣr, to the N. of the castle of Siwah, near the date-magazine and the dome of *Sidi Slimân.* Siwah and *Akermi*, the chief towns situated like castles upon steep rocks, lie about 3 M. apart. The streets of both are narrow. Siwah belongs to the *Lifayah* and only the portion of the oasis to the S.W. of it belongs to the *Rharbyin*, including Akermi. The Lifayah are forbidden to enter Akermi, in consequence of their having suddenly seized the town about 40 years ago, though they were afterwards repelled by the Rhar-byin. Shêkh *Mohammed Djari*, the richest man in the oasis, resides at Akermi as head of the natives.

The ruins now to be found are very scanty. The triple-walled castle described by Diodorus (see p. 345) appears to be identified with the loftily situated Akermi, also called *Sharkiyeh.* An early Egyptian structure, discovered here in 1853 under some modern houses by the Scottish traveller *James Hamilton*, was easily recognized as the fore-court and chamber of a temple or palace. The interior walls were covered with hieroglyphics, but so blackened with smoke that the kings' cartouches could not be recognized. In the thickness of the wall was a narrow passage, 6 ft. long and 2 ft. wide. In an adjoining street was a colossal Egyptian gate. *Rohlfs* confirmed this discovery in 1869. Passing along a narrow, winding passage, he observed a building with foundation-walls of hewn stones, and to the W. of it he came upon the large edifice, the outer walls of which are visible from outside the village, while the inner wall extends to the great square of Akermi. A rough passage admits to a fore-court, 15 ft. long and 10 ft. broad. Two large Egyptian gateways (18¹/₂ ft. high) lead to the holy of holies, which is entirely ob-structed by houses; the gateways can be passed only through the houses. Rohlfs found a large number of pictures and inscriptions here, and copied some of them by candle-light. The cella was 50 ft. long, 18¹/₂ ft. broad, and 18¹/₂ f_t. high. A secret passage, 2 ft. wide, within the E. wall communicated w_ce the great well of Akermi.

About 300 pa_s to the S. of Akermi lie the ruins of *Umm el-Bédâh* (white mother), facing the town and lying from N. to S. In the time of Cailliaud and Minutoli the ruins consisted of the left wing of the gate-way and a covered portion behind. The former, which has now dis-appeared, contained the representation of a king offering to the ram's-headed Ammon and his female companion. The other portion, which still remains, is 14¹/₂ ft. long (at places only 10¹/₄ ft.) and about 25 ft. high, with a passage 16¹/₂ ft. wide. On the right and left sides are pro-cessions of gods in several rows, with the above-mentioned ram's-headed Ammon as the chief deity. Above these gods are numerous vertical lines of hieroglyphics—55 on the W. wall, 53 on the E. (left)—of which we unfortunately possess no copies. The ceiling consists of three (before the earthquake in 1811 of five) massive stone blocks, 28 ft. long, 5 ft. broad, and 3 ft. thick, decorated with vultures (the symbol of lordship) and stars. Curtius states that the figure of the god was like a navel; round it were emeralds and other precious stones. The extant remains date from a late period; a fragment bearing a royal cartouche appears to date from Nectanebus I.

Minutoli farther mentions the corner-stones of a *Girdle Wall* near the temple; they are still to be found at the N.E. angle. The girdle-wall was 77 paces long and 66 paces broad. It apparently belonged to the second temple mentioned by Diodorus (see p. 345), for in a pretty palm-grove only about ¹/₂ M. to the S.E. of it is the *Sun Spring*, known also to Herodotus (IV, 181). This oval spring, about 110 paces in circumference, is now called *'Ain Hammâm.* The story of the peculiar properties of this spring, repeated by all the ancient writers, in virtue of which its temperature varied at different periods of the day, rests upon error. For the water has a uniform temperature of 73¹/₂° Fahr., though it may sometimes appear warmer than it really is, in the often very cold nights, while at midday it may seem almost cold in contrast to the heat of the burning sun.

Rohlfs failed to find in Siwah any confirmation of the statements of the natives, reported by St. John, that some of the houses rest upon more ancient buildings.—To the N. of Siwah is the *Gebel Mûtâh*, or hill of the dead, a limestone hill about 150 ft. high and 1600 yds. in circumference, perforated with hundreds of vaults, graves, and catacombs. Some of the vaults are large enough for a hundred or more corpses. All the graves have been rifled, and heaps of skulls and shattered skeletons lie around. Half way up the hill, on the E. side, is a solitary tomb of more pretensions, with its entrance adorned with pilasters. Beyond a fore-court is a spacious sepulchral chamber, with two side-rooms, and adorned with a vivid green garland of vine-leaves on a blue ground. In the background are some defaced chiselled figures. At *Beled er-Rûm*, to the W. of Siwah, is another cemetery excavated in a hill. Here also are the remains of an ancient Egyptian temple (*Kasr er-Rûm*), 62 ft. long by 15¹/₂ ft. broad, without any hieroglyphics. A little to the N. of this temple are some scanty remains of a late period, on the hill *'Amûdên* (Two Columns). At *Bâb el-Medineh*, 3 M. to the S.W. of Siwah, Rohlfs discovered a marble ram, now in the museum at Berlin.—The *Lake of Arakhiyeh*, about 60 M. to the N.W. of Siwah, is of little importance, though the French colonel *Bertin* was induced by the wonderful tales of the Arabs to bring a boat for the purpose of exploring it.

On the return from the oasis to *Terâneh*, or to *Kafr Dâwud* (Vol. I., p. 225), a station on the railway from Têh el-Bârûd to Bûlâk el-Dakrûr, and the Nile, the traveller should not omit to visit the Natron Monasteries. Leaving Siwah we journey viâ *el-Karah* (*Umm es-Soghér*, 2 days), *el-Gatarah*, *el-Libbah* (*Bir Lebûs*, 3 days), and *el-Mághrah* (1 day), and on the eighth day reach the depression known as the *Bahr belah mâh* or 'River without water', which has various branches, as e.g. the *Bahr el-Fârir* to the S., in the direction of Sakkârah. Zittel and Jordan have demonstrated that the valleys grouped under the name of Bahr belah mâh could never have been occupied by side channels of the Nile as was at one time supposed. A somewhat steep slope separates this depression from the Wâdi Natrûn (20 M. long, 1¹/₂-5 M. broad), the district called *Nitria* or *Nitriotis* by the Greeks, where, according to Strabo, *Serapis* was worshipped. The Coptic name of Nitria was *P mam pi hosem*, the Egyptian name

Pi ma en pi hesmen or 'place of salt'. It owes its name to the natron which is obtained here in great quantities by evaporation; natron being in fact a salt containing, with 52% of common salt and 11% of sulphate of sodium, about 23% of carbonic natron. The preparation of the natron is carried on at the expense of government, and constitutes an important industry, though somewhat injured by the manufacture of artificial soda. About 2 hrs. to the E. of Wâdi Naṭrûn (comp. the Map at the beginning of Vol. I.) are four Coptic **Monasteries**, a visit to which is interesting. The monasteries owe their origin to *Macarius* of Alexandria (d. 394), a hermit who first retired to the Theban desert in 335, and afterwards, about 373, took up his abode in a lonely cell in this spot. He was the founder of an order that won numerous disciples. The monks fast all the year round, except on Sundays and between Easter and Whitsuntide. *Rufinus* mentions fifty monasteries of ascetics, who numbered 5000 in all. In the year 800 the ruined monastery of *St. Macarius* was repaired and fortified by *Sanutius*, patriarch of Alexandria. The next most interesting monastery is that of *Syriâni*, built by a saint named *Honnes* or Johannes the dwarf. It has 30-40 monks and 3 churches. *Curzon* and afterwards *Tattam* and *Pacho*, who visited the monastery twice, here found most valuable collections of Syrian MSS., acquired between 1840 and 1850. These MSS., in 371 vols., of which the oldest are one by *Eusebius* of Edessa (411 A.D.) and twelve of the 6th cent., included the Theophany and other writings of Eusebius of Caesarea, the *Recognitiones* of Clemens, a treatise against the Manichæans by *Titus of Bosra*, etc. This monastery contains also an *Abyssinian* college with a library.—There is little chance of discovering any more valuable MSS. here, as all except those required for the religious services have been transferred to the library of the Coptic patriarch at Cairo.

A visit to the remaining monasteries, of *Baramus* (Coptic liturgical MSS.) and *Amba Biskhai*, with three small churches, scarcely repays the trouble, and is not recommended on account of the vermin. — Interesting accounts of these and other monasteries in the Levant are contained in *R. Curzon's* Visits to the Monasteries in the Levant (London, 1849), and in *Quatremère's* Mémoires Géographiques, Vol. I. pp. 451 seq. (Paris, 1811).

II. The Oases of Baḥriyeh and Farâfrah.

The visit to the oasis of Baḥriyeh (the Northern Oasis), called by Strabo δεύτερα, '*the Second*', and by Ptolemy ὄασις μιχρά, '*the Small Oasis*', is of interest only to the naturalist, for its antiquities are few and unimportant. The latter include a small Roman triumphal arch (Cailliaud, Meroë, II. Pl. 39, 40, 42) and a stele of the reign of Tutmes III., besides the scanty remains of a temple at *Bawîtî* (Ascherson).

The oasis of **Farâfrah**, probably the *To aḥe*   or

Cow-land of antiquity (temple of Edfu), as the latter is described as to the N.W. of *Kenem*, the great oasis, is of importance merely as an intermediate station between the oases of Siwah and Dâkhel, or the oases of Baḥriyeh and Dâkhel. It contains no antiquities, but some catacombs in a cliff to the W. suggest that there was at one time a Christian settlement here. The oasis which has only 320 inhab., has been since 1860 entirely in the hands of the *Senûsi*, a rigid Mohammedan sect, founded by *Mohammed Senûsi* of Algiers (Vol. I., p. 67). The people are suspicious of and hostile to strangers. The chief village is *Sarabûb*, two days' journey to the W. of Siwah.

III. The Oasis of el-Khârgeh.

Authorities. *Cailliaud*, Voyage à l'Oasis de Thèbes 1821. *Hoskins*, Visit to the Great Oasis of the Libyan Desert, 1837. *Rohlfs*, Drei Monate in der libyschen Wüste, 1875. *H. Brugsch*, Reise nach der grossen Oase el-Khârgeh, 1878.

A journey to the oasis of *el-Khârgeh* is much more interesting and less difficult than that to the oasis of Jupiter Ammon, and it may be combined with a visit to Dâkhel. El-Khârgeh may be reached in 4-5 days from Assiût (Drovetti, Schweinfurth), from Sohâg, Girgeh, Farshût (above Beliâneh), from Rizakât near Erment (Hoskins), or from Esneh

(Cailliaud; Rohlf's return journey). Sohâg, Girgeh, and Esneh are the preferable starting-points, as they are towns of some size where the necessary number of camels is easily obtained. About 40 hrs. are required from Sohâg or Girgeh; while 50-52 are required from Esneh, because the road leads chiefly over rocky soil, and is therefore more exhausting for the camels. Camels, water, provisions, fire-arms, etc. must be provided as mentioned on p. 343.

This oasis was visited by Poncet in 1690, by Browne in 1793, and in the present century by Cailliaud (1818), Drovetti (1832), Hoskins (1835), P. W. Grey (1843), Rohlfs, with Zittel, Jordan, Ascherson, and Remelé (1874), and Brugsch (1875). The excellent photographs taken by Remelé have contributed largely to our knowledge of the temple of el-Khârgeh.

The oasis of **el-Khârgeh** (the *outer*, in contrast to Dâkhileh, the *inner*, i.e. farther into the desert) is named *Kenem* in the inscription at Edfu referring to the oases, while in an older inscription in the tomb of an official of Tutmes III. it is called the *South Oasis*, *Ut res*, in contrast to el-Bahriyeh, the *North Oasis*. Olympiodorus names it ὄασις μεγάλη ἐξωτέρω, the *Great Outer Oasis*, Strabo ἡ πρώτη αὔασις, the *First Oasis*, and Ptolemy, the *Great Oasis*. It is also referred to as the *Oasis of the Thebaïd*. The ancient name of the town with the temple was *Hib*, also written ⟨hieroglyphs⟩, *Town of the Plough*, whence its garrison is mentioned in the Notitia Dignitatum as 'Ala prima Abasgorum Hibeos Oaseos Majoris'.

Like all the oases el-Khârgeh is surrounded by a tolerably steep chain of cretacious limestone hills, which rises in terraces to the height of 1475 ft. on the side next the desert, and sinks down again towards the oasis (Katabathmus, descent). The oasis stretches from N. to S. for about 90 M. (34 hrs. travel), and from E. to W. only 12 M. (4-5 hrs.), and its population was estimated by Schweinfurth at 6340. The natives who pay an annual tribute of 300 purses (500 piastres or 104s. each), or 1560l., to the Egyptian government, are of a dark complexion and are far from good looking. Every summer they are subject to an intermittent fever, which is fatal to many. They speak Arabic though they are not pure fellâhin from the Nile but are mixed with the Libyan race. The oasis is ruled by an Egyptian governor (*Hâkim*). The chief town *el-Khârgeh* has about 3000 inhabitants. *Gennah* and *Bûlâk*, to the S., have each about 250, *Bérys* 600, *Dûsh* and *Maks* each 100, according to the moderate estimates of Cailliaud. — There are about 150 springs in the oasis, most of them issuing freely from clefts in the cretaceous marl. Several were discovered by boring, and in this way the fertility of the oasis was increased. Some of them are warm (88°-97° F.) and are strongly impregnated with iron. The chief wealth of the oasis consists in its date-palms, 65,000 in number.

The town of **el-Khârgeh** lies in lat. 25° 56′ N., and long. 30° 40′ E. of Greenwich, at a height of about 245 ft. above the sea-level (Esneh 345 ft.). The chief object of interest is the temple lying a full hour to the N.E. of the town. Immediately on quitting the brick wall that encircles the town, we see on the right the domed tombs of some Arab shêkhs. Our route leads past some enclosed palm-groves and crosses some dry water-courses. The ruins of the small building like a temple, but destitute of hieroglyphics, which Cailliaud discovered half-way between the town and the large temple, seem now to have disappeared, as has also a still smaller building with a sunk doorway to the S. of the temple.

The *Large Temple* of el-Khârgeh, 150 ft. long and about 60 ft. broad, is a well-preserved structure built of a reddish sandstone, which Zittel believes to have been quarried in Lower Nubia. Its axis runs E. and W., with a slight inclination to the N. In front of the temple is a fore-court and three successive gateways at irregular distances. Remains of both the wings of the outermost gateway are left. On the right wing, at the top of the E. side, a space 8 ft. high and 6 ft. broad, is occupied by a long inscription of 66 lines, reported both by Cailliaud and Hoskins. In this inscription, which dates from the 2nd year of the emperor *Galba* (69 A.D.), *Julius Demetrius*, governor of the oasis, communicates the answer of the provincial governor (ἡγεμών), *Tiberius Julius Alexander*, to the complaints of the inhabitants of the oasis against the illegal exaction of taxes, etc., to the effect that future extortion is forbidden under penalties and that what has been unjustly exacted will be restored. On the left side also, lower down, are some shorter Greek inscriptions. One of these, by the general (στρατηγός) *Posidonius*, dated the 7th Mekhir of the emperor Tiberius Claudius, directs attention to a decree by the provincial governor *Gnœus Virgilius Capito*, inscribed below. This decree warns against payments to unauthorized extorters of money, and threatens the latter with severe punishment, viz. the payment of ten times the extorted sum as penalty besides restitution fourfold to the victim. — Traces of an avenue of sphinxes exist between the first and second gateways, which are 50 ft. apart. Only a fragment of the left (S.) wing of the *Second Gateway* is standing. Some crudely executed representations on its inner side depict an unnamed emperor (the cartouche is empty) before Ammon-Ra, Muth, and Tum, lord of *Hib* (*i.e.* el-Khârgeh). The *Third Gateway*, 140 ft. from the second, is still entire. It is 18 ft. long and nearly 20 ft. broad. Beneath the cornice appears the well-known winged sun-disc with the serpents of both lands. The lintel below has two representations on the right side: an unknown king before Ammon-Ra and Khnum, and then before Harmachis; on the left the same king appears before Tum, then before Ammon-Ra, Uaz, and Month.

The next two fields on the right and left are destroyed. Then on the right, Darius II. (? 425-405 B.C.) ⟨cartouche⟩ appears thrice, viz. before Auber and Tefnut, before Isis and Nephthys, and before Horus, Isis, and Nephthys. On the left the same king appears before Osiris, Horsi-isis, and Isis, then before Khnum, and finally before Thoth in *Hib* and the gods of his cycle. On the inside of this doorway, Darius appears on the left with the figure of Ma before Ammon-Ra, lord of *Hib*, and on the right (where his name is almost illegible) before Ammon-Ra, the husband of his mother, presenting to him two palm-trees. Two vertical inscriptions on the exit from this pylon (right and left) are also noteworthy. These refer to the above-mentioned *Darius* as 'the beloved of Ammon-Ra, *Lord of Hib*, the great god, strong with the sword', and continue: 'He has built the walls *(umt)* of good white stone for a *meska* (dwelling) of the god, its doors of acacia-wood, covered with Asiatic brass in excellent enduring workmanship. May (the gods) grant him innumerable festivals on the seat of Horus'. The designs on the W. side of the pylon are no longer distinguishable. About 40 ft. behind this third gateway is the *Fore-court*, 52 ft. deep and 30 ft. broad, the front of which has fallen. It contained four engaged columns, two at the front corners and two at the sides, and had also a door on each side, of which that to the right (N.) is still entire. This latter bears the cartouches of king *Nekhthorheb* (Nectanebus I.), of the 30th Dyn. (378-364 B.C.), on the right before Tum, on the left before Month. This king was the builder of the fore-court, and his cartouches also appear on the side-doors in the following portal, the architrave of which is imperfect. To the left Nekhthorheb appears before Ptah and Sekhet, then, below, before Month and Uaz, and finally before Ammon-Ra, Muth, and Khnum; to the right he appears before Osiris and Isis, then before Thoth and *Mehemaut*, and finally before the ram's-headed Ammon and Muth. The gods are styled lords of *Hib*

⟨cartouche⟩ or presidents (⟨glyphs⟩) of that town. The following *First Hall*, with 12 fan-palm columns, is believed by Brugsch to be a late (Roman?) restoration of a former hall destroyed by an earthquake. He describes it as being without inscriptions or representations, though Hoskins reports otherwise. In the N. and S.W. angles are two separate spaces with double chambers, one above the other. The next room is the most remarkable part of the temple. This is the *Sacrificial Chamber*, a narrow apartment with a row of four columns supporting the roof, while four others are engaged in the entrance-wall. The builder was Darius, who is here named in a second cartouche, 'the beloved of *Ammon* of Hib, the strong-sworded', whilst elsewhere he is usually styled 'the beloved of Ra and Ammon' (see below). On the inside of the entrance-wall, to the right, the king is shown kneeling and presenting two vessels of wine, before the ram's-headed Ammon, lord of Hib, Muth, and Month. Two finely carved lines of hieroglyphics beside this scene state: 'This is *Ammon of Hib*, the great god, strong with the sword; may they (the gods) grant constant peaceful life'. Beneath is the empty cartouche of the king. On the left side the cartouche beneath a similar inscription is filled in with the king's name; while the accompanying representation shows the king presenting wine (of the oasis) to *Osiris*, Horus, Isis, and Nephthys. The highly interesting inscriptions and representations on the walls of the narrow chamber lend it a peculiar importance. Thus at the top, to the left, of the S. wall is the Persian king in an attitude of worship, presenting a rich offering to the deities. Between him and the gods is a long list of offerings, in horizontal lines. Beneath this scene, and beginning in the N.E. corner, is a *Song of Praise*, composed by the king in honour of the sun-god Ra in very pantheistic terms. This song, in 46 lines, was first published after copies by *Robert Hay*, the companion of Hoskins, and translated by *S. Birch* (Transactions of the Bibl. Arch. Society, Vol. V, London 1876), then more completely by *Brugsch* in his 'Reise nach der großen Oase' (pp. 276 seq., Plates XIV, XXV-XXVII). On the *E. Wall* (back-wall) are sacrificial scenes on both sides, corresponding to each other, to Ammon-Ra, Muth, and Khunsu. Ammon has the ram's head like the god of the Oasis of Ammon. Towards the N.W. corner of this wall is a mystic inscription, with the title above it: 'The mysterious sayings of Ammon which are on the tables of mulberry-wood.' This text refers to the secret character of Ammon, the pantheistic god of the oasis, whose oracular importance appears from the passage 'his voice is heard, but he is not visible to all who draw breath' (line 33). On the door-posts on each side of the entrance to the next room is an inscription in the so-called *enigmatic* (*i.e.* secret) characters, of which a duplicate is found on the outside of the S.W. wall of the temple. This next room has four columns, and on each side are two side-rooms. The builder was again Darius. The central door in this room admits to the *Sanctuary*, the small door on the right to another room, which evidently was once connected with the sanctuary, for the mystic representations of the two rooms, as reported by Hoskins, are parts of one whole. The partition-wall must be a later addition. The door to the left admits to a staircase, leading straight on to a crypt, and ascending to the left to the Osiris rooms, which are on the temple-roof as at Philæ, Denderah, and Edfu. Opposite the last flight of steps is a finely-executed inscription: 'List of the sacrifices made by King Darius in the golden hall for Ammon of Hib, the great god, strong with the sword'. Another list beneath contains a catalogue of the sacrificial wines from the various districts of Egypt; at the top the *Wine of the Oasis*. Of the three Osiris rooms, the middle one contains the most interesting representations. At the top of the N. wall is Osiris lying on a bier, beneath him are four canopi, to the right Isis and Nephthys; in the section below the *Dead Osiris* lies on the ground with Isis and Nephthys kneeling beside him. The latter are represented as saying: 'Thou art in millions of years, thy soul is raised to heaven with the soul of Ra. I am the light by day, thou art the moon at night'. To the right is the bull *Apis*, running with the Osiris-mummy on its back; to the left is a frog (hakt) as the representative of Osiris. At the bottom is Osiris resting in the grave as *Khem of Koptos*, with Khem, Isis, and Nephthys beside him. — A fragment of an inscription on the outside of the W. wall of the temple (be-

side the figure of a king) is noteworthy from the fact that it assigns
another prænomen to Darius, viz. *Settura* ⟮ ⊙ 𓂉 ⟯ , which closely
resembles one of the names of Ramses II. ⟮ 𓂉 ⟯. Lepsius
proposes to recognize in this the name, not of the builder of the inner
chambers, but of *Darius I.* (521-486 B.C.); but as this king is expressly
styled the 'beloved of Ammon Ra, lord of Hib, strong with the sword',
he is doubtless to be identified with Darius II. who is mentioned within
the temple. Beneath, Darius, accompanied by Hathor with a sistrum and
year-rings, offers to Ammon Ra, lord of the thrones of both the lands of
Apt-asu (Thebes). On the outside of the N. wall of the temple is another
cartouche of Darius ⟮ 𓂉 ⟯ *Ammon Rameri.* Whether this belongs to another Darius than that named in the other cartouches, perhaps
Darius I., or whether this belongs to Darius II. and the name *Settura* to
Darius I., must remain undecided.

H. Brugsch has proved from an inscription found at Luxor (Stele
Maunier), of the 25th year of Pinozem I. (1033 B.C.), that the oasis was
used from an early period as a place of banishment. In Christian times
the schismatic *Nestorius* (435 A.D.) was banished hither (p. 50). Christian
monks settled here, protecting themselves against the attacks of the Beduins from a place of refuge on the top of the temple, traces of which
were seen by Hoskins.

At *Nadurah*, a little to the S.E. of the great temple, are the ruins of
a temple of the Roman period, 9 paces long by 12 broad. It has three
doors, above the central and more carefully built of which is the winged
sun-disc. Within the little building is [found the name of the emperor
Antoninus, which also occurs at *Kasr ez-Zayân* (see below). He is here said
to conduct to the god the land of Kuu or Huu with its possessions and
the W. land with its wines. On the outside are a few Coptic names.

Fully an hour to the N. of the town of Khârgeh, 1/4 hr. from the
great temple, lies the extensive Christian *Necropolis*, resembling a city
with its regularly laid out streets, but now utterly devastated. At the
most only a few mortuary chapels are worth visiting. Some of the smaller
of these may have been the mausolea of particular families, but the larger
were probably sepulchral chapels in which religious services were held
in memory of the dead. About 1/4 hr. to the N.W. of the necropolis is
Kasr Mustafâh Desh, an ancient Christian monastery, built entirely of brick
except the main portal, which is of hewn stone. To the N. of it is a
Hypogeum, 36 ft. long by 16 ft. broad, with three chambers on each side.

About 2 hrs. to the S. of Khârgeh is the little village of *Gennâh*, with
250 inhabitants. The houses are covered with branches of the orange-tree
and pomegranate-tree in place of roofs. The streets are so narrow as to
make it difficult for a laden camel to pass through them. About 1³/₄ hr.
from the village are the ruins of a temple, dating from the time of the
Ptolemies (Euergetes, Philopator, and Lathyrus), and dedicated to the
Theban triad, Ammon-Ra, Muth, and Khunsu. The ruins, prettily situated
on a hill, are now known as *Kasr Gaitah* or *Kasr Wali* (drawings of it,
see Hoskins, plates xvii-xix, and Cailliaud, pl. xiv). About 1³/₄ hr. farther is the picturesque ruin of *Kasr ʿAin ez-Zayân*, a temple, enclosed by
a rough brick wall, 230 ft. long and 83 ft. broad. The entrance is on the
S. side. Within the wall is a kind of court, of unburnt bricks, 50 ft.
long and 17 ft. broad, at the approach to which are fragments of stone
with part of a Greek inscription. In this court is situated the temple,
13 ft. from the girdle-wall, and entered through a pylon, 24 ft. broad, with
the winged sun-disc, facing the S. The doorway, which is 4¹/₂ ft. wide,
is adorned with representations of the emperor Antoninus making offerings

to the ram's-headed Ammon, Osiris, Isis, and Horus. According to the Greek inscription here, the temple was dedicated to *Amenebis*, *i.e.* the Ammon of Hib, god of *Tkhonemyris*, *i.e.* *Ta-khnum-ra* 'belonging to Khnum', the name of the place. This inscription relates to a rebuilding of the sanctuary (σηκός) and of the vestibule (πρόναος), carried out in the 3rd year (140 A.D.) of the emperor Antoninus Pius (εὐσεβής). under the prefect *Avidius Heliodorus*, the military commandant *Septimius Macro* and the general (strategos) *Paenias Caepio*. The celebrated rhetorician *Aristides* came to Egypt in the prefecture of Heliodorus, who was a famous orator. The entrance-portal admits to the first hall, 26¹/₂ ft. long by 19¹/₂ ft. broad, which is adjoined by the *Sanctuary*, 16 ft. by 7¹/₃ ft. A niche at the back was probably intended for the statue of a god. To the W. of the sanctuary is another chamber, 10 ft. long by 2³/₄ broad. The total length of the temple was 44 ft.

The village of *Bûlâk* (3-400 inhab.) is only 1¹/₂ hr. to the S. of Kaṣr ez-Zayân, and 7 hrs. to the S. of Bûlâk is the deserted village of *Dakâkîn*. A route leads viâ *Hadegageh*, with a good spring and fine date-palms and dûm-palms, to *Berys* (600 inhab.; 13 hrs. from Bûlâk), situated on a hill, with numerous date-palms and surrounded with fields of grain (chiefly dura), abounding in springs. *El-Maks* (100 inhab.), 3 hrs. farther, is the most southerly point in the oasis. The caravan-route leads hence in 25 days of *Darfûr*. About halfway between Berys and Maks, but a little to E. of the road, lies the temple of *Dûsh el-Kal'ah*. This temple also was once surrounded with a high wall of unburned bricks, furnished on the inside with stairs and galleries. Two propylons stand in front of the temple which faces the N.; the first and larger of these is 14³/₄ ft. broad and 13³/₄ ft. long. On the architrave of the portal is a Greek inscription (published by Cailliaud) of the 19th year of the emperor *Trajan* (116 A.D.), in which the inhabitants of *Kysis* (οἱ ἀπὸ τῆς Κύσεως; comp. *Kus*, the above-mentioned hieroglyphic name of the oasis) record the building of this pylon, under *Marcus Rutilius Lupus*, prefect of Egypt. On the left wall of the same pylon is another but hardly decipherable Greek inscription in which the name ἐνὶ κύσι recurs. Behind the propylon are some remains of columns, so that a colonnaded gallery must be supposed to have existed between the first and second pylons, which are 100 ft. apart. The *Second Pylon*, only 13 ft. broad and 13¹/₂ ft. long, is united by a brick wall with the girdle-wall. The poor sculptures upon it represent a king whose name is not legible. About 38 ft. farther back is the temple proper, its first portion being a kind of *Vestibule*, on the sides of which a *Roman* emperor presents offerings to Serapis, Isis, and Horus. The hieroglyphics, however, are scarcely legible. This vestibule, with two columns at the entrance, is only 22 ft. broad and 13³/₄ ft. deep. Beyond it is a portico with four columns, the capitals of which are much damaged. A door in the right (W.) wall seems to have led to a staircase. At the back of the portico is a large door between two smaller ones, the former leading into the sanctuary which is divided into two chambers, the latter into corridors. The method of lighting the sanctuary chambers by windows at the top of the walls, like those in the great temple of Karnak, and the vaulted roof should be noticed. Over the doors appears the winged sun-disc, and on each side are hieroglyphics. The S. (back) wall of the temple is also covered with reliefs, one representing the emperor Domitian, sacrificing to Horus, son of Isis, and to Osiris.

About 60 ells from this temple are the ruins of another noteworthy structure, wholly of brick, apparently also a temple. The entrance is formed by a pointed Gothic arch, and the three following chambers have doors of the same form, on which the winged sun-disc is still to be seen. Hoskins refers this building to the Romans.

IV. The Oasis of Dâkhel.

The ancient Egyptian name of this oasis was

Zeszes, *i.e.* 'Place of the Two Swords', probably a mythological allusion.
The temple at Ḳaṣr ed-Dâkhel was. called   *Ast abt, i.e.* Seat
of the moon, and also (Brugsch)   *Ha ša en suten*
neteru, *i.e.* 'Place of the going out of the King of the Gods'. Under the
Romans the oasis was named *Oasis Minor* and was garrisoned by the Ala
prima Quadorum. The present name *el-wâḥ ed-dâkh'leh* means 'inner oasis'.

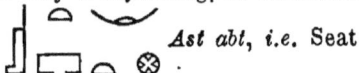

Ed-Dâkhel lies 4-5 days' journey from Farâfrah (Cailliaud, Rohlfs),
5 long days' journey from Assiût (Edmonstone), and 3, or at most 4, from
el-Khârgeh. The last-named route is described below.

The oasis was visited in 1818 by Drovetti, in 1819 by Edmonstone,
and in 1873 by Rohlfs, with Zittel, Jordan, and Ascherson, starting from
Farâfrah. The ascent amid the picturesque cliffs of the so-called *Bâb
el-Cailliaud*, on the last mentioned route, is very impressive.

The oasis has at present about 17,000 inhabitants It is very rich in
date-palms and olive-trees, and produces wheat, barley, rice, dura, and
dukhn, though not sufficient. for its own consumption. Large acacias
(sunt-trees), and fruit-trees, such as apricot and walnut trees, flourish.
The chief villages are *el-Ḳaṣr*, *Kalamûn*, and *Budshulu* (see below).

The route from el-Khârgeh leads N.W. to (15 hrs.) *'Ain
Amûr*, there turns due W. to (15½ hrs.) *Tenidah*, at the E. extremity of
the oasis, and proceeds viâ (4 hrs.) *Balad*, (4¼ hrs.) *Smint*, and (3½ hrs.)
Mut. Finally it bends to the N. viâ *Rashidah* and *Budshulu* to (7 hrs.)
el-Ḳaṣr, which we thus reach 18¾ hrs after leaving Tenidah.

In 1¼ hr. after leaving el-Khârgeh we pass the ruins of *Ḳaṣr eṭ-ṭârif*,
in 7 hrs. more those of *Ḳaṣr el-fâkhûrah*, and in 5¼ hrs more reach the
foot of the *Gebel Amûr*. An ascent of ¾ hr. brings us to the middle of
the mountain-slope, along which we ride for ½ hr. to *Ḳaṣr 'Ain Amûr*.
Here are the shattered remains of a small temple in the Gracco-Egyptian
style, on which Wilkinson discovered the name Caesar. According to
Cailliaud's measurements the temple is 71½ ft. long and 31 ft. broad. It
consisted of a vestibule, and a larger room with a smaller one behind it,
with three doors leading to three other chambers, the central one being
the adytum (Plan in Cailliaud's Voyage à Meroë II, XLII, 1). Inside the
girdle-wall of the temple is a scanty spring with a somewhat unpleasant
taste. We continue our journey in a steep gorge, which leads in ½ hr.
to the top of the *Gebel Amûr* (1765 ft. above the sea-level). Thence the
route leads to the W. along the height to (5 hrs.) *el-Gawâzi*, beyond
which a rocky path (limestone), very difficult for camels, leads to (3½ hrs.)
Abu Turtur, an isolated peak rising from the plateau. Our descent (¾ hr.)
begins at (3 hrs.) *'Akabet esh-Shêkhâwi*. We begin a second descent at
(2½ hrs.) *'Akabet es-Sâbûn*, which brings us in 10 min to the valley of
Dâkhel. From this point the oasis of Dakhel stretches towards the W.,
interrupted twice by the desert, so as to form, strictly speaking, three
oases. The last of these lying N. and S., is the most considerable. After
passing two springs, *'Ain Segah* and *'Ain Ansorah*, we reach the considerable
village of *Tenidah*, with 600 inhab., largely employed in the production of
indigo. The manufacture is carried on in the open air under palm-leave
sheds. The dried leaves are placed in earthen pots with boiling water,
which is stirred with a stick until the dye-stuff has been separated from
the leaves. The blue liquid is then poured into shallow holes in the
earth, and the water allowed to evaporate. To the left of the route, near
the spring of *'Ain el-Birbeh*, about 1 hr. beyond Tenidah, are the remains
of a square vaulted temple or a Roman fort, consisting of three main

chambers and two side-rooms. Farther on we pass the little village of *Shêkh Besendi*, with sunt-trees watered by two brooks, then *Ḳaṣr 'Ain Amîr*, with an ancient edifice, perhaps a temple, and in ³/₄ hr. reach *Balad*, with over 800 inhab., the largest village but one in the oasis. With the immediately adjoining villages (*nezleh*) it counts 3000 inhabitants. To the N. of the town, which contains two mosques, are several large tombs of shêkhs. At the entrance to the town (from the E.) is a vault containing some water-vessels, which are kept always full for the use of travellers, by the beneficence of a Shêkh Muṣṭafâh.

Beyond Balad the first division of the oasis ends, and we cross a desert strip (2³/₄ hrs.), inappropriately named *Baḥr belah mâh* (comp. p. 347). After ¹/₂ hr.'s ride in the second part of the oasis, we reach *Ḳaṣr el-ḥalaḳah*, a large building surrounded by a vaulted gallery, the remains of a temple. About ³/₄ hr. farther is a ruined town, called *Isment el-Kharâb* or the 'destroyed Sment', containing a sandstone structure, known as *ed-Dêr* (the monastery), 19 paces long by 9 broad, with two chambers in a very ruinous condition. Beside it is a small building. The modern village of *Smint* lies ³/₄ hr. farther; it is surrounded by a high wall and most of the houses have two stories. To the S. of our road lies *Ma'ṣarah* (250 inhab.), near which is a ruined temple, called *Kharâbet el-yazîdi*. Straight on is (1¹/₂ hr.) the village of *Mut*, the residence of *Hasan Effendi* (see below), on an eminence among date-palms. A ruined temple is found here also. In the neighbouring hills is an alum-mine. Hence we proceed to the N.W. to *el-Hindau*, and then cross the last strip of desert to (2¹/₂ hrs.) *Ḳalamûn*, a small place with houses of three stories. Ḳalamûn is the residence of the Ḳâimmaḳâm or governor of the oasis. This village is mentioned by *El-Bekri;* its name perhaps signifies 'Castle of Ammon'. The Shurbagi who are settled here claim to have ruled the oasis since the days of the sultan Selim (1517), though they were first placed here only about 100 years ago by the mameluke government of that time as e guard against the incursions of the predatory nomads (the *Bideẓât*). About 2 hrs. to the N.E. of Ḳalamûn is *Rashidah*, a flourishing village with numerous palm-trees and said to have 1000 inhabitants. A route leads direct N. from Ḳalamûn viâ the village of *Mushîyeh*, surrounded by gardens, to *el-Ḳaṣr*. About 1 hr. farther is *Budshulu*, with 2400 inhab. and 8000 palm-trees, which yield an annual harvest of 4-5000 camel-loads. There are also rich olive-plantations. The hospitable shêkh is one of the richest landowners in the oasis. El-Ḳaṣr, also called *Medinet el Ḳaṣr ed-Dâkhel*, the capital of the oasis, lies 2 hrs. to the N., in lat. 25° 42' N. and long. 29° E. of Greenwich. Its chief spring is 360 ft. above the sea-level. The town contains at least 2000 inhab., or including the adjacent settlements (*nezleh*), 6000. Its outward appearance is handsome, and it contains several large and fine houses, nearly all of them two-storied, besides four mosques and a *Zawîyeh* or seminary of the *Senûsi* (P. 348). In the midst of the town is a thermal spring ('*Ain Ḥamrâh*; 96° Fahr.), strongly impregnated with iron and sulphur, and several others are to be found in the neighbourhood. *Hasan Effendi*, now in Mut (see above), a native of the Nile valley and formerly a servant of *Lefèvre*, the French mining-engineer, has bored about 50 new wells in the oasis within the last 30 years. The inhabitants employ themselves in a great variety of industries, their employments being hereditary. In their mild and amiable disposition they are a complete contrast to the natives of Farâfrah.

Archæologists find an object of interest in the temple known as °*Dêr el-Hegâr*, *i.e.* monastery of the stones, lying about 2 hrs. to the S.W. of Ḳaṣr. It is almost entirely covered with sand and fallen blocks, and had to be cleared by Rohlfs. It lies from E. to W., and is 51 ft. long by 23¹/₂ ft. broad, excluding the external vestibule. This vestibule, which is completely covered with stones, had originally 8 columns, of which only one is now standing. The only relic of the entrance to the temple is the portal with the winged sun-disc, beneath which the emperor *Titus* is represented worshipping the ram's-headed Ammon-Ra, Muth, and Khunsu on the right, and the same with the ibis-headed Thoth on the left. The first hall, 24 ft. long by 20 ft. broad, has four columns, and

contains representations of the ram's-headed Ammon, Isis, and Anubis.
The second room is entered by a narrow door, on which are sacrificial
scenes before the ram's-head Ammon and other deities. The name of
the worshipping king is unfortunately not added and only the word *Kisres*
is legible in the second cartouche. Above is the winged sun-disc. This
room is only half as long as the preceding and is destitute of all ornament
except on the central door leading to the *Sanctuary.* Remelé's measurements of the latter give the breadth at 7¹/₂ ft., the depth at 11 ft., and
the height at 10 ft. The photographs taken by him indicate that the
temple was built by *Nero* (?), *Vespasian,* and *Titus.* It was dedicated to
Ammon-Ra, who is frequently represented with the ram's-head and usually
accompanied by Muth. Once he is styled *Lord of Heb*, but his usual

designation is 'Dweller in   *Ast ab*', *i.e.* the seat of the

moon. Ast ab appears to be the name of the site of the temple, for the
same designation is here used for Shu, son of Ra, and for other gods. —
The above-mentioned door to the sanctuary had scenes of worship on
both its wings, and a six-line dedication-inscription. On passing through
it into the cella, we see on the left, above, Vespasian offering to Ammon-
Ra, Muth, and Khunsu; beneath, on the left, the same emperor offering
to the ram's-headed Ammon-Ra with his family, and on the right, to Khem
and Osiris Unnofer. In the bottom rows on the side-walls are depicted
Nile-gods, bringing offerings. — On the right wall of the cella Vespasian
makes offerings to the ram's-headed Ammon-Ra, Muth, and Khunsu, then
to Shu, son of Ra, and to Tefnut, and finally to Shu, Osiris, and Isis.
The ceiling was occupied by a rude astronomical representation, but
most of the blocks have fallen. The back-wall of the cella is divided
in halves, each containing 3 fields. In all 6 fields there appears an
emperor sacrificing to the gods, among whom the ram's-headed Ammon is
twice represented. The emperor's name seems to be Nero (or more probably Nerva) Kisres Germanicus. — The platform of the temple commands an excellent *View towards the long *Table Mountain* mentioned by
Edmonstone. About 120 ft. in front of the fore-court of the temple is a
stone gateway, with various representations now barely visible. The
entire temple is surrounded by a brick wall.

INDEX.

Ranebkher 255.
Raneferka 71.
Raneferu 269.
Ranubkau 16.
Ranubkaunekht, Tomb of 269.
Rasankhka 255.
Rasekhem 243.
Rashidah 355.
Raskenen 195. 229. 230.
Ratati 230.
Rayân 344.
Red Convent, the 49.
Redêsîyeh 253.
—, Temple of 78. 254.
Re'îs xx-xxii.
Rekh-ma-ra, Tomb of 191.
Rênaneh, Canal of 53.
Renni, Tomb of 242.
Renpet 60.
Retennu 128. 310.
Rhampsinitus 182.
Rharbyin, the 346.
Rhodopis 223.
Ri'at el-Khêl 77.
— el-Ghazal 77.
— el-Hamrah 77.
Rikkah 2.
Rizagât 231.
Rôdah 1. 18.
Rohannu 76.
Rohlfs 344. 346. 347. etc.
Rosellini 16. 182.
Rougé, E. de 112. 239. 244.
el-Rubayât 40.
Rufinus 348.
Russegger 325.

Sa 200.
Sabagûrah 316.
Saben, Tomb of 269.
Safekh 64. 166. 167. 234.
Sahâra, the 35. 41.
Sâhel 48.
Sakêt el-Kiblah 78.
Sâkiyehs 37. 324. etc.
Salâmat 154.
Salamîyeh 231.
Samallût 1. 7.
Samhûd 70.
Samunt 77.
Santaria 345.
Sarabub 348.
Sarras 341. 342.
Sati 275. 283. 298. 311. 329. 330.
Scarabæus 200.
Seb 59. 263.
Sebek 7. 36. 256. 257. 258. 262. 263. 275.
Sebekhi, Tomb of 243.
Sebekhotep II. 114.

Sebeknefru, Tomb of 242.
Sebti 210.
Sebû'ah 322.
Sedfeh 46.
Sefian 243.
Sehêl 273. 298.
Sekhet 96. 148. 319.
Sekhet Amu 345.
Seleh 41.
Selk 187.
Sembrites 302.
Semites 17. 171.
Semueh 342.
Semnes, Tomb of 270.
Senâd 231.
Senemt 297.
Sennâr 303.
Senhûr (Fayûm) 43.
— (near Kûs) 100.
Sen-nefer, Tomb of 192.
Senrû 42.
Sennsi, the 348. 355.
Sept. Severus 156. 233. 306.
Serapis 347.
Serpents 87. 201. 205. 208.
Serreh 341.
Sesebi 342.
Sesoosis 311.
Setau 331. 339.
—, Tomb of 240.
Setep-en-Ra 166.
Seth 99. 109. 140. etc.
— Typhon 234.
Seti I. 11. 56. 57. 60. 61. 66. 114. 124. 125. 126. 127. 129. 146. 151. 186. 229. 230. 238. 260. 269. 316. 326.
— I., Tomb of 217.
— II. Merenptah 7. 114. 117. 119. 120. 132. 137. 333.
— II., Tomb of 217.
—, prince 166. 339.
Set-nekht 172. 188. 215.
Seyâleh 322.
Shabako 114. 132. 137. 141. 143. 301.
Shalmah 160.
Sharkîyeh 346.
Shas-hotep 46.
Shataui 340.
Shatt er-Regâl 255.
Shêkh 'Abâdeh 19.
— 'Abd el-Kurnah 190.
— Abu Hamed 41.
— Amrân xv.
— Besendi 355.
— el-Fadhl 7.
— Gaber 47.
— Hamed 49.
— Kekâb 74.
— Sa'îd 22.

esh-Shekilkil 29.
Shellâl 279. 273.
Shendawîn 48.
Shendi 302.
Shepenapt, Tomb of 223.
Sheshenk I. 122. 123. 137. 256.
Shet 35.
Shishak 123.
Shu 59. 206. 233. 263. 283.
Shunet ez-Zebib 69.
Shuteb 46.
Sigajah 341. 342.
Silko 302. 308.
Sinjerli 164.
Siptah 215. 257.
Si Renput, Tomb of 270.
Sitra, Queen 187.
Siût see Assiût.
Siwah, oasis of 344. 346.
Smint 355.
Snefru 2.
Sohâg 48.
Sokar-Osiris 61. 65. 67. 166. 181.
Soldiers' Tomb, the 34.
Soleh 301. 342.
Sopt 319.
Speos Artemidos 11.
Sphinxes, Avenues of 116. 143. 147. 149. 224. 322. 350.
Sruptikhis 306.
Stahl 'Antar 11. 33.
Stephanus of Byzantium 71.
Stern 192. 258. 259.
Strabo 4. 7. 36. 40. 52. 54. 98. 99. 108. 153. 155. 200. 231. 233. 243. 272. 277. 302. 347. 348.
Stuart's Tomb 191.
Sûdân 169. 266. 300. 303. 342.
Suez Canal, ancient 129.
Sugar-factories 6. 230. etc.
es Sulêhîyeh 236.
Sun, Spring of the 345. 347.
Sun-disc, winged 24. 262. 313.
Surarîyeh 7.
Suyuti 8.
Syene 267.
Syenite 276.
Syringes 200.

Tabenna, Tabennesus 72.
Table Mountain 356.
Tablet of Abydos 65.
— Karnak 140.
Tacitus 155.
Tafeh 306.